FROM CRIME
TO
PUNISHMENT

An Introduction to the Criminal Law System

SEVENTH EDITION

Edited by

Joel E. Pink B.A., LL.B., Q.C.

and

David C. Perrier Ph.D.

with a Foreword by

The Honourable Justice Thomas A. Cromwell

CARSWELL®

A cataloguing record for this publication is available from Library and Archives Canada.

ISBN 978-0-7798-2801-2

 **THOMSON REUTERS**

CARSWELL, A DIVISION OF THOMSON REUTERS CANADA LIMITED

One Corporate Plaza
2075 Kennedy Road
Toronto, Ontario
M1T 3V4

Customer Relations:
Toronto 1-416-609-3800
Elsewhere in Canada/U.S. 1-800-387-5164
Fax 1-416-298-5082
www.carswell.com
E-mail www.carswell.com/email

Dedication

To my wife Rita, my children, Jennifer, Leah and Daniel, and my grandchildren, Freya and Joshua.

Joel E. Pink, Q.C.

To my wife Colline, my children, Suzanne, Christine and David, and my grandchildren, Nicholas, Lauren, Kyle, Zachary and Jack.

David C. Perrier, Ph.D.

Preface

This is the seventh edition of *From Crime To Punishment* and a little over two decades since the first edition was published. Our objectives over this period have not changed: to provide a book about the basic principles and procedures of criminal law that is both readable and interesting to students, practitioners and members of the general public. To that end, we have incorporated a wide variety of exceptional and experienced practitioners, from judges to prosecutors, including legal experts and researchers, to describe as succinctly as they can the various elements of contemporary criminal law. In doing so, our contributors, where appropriate, have referenced specific cases which supplement their descriptive material that our readers can further investigate, should they so wish. Throughout each chapter, our authors have included numerous examples to illustrate their work and have kept faith with our overriding principle of ensuring their material is "user friendly" and reflects how criminal law operates in real-life situations. The chapters and their content have been selected in a way that reflects the exercise of criminal law in our present criminal justice system.

The present text begins with the history and principles of criminal law, followed by the classification of offences and then describes who can be charged with an offence. What follows is a discussion of the arrest of an accused, the manner in which an accused is either brought before the courts and possibly released, the nature of guilt before the courts, and a description of exceptional cases where mental disorder or the age of the accused may impact on the legal process and criminal proceedings. Then the adversary system of justice is analyzed with a focus on trial procedures, the principles of evidence and the impact of modern technology such as electronic surveillance for securing evidence before the courts. Finally, the trial process is explained with an emphasis on jury trials, the principles and powers of sentencing vested in our judiciary and the appeal process. This final section also highlights the areas of search and seizure, proceeds of crime and money laundering, the *Canadian Charter of Rights and Freedoms*, solicitor/

client privilege, bans on publication and media restrictions, dangerous offenders, eyewitness testimony and how judges decide on the credibility of witnesses that appear before them. The authors have attempted to chronicle these chapters in a manner as to describe how the criminal law operates from the time a crime is committed to its final conclusion when a person is found guilty and sentenced accordingly.

As authors and editors, we acknowledge that this work could not have been accomplished had it not been for the dedication of our contributors many of whom have continued to work with us over the past two decades. As a testimony to their knowledge and contributions, many of our earlier contributors have achieved success in being appointed to the bench and, in one case, to the Supreme Court of Canada. To Thomson Carswell and their staff, we extend a special thanks for their continuing support of our efforts to better educate and inform others of the elements that comprise our criminal law enterprise.

Joel E. Pink, Q.C.
David C. Perrier, Ph.D.
March 2010

About the Authors / Editors

Joel E. Pink, Q.C. is a criminal lawyer in Halifax, Nova Scotia, practicing exclusively in the field of criminal and quasi-criminal law. For 31 years he was a member of the faculty of the National Criminal Law program. Mr. Pink has taught criminal trial practice and evidence at Dalhousie Law School and in the Halifax Regional Police Recruit Training Program. He was the president of the Nova Scotia Barristers' Society for 2008 and 2009. He is a fellow of the International Society of Barristers and a Fellow of the American College of Trial Lawyers. He has also appeared on several occasions before the Supreme Court of Canada.

Dr. David C. Perrier is an Associate Professor in the Department of Sociology and Criminology at Saint Mary's University in Halifax, Nova Scotia with 38 years teaching experience. His current research and teaching interests include Criminology, the Canadian Criminal Justice System, Policing and Society, Police Accountability, Penology, Regulatory Enforcement in the Fishing Industry and Gambling and its Social Impacts. As one of the founders of the only Criminology Undergraduate and Graduate Programs in Nova Scotia, he continues to contribute to numerous published articles, reports and conference papers in the area of gambling studies and regulatory enforcement. Having worked with the Royal Canadian Mounted Police Auxiliary program and chaired the Nova Scotia Police Commission, he continues to teach in the Halifax Regional Police Recruit Training Program and serve on numerous educational and community committees.

Foreword

In 1988, a senior criminal defence lawyer and a highly respected criminologist teamed up to present a readable, layperson's guide to criminal justice. Seven editions and over 17,000 copies later, *From Crime to Punishment*, remains true to its goal of making criminal law and the criminal justice system more clearly understandable to anyone who cares to read it. Mr. Pink and Dr. Perrier have assembled a team of first-rate contributors whose command of their subjects is matched by their gift for providing accessible explanations of complex material. From the history and basic principles of criminal law to sentencing, the reader will find concise, carefully constructed and readable chapters on all the main topics of criminal procedure, evidence and criminal justice.

This book is a wonderful resource for anyone wishing to have a thorough yet readily understandable overview of how our criminal justice system operates. To Mr. Pink and Dr. Perrier and to all of the contributors, I say "bravo" and "encore".

The Honourable Justice Thomas A. Cromwell
Justice of the Supreme Court of Canada

Contents

The Queen v. John Doe—A Case Study

John Doe, as he was known to his friends, had a number of trouble-some years in the Province of Ontario where he accumulated a host of criminal convictions: assault causing bodily harm; common assault; wounding with intent and discharging a firearm for which he was sentenced to two years less one day; and theft under $200.

In the mid 1980s, John Doe decided to turn his life around and returned to his native home in Nova Scotia to embark on a new beginning. Upon returning to his home community his dream was to be a homeowner in an area where his parents and grandparents once lived.

In August, after having accumulated a few dollars, Mr. Doe was able to partially realize his dream by purchasing a piece of property at a tax sale. The parcel of land consisted of two acres that was once used as a garbage dump by some local residents; however, there was a clear patch of land, which he developed. On this parcel of land he placed a mobile home. Once John settled in, his troubles began.

John's neighbors were Mark Smith, Jim Lane, and Brian Lane. They all lived within one or two kilometers of John. Over the next 18 months, for reasons unknown to Mr. Doe, Mark Smith, Jim Lane and Brian Lane relentlessly violated the peace and tranquility that Mr. Doe desired by continually harassing him both as a group and individually. The three individuals collectively and individually:

1. dumped garbage on his property;
2. tore up his front lawn and garden with an All Terrain Vehicle;
3. threatened to cause him death;
4. chained and nailed his back door so he could not get into his residence;
5. committed a break and enter into his residence;
6. knocked on his back door during the early morning hours to awaken him;
7. dismantled his propane tank;
8. bulldozed his driveway;

9. tore down his front gate;
10. captured his dog, put it on a rope and dragged the dog down the dirt road behind an All Terrain Vehicle eventually killing it;
11. placed stolen property on his property and then called the RCMP on him;
12. killed his cat and left it on his back steps;
13. shot holes in his mailbox; and
14. fired gunshots in the vicinity of his trailer.

Mr. Doe lived in constant fear of Mark Smith, Jim Lane, and Brian Lane.

John pleaded with all three men to stay off his property. The three men ignored and laughed at him. They took advantage of Mr. Doe at every opportunity as he was a meek and mild man. These three men made life so miserable that it would have driven most people to move elsewhere. John, however, never gave in to their cruel acts.

John Doe felt he had every right to live peacefully wherever he wanted and he wanted to live in his hometown and he refused to be forced out by these three men. The harassment became so intolerable that Mr. Doe slept on his trailer floor with his prayer beads, hoping that bullets being fired in the vicinity of the trailer would not hit him.

John Doe turned to alcohol to calm his nerves. For the six weeks prior to June 1989, Mr. Doe never saw a sober day.

On June 23, 1989, Mr. Doe drank alcohol most of the day with his friend, Bill Jones. According to a forensic toxicologist, John's blood/alcohol concentration at 4:30 a.m. on June 24, 1989, would have read a low of 281 milligrams of alcohol per 100 millilitres of blood to a high of 330 milligrams of alcohol per 100 millilitres of blood.

Between 3:30 a.m. and 4:00 a.m. on June 24, 1989, Susan, the wife of Mark Smith, heard gunshots. Not realizing the significance of what she had heard she drifted back into a sound sleep without her husband beside her, until morning.

A neighbour, George Mont, on June 24, 1989, heard three shots at 4:17 a.m. and then heard another two shots at 4:58 a.m. and approximately 30 seconds later heard two more shots. On each occasion that he heard the shots, he testified, he looked at the clock in his bedroom. According to this neighbor, it was not unusual to hear gunshots in this town at any hour of the day or night.

Bill Jones was staying with John on June 24, 1989, at his trailer. He woke up between 4:30-4:45 a.m., according to his watch, and he saw Mr. Doe sitting at the kitchen table with a beer in his hand.

In the early morning hours of June 24, 1989, Susan Smith discovered the body of her husband on their front lawn and called the RCMP. Upon notification the RCMP responded to the scene immediately. They discovered Mark Smith, deceased, on his front lawn. Upon further investigation in the area, the body of Jim Lane was discovered, deceased, in his bed from gunshot wounds, and at the house diagonally across the road the police found Brian Lane, in his truck, fatally injured from a gunshot wound. He died from his injury a short time later.

The RCMP sent in a veteran and experienced investigator to assist Cst. Darrell in the investigation. This investigator arrived at the scene at 10:45 a.m. and was directed to the residences of Mark Smith, Jim Lane, and Brian Lane.

It was determined that John Doe was likely their prime suspect because of the many reports of harassment.

The police spent the entire day gathering evidence at the scene. During the day John Doe's well was drained and the RCMP located a pair of shoes and a 22-calibre gun, which later proved through forensic testing to be the murder weapon used in the shooting of the three men.

At approximately 7:30 p.m., the RCMP obtained a search warrant and went into the residence of Mr. Doe. They found a 22-calibre rifle but quickly determined that the gun had not been fired.

As a result of information received, an RCMP Corporal and Sergeant proceeded to a residence in the small community. There they located John Doe at 8:41 p.m. The RCMP described Mr. Doe, when they first saw him, as a person "who had been drinking heavily." They immediately placed him under arrest for the murders of Mark Smith and Jim Lane and the wounding of Brian Lane. John Doe was given the police caution and read his rights under the *Charter* and then he was escorted back to the detachment. A statement was not taken from him at this time due to his level of impairment. Mr. Doe was remanded to the County Correctional Centre.

On June 25, 1989, at 9:46 a.m., the RCMP summoned John Doe from his cell and he was taken to an interrogation room in the Superintendent's office at the Correctional Centre. The RCMP Sergeant repeated the standard police warning:

> You need not say anything. You have nothing to hope from any promise or favour, nothing to fear from any threat whether or not you say anything, but anything that you do say may be used as evidence.

Mr. Doe was again advised of his right to retain and instruct counsel and that if he could not afford a lawyer he could contact Legal Aid and counsel would be provided for him.

The interview began at 9:46 a.m. and was completed at 10:37 a.m. At 10:05 a.m. John Doe requested to phone his sister to see if she could contact a lawyer for him. The phone call was made and the Sergeant was informed that a Legal Aid lawyer would be arriving shortly. The Legal Aid lawyer arrived at approximately 10:37 a.m. Between the hour of 10:05 a.m. and 10:37 a.m. the Sergeant did not remove himself from the interrogation room. The police knew that John Doe was a talkative person and would converse freely if the opportunity was presented and he did.

In Nova Scotia if one is charged with murder he/she has the right to request counsel of his/her choice. Mr. Doe did not wish to accept the services of Nova Scotia Legal Aid. It was after June 25 that I received a call from Legal Aid requesting my services.

The RCMP charged John Doe with three counts of first-degree murder.

Shortly after I was contacted I was informed that John Doe had made a statement to the police between the hours of 9:46 a.m. and 10:37 a.m. and he had made a statement to his friend Bill Jones.

How was the defence ever going to maneuver around the admissions that John made in his statement to the police and to Bill Jones, and the police finding the murder weapon and the shoes in John's well, and still try to establish the legal defences of provocation and drunkenness?

The words of Viscount Sanky in the English murder case of *Woolmington v. The Director of Public Prosecution* rang loud and clear, where he states:

> Throughout the Web of English Criminal Law one golden thread is always to be seen, that it is the duty of the prosecution to prove the prisoner's guilty subject ... to the defence of insanity, and subject also to any statutory exception. If, at the end of and on the whole of the case, there is no reasonable doubt created by the evidence given by either the prosecution or the prisoner, ... the prosecution has not made out the case, the prisoner is entitled to an acquittal.

The Queen v. John Doe was the case to put to the test the three basic legal principles of law: the presumption of innocence, burden of proof, and proof beyond a reasonable doubt. These fundamental rights guaranteed under our *Charter* would be confidently put to a jury, who would make every effort under the terms of their oath, to reach a verdict that was fair, just, and in accordance with the evidence and the law.

The presiding judge was a senior judge of the Trial Division of the Supreme Court of Nova Scotia and an experienced trial judge.

During the *voir dire* to determine the admissibility of the statements, the police painted a picture of John Doe as a sober individual who was fully aware of his surroundings and a person willing and eager to talk. Even after he requested a lawyer John Doe kept on talking without any promises, inducements, or threats from the police. As far as the Crown was concerned, any statements made by Mr. Doe were freely and voluntarily given.

The defence, however, had to portray a different picture: a person who was an alcoholic; who had not been sober for six weeks, and who was extremely hungover. My task was to try and develop a theory that any information elicited from John Doe was not from a person with "an operating mind." It was at this juncture that I decided to throw in a possible *Charter* violation—the right to remain silent (after the police were informed that counsel was on their way).

After hearing defence evidence tendered at the *voir dire* from the forensic toxicologist, a psychiatrist, and from Mr. Doe, the trial judge made the following ruling:

> The two experts were given hypothetical questions consistent with the accused's evidence of his condition, and they were of the opinion that these conditions were consistent with symptoms of alcoholic withdrawal. Neither expert, of course, was present with the accused on June 25th. They both admit that between individuals there is a great difference between the affects of alcohol withdrawal; that is, they do not have the same withdrawal affects.
>
> As stated by one Doctor when asked what happens to a person who is going through the initial stages of withdrawal from alcohol, he replied:
>
> > It's one of the most uncomfortable states I'm sure known to man. There are a progression of symptoms not necessarily the same in each individual over a period of time.
>
> At another point in his evidence when asked if alcohol withdrawal varies greatly from individual to individual, he replied in the affirmative once again.
>
> In light of such a scenario, I am unable to accept the opinions of these experts as to the lack of ability of the accused on June 25th to appreciate the consequences of making incriminating statements to the police and giving up the right to counsel.

Having also had the opportunity to assess the evidence given by the accused, it has buttressed my decision to reject the above noted opinions. Despite being an alcoholic, he is clearly not a man of low intelligence. During his testimony, he exhibited a very selective memory capacity when it suited his purposes. As a consequence, I find his evidence suspect in many respects. . .

The presiding judge continued:

I accept the evidence of two experienced RCMP police officers, that on June 25th the accused was sober and alert and aware of what was going on. Their handling of the accused was adjudicatively fair as well as meeting the test set forth by Justice MacIntyre in *Clarkson v. The Queen*; that is, with respect to those statements made by the accused to the police on June 25, 1989 between 9:46 a.m. and 10:05 a.m. at which latter time the accused exercised his right to retain legal counsel.

Although no questions were asked of the accused subsequent to 10:05 a.m. (that is when the accused asked to retain counsel) the continued presence in the same room with the accused of the police could be taken in this instance as urging the accused to continue talking. In my opinion it could be considered adjudicatively unfair and such statements are therefore inadmissible.

So to recap, the statements made between 9:46 a.m. and 10:05 a.m. are admissible, those subsequent to that time are not. . . .

The Crown had thrown the first pitch and it was a swing and a miss for the defence. However, you must remember that there has to be three strikes before you are out.

I, as defence counsel, never gave up hope. You just never know as a case unfolds when there might be a new development that may be beneficial to your client. Most importantly, Mr. Doe had the benefit of having his case heard by a jury who I felt would be sympathetic towards him.

What was the jury going to hear as a result of the judge's ruling on the *voir dire*?

The learned trial judge's ruling allowed the jury to hear the content of the statement of John Doe, which he made to the police between 9:46 a.m. and 10:05 a.m. It was transcribed as follows:

I think they are dead. They never leave me alone, the xxxx. I told them to stay away from my property but that xxxx, Mark Smith landed up the other night ... told them to stay away from my property. I told them to stay away from my property but the xxxx Mark Smith landed up the other night when Bill Jones trying to let on, he dropped a rock on his foot. He came looking for beer. Then he left and around 3 a.m. that xxxx Brian Lane came to the door. I told him to f— off, that I was asleep. Then I guess it started bugging me and I snapped and I went down and shot them. First down to Mark Smith's place and I couldn't see him. Then he came out and started shouting: *What are you doing around here?* I said: *I came to kill you, you xxxx,* and I shot him.

The RCMP Constable then asked: *How many times?* and John Doe replied:

I don't know perhaps five. I figured I shot one I might as well do them all. Then I went up to Brian Lane's and wrapped on the door. I heard a moan. He was in the truck, drunk so I put two in the xxxx. Then I went up to Jim's. He wouldn't open the door so I put three in him through the door. Then I went in and finished him off. I was going to shoot myself but I wanted to get another drink so I ran home.

Cst.:	What did you do with the bullets?
Answer:	Threw them in the woods.
Another Comment:	I put the gun in the well and dress shoes in the well.

Some of the facts as related by Mr. Doe in his statement could be proven to be inaccurate, *e.g.*, how many shots were fired.

How was the defence going to overcome the comments made to Bill Jones at approximately 4:40 a.m. on the day in question? The following is an excerpt of Bill Jones's testimony at trial when he was asked by the Crown Attorney about his conversation with John Doe:

Q. And what can you say—any conversation with him?

A. Not too much right then because I didn't stir too much. I just woke up. I got up on my elbow and I could see John sitting at the end of the table.

Q. And any ... when ... did you have any conversation with any, with John Doe?

A. Well, I got up—no. I don't know when he ... it'll be quarter to five or something like that and he came in and he told me that he got the *three son's of whores last night.*

Q. Okay, what did you say to that or was there any further conversation?

A. No there wasn't too much more conversation. I told him I didn't want to hear about it at all. But I just figured it was just a dream or something he was reacting. He's a pretty good storyteller and he acts the stories out.

Q. How many times did he tell you this?

A. Oh maybe twice before I faced him. I went eye to eye with him and I said: *John, tell me this is not the truth or say something to that effect* and he said: *no, brother, it's not true.*

. . .

On cross-examination I somehow had to minimize Bill Jones's evidence. I asked Mr. Jones the following questions on cross-examination:

Q. My learned friend asked you about conversation that you had with John Doe in the morning. As I understand it, after he made some initial comments, immediately thereafter, he, in fact, he told you he didn't know whether or not it was a dream. Is that not true?

A. He did, yeah.

Q. And then when you pushed him a little further, he said, *no brother, it is not true.*

A. That's correct.

Q. In fact, John Doe when he's been drinking has been known to talk a lot of nonsense. Would you agree with that sir?

A. Story after story.

Q. In fact, you've told the jury about other problems that he may have been having, that he said on some other occasions he was going to shoot them, and then he was going to take his own life, he was drinking at that time, wasn't he?

A. Oh, every, every time he told me that.

Q. But you didn't take him seriously?

A. I told him one time—an occasion, *John that would be a very poor trade.*

Q. And in fact, you did not take him seriously?

A. I did not, no, no.

Q. Let's face facts, Mr. Jones, when you are drinking and drinking to state you were drinking on this particular day, your memory of the events are clouded and you cannot honestly say for sure what John Doe told you during the early morning hours of June 24, 1989?

A. No, not really. I could recollect some stuff but it's possible that a lot of the stuff he said but it's possible that a lot of the stuff he said I can't remember. I didn't.

. . .

Q. John Doe was, or is a private person who likes to be alone and to basically be with nature. Would you agree with me there?

A. Yes very much so.

Q. And in fact, during the afternoon of the 23rd you in fact together with John took some peanuts and went down to feed the squirrels?

A. Yeah he has a squirrel station down in the woods just a little ways down and he feeds them.

Q. He not only had a squirrel station but he also had a calf, a little baby calf?

A. Right.

I figured that now some of the bluster had been taken out of the direct examination and I would have to deal with my client's statement to Bill Jones during my final address to the jury.

Another hurdle that the defence had to overcome was the evidence of Susan Smith. She portrayed her husband as a well-liked man who was a good neighbour who would never cause harm to anyone. She portrayed her husband as a good friend of Mr. Doe.

I had to discredit her without allowing the jury to feel sorry for the grieving widow. Throughout her evidence she was tearful. Susan Smith would not succumb to my suggestion that Jim and Brian Lane and her husband were best friends. All that she would state is that they were casual acquaintances but on the other hand Jim and Brian Lane were good friends of John Doe.

I started my cross-examination by stating:

Q. Would you agree that friends would not harass one another and then use the trailer—their tractors, to dig up another's driveway?
A. That's right.
Q. Would you also agree with me that friends would not tear down one's gate that was erected to keep persons off of one's property?
A. That's right.

. . .

Q. And would you agree that one would not take another's animals such as a cat and kill it?
A. Yes.
Q. And would you also agree with me that another friend would not take a friend's dog, drag it behind an All Terrain Vehicle and kill it because the All Terrain Vehicle outran the dog and then dump it on one's lawn—would you not agree that that would not be a friend?
A. Right.

. . .

Q. If in fact, Mrs. Smith, either your late husband, Mark Smith, Brian Lane or Jim Lane, did any of these things would you not agree that they would not be the acts of a friend?
A. No, I say that they'd be acts of an enemy.

The one thing that John Doe had in his favour was the jury: 12 men and women who would apply common sense to the issues. I kept reminding myself of the three basic principles of law: presumption of innocence, burden of proof, and proof beyond a reasonable doubt.

I tested John Doe during the *voir dire* and he did not make a good impression on the trial judge. That was most unfortunate; however, the real test would be whether the jury would believe him or be left in reasonable doubt after hearing his evidence.

John did testify before the jury and he presented his evidence in a credible manner. He testified before a full courtroom. In fact, the Sheriff's Department brought in the Fire Marshall to enforce the fire regulations and the overflow of spectators were escorted from the courtroom. The following is a portion of John's testimony:

Q. Now Mr. Doe what was your condition as you eventually went to sleep on the floor that night?

A. Well I passed out, Sir, from that moment I hit the floor to—I—the next—I was awakened at five after three with a lot of kicking and banging at my door. I looked at my clock, I have a little battery electric clock on a mantelpiece, to see what time somebody would be coming bugging me. I could tell by the time who was there actually, because none of my people ever came at that hour of the morning. It was five after three a.m. that morning—the morning of the 24th.

Q. Who was it?

A. It was Jim Lane and I told him to go away we're sleeping, leave us alone. And he slammed the door. There was talking and cursing going on and then he—I laid back on the floor, I didn't get up and I didn't look out the window but I did hear people's voices, I did hear bottles rattling and I did hear motors revving up and I did hear tires spinning and gravel flying in my driveway and I don't know how long this took place, maybe 10 minutes, but they eventually left.

. . .

Q. Now what affect did this, of course, have upon you?

A. Well I—like I said I never got up off the floor. I tried to get back to sleep because Bill Jones and I had plans at 7 o'clock in the morning. We were going to go down to St. Augustine's in Monastery to the Shrine, and we were going to meditate and pray and I was—I had no intentions of staying drunk that day. I was going to sober up because I had to be to work Monday morning, Sir. So while I was trying to get back to sleep on the floor I—I was thinking about all the problems that I was having, all the persecution with these people, and I could not get back to sleep. So I did get up, and I said I'll go to sleep now and I grabbed a mickey of rum I had, Captain Morgan Light, and I drunk four good big mouthfuls in me and then I opened up a bottle of MacEwin's Ale and I used that for a chaser and then I went and laid back on the floor thinking I'd be—I'd go to sleep now. I continued to stay awake and these things of harassment and torture kept running through my mind, so I said there's one alternative to this, I've got stronger alcohol than rum. I went into the washroom, I dumped out a good shot of Aqua Velva, which I know is 70 proof alcohol and I put some juice in it—out—out to the kitchen with it and I put juice in it, and I drunk it down very fast so I couldn't smell it and taste it and I opened up a beer for a chaser and I laid down on the floor again at that time, Sir.

. . .

Q. What happened after you took the swig of Aqua Velva?

A. Well after I took this Aqua Velva, I opened up a beer and I laid down on the floor and the next thing I can honestly remember is waking up on the floor. I don't know how much time was involved. I had a cap on my head. I had a coat—a small jacket on me. I had shoes on my feet and I had the idea that I have seen bodies on my street that night.

Q. And what bodies had you seen on your street that night?

A. Well to the best of my knowledge I—I thought it was a dream, and I thought I seen Mark Smith, Jim Lane and Brian Lane. I thought—this is what I thought I seen, Sir.

Q. What's the next thing you seen, Mr.—the next thing you saw, Mr. Doe?

A. The next thing I—well this was disturbing to my mind. So I got up off of the floor and the first thing I seen was a 22 pistol was laying on my counter and I had—if it had've been given back to me or not, I wasn't sure. The last time I seen it, it was taken from me and Mrs. Smith—before I entered Susan Smith's car. So I—I went to the fridge and I—I sat down and I was thinking, the gun is there and I think—I think I've seen bodies. If I walked by bodies and if the gun is here, it looks very much, whether I'm guilty or innocent, I'm going to be blamed anyway, because I'm number one suspect, kind of the feuds that we've been having. So I seen Bill Jones kind of make a turn on the chesterfield. I went over and I talked to him. I told him what I—what I dreamt. He said, "You're absolutely crazy," he said, "you never left this house," he said. Well I said, "I pray to God I didn't Bill, but," I said, "the pistol is on the counter and I don't remember seeing the pistol for the last 12 days. I was fighting with Smith to get the pistol back." And over that conversation with Smith, he said, he was talking to an RCMP Corporal and he said, "Yes, he knows Doe got the pistol." He said, "I'm going up Doe's place to get the pistol"—Smith told me this, and he said, "Susan is not giving you back the pistol until the police raid your place and until you sober up off of this drunk." So I told this to Bill Jones and I said, "There's the pistol, and I think I seen bodies. I walked by bodies. I'm going to definitely be first number one suspect." So I said, "Bill, do you think it's wise if I get rid of the shoes and the pistols if I walked by bodies?" He said, "I—I—it's up—I don't know Johnny." He thought I was fooling. He said, "it's up to you," he said, "I guess so." So I was in no state of mind to reason. If I thought I saw bodies, the most reasonable thing to do would be to phone help—help for these people, but I did. I don't remember throwing the gun and the shoes in the well. I didn't know I put them there until R.C.M.P. told me in the lockup.

Q. Tell me, Sir, in the early morning of June the 23rd, today, do you have any recollection of shooting Mark Smith, Jim Lane and of Brian Lane?

A. I have no recollection whatsoever of shooting these men, and I examined it in my conscience very much since. That is why I insisted to be put in the Hospital. It was my idea to go there so I could talk to psychologist, psychiatrist to see if such a thing did happen. I did see the bodies some way or another. I've talked to these people and I still—I've been told by professional people that I don't...

Q. Okay. The question is, do you have any recollection today?

A. No, I do not, Sir. And I do not have the nature to kill people under any circumstances, animals or humans.

It is not the role of defence counsel to judge his/her client's story but this is the role of the jury. It was my goal to present to the jury a case that would leave them in reasonable doubt as to John Doe's guilt. If the jury was convinced beyond a reasonable doubt that it was John Doe who fired the gunshots then the jury would still have to deal with the issues of provocation, drunkenness, and the offence of manslaughter.

The Crown did not call any rebuttal evidence to refute Mr. Doe's evidence about the gun. It was then left for me to try to convince the jury that there was a reasonable doubt about who in fact fired the shots. I decided to approach the issues before the jury in the following manner:

> There are some real questions, however, in this case which I must leave with you to consider. First of all, has the Crown proved beyond a reasonable doubt that it was John Doe who actually did the shooting? If you should so conclude this, then you may proceed on to answer these other questions.

I then listed the other questions for them to consider. My jury address continued as follows:

> Going back to the first question of: *Who did it?* It's not a matter of looking at the evidence and saying to yourselves: *In light of all the evidence, who else could have done it?* That is not the issue. The issue is: *Has the Crown proved beyond a reasonable doubt that, in fact, it was John Doe who in fact, shot Mark Smith, Jim Lane and Brian Lane?*
>
> In light of the evidence that you have heard in this courtroom, can it be said that the Crown have met that burden.
>
> The Crown has called 2 witnesses in which they will try to tell you, that from their evidence you can, you can conclude it was in fact John Doe.
>
> Well do you remember the two witnesses called?
>
> George Mont was the neighbor that stated that he placed the time of the first shot at 4:17 a.m. and the second set of shots at 4:58 a.m. and the

third set of shots a few minutes later. He also stated to you that he heard gunshots in the early morning on several other occasions and it was not an unusual happening in this area to hear gunshots.

He also said that there were differences in what he, in fact, heard. The Crown wants you the jury, to infer that these were in fact the times of the shootings. But, you cannot be unmindful of the evidence of the Crown's other witness, Bill Jones, who said that when he woke up at 4:45 a.m. and he looked at his clock, John Doe was in the trailer. So if he was in the trailer at 4:45 a.m. who in fact fired the other shots at 4:58 a.m. and a few minutes later?

To be precise, Bill Jones looked at his watch again at 5:03 a.m. and John was sitting at the table drinking a beer.

Accepting what both of these Crown witnesses have said, can it be said beyond a reasonable doubt so that you can say that you are sure that it was John Doe who shot these three men?

There was no evidence to refute what John Doe said that Susan Smith was the last person to be in possession of the gun. In fact, the unrebuted evidence is that in the week before, John Doe could not find his gun. I'm sure the Crown's going to say to you Mr. Foreman and Ladies and Gentlemen: *Well how did the gun get into the trailer?* Well that is not for us to answer, that is for them to prove. Sure they can prove that it was that gun that in fact killed those 3 people but they still have to put John Doe behind the gun with his finger on the trigger before you can say that, in fact, he committed any type of homicide which His Lordship will define.

In light of the evidence of George Mont who said that at 4:58 a.m. he heard the second shots, the Crown would have you infer that that's when John shot Brian Lane, but keep in mind the evidence of Bill Jones, another Crown witness, when he states that he was at home. And a few minutes later the third series of shots, and the Crown would have you believe that's when John shot Jim Lane. But there's also the evidence of Bill Jones who said that at 5:03 a.m. when he looked at his clock, John Doe was at home drinking. That's the evidence.

. . .

The first question to be addressed is "Has the Crown proven beyond a reasonable doubt that John Doe fired the gunshots that claimed the lives of Mark Smith, Brian Lane and Jim Lane?"

When dealing with John Doe's statement I decided to remind the jury that once a statement has been ruled admissible, it is in the same position as any other evidence and they (jury) may accept it or reject it in whole or in part.

The same can be said about any statement that John Doe made to

Bill Jones. It was the jury's prerogative after examining all of the evidence to decide whether they will accept the evidence in whole or in part or not at all. The opinions of the judge, the Crown or Defence are not pertinent.

At the end of my address I declared:

> As I commenced my address so will I end it by stating that the mere fact that John sits before you does not mean that he must be guilty. There is no burden upon John to prove that he is innocent. The burden is solely upon the Crown and that burden never shifts.

I completed my address by stating:

> Ladies and Gentlemen of the jury, when you listen to His Lordship's instructions concerning reasonable doubt and you hear his instructions regarding the Crown's burden of proof, these are not empty slogans. They are the foundation of the criminal justice system in Canada. They are what our system offers my client as a way to answer such a serious allegation, a way to make a defence. Not only because of the great impact a conviction would have in these circumstances on my client and those close to him, but also because it is necessary for the law to recognize the errors and inaccuracies and the misconceptions that sometimes result. When we try to judge the truth of what a person says or what we try to infer, where there are gaps in the evidence as they clearly are here, then the words *reasonable doubt* will have a significant meaning. Listen carefully to His Lordship's instructions.

I aspired for a favourable jury charge by the trial judge.

The Honourable Justice in his jury address made some very pertinent remarks that a jury could grasp at in deciding whether the Crown had proven their case beyond a reasonable doubt. The judge's charge to the jury was fair and well-balanced. His Lordship stated:

> A reasonable doubt is an honest doubt, a fair doubt based on reason and common sense. It is not an imaginary or frivolous doubt that you might use to avoid your responsibility as jurors. The accused is entitled to the benefit of a reasonable doubt on the whole of the case with respect to each count and on each and every issue in the case.

> In this case the accused himself gave evidence. He is in the same position as any other witness as far as his credibility is concerned... Shortly I will instruct you how to weigh testimony, but for the present let me tell you that if you believe the accused that he did not commit the offence or what he did lacks some essential element of the offence, which I will describe later, or if the evidence of the accused, either standing alone or taken together with all the other evidence, leaves you in a state of reasonable doubt then you must acquit him.

In dealing with the statements of the accused the Provincial Justice stated:

> You've heard the evidence [of the RCMP Sergeant and Constable] regarding statements ... made by the accused to them on June the 25th. The fact that evidence of this—these statements were given does not mean that they were made or that they were true. That's up for you to decide. It's for you to decide whether the statements were made and if you have a reasonable doubt about whether or not a particular statement was made in whole or in part, you must reject it entirely or reject those parts as to which you have a reasonable doubt as the making. If you find the statements were made, you may believe all of the statement, part of it, or you can reject them entirely... Here we recall that the accused is saying he doesn't remember anything of what happened, ... that these statements he gave is what he had heard from other people. If you decide to accept part or all of it, it will be considered by you with the other evidence you decide to accept. You, of course, must reach your verdict on the whole of the evidence that you decide is worthy of belief. The accused, as a witness, you can accept earlier testimony as the statement that the police—the Crown alleges he made to the police. You can accept that as the truth of what happened ... as opposed to what he said in court... If you find that his evidence at trial represented the true facts, or if you have any reasonable doubt about it, you will reject entirely the earlier statement.

In reviewing the evidence of Bill Jones the learned Justice stated:

> ... It's obvious that certainly at 4:45 a.m. there's no doubt that the accused was at the trailer.

> Keep in mind the times that other people said about hearing shots and so on. It's up to you to decided just what significance you put to those—those times. You can—how well you can rely on when people tell you times and so on. Use your own common sense in judging the weight you give to that evidence.

The Judge's charge to the jury lasted four-and-a-half hours.

The jury returned at 4:30 p.m. on the first day of deliberation to rehear the evidence of Bill Jones, Susan Smith and George Mont. The jury deliberated for two-and-a-half days and at 2:23 p.m. of the third day a verdict was reached.

The townspeople crowded into the courtroom. There were people outside waiting for the verdict.

Clerk:	Members of the jury have you agreed upon your verdict?
Mr. Foreman:	We have.
Clerk to the Foreman:	What's your verdict on the first count?

A.	The verdict on the first count is not guilty.
Q.	What is your verdict on the second count?
A.	The verdict on the second count is not guilty.
Q.	And what is your verdict on the third count?
A.	The verdict on the third count is not guilty.
Clerk:	Members of the jury, you have found the accused not guilty, are you in agreement?
Body of Jurors:	Yes.

The Crown Attorney then requested that the jury be polled.

Clerk:	Asking each juror: Your verdict on all three counts?

Each responded not guilty.

Those in attendance applauded and the judge, without thanking the jury or discharging the accused, said: "Well, the court stands adjourned."

John Doe was free to return home. Upon exiting the court there were townspeople clapping and cheering for my client.

I gave Mr. Doe a ride home to his sister's residence and in the car he thanked me for my assistance but said that it was not my work that had him acquitted it was G-d's wishes. Mr. Doe became a very religious person. I accepted his words without comment. We shook hands and I returned to my office to wait and see if the Crown would appeal.

The date of the acquittal was April 20, 1990 and on May 17th, just three days before the 30-day time limit would have expired the Crown appealed the verdict. There were 11 grounds of appeal. The appeal was heard on February 13, 1991 before a panel of three justices of the Nova Scotia Court of Appeal.

On April 11, 1991, the Court of Appeal handed down its 108-page decision. The majority found an error in law and allowed the Crown appeal and sent the matter back for a new trial. One Justice dissented. (See 64 C.C.C. (3d) 336, 103 N.S.R. (2d) 91.)

When I reported the decision to my client I informed him that I did my best but it must have been G-d's wish that he have a new trial.

It was Mr. Doe's decision to appeal the matter to the Supreme Court of Canada. On April 22, 1991, I filed a Notice of Appeal based on the following questions of law from the dissenting Judge of the Nova Scotia Court of Appeal:

1. That the Learned Trial Judge erred in law in instructing the jury that the appellant's out of court culpatory statement must be rejected entirely if the appellant's testimony at trial raised any reasonable doubt

about it thereby misdirecting the jury on the doctrine of reasonable doubt and the proper method of deliberating on the evidence as a whole;

2. That the Learned Trial Judge erred in law in excluding from evidence certain statements made by the accused to police officers on the basis that the appellant had exercised his right to retain legal counsel and the taking or admission of these statements would be considered "adjudicatively unfair";

3. That the majority erred in law in holding that the verdict might have been different therefor usurping the function of the jury which amounted to an error in law.

After presentation of the arguments the Supreme Court of Canada reserved its decision.

The Court narrowed in on the issues dealing with Mr. Doe's statement and the trial judge's instructions pertaining to it. The Court closely examined the trial judge's instructions to the jury, in particular, where he stated that, "... they must *reject* the accused's statement if they had a reasonable doubt as to whether the statement was made." And further when the trial judge, "... invited the jury to reject the statement if they had a reasonable doubt as to its veracity."

As stated by one Justice at p. 212-213:

> In my view, it is acceptable for a trial judge to focus the jury's attention on the vital issues of its inquiry. Perhaps the jury should not be directed to compartmentalize their deliberations, but at the same time it is unrealistic to view a jury's decision as some epiphanic pronouncement of guilt or innocence; rather, the jurors engage in a deliberate process of evaluating the evidence presented to them. In this case, the jury deliberated for two days on evidence from a trial that lasted more than three weeks. To restrain jurors from rejecting evidence during this process is to impose an artificial constraint on their mandate. Having said this, a trial judge should proceed with the utmost caution in advising the jury that certain evidence may be "rejected". If the trial judge ventures into this realm, then the advice must be complete—he or she must go on to stress to the jury that this rejection must not be done in isolation—the evidence is not to be evaluated in a piecemeal fashion.

> ... As in this case, where a statement by an accused at trial is entirely at odds with a previous out-of-court statement by the accused, and the jury believes the statement at trial, or is left in reasonable doubt that it is true, then the jury must reject the out-of-court statement; the accused must be given the benefit of the doubt. In arriving at that conclusion, the jury should, of course, give consideration to the evidence as a whole.

. . .

The contradictory statements of the accused were a key element of this trial, and the judge was entitled to give the jury some guidance on how to handle this discrepancy in the evidence. As a matter of logic, the two stories could not be reconciled, and the advice to reject one of them is one way to deal with the dilemma. When a judge ventures into this kind of instruction, a reviewing court will have two concerns: (1) the jury must know that their job is not to choose the most believable of the versions, but that the version most favourable to the accused is entitled to the benefit of the doubt, and (2) the two versions cannot be simply pitted against one another in isolation, rather all of the other evidence must also be considered.

The Supreme Court of Canada relied upon their decision in *R. v. Morin* (1988), 44 C.C.C. (3d) 193, and stated:

Morin demonstrates that it is both acceptable and desirable for a trial judge to focus the jury's attention on vital issues, and to direct their minds to the proper burden of proof on those discrete questions... In my view, this is exactly what the trial judge has done in the present case. As Freeman J.A. commented in the court below, at p. 389: "... the words of Mr. Justice MacIntosh referred to above, to say nothing of his instructions as a whole, would have left the jury in a state of mind no different than if he had charged them in the words of Mr. Justice Lamer in *Nadeau*."

Chief Justice Lamer in his judgment stated at p. 197-198:

However, the jury can and must decide whether the whole of the evidence establishes, beyond a reasonable doubt, the individual facts necessary to support a conviction. This must, of necessity, be done in a sequential manner, and I agree with La Forest J. that it is unrealistic to expect the jury to have an "epiphanic" experience in rejecting its verdict. In *Morin*, Wilson J. stated (at p. 199) that the process of the jury's deliberation with respect to the Crown evidence "requires a fact elicited through the mouth of a witness to be assessed by the jury in the context of all the evidence and to be rejected if it has not been proved beyond a reasonable doubt". Therefore, while the jury never rejects evidence, it can and must decide whether to accept or reject the factual assertions made by that evidence before it uses those factual assertions to support or infer other factual assertions towards reaching its verdict. Such factual assertions can only be accepted and used by the jury to convict the accused if they are established by the evidence beyond a reasonable doubt. Facts which are not so established cannot corroborate or be allowed to "bootstrap" other doubtful facts. Any lower standard would present the possibility that an accused could be convicted on the basis of facts which are established as matters of conjecture only.

An analogy I often used in charging juries, especially in cases where the Crown's case was circumstantial, was that of a fisherman's net. The evidence presented at trial by the Crown seeks to establish factual propositions. Once established, facts may be used to infer other facts. In this

The Law—And The Lawyers

The first thing we do, let's kill all the lawyers.
— WILLIAM SHAKESPEARE (1564-1616), **King Henry VI, Act IV, Scene II**.

Reason is the life of the law, nay the common law itself is nothing else but reason.
— SIR EDWARD COKE(1552-1634), **Institutes, Commentary upon Littleton, First Institute, #80**.

Custom, that unwritten law. By which the people keep even kings in awe.
— CHARLES DAVENANT (1656-1714) **Circe, II, iii**.

The law's made to take care of raskills.
— GEORGE ELIOT (1819-1880), **The Mill on the Floss**.

In no country perhaps in the world is the law so general a study... . This study renders men acute, inquisitive, dexterous, prompt in attack, ready to defence, full of resources. . . .
— EDMUND BURKE (1729-1797), **Speech on Conciliation with America, 1775**.

Bad laws are the worst sort of tyranny.
— EDMUND BURKE, **Speech at Bristol, 1780**.

The people have nothing to do with the laws but to obey them.
— BISHOP SAMUEL HORSLEY (1733-1806), **Speech in the House of Lords**.

A lawyer has no business with the justice or injustice of the cause which he undertakes, unless his client asks his opinion, and then he is bound to give it honestly. The justice or injustice of the cause is to be decided by the judge.
— SAMUEL JOHNSON (1709-1784), **Tour to the Hebrides, 15 August 1773**.

We must not made a scarecrow of the law, Setting it up to fear the birds of prey And let it keep one shape, till custom make it Their perch and not their terror.
— WILLIAM SHAKESPEARE, **Measure for Measure, Act II, Scene I**.

1

An Introduction to Criminal Law

David C. Perrier, Ph.D.[*]

For the ordinary person one of the most interesting and fascinating topics of discussion is that of law and order. Law and order has become the subject of books, articles, and television programs which are read or viewed by people as they go about their daily lives. However, the relationship between law and order is not all that apparent to many people and it is for that reason this chapter begins with an analysis of the role of criminal law as one means of maintaining social control, and hence order, in our society.

To many people, the term "criminal law" simply refers to society's prohibitions against acts that threaten its very existence—acts such as murder, assault and theft. In the same vein, "crime" simply means the breaking of these laws, and the "criminal" is the person who has broken them. Criminal law, then, may be seen as one form of social control—a term encompassing all kinds of pressure upon individuals to do what is customarily considered the right thing in a given society. Social control, of course, also resides in many other mechanisms, including customs, peer group pressure, and institutional patterns of behaviour.

Criminal law, however, as distinct from these other forms of social control, tends to be more specific about the behaviour defined as an offence and about the nature of the punishment to be imposed if it is violated. Criminal law is also distinguished from mere custom in that it endows selected individuals with the privilege or right of applying the sanction of physical coercion, if need be. In addition, within the confines of a given society, criminal law tends to be perceived as universal in scope. One has to remember that customs tend to have an optional character and that there are a wide variety of customs existing within the boundaries of a single society. Furthermore, unlike customs that arise spontaneously out of the necessity of group living, criminal laws are formal enactments normally contrived by legislative bodies. Con-

* B.A., Saint Mary's University, Halifax, Nova Scotia; M.A., Dalhousie University, Halifax, Nova Scotia; Ph. D., York University, Toronto, Ontario; Associate Professor in the Department of Sociology and Criminology at Saint Mary's University, Halifax, Nova Scotia.

sequently, the criminal law is a list of specific forms of human conduct outlawed by political authority which applies uniformly to all persons living under that political authority, and which is enforced by punishment administered by the state. At the core of any body of criminal law are rules that prohibit certain acts whose harm is plain, grave, and universally unwelcome. Rules relating to personal safety and security of property are the criminal law's first order of business.

The earliest form of criminal law originated as essentially a private matter in which individuals and families exacted retribution against those who had wronged them. In early history the tendency was to allocate authority to the party who was directly injured. This early concept of personal justice is clearly visible in all early laws such as the Code of Hammurabi, the Roman Tablets of Laws, as well as the Mosaic Code. With the passage of time, however, and through a series of developments in the law, the group or society took charge, and the wrongs came to be regarded as injuries to the group or to the state.

As time passed, formal political organization was substituted for kinship systems of justice and the character of early criminal law and procedure changed. For example, with the introduction of feudalism in England there came an emerging court system that placed the administration of justice in the hands of landowners, religious elites and, eventually, a centralized government under a king. Rules abolishing violence or feuding soon became the general laws of the land and were strictly administered by justices of the King's Court. Often this was referred to as "keeping the King's Peace." To some extent it was the state as the representative of society that became the victim of law violations, and not the private offended party, and the state took the initiative in seeing that justice was carried out. The Crown kept the peace through its courts, assisted by such alternative modes of punishment as fines, mutilation, transportation and death.

By the reign of Henry II (1154-1189), England had developed a strong centralized government and feudal lords had lost control over the administration of justice. Under Henry's tutelage, England established a court system in which peasants—the commoners—could obtain justice from the King. Thus began a system of common law available to all, regardless of rank, and administered in the name of the central government.

Consequently, common law originated in England. Our Canadian legal system is a direct descendant. As a major source of criminal law, common law may best be understood as a system of guidelines that emerged from the decision-making process of courts. At first, common law referred to the customs common to particular localities. Gradually it came to mean customs common to all England and eventually was called "the law of the land". No one knows exactly how and when certain principles, which judges enforced through the powerful royal courts, came to be accepted as English common law. But it is clear that customs were the source of common law, rather than statutes, as is the case today. Initially, judges would make decisions on cases coming before them; these decisions in turn would be recorded and referred to by others when deciding later cases. These prior decisions are called *precedents*.

With the passage of time, hundreds of judicial decisions made the nature of many kinds of offences, including criminal offences, more and more precise. Judges gradually came to feel bound by prior decisions and often refused to set these decisions aside and break new ground. When a court had decided a case through its application of some legal principle, the assumption was that all similar cases that appeared in the future would be decided on the same basis, unless there were unusual reasons for changes in the rules. This binding quality of prior decisions is called *stare decisis*, which lawyers are fond of referring to as "letting the decision stand." Although it reflects a very conservative stance, this process is often defended, based upon the belief that it ensures fairness, consistency, and predictability in judicial decision-making. In the deliberations of the Supreme Court of Canada, precedents established in prior cases continue to play a significant role.

Criminal law was the product of a long political process in medieval England. Originally there were no criminal codes; justice was administered through many court decisions and some statutes. Over the centuries, common law principles became dated and increasingly inadequate. This resulted in statutes being passed to clarify or augment common law principles. The process of incorporating common law offences and statutes into a single document called the *Criminal Code* serves to highlight the changing nature of criminal law and its close correspondence with custom and tradition.

Both common and statutory law have been important sources in the evolution of Canadian criminal law. Currently in Canada, however, there are no common law offences and people who become involved with the law are normally in violation of the *Criminal Code* or one of the statutes. A statute overrides all the common law dealing with the same point; consequently, when reference is made to a statute there is normally no need to examine decisions reached in cases prior to the time when the statute was passed.

The primary source of Canadian criminal law is our *Criminal Code*, first drafted but never enacted in England. This *Criminal Code* was enacted by the Canadian Parliament in 1892, revised in 1955, and amended on many occasions over past decades.

To ordinary citizens, the *Criminal Code* is confusing, overly complicated and difficult to understand. Its language is unfamiliar, which may make it difficult for people to obey, and should they have the opportunity to serve as jurors, difficult for people to apply. Our *Criminal Code* today is a lengthy document, consisting of enactments of general principles, followed by sections dealing with offences against the person, property and the state, as well as with procedural matters such as police powers, bail and rights to appeal.

All offences under the *Criminal Code* can be categorized according to the procedure employed for trying the case. Crimes are divided into classes: "summary" (an offence which can be tried by the summary conviction procedure) or "indictable" (an offence which can be tried by indictment). Some offences can be classified in a particular instance as either indictable or summary, depending upon the decision of the Crown Attorney (i.e., the Crown having the choice of procedure). Consequently, the procedures the accused is entitled to, and the punishments handed down upon conviction, vary depending upon the offence committed. Canada, unlike the United States and England, has abolished the distinction between a felony and a misdemeanour.

Although the original *Criminal Code* has served Canadians well for over a century, if we are to reflect our identity as a nation and our common values as a people, changes are indeed necessary from time to time. It is important, for example, that our *Criminal Code* be in harmony with newly created legislation such as the *Canadian Charter of Rights and Freedoms,* as well as being responsive to the needs of modern Canada. In fact, as illustrated lately within Canadian juvenile justice, any statutory change created by Parliament should promote improvements while being consistent with our current perceptions of justice and rights.

With the introduction of the *Young Offenders Act* in April of 1984, we witnessed a fundamental change in approach to juvenile justice in this country. Under the former legislation (*Juvenile Delinquents Act*), the *parens patriae* doctrine governed, which meant that the state assumed the role of a protective parent. The primary role of the courts was to extend guidance, care and assistance to misdirected youth. The juvenile courts exercised broad discretionary powers and were not obliged to confine their intervention to children committing acts considered criminal by adult standards, nor was it felt necessary to confine the intervention to circumstances where the youth had been found guilty of the alleged offences according to fundamental principles of justice. Juvenile courts did not provide procedural safeguards to the same extent or degree as the adult court system.

Thus, the criminal law jurisdiction was invoked to effect social welfare purposes. This was very contentious. In addition, there were inadequate checks and balances in the exercise of discretion and authority over young persons by police, the courts and those who administered court dispositions. The *Young Offenders Act* that was introduced removed the inequities of the *parens patriae* approach to juvenile justice and, at the same time, ensured that all the due process protections accorded adults were equally available to young people. State intervention was limited by this new legislation and it is now consistent with the *Charter of Rights and Freedoms.* Insofar as our legal system is a direct descendant of the English experience, it is important to keep in mind that criminal law embodies a particular set of rules whose content has varied according to time and place. To some extent criminal law reflects constantly changing public opinions and moral values, albeit such changes in law are often slow in coming. Then, in 2003, parliament replaced the *Young Offenders Act* with the *Youth Criminal Justice Act* (YCJA). This new legislation addressed some of the problems that plagued the youth justice system such as the lack of a coherent youth justice philosophy; the largest youth incarceration rate in Western societies, the extensive use of courts for minor cases better dealt with outside the court system, sentencing disparities, unfairness in transfers to the adult system and lack of concerns of victims.

Our laws and legal system also share a number of interesting characteristics with the English common law from which they are directly descended. Our system of justice, for example, is an adversarial one, as was early English common law. The adversarial process implies that two parties assume antagonistic positions in debating the guilt or innocence of an accused person. In such a contest judges are supposed to be neutral, as if umpiring a football game in which the prosecution and the defence are contestants. Each side, of course, is hoping to win. When the two parties take opposing positions, debate the merits of each position and introduce evidence supporting their own position, all relevant facts should emerge. It is assumed within the adversarial model that, in order that truth be known, a combative process is more effective than a co-operative one. Furthermore, within our adversarial system of justice, the process of discovering the truth is more important than the truth itself. Consequently, our adversarial system places emphasis on the "rules of the game" and the "rights of the accused."

One of the "rules of the game" is often referred to as "due process of law." Not only is the offender who is caught entitled to a legal defence, but in order for a conviction to be registered, prosecutors are required to prove all the material elements of the crime beyond a reasonable doubt, while at the same time complying with rights accorded the defendant. Prosecutors must prove enough facts to convince jurors that the defendant is guilty. Often this is referred to in criminal cases as the state's burden of proof. This rule is based on the firmly entrenched principle of common law often called the presumption of innocence, in which the criminal defendant is assumed to be innocent until proven guilty. Consequently, the adversarial process is structured in such a way as to provide the accused with a skilled lawyer who will maintain the presumption of innocence until all legal avenues have been exhausted and all appeals have been lost.

It has long been recognized that it would be repugnant in principle to empower police as agents of the state to compel statements or answers from persons suspected of committing crimes. Such an authority would constitute a power to compel incriminating admissions or confessions of guilt. The absence of any obligation to answer questions (notwithstanding s. 5(1) of the *Canada Evidence Act*) is described positively as the right to remain silent. Consequently, the authority to ask questions (by agents of the state) is balanced by the freedom to keep quiet (suspect or accused). The police, as well as the prosecution, cannot expect a suspect or an accused to assist in the preparation and proof of the case against him or her. In our adversarial system of law this principle is as fundamental as the presumption of innocence. To balance the interests of the police to investigate crime with that of the accused or suspect to remain silent, common law courts developed rules of evidence to govern the admissibility of extra-judicial statements. Herein lies the important principle of voluntariness as a rule of evidence. According to this principle, no statement by an accused is admissible in evidence against him unless it is has been demonstrated by the prosecution to have been a voluntary statement.

In general, the adversarial process ensures that a number of safeguards are built into our criminal justice system in order to reveal the truth: (a) it provides a vehicle for examining the evidence; (b) it distributes power among various actors via a system of checks and balances; and (c) it provides for the rights of the accused by delegating that responsibility to a defence lawyer.

In general, most Canadians are unfamiliar with Canadian criminal procedure or are unaware of what happens to a person when he or she is charged with a criminal offence. A person who has violated and been accused of an offence against the *Criminal Code* may be either summoned or arrested with or without a warrant. For a summons or an arrest with a warrant the complainant would first have gone before a justice of the peace to initiate proceedings; an arrest without a warrant requires no judicial authorization.

Within our adversarial system one may logically assume that responsibility for charging people who have violated the *Criminal Code* rests solely with the Crown. However, as in early English common law, tradition recognizes the duty of a citizen to bring offenders to justice, and consequently, under the *Criminal Code* "any one who, on reasonable and probable grounds, believes that a person committed" an offence may lay an information before a justice. The laying of an information before a justice of the peace is a vital step in the criminal justice process in that it effectively sets the machinery of the court system into operation. An information is simply a written allegation, made upon oath, that an individual has committed an offence. Although in practice the majority of cases involving the laying of an information are carried out by official representatives—namely, the police—the role of the private individual in the charging process is still recognized in Canadian law.

Just as the justices of the peace played an important role in the administration of early English courts, so did they continue to perform a vital function within the early system of Canadian criminal justice. It was before a justice of the peace that an information was laid detailing the nature of the offence committed by an individual. The responsibility for deciding whether or not to issue an arrest or search warrant, to confirm an appearance notice issued by a peace officer, or to compel the accused, by means of a summons, to appear for trial, rested with the justice of the peace. Also invested in his office was the responsibility for decisions surrounding, in some cases, the granting of bail. Their role should not be confused with that of provincial court judges (formerly called magistrates) whose statutory authority allowed them to try all but the most serious offences under the *Criminal Code* and other criminal legislation.

Traditionally, the powers of the police in Canada have always been extremely broad when compared, for example, with those granted to law enforcement officers within the United States. Police authority to make an arrest derives from legislation, with the most significant source of power being the Canadian *Criminal Code*. Specific powers of arrest may also be granted to police under other statutes, such as the provincial *Highway Traffic* and *Liquor Acts*. With the enactment of the *Bail Reform Act* in 1971, restraints as contained in the *Criminal Code* were placed on police detention of individuals in that only where the public interest would best be served or the accused's appearance in court guaranteed could the police officer's power be exercised.

In addition, more recent legislative initiatives in our new Canadian Constitution serve to highlight profound changes that have influenced police authority and procedure. The Constitution of Canada is, of course, the supreme law of Canada and any law that is inconsistent with the provisions of the Constitution is, to the extent of the inconsistency, of no force or effect. The inclusion in 1982 of the *Canadian Charter of Rights and Freedoms*, a far more sweeping document than is the United States Bill of Rights, has given the courts and legal profession an opportunity to open up to legal challenge a plethora of issues involving legislated police powers. The *Charter* may be used to challenge the legislation and exercise of police investigative and arresting powers, particularly those involving search and seizure, fingerprinting, informing individuals of the reasons for their arrest, and allowing retention and instruction by counsel. To illustrate, until the proclamation of the *Canadian Charter of Rights and Freedoms*, the police in Canada had not been obliged to issue a warning of any kind to persons whom they wished to question, although most police forces had done so as a matter of practice for many years. Sections 10 and 11 of the *Charter* require the police to inform persons who are arrested, detained or charged with an offence, of certain constitutional rights. With the introduction of the *Charter*, there is greater emphasis being placed upon "due process" values, whereby the likelihood now exists of setting appropriate limits on police powers over the individual citizen. No doubt the exercise of police powers will come more frequently under scrutiny by the courts in the process of protecting the rights of the individual.

Under the *British North America Act*, power to create courts was vested in the Parliament of Canada and the administration of the courts was left to the provincial legislatures. Accordingly, the federal Parliament has created three courts under its authority, undoubtedly the most important being the Supreme Court of Canada, established in 1875. The other courts created by federal Parliament are the Federal Courts of Canada and the Tax Court of Canada which deal with matters relating to the better administration of the laws of Canada (federal laws). At the provincial level, the traditional practice has been to provide for either two or three levels of trial courts and a supervising body in the form of a court of appeal. All provinces have a provincial court, with provincially-appointed judges. In addition, all provinces have a court of general jurisdiction, sometimes referred to as a supreme, a superior or a high court. In addition, each province also provides for a court of appeal to hear appeals from one or more of these trial courts. Usually a case is heard at trial by one level of trial court and appealed to the Supreme Court or the court of appeal.

The labyrinthine nature of the formal structure of the criminal court process may be confusing to many people. The proper court for a criminal trial, however, depends on the offence for which the accused person has been charged. If a person is charged with an offence punishable upon summary conviction, the trial will be held in provincial court and presided over by a provincial court judge. A provincial court also has the power to hear cases involving violations of provincial statutes and municipal by-laws. This ultimately means that while the federal Parliament created the *Criminal Code*, a great deal of penal law is to be found in provincial statutes and municipal by-laws. In fact, a very small proportion of convictions for contravention of penal statutes is concerned with indictable and summary offences under national legislation. Offences consist mainly of violations of municipal by-laws and provincial statutes. Combined with the fact that many indictable offences can be tried only by a provincial court judge in provincial court, it becomes readily apparent that the bulk of criminal cases flowing into the court system are ultimately disposed of within the provincial court. Although the criminal trial is often seen as involving a judge and jury, the reality is that only a very small proportion of accused persons proceed to jury trial in a higher court.

Most indictable offences may be tried in one of three ways: by judge and jury, by judge without jury (Supreme Court judge), or superior court judges or by provincial court judge. Certain indictable offences, two of which are treason and murder, must be tried only by a superior court judge with a jury; others may only be heard by a provincial court judge alone (*Criminal Code*, s. 553); while the residual group of indictable offences may, at the option of the accused, be tried in any of the three ways. Most people, when envisaging our court process, think of a trial by jury, with prosecution and defence attorneys assuming adversarial roles in a battle for justice. A further examination of the actual occurrences of jury trials may be surprising in that few criminal cases follow this adversarial pattern. In fact, the majority of trials in Canada in any given year are conducted before a judge who acts as trier of both fact and law.

Trials, especially by jury, have important functions for the court inasmuch as they maintain the legitimacy of the criminal justice process. They are public events, allowing outside scrutiny of what the public believes to be the major decision-making point in the system. They also reaffirm the principle underlying our adversary system—that defendants are presumed to be innocent until proven guilty. The presumption of innocence at the pretrial stage of the criminal process is not all that apparent. For example, a peace officer who arrests a defendant does not presume his or her innocence, nor does the justice of the peace who issues a warrant of summons for compelling the defendant's attendance in court.

Jury trials also allow members of the community to participate as jurors. Ordinary citizens serving as jurors validate the system of justice, uphold current laws and reaffirm legal precedent by their compliance with court instructions to render a verdict based on the facts as presented, rather than on the correctness of the law at issue. Many of these functions associated with trials, with or without juries, are symbolic in nature but serve to reaffirm the basic principles of our criminal justice system.

However, with respect to jury trials, people in general know very little about the role of juries, their selection and the problems they encounter. The task facing juries is to render a "correct" verdict based upon facts as presented and applied to the law as stated in the judge's instructions to the jury. For that reason the jury is often called the "trier of fact." On the other hand, the judge decides all questions of law. At best, the task facing a jury is a difficult one. Laypeople serving on juries may have problems in understanding the facts within a legal context, the judicial instructions, or the knowledge arising out of conflicting testimony of various professional or expert witnesses. Moreover, jurors are subject to the influence of such non-legal factors as irrelevant testimony, empathy for the victim or offender, and behaviour of prosecutors and defence attorneys.

To some people, the jury trial may even represent a game of deception in which participants are coached and appearances managed. This harms the integrity of the trial process and undermines both our sense of justice and our justice system. Added to these concerns is the inevitable question of whether verdicts in jury trials are based more on the composition of the jury itself than on the strength and weakness of the evidence before the courts. Jury selection and the procedures surrounding it may be important in rendering a fair and impartial verdict, yet most people are unaware of the selection procedures themselves.

The criminal trial is the institution through which persons accused of wrongdoing are either brought to account or exonerated. Its procedure, as we have seen, is adversarial, structured as a dispute between society and the accused and arbitrated by an impartial judge. The presence and participation of the accused is essential, for he or she is an active party, answering the charge, engaging and dismissing counsel and suffering the consequences if convicted. Often, newspapers will report accounts of trials where people admit that they committed the act, but are subsequently found not guilty of the crime. This may occur because the prosecutor has not proven that their behaviour falls within the legal definition of a crime. To fulfill the legal definition, all elements of the crime must be proven.

There are two basic elements which must be present at the same time for an act to be considered criminal. The first element is the *actus reus* (guilty act) which is the criminal act itself. The second element, the *mens rea* (guilty mind), refers to the state of mind of an individual at the time the act is done or, more specifically, the person's intent to commit the crime. Regarding the latter concept of criminal responsibility or mental intent, this doctrine says that we do not qualify as law-breakers without some intention, knowledge, recklessness or negligence. Provided we do not knowingly commit the act the law forbids, the law will, in essence, stay away from us. Without a doctrine of *mens rea* the law could intervene whenever we did the act proscribed, whether we were unaware or aware that the act was prohibited. Dropping the requirements of *mens rea* in defining an act as a crime would therefore widen the ambit of the criminal law, extend the scope of its intervention, and restrict our liberty. Where crimes created by statute do not require *mens rea*, they are often referred to as strict-liability crimes. In actual practice, many offences—especially regulatory offences (i.e., the *Food and Drugs Act*)—are of this type, whereby one can be guilty without intention, knowledge or even carelessness. However, before a violation of the criminal law can be considered a criminal act, the person acting in violation of the law must have had in mind the intention to carry out the behaviour.

If a person whose mental state is affected commits a criminal act, it is possible for the person to defend his or her illegal actions. The individual is said to have a legally acceptable justification, defence, or excuse in that the intent required, if he or she is to be held criminally responsible for his or her actions, is lacking. Among the excuse-type defences are mental disorder, intoxication, necessity, and duress. Another type of defence is that of justification, whereby an individual commits the act, but maintains the act was justified as in the case of self-defence. Of all the defences, insanity is probably the most controversial. If such claims are accepted by a judge or jury, then the accused person cannot be held responsible for violating the law, and will usually be found "not guilty".

However, from conviction flows punishment and sentencing, the final stage of the criminal process. Judges have enormous discretionary power in relation to the dispositions which they may choose, since the *Criminal Code* is characterized by high maximum penalties and few criteria to guide them in sentencing. Sentencing refers to that process in which the court or officials, having inquired into the alleged offence, give a reasoned statement, making clear what values are at stake and what is involved in the offence. The disposition, on the other hand, refers to the actual penalty or sanction imposed in sentencing. Punishment, retribution, rehabilitation, treatment, deterrence, restitution, or incapacitation have all been used at one time or another as justifications for imposing a criminal sanction. With maximum penalties provided in legislation, it is left entirely to the courts to decide, within limits, what sanctions or penalties should be imposed and, more important, for what reasons. Indictable offences, for example, carry maximum sentences of imprisonment ranging from two years to life imprisonment. On the other hand, summary conviction offences carry a maximum sentence of imprisonment for a period of six months unless otherwise stated, a fine of up to $2,000, or both. The punishments authorized under the criminal law and available to judges include a wide range of types of sentences, from discharges to imprisonment.

The courts, as a result of our common law heritage and the developments in case law precedents, are given a great deal of guidance in determining the guilt or innocence of an accused, but, insofar as sentencing is concerned, lack a clearly articulated sentencing policy. This situation makes judicial sentencing a very lonely and onerous task and will inevitably result in inconsistency among courts in the application of sentencing principles and in the levying of penalties.

Like death and taxes, most citizens take law for granted. We are also inclined to think that, like death and taxes, law is an inevitable feature of human life. For that matter, when we think of our daily lives, it would be difficult to conceive of any situation in which a set of rules does not operate. Whether attending a school or driving a car we are confronted by rules. We may at times be ignorant of the rules, but the rules are there nevertheless. But of all the sets of rules imposing order on our lives, few are as essential as the *Criminal Code*. The *Criminal Code* represents the model of behaviour deemed necessary for the continued existence of society.

Whether or not we agree with the prescriptions of criminal law, it is clear that no member of society can escape the law's effects. Few people are aware of the nature of criminal law, of criminal procedure, or of the criminal process itself. Others are cynical and contemptuous of its principles and functioning. However, each of us should be more familiar with criminal law and the processes surrounding it, if only because it involves society's most destructive and intrusive form of intervention against the individual. *From Crime to Punishment* is an examination of society's ultimate weapon to protect itself and its citizens from possible harm.

2

A Brief History of Canadian Criminal Law

The Honourable Graham J. Steele*

INTRODUCTION

History has a central place in Canadian law. The major reason for the centrality of history is that the common law, which consists of principles that can be deduced from prior court decisions, puts a great deal of weight on *precedent*.[1] That is why every lawyer and judge has available, either in his or her office or in the local law library, volumes and volumes of old judgments, some going back as far as the 14th century. These law books are also history books—they recount cases of centuries of thieves and traitors, fools and heroes, greed, anger and revenge—and they turn everyone who uses them into an historian.

History also matters because the historical background of a statute enacted by Parliament can offer important clues about how it should be applied in a particular case. This reason takes on special importance in Canadian criminal law, because, since 1892, almost all of our criminal law and procedure has been gathered together in one comprehensive statute—the *Criminal Code of Canada*.

The history of Canadian criminal law, or at least that part of it that is specifically Canadian, is not a story of battle or bloody revolution, but more a story of quiet hard work and perseverance. Even if that kind of history does not interest you, remember that the history of our criminal law also includes the cruel severity of early English penal law, and that the entire history of our criminal law reverberates in every decision made by a criminal court judge today.

If we are ever tempted to take for granted any part of our criminal law and procedure, the cure for complacency is to look to the roots of our criminal law in England. The most basic principles, such as the

* B.A., University of Manitoba, Winnipeg, Manitoba; B.A., University of Oxford, Oxford, England; LL.B., Dalhousie Law School, Halifax, Nova Scotia; Member of the Nova Scotia Barristers' Society; presently sits as a member of the Provincial Legislature and is presently Minister of Finance for the Province of Nova Scotia.

right to be tried by a jury of one's peers, the right of the accused to mount a defence, and the right to humane punishment, have all been forged by slow degrees over many centuries and in the wake of cruel injustice.

"CRIMINAL" LAW: SCOPE, PURPOSE, CONTEXT

Every civilized society must have a set of conduct-guiding rules, or else it hardly merits the adjective "civilized". In a memorable phrase, the English philosopher Thomas Hobbes described life without such rules as having:

> No arts; no letters; no society; and which is worst of all, continual fear and danger of violent death; and the life of man, solitary, poor, nasty, brutish, and short.[2]

But not every social rule is "criminal" in nature. In order to write a history of "criminal" law, then, it is necessary first to draw a line between the social rules which are "criminal" and those which are not.

The plain fact is that a line between the criminal and the non-criminal is impossible to draw firmly. Any line-drawing has more to do with the semantics of our language, and artificial legal categorization, than the inherent nature of the rule. For example, the early history of English law shows that punishment for breach of the social rules that we would characterize today as "criminal" (do not kill, do not steal, etc.), were enforced privately, like a debt owed by one clan to another, and so are missing the public element that today we consider essential to true "criminal" law. To give another example, there is presently a multitude of federal and provincial regulatory offences for the breach of which fines and even imprisonment can be imposed, but we do not generally include these offences under the rubric of "criminal" law. A final example might be the laws against procuring a miscarriage, otherwise known as abortion. The debate about whether these laws are, or should be, "criminal" is truly endless, because a conclusive answer would require a conclusive line between criminal and non-criminal conduct. Such a line does not exist.

The reader is therefore warned that this "history" is really only a history of criminal law as that term is presently understood in late 20th century Canada.[3]

Besides a recognition of the artificial boundaries of "criminal" law, a proper grasp of criminal law history also requires some notion of the *purpose* of criminal law. On the simplest level, the purpose of criminal law throughout history has been to deter and punish anti-social acts. There are, however, deeper purposes at work. The French writer Anatole France made ironic reference to some of these deeper purposes of criminal law when he wrote of:

> The majestic egalitarianism of the law, which forbids rich and poor alike to sleep under bridges, to beg in the streets, and to steal bread.[4]

Criminal law history becomes much more than a bare recitation of facts and dates when we consider who, in each society, was empowered to define "criminal" acts, set punishments, and direct the investigative and enforcement branches of government. Knowing more about who wielded political and judicial power may offer important clues about the purposes at various times of, for example, the laws against theft, or vagrancy, or prostitution.[5]

It is evident, then, the history of criminal law cannot be understood outside the broader historical *context*. It is easy to marvel at or mock the laws and procedures that were applied in past centuries, some of which will be mentioned later. Some cannot be excused—by any standard, they were barbarous and cruel. At the same time, the apparent severity of other times must be understood in the context of those times, when, for example, there was no organized police force and the government was not as stable as it is today.

THE CRIMINAL LAW OF ENGLAND[6]

"Crime" was, in the times before the Norman Conquest in 1066, a matter of private vengeance between the injured person or his clan, and the wrongdoer or *his* clan. The main deterrent to crime was, therefore, the fear of private war, which could degenerate into blood feud and virtual anarchy. The first criminal laws were those by which the king attempted to regulate these private wars in the interests of public peace, later generally proclaimed as "the King's Peace".

Generally speaking, by the time of the Conquest most first offences were punishable by an elaborate system of fines. *Were* was a price set upon a person according to his rank; for example, a slave's life was deemed to be worth less than that of a free man. *Bot* was the compensation paid to a person injured by a crime. It might be either a fixed or market rate, and in the case of murder would be the same as the *were*. *Wite* was a fine paid to the king or other lord in respect of an offence. Second offences, and some first offences, were "*bot*-less", meaning they could not be satisfied by a fine, and were generally punishable by death, mutilation, or flogging. In still further cases, notably adultery and theft, the injured husband or property owner had a right of summary execution—*infangthief*— if he caught the wrongdoer in the act.

The central concern of the Anglo-Saxon system, then, was compensation to the victim. This concern sometimes went to absurd lengths, as when a law of Alfred provided that the *bot* for loss of a toe was, in order from the big toe to the little toe, 20, 15, 9, 6 and 5 shillings. The concern for compensation also meant that moral culpability was a secondary concern. For example, if a man accidentally impaled himself on a spear being carried over another's shoulder, the spear-carrier was still subject to payment of the *were*, though he was forgiven the *wite*.

A further refinement of the fine system was the Conquest-era requirement that men form themselves into groups of 10, called "frank-pledges". Each member of the group was responsible for the actions of the rest, and could be called upon to produce an accused, and to pay any fines.

Supervision of the system of fines and frank-pledges fell to the local courts, which were really more in the nature of a municipal council. These courts corresponded to the units of local government, which were the shire or county (headed by the "shire-reeve" or sheriff), the "hundred" (a group of townships headed by the bailiff), and the "tithing" (a single parish or township headed by a reeve assisted by four others). The chief officers of each unit were responsible for the administration of justice, and were, in effect, the first police officers. It was their duty to arrest criminals, to recover stolen property, and, where a culprit was not immediately found, to "raise the hue and cry", which was a call to the citizenry to assist in the apprehension of a criminal.

The officers of the local administration were the "judges" of the courts. Thus, the hundred court consisted of the parish priest, the reeve and the reeve's four assistants. The county court consisted of each member of the hundred courts, together with all lords and public officers of the county. Since the result would be an unwieldy number of judges, it appears that from early days the county court chose a representative body of 12 to sit as a judicial committee. For criminal cases the county court was known as the sheriff's *tourn*, or circuit, and it had jurisdiction over each hundred in which it appeared. The King's Court could, but rarely did, choose to hear a case itself.

"Hearing" a criminal case was, however, a most peculiar procedure. If any man were accused of a crime, and denied that he committed it, the only question at trial was his character. Strange as it seems, the facts of the alleged crime appear not to have mattered. Proof of character was sworn to in general terms by witnesses, usually the members of his frank-pledge. The success of the oath depended on having the right number and quality of witnesses in one's favour. If the right number could not be found, or would not swear, or swore the accused was of bad character, he was made to undergo trial by ordeal. The most common ordeals were handling a piece of red-hot iron, or plunging an arm into boiling water.

The point of trial by ordeal was that, if the accused were innocent, God would surely demonstrate that fact by working a miracle. If the wound did not heal cleanly, the accused was deemed to be guilty. Depending on the offence and whether it was his first or second conviction, he paid the applicable fine, or was killed or mutilated.

This, then, was the general state of the law in the Anglo-Saxon and early post-Conquest eras. A great deal of weight was placed on the mere fact of sworn accusation (a state of affairs that did not change for centuries), and guilt or innocence was decided by oaths to the accused person's character, and by the justice of God.

Trial by ordeal apparently fell into disuse by the 13th century, and in its place arose a method of procedure known as trial by jury. There were two kinds of jury: the "grand" and the "petit" (pronounced "petty").

The "grand" jury was the body responsible for making accusations when the King's Court arrived on circuit. After the Conquest, the King's Court exercised its supervisory jurisdiction much more frequently, and its various branches eventually superseded the local courts for all serious crimes. The old county court took on a modified form, in which the sheriff called just enough qualified men to form the grand jury.[7]

By degrees, and presumably in reverse proportion to the use of trial by ordeal, the determination of questions of fact by a "petit" jury (which corresponds to the modern jury) came into general use in criminal cases. The procedure was borrowed from the "inquest", which had been used since pre-Conquest times for the determination of certain questions of fact in civil cases, such as ownership of land. The first petit juries were composed of witnesses who were acquainted with the facts in issue, and could even include members of the grand jury that made the accusation. The transition from a jury composed of witnesses to an impartial jury that judged the evidence of others cannot be traced with any exactness, but it certainly had taken place by the middle of the 15th century.

Trial by jury gave English criminal trials their characteristic form, but the system was many centuries away from producing anything that we would call "justice". A prisoner was faced with a number of obstacles, both procedural and substantive.[8] The tumultuous period surrounding the English civil war saw a large number of major trials in the period 1640-1678, as first one side and then the other tried its opponents for treason. Out of this tumult, or perhaps in response to the gross injustice of some of the trials, the rights which we now recognize as fundamental to a fair trial were developed.

In the century leading up to the English civil war the prisoner was generally kept in isolation until his or her trial, and had no notice beforehand of the charge or evidence against him or her. It was not until 1695 that prisoners were permitted to receive a copy of the formal accusation before the trial, and even then it applied only to cases of treason. Thirteen years later, in 1708, the prisoner was permitted to receive a copy of the list of jurors, and the list of witnesses who would be called against him or her. Stephen says this legislation was perceived at the time to be extraordinarily liberal, but suggests the legislators may have recognized that treason was a crime for which they, or their friends or connections, might be tried. It was not until 1836 that all prisoners won the right to inspect sworn statements taken against them.

Prior to the civil war the prisoner was not allowed to call evidence on his or her behalf. The judges reasoned that if the sworn evidence given against the accused were sufficient to support a conviction, the accused would only be lying if given the opportunity to contradict the evidence. This peculiar rule appears to have been given up by 1660, at least in cases of treason. Witnesses for the accused could not be sworn until 1702, and even then the rule applied only to trials for treason.

The next impediment was the lack of a right to counsel. Originally an accused had no right to counsel at all. The rule was gradually relaxed, until by the mid-18th century it seems to have been accepted, though not universally, that counsel could do everything on the prisoner's behalf except address the jury. It was not until 1837 that an accused was entitled to a full defence by counsel.

The accused also laboured under a lack of evidentiary rules, which meant that evidence of the flimsiest kind could come before the court and form the basis for a conviction. Stephen offers, as a prime example of the injustice wrought by the lack of evidentiary rules, the 1665 "Suffolk witches" case. Two women were put on trial for bewitching several children. The "evidence" was that the accused had arguments with the children's parents, and the children afterward had fits and declared that the accused were tormenting them, and that they saw the accused in apparitions. On such flimsy evidence, and the most foolish conjecture of other witnesses, the women were convicted, and hanged.

Finally, the best system of criminal justice in the world is of no avail unless its officers are honest; and the individuals who staffed the early English criminal justice system seem to have been rather prone to corruption. Juries were notoriously corrupt, being very much subject to the demands of the leading landowners, as well as political and religious prejudice. It did not help matters that the process of "attaint", which was the only means by which a corrupt jury could be punished or its verdict impeached, was itself subject to trial by jury. Juries could be fined for a "bad" verdict, a practice which did not end until 1670. Since the prisoner had only limited means of testing the evidence of his or her accusers, and cross-examination was reserved for the judges, there was no reliable method for detecting perjury. The courts of 17th-century England were not ennobled by the black perjury on which they sometimes relied.[9]

I will allow Stephen, on whom I have so much relied, to sum up the English criminal justice system of the civil war period in his own words:

> The impression made upon my mind by these trials is, that when neither political nor religious passions or prejudices were excited, when the matters at issue were very plain and simple, when the facts were all within the prisoner's knowledge, and when he was not kept in close confinement before his trial, and was able to consult counsel, and to procure witnesses if he had any, trials were simple, fair, and substantially just, though little or no protection against perjury was afforded; but when any of these conditions was not fulfilled, the prisoner was at a great disadvantage.[10]

He adds elsewhere that the gross injustice apparent at some of the treason trials, where the defendants (and judges) were men of education and means, can only mean that "a great amount of obscure injustice and misery" must have been produced in the courts for common criminals.

There can be no question about the cruel severity of early English penal law, nor that gross injustices occurred merely because of a lack of basic procedural and evidentiary rules. Nevertheless, there were certain mechanisms by which the severity of the law was mitigated, albeit in a generally crude and capricious way.

The early legislators were not oblivious to the defects of the system, particularly the grosser forms of corruption. The Court of Star Chamber, which corresponds roughly to the modern Cabinet, assumed from the earliest days a criminal jurisdiction, commonly including cases of forgery, perjury, riot, conspiracy and fraud. This court was able to exercise a salutary control over landowners who interfered with the workings of the common law courts.

In later times, however, the Court of Star Chamber was itself corrupted and became an intensely political court. This latter part of its history has made its name a watchword for cruel abuse of judicial power. Most notoriously, it required prisoners to give evidence against themselves. When John Lilburn refused to do so just before the civil war, he was whipped more than 500 times and made to stand in the pillory for two hours immediately thereafter.[11] Largely in response to such abuses, the Court of Star Chamber was abolished in 1640.[12]

The law was also tempered, probably unconsciously and certainly irrationally, by an excessive technicality. For example, there was a strict reliance on rules relating to the drafting of documents. A prisoner could be acquitted if the accusations and proof were not exactly right. Stephen cites a case from 1790, in which a man who had stabbed a woman was accused of "maliciously assaulting her with intent to cut her clothes", which at the time was punishable by death. The accusation stated that the accused had assaulted the victim with intent to cut her clothes, and that he did cut her clothes. An objection was made that the indictment did not state that the accused cut the victim's clothes *then and there*. Looking strictly at the words of the accusation, it was possible that he cut the clothes some time later. On that basis the charge was held invalid, and the accused was acquitted.

Another example of the strange mercy of the law was the doctrine known as "benefit of clergy" or simply "clergy", which over centuries developed into a general doctrine of the "second chance". The histories of capital crimes (*i.e.*, crimes punishable by death) and benefit of clergy really go hand in hand. At least in theory, until 1826 all felonies except petty larceny and mayhem were punishable by death. The law needed to develop a mechanism for softening the harshness of the law, and "clergy" was the answer.

"Benefit of clergy" began as a demand by the Church that any clergyman accused of a crime be tried in the ecclesiastical courts, where punishment, if any, was light. A 1350 statute extended the privilege to all clerks, being everyone in any way connected with the Church, including doorkeepers and exorcists. This statute was eventually interpreted to extend benefit of clergy to every man who could read.[13] By the reign of Henry VI it was settled that clergy could be claimed only after conviction.

In 1487, a law was passed that a murderer who pleaded his clergy was to be branded on the thumb with an M, and a thief with a T, and that no-one except true clergy could plead clergy more than once. Strange but true, until 1487 an educated man could commit a felony as often as he pleased, with no greater risk than of being delivered to the ecclesiastical court. Even after that date, and before transportation was instituted in 1717, he could commit murder or theft once with no greater punishment than being branded on the hand. The availablity of clergy dramatically reduced the number of death sentences that were actually carried out; yet clergy notwithstanding, it has been estimated that some 800 convicts were hanged in England in 1598.[14]

Throughout the 17th and 18th centuries more and more offences were declared by the courts or by statute to be "unclergyable". The severity of the law increased accordingly, although it became common for a pardon to be granted conditional on transportation to the colonies, first America and then Australia. Benefit of clergy was finally abolished entirely in 1827. It is no coincidence that the statute abolishing clergy put restrictions on cases in which the death penalty could be imposed, and the number of capital crimes decreased substantially in the following years.

Stephen concludes his account of the history of criminal law by saying that all the essential elements of the criminal law of his day (1880) were in place by 1760. And so 1760, or thereabouts, is a convenient place to turn to the early development of criminal law in the colonies that would become Canada.

THE EARLY HISTORY OF CANADIAN CRIMINAL LAW[15]

By the late 18th century, the penal law of England was "cruel, capricious, and obscure".[16] Unfortunately, it was precisely in this period that Britain was settling its North American colonies in earnest, and the courts had decreed that colonists took the law of England with them.

All the colonies faced a difficult question: What exactly was the law they had brought? Certainly English common law was accepted as authoritative, adapted of course to the conditions of the colonies. At least in Nova Scotia, the law of the New England states was thought to be helpful. The question became more difficult when it came to statute law. The rule was that the statute law of England as of the date of discovery became the law of the colony, unless a later law was: (a) introduced by charter or commission from the Crown, (b) expressly adopted by the Assembly, or (c) declared to be law by the courts.

If that sounds complicated, it was. One consequence of the rules was that each of the colonies in British North America had a different "reception date" for English law. For Nova Scotia it was 1497, the year Cabot claimed Acadia.[17] The reception date was never settled in New Brunswick. In 1800 the legislature of Upper Canada decreed the reception date to be 1792. British Columbia adopted the law as of 1858. Lower Canada was a special case, since it was the only colony acquired by conquest confirmed by treaty. The reception date was therefore fixed at 1763, the date of the Royal Proclamation. The criminal law that had been developed under French rule was abolished as of that date and replaced by English law, which, as we know, was then savagely repressive.

Of course the colonists were not foolish enough to import holus-bolus the law of the mother country. English law regulating the shooting of game or cutting trees, for example, was not particularly suited to colonial conditions. Perhaps the following comment, made in relation to the first American settlers, could apply equally to the colonists at Chebucto Bay in 1749:

> That a hundred settlers huddled on an island near what is now the city of Newport, or freezing in the Plymouth winter, should have reproduced this [English court] system exactly, would have been both miraculous and insane.[18]

The early settlers took a liberal attitude to precedent and, at least in Nova Scotia, freely adapted the examples set by the New England colonies. In this way they were able to develop a system of law that was suitable to colonial conditions while respecting the common law.

The confusion engendered by these rules had a number of practical consequences, and ultimately may have been the decisive spur to codification in 1892. For example, Nova Scotia inherited the statute law of 1497, which was relatively benign in terms of capital crimes. Lower Canada, in contrast, inherited the hundreds of capital crimes of 1763. The harshness of Lower Canadian law was brought into sharp relief when Upper and Lower Canada were unified in 1841. The law of Upper Canada at the time was mostly "home-made", and was relatively liberal—it included only 11 crimes punishable by death. Since the Act of Union provided that the law of each province was to continue in force until changed by the new Assembly, the Assembly had to move quickly to ensure that two widely different standards of justice did not co-exist in the same jurisdiction.

Doubtless a similar desire animated the Fathers of Confederation as they negotiated the division of powers in the years leading up to 1867. Section 91(27) of the *Constitution Act, 1867* granted exclusive jurisdiction to the Parliament of Canada over all matters coming within the subject of "the Criminal Law, except the Constitution of Courts of Criminal Jurisdiction, but including the Procedure in Criminal Matters."

The first post-Confederation Parliament moved quickly to use its new power. One hundred and ten criminal enactments of the colonies were repealed, and 19 Dominion-wide statutes were enacted. The provincial legislatures no longer had power to enact new criminal law, but any criminal laws not repealed or overridden by federal law remained in force. Provincial criminal offences were not finally abolished until 1955.

THE CRIMINAL CODE OF 1892

Of all the sins of early English criminal law, perhaps the greatest was its obscurity. It was difficult to know which statutes were in force and which were not, which statutes would be enforced and which would not, and, in many situations, what exactly was forbidden. One of the principal reasons for the obscurity was the fact that statutes were not officially published. It was virtually impossible for lawyers, and Parliament itself, to know what had been enacted. The common law too was a barrier to clarity in the law, because it was composed of layers of judicial decisions which were difficult to systematize, and if they were systematized it was in textbooks available only to lawyers.

Criminal law reform can be traced to a simple event: the publication between 1811 and 1824 of all English statute law. As a result of the publication of the laws, it was possible as early as 1826 to consolidate into one statute the law of larceny, which was at the time a maze of old laws including 20 separate statutes relating to theft of or wilful damage to trees. By 1830 over half of criminal law had been consolidated into topical statutes.

In 1833, the Lord Chancellor, Henry Brougham, commissioned a few eminent jurists to inquire into the possibility of consolidating the entire criminal law into a single statute. This work progressed steadily, though slowly, and resulted in the presentation to Parliament of a draft code of indictable offences (1843) and procedure (1845). These drafts, and revisions submitted in the next few years, foundered on the same objections that were heard throughout the next four decades in England and in Canada: principally, that Parliament had been insufficiently involved in the drafting, and especially that the wisdom of the common law would be lost if it were codified or modified by statute. The project of codification stalled until, in August 1877, it fell into the hands of Sir James FitzJames Stephen.

By the time he was commissioned to draft a criminal code, Stephen had already devoted an enormous amount of work to the criminal law and was a prodigious writer. He had written a substantial amount of the criminal law of India as well as a comprehensive *Digest of the Criminal Law,* and he later wrote a lengthy history of English criminal law. He set to work with vigour, and, using his *Digest* as a guide, completed a draft code by October. The result was a model of clarity.

Unfortunately, neither Stephen nor the sponsor of the bill, Attorney General Sir John Holker, devoted as much attention to the politics of passing the bill as they did to its substance. Members of Parliament were indignant that the draft code proposed to do away with the common law, suspicious about changes such as deletion of the term "felony" in favour of the undefined "indictable offence", and wary of unmentioned amendments that might be hidden in the massive bulk of the draft code.

The bill was eventually withdrawn and submitted to a Royal Commission, of which Stephen was a member. After six months of sittings, ending in April 1879, the Commission made a number of amendments and submitted a new draft code. Not long after debate on the new code began—during which the Opposition raised the same objections as before, but more strongly—Parliament was dissolved, the Disraeli government lost the election, and the code disappeared forever from the British political agenda.

The failure of codification in England was just the beginning in Canada. Confederation had enlarged the need for a comprehensive national criminal law, and by the late 1880s a proposal for codification had been brought to the attention of the Attorney General, and future Prime Minister, Sir John Thompson. Thompson liked the idea, and discussed the matter extensively with George Burbidge of New Brunswick, an advisor and recently-appointed judge of the Exchequer Court.

Burbidge had already drafted a digest of Canadian criminal law modelled on Stephen's English version, as well as a draft code in 1884, so the subject was well familiar to him. With the continuing encouragement of Thompson, Burbidge set about drafting a criminal code bill with the assistance of Robert Sedgewick, the deputy Minister of Justice, and Charles Masters, a reporter in the Supreme Court.

The draft code was introduced into Parliament in 1891, and a slightly modified version was re-introduced in 1892. The drafters had certainly benefitted from Stephen's scholarship and the various drafts submitted to the British Parliament, but their version was not just a slavish copy. Of the 530 substantive sections, 209 were taken from the English version and 321 were taken from Canadian models or were new. On the procedural side, only 81 of 475 sections were English.

Thompson, a shrewd Parliamentary tactician, was also able to benefit from the mistakes of Stephen and Holker in the British Parliament. For example, there was no mention in the bill of the abrogation of the common law, even though nearly the same result would be achieved in practice. Whether by accident or design, printing of the 300-page bill was held up so that members did not have a copy by the time of second reading. Thompson's speech on second reading was masterly, cloaking the new bill with the authority of the British legislation, downplaying the contribution of the Canadian drafters and disavowing any intention to do away with the common law.

The draft bill received some critical attention at the committee stage, where the bill was examined section by section. But Thompson took a non-confrontational stand, and dropped any section, such as the definition of sedition or the restricted role given to the grand jury, that seemed controversial.

It was in the Senate, where Thompson could not defend it, that the bill took its heaviest attack. Senator Scott, who alone among the Opposition appears to have made a detailed study of the bill, decried the substantial changes the bill would make to the law. He also recognized the important alterations the bill would make to the common law:

> [F]or the first time in our history [Parliament] is ... going to depart in so important a subject matter as the criminal law of the old country from the usages of England and Great Britain and Ireland—usages which have grown up from time immemorial. We have a great many writers on criminal law who have compiled and crystallized from time to time decisions of learned judges, and it is upon those decisions that the law largely depends. When this code is passed a large portion of the learning and experience of ages will be laid aside. Instead of looking to the text books for definitions of important crimes—homicide and murder—to the writings of learned judges who have laid down well defined principles gathered after much labour from the decisions of centuries, we shall have to take up our code and ascertain what is the interpretation of the language used in the statutes we are now about to consider.[19]

Senator Scott had been named as a member of the joint committee, and if he had made his objections known there the bill might never have been enacted at all. However, he failed to attend a single meeting. Perhaps that made his colleagues less supportive, or perhaps his objections came simply too late; in any event, the bill survived, received royal assent on July 9, 1892, and came into force on July 1, 1893, Canada's 26th birthday.

MODERN DEVELOPMENTS

Although enactment of the *Code* is of the first historical importance, the history of Canadian criminal law did not end in 1892. Changes in social thought and technological change have made necessary numerous changes to the code over the years, such as repeal of the punishment of whipping and inclusion of crimes like aeronautical piracy, driving while impaired, and money-laundering.

The *Code* was extensively revised and rationalized in 1953, and the revisions came into effect in 1955. A significant addition was s. 8, which expressly abolished all offences at common law, under a law of Britain, or under a law of a province in force before Confederation, all of which arguably still existed. The effect, of course, was to abolish all criminal offences except those specifically enumerated in the *Code*.[20]

There are at least two more recent developments that will, I believe, take a front rank in any future history of Canadian criminal law.

The first is the *Canadian Charter of Rights and Freedoms*, which came into force in 1982. Sections 7-14 of the *Charter* deal specifically with legal rights, and are directly applicable to the criminal justice system. Because of the status of the *Charter* as part of the supreme law of Canada, the *Charter* has had and will continue to have a profound effect on criminal law and procedure. The *Charter* will be discussed at length in a later chapter of this book.

A second major recent development is the institution of native justice systems. Readers will no doubt have remarked on the glaring omission of First Nations history in the foregoing account of "Canadian" criminal justice. However, that is no more than a reflection of the fact that our criminal law has historically ignored native justice concerns. A recent series of well-publicized miscarriages of justice has put native justice issues, including the creation of native criminal tribunals, on the political agenda. The possibility of incorporating traditional native justice into the wider criminal justice system poses a challenge to natives to reconstruct accurately their own history, since the legitimacy of the new tribunals may depend in part on the historical resonance the tribunals have for the participants.

We like to think of the history of criminal law, in my opinion mistakenly, as being a linear progression towards a more just system. Even if it were possible to define with exactness what we mean by "just" (which is doubtful), such a view disregards the broader context of our times. The modern system of Canadian criminal justice has been developed in the context of a stable government with unprecedented power. Such a context explains, for example, why so much emphasis is placed by us on the rights of the accused. It is not hard to imagine that in different circumstances, such as war or rebellion, or the ascendancy of some non-governmental power, we might well revert to many of the ancient practices that today we find distasteful.

Notes

1. In the civil law tradition of Quebec (which does not apply in criminal cases), the doctrine of binding precedent is rejected. "The decisions of the courts are determined by authority of reasons, not by reason of authority": J.-G. Castel, *The Civil Law System of the Province of Quebec* (Toronto: Butterworths, 1962) at 218. For more information on the common law, see H.P. Glen, "Common Law in Canada" (1995) 74 Can. Bar Rev. 261.

2. *Leviathan* (1651), pt. 1, c. 13.

3. What does "criminal" mean today? The offences set out in the *Criminal Code* appear to share certain common elements, but our courts have had a great deal of difficulty defining what they are. It is clear enough that a "criminal" law includes a prohibition, and a punishment if the prohibited act is committed, but that is obviously not enough. The third essential element has been vaguely defined as "a typically criminal public purpose": Peter Hogg, *Constitutional Law of Canada* (Toronto: Carswell, 1977) at 280, paraphrasing *Canadian Federation of Agriculture v. Quebec (Attorney General)*, [1951] A.C. 179 (P.C.), affirming (*sub nom. Reference re Validity of S. 5(a) of Dairy Industry Act (Canada), (Margarine Case)*) [1949] S.C.R. 1. The cases demonstrate that typically criminal public purposes include, but are not limited to, public peace, order, security, health, and morality.

4. *Le Lys Rouge* (1894) c. 7.

5. This point is amply illustrated in a recent volume of essays on Nova Scotia legal history: Philip Girard and Jim Phillips (eds.), *Essays in the History of Canadian Law: Volume III, Nova Scotia* (Toronto: Osgoode Society, 1990). Among the 10 essays, Clara Greco provides a fascinating collective portrait of the men (and only men) who staffed the superior courts from 1754-1900; Jim Phillips describes the use of vagrancy laws as a means of social control in the late Victorian era; and Jane Price describes the female criminal underclass of Halifax in the same era. The latter two argue persuasively that the vagrancy and prostitution laws simply criminalized poverty. See also F.M. Shaver, "The regulation of prostitution: avoiding the morality trap" [1994] Canadian Journal of Law and Society 123.

6. The principal source for the section "The Criminal Law of England" is Sir James FitzJames Stephen, *A History of the Criminal Law of England* (3 vols., 1883; republished by Burt Franklin, New York, 1964).

7. Grand juries remained an important part of the Canadian criminal justice system until the mid-19th century, and in a modified form until this century; and they still exist in some American states.

8. Early trial reports relate almost entirely to trials for sensational, political crimes

like treason, and so it is impossible to know exactly how the "common" criminal was treated (the earliest full non-treason trial report is from 1664). However, given the seriousness of treason, and the fact that those accused of it weregenerally well-educated and well-connected, it is probably safe to say that prisoners accused of treason were treated more liberally than the common criminal.

⁹ *Supra*, note 6, vol. 1 at 402. Sir James FitzJames Stephen puts it thus: "A perjurer in those days was in the position of a person armed with a deadly poison which he could administer with no considerable chance of detection".

¹⁰ *Ibid.*, vol. 1 at 381-382.

¹¹ The modern right against self-incrimination was born as a reaction to such excesses: see *R. v. Hebert*, 1990 CarswellYukon 4, 57 C.C.C. (3d) 1 (S.C.C.), in which the Supreme Court of Canada reviewed the history of the Court of Star Chamber.

¹² A direct descendant of the Court of Star Chamber is the Judicial Committee of the Privy Council, which until 1949 was the final court of appeal for Canada and is still the highest court for other former colonies such as New Zealand.

¹³ Clergy was not extended to women until 1692, and the requirement of reading was not abolished until 1705. The reasoning behind the exclusion of women was that since they could not be ordained, they should not be allowed to plead clergy. It seems not to have occurred to lawmakers that the whole doctrine of clergy was a patent fiction in any event. It is not difficult to see who benefited from a doctrine excusing only educated men.

¹⁴ See Sir James FitzJames Stephen, *supra* note 6, vol. 1 at 467-468.

¹⁵ Most of the history recounted in this section and the next is taken from Desmond H. Brown, *The Genesis of the Canadian Criminal Code of 1892* (Toronto: Osgoode Society, 1989). Readers wishing to pursue the topic further may wish to look at R.C. Macleod (ed.), *Lawful Authority: Readings on the History of Criminal Justice in Canada* (Toronto: Copp Clark Pitman Ltd., 1988). The 100th anniversary of the *Criminal Code* in 1992 led to several interesting reflections on its history. Among them are J. Wood and R. Peck (eds.), *100 Years of the Criminal Code in Canada* (Ottawa: Canadian Bar Association, 1993), a collection of essays; and Martin Friedland, "Canadian criminal justice 1892-1992" (1993) 42 University of New Brunswick Law Journal 175.

¹⁶ See *ibid.*, Desmond H. Brown at 3.

¹⁷ *Ibid.*, Desmond H. Brown at 43. This date is controversial, and other writers put it at 1758, the date of the first sitting of the Nova Scotia legislature.

¹⁸ Lawrence Friedman, *A History of American Law* (New York: Simon and Schuster, 1973), at 32.

¹⁹ See Desmond H. Brown, *supra*, note 15, at 144.

²⁰ The only remaining common law offence is criminal contempt of court.

3

Basic Principles of Criminal Law

Heather E. MacKay*
(edited for the 7th edition by Joel E. Pink, Q.C.)**

The Canadian criminal justice system is derived from its English counterpart. The fundamental principles of that system arose to protect individuals against the vast resources of the state. There are four cornerstones which form the foundation of the criminal law:

(1)   the presumption of innocence;
(2)   the burden of proof is on the Crown;
(3)   proof of guilt beyond a reasonable doubt; and
(4)   proof is made during a fair and public hearing.

Unless these principles are met by the state, the accused cannot be convicted. In a criminal trial, the law offers these basic protections to an accused to ensure both the verdict and the process in reaching it are fair. It is an old legal adage that justice must not only *be* done but *be seen to be* done.

Until the *Canadian Charter of Rights and Freedoms* was enacted in 1982, the Canadian criminal justice system relied upon these tenets of common law passed on from England. Their origin can be traced to the abolition of the Star Chamber which was a secret court of the King first established by Henry VIII and finally outlawed by Parliament in 1641. During the reign of the Tudors, the Star Chamber could try a person based on rumours and also employ torture. It was used, in particular, against "traitors" (usually anyone who attracted the King's ire). The person so accused was presumed guilty and had to prove his innocence. The unfairness of this process was worsened because the hearings were held in secret in front of a biased tribunal. Unfortunately, those rules are still applied today in police states found in places such as Central

*   B.Sc. (Honours), Mount Allison University, Sackville,NewBrunswick; M.B.A.,Dalhousie University, Halifax, Nova Scotia; LL.B., University of New Brunswick, Federicton, New Brunswick.
**B.A., Acadia University, Wolfville, Nova Scotia; LL.B., Dalhousie Law School, Halifax, Nova Scotia; practices law in Halifax, Nova Scotia.

America and in China. Thus, in Canada, we are fortunate to have a system based on the presumption of innocence and proof by the Crown beyond a reasonable doubt. These principles were given added weight in 1982 when they were enshrined in the *Charter*, particularly under s. 11(*d*) which states:

> **11.** Any person charged with an offence has the right
>
> . . .
>
> > (*d*) to be presumed innocent until proven guilty according to law in a fair and public hearing by an independent and impartial tribunal;
>
> . . .

This section ensures that the common law principles continue to be the foundation of the Canadian criminal justice system.

PRESUMPTION OF INNOCENCE

An accused is presumed innocent until proven guilty. What does this mean? Innocence forms a cloak protecting the person against the accusations of the state. This cloak exists from the moment the person is charged until the conviction is stated in open court. During the entire process, the presumption never changes no matter what evidence is presented in court. Until the court, either a judge alone or a judge and jury, pronounces a person guilty according to law, that person, through the presumption, is as innocent as his or her unaccused fellow humans.

In practical terms, the presumption of innocence means an accused need not reply to the charge. The accused does not have to say, "I am innocent." Failure to speak cannot be held against an accused at trial. No adverse inferences can be drawn by the Crown or the court from the mere fact that the accusation was made; if it is, an accused is entitled to a new trial. Nor can the prosecution base its case on the fact that the accused has done nothing to prove his or her innocence. The prosecution must overcome the presumption and prove an accused guilty with its own independent evidence. This protects an accused from ill-founded accusations or abuses, by the state, of its power and resources.

BURDEN OF PROOF

The presumption of innocence leads to the second basic principle recognized in the criminal trial: the burden of proof is always and ultimately on the Crown. The case for guilt must be made by the prosecution; that is their responsibility in law. While the state has the power to accuse someone, it must prove guilt independent of the accused in order to obtain a conviction. That, of course, is not to say the Crown cannot use a legally obtained confession against the accused, nor does it mean an accused does not produce evidence when relying on a defence.

During a criminal trial, there co-exist two different burdens of proof: the "legal" burden and the "evidentiary" burden. The legal burden requires that the Crown prove guilt beyond a reasonable doubt (which will be discussed later), whereas an evidentiary burden only requires that some evidence acceptable to the court be presented on an issue.

Evidentiary burden can shift back and forth between the prosecution and the defence throughout the trial. When the Crown's case is so overwhelming that the accused may be convicted, then it can be said the defence faces an evidentiary burden to raise a reasonable doubt. However, this does not require an accused to present his or her own evidence. Because of the presumption of innocence and the legal burden on the Crown, it can be done by challenging the Crown's evidence, in cross-examination, enough to raise a reasonable doubt.

The legal burden overlays the entire court process and never shifts from the Crown. For example, when an accused wants to rely on self-defence in a murder case, there is an evidentiary burden on the defence. There is, perhaps, a natural inclination to think that when mention is made of the "defence of self-defence" (or other defences), there rests upon the accused some legal onus or obligation of proof in connection with it. It must be clearly understood that no such obligation exists. However, from a "trial tactics" point of view in order for self-defence to be considered by the court, some evidence needs to be presented. Once some admissible evidence of self-defence is adduced, due to the legal burden imposed on the Crown an evidentiary burden shifts to the Crown to show beyond a reasonable doubt that the defence is not available in the circumstances of the case.

Because the prosecution carries the legal burden of proof of guilt, each and every essential ingredient of the offence charged must be proven. If these ingredients, which include place, identity and mental and physical aspects of the crime, are not proven beyond a reasonable doubt, the Crown's case will fail. It is not always necessary for the Crown to prove every detail due to statutory presumptions.

The *Criminal Code* contains provisions where, once certain facts are proven, presumptions or inferences can be drawn from them. Where the provision creates a presumption, it is referred to as a "reverse onus clause". When such provisions are relied upon, the accused is faced with an evidentiary burden to rebut the presumption or inference. If the effect of the reverse onus clause is either to shift the legal burden of proof to the accused or that a conviction would occur despite a reasonable doubt as to guilt, the clause will violate the presumption of innocence protected by s. 11(d) of the *Charter*. The Crown would then not be able to rely on that unconstitutional presumption.[1]

To prove the offence of break, enter and theft, the Crown usually would have to prove the "break", the unlawful entry and the intent to commit theft once inside the premises, plus elements that always have to be proven for every offence (e.g., place). However, under the same section that defines the offence, a statutory presumption is created by s. 348(2)(a) of the *Code*. Under that section, if the Crown proves there was an unlawful entry into a house, then it is presumed that the entry was "to commit an indictable offence therein", such as theft. Without evidence to the contrary, the accused can be convicted because proof of the entry, beyond reasonable doubt, proves the entire offence. It is unnecessary for the Crown to prove the accused had the intent to steal. If the accused presents evidence that he or she was drunk at the time, the requisite specific intent tends to be negated. The onus is then on the Crown to prove the necessary intent beyond a reasonable doubt without the benefit of the presumption.[2]

Another presumption, set out in s. 16 of the *Code*, is that "every one shall, until the contrary is proved, be presumed to be and to have been sane" at the time of an alleged offence. This means the Crown does not have to prove a person was sane as part of its case, the proof of which would be an administrative nightmare. The presumption of sanity also recognizes that an accused is in a better position to show he or she was not sane at the time of the offence. An accused who wishes to use the defence of insanity has an evidentiary burden that is heavier than usual for a defence. The accused must show, on the evidence as a whole, that it is more probable than not, that she or he was not sane at the time of the offence. This standard of proof, known as proof on "a balance of probabilities", is however less onerous than proof beyond a reasonable doubt. Basically, enough evidence must be presented to just "tip the scales" in the accused's favour on the insanity defence. As always, the Crown still carries the legal burden on the case overall.

In summary, while the legal burden of proof of guilt remains with the prosecution, an accused may find it necessary to introduce evidence:

(1) to support a particular defence; or

(2) to rebut presumptions or inferences raised by proven facts or else find that they will prevail against him or her.

An evidentiary burden exists only in regards to those limited issues and the standard of proof is much less onerous than that imposed on the Crown.

REASONABLE DOUBT

In order for the prosecution to obtain a conviction, the Crown must prove each and every one of the essential elements of the crime "beyond a reasonable doubt". What is meant by "proof beyond a reasonable doubt"? It has been said that the term explains itself. It is achieved when the trier-of-fact, be it a judge or jury, feels sure of the guilt of the accused.

In *R. v. Lifchus*,[3] the Supreme Court of Canada was asked to consider this basic question. Mr. Justice Cory sets out suggested instructions that should be used in all criminal cases. He states, "Instructions pertaining to the requisite standard of proof in a criminal trial of proof beyond a reasonable doubt might be given along these lines":

> The accused enters these proceedings presumed to be innocent. The presumption of innocence remains throughout the case until such time as the Crown has, on the evidence put before you, satisfied you beyond a reasonable doubt that the accused is guilty.

> What does the expression "beyond a reasonable doubt" mean? The term, "beyond a reasonable doubt" has been used for a very long time and is a part of our history and tradition of justice. It is so engrained in our criminal law that some think it needs no explanation, yet something must be said regarding its meaning. A reasonable doubt is not an imaginary or frivolous doubt. It must not be based upon sympathy or prejudice, rather, it is based on reason and common sense. It is logically derived from the evidence or absence of evidence.

> Even if you believe the accused is probably guilty or likely guilty, that is not sufficient. In those circumstances, you must give the benefit of the doubt to the accused and acquit because the Crown has failed to satisfy you of the guilt of the accused beyond a reasonable doubt.

> On the other hand, you must remember that it is virtually impossible to prove anything of an absolute certainty and the Crown is not required to do so. Such a standard of proof is impossibly high.

> In short, if, based upon the evidence or lack of evidence, you are sure that the accused committed the offense, you should convict since this demonstrates that you are satisfied of his guilt beyond a reasonable doubt.

In *R. v. Starr*,[4] Mr. Justice Iacobucci states:

...As was emphasized repeatedly in *Lifchus* and again in *Bisson*, a jury *must* be instructed that the standard of proof in a criminal trial is higher than the probability standard used in making everyday decisions and in civil trials. Indeed, it is this very requirement to go beyond probability that meshes the standard of proof in criminal cases with the presumption of innocence and the Crown's onus...

In my view, an effective way to define the reasonable doubt standard for a jury is to explain that it falls much closer to absolute certainty than to proof on a balance of probabilities. As stated in *Lifchus*, a trial judge is required to explain that something less than absolute certainty is required, and that something more than probable guilt is required, in order for the jury to convict. Both of these alternative standards are fairly and easily comprehensible. It will be of great assistance for a jury if the trial judge situates the reasonable doubt standard appropriately between these two standards. The additional instructions to the jury set out in *Lifchus* as to the meaning and appropriate manner of determining the existence of a reasonable doubt serve to define the space between absolute certainty and proof beyond a reasonable doubt. In this regard, I am in agreement with Twaddle J.A. in the court below, when he said, at p. 177:

> If standards of proof were marked on a measure, proof "beyond reasonable doubt" would lie much closer to "absolute certainty" than to "a balance of probabilities". Just as a judge has a duty to instruct the jury that absolute certainty is not required, he or she has a duty, in my view, to instruct the jury that the criminal standard is more than a probability. The words he or she uses to convey this idea are of no significance, but the idea itself must be conveyed.

Whenever a reasonable doubt arises, it must be resolved in the favour of the accused. As previously discussed, there is no legal obligation of proof imposed on an accused who raises a defence or on any other issue. It falls to the Crown to prove beyond a reasonable doubt the accused's defence does not apply to the case. It is not necessary for a judge or a jury to believe the accuser's defence is true to harbour a reasonable doubt; rather, it is only necessary that the defence is reasonably or possibly true.[5] If so, the burden is on the Crown to negate the defence.

The reasonable doubt doctrine applies to the trial from start to finish. If the court is satisfied beyond a reasonable doubt on all issues except one, it must acquit. The court looks at all the evidence but must find certain facts were proven before it can say the accused is guilty.

Here is an example to illustrate. Mrs. B.Z. Body has her microwave stolen while she is out visiting a neighbour for an hour. Immediately before leaving, Mr. Shifty was visiting her brother at her house. The three left at the same time and went their separate ways. Mrs. Body receives a call two days later from a man who she thinks is Mr. Shifty. The caller says if she drops the charges, he will bring back her microwave. Mrs. Body's back door was left unlocked as it usually was. There is no physical evidence (like fingerprints) tying Mr. Shifty to the scene nor was the oven ever found in his possession. Although the phone call is suspect, another reasonable inference is that the accused knew who stole the oven but did not do it himself. That is the inference that the court must draw because it gives the benefit of the reasonable doubt to the accused. The call alone without proof of exclusive opportunity to gain access to the home is not enough. While a court presented with this evidence may be suspicious of the accused and might even think he "probably" did it, the theft charge is not proven because identification is not proven beyond a reasonable doubt.

This example demonstrates the importance of the Crown's case being built on strong and unequivocal evidence that links together logically. The Crown's case is only as strong as the weakest link in the chain of proven facts. The court is not allowed to jump to conclusions. It must reach its conclusion based on logical reasoning. That reasoning can only lead to a conviction when the Crown has satisfied the court with proof beyond a reasonable doubt of all the elements of the crime.

FAIR AND PUBLIC HEARING

The process of a criminal trial has developed to ensure fair and impartial treatment of the accused. Besides the above principles, there are numerous procedural and evidentiary rules that are applied to protect the accused from being overwhelmed by the state's resources. These rules and procedures are often called "technicalities". That is an unfortunate and inaccurate term as it implies that somehow procedures are not important and do not form an integral part of the way our society dispenses justice. To reiterate, "justice" in our system encompasses the process as well as the verdict.

Persons who would override these procedural protections with little thought or because the crime is serious, forget their purpose. Fairness and impartiality cannot be sacrificed for the sake of societal revenge; that would make our justice system one where the end justifies the means. Such result-oriented decision-making is what basic principles of criminal law, such as the presumption of innocence and proof beyond a reasonable doubt, are designed to avoid. Procedures go a long way to ensuring the accused is treated fairly and impartially. Society, as well as the accused, is served through the open process in the form of a public hearing which is another way to protect impartiality.

The criminal justice system works best for the individual accused and for society as a whole when all its parts perform their own functions. Police should conduct their investigations with proper care and attention to procedures and to the accused's rights. Prosecutors are under a duty to provide full and proper disclosure of the case against the accused and seek justice when presenting the state's case. Defence counsel's role is to challenge the Crown's case, ensuring the accused's rights are protected, procedures are followed and that the Crown meets its legal burden of proof. The court allows Crown and defence counsel to run their own cases, sees that procedures and evidentiary rules are followed and determines whether the Crown has proven its case. It then renders the appropriate verdict, be it conviction or acquittal.

Most often, a Crown case fails when the state does not follow the principles and rules or the persons involved do not properly perform their roles; then the accused obtains the protection to which he or she is entitled. Acquittals are not based on "technicalities"; they are based on legitimate procedural and substantive defences. When our criminal justice system follows the long-standing and basic principles and the players perform their own parts, to modify a line of Shakespeare's, the quality of justice will not be strained.

Notes

[1] *R. v. Oakes*, 1986 CarswellOnt 95, 1986 CarswellOnt 1001, 24 C.C.C. (3d) 321, [1986] 1 S.C.R. 103, 26 D.L.R. (4th) 200, 65 N.R. 87, 14 O.A.C. 335, 50 C.R. (3d) 1, 19 C.R.R. 308, 53 O.R. (2d) 719 (S.C.C.).

[2] *R. v. Campbell*, 1974 CarswellOnt 1037, 17 C.C.C. (2d) 320 (Ont. C.A.).

[3] *R. v. Lifchus*, 1997 CarswellMan 392, 1997 CarswellMan 393, 118 C.C.C. (3d) 1, 216 N.R. 215, 150 D.L.R. (4th) 733, 9 C.R. (5th) 1, 118 Man. R. (2d) 218, 149 W.A.C. 218, [1997] 3 S.C.R. 320, [1997] 10 W.W.R. 570 (S.C.C.), at para. 39, amended (1998), 120 C.C.C. (3d) vi (S.C.C.).

[4] *R. v. Starr*, 2000 CarswellMan 449, 2000 CarswellMan 450, 2000 SCC 40, 147 C.C.C. (3d) 449, 36 C.R. (5th) 1, 190 D.L.R. (4th) 591, [2000] 2 S.C.R. 144, [2000] 11 W.W.R. 1, 148 Man. R. (2d) 161, 224 W.A.C. 161, 258 N.R. 250 (S.C.C.), at p. 544 [C.C.C.].

[5] *Kearney v. R.* (1957), 119 C.C.C. 99 (N.B. C.A.).

4

Classification of Criminal Offences

Denise C. Smith*

Whether certain conduct is prohibited in Canada by law is a matter determined by our legislators, be they municipal councils creating bylaws, provincial legislatures creating provincial offences, or Parliament creating criminal offences. Under our Constitution, only Parliament has the authority to create criminal offences, and thus all offences created by other legislators are considered "quasi-criminal". In some instances, conduct may be prohibited by both a federal and a provincial enactment. For example, an episode of reckless driving could result in a charge under either a provincial motor vehicle statute or the *Criminal Code*. In such a case, a police officer or a Crown Attorney exercises discretion as to which charge should be laid, depending on the seriousness of the conduct.

Criminal and quasi-criminal offences are classified according to their gravity. American television has probably familiarized most of us with the terms "felony" and "misdemeanour". In Canada, offences created under a provincial statute or municipal ordinance are known as "summary conviction offences". Offences created by Parliament, in the *Criminal Code* or in a federal statute are either "summary conviction", or "indictable" or "hybrid" offences. How a particular offence is classified has implications for the investigation, trial, sentencing, and appeal procedures employed to deal with the offence.

SUMMARY CONVICTION OFFENCES

Summary conviction offences are considered less serious than indictable offences. Examples of summary conviction offences created by a municipal government include parking restrictions and noise bylaws; examples of summary conviction offences created by a provincial legislature include traffic offences, such as speeding or failing to stop at a stop sign. An example of a summary conviction offence under a fed-

---

* B.A. (*cum laude*), Dalhousie University, Halifax, Nova Scotia; LL.B, Osgoode Hall Law School, Toronto, Ontario; presently Chief Crown Attorney—Halifax Region, Public Prosecution Service, Halifax, Nova Scotia.

eral statute is failing to have sufficient life jackets on a boat under the *Canada Shipping Act*. Examples of summary conviction offences under the *Criminal Code* include impersonating a peace officer and interfering with boundary lines.

At the investigation stage, classifying an offence as summary conviction has implications, for example, by limiting the powers of a peace officer to make an arrest without warrant.

The trial procedures for federally created summary conviction offences are prescribed in the *Criminal Code* and in a few other federal statutes. The trial procedures for municipal or provincial summary conviction offences are often contained in a provincial statute. That statute will have different names in different provinces (e.g., the *Summary Proceedings Act* or the *Provincial Offences Act*), and the procedures may vary slightly from province to province. In some cases, the statute will simply adopt the summary conviction procedures contained in the *Criminal Code*.

Limitation periods apply to summary conviction offences. A limitation period is a time frame following an alleged wrongful act during which a charge must be laid in order to be valid. As a general rule, the *Criminal Code* prescribes a six-month period of limitation, but some provinces provide for longer limitation periods for provincial offences.[1]

A person charged with a summary conviction offence will be summonsed to appear in court before a Justice of the Peace or a Provincial Court Judge, as the case may be, depending on the source of the charge. This will be the same court before which the person will be tried. The person may choose to appear in court in person, or by agent or counsel. The maximum penalty upon conviction will most often be stipulated in the statute creating the offence. Generally, punishment for a summary conviction offence can include a period of incarceration, a fine, or both. The *Criminal Code* provides for punishment of up to six months imprisonment and/or a fine of up to two thousand dollars unless a different (greater) maximum penalty is specified.[2]

Particular procedures apply to appeals involving summary conviction offences. These procedures will be discussed in Chapter 19.

INDICTABLE OFFENCES

An indictable offence is the most serious classification of offence in Canada. Almost all indictable offences are found in the *Criminal Code*, although other federal statutes, such as the *Controlled Drugs and Substances Act*, contain indictable offences.

Examples of indictable offences under the *Criminal Code* include possession of counterfeit money, theft from mail, and murder. Examples of non-*Criminal Code* indictable offences include trafficking in certain types of narcotics (e.g., cocaine, morphine).

The trial procedures for indictable offences are prescribed by the *Criminal Code*. There is no limitation period applicable to indictable offences.[3] There are three trial procedures applicable to indictable offences. First, offences listed in s. 469 of the *Criminal Code* are triable only in the superior court of a province (Supreme Court, Court of Queen's Bench, General Division). This list of offences includes the most serious charge known to the criminal law—murder—but also some curious not-oft found offences, such as "alarming Her Majesty" and "Inciting to Mutiny". Second, offences listed in s. 553 of the *Criminal Code* are in the absolute jurisdiction of the provincial court, meaning that the person charged with one of these enumerated offences does not have the right to choose where he or she will be tried. An example of an indictable offence that is within the absolute jurisdiction of the provincial court is keeping a common gaming house.

The third trial procedure applicable to indictable offences relates to all those offences not specified in either s. 469 or s. 553 of the *Criminal Code*. This is the vast majority of indictable offences. For these offences, the person charged has a right to elect how he or she will be tried: before a Provincial Court Judge without a preliminary inquiry; before a Supreme Court Judge with a preliminary inquiry; or before a judge and jury with a preliminary inquiry. Unlike summary conviction offences, a person charged with an indictable offence must appear before the court in person, unless the accused appoints counsel to appear on his behalf and that counsel files a designation with the court.[4]

The maximum penalties for indictable offences vary according to the offence, but can be as long as life imprisonment for some offences.

Appeal procedures for indictable offences will be discussed in Chapter 19.

HYBRID OFFENCES

Sometimes called "dual procedure" or "Crown option" offences, hybrid offences are federal offences that may be prosecuted by summary conviction or by indictment, at the choice of the Crown Attorney. Once that choice has been made, the charge proceeds in the same manner as any other summary or indictable offence, as the case may be. The choice is made by the Crown Attorney announcing his or her election in open court. If no choice is specifically declared, then the offence is presumed to be by summary conviction.

No law prescribes what factors influence a Crown Attorney's decision whether to proceed summarily or by indictment.[5] An obvious factor is the six-month limitation period applicable only to summary offences, but factors may include the seriousness of the offence and the prior criminal record of the person charged. Since the maximum penalty for the same offence prosecuted by indictment will be higher than when prosecuted by summary conviction, an assessment of the appropriate penalty upon conviction may form part of the Crown Attorney's consideration as to in which manner the charge should proceed.

Under the *Interpretation Act*, a hybrid offence is considered to be an indictable offence until the Crown Attorney's election is made in court.[6] Thus, for the purposes of all investigative measures, the procedures applicable to indictable offences are available to peace officers.

One of the means Parliament has to respond to changing societal values is to alter an offence's classification from summary to indictable or hybrid, or *vice versa*, along with modifying stated maximum penalties. From time to time, the *Criminal Code* is amended in this manner, along with having new crimes created or old ones abolished.

In this chapter, we have seen how classifying an offence as summary or indictable can impact in which court that charge will be tried. One exception to the general rule stated above is with respect to offences alleged to have been committed by a person between the ages of 12 and 17. In Canada, all charges against young persons, whether summary or indictable, are tried in Youth Justice Court.

Notes

[1] *Criminal Code*, subs. 786(2). In 1997, the *Code* was amended to enable a case to proceed by way of summary conviction where the subject matter is more than six months old in instances where "the prosecutor and the defendant so agree."

[2] *Criminal Code*, subs. 787(1). A number of summary conviction offences are now punishable by 18 months imprisonment, instead of six.

[3] While there is no limitation period applicable to indictable offences, other factors can influence the decision to proceed with a dated charge, including problems of proof and the right of the accused to trial within a reasonable time under the *Canadian Charter of Rights and Freedoms*.

[4] *Criminal Code*, s. 650.01. Even so, there are some proceedings for which the accused must personally appear. See also, subs. 650(1.1) and (2).

[5] While the law does not prescribe the factors influencing the exercise of discretion, a Prosecution Service may have internal policies about same.

[6] *Interpretation Act*, R.S.C. 1985, c. I-21, subs. 34(1).

5

Who Can Be Charged With a Crime?

*Shane G. Parker**

There is a wide net that captures various degrees of criminal liability. All those who take part in crime with guilty intentions are criminally liable whether they actually perpetrate the act (principals), aid the principal, abet (encourage or "cheer on"[1] the principal), counsel (procure, solicit, or incite[2] the principal), or are accessories (receive, comfort, or assist[3]) after the fact. One can also be guilty as a conspirator. Finally, one may attempt to commit a criminal act, but fail to complete it and still be liable.

PEOPLE AND CORPORATIONS MAY BE CHARGED

Criminal law governs the actions of individuals and corporate bodies that are contrary to the order, peace, and well being of society and its objective is to punish a public offence.[4] Section 2 of the *Criminal Code* defines "everyone, person and owner", which includes a corporation. The Federal *Interpretation Act* defines "person" as including a corporation; however, a corporation can be convicted only as a party and not under the civil legal concept of "vicarious liability".[5]

A BRIEF HISTORY OF PARTIES TO A CRIMINAL OFFENCE

Modern Canadian criminal law statutorily defines the parties to an offence. The genesis for Canadian definitions is founded in the common law of England. English law distinguished between first and secondary principals, aiders and abettors, and accessories before and after the fact. It is worthwhile to review briefly the common law to gain an understanding of how the definitions have developed in statute and modern-day judicial interpretation.

Principals in the first degree were those who actually committed the act. A principal in the second degree was defined as anyone who

---

* B.Sc. (Hons), University of Waterloo; M.P.E., University of New Brunswick; LL.B., Dalhousie Law School, Halifax, Nova Scotia; Crown Attorney with the Nova Scotia Public Prosecution Service; currently a Crown Attorney practicing in the Province of Alberta.

guilty of manslaughter, even though Joel only went there to rob the store and had nothing to do with Frank's actions.

AIDERS AND ABETTORS

Aiding and abetting are defined under section 21(1)(b) and (c) of the *Criminal Code* respectively.

> **21. (1) Parties to offence** — Every one is a party to an offence who
>
> ...
>
> (b) does or omits to do anything for the purpose of aiding any person to commit it; or
> (c) abets any person in committing it.

Aiding typically relates to assisting in the actual physical act of the principal. In contrast, abetting, or encouraging, relates to affecting the *mens rea* of the offender. If, in the example above with the gang, Joe hands a rope to one of the gang's members, then Joe is aiding. Whereas, if Joe is a bystander but cheering on the gang while they beat the little old lady, by encouraging them, he is abetting.

The Crown must prove that the aider/abettor also had the requisite *mens rea*. *Mens rea* is a person's intent and knowledge. Desire to see something occur is not the same as "intent". The perpetrator's intention to kill the victim must be known to the aider or abettor; it need not be shared. The aider or abettor need not have the same *mens rea*. Justice Charron, in *R. v. Briscoe*,[13] states (at para. 18):

> It is sufficient that he or she, armed with *knowledge* of the perpetrator's intention to commit the crime, acts with the intention of assisting the perpetrator in its commission. It is only in this sense that it can be said that the aider and abettor must intend that the principal offence be committed.

The Crown must prove that the purpose was to assist the principal. Inadvertent assistance, being unwittingly of assistance as an innocent dupe, is not aiding. The aider must have knowledge of the general offence that is intended and the Crown must be able to prove that knowledge. The Crown must also prove the aider possessed a purpose, or intended the consequences that flowed from his or her assistance to the principal.[14] The old common law rule requiring presence at the scene no longer applies.

The aider may still be liable if he should have known what was going to occur. In *R. v. Briscoe*, it was held that if an accused is willfully blind, or is "deliberately ignorant" then *mens rea* has been met.

Wilful blindness does not define the *mens rea* required for particular offences. It can substitute for actual knowledge whenever knowledge is a component of the *mens rea*. The doctrine of wilful blindness imputes knowledge to an accused whose suspicion is aroused to the point where he or she sees the need for further inquiries, but *deliberately chooses* not to make those inquiries. Wilful blindness involves an affirmative answer to the question: Did the accused shut his eyes because he knew or strongly suspected that looking would fix him with knowledge?

The present law, in contrast with the common law, captures as aiders those who have a legal duty to act, to be aiding in a crime if they fail to act, or "omit to act". This broadens the scope of criminal liability to those who by statute are required to act in specific situations. An example could be a provincial child care worker, who by statute must report suspected abuse and fails to do so, may be charged as an aider in future charges of parental assault involving the child.

Abetting requires instigating or promoting or procuring the offence with the intention that the crime be committed. Again, the Crown must prove that there was knowledge of the general circumstances of the crime contemplated. The encouraging can occur in the preparation stage and up to and during the commission of the offence. The Crown must prove that it was the abettor's intention that his or her words or actions would encourage the principal.[15]

As an example, a leader of a disreputable motorcycle gang encourages two members to disrupt the administration of justice by killing correctional officers and other members of the justice system. The leader even confers favours upon them by promoting them through the ranks for doing this. Finally he praises them after they have killed two of the correctional officers. That may be said to be abetting.

COUNSELLING

Counselling is much like abetting. Counselling is defined under s. 22 of the *Criminal Code* as to procure, solicit and/or incite. It has also been defined as "active inducement" or "encouragement".[16] Section 22 of the *Criminal Code* states:

> **22. (1) Person counseling offence** — Where a person counsels another person to be a party to an offence and that other person is afterwards a party to that offence, the person who counselled is a party to that offence, notwithstanding that the offence was committed in a way different from that which was counselled.

> **(2) Idem** — Every one who counsels another person to be a party to an

offence is a party to every offence that the other commits in consequence
of the counselling that the person who counselled knew or ought to have
known was likely to be committed in consequence of the counselling.

(3) Definition of "counsel"— For the purposes of this Act, "counsel"
includes procure, solicit or incite.

However, under s. 464 of the *Criminal Code*, if a person counsels
another to commit a crime, but that crime is not completed, he or she
is still guilty and liable to the same punishment as if it had been a completed act. An example would be the man who seeks to hire a hit man to
kill his wife. Unknowingly, he counsels an undercover police agent to
act as the hit man. The husband is guilty under s. 464 of the *Code*, even
though the undercover officer takes no steps to carry out the plan. Section 23.1 states that even if the principal cannot be convicted the person
who counseled the offence may still be convicted. Counselling is typically charged when the person is not present at the crime and when the
counselling was done prior to the offence.[17] The example above with
the motorcycle gang may also be considered counselling.

There is no statutory increase to the maximum penalty for counseling a person to commit a crime.

CONSPIRACY

Section 465 of the *Criminal Code* is the penalty provision and clarifies the territorial jurisdiction to charge conspiracy. Conspiracy is not
restricted in concept to the *Code* and applies to offences under the *Controlled Drugs and Substances Act*. Conspiracy can be completed before
anything overt is done or before the common design can be put into effect. The decision in *R. v. Maugey*,[18] directs that a three step process be
followed. First, the court must be satisfied beyond a reasonable doubt
of the existence of a conspiracy. Secondly, the judge must determine
whether the accused was probably a member of the conspiracy based
only on his own acts and declarations directly admissible against him. If
the court is satisfied on this point, it may find the words and acts of other
probable members of the conspiracy as evidence against the accused
and consider any acts and words which move the conspiracy forward.
Thirdly, the court must find on the criminal standard, the accused was a
member of the conspiracy.

In *R. v. Cotroni*,[19] Justice Dickson said:

The word "conspire"'derives from two Latin words, "con" and "spirare"
meaning "to breathe together". To conspire is to agree. The essence of

criminal conspiracy is proof of agreement. On a charge of conspiracy the agreement itself is the gist of the offence ... The *actus reus* is the fact of agreement ... The agreement reached by the co-conspirators may contemplate a number of acts or offences. Any number of persons may be privy to it. Additional persons may join the ongoing scheme while others may drop out. So long as there is a continuing overall plan there may be changes in methods of operation, personnel, or victims, without bringing the conspiracy to an end. The important thing is not as to the acts done in pursuance of the agreement, but whether there was, in fact, a common agreement to which the acts are referable and to which all the alleged conspirators were privy. In *R. v. Meyrick*, [1929] 21 Cr. App. R. 94 (C.C.A.) at 102, the question was asked whether the "the acts of the accused were done in pursuance of a criminal purpose held in common between them", and in 11 Halsbury (4th ed.) 44 it said:

> It is not enough that two or more persons pursued the same unlawful object at the same time or in the same place; it is necessary to show a meeting of minds, a consensus to effect an unlawful purpose.

There must be evidence beyond a reasonable doubt that the alleged conspirators acted in concert in pursuit of a common goal.

It is always possible that isolated acts and statements may have little or no value viewed out of context, but when viewed as part of a total picture and interwoven, they may allow the judge to infer a concerted purpose. It is common sense that criminal agreements are never reduced to writing and that those involved would be cautious about orally broadcasting details of illegal agreements among themselves.

In the law of conspiracy there is a blurring between modes of criminal liability. Conspiracy is more preliminary to a crime than an attempt. The offence of conspiracy is complete before any preparatory steps are taken. For conspiracy, the Crown must prove that there was a meeting of the minds with regard to a common design to do something unlawful.[20] Conspiracy is made out once there is an agreement between two or more people to do *something unlawful*. There can be more than one objective. It does not matter that the agreement was not carried out or impossible to carry out. It is not a defence that a person having entered into the agreement later "quits" the conspiracy.[21] "Attempted conspiracy" is a nuanced issue that is not settled and may apply in specific offences in the *Code*.

Conspiracy prosecutions are very complex and have difficult evidentiary hurdles. They typically involve electronic evidence and/or evidence from co-conspirators who become co-operative witnesses, or undercover police officers.

ACCESSORY AFTER THE FACT

Criminal liability does not end once the crime has been committed. Those who knowingly provide comfort or assistance to a criminal for the purpose of allowing him or her to escape, may be charged separately under s. 23 of the *Criminal Code*, which states:

> **23. (1) Accessory after the fact** — An accessory after the fact to an offence is one who, knowing that a person has been a party to the offence, receives, comforts or assists that person for the purpose of enabling that person to escape.
>
> **(2)** [Repealed: S.C. 2000, c. 12, s. 92, effective July 31, 2000 (SI/2000-76)].
>
> R.S.C. 1985, c. C-46, s. 23; S.C. 2000, c. 12, s. 92.
>
> **23.1 Where one party cannot be convicted** — For greater certainty, sections 21 to 23 apply in respect of an accused notwithstanding the fact that the person whom the accused aids or abets, counsels or procures or receives, comforts or assists cannot be convicted of the offence.

For example, Ruth is the girlfriend of a man who is wanted by the police for escaping lawful custody of an officer after being charged with aggravated assault in connection with a vicious bar room brawl. Ruth, by allowing him to hide in her trunk to help get him to the nearby big city to flee the jurisdiction, is guilty of being an accessory after the fact. If Ruth also washes his blood-stained clothes so as to destroy the evidence, and thus escaping from the crime, is guilty of being an accessory after the fact.

The Crown must prove the "accessory" (1) *knew* the person he or she was assisting had been a party to an offence; (2) received, comforted, or assisted the offender (the *actus reas* of the offence of being an accessory after the fact); and (3) did so for the purpose of enabling that person to escape (*mens rea* for the offence of accessory after the fact).

There must be some aid provided that makes his or her apprehension more difficult. "Escape" means to escape "from justice",[22] including apprehension by police and conviction following prosecution. Simply failing to notify the police that a person was involved in a crime is not sufficient to prove the *actus reas*.

There are other specific *Criminal Code* sections for accessory after the fact to murder[23] and manslaughter.[24]

All of the modes of criminal liability, including accessory after the fact, do not require the *conviction* of the principal as stated in s. 23.1 of the *Criminal Code*, but the Crown must prove the underlying offence.

The rationale is that the case against the principal may have problems with admissibility of evidence, or may have a legal justification for the act. This does not bar the state from criminalizing the separate conduct of the accessory after the fact. A conviction or a guilty plea by the principal is the best evidence and certainly goes a long way in proving this element of the offence!

ATTEMPTS

Finally, a person is criminally liable if he or she attempts to commit a crime but does not complete it. Section 24 of the *Criminal Code* states:

> **24. (1) Attempts** — Every one who, having an intent to commit an offence, does or omits to do anything for the purpose of carrying out the intention is guilty of an attempt to commit the offence whether or not it was possible under the circumstances to commit the offence.

> **(2) Question of law** — The question whether an act or omission by a person who has an intent to commit an offence is or is not mere preparation to commit the offence, and too remote to constitute an attempt to commit the offence, is a question of law.

Section 24 of the *Code* covers every *Criminal Code* offence. There are also specific sections of the *Code* that provide for attempts in their definition. Assault, as an example, is defined by s. 265, as contemplating the offence through merely attempting.[25] The gravamen to the offence of attempt is the *mens rea* or intent of the offender coupled with the physical preparatory steps to commit the act. The caveat upon the acts to prepare is that there must be some connection in time and that they are not too remote to commit an attempt. As stated in subs. 24(2) of the *Code*, this is a question of law. The distinction between an attempt and preparation is a qualitative one and one must look to nature and quality of the act compared to the completed ac

Canadian law does not recognize a difference between legal and factual impossibilities. Only attempts at "imaginary crimes" falls outside the *Criminal Code*.[26]

As an example, Rod was upset that his ex-wife as taken up a common-law relationship with a new man. In his jealous rage, Rod drove his car at a high rate of speed towards the new man. Rod narrowly missed the man after a bystander moved the new man out of the way. Rod attempted to assault the new man with a weapon, even though he failed run him over. The Crown would ask the Court to infer Rod's intent by his animus towards the new man and Rod's driving behaviour (including accelerating and the close call causing the bystander to feel the need to pull the new man away). The steps taken to get the car, turn on the ignition, and aim it towards the new man would be all the physical steps that need to be considered to prove the elements for an attempt with a weapon.

CRIMINAL ORGANIZATIONS AND TERRORISM

The *Criminal Code* was amended in 2001 to respond to two different social ills. Parliament's response to widely expand the net of criminal liability was similar to address both problems. Parliament created a crime for being a member, or facilitator of an organization.

In response to the tragic events of September 11, 2001, Parliament enacted sections 83.01 through 83.33 to create a comprehensive subsection of the *Code* targeting terrorism. Section 83.01 defines "entities" to mean a person, group, trust, partnership or fund or an unincorporated association or organization that commit "terrorist activities" inside or outside of Canada.

Subsections 83.02 and 83.03 of the *Code* creates offences for those who provide property (i.e., financial support), or services to a terrorist group knowing it would be used for such a purpose. The Minister of Public Safety and Emergency Preparedness provides a list of "entities" based on, or on reasonable grounds to believe meets, the criteria to the Governor in Council to add to the regulations the names of outlawed organizations or associations. Subsections under 83.18 specifically define the liability that extends to anyone who facilitates, contributes (directly or indirectly), trains, recruits for, or participates in, a terrorist group whether or not the act is completed, could be completed, or knew the specific nature of the act. Conceivably, even pretending to be a terrorist entity is also an offence (s. 83.231). Unique to this section of the *Code* is a sunset clause, whereby Parliament must reconsider the provisions by December 31, 2006, or extend the provisions for a period not to exceed 5 years before another review is to take place.

Parliament used a similar strategy to encompass organized crime by casting a wide net to capture criminal liability. Section 467.1 defines a criminal organization as a group of 3 or more people that has a main activity to commit serious indictable offences that benefit the group materially, or financially. The law excludes people who randomly form for the immediate commission of a single offence. Facilitating also appears within the purview of liability and does not require the Crown to prove knowledge of an actual crime, real or intended. "Facilitation" has been upheld by the Ontario Court of Appeal to mean, "make easy, or easier" and "in association with" to mean, "the accused commit[ted] a criminal offence in connection with the criminal organization."[27] Anyone who directs or instructs a criminal act for the benefit of the criminal organization is also liable under s. 467.13. The maximum penalty for instructing or directing an offence is life imprisonment versus a maximum of 14 years for the person who actually commits the offence. When not dealing with a organized crime, there is not the statutory increasing maximum for counseling.

Therefore, liability attaches to those who: counsel the commission of a crime for the benefit of the organization, commits the crime (principal, aider or abettor), or facilitates a criminal organization (anyone who helps such an organization). The constitutionality of the criminal organized crime sections 467.1, 467.12 and 467.13 have been upheld by courts in Ontario, British Columbia, Quebec and Saskatchewan.[28]

Notes

[1] Section 21(1)(a) of the *Criminal Code*, R.S.C. 1985, c. C-46, s. 21, sets out the authority that includes the principal as the one who actually commits, section 21(1)(b) does or omits to do anything for the purpose of aiding any person, and section 21(1)(c) provides for the liability for those who "abet".

[2] Subsection 22(3) of the *Criminal Code*, as am. R.S.C. 1985, c. 27 (1st Supp.), s. 7(1).

[3] Section 23(1) of *Criminal Code*, as am. S.C. 2000, c. 12, s. 92.

[4] Halsbury, *The Laws of England*, 3d ed. (Butterworths: London, 1955) vol. 10 at 271.

[5] May be defined as imputed negligence. The employer, under certain legal constructs, is liable civilly for the actions of its employee. Vicarious liability exists if it is a "regulatory offence" (E.G. Ewaschuk, *Criminal Pleadings & Practice in Canada*, 2d ed. (Aurora: Canada Law Book Inc., looseleaf series)); see *R. v. McNamara (No. 1)*, 1985 CarswellOnt 96, 1985 CarswellOnt 939, (*sub nom. Canadian Dredge & Dock Co. v. R.*) 45 C.R. (3d) 289, (*sub nom. Canadian Dredge & Dock Co. v. R.*) 19 C.C.C. (3d) 1, (*sub nom. Canadian Dredge & Dock Co. v. R.*) 59 N.R. 241, (*sub nom. R. v. Canadian Dredge & Dock Co.*) [1985] 1 S.C.R. 662, (*sub nom. Canadian Dredge & Dock Co. v. R.*) 9 O.A.C. 321, (*sub nom. Canadian Dredge & Dock Co. v. R.*) 19 D.L.R. (4th) 314 (S.C.C.))

[6] *Supra.*, note 4, at 297.

[7] *R. v. Coney* (1882), 8 Q.B.D. 534, 30 W.W.R. 678, 15 Cox C.C. 46, 51 L.J.M.C. 66 (Eng. Q.B.).

[8] S.C. 1892, c. 29.

[9] *R. v. Biniaris*, 1998 CarswellBC 548, 124 C.C.C. (3d) 58, 104 B.C.A.C. 203, 170 W.A.C. 203 (B.C. C.A.); reversed on other grounds by the Supreme Court of Cana-

da 2000 CarswellBC 753, 2000 CarswellBC 754, 2000 SCC 15, 134 B.C.A.C. 161, 219 W.A.C. 161, 32 C.R. (5th) 1, 184 D.L.R. (4th) 193, 143 C.C.C. (3d) 1, [2000] 1 S.C.R. 381, 252 N.R. 204 (S.C.C.); reconsideration refused 2000 CarswellBC 1992, 2000 CarswellBC 1993 (S.C.C.).

[10] *Macklin, Murphy & Others, Re* (1838), 2 Lewin 225, 168 E.R. 1136.

[11] *R. v. Schell*, 1977 CarswellOnt 982, 33 C.C.C. (2d) 422 (Ont. C.A.).

[12] *R. v. Rowley*, 1999 CarswellOnt 3682, 140 C.C.C. (3d) 361, 127 O.A.C. 35 (Ont. C.A.).

[13] *R. v. Briscoe*, 2010 CarswellAlta 588, 2010 CarswellAlta 589, 2010 SCC 13 (S.C.C.).

[14] *R. v. Greyeyes*, 1997 CarswellSask 271, 1997 CarswellSask 272, [1997] 2 S.C.R. 825, 8 C.R. (5th) 308, 116 C.C.C. (3d) 334, 214 N.R. 43, 148 D.L.R. (4th) 634, 152 Sask. R. 294, 140 W.A.C. 294, [1997] 7 W.W.R. 426 (S.C.C.).

[15] *R. v. Curran*, 1977 CarswellAlta 256, [1978] 1 W.W.R. 255, 7 A.R. 295, 38 C.C.C. (2d) 151 (Alta. C.A.); leave to appeal refused (1978), 38 C.C.C. (2d) 151n (S.C.C.).

[16] *R. v. Sharpe*, 150 C.C.C. (3d) 321, 2001 CarswellBC 82, 2001 CarswellBC 83, 39 C.R. (5th) 72 (S.C.C.).

[17] *Supra*, note 5, at 15-26.

[18] *R. v. Maugey*, 2000 CarswellOnt 2257, 146 C.C.C. (3d) 99, 133 O.A.C. 255 (Ont. C.A.).

[19] *R. v. Cotroni*, 1979 CarswellOnt 48, 1979 CarswellOnt 78, [1979] 2 S.C.R. 256, 93 D.L.R. (3d) 161, 7 C.R. (3d) 185, 11 C.R. (3d) 150, 26 N.R. 133, 45 C.C.C. (2d) 1 (S.C.C.).

[20] *United States v. Dynar*, 1997 CarswellOnt 1981, 1997 CarswellOnt 1982, [1997] 2 S.C.R. 462, 8 C.R. (5th) 79, 213 N.R. 321, 115 C.C.C. (3d) 481, 147 D.L.R. (4th) 399, 44 C.R.R. (2d) 189, 33 O.R. (3d) 478 (headnote only), 101 O.A.C. 321 (S.C.C.).

[21] *R. v. O'Brien*, 1954 CarswellBC 2, [1954] S.C.R. 666, 19 C.R. 371, 110 C.C.C. 1, [1955] 2 D.L.R. 311 (S.C.C.).

[22] *R. v. Vinette*, 1974 CarswellQue 46, 1974 CarswellQue 46F, 4 N.R. 181, 19 C.C.C. (2d) 1, 50 D.L.R. (3d) 697, [1975] 2 S.C.R. 222 (S.C.C.).

[23] Section 240 of the *Criminal Code*.

[24] See *R. v. Webber*, 1995 CarswellBC 1301, 102 C.C.C. (3d) 248, 65 B.C.A.C. 161, 106 W.A.C. 161 (B.C. C.A.).

[25] Section 265(1)(b) of the *Criminal Code*.

[26] *United States v. Dyner*, *supra*, note 20.

[27] *R. v. Lindsay*, 2009 CarswellOnt 3687, 2009 ONCA 532, 68 C.R. (6th) 279, 245 C.C.C. (3d) 301, 251 O.A.C. 1, 97 O.R. (3d) 567 (Ont. C.A.).

[28] *Ibid; R. v. Terezakis*, 2007 CarswellBC 1669, 2007 BCCA 384, 245 B.C.A.C. 74, 405 W.A.C. 74, 223 C.C.C. (3d) 344, 51 C.R. (6th) 165 (B.C. C.A.); *R. v. Smith*, 2006 CarswellSask 180, 2006 SKQB 132, 280 Sask. R. 128 (Sask. Q.B.); and *R. v. Joseph* (2006) (Que. S.C.).

6

Arrest and Compelling the Appearance of the Accused

*The Honourable Judge Frank P. Hoskins**

The initial step in prosecuting anyone accused of having committed a criminal offence is the commencement of proceedings by a peace officer or a private citizen to ensure the accused's appearance in court. Despite the laudable efforts of Parliament in reforming the provisions of the *Criminal Code* dealing with the powers of arrest and interim release of the accused, they remain to be very detailed and difficult to follow. As one legal commentator observed:

> The provisions relating to police powers of arrest and detention are among the most detailed and complex in the *Criminal Code*. They have recently come under harsh attack for this reason by the Law Reform Commission of Canada. Part of the problem stems from the number of variables that are involved. This area can be approached from a number of perspectives, according to the type of offence under consideration, the status of the person who is dealing with the accused (*i.e.*, a *peace officer* or the *officer in charge*), ... or the particular type of form of release being used. These provisions are reviewed according to the status of the person the accused encounters as he or she experiences the release process—first the peace officer and then the officer in charge.[1]

Accordingly, this chapter is intended to provide an overview of the law in an effort to impart a greater appreciation and understanding of the procedural safeguards inherent in the structure of these complex provisions. These provisions are predicated upon the notion that the purposes of the criminal law should be carried out with no more interference with the freedom of individuals than is necessary.[2] Indeed, the law recognizes the general duties of peace officers as having limited powers that entitle them to interfere with the liberty and property of the citizen only where such interference is authorized by law.

* B.A., B.Ed., St. Mary's University, Halifax, Nova Scotia; LL.B., Dalhousie Law School, Halifax, Nova Scotia; Provincial Court Judge for the Provincial Court of Nova Scotia.

ARREST

What Constitutes an Arrest

Although the word *arrest* is not defined in the *Criminal Code*, the Supreme Court of Canada has interpreted it to mean consisting of the actual seizure or touching of a person's body with a view to his or her detention. The mere pronouncing of words of arrest is not an arrest, *unless* the person sought to be arrested submits to the process and goes with the arresting officer.[3] Hence, an arrest may be effected in one of two ways:

1. the actual seizure or touching of a person's body with a view to his or her detention; or
2. by verbally expressing to the person that he or she is under arrest, and the person voluntarily submits to the arrest and goes with the police officer.

It should be noted that the person being arrested must be informed that he or she is being arrested and the reasons therefor. Until it has been made clear to the person that he or she is under arrest, the arrest is not complete in law.[4] Indeed, the essence of an arrest includes the power to ensure that the person being arrested submits to the control and custody of the arrestor.

The purposes of arrest may be for *preventive or protective* reasons. It may be preventive in order to prevent a *breach of the peace*[5] or to prevent the continuation or repetition of an offence. It may also be necessary for the protection of the person being arrested where that person is in need of assistance; for example, medical treatment. An arrest is also effected for the *protection of the public* and to ensure that the accused will answer for an offence he or she is alleged to have committed, or one where it is believed on reasonable grounds he or she is about to commit.

Authority to Arrest

The law defines with reasonable precision the circumstances in which a private citizen and/or a police officer have the legal right to effect an arrest.

Historically, the common law powers of arrest are derived from the rights and duties of ordinary citizens in relation to the maintenance of the *King's Peace*.[6] In early times, before the advent of professional police forces, the ordinary citizen not only enjoyed the right to make arrests, but was duty-bound in certain cases to do so.[7] Citizens were expected to preserve the *King's Peace* and thus were granted powers to arrest persons they found committing felonies.[8]

The general principles of the common law powers of arrest in relation to warrantless arrest have been set out in the case law and subsequently codified in the *Criminal Code.*

Accordingly, the powers of arrest without warrant for *citizens* and *peace officers* are prescribed in the *Criminal Code.*

CITIZENS' POWERS OF ARREST WITHOUT WARRANT

Section 494 of the *Criminal Code* defines the circumstances in which a citizen or a peace officer is empowered to arrest another person without a warrant. The section provides:

> **494. (1) Arrest without warrant by any person**—Any one may arrest without warrant
>> (a) a person whom he finds committing an indictable offence; or
>> (b) a person who, on reasonable grounds, he believes
>>> (i) has committed a criminal offence, and
>>> (ii) is escaping from and freshly pursued by persons who have lawful authority to arrest that person.
>
> **(2) Arrest by owner, etc., of property**—Any one who is
>> (a) the owner or a person in lawful possession of property, or
>> (b) a person authorized by the owner or by a person in lawful possession of property
>
> may arrest without warrant a person whom he finds committing a criminal offence on or in relation to that property.
>
> **(3) Delivery to peace officer**—Any one other than a peace officer who arrests a person without warrant shall forthwith deliver the person to a peace officer.

There are *three* defined circumstances as set out in s. 494 that provide a citizen authority to arrest another citizen *without warrant*. They are:

1. a person whom the citizen *finds committing* an *indictable* offence;
2. a person whom the citizen believes on *reasonable grounds* has committed a *criminal offence*, and is *escaping* from and freely *pursued* by persons who have lawful authority to arrest that person; and
3. a citizen who is the *owner* or a person in *lawful possession of*

property, or a person *authorized by the owner* or a person in lawful possession of property.

Finds Committing an Indictable Offence

The citizen must find the offender committing an *indictable* offence. The expression *finds committing* has been interpreted by the case law to mean *apparently committing*.[9] Where a citizen makes an arrest, the validity of that arrest does not depend upon a subsequent conviction, but rather upon the circumstances that were *apparent* to the citizen at the time the arrest was made.[10] It is not sufficient for the arresting citizen to have *reasonable grounds* to believe that an offence had been committed. It must be clearly established that the citizen found a situation in which a person was apparently committing an *indictable* offence.[11] In other words, the citizen's powers of arrest are based on his or her own discovery of an *indictable* offence actually being committed.[12]

It is important to note that under subs. 494(1)(a) the citizen must find the offender committing an *indictable* offence. An *indictable* offence for the purposes of this section includes *dual* or *hybrid* offences. *Dual* or *hybrid* offences are deemed to be *indictable* offences until the crown makes its election.[13]

Believes on Reasonable Grounds has Committed a Criminal Offence and is Escaping from and Being Freshly Pursued

A citizen has the authority to arrest *without warrant* a person whom he or she has *reasonable grounds* to believe has committed a *criminal offence, and is escaping from and freshly pursued by persons who have the lawful authority to arrest that person.*

There are several preconditions that must exist in order for a citizen to effect a valid arrest under subs. 494(1)(b). First, the citizen must possess *reasonable grounds* to believe that a *criminal offence* had been committed. A *criminal offence* is defined broadly to include summary conviction offences and indictable offences. The meaning of the phrase *reasonable grounds* imports both a *subjective* and *objective* assessment of the circumstances of whether or not the requisite grounds exist. The *subjective* (or personal) belief of the citizen making the arrest is *not* enough. Rather, it must also be shown that a reasonable person, standing in the shoes of the citizen making the arrest, would also come to the same conclusion that grounds exist to effect an arrest.[14] Second, the citizen must believe that the offender is *escaping* from and is being *freshly* pursued by those who have authority to arrest the offender.

Fresh pursuit or *hot pursuit* means that it must be continuous pursuit conducted with reasonable diligence, so that pursuit and capture along with the commission of the offence may be considered as forming part of a single transaction.[15]

The Owner or Person in Lawful Possession of Property

Subsection 494(2) authorizes anyone who is either the *owner* of, in *lawful possession* of, or has been authorized by the owner or the person in lawful possession of property, to arrest without warrant a person whom he or she finds committing a *criminal offence* on or in relation to that property.

This section is often relied on by commercial enterprises to engage private security to protect their property.

DUTIES UPON ARREST

A citizen who effects an arrest must deliver the arrested person *forthwith* to a peace officer. *Forthwith* means as soon as is reasonably practicable under all the circumstances.[16]

PEACE OFFICERS' POWERS OF ARREST WITHOUT WARRANT

Section 495 of the *Criminal Code* defines the circumstances in which a peace officer is authorized to arrest without warrant and defines the *limitations* therein. It provides:

> **495. (1) Arrest without warrant by peace officer**—A peace officer may arrest without warrant
>> (a) a person who has committed an indictable offence or who, on reasonable grounds, he believes has committed or is about to commit an indictable offence;
>> (b) a person whom he finds committing a criminal offence; or
>> (c) a person in respect of whom he has reasonable grounds to believe that a warrant of arrest or committal, in any form set out in Part XXVIII in relation thereto, is in force within the territorial jurisdiction in which the person is found.

Section 495 prescribes *broader* powers of arrest for *peace officers* than those conferred on *citizens* as describ/ed above in s. 494. For obvious reasons, law enforcement officers have additional powers of arrest to those set out in s. 494. In addition to those powers of arrest contained in s. 494, a *peace officer* has authority pursuant to s. 495 to effect an arrest without warrant if any one of the circumstances described in subs. 495(1)(a), (b) or (c) exist.

The Commission of an Indictable Offence or Reasonable Grounds to Believe that an Indictable Offence has been Committed or is about to be Committed

Section 495(1)(a) authorizes a peace officer to arrest *without warrant* a person who has committed an *indictable* offence or who, on reasonable grounds, he or she believes *is about to commit* an indictable offence. The peace officer does not have to discover the offender committing an indictable offence. Thus, if a peace officer observed an intoxicated driver about to enter his or her motor vehicle with the intent to operate it, the officer could effect a valid arrest. The peace officer does not have to wait for the offender to commit the offence. Although this offender would not be charged with committing an offence, he or she nonetheless was prevented from committing one.

Finds Committing a Criminal Offence

A peace officer has authority pursuant to subs. 495(1)(b) to arrest a person whom he or she *finds committing a criminal offence*. Thus, a peace officer is permitted to arrest a person whom he or she finds committing a *summary conviction offence*.

Reasonable Grounds to Believe that a Warrant Exists

Section 495(1)(c) provides that if a peace officer has *reasonable grounds* to believe that there is an *outstanding arrest warrant* or *committal* for a person within the territorial jurisdiction in which the person is found, then the peace officer has authority to effect an arrest upon that person to ensure his or her attendance before a justice in order to be dealt with according to law.

Additional Powers of Arrest Without Warrant

In addition to the powers contained in s. 495, peace officers may effect an arrest without a warrant in the following circumstances:

1. where the peace officer or anyone assisting the peace officer *finds* a person committing a *breach of the peace* or a person the officer reasonably believes is about to join or renew the breach;[17]

2. where the peace officer has reasonable grounds to believe that an accused has contravened or is about to contravene any summons, appearance notice, promise to appear, *undertaking or recognizance* that was issued or given to him or her or entered into by him or her;[18]

3. where the accused has committed an *indictable offence* after any *summons, appearance notice, promise to appear, undertaking or recognizance* was issued or given to him or her or entered into by him or her;[19] or

4. where a peace officer has reasonable grounds to believe that the accused has contravened or wilfully failed to comply with the disposition or any condition of it made pursuant to the *mental disorder provisions* of the *Criminal Code*.[20]

LIMITATIONS ON THE POWERS OF ARREST

Subsection 495(2) imposes a *duty* upon a peace officer *not* to arrest a person without a warrant for:

. . .

(a) an indictable offence mentioned in section 553,

(b) an offence for which the person may be prosecuted by indictment or for which he is punishable on summary conviction, or

(c) an offence punishable on summary conviction,

in any case where

(d) he believes on reasonable grounds that the public interest, having regard to all the circumstances including the need to

(i) establish the identity of the person,

(ii) secure or preserve evidence of or relating to the offence, or

(iii) prevent the continuation or repetition of the offence or the commission of another offence,

may be satisfied without so arresting the person, and

(e) he has no reasonable grounds to believe that, if he does not so arrest the person, the person will fail to attend in court in order to be dealt with according to law.

Unfortunately, the wording is not clearly drafted in subs. 495(2). Arguably, it requires a peace officer to exercise restraint in exercising his or her discretion in making an arrest without warrant. The peace officer has a duty *not* to arrest without warrant *unless* he or she believes on *reasonable grounds* that it is necessary in the *public interest* for any one of the following reasons:

1. to establish the identity of the person;
2. to secure or preserve evidence of or relating to the offence;
3. to prevent the continuation or repetition of the offence or the commission of another offence, or
4. to ensure the attendance of the person in court to be dealt with according to law.

The failure of a peace officer to comply with subs. 495(2) does not automatically provide a defence for a charge of obstruction of justice arising from the unlawful arrest. Subsection 495(3) states that:

> **(3) Consequences of arrest without warrant**—Notwithstanding subsection (2), a peace officer acting under subsection (1) is deemed to be acting lawfully and in the execution of his duty for the purposes of
>> (a) any proceedings under this or any other Act of Parliament; and
>> (b) any other proceedings, unless in any such proceedings it is alleged and established by the person making the allegation that the peace officer did not comply with the requirements of subsection (2).

This section provides that a peace officer is deemed to be acting lawfully and in the execution of his or her duties for the purposes of any proceedings under the *Criminal Code* or any other Federal Act. This deeming provision also extends to all other proceedings, unless it is established that the peace officer did not comply with subs. 495(2).[21]

RIGHTS AND DUTIES UPON ARREST

Reasons for Arrest

There are legal obligations upon the person who makes an arrest, regardless of whether or not the arrest is *with* or *without* a warrant. As previously mentioned, when a *citizen* makes an arrest he or she must deliver the arrested person forthwith to a peace officer. When a *peace officer* makes an arrest, he or she must inform the arrested person of the *reasons for the arrest*. Historically, the common law imposed a duty upon the person making an arrest to inform the arrested person of the reasons for the arrest, the failure of which would have resulted in justification to resist the arrest.[22] With the advent of the *Canadian Charter of Rights and Freedoms,* these duties have become substantive rights of every person arrested or detained.[23] Thus, s. 10 of the *Charter*[24] states:

> Everyone has the right on arrest or detention
>> (a) to be informed promptly of the reasons therefor;

(b) to retain and instruct counsel without delay and to be informed of that right; and

(c) to have the validity of the detention determined by way of *habeas corpus* and to be released if the detention is not lawful.

The arresting peace officer is under a duty to ensure that the arrested person is informed of the reasons of the arrest. If the peace officer does not inform the person of the reasons for the arrest then the arrest is *invalid* and thus *unlawful*. An unlawful arrest entitles the person to resist the arrest by reasonable force.[25] However, the courts are mindful of the difficult circumstances that can arise for peace officers in their efforts to discharge their duty. The courts have given peace officers leeway in cases where the arrested person made it very difficult for the peace officer to inform the arrested person of the reasons. These are cases wherein the arrested person was trying to escape, resisting arrest, or was too intoxicated to understand.[26]

A peace officer must provide the arrested person sufficient factual details for the arrest. The arrested person is entitled to know the extent of his or her legal jeopardy to enable him or her to make an informed and appropriate decision as to whether to speak to a lawyer or not. The arrested person need not be aware of the precise charge faced. Nor need he or she be aware of all the factual details of the case. What is required is that he or she be possessed of sufficient information to allow an informed and appropriate decision to be made.[27]

Section 29 of the *Criminal Code* outlines the duties imposed upon those who execute a warrant or an arrest. The section provides:

(1) Duty of person arresting—It is the duty of every one who executes a process or warrant to have it with him, where it is feasible to do so, and to produce it when requested to do so.

(2) Notice—It is the duty of every one who arrests a person, whether with or without a warrant, to give notice to that person, where it is feasible to do so, of

(a) the process or warrant under which he makes the arrest; or

(b) the reason for the arrest.

(3) Failure to comply—Failure to comply with subsection (1) or (2) does not of itself deprive a person who executes a process or warrant, or a person who makes an arrest, or those who assist them, of protection from criminal responsibility.

It is the duty of everyone who executes a process or warrant to have it in their possession for inspection, where it is feasible to do so, and to produce it when requested to do so and to allow the person a reasonable amount of time to examine the document. The executor of the process or warrant is also required to provide *notice*, where it is feasible to do so, of the process or warrant under which the arrest is made or the reason for the arrest.

Right to a Lawyer

As previously mentioned, s. 10 of the *Charter* imposes a duty on anyone making an arrest to inform the person of the right to obtain and instruct legal counsel without delay. Indeed, there are correlative duties that include the following:

1. The person must be informed of the availability of free legal and immediate legal assistance through Legal Aid or duty counsel;[28]
2. A reasonable opportunity to contact counsel must be provided unless compelling circumstances exist that require the police not to hold off in their attempts to obtain incriminating evidence.[29] The police must cease questioning or otherwise attempting to obtain evidence until the arrestee has had a reasonable opportunity to retain and instruct counsel. However, the arrested person must be reasonably diligent in attempting to contact counsel if he or she wishes to do so.[30] The duty to facilitate contact with counsel includes providing access to a telephone and privacy to consult with counsel;[31] and
3. The person has a right to choose his or her counsel and it is only if the lawyer chosen cannot be available after a reasonable delay that the arrested person should be expected to exercise the right to counsel by calling another lawyer.[32]

Right to Enter Private Dwellings to Make Arrest

The right of the police to enter a private dwelling to effect an arrest without a warrant exists only where there are exigent circumstances that make it impracticable to obtain a warrant. A peace officer is permitted to enter a private dwelling, by force if necessary, to prevent the commission of an offence that would cause immediate and serious injury to any person; to prevent destruction of evidence; or to arrest someone in the act of hot pursuit, if the officer believes on reasonable grounds that the person is in the dwelling house, and the conditions for obtaining a warrant exist.[33]

Prior to May 22, 1997, the law permitted the police to enter and arrest a person in a dwelling without having met the above preconditions. On May 22, 1997, the Supreme Court of Canada released a ruling that had a profound impact upon the law governing arrests of persons in dwellings.[34] The Court held that the privacy interest outweighs the law enforcement interest and, thus, warrantless entry into dwellings is prohibited unless exigent circumstances exist. The initial impact of the Supreme Court's judgment was widespread and profound, as the police were forced to change entrenched police practice.[35] It was unclear as to how compliance with the Supreme Court's judgment was going to be achieved because of the lack of statutory authority.[36] Parliament responded by amending the *Criminal Code*. On December 18, 1977, ss. 529 to 529.5 of the *Criminal Code* came into force. These provisions authorize justices of the peace to issue warrants permitting the entry into dwellings for purposes of arrest. The justice must be satisfied that there are reasonable grounds for the arrest and reasonable grounds to believe the person will be found at the named location, before giving the police the authority to enter. Subsection 529.3(1) provides that an officer may enter a dwelling for the purposes of arrest without warrant, if there are reasonable grounds to believe that a person is present in the dwelling and the conditions for obtaining a warrant exist, but by reason of exigent circumstances, it would be impracticable to obtain a warrant. Also, as earlier mentioned, an exception that authorizes warrantless entry of dwellings is the doctrine of *hot* or *fresh* pursuit. In cases of *hot pursuit* society's interest in effective law enforcement takes precedence over the privacy interest and the police are permitted to enter a dwelling to make an arrest without warrant.[37] *Hot* or *fresh* pursuit (pursuit is continuous pursuit), conducted with reasonable diligence, may be considered as forming part of a single transaction.[38]

Use of Force in Making Arrest

A peace officer or a citizen is entitled to use force to effect an arrest with or without warrant. Section 25 of the *Criminal Code* authorizes *anyone* to use force who is required or authorized by law to administer or enforce the law. A person authorized to use force to effect an arrest is justified in using *as much force as is necessary* for that purpose. The court, in determining whether the force used was necessary, will consider the all the circumstances including the nature and degree of the force used, the gravity of the offence for which the arrest was made, the conduct of the person being arrested and the possibility of effecting the arrest by other alternative means than the use of force. A person is not entitled to use *excessive force* in effecting an arrest.

It should be noted that subs. 25(3) provides that a person is not justified in using force that is *intended or is likely to cause death or grievous bodily harm* unless the person *reasonably believes* that such force is necessary to preserve himself or anyone under his protection from *death or grievous bodily harm*. Subsection 25(4), however, does provide authority for a peace officer, or anyone lawfully assisting the peace officer, to use force that is *intended or likely to cause death or grievous bodily harm* to a person to be arrested provided that the following preconditions are exist:

. . .

(a) the peace officer is proceeding lawfully to arrest, with or without warrant, the person to be arrested;
(b) the offence for which the person is to be arrested is one for which that person may be arrested without warrant;
(c) the person to be arrested takes flight to avoid arrest;
(d) the peace officer or other person using the force believes on reasonable grounds that the force is necessary for the purpose of protecting the peace officer, the person lawfully assisting the peace officer or any other person from imminent or future death or grievous bodily harm; and
(e) the flight cannot be prevented by reasonable means in a less violent manner.

Notwithstanding the above-noted, s. 26 imposes *criminal liability* for the use of *excessive force* in effecting an arrest.

Search or Seizure Incidental to Arrest

A peace officer (or a citizen) has the authority at common law to search a person incident to a lawful arrest.[39] The right to search incident to an arrest derives from the fact of arrest or detention of the person and thus a search or seizure may be conducted before or after the arrest.[40] The Supreme Court of Canada has stated that the exercise of this power is not unlimited and consideration must be given to the following underlying interests:

1. This power does not impose a duty. The police have some discretion in conducting the search. Where they are satisfied that the law can be effectively and safely applied without a search, the police may see fit not to conduct a search. They must be

in a position to assess the circumstances of each case so as to determine whether a search meets the underlying objectives.

2. The search must be for a valid objective in pursuit of the ends of criminal justice, such as the discovery of an object that may be a threat to the safety of the police, the accused or the public, or that may facilitate escape or act as evidence against the accused. The purpose of the search must not be unrelated to the objectives of the proper administration of justice, which would be the case, for example, if the purpose of the search was to intimidate, ridicule or pressure the accused in order to obtain admissions.

3. The search must not be conducted in an abusive fashion and, in particular, the use of physical or psychological constraint should be proportionate to the objectives sought and the other circumstances of the situation.[41]

These broad propositions help define the scope of the common law power of search incidental to an arrest. These propositions are to be construed in a restrictive manner.[42] There are no readily ascertainable limits on the scope of the common law power of search incidental to arrest and it is, therefore, the court's responsibility to set boundaries that allow the state to pursue its legitimate interest, while vigorously protecting the individual's right to privacy. The scope of the search incident to arrest can refer to many different aspects of the search. It can refer to the items seized during the search and/or the place to be searched. Scope can also refer to the temporal limits on the power of search.

The authority of the search does not arise as a result of a reduced expectation of privacy of the arrested person. Rather, it arises out of the need for the law enforcement authorities to gain control of things or information that outweigh the individual's interest in privacy. In other words, the search is only justifiable if the purpose of the search is related to the purpose of the arrest.

A search that does not meet the above-noted objectives could be characterized as unreasonable and unjustified at common law and thus could be a breach of s. 8 of the *Charter*.

COMPELLING THE APPEARANCE OF THE ACCUSED

Without Arresting the Accused

As previously mentioned, the *Criminal Code* imposes a *duty* upon a peace officer *not* to arrest without warrant *unless* he or she has reasonable grounds to believe that it is necessary in the *public interest.* Accordingly, s. 496 provides authority for the peace officer to issue an *appearance notice* where the officer decides *not* to arrest because the offence is

(a) an indictable offence mentioned in s. 553;
(b) a hybrid or dual procedure offence; or
(c) a summary conviction offence.

An *appearance notice* issued by a peace officer is a piece of paper that compels the accused to appear in court at a stated time and place. Section 501 states that the *appearance notice* must contain the following:

1. the name of the accused;
2. the substance of the charge;
3. the date and place where the accused is to attend court; and
4. the text of subs. 145(5) and (6) and s. 502 of the *Criminal Code.*

The accused is required to sign the *appearance notice* and then a copy is provided to him or her. The accused's refusal or failure to sign it does not invalidate the appearance notice.[43]

An *appearance notice* may also require an accused to appear at a time and place stated in it for the purposes of the *Identification of Criminals Act,*[44] where the accused is alleged to have committed an *indictable offence.* This provision allows the police to fingerprint and photograph the accused.

By Arresting the Accused

The *Criminal Code* imposes prescribed duties upon a person who makes an arrest. As stated, a citizen making an arrest must deliver the accused forthwith to a peace officer upon arrest.

Section 503 imposes a duty upon a peace officer, who makes an arrest with or without warrant, to take the arrested accused before a *justice* within *24 hours* of arrest or if a justice is *not* available, as soon as possible thereafter, *unless* at any time before the expiration of time prescribed above:

1. the peace officer or officer in charge releases the person under any other provision of the *Criminal Code*; or
2. the peace officer or officer in charge is satisfied that the person should be released from custody, whether conditionally or unconditionally, and so releases him or her.

Arrest for Offence Committed Outside Province

Where an accused has been arrested without a warrant for an *indictable* offence alleged to have been committed in *another province*, he or she may not be released by a *peace officer* or the *officer in charge*, but must be taken before a justice as in accordance with subs. 503(3). If the justice is *not* satisfied that there are reasonable grounds to believe that the accused is the person alleged to have committed the offence, the justice must release him. However, if the justice is satisfied that there are reasonable grounds to believe that the accused is the person alleged to have committed the offence, then the justice may remand the accused to the custody of a *peace officer* to await the execution of a warrant for the arrest of the accused. The warrant must be executed within *six days* after the accused was remanded to the custody of a *peace officer*. After the elapse of *six days*, the justice *must* release the accused.

RELEASE BY ARRESTING OFFICER

A peace officer who arrests a person without warrant for an *absolute indictable offence*, a *criminal offence*, or a *summary conviction offence*,[45] must *as soon as practicable*,

(a) release the accused from custody and compel his or her appearance by issuing a summons; or
(b) issue an appearance notice and release him or her.

However, a peace officer shall *not* release an accused, if the officer believes, on reasonable grounds, that it is necessary in the public interest to detain the accused in custody, which includes, for any of the following reasons:[46]

. . .

(i) establish the identity of the accused,
(ii) secure or preserve evidence of or relating to the offence,

> (iii) prevent the continuation or repetition of the offence or the commission of another offence, or
> (iv) ensure the safety and security of any victim of or witness to the offence; or
>
> (b) ... the [accused] will fail to attend court ...

RELEASE BY THE OFFICER IN CHARGE

An accused arrested without warrant and delivered to an *officer in charge*[47] must be released from custody, as soon as practicable, by way of:

1. a summons;
2. promise to appear;
3. a recognizance without sureties in an amount not exceeding $500 without deposit of money or other valuable security; or
4. a recognizance without securities in an amount not exceeding $500 or if the officer directs on depositing with the officer a sum of money or other valuable security not exceeding in amount or value of $500; if the accused is not ordinarily a resident in the province in which he or she is in custody or does not ordinarily reside within 200 kilometers of the place in which he or she is in custody.[48]

An *officer in charge*, however, shall *not* release an accused where there are reasonable grounds to believe that it is necessary in the *public interest* to detain the accused in custody which includes for any of the following reasons:

> . . .
>
> (i) establish the identity of the accused,
> (ii) secure or preserve evidence of or relating to the offence,
> (iii) prevent the continuation or repetition of the offence or the commission of another offence, or
> (iv) ensure the safety and security of any victim of or witness to the offence; or
>
> (b) ... the [accused] will fail to attend court ...

A *peace officer* or *the officer in charge* is not permitted to release an accused who has been arrested without warrant by a peace officer for an indictable offence committed in a different province.[49]

The powers of the *officer in charge* are broader than those of an *arresting peace officer*. Unlike the *arresting peace officer*, the *officer in charge* has the authority to release an accused who has been arrested on a warrant *endorsed* by a justice. A warrant *endorsed* by a justice means that the *officer in charge* has been given the authority to release the accused. An *unendorsed* warrant compels the appearance of the accused before a justice of the same jurisdiction. The *officer in charge* has no authority to release an accused arrested on an *unendorsed* warrant.

APPEARANCE OF ACCUSED BEFORE JUSTICE

As previously mentioned, section 503 of the *Criminal Code* requires a police officer to ensure that a person arrested with or without a warrant be brought before a justice. Where a justice is available, that arrested person must be taken before the justice without unreasonable delay and, in any event, within 24 hours. Where a justice is not available within a period of 24 hours after the person has been arrested by, or delivered to, the peace officer, the person shall be taken before a justice as soon as possible.

RELEASE BY PEACE OFFICER OR OFFICER IN CHARGE

Subsection 503(2) provides a peace officer or an officer in charge with authority to release if he or she is satisfied that an arrested person should be released from custody conditionally. The officer may, unless the person is detained in custody for an offence mentioned in s. 522 (i.e., murder), release that person on the person's giving a promise to appear or entering into a recognizance in accordance with subs. 498(1) (b) to (d) and subs. 503(2.1).

In addition to these conditions referred to in subs. 503(2), the peace officer or officer in charge may, in order to release the person, require the person to enter into an undertaking in which the person undertakes to do one or more of the following things:

> (a) to remain within a territorial jurisdiction specified in the undertaking;
> (b) to notify the peace officer or another person mentioned in the undertaking of any change in his or her address, employment or occupation;
> (c) to abstain from communicating, directly or indirectly, with any victim, witness or other person identified in the undertaking, or from going to a place specified in the undertaking, except in accordance with the conditions specified in the undertaking;
> (d) to deposit the person's passport with the peace officer or other person mentioned in the undertaking;
> (e) to abstain from possessing a firearm and to surrender any firearm in the possession of the person and any authorization, licence

or registration certificate or other document enabling that person to acquire or possess a firearm;

(f) to report at the times specified in the undertaking to a peace officer or other person designated in the undertaking;

(g) to abstain from

(i) the consumption of alcohol or other intoxicating substances, or

(ii) the consumption of drugs except in accordance with a medical prescription; or

(h) to comply with any other condition specified in the undertaking that the peace officer or officer in charge considers necessary to ensure the safety and security of any victim of or witness to the offence.

Subsection 503(2.2) provides that a person who has entered into an undertaking under subs. 503(2.1) may, at any time before or at his or her court appearance, apply to a justice to replace his or her undertaking with such modifications as the circumstances require. This section permits a person to apply to a justice to have his or her release mechanism replaced with less onerous conditions. Similarly, subs. 503(2.3) provides authority for the Crown to make an application to have more or fewer restrictions imposed.

As previously mentioned, where a person has been arrested without warrant for an indictable offence alleged to have been committed in Canada but outside the territorial jurisdiction where the arrest occurred, the person must be taken before a justice within the arresting jurisdiction within 24 hours of the arrest or as soon as possible thereafter. If the justice is satisfied that there are reasonable grounds to believe that the person arrested is the same person alleged to have committed the offence, the justice may remand the person arrested to the custody of the peace officer to allow an arrest warrant to be executed in accordance with s. 528. Any such remand is valid for six days and if no such warrant is executed the person shall be released.

If, however, the person is arrested in the same province where the offence is alleged to have been committed, the justice may order the arrested person to be taken before a justice having jurisdiction with respect to the offence.

Subsection 503(3.1) provides authority for a justice, with the consent of the Crown, to order the arrested person to be released pending the execution of a warrant of arrest.

Subsection 503(4) directs that a peace officer or an officer in charge, having custody of a person who has been arrested without warrant, as a person *about to commit an indictable offence*, shall release that person unconditionally as soon as practicable after he or she is satisfied that the continued detention of that person in custody is no longer necessary to prevent the commission by him or her of an indictable offence.

JUDICIAL AUTHORITY TO COMPEL THE APPEARANCE OF THE ACCUSED

Section 504 of the *Criminal Code* provides that *anyone*, who has reasonable grounds, to believe that a person has committed an *indictable* offence may lay an *information* in writing and *under oath* before a justice, and the justice is required to receive that *information*, upon being satisfied of the following:

> (a) that the person has committed, anywhere, an indictable offence that may be tried in the province in which the justice resides, and that the person
>> (i) is or is believed to be, or
>> (ii) resides or is believed to reside,
>> within the territorial jurisdiction of the justice;
> (b) that the person, wherever he may be, has committed an indictable offence within the territorial jurisdiction of the justice;
> (c) that the person has, anywhere, unlawfully received property that was unlawfully obtained within the territorial jurisdiction of the justice; or
> (d) that the person has in his possession stolen property within the territorial jurisdiction of the justice.

An *information* is a document that contains the allegation that forms the substance of the charge against an accused. The *laying of an information* signifies the initiation of the prosecution. An *information* may consist of more than one charge; it is permissible to have multiple charges on an *information*. The accused is not required to respond in writing, but is called upon in court to enter an oral plea to the charge(s). The Crown has the right to withdraw an *information* from the judicial process at any time before the accused enters a plea. Once the accused enters a plea, the court is seized with the matter and it must be dealt with accordingly.

Where an accused has been released from custody under an *appearance notice* issued by a peace officer as in accordance with s. 496 or under a *promise to appear*[50] or *recognizance*[51] pursuant to s. 497 or s. 498, the *information* must be laid before a justice *as soon as practicable thereafter* and, in any event, prior to the first court appearance of the accused in court.

An *information* is a written complaint or allegation on oath that he or she has personal knowledge or reasonable grounds to believe that the person named in the information has committed a criminal offence. As previously mentioned, an *information* is sworn before a justice, who must receive the *information* if it contains any of the allegations set out in subs. 504 (a), (b), (c) or (d).

It is important to note that subs. 786(2) of the *Criminal Code* provides that an *information* in respect to a *summary conviction offence* must be laid within *six months* from the date of the alleged offence. In other words, no summary conviction proceedings shall be instituted more than *six months* after the time when the subject matter of the proceedings arose.

With respect to *indictable offences*, there is *no time limitation period* that must be met as between the date of the offence and the laying of the *information*.

COMPELLING APPEARANCE BY SUMMONS OR WARRANT

The Issuance of a Summons

Section 507 of the *Criminal Code* sets out the procedure that must be followed when a justice receives an *information* other than an *information* laid under s. 505. Section 507 provides that *except* where an accused has already been arrested, the justice must hear and consider the allegations of the informant and the evidence of witnesses, where he or she considers it desirable or necessary to do so. Where the justice considers that a case for doing so is made out, he or she shall issue a *summons* or a *warrant* for the arrest of the accused.

Subsection 507(2) states that no justice shall refuse to issue a *summons* or *warrant* by reason only that the alleged offence is one for which a person may be arrested without warrant.

It is important to note that subs. 507(4) states that a *summons* is to be issued rather than a *warrant*, unless the allegations or evidence discloses *reasonable grounds* to believe that it is necessary in the *public interest* to issue a *warrant* for the arrest of the accused.

A *summons* issued under s. 507 is directed to the accused, sets out briefly the offence charged, and requires the accused to attend court at a stated time and place. The *summons* must be served by a peace officer *personally* upon the accused or, if that person cannot conveniently be found, shall leave it for him or her at his or her last or usual place of abode with some person thereof who appears to be at least 16 years old.

Where the accused fails to appear in court as directed in the *summons*, the Crown will usually apply for a warrant for the arrest of the accused, providing it can prove that the *summons* was *personally* served upon the accused or that the accused is *evading service*. Upon being satisfied that the Crown has discharged its burden, the court will usually issue the warrant for the arrest of the accused.

The Issuance of a Warrant

The power to issue an arrest *warrant* applies at any stage of the proceedings and not only at the time the justice initially receives an *information*.[52]

The *Criminal Code* prescribes the contents of a *warrant* to arrest an accused under subs. 511(1), which states that a warrant shall:

> (a) name or describe the accused;
> (b) set out briefly the offence in respect of which the accused is charged; and
> (c) order that the accused be forthwith arrested and brought before the judge or justice who issued the warrant or before some other judge or justice having jurisdiction in the same territorial division, to be dealt with according to law.

Unlike a summons, the *warrant* permits a description of the accused as an alternative to naming him or her. This provision contemplates situations in which the name of the accused is unknown, but there is an actual description of the accused with enough particularity to ascertain identification.

The *warrant* directs the police to arrest the accused and bring him or her before the issuing justice or some other justice of the same jurisdiction to be dealt with according to law.

Subsection 511(2) provides that the *warrant* remains in effect until it is executed and need not be made returnable at any particular time. Thus, a *warrant* remains outstanding for an accused until he or she is arrested and brought before a justice. However, a justice is empowered to *hold* the *warrant* for a specified time to allow the accused to surrender voluntarily into custody.[53] Where the accused appears voluntarily for the offence in respect of which the accused is charged, the warrant is deemed to be executed.[54]

A justice may issue a *warrant* for the arrest of the accused, where the justice has *reasonable and probable grounds* to believe that it is necessary in the *public interest*; notwithstanding that:

> (a) an appearance notice or a promise to appear or a recognizance

entered into before an officer in charge or another peace officer has
been confirmed or cancelled ...;

(b) a summons has been previously issued ...; or

(c) the accused has been released unconditionally or with the intention of compelling his or her appearance by way of summons.[55]

Also, a justice may issue a warrant for the arrest of the accused where any of the following circumstances exist:

(a) service of a summons is proved and the accused fails to attend court in accordance with the summons;[56]

(b) an appearance notice or a promise to appear or a recognizance entered before the officer in charge or another peace officer has been confirmed and the accused fails to attend court;[57]

(c) it appears that the summons cannot be served because the accused is evading service;[58]

(d) fails to appear for the purposes of the *Identification of Criminals Act*;[59]

(e) has violated or there are reasonable grounds to believe that the accused is about to violate his promise to appear, undertaking or recognizance;[60] or

(f) has committed an indictable offence after his or her release.[61]

EXECUTION OF WARRANT WHERE ACCUSED IS IN ANOTHER PROVINCE

A warrant may be *executed* by arresting the accused wherever he or she is found within the territorial jurisdiction of the justice, judge or court by whom or by which the warrant was issued.[62] Thus, the warrant may be executed anywhere in that issuing province. However, an accused can be arrested wherever he or she is found in Canada, in the case of *fresh or hot pursuit*.[63] In other words, in the process of executing a warrant in the issuing province, the officer is permitted to *pursue* the accused into another province to effect the arrest.

The *Criminal Code* also authorizes a process for which a peace officer is permitted to execute an arrest warrant outside the province from which the warrant was issued.[64] The following procedure is recommended in cases where a warrant has to be endorsed in another province:

1. the peace officer should have the warrant with him or her

when they appear before the justice of the other province who has jurisdiction to endorse the warrant;

2. the peace officer must be prepared to prove the signature of the justice who issued the warrant, either by sworn evidence or by affidavit; and

3. the peace officer should accept or accept assistance of local peace officers to execute the warrant within the endorsing court's jurisdiction.[65]

CANADA-WIDE WARRANT

A Canada-wide warrant can only be issued by a *federally* appointed judge such as a Superior Court judge.[66] A Canada-wide warrant authorizes the arrest of the accused anywhere in Canada. Thus, a peace officer is not required to follow the above-noted procedure of having a warrant endorsed in another province.

Notes

[1] See Gary T. Trotter, *The Law of Bail In Canada*, 1st ed. (Toronto: Carswell, 1992), at pp. 38-39.

[2] See Clay M. Powell, *Arrest and Bail in Canada*, 2nd ed. (Markham: Butterworths, 1976).

[3] *R. v. Whitfield*, 1969 CarswellOnt 138, 1969 CarswellOnt 138F, [1970] 1 C.C.C. 129, 9 C.R.N.S. 59, 7 D.L.R. (3d) 97, [1970] S.C.R. 46 (S.C.C.), at p. 130 [C.C.C.].

[4] *R. v. Delong*, 1989 CarswellOnt 77, 47 C.C.C. (3d) 402, 69 C.R. (3d) 147, 31 O.A.C. 339 (Ont. C.A.), at p. 417 [C.C.C.].

[5] *Criminal Code*, R.S.C. 1985, c. C-46, s. 31.

[6] Second Statute of Westminster, (13 Edw. 1), ss. 1, 2, 4, 5 and 6, passed in 1285.

[7] See *R. v. Asante-Mensah*, 2001 CarswellOnt 3369, 157 C.C.C. (3d) 481, 204 D.L.R. (4th) 51, 150 O.A.C. 325 (Ont. C.A.), leave to appeal refused 2002 CarswellOnt 646, 2002 CarswellOnt 647 (S.C.C.), affirmed CarswellOnt 2667, 2003 CarswellOnt 2668, 174 C.C.C. (3d) 481, 11 C.R. (6th) 1, 227 D.L.R. (4th) 75, [2003] 2 S.C.R. 3, 306 N.R. 289, 39 M.V.R. (4th) 155, 2003 SCC 38, 175 O.A.C. 317 (S.C.C.), wherein Macpherson and Sharpe J.J.A. reference Holdsworth, *A History of English Law*, vol. III, 2nd impression (1973) at 598-600.

[8] E.G. Ewaschuk, *Criminal Pleadings & Practice in Canada* 2nd ed. (Aurora: Canada Law Book, 2003) at vol. 1, c. 5.

[9] *R. v. Biron*, 1975 CarswellQue 2, 1975 CarswellQue 34F, 23 C.C.C. (2d) 513, 30 C.R.N.S. 109, 59 D.L.R. (3d) 409, [1976] 2 S.C.R. 56, 4 N.R. 45 (S.C.C.).

[10] *Ibid.*, at p. 524 [C.C.C.].

[11] See Greenspan & Rosenberg, *Martin's Annual Criminal Code 2003* (Aurora: Canada Law Book, 2002), at cc/875.

[12] *R. v. Biron, supra*, note 9, at 524 [C.C.C.].

[13] See *Interpretation Act*, R.S.C. 1985, c. I-21, subs. 34(1)(a).

[14] Greenspan & Rosenberg, *supra*, note 11, at cc/874; see also *R. v. Storrey*, 1990 CarswellOnt 78, 1990 CarswellOnt 989, [1990] 1 S.C.R. 241, 75 C.R. (3d) 1, 53 C.C.C. (3d) 316, 47 C.R.R. 210, 37 O.A.C. 161, 105 N.R. 81 (S.C.C.).

[15] See *R. v. Macooh*, 1993 CarswellAlta 411, 1993 CarswellAlta 563, 82 C.C.C. (3d) 481, 22 C.R. (4th) 70, 16 C.R.R. (2d) 1, 105 D.L.R. (4th) 96, 141 A.R. 321, 46 W.A.C. 321, [1993] 2 S.C.R. 802, 155 N.R. 44 (S.C.C.), at p. 491 [C.C.C.], wherein Lamer, C.J.C., as he then was, quoted with approval R.E. Salhany's definition of hot pursuit; see R.E. Salhany, *Canadian Criminal Procedure*, 5th ed. (Aurora: Canada Law Book, 1989), at p. 44.

[16] *R. v. Cunningham*, 1979 CarswellMan 243, 49 C.C.C. (2d) 390 (Man. Co. Ct.).

[17] *Criminal Code*, s. 31.

[18] *Criminal Code*, subs. 524(2)(a).

[19] *Criminal Code*, subs. 524(1)(b).

[20] *Criminal Code*, s. 672.91.

[21] Greenspan & Rosenberg, *supra*, note 11, at cc/874.

[22] See *R. v. Acker*, 1970 CarswellNS 22, [1970] 4 C.C.C. 269, 9 C.R.N.S. 371, 1 N.S.R. (2d) 572 (N.S. C.A.).

[23] See *R. v. Therens*, 1985 CarswellSask 368, 1985 CarswellSask 851, 18 C.C.C. (3d) 481, 45 C.R. (3d) 97, 38 Alta. L.R. (2d) 99, [1985] 1 S.C.R. 613, 13 C.R.R. 193, [1985] 4 W.W.R. 286, 18 D.L.R. (4th) 655, 59 N.R. 122, 40 Sask. R. 122, 32 M.V.R. 153 (S.C.C.), wherein the Supreme Court of Canada defines the purpose of s. 10 of the *Charter*. Its purpose is to ensure that in certain situations a person is made aware of the right to counsel and is permitted to retain and instruct counsel without delay. Detention within s. 10 applies both to a deprivation of liberty by physical constraint other than arrest in which a person may reasonably require the assistance of counsel, and when a police officer or other agent of the state assumes control over the movement of a person by a demand or direction that may have significant legal consequences and that prevents or impedes access to counsel. It is not the intent to discuss the jurisprudence surrounding the issues relating to s. 10 of the *Charter*, as it would clearly exceed the scope of this chapter.

[24] Part 1 of the *Constitution Act, 1982*, being Schedule B to the *Canada Act, 1982* (U.K.), c. 11.

[25] *R. v. Macooh, supra*, note 15.

[26] See *Christie v. Leachinsky*, [1947] A.C. 573, [1947] 1 All E.R. 567 (U.K. H.L.).

[27] See *R. v. Smith*, 1991 CarswellNS 29, 1991 CarswellNS 414, 63 C.C.C. (3d) 313, 4 C.R. (4th) 125, 104 N.S.R. (2d) 233, 283 A.P.R. 233, 122 N.R. 203, 3 C.R.R. (2d) 370, [1991] 1 S.C.R. 714 (S.C.C.).

[28] *R. v. Brydges*, 1990 CarswellAlta 3, 1990 CarswellAlta 648, 53 C.C.C. (3d) 330, 74 C.R. (3d) 129, [1990] 2 W.W.R. 220, 46 C.R.R. 236, [1990] 1 S.C.R. 190, 103 N.R. 282, 71 Alta. L.R. (2d) 145, 104 A.R. 124 (S.C.C.).

[29] *R. v. Prosper*, 1994 CarswellNS 438, 1994 CarswellNS 25, 92 C.C.C. (3d) 353, 33 C.R. (4th) 85, 118 D.L.R. (4th) 154, 133 N.S.R. (2d) 321, 380 A.P.R. 321, 172 N.R. 161, 6 M.V.R. (3d) 181, [1994] 3 S.C.R. 236, 23 C.R.R. (2d) 239 (S.C.C.).

[30] *R. v. Tremblay* (1987), 1987 CarswellOnt 111, 1987 CarswellOnt 972, 60 C.R. (3d) 59,, 37 C.C.C. (3d) 565 [1987] 2 S.C.R. 435, 45 D.L.R. (4th) 445, 79 N.R. 153, 25 O.A.C. 93, 32 C.R.R. 381, 2 M.V.R. (2d) 289 (S.C.C.).

[31] *R. v. Manninen* (1987), 1987 CarswellOnt 967, 1987 CarswellOnt 99, 34 C.C.C.

(3d) 385, 58 C.R. (3d) 97, 76 N.R. 198, 38 C.R.R. 37, 21 O.A.C. 192, [1987] 1
S.C.R. 1233, 41 D.L.R. (4th) 301, 61 O.R. (2d) 736 (note) (S.C.C.).

[32] *R. v. Leclair*, 1989 CarswellOnt 67, 1989 CarswellOnt 953, 67 C.R. (3d) 209, 31
O.A.C. 321, 91 N.R. 81, (*sub nom. R. v. Ross*) 46 C.C.C. (3d) 129, (*sub nom. R. v.
Ross*) [1989] 1 S.C.R. 3, (*sub nom. R. v. Ross*) 37 C.R.R. 369 (S.C.C.).

[33] *R. v. Feeney* (1997), 1997 CarswellBC 1015, 1997 CarswellBC 1016, 115 C.C.C.
(3d) 129, 7 C.R. (5th) 101, 212 N.R. 83, [1997] 2 S.C.R. 13, [1997] 6 W.W.R. 634,
146 D.L.R. (4th) 609, 91 B.C.A.C. 1, 148 W.A.C. 1, 44 C.R.R. (2d) 1 (S.C.C.),
reconsideration granted 1997 CarswellBC 3179, 1997 CarswellBC 3180, [1997] 2
S.C.R. 117 (S.C.C.).

[34] See Reneé M. Pomerance's article entitled, "Entry and Arrest in Dwelling Houses"
(1998), 13 C.R. (5th) 84.

[35] *Ibid.*

[36] *Ibid.*

[37] *R. v. Macooh, supra,* note 15.

[38] *Ibid.*

[39] *Cloutier c. Langlois*, 1990 CarswellQue 8, 1990 CarswellQue 110, 53 C.C.C. (3d)
257, 74 C.R. (3d) 316, [1990] 1 S.C.R. 158, 105 N.R. 241, 46 C.R.R. 37, 30 Q.A.C.
241 (S.C.C.).

[40] *R. v. Debot*, 1989 CarswellOnt 111, 1989 CarswellOnt 966, 52 C.C.C. (3d) 193,
73 C.R. (3d) 129, [1989] 2 S.C.R. 1140, 102 N.R. 161, 37 O.A.C. 1, 45 C.R.R. 49
(S.C.C.).

[41] *Cloutier c. Langlois, supra,* note 39, at p. 278 [C.C.C.].

[42] *R. v. Caslake*, 1998 CarswellMan 1, 1998 CarswellMan 2, 13 C.R. (5th) 1, 121
C.C.C. (3d) 97, 48 C.R.R. (2d) 189, [1998] 1 S.C.R. 51, 123 Man. R. (2d) 208, 159
W.A.C. 208, [1999] 4 W.W.R. 303, 155 D.L.R. (4th) 19, 221 N.R. 281 (S.C.C.), at
p. 17 [C.R.].

[43] See *Criminal Code*, subs. 501(2), (3) and (4).

[44] R.S.C. 1985, c. I-1.

[45] *Criminal Code*, subs. 497(1)(a), (b).

[46] *Criminal Code*, subs. 497(1.1), (2).

[47] See *Criminal Code*, s. 493, which defines "officer in charge" as the officer for the
time being in command of the police force responsible for the lock-up or other place
to which an accused is taken after arrest or a peace officer designated by him or her
for the purposes of this part who is in charge of that place at the time an accused is
taken to that place to be detained in custody.

[48] *Criminal Code*, subs. 498(1)(a), (b), (c) and (d).

[49] *Criminal Code*, subs. 498(2).

[50] A *promise to appear* is a release form given to the accused, signed by him or her
and by the officer in charge, at the time of his or her release from custody.

[51] Gary T. Trotter, *supra,* note 1, at p. 161. A recognizance is the formal record of an
acknowledgment of indebtedness to the Crown that is defeasible upon the fulfil-
ment of certain conditions, the primary one being attendance in court for trial. The
actual document that is executed, the recognizance, does not create the obligation,
but merely records it.

[52] Gary T. Trotter, *supra,* note 1, at p. 40.

[53] *Criminal Code*, subs. 511(3).

[54] *Criminal Code*, subs. 511(4).

[55] *Criminal Code*, subs. 512(1).

[56] *Criminal Code*, subs. 512(2)(a).

[57] *Criminal Code*, 512(2)(b).

[58] *Criminal Code*, subs. 512(2)(c).

[59] *Criminal Code*, s. 502.

[60] *Criminal Code*, subs. 524(1)(a).

[61] *Criminal Code*, subs. 524(1)(b).

[62] *Criminal Code*, subs. 514(1)(a).

[63] *Criminal Code*, subs. 514(1)(b).

[64] *Criminal Code*, s. 528.

[65] See J.E. Pink and H. MacKay, *Power of Arrest and Compelling Appearance* (Paper prepared for the Federation of Law Societies, 1992 National Criminal Law Program, University of Saskatchewan, Saskatoon, Saskatchewan) at section 1.1.

[66] Section 2 of the *Criminal Code* defines a *superior court of criminal jurisdiction* as meaning:

> (a) in the Province of Ontario, the Court of Appeal or the Superior Court of Justice,
> (b) in the Province of Quebec, the Superior Court,
> (c) in the Province of Prince Edward Island, the Supreme Court,
> (d) in the Provinces of New Brunswick, Manitoba, Saskatchewan and Alberta, the Court of Appeal or the Court of Queen's Bench,
> (e) in the Provinces of Nova Scotia, British Columbia and Newfoundland, the Supreme Court or the Court of Appeal,
> (f) in Yukon, the Supreme Court,
> (g) in the Northwest Territories, the Supreme Court, and
> (h) in Nunavut, the Nunavut Court of Justice.

7

Release After Arrest

*Shane G. Parker**

BASIC PHILOSOPHY

The philosophy of the release provisions of the *Criminal Code* pursues two objectives. First, society deserves to be protected from those who will predictably act in an anti-social manner when in the community. Second, our prisons should not be used to warehouse individuals who have not been proven criminals, who will probably show up for trial, and who will respond to specific liberty restraints in the period between release and trial.

HISTORY

The common law of England recognized from its earliest beginnings the right of a prisoner to be permitted bail where appropriate. Enforcement of this right was through the writ of *habeas corpus*. On the other hand, this "right" to bail had many restrictions. In fact, a person arrested was only entitled to be released with respect to minor crimes regarded as "misdemeanors". Release was discretionary in relation to the more serious "felonies" and treason. In cases of homicide, release was not available at common law.

In Canada, after 1869, release pending trial was discretionary regardless of the offence charged. Until the *Bail Reform Act* of the 1970s, the burden was on the person accused to demonstrate that he or she would likely appear at trial. The appropriate court would assess the request for release in light of three criteria:

(1) the nature of the crime;
(2) the probability of conviction; and
(3) the severity of the penalty.

---

*   B.Sc. (Hons), University of Waterloo; MPE, University of New Brunswick; LL.B., Dalhousie Law School, Halifax, Nova Scotia; Crown Attorney with the Nova Scotia Public Prosecution Service; currently a Crown Attorney practicing in the Province of Alberta.

If release was to be contemplated, the usual mechanism was to give the accused, or his or her sureties (persons who would vouch for his or her reappearance at trial), a financial incentive to obey the terms of release. Thus, a cash figure was set that the accused or his or her sureties would have to deposit, and would forfeit in the event of non-appearance. That deposit of money is the source of the concept of release as "bail".

Since the *Bail Reform Act*, the question of release prior to trial has evolved to focus on a number of concurrent objectives. First, conditions of release must ensure the accused attends trial. Secondly, release conditions should seek to prevent the commission of further offences while the accused is released awaiting trial. Thirdly, release conditions must prevent harm to the integrity of the prosecutorial process while the accused is awaiting trial. The release is to maintain the public confidence in its security while the possible criminal awaits trial.

Now, the law interpreting release and detention provisions is governed by ss. 9 and 11(e) under the *Canada Charter of Right and Freedoms*. Section 9 of the *Charter* states, "Everyone has the right not to be arbitrarily detained or imprisoned." Subsection 11(e) of the *Charter* states, "Any person charged with an offence has the right not to be denied reasonable bail without just cause".

The *Bail Reform Act*, incorporated in the *Criminal Code*, has changed the terminology from "bail". Bail is not referred to in the *Code* but rather a broader term of "judicial interim release".

One also must consider the difference between the American style of justice and Canadian criminal law. Many will be familiar with the American criminal justice system, which has bail bondsmen, essentially third parties that can post bond or bail. This is specifically outlawed under the *Criminal Code*. In Canada "sureties" must have some connection to the offender.

RELEASE PRIOR TO ATTENDANCE IN COURT

An individual may lose his or her liberty by being arrested. Where an offence committed or observed is an indictable offence, s. 507 of the *Criminal Code* requires release before a justice, unless the warrant is endorsed. Greater latitude is now provided to a peace officer to release when making an arrest without a warrant. A peace officer may only detain if it is necessary:

(1) to establish identity;

(2) to secure or preserve evidence; or

(3) to prevent the continuation or repetition of the offence or another offence.

A person may also be justifiably detained if there are reasonable grounds to believe the person will fail to attend court in order to be dealt with according to law (s. 495).

If the offence allegedly committed is a summary conviction or a hybrid offence, or one of those within the absolute jurisdiction of the provincial court, the arrested person should be released as soon as the reason for the arrest is satisfied. The only consideration at this stage is whether it satisfies the public interest and the officer is satisfied or is assured that the offender will attend court. This is the only criteria that need be assessed at this time. This assessment may be done by the arresting officer with the issuance of an Appearance Notice.

The Appearance Notice may precede the laying of any charge. It sets out the substance of the offence that may be charged and requires the person to attend court at a particular place and at a particular time. The Appearance Notice may also require the person to appear at another place and time for purposes of the *Identification of Criminals Act*.

Failure to comply with this police direction from the Appearance Notice of either attendance of court or for *Identification of Criminal Act* is an offence itself under s. 145(5) of the *Criminal Code*. It should be noted that an Appearance Notice is in substance no different than a summons except that a summons may only be issued after a charge has been laid.

In the event the arresting police officer is unwilling or unable to release an arrested person, the matter may be dealt with by the police officer in charge. The officer in charge is permitted to act in the time prior to an appearance before a justice of the peace or provincial court judge as described in the *Criminal Code* as a "justice". The *Code* contemplates that a person not released by the police will be in front of a justice as soon as practical within 24 hours, or as soon as possible thereafter (s. 503).

"Officer in charge" is not defined in the *Criminal Code*. In *R. v. Gendron*,[1] the issue was whether the staff sergeant was the officer in charge. Since *Gendron*, the *Code* was amended in 1998, which changed the language to "officer in charge or another peace officer". To date there has been no judicial decision defining how to interpret the amendment that is broader than what the Court had to address in *Gendron*. It is arguable that the plain meaning of the amended section is that a different police officer with a fresher perspective would satisfy the provision of the *Code*; logically this has some appeal.[2]

The other important concept to contemplate is the provision of 24 hours. It is a common mistake that the police have 24 hours with the accused before he or she must go before the justice of the peace; this is only partially correct. Section 503(1)(a) of the *Criminal Code* outlines that where a justice is available within a period of 24 hours after the person has been arrested by or delivered to the peace officer, the person shall be taken before a justice without unreasonable delay. What the section further contemplates is that there will not be an unreasonable delay in getting the offender before a justice of the peace. The 24 hours is simply a maximum time limit but should not be used as the norm.

The officer in charge who chooses to release an individual may simply release him or her without documentation, or may require a "Promise to Appear" or a "Recognizance". The Promise to Appear involves a promise by the detained person to appear in a particular court on a particular day, and may also involve an appearance for the purposes of the *Identification of Criminals Act*. Unlike the Appearance Notice, which may be signed by a potential accused, but does not have to be, the Promise to Appear does require an acknowledgment by the person detained. Having said that, the promise may be made orally and there does not need to be an actual signature on the document. Failure to appear in response to a Promise to Appear is an offence. The offence is punishable on a more serious note indicating that the *Criminal Code* recognises that more serious offences require more careful considerations about permitting release.

Given the ascending concerns with respect to release as the seriousness of the offence increases, the officer in charge may require more than a simple promise from the detained person. A Recognizance requires both a promise to appear and a promise that if the individual fails to appear, he or she will owe the Crown up to $500 in value. If the person detained is not ordinarily a resident in the province or within 200 kilometers of the place of detention, the officer can take the further precaution of requiring the promise to attend, the promise to owe up to $500 to the Crown in the event of non-appearance, and the actual deposit of cash or other valuable security up to $500. In addition to these monetary consequences, failure to abide by a Recognizance is itself a criminal offence.

Officers in charge have been given the ability to require special release conditions where a person is "picked up" on a warrant or delivered to the officer in charge, assuming that the offence is not under s. 469.

The officer in charge may require the accused, in order to be released, to enter into an undertaking to remain within the territorial jurisdiction, to notify of changes in address or employment, to deposit any passport, and to abstain from contact with specified people or places except on further condition. For there to be this kind of release, there must have been a warrant, and therefore there must already be a charge. As a practical matter, conditions for such undertakings usually get formulated in rather coercive circumstances without access to or advice from counsel, and it can be difficult to relax them later since the accused was at one point prepared to make the promises. Where conditions additional to those set out in s. 499(2) are advisable to meet the objectives of protecting the society, the detained person will likely be held until dealt with by a justice of the peace or a provincial court judge.

RELEASE BY A JUSTICE OF THE PEACE OR PROVINCIAL COURT JUDGE

A justice of the peace or a provincial court judge has, by virtue of s. 2 of the *Criminal Code*, the same powers of release. As a judicial officer, the "justice" has the authority to release individuals charged with any but the most serious criminal offences (for instance, those set out in s. 469). A justice may also confirm detention and remand those who are alleged to have committed offences elsewhere in Canada pending execution of a warrant.

The equality of the justice of the peace with provincial court judges has allowed for creation of a "telebail" system in various jurisdictions. Prior amendments to s. 515 have included ss. 515(2) and (2.3) of the *Code*. Bail hearings can be preformed over the phone between police, accused, and a justice of the peace. This is a growing trend across Canadian jurisdictions, particularly in off-hours or on weekends.

The tools that a justice may use in providing for release, while at the same time attempting to meet the objectives of protecting society, are "Undertakings" and "Recognizances".

An Undertaking is a promise given to the court by an accused to attend at a particular time and place. Unlike the police Promise to Appear, an Undertaking may or may not include conditions such as regular reporting, refraining from contact with particular persons, surrendering a passport, and so on. The other main distinction of an Undertaking from a Promise to Appear is that a charge must actually have been laid prior to the giving of an Undertaking. It is an offence not to comply with an Undertaking.

A higher form of release is a Recognizance. As described above, a Recognizance is a promise by the accused person to appear and to acknowledge the forfeiture of money in the event of a failure to appear. Recognizances may be in various forms and various amounts. Unlike the police Recognizance, there may be additional conditions designed to ensure the accused's attendance, or designed to reduce the opportunity to commit further crime pending reappearance. Sureties, persons to vouch for the detained person's compliance with conditions, may be required. Sureties themselves sign the Recognizance and promise to pay a sum of money to the Crown in the event the detained person does not continue to comply with the terms of the release. The Recognizance may or may not require the actual deposit of money by the detained person or the sureties. The court may or may not choose to determine who may act as sureties for the detained person.

An important concept is the "ladder". Normally, the least restricted release mechanism is to be applied under s. 515(2). A careful review of paragraphs (a) to (e) show increasing restrictions of liberty.

Section 515(2) of the *Code* states:

> Where the justice does not make an order under subsection (1), he shall, unless the prosecutor shows cause why the detention of the accused is justified, order that the accused be released
>> (a) on his giving an undertaking with such conditions as the justice directs;
>> (b) on his entering into a recognizance before the justice, without sureties, in such amount and with such conditions, if any, as the justice directs but without deposit of money or other valuable security;
>> (c) on his entering into a recognizance before the justice with sureties in such amount and with such conditions, if any, as the justice directs but without deposit of money or other valuable security;
>> (d) with the consent of the prosecutor, on his entering into a recognizance before the justice, without sureties, in such amount and with such conditions, if any, as the justice directs and on his depositing with the justice such sum of money or other valuable security as the justice directs; or
>> (e) if the accused is not ordinarily a resident in the province in which the accused is in custody or does not ordinarily reside within two hundred kilometres of the place in which he is in custody, on his entering into a recognizance before the justice with or without sureties in such amount and with such conditions, if any, as the justice directs, and on his depositing with the justice such sum of money or other valuable security as the justice directs.

Section 515(2.1) of the *Code* states:

> Where, pursuant to subsection (2) or any other provision of this Act, a

justice, judge or court orders that an accused be released on his entering
into a recognizance with sureties, the justice, judge or court may, in the
order, name particular persons as sureties.

Subsections 515(2) and (2.1) are critical to the understanding of
bail and release by a judge or justice of the peace. What is seen in s.
515(2) is first, the use of an Undertaking; moving to a Recognizance
without sureties; moving to a Recognizance with sureties, but without
deposit of money; to a Recognizance with sureties with deposit of money or valuable security as the justice directs. Subsection (e) is simply a
condition for those that are outside of the jurisdiction.

Should an offender breach a lower form of release, if the person is
then been picked up and charged for the breach, a consideration is usually made to the next higher form of release. It is a common law rule
that before a person is simply remanded, the other considerations higher
up on the ladder are considered. For instance, if a person breaches an
undertaking by having contact with a person they are not supposed to,
they are held to be released typically before a justice of the peace. The
justice of peace or provincial court judge will consider whether the
person should be remanded in custody until the time of the trial or be
released on a higher form of release such as a Recognizance or a Recognizance with sureties.

To this point we have reviewed release by the officer, by the officer
in charge, and by the justice of the peace or provincial court judge. As
can be seen, the release and restrictions upon liberty while awaiting trial
and disposition become much more restrictive and more encompassing
depending on the person who is, in a sense, making the release. There is
greater discretion, for obvious reasons, for release by a provincial court
judge then by, for instance, the arresting officer. More serious matters
often necessitate that those with greater discretion and can provide
greater controls upon a persons liberty to affective attendance at trial or
to ensure that there will not be a substantial likelihood of re-offending
that these people go to a provincial court judge.

It is critical for the system to work properly that all of those use
their discretion properly. It would be a waste of judicial resources and a
deprivation to a person's liberty interest if, for instance, a first-time offender is caught stealing a bicycle. Release in that case should be done
by an officer in charge. To hold a person in such circumstances to be
held before a judge, which may take up to 24 hours or, in some cases,
slightly longer than that until the justice of the peace or a provincial
court judge can be located and the person can actually be brought be-

fore them, is a intrusion upon their liberty interest and runs counter to ss. 9 and 11(e) of the *Charter*.

RELEASE BY JUDGE ONLY

An individual arrested and charged with one of the more serious offences in the *Criminal Code*, including treason and murder that are governed under s. 469, must be held in custody by the police. The detainee must also be remanded to custody upon appearance before a justice. Such persons may only be released by a judge of the provincial superior court of the criminal jurisdiction. This means the superior court of criminal jurisdiction (defined in s. 2) is the only capable court when it comes to release for serious offences under s. 469. Since the *Criminal Code* procedure for dealing with such serious offences does not automatically result in an appearance before the court capable of providing release, any initiative in this regard generally has to come from the detained person. Like a justice, the tools available to a judge of the superior court of the criminal jurisdiction are the Undertaking and any of the appropriate forms of Recognizance that are outlined previously under ss. 515(2) and (2.1).

ISSUES AT THE RELEASE HEARING

The release hearing is often called a "show cause" or "bail hearing". There is little difference in substance or in procedure if the issue of release comes before a provincial court or the superior court of criminal jurisdiction in the province. Typically, the Crown has the burden of showing on a balance of probabilities why the detained person should be kept in custody.

Section 515(6) of the *Criminal Code* put the burden on the accused in certain circumstances. Where the accused bears the burden on a balance of probabilities is when the accused is charged with:

1. An indictable offence, other than ones listed in section 469, and the person is not a resident of Canada;
2. is charged with an indictable offence and is on judicial interim release for an indictable offence;
3. a criminal organization, terrorism, or specified provisions of the *Security of Information Act* offence;
4. firearm trafficking offences;
5. Using a firearm to commit robbery, extortion, serious sexual assaults, confinement/kidnapping, attempted murder or dis-

[handwritten: 10. Subsequent n×6n10 / indictable offences]

charging a firearm with the intent to commit aggravated assault;

6. used, or the subject matter is, a firearm and was under a prohibition order from possessing one at the time;

7. charged with a breach of a release condition under section 145; or

8. A life imprisonment offence under ss. 5(3), 6(3), or 7(2) of the CDSA. *[handwritten: – Inafficially News...]*

[handwritten: 9 – Fauure to Appean]

In these situations it is called a "reverse onus" whereby the accused bears the burden on a balance of probabilities of why he or she should be released. There is some debate in practical terms whether reverse onus on the accused truly changes the eventual judicial determination.

Canadian jurisdictions vary in practice whether the accused will call evidence or not. In some eastern parts of the country the accused will routinely call evidence, where generally in western provinces counsel for the accused will make representations on behalf of the accused, including a description of the surety's connection and financial background. More will be said about the conduct of the hearing.

There are three relevant issues at a bail hearing under s. 515(10):

> (a) where the detention is necessary to ensure [the accused's] attendance in court ...;
> (b) where the detention is necessary for the protection or safety of the public, ... including any substantial likelihood that the accused will, ... if released, commit a criminal offence or interfere with the administration of justice; and
> (c) if the detention is necessary to maintain confidence in the administration of justice, having regard to all the circumstances, including
>> (i) the apparent strength of the prosecution's case,
>> (ii) the gravity of the offence,
>> (iii) the circumstances surrounding the commission of the offence, including whether a firearm was used, and
>> (iv) the fact that the accused is liable, on conviction, for a potentially lengthy term of imprisonment or, in the case of an offence that involves, or whose subject-matter is, a firearm, a minimum punishment of imprisonment for a term of three years or more.

Paragraphs (a) and (b) have remained the same for decades. In 2008 Parliament re-crafted paragraph (c) by adding subparagraphs (iii)—use of a firearm—and (iv)—the subject-matter is a firearm where the accused may be liable to a mandatory minimum of 3 years if convicted.

This was in response to growing public outrage over the use of handguns by urban street gangs.

The party bearing the burden must do so on balance of probabilities and not on the juridical standard of proof beyond reasonable doubt.

For the Crown to show cause for the burden, they only need prove that on one of those three, either (a), (b), or (c) under s. 515(10), is grounds for detention or remand.

THE PRIMARY GROUND

The issue of whether a detained person will appear for upcoming steps in the criminal trial process is an issue that courts considering release have dealt with for centuries. This is a common issue in deciding whether the accused should have bail in the United States and the United Kingdom as well. A reasonably stable list of factors are assessed, each of which points towards or against the likelihood of the accused person remaining in the locality where the criminal trial process will take place and showing up for trial. These factors include:

(1) usual residence in the province;
(2) a fixed place of abode in the province;
(3) employment;
(4) close friends and relatives;
(5) family status;
(6) personal history;
(7) evidence as to character;
(8) previous criminal record; and
(9) the nature of the offence.

Some of these considerations will obviously be considerations under the secondary or tertiary grounds as well. Evidence of these is not inclusive but all go toward showing that ultimately the person will attend court or, depending on the burden, will not attend court and should justify detention.

From a practical point of view, where there is some established residence and no established criminal or probationary record for failures to appear in response to the requirements of the justice system, there is little basis to conclude that detention is necessary to ensure attendance in court. The likelihood of a released individual responding to appearance obligations is enhanced where the individual has all or essentially all of his or her relatives, as well as employment, in the community of where the offence is alleged to have occurred. In the event of concerns that are not substantial enough to make detention necessary, conditions may be imposed that reduce the likelihood of non-appearance (i.e., the ceasing of a passport; depositing large amounts of money by recognizance; reporting to particular police detachments on a regular basis; curfews). Essentially any conditions that allow for a person to stay in the jurisdiction and have this monitored or checked will satisfy the court that this is appropriate.

Sureties also play a pivotal role and are very appropriate in dealing with concerns under s. 515(10)(a). Sureties ensure that individuals in the community who are not directly connected with the justice system and who have some reasonable association with the accused will also have an incentive to ensure that the accused appears as required because they have a financial stake. The sureties thus become the eyes and ears for the court to ensure re-attendance once the accused leaves the courtroom.

The Court does not necessarily have to pre-approve named sureties. The Justice who later on in executing the recognizance under s. 519 may be in a position to approve or disapprove any surety. As an example, the Court may agree to release Mr. Smith on a recognizance with a surety to pledge $5000.00, but not name a surety. Mr. Smith will remain in custody until he can find a person to come forward and pledge the money ("justify" the amount). Once Mr. Smith finds the person who financially is in a position to comply, and is willing to act as a surety, then both the surety and Mr. Smith will go before a Justice of the Peace to enter into a recognizance (essentially, sign a "contract" with the Court). There is no provision under the judicial interim release sections that a surety must attend court and present himself or herself as a witness.[3] In practice, it may very well be necessary to satisfy the Court of the wisdom of the proposed release plan.

Subsection 515(2.1) is important in that the court can name sureties. Often at a show cause or bail hearing the court will give great consideration as to whether the proposed sureties are appropriate. Courts are not only looking at whether they can be financial safeguards and provide appropriate feelings of security assessed by the public interest and attendance in court, but are also looking at whether the sureties can, in some term, be used as "modern jailers". A surety not only has a financial responsibility, but also often has some responsibility in helping the offender abide by the conditions that have been put in place by the court.

THE SECONDARY GROUND

If the court dealing with the release decides that the attendance of the accused can be assured, it will then turn to the secondary ground under s. 515(10)(b) of the *Code*, which is concerned with the interests of the community at large during the time the individual is on release. The integrity of the prosecutorial process has to be protected by preventing possible interference with witnesses, and the community should be given the confidence that it will not be subjected to further criminal activity by this individual while he or she awaits trial. Similarly worded provision is also in the *Criminal Justice Act 2003* in the United Kingdom.

The releasing court cannot guarantee that a person released will not, in fact, commit other criminal offences if released. Therefore, the court on the secondary ground for detention considers whether there is a substantial likelihood the community will suffer further wrongs at the hands of the particular individual. Most bail hearings are fought on this ground.

The courts have consistently been concerned with clear evidence of participation by the accused in on-going criminal activities or patterns of criminal activity. The Crown may be able to offer evidence that at the time of the arrest the accused was contemplating or participating in some more serious criminal activity than the offence for which he or she was being held. For example, an individual arrested for the possession of narcotics may be shown, as a result of wiretap, to have been preparing to import narcotics.

The court may infer a continuing inclination to participate in criminal activities where a record of previous convictions exists, and particularly if it is lengthy and without gaps. Such an inference will be compelling where the record is recent. Obviously, a record with recent convictions for offences similar to the ones charged in the case before the court may be extremely persuasive that the release will only lead to further offences of the same nature. Also persuasive for the court is whether the person has a history of breaching undertakings or recognizance in the past.

The considerations on the secondary ground are not limited to an individual's prior record and current trouble. The court is required to consider "all the circumstances". Described by one court as taking into account "the plain lessons of human experience", it is important to focus on and be wary of releasing those who have "proceeded with depressing regularity from one conviction to the next".

In situations where the appropriateness of release on this ground is seriously questioned, the court is also disposed to consider the causes of past and current difficulties with the law with a view to, perhaps, mold or draft conditions that will prevent or ensure that there will not be a substantial likelihood of re-offending. For example, an individual arrested for murder is known to have been drunk at the time of arrest. He has a record for two or three impaired driving convictions over the previous five years. The circumstances of the offence and the nature of the offences themselves may speak to the fact that the accused has a problem in controlling his actions while using alcohol. The court will consider what conditions can be imposed to curtail the use of alcohol, which may be one of the criminological precursors.

The court is also going to be concerned with how much time is going to be involved in awaiting the trial. Often if the person is remanded there will be an attempt to have an earlier trial date so the person is not kept in custody. Sometimes that simply is not practical and a lengthy period between custody will require the court to look more seriously at trying to draft conditions to curve the substantial likelihood of re-offending or interfering with Crown witnesses.

Other conditions that can be used to satisfy s. 515(2)(b) concerns, rather than remanding, are curfews; sureties; having no contact with specified persons or places; and even forms of house arrest.

THE TERTIARY GROUND

The premise of the tertiary ground is to protect the public's confidence in the administration of justice. The public commands that a proper and fair trial is conducted. There must not be tampering with evidence or manipulating witnesses in how they will deliver their testimony at trial and the accused must appear at trial to answer to the charges. Those concerns are addressed in the primary and secondary grounds. The tertiary ground is different. It could be argued that the tertiary ground moves closer to the United States federal—and some State law—Code, Title 18, where an accused is detained if they are charged with listed serious violent offences, drug offences which carry maximums over 10 years and repeat felons. The other consideration is whether the accused will abscond or show up for his trial (our primary concern). It is tempting to classify the tertiary ground as a residual category, but properly it must be considered a distinct consideration applied in appropriate cases, like serious violent offences, or sophisticated, organized crime.

As presented above, s. 515(10)(c) states:

> (c) if the detention is necessary to maintain confidence in the ad-
> ministration of justice, having regard to all the circumstances, in-
> cluding
>> (i) the apparent strength of the prosecution's case,
>> (ii) the gravity of the offence,
>> (iii) the circumstances surrounding the commission of the
>> offence, including whether a firearm was used, and
>> (iv) the fact that the accused is liable, on conviction, for a
>> potentially lengthy term of imprisonment or, in the case of
>> an offence that involves, or whose subject-matter is, a fire-
>> arm, a minimum punishment of imprisonment for a term of
>> three years or more.

The tertiary ground has undergone an evolution over the last 20 years. Section 515(10)(c) of the *Code* was a response to the Supreme Court of Canada decision in *R. c. Morales*,[4] where the Court struck down the term "in the public interest" as vague and therefore unconstitutional and more recently by adding offences where firearms are used as a response to gang gun violence.

The main principle to understand about the tertiary ground is that the accused person's detention is necessary to maintain confidence in the administration of justice. It is the confidence of a reasonable, informed and dispassionate public that provides the measure of this ground. As such, the public would understand that the applicant has re-acquired the presumption of innocence as a result of the decision of this court. Further, as stated by the Ontario Court of Appeal, the public's interest in the continued incarceration of an individual charged with the most serious offence known to the law must be balanced against the public's interest in seeing that no person be unjustly punished.

R. v. Hall[5] offered the Supreme Court of Canada the first opportunity to question the constitutionality of s. 515(10)(c). In 1999, Peggy Jo Barkley-Dubé's body was found dead in her home in Sault Ste. Marie from massive bleeding resulting from 37 stab wounds. One month later the victim's husband's second cousin was charged with the slaying. Evidence linking his involvement included his blood at the scene, foot-print impressions containing the victim's blood, and a matching type of shoes worn by Mr. Hall. A surveillance tape from a local convenience store showed Mr. Hall was wearing these shoes on the night of the mur-der, although he denied such. Evidence at the bail hearing showed the fear in the community and by the immediate family members in the one month proceeding his arrest.

The justice at the bail hearing held that the evidence did not support denying bail on the first two grounds. Justice Bolan found there were adequate conditions to ensure Mr. Hall's attendance and there was no reason to believe Hall would commit another offence.

Justice Bolan did find that Hall should be remanded in custody in order to maintain confidence in the administration of justice on the tertiary ground under s. 515(10)(c). Bolan, J. reasoned that the heightened fear in the community, the nature of the offence, and the strong Crown case supported the tertiary ground. The majority held that the phrase that begins s. 515(10)(c): "on any other just cause being shown" was vague and offended s. 11(e) of the *Charter* (not to be denied reasonable bail without just cause). Without the phrase, "any other just cause being shown", the remainder of s. 515(10)(c) was and is constitutional.

Chief Justice McLachlin held that the remaining section is narrower and more precise then the old "in the public interest" grounds struck down earlier by the court in the *Morales* decision. Mr. Justice Bolan's decision stands; Hall was to remain in custody.

The point to be made is that the accused must show that his detention is not necessary to maintain confidence in the administration of justice. It is *the confidence of a reasonable, informed and dispassionate public* that provides the measure of this ground. The public must equally be informed and consider the presumption of innocence. The public's interest in the continued incarceration of an individual charged with the most serious offence known to the law must be balanced against the public's interest in seeing that no person be unjustly punished.

In *R. v. Broderick*,[6] Kowarsky J.P. for the Ontario Court of Justice reviewed the latest amendments to paragraph (c) and made the following well reasoned observations:

[55] ... Parliament recently chose to address the issue of bail and firearms specifically by enacting the amendments to section 515 (10) (c) of the Criminal Code. It seems to me that Parliament would have more likely added the firearms provisions to the secondary rather than the tertiary ground since it is the secondary ground which is primarily concerned with public safety. However, having regard to the epidemic of gun violence in the country, it appears that Parliament was especially concerned with maintaining confidence in the administration of justice.

[56] It is safe to infer, therefore, that the intention of Parliament in amending the tertiary ground was clearly to ensure that people charged with firearms offences will face severe scrutiny by members of the public; even by those who are "properly informed about the philosophy of the legislative provisions, Charter values and the actual circumstances of the case." See *R. v. Nguyen* (1997), 119 C.C.C. (3d) 269 (B.C. C.A. [In Chambers]) quoted with approval by Chief Justice McLachlin in *R. v. Hall*, [2002] 3 S.C.R. 309 (S.C.C.). In my view, these informed members of the public

expect the government to pay special attention to people charged with firearms offences so as to protect the integrity of the justice system. I believe that in light of the perpetual cycle of violence involving guns, drugs and gangs in the country, Parliament wanted to send a strong message to people charged with such offences.

[57] While I am fully aware that it is not the role of the Justice presiding in a Bail Court to pander to the hysteria and outrage of the community (See *R. v. B. (A.)*, [2006] O.J. No. 394 (Ont. S.C.J.)), there are times such as these, when the surrounding circumstances of cases include an ongoing epidemic of gun violence, death, injury and destruction. Statistics reveal that the vast majority of gun related crimes are committed by people whose guns are illegal and unregistered. It is paramount that these illegal firearms are eradicated from our streets, and the people who steal, import, distribute and use them must be held accountable even at the pre-trial stage of the criminal justice system.

[58] ... The recent elimination of the words "the nature of" from the tertiary ground suggests that Parliament wanted to clarify that it is not necessarily the type of offence with which the accused is charged, but rather the "gravity" of the offence itself regardless of the nature of the offence itself. I find great support in this contention by the words of the Chief Justice of the Ontario Court of Appeal in *R. v. S. (B.)*, [2007] O.J. No. 3046 (Ont. C.A.). Winkler C.J. said the following at paragraph 10:

> The tertiary ground continues to apply to all persons seeking judicial interim release, whether charged with relatively minor, non violent offences or whether charged with murder ... as the nature of the offence and the surrounding circumstances become more serious, the consideration of the tertiary ground will become more relevant.

However, law professor, Don Stuart, who reviewed the Ontario Court of Appeal decision of *R. v. S. (B)*,[7] may disagree. Professor Stuart provided the following commentary as to the realities of how judges are typically applying the tertiary ground despite the decision in *R. v. Hall*:

> The Chief Justice in *S. (B.)* and Justice Juriansz before him in *M. (E.W.)* (2007), 41 C.R. (6th) 259 (Ont. C.A.) have chosen to ignore and/or discount a clear trend in decisions by trial judges holding that the tertiary ground of denying bail to maintain public confidence in the administration of justice is to be used sparingly ... The tertiary ground to be used rarely and even more rarely in the case of a youth ...
>
> Many of the above judges [cases omitted] have placed great emphasis on McLachlin C.J.C.'s acceptance that the reasonable person, in making the assessment of the need to maintain public confidence, must be properly informed about the philosophy of the legislative provisions, *Charter* values

and the actual circumstances of the case. In the context of murder superior court judges have in fact often distinguished *Hall* as a particularly brutal and inexplicable murder case involving attempted decapitation where there was evidence that the community was fearful about such a vicious killer being on the loose. In seeking to restrict the application of *Hall* these many trial judges appear to share the perspective of the dissenters in *Hall* who suggested that it was unjust to rely on the tertiary ground to detain where there is no flight risk or public safety concerns under s. 515(10)

Justice Cronk in *LaFramboise*, 2005 CarswellOnt 8335 (C.A.) (in Chambers), and Justice Monnin in *Trout* (2007), 41 C.R. (6th) 254 (Man. C.A.) added appellate authority to the view that the tertiary ground should be used sparingly. Justice Cronk reads *Hall* as requiring that the tertiary ground be used sparingly and rarely as the sole basis for detention and emphasizes the presumption of innocence. Justice Monnin holds the same view. He worries about the lengthy pre-trial detention that would result in the case before him before the preliminary inquiry and points to a release plan which would not send the accused back to the small community in which the killing took place.

Ascertaining the true reality of the use of the tertiary ground since *Hall* would require expensive empirical research given that so many bail decisions are made by provincial judges and justices of the peace and not recorded in available data bases. An early survey (Don Stuart and Joanna Harris, "Is the Public Confidence Ground to Deny Bail Used Sparingly?", (2004) 21 C.R. (6th) 232 examined 64 higher level decisions turning on the tertiary ground. It found that it was used to deny bail in 35 cases. This suggested that the ground was not being used sparingly. The trend was, however, already different in murder cases where detention on the tertiary ground was denied in 11 of 17 cases.

Judicial debate will continue as the provision and the amendments are, in court time, recent. It takes time for the debate to continue and over time consensus will be achieved, or the Supreme Court of Canada will weigh in giving clarity.

HEARING AND REVIEW

The hearing may take many forms. It may resemble a trial in that witnesses are called, documentary evidence introduced, and lengthy submissions made by counsel. As an alternative, a hearing may take place over the telephone, replacing a live hearing under s. 515(2.1). Most often release is dealt with simply through representations made by both Crown counsel and defence counsel after the essential facts have been agreed to and read in by the Crown, or put before the court through affidavits.

Bail hearings are to be expeditious so as not to further detain the accused. Rules of evidence at a trial are loosened. For instance, hearsay is permissible if it is credible and trustworthy. Another difference is on the focus of the accused's character. Contrast this with a trial where there is much evidentiary exclusion as to what the prosecutor can lead in terms of the accused's character.

In order that the release hearing does not become a trial in advance, and the integrity of the actual trial is not prejudiced, some special provisions apply. The accused may not be cross-examined with respect to the crime charged unless the accused testifies "respecting the offence", but this ability to question does not extend to the justice conducting the release hearing (see s. 515(b)). The justice may also order that a publication ban be put in place where the representations by counsel and any evidence heard will not be released, thus prejudicing the right to a fair trial.

Another focus of the bail hearing is the suitability of proposed sureties. Is the surety well suited to be the accused's "jailer" in the community and be financially responsible for his or her release? Accomplices (those with serious criminal records) or the accused's lawyer cannot be sureties at a bail hearing. A person who is already a surety is not a suitable surety. Good character for a surety is a critical issue; will the surety contact authorities if the accused is going to breach a condition or after breaching a condition? If an accused breaches a recognizance, or a third party is a surety, he or she will be liable to the Crown for the amount justified. Should a surety render (quit) the offender is back in custody until another suitable surety can be found?

The justice may adjourn the release hearing from time to time, and is initially required (if asked) to permit the Crown up to three "clear" days in order to prepare to show cause why the individual should not be released. An order of release can be varied on consent as circumstances require. If contested, the variation may be brought before the court initially capable of granting release, or the trial court if proceedings have put the accused in the jurisdiction of some court other than the provincial court.

If the Crown or defence is concerned about the order made by the justice of the peace or provincial court judge, there are provisions under the *Criminal Code* where a judge of a superior court of criminal jurisdiction can review the order. Success of reviews may be sought more than 30 days after the first review. The question on review is to show cause why the order previously made should be vacated or changed. Cause may include circumstances having been changed since the previous hearing, misconception of the facts at the previous hearing, or an error of law at the previous hearing. The review court may substitute its own discretion for that of the previous court dealing with the matter. As a practical matter, if there is nothing new since the previous hearing by way of additional evidence, and no demonstrable error on the part of the previous judge or justice, the original decision will be left intact. The discretion of the reviewing judge is intentional because of the importance of the competing interests: on the one side is the liberty of an accused person who has not been found guilty; on the other is the interest of the community of not being exposed to the high risk of criminal activity.

CONCLUSION OR SUMMARY

It is important to remember that when a person is arrested they are still presumed to be innocent. It is critical that release or detainment be in the least restrictive forms possible given this presumption. Release can be made under certain conditions for less serious offences by the arresting officer, for slightly more serious offences by an officer in charge, or where there is a concern about the circumstances of the alleged offender. For more grave concerns about the person who is in custody, or the nature of the offence, release can be by way of a justice of the peace or a provincial court judge. A justice of the peace or provincial court judge has greater discretion as to the mechanisms of release, such as an undertaking, a recognizance, a recognizance with sureties, and a recognizance with sureties and with a cash deposit. They can also have greater latitude in the conditions that they will try and draft to satisfy the three grounds of detainment under s. 515(10)(a), (b), or (c). If contested in a bail hearing or show cause, the concerns are: (a) if this person is going to attend court; (b) is there a substantial likelihood of this person committing another criminal offence or interfering with witnesses; or (c) to maintain confidence in the administration of justice in regards to all circumstances including the circumstances surrounding the offence and the strength of the Crown's case.

No doubt bail or judicial interim release will continue to evolve. The competing interests are the presumption of the accused's innocence and the right not to be detained by the state any longer than it is absolute necessary and the right to bail versus concern for the public's safety and concern for the proper administration of justice. Underscoring the concerns is that having a person in more restrictive conditions than are necessary will influence whether that person will receive a fair trial and whether the administration of justice will be properly carried out.

Conditions in remand are harsh and the deprivation of liberty no doubt affects the person's ability to properly prepare for trial.

Notes

[1] 1985 CarswellOnt 1372, 22 C.C.C. (3d) 312, 10 O.A.C. 122 (Ont. C.A.).

[2] Gary T. Trotter, *The Law of Bail in Canada*, 2d ed. (Toronto: Carswell, 1999).

[3] *R. v. Brooks*, 2001 CarswellOnt 1423, 153 C.C.C. (3d) 533 (Ont. S.C.J.); *R. v. Villota*, 2002 CarswellOnt 854, 163 C.C.C. (3d) 507, 3 C.R. (6th) 342 (Ont. S.C.J.).

[4] 1992 CarswellQue 18, 1992 CarswellQue 121, 17 C.R. (4th) 74, 12 C.R.R. (2d) 31, [1992] 3 S.C.R. 711, 77 C.C.C. (3d) 91, 144 N.R. 176, 51 Q.A.C. 161 (S.C.C.).

[5] 2002 CarswellOnt 3259, 2002 CarswellOnt 3260, [2002] S.C.J. No. 65, 4 C.R. (6th) 197, 217 D.L.R. (4th) 536, 167 C.C.C. (3d) 449, 97 C.R.R. (2d) 189, 293 N.R. 239, [2002] 3 S.C.R. 309, 2002 SCC 64, 165 O.A.C. 319 (S.C.C.).

[6] 2009 CarswellOnt 1983, 2009 ONCJ 152 (Ont. C.J.).

[7] 2007 CarswellOnt 5288, 2007 ONCA 560, 49 C.R. (6th) 397, 228 O.A.C. 24 (Ont. C.A.).

8

Guilty in Fact—Not Guilty in Law

Brian Casey*

Perhaps the most important characteristic of the common law is that guilt depends on intention. A pedestrian who is hit by a car and killed may have died accidentally, or the driver may be guilty of manslaughter or murder. We treat the person who has deliberately planned to kill someone differently than we treat someone who has accidentally killed someone through negligence, and differently again from someone who has accidentally killed someone without any fault at all.

Sometimes an accused person is acquitted because there is no proof of guilt, an issue that is discussed elsewhere in this book. But often a person is acquitted because of the difference between guilt in fact and guilt in law. In this chapter, we examine circumstances where the accused is apparently guilty in fact—he or she has done something the law prohibits, but not guilty in law—the circumstances (normally the intention) necessary to make it an offence do not exist.

Many circumstances excuse, or partly excuse, what an accused has done. We recognize this principle when we deal with children. A child may say, "he hit me first" or "it was an accident" to explain why his brother is crying. Another child may be comforted when a parent explains that baby brother "didn't realize what he was doing." These are examples of circumstances that we acknowledge can excuse or partly excuse a child's behaviour. Those same circumstances may excuse the behaviour of a person accused of a crime. In the case of a person accused of a crime, however, the analysis is a little different. It is not a case of circumstances excusing conduct; the act done is simply not an offence in the circumstances in the first place.

It is not exactly clear why some circumstances do excuse behaviour. To return to our discussion of children, if Robert accidentally hits his sister, she may well think it appropriate to hit him back—even though it was an accident. We could probably design a criminal justice system on the same principle, and punish people who commit certain acts, regard-

---

* B.A., University of British Columbia, Victoria, British Columbia; LL.B., Dalhousie Law School, Halifax, Nova Scotia; practicing law in Dartmouth, Nova Scotia.

less whether the act is intentional or accidental, in self-defence, or not, and regardless whether the accused is responsible for what he or she has done. In fact, historians believe that until the 12th century, that was the way English law proceeded. Now, however, we normally penalize people only if they have the necessary degree of intention for their actions, and are therefore guilty in law. By contrast, many lay persons tend to focus on guilt in fact, and not on guilt in law. When an accused is acquitted because he or she is not guilty in law, we sometimes think that the accused "got off on a technicality." We should recognize, however, that he or she has not gotten off because of the excuse; because of the excuse the accused was never guilty in the first place.

MENS REA AND ACTUS REUS

In analyzing whether a crime has been committed, it may be helpful to divide the criminal conduct into two categories, generally what the accused did, and what his or her intention was at the time. More precisely, the first category covers the existence of a certain event or state of affairs that is forbidden by the criminal law, which we call the *actus reus*, and the second category covers the prescribed state of mind, which we call the *mens rea*.[1] If either element is missing, the particular offence is not committed. For instance, someone who intends to murder another has the *mens rea* of murder, but unless he or she does something, no offence is committed. Similarly, every killing is not first degree murder; it may be an accident or manslaughter. Even though the *actus reus* is present (a person has died), without the requisite degree of intention, the offence is not committed.

Of course, the court is only concerned with whether a crime has been committed. The distinction between the *actus reus* and *mens rea* is useful for our purposes in analyzing a crime and explaining the different defences available, but you should appreciate that the court does not formally divide the offence into actus and mens during a trial.

In the discussion that follows, we consider a number of different kinds of "defences." This is not an exhaustive list of all the circumstances that allow an accused to avoid liability, but it attempts to describe the most important general defences, those that are relevant regardless of the offence. It is possible to combine different defences in some circumstances.

There are really only two categories of defences. These can be set out as follows:

1. No *mens rea*
   (a) Mistake
   (b) Intoxication
   (c) Mental Disorder
2. No *actus reus*
   (a) Automatism
   (b) Provocation
   (c) Necessity
       (i) Duress
       (ii) Necessity
       (iii) Self-defence
       (iv) Defence of Property

In fact, however, these so-called defences are only particular illustrations of the fundamental rule of criminal liability: if the accused acted without *mens rea*, or the acts of the accused do not voluntarily amount to the *actus reus* of an offence, he or she is not guilty. The accused says that because of a mistake, intoxication, or mental disorder, he or she did not have *mens rea*. Or the accused says that because of automatism, provocation, or some necessity, he or she did not voluntarily commit the *actus reus* of an offence. The different defences are only particular examples of the general principle that before an offence is committed there must be an *actus reus* accompanied contemporaneously by the prescribed *mens rea*. There are then, in reality, only two defences: "No *mens rea*" or "no *actus reus*."

The fact that the defence is "no *mens rea*" and not, for example, "intoxication," is vitally important: intoxication is irrelevant unless the drunkenness has precluded the accused from having the necessary *mens rea*. An accused who is drunk but has *mens rea* is still guilty. So the question is always, "Was there *mens rea*?" "Was there an *actus reus*?" The specified defences are only instances of the general principle.

We are not concerned here with proof. It will frequently be difficult to establish that the facts giving rise to a particular defence exist. This chapter is concerned only with the defences themselves in a legal way; concerns of proof and whether an accused can establish a defence are dealt with elsewhere in this book. Whether an accused has a legal defence, and whether he or she can prove it, are separate questions.

INTENTION AND DIFFERING DEGREES OF MENS REA

Our starting point is intention: what did the accused mean to do? In our discussion, we use the term intention in a special way. To be guilty, a person does not have to intend to commit a crime. The accused may not know he or she is breaking the law. But the person must intend to do something that the law defines as a crime. For example, a person might believe there is nothing illegal about using a flashlight to assist with his night-time hunting. If it is illegal, however, then so long as the accused is deliberately using the flashlight for that purpose, we say he intended to do what he did—and thus has the necessary *mens rea*—even though he may not know he is breaking the law.

Put another way, a desire to break the law is never a prerequisite to guilt or an element of the offence. If an accused deliberately uses a flashlight not knowing it is illegal, he is not only guilty of the offence, he has *mens rea*. Equally, motive is irrelevant. The accused may be hunting to feed his family, but that good motive will not negate *mens rea*.[2]

The criminal law distinguishes between differing degrees of *mens rea*. Sometimes an accused intends the *actus reus* to occur, sometimes he foresees it as possible and is reckless whether it happens or not, sometimes he does not foresee it, but a reasonable man would have, and in a final category, sometimes he does not intend it to happen at all and is not unreasonable in his conduct. These distinctions can be difficult to make in practice. Let us take an example.

If a woman drives her car fast, she can intend to speed. If she knows the speed limit, and intentionally goes faster than permitted, she is intentionally speeding. However, not every person who drives fast intends to speed. A woman may drive her car fast, knowing the speedometer is broken. She may not know for sure she is speeding, but if she recognizes that the speedometer is broken and does not take care to stay within the speed limit, she is reckless.

Sometimes a person can speed negligently: without foreseeing that she might be speeding, in circumstances in which a reasonable person would know better. She might not realize that her speedometer is broken, even though if she had paid more attention she would see that it never went above 30 km/h no matter how fast she was driving.

Finally, a person can speed inadvertently. Someone who has just had her speedometer calibrated, who deliberately tries to drive within the speed limit, may inadvertently speed if the calibration was faulty. If there was nothing to put her on notice of the fact the calibration was defective, her speeding is inadvertent.

Because the same action can be committed with different mental states, the law must decide what mental state will make an accused guilty for each offence. Is negligence or inadvertence enough? Must the actions be intentional or reckless? As a general guide, very serious offences can only be committed when the accused intends the act, or is reckless; less serious offences can be committed through negligence or inadvertence.

As the illustration at the beginning of this chapter shows, frequently the same act—running over a pedestrian—will have different consequences depending on the driver's intention. The difference between manslaughter and murder will normally be what the accused's intention, or *mens rea* was. In each case the *actus reus* may be the same— causing the death of another person. What often distinguishes the offences is the mental state of the accused accompanying the killing. If I deliberately run over a pedestrian, I may be guilty of murder; if I negligently run over a pedestrian, I may be guilty of manslaughter. If it happened inadvertently, without negligence, I may not be guilty of any offence.

Many offences have a compound *mens rea* and compound *actus reus*. In the case of murder, for instance, the *mens rea* is satisfied if the accused intends to cause the victim bodily harm that he or she knows is likely to cause death and is reckless whether death ensues. The accused must commit an assault of some kind, and death must result. Before an accused can be guilty of the most serious offences, he or she must have intended an essential part of the *actus reus* or been reckless about its occurrence. However, he or she does not need to intend every part of the *actus reus*. A person who deliberately beats another to intimidate the victim may be guilty of murder if the victim dies—even if the accused did not intend to kill, simply to cause very serious harm that was likely to cause death.

The law normally defines only a certain core portion of the *actus reus* that requires intention or recklessness. In the example just given, an intention to cause serious bodily harm, knowing that it is likely to cause death, is sufficient intention for murder. The accused does not have to intend to cause death. For less serious offences (including all provincially created offences), a *mens rea* of negligence or inadvertence may be sufficient. A person who carelessly speeds, without meaning to do so, may be guilty of speeding depending on the intention required by the provincial motor vehicle legislation. The *mens rea* for distinct elements of each offence ranges between intention and inadvertence.

So there are four different degrees of *mens rea*, and their presence or absence can control what crime, if any, is committed. The *actus reus* of even a single offence may involve different elements with differing degrees of *mens rea* for each.

Mistake

> A mistake that prevents the accused from having the *mens rea* for the offence will excuse him.

The first example of the "no *mens rea*" defence we will consider is mistake. A relevant mistake of fact prevents an accused from having the *mens rea* necessary to commit an offence. The accused says, in effect, that because of a relevant mistake of fact, he or she did not have the *mens rea* of the offence. (A mistake of fact is irrelevant unless it precludes *mens rea*.) It is important to note that for most offences, a mistake of law is no defence: a person must make a mistake of fact to be entitled to an acquittal.

Consider the example of someone possessing narcotics. The accused can make two mistakes:

(1) the accused may know that he has psilocybin, but not know that it is illegal in Canada to possess psilocybin (mistake of law); or

(2) he may believe that he has powdered milk and not know that the package has been switched for one containing psilocybin (mistake of fact).

The accused in the first example is guilty of an offence under the *Controlled Drugs and Substances Act*; the accused in our second example is not guilty of any offence. In each case the *actus reus* is the same-the accused has the same package in his or her possession. The only difference is what the accused's intention was at the time of possession. The example illustrates that an intention to break the law is not required to be guilty of an offence. In the first case, the accused has the necessary *mens rea* while committing the *actus reus*, and so an offence is committed. The accused *intentionally* possessed the drug. In the second case, there is no *mens rea*.

In analyzing what the accused have done, we ask two questions: What did they intend to possess? What did they possess? The first accused intended to possess psilocybin. He did possess psilocybin. The second accused intended to possess powdered milk. He in fact possessed psilocybin.

It is not normally a defence for a person to say that he or she made a mistake of law. If it were, a lot of people might possess prohibited drugs and claim they did not realize the drug was illegal. "Ignorance of the law is no excuse."[3]

One category of mistake of law is treated differently, and that is mistake of regulation. This is not a *mens rea* defence at all, but a concession to the difficulty of determining what the myriad of regulations provide. Although all persons are presumed to know the law (meaning that mistake of the criminal and quasi-criminal law is no excuse) regulations are different. If an accused was unaware of a regulation and could not reasonably have known about it, he or she may have a special defence.

A mistake of fact that is not innocent will not negate *mens rea*. Consider an accused who intends to sell mescaline, but in fact sells LSD. She has the *mens rea* of one offence (intent to sell mescaline) and the *actus reus* of another offence (selling LSD). As a matter of law, however, she is guilty of selling LSD, probably because she intends to sell that particular substance (which is a proscribed substance) and is reckless whether it is LSD or mescaline.

Mostly this is just good sense. If I go to a party and on leaving take your coat mistaking it for mine, I make a mistake of fact. If I really had taken my own coat, I would have committed no crime. So, if I mistake your coat for mine, I do not commit an offence when I take it.[4]

When we say a mistake of law is no excuse, we mean a mistake of the criminal law: a mistake of the civil law can negate the *mens rea* of the offence. If I find your coat and then think that it belongs to me ("finders keepers") and that I can sell it, I make a mistake about property law. That still excuses my conduct because I do not intend to sell someone else's coat; I intend to sell a coat that now belongs to me. I am mistaken—it is not in fact my coat. But that mistake of the property law prevents me from having the *mens rea* necessary to commit the offence.

So the rule is that a mistake that prevents an accused from having the *mens rea* of the offence will excuse him or her.

Mistake of fact or the civil law that precludes *mens rea* is a complete defence to a charge, which applies to all offences requiring intention or recklessness as the *mens rea*. A reasonable mistake of fact is a defence to offences that require only negligence as the *mens rea*.

Intoxication

An accused who, as a result of involuntary intoxication does not form the *mens rea* of the offence is not guilty.

An accused who, as the result of voluntary intoxication to a point akin to insanity, is not guilty of the offence.

An accused who, as the result of voluntary intoxication short of a condi-

> tion akin to insanity, does not form the *mens rea* of an offence requiring specific intent is not guilty of the offence, but may be guilty of a related general intent offence.
>
> An accused who has *mens rea* but does something while drunk that he would never have done while sober has no defence.

People behave differently when they drink or use drugs (whether prescription medication or non-prescription drugs). Often, inhibitions are reduced; sometimes judgment and motor skills will be impaired. Finally, in extreme cases, intoxication can produce a state akin to insanity.

Drinking and drug-related crime is widespread. Most drinking and drug taking is voluntary. To recognize drinking or drug taking as a defence would allow people to escape criminal responsibility for something that in a sense is voluntarily undertaken, and would fail to protect the public from a large proportion of all crime.

Our criminal justice system is based on the premises of intention and responsibility, that people should only be punished for acts that they intend. And people behave differently drunk than sober. So some special treatment ought to be accorded to those who are intoxicated when an offence is committed: the offence would surely be more serious if committed while they were sober and could fully appreciate what they were doing.

It is the tension between these competing principles that is responsible for the special rules concerning intoxication by alcohol or drugs. The courts have therefore developed very specialized rules to deal with intoxication.

Involuntary Intoxication

In Canada, people go to considerable lengths to become intoxicated. Most intoxication is entirely voluntary. Occasionally, a person will be involuntarily intoxicated (for example, when a non-alcoholic drink has been spiked or when a person becomes intoxicated from an anaesthetic or a prescription drug, which they were unaware would produce that effect). Involuntary intoxication is relevant in two circumstances.

Some offences consist of conduct while intoxicated. (For example, impaired driving, being drunk in public).A person who is not knowingly intoxicated has a defence to those charges. (The defence is mistake of fact. "I did not realize that the needle the dentist gave me made it unsafe for me to drive.") Where the accused has ignored warnings about the effect of a drug, then the intoxication is treated as voluntary and the usual rules apply.

For all other offences, involuntary intoxication is a defence only if the accused did not have *mens rea* of the offence. If so, then involuntary intoxication is a complete defence to the charge.

Voluntary Intoxication Short of Insanity

Because voluntary intoxication often accompanies criminal behaviour, the courts have determined that it will not be a complete defence. Instead, it will reduce certain criminal offences to lesser criminal offences, if the accused did not have the *mens rea* required to commit the more serious offence. The courts have (somewhat arbitrarily) divided offences into those that can be committed while intoxicated (called "general intent offences"), and those that cannot be committed while intoxicated (called "specific intent offences"). For example, it has been held that robbery requires a specific intention to steal. Therefore, a person who commits robbery while drunk (to the point that he or she did not form the specific intention to steal) can only be convicted of the included offence of assault.

No precise definition of what constitutes a specific intent offence has been promulgated by the courts. The courts seem to be concerned that drunkenness be a defence to serious crimes only. Although serious crimes often require a *mens rea* of intention or recklessness (rather than negligence or inadvertence), they do not necessarily have any requirement for a specific intent. The courts have therefore had difficulty deciding which crimes are specific intent offences and which are general intent offences. It comes down to a policy decision by the court whether the offence is serious enough to justify a defence of no *mens rea* because of drunkenness.

If I murder someone while so drunk that I cannot form the *mens rea* of murder, I am not guilty of murder (which is a specific intent offence). But I am guilty of a general intent offence (manslaughter) because lack of *mens rea* because of drunkenness is no defence to a general intent offence. Lack of *mens rea* because of drunkenness is therefore rarely a complete defence; there will almost always be a lesser offence that is available to the Crown to which drunkenness is no defence.

This so-called defence is really no different than the ordinary rule in all criminal trials. If someone commits robbery, it is always open to him or her to say "I did not mean to steal." If the court has a reasonable doubt that the accused did not intend to steal, then the accused can be convicted of assault, but not robbery. A person does not have to be drunk to rely on this defence.

So there is in fact no "defence" of drunkenness. All the accused is saying is, "I didn't intend to commit the offence." The explanation that the accused was drinking only serves to make the claimed lack of intention easier to believe. Someone who opens the door to his neighbour's house, and goes to sleep on his couch may be believed when he says that he was so drunk he thought he was in his own house. The same person sober may not be believed at all.

Intoxication Akin to Insanity or Automatism

Finally, there is the case of a person who has voluntarily become intoxicated to the point where he or she is akin to being insane. In those circumstances, the accused is entitled to be acquitted.

The *Criminal Code* contains an exception to this general rule in s. 33.1, which provides that the defence does not apply to offences where the accused, "assaults or interferes, or threatens to interfere" with the bodily integrity of another person. It remains to be seen if this exception is contrary to the *Charter*.

Mental Disorder

> An accused who, because of a mental disorder does not appreciate the nature and quality of his acts, or does not know they are illegal, does not have the *mens rea* of an offence. He is instead to be dealt with under the Code provisions relating to the not criminally responsible.

A particularly controversial defence is the plea of not criminally responsible. If the court finds that because of a mental disorder the accused lacked the *mens rea*, then the accused is entitled to be acquitted. (The finding of not criminally responsible by reason of a mental disorder may lead the accused to be detained, however, if he or she is found to be dangerous by a Review Board or on a Disposition hearing).

In Canada, persons who suffer from a mental illness as a result of which they do not know the nature and quality of their acts, or as a result of which they do not know that what they are doing is illegal, have the defence of not criminally responsible by reason of mental disorder. However, the defence is also available in appropriate cases for persons who are mentally retarded, for those suffering from delirium tremens, and for those in a cocaine psychosis.

It should first be appreciated that whether a person is not criminally responsible because of mental disorder is a legal, not a medical, question. The court is not interested in whether, according to medical standards, the accused is responsible; the court wants to know whether the accused meets the legal test. That test considers whether at the time of the act the accused appreciated the nature and quality of the act, or knew it was illegal.

ACTUS REUS DEFENCES

In addition to the foregoing *mens rea* defences, there are a number of *actus reus* defences, cases where the accused says either there was no voluntary act, or it was done under circumstances of necessity. If A overpowers B, and pushes him into C, then A is guilty of assaulting C but B is not. Criminal liability requires first that there be a voluntary act by the accused. In the example, B does no voluntary act, which is an essential part of the *actus reus*; so too if B acts out of necessity. The act is not "truly" voluntary.

Automatism

An accused who performs an act while unconscious or which is otherwise involuntary (not caused by drinking, drug taking or a disease of the mind), does not commit the *actus reus* of an offence.

In keeping with the rule that involuntary behaviour is not culpable, the criminal law gives an accused a defence where he acts unconsciously, or while his consciousness is impaired. The term has been defined in Canada to mean:

a state of impaired consciousness, rather than unconsciousness, in which an individual, though capable of action, has no voluntary control over that action.[5]

The defence is available for all offences, and if successful results in a complete acquittal. It is therefore a much more attractive defence than either intoxication (which can result in a conviction for a lesser, general intent offence), or a verdict of non-criminally responsible (which can result in a detention order, despite the acquittal). Because the defence offers a complete acquittal if accepted, the courts have placed very strict limits on its use. If the accused was in an automatic state as a result of voluntary intoxication, the only defence is drunkenness. If the accused is in an automatic state as a result of a mental disorder, the only defence is insanity. Automatism therefore comprises the residual automatic behaviour that is neither produced by voluntary intoxication nor by a mental disorder.

Despite these limits, conditions caused by a concussion, physical blow, hyperglycaemia, sleepwalking, epilepsy, cerebral tumour, arteriosclerosis, and dissociative states have been found to reduce persons to an automatic state.[6]

Automatism is a particular instance of the rule that a voluntary act is a prerequisite to criminal liability.

Provocation

> An accused who kills a person when suddenly provoked by the deceased's wrongful act or insult is guilty of manslaughter but not murder.

One factor that each of us recognizes affects our conduct is the provocation which we receive at the hands of others. A child who is teased is far more likely to strike out. At the same time, we are expected to resist provocation and not lose our tempers. It would be a violent world if every provocation was avenged. Provocation does not deny *mens rea*, but only explains it. It is therefore generally not a defence, although it may go in mitigation of the sentence an accused would otherwise receive.

There is one exception to this, however, in the case of murder. An assault that would otherwise be murder will be manslaughter if the accused acted under provocation. The law stems from a time when the penalty for murder (but not for manslaughter) was capital punishment; someone who killed while provoked ought not to be hanged. Provocation is not a defence to any other crime, not even attempted murder. Because it reduces the offence to manslaughter, rather than resulting in a complete acquittal, it is only a partial defence.

Any legal system that recognizes provocation as a defence must confront two questions: what kind of act is sufficient to constitute "provocation" in a legal sense; and to what extent must the accused be affected? If provocation reduces murder to manslaughter, then everyone charged with murder will raise provocation as a defence if he or she can. What limits do we place on this?

The criminal law has said, first, that the provocation must be sudden (unexpected): one's reaction (in which you kill your victim) must happen so soon after the provocation that the accused does not have a chance for his or her passion to cool.

Second, only a wrongful act or insult can in law amount to provocation sufficient to enable an accused to raise this defence. An act that the deceased was entitled to do cannot amount to provocation. A person who marries your ex-wife commits no wrongful act. His act cannot amount to provocation in law. The act or insult must also be such as would have deprived an ordinary person with the physical characteristics of the accused of his or her self-control. The law does not make the defence available to irrational emotional people who take offence in circumstances in which no one else would. The law does take account of the fact that "pegleg" is an insult to an amputee but would not be to a person with all his or her limbs. Of course, the particular accused must also be, for the time, deprived of his or her self-control. The provocation does not give the accused a licence to punish, but excuses uncontrolled behaviour.

Necessity

Most of the remaining *actus reus* defences are, broadly speaking, necessity defences. The accused says that exigent circumstances made it necessary to behave as he or she did. One defends oneself or one's property or otherwise breaks the law because it is necessary to do so. The conduct is not involuntary—the accused always has a choice whether to defend himself, or his property, for instance—but we give the accused a defence just the same, out of recognition that what was done is not morally culpable. This general category of defences should be distinguished from the special subspecies of compulsion, which is also called necessity.

Compulsion

The law recognizes two special defences for conduct under compulsion: the defence of duress and the defence of necessity. The defence of duress arises when another person forced an accused to do what was done; the defence of necessity arises when circumstances force an accused to do what was done. If a hitchhiker takes a car driver hostage at knife point, duress excuses the fact that the driver speeds or runs a red light. If you steal a car to rush an injured pedestrian to hospital, the defence of necessity excuses you.

Let us consider each of these in turn.

Duress

An accused who assists in or commits an offence is not guilty if he acts under a continuing threat of death or serious injury to himself or a third person in circumstances where it was not reasonably possible to escape.

The law excuses involuntary conduct and conduct when an accused is not responsible for his or her actions. Speaking strictly, duress is not an example of involuntary conduct. If a terrorist threatens your life unless you comply with his or her demands, you have a choice—to resist or submit to the threat. The conduct is not involuntary in the same way that an accident is involuntary, and you are not bereft of responsibility in the same way as an accused who is drunk or suffering from a mental disorder. But the law concedes you should be treated differently than an accused who acts freely.

The law confronts a difficult problem in the defence of duress: at what point must an innocent hostage refuse to comply with a terrorist's demands at the risk of his own life? If the hostage is blameless under the criminal law, then the terrorist can force him to commit one offence after another; if the hostage is blameworthy under the criminal law, then we penalize him for doing what almost every one of us would do in the same circumstances. What is the purpose of punishment in these circumstances when it will almost never deter an accused?

Sir James Fitzjames Stephens, an English judge who wrote what became our *Criminal Code*, described the problem this way:

> Criminal law is itself a system of compulsion on the widest scale. It is a collection of threats of injury to life, liberty, and property if people do commit crimes. Are such threats to be withdrawn as soon as they are encountered by opposing threats? The law says to a man intending to commit murder, if you do it I will hang you. Is the law to withdraw its threat if some one else says, If you do not do it I will shoot you?[7]

The law must therefore impose limits on what circumstances are severe enough to justify excusing conduct for this reason. In 2001, the Supreme Court of Canada found some of the statutory provisions in the *Criminal Code* relating to duress unconstitutional, because they deny the defence of duress in circumstances in which someone has acted without moral culpability. As a result, it is difficult to know the limits that the court will uphold on the defence of duress.

It seems the following are the requirements:

- there must be an actual threat, not merely fear;
- the threat that creates the duress must be one that would have caused a reasonable person to act as the accused did;
- the threat must have been of imminent or immediate harm to the accused or to a third person;

- duress is not available if a reasonably safe alternative course of conduct was available;
- the act committed cannot be disproportionate to the threat. A threatened spanking cannot justify a murder.

Necessity

> An accused who, in the face of imminent peril acts in good faith believing that a failure to act could endanger life or health and that compliance with the law is impossible, does not commit an offence if his act is proportionate to the harm avoided.

As already suggested, necessity is a legal doctrine that encompasses all of the self-defences and defence of property defences too. A man can defend himself and although the act would otherwise be an offence, the necessity of defending himself justifies it.

We speak of necessity, however, as a separate defence as well, because particular instances of it, such as self-defence, are separately outlined in the criminal law.

Philosophers have recognized from the earliest times that necessitous circumstances will excuse an act that would otherwise be wrongful. The courts, however, have found it difficult to determine when particular circumstances are sufficient to justify particular conduct, and when an accused has simply ignored the law to satisfy his own views of right and wrong. Some writers worry that once the doctrine is allowed to flourish it will be impossible to stop.

The decided cases establish the theoretical framework for necessity as a defence, but they have not done much to define its particular application in particular circumstances. May a bus driver save nine passengers at a cost of two pedestrians?

Before the defence is available, there must be no lawful way of avoiding the harm: if there is, the accused is obliged to rely on the lawful means.

Self-defence

> An accused who uses no more force than necessary to defend himself or someone under his authority commits no offence even if he causes death or serious bodily harm, unless he commenced the assault with intent to cause death or serious injury.

The criminal law recognizes that a person may defend one's self if assaulted. Self-defence is accordingly a defence to all crimes. The law privileges the accused to use force and judges the force that the accused intended to use, not the damage that actually results. This is no different than the child's assertion, "he hit me first." The rules excusing criminal liability when defending one's self try to deal with several different problems. Speaking generally, the law distinguishes between four types of self defence:

(a) when you think you or someone under your protection will be assaulted;
(b) when you have been unlawfully assaulted;
(c) when you have been assaulted (after provoking the assault or assaulting another) and apprehend death or serious bodily harm; and
(d) when you have been unlawfully assaulted and apprehend death or serious bodily harm.

These distinctions only illustrate the general principle stated above but are important: the law will justify more force when you apprehend death than when the assault you expect is quite trivial. You will receive less protection when you have started or provoked the assault.

When you think you or someone under your protection will be assaulted

As children we expected a right to retaliate: if someone hit us, we hit him back. That is *not* what the criminal law authorizes. If we apprehend that someone will assault us or someone under our protection, then we can assault him or her to prevent the assault from taking place. It is not a rule of punishment, but of prevention. If the assailant has broken off the attack, this does not give us any right to hit him or her. If we fear that we will be assaulted, or fear that an assault will be repeated, then we are entitled to attempt to prevent that assault by the use of force. The force we use must be proportionate to that we are preventing: we cannot murder someone to avoid a spanking. At the same time, the criminal law makes allowance for victims of an assault trying to protect themselves: although the force used must be roughly proportionate, one is not required to "weigh to a nicety" the amount of force used in self-defence. It does not normally lie in the assailant's mouth to complain that you hit him or her a little harder than you should have.

When you have been unlawfully assaulted

When an assault has actually occurred, you are entitled to defend yourself, and this encompasses what we normally think of as self-defence. For your actions to be lawful, you must not use fatal force or force that you intend to cause serious bodily harm. Arguably, you can use more force than your assailant, but it cannot be intended to cause death or serious injury. Again, the fact that you have been assaulted does not give you licence to maim or kill your assailant. It must be no more force than necessary to enable you to defend yourself.

When you have been assaulted (after provoking the assault or assaulting another) and apprehend death or serious bodily harm

If one has provoked an assault, either by words or gestures or by assaulting another person, the law gives a much more limited right of defence. You are chiefly to blame for what has happened and you must be very careful not to escalate the assault. You cannot pick a fight, let someone else land the first punch, and then kill him. At the same time, what starts as a shouting match may get out of hand, and even though you started the shouting, you may have to defend yourself. Even a robber who is overpowered in the course of a robbery is entitled to kill in self-defence if the original assault he or she committed was not intended to cause death or serious bodily harm. Before one is entitled to defend oneself in these circumstances, the assault earlier committed must not have been with the intent to cause death or serious injury. If it was, this defence is unavailable.

When you have been unlawfully assaulted and apprehend death or serious bodily harm

By contrast, if you have not started the fight, then you are given a much freer hand to defend yourself from fatal force or serious injury. If you reasonably apprehend death or serious injury, then you can use fatal force or cause serious injury, if there is no other means of avoiding serious injury or death.

In each case, where the circumstances already described are present so as to make one of the four types of self-defence available, the accused is entitled to an acquittal. What he or she has done is justified in the circumstances. Although each of the four sections gives a different right to defend one's self, one must use no more force than is necessary. Does this mean you have an obligation to break off the fight and retreat if you can do so? The answer to that is not clear, but it is submitted that if it would be reasonable to retreat, then you cannot continue to forcibly defend yourself.

Defence of Property

> An accused who used no more force than necessary to defend his property commits no offence.

The criminal law gives the lawful owner of property a right to defend it, and in more limited circumstances, the right to retake possession of it.

Movable property

The law gives protection to someone defending moveable property (in distinction to real property or land). Protecting your television set does not justify the same force as defending your house. In defending your moveable property, one is justified unless one strikes or causes bodily harm to the trespasser. If one is in peaceable possession of the property, and a trespasser lays hands on it, the full self-defence provisions earlier described become available to the accused as if assaulted.

Dwelling

Any necessary force including fatal force may be used to prevent someone from unlawfully entering a dwelling.

Real property

Any necessary force may be used to prevent a trespass or remove a trespasser from real property and if the trespasser actively resists, the full self-defence provisions already described are available to the accused as if assaulted. If the trespasser does not resist being removed, or agrees to leave the property, there is no right to use force, as there is no necessity to do so.

The effect of these provisions is that if one is not in peaceable possession of property, the law does not extend the same protection to you to recover your property as to defend it. This is to discourage people from retaking property by force.

REVIEW AND SELF TEST

Read through the following cases and try to answer the questions that follow.

A. David goes to a party one evening, where he consumes a quantity of alcohol. He returns home to his apartment, opens the door (which is unlocked), and falls asleep on the couch. In the morning, he wakes up and finds himself confronted by Linda. It seems he has gotten off the elevator one floor early and has fallen asleep on her couch by accident. She orders him out.

In these circumstances, does David have a defence to trespassing in Linda's apartment? How much force would she be entitled to use to eject him?

B. Geoff and Sally come home from the same party and surprise a burglar in the midst of rifling their apartment. He pulls out a gun and forces Geoff to tie Sally to the rocking chair. He then ties Geoff up. He verbally abuses Geoff and Sally, and then goes into another room to continue his looting. After 15 minutes of struggling, Sally escapes. She sneaks up on the burglar and clubs him to death.

Under these circumstances, what entitles Geoff to tie Sally up? Does Sally have a defence to a charge of causing the burglar's death?

C. Phil comes home from the same party with his wife Ruth. He, too, has had a lot to drink. After getting ready for bed, he hears a commotion in the next apartment. Sally knocks on his door, and asks him to drive her to the police station to report the incident described in B. On the way, Phil is stopped for driving while impaired.

Does his driving Sally to the police station afford him a defence?

D. Dianne and Charlotte are also at the party. During conversation, Dianne discovers that Charlotte's new boyfriend, Ted, is Dianne's husband, who is evidently having an affair. Dianne goes into a blind rage and the next thing she remembers is seeing Charlotte dead.

Does Dianne have a defence in these circumstances?

Answers

A. David has apparently made a mistake of fact that precludes him from intending to enter Linda's apartment. That would be a complete defence to the charge. In these circumstances, he does not need to rely on drunkenness, which helps to explain how he could walk into the wrong apartment without realizing it. Linda is not entitled to use force to eject David unless he resists; if he goes quietly when requested, she may not use force. If he physically resists her efforts to remove him, then she can use as much force as necessary to eject him.

B.   Geoff has the defence of duress. Sally may not have a defence to killing the burglar. Although the earlier comments may have provoked her, it is not clear that it was sudden enough to qualify as provocation. In any event, it would seem that Sally uses more force than necessary to subdue the burglar; clubbing him is perhaps justified to prevent the burglary, but killing him is not. If she only intended to render him unconscious (and his death was an accident) then she may have a defence.

C.   Probably no defence. Sally could probably have driven his car, or the incident could have been reported by phone, or Ruth or Geoff might have been able to drive.

D.   The defence of automatism is normally not established by a psychological blow alone. Similarly, Dianne is unlikely to establish that she is not criminally responsible, because there is no obvious mental disorder to explain her behaviour. Provocation may be available, depending on whether this is a clear enough "insult" that Charlotte had no right to make.

Notes

[1] J.C. Smith and Brian Hogan, *Criminal Law*, 4th ed. (Markham: Butterworths, 1978), at p. 31.

[2] The accused's *actus reus* might not amount to an offence, however, if the elements of necessity are made out.

[3] Of course, as we have seen, ignorance may prevent an offence from occurring if there is no *actus reus* because the conduct does not amount to an offence.

[4] I may commit an offence, however, if I try to sell the coat when I discover the mistake.

[5] *R. v. Stone*, 1999 CarswellBC 1064, 1999 CarswellBC 1065, 134 C.C.C. (3d) 353, 24 C.R. (5th) 1, 239 N.R. 201, 63 C.R.R. (2d) 43, 123 B.C.A.C. 1, 201 W.A.C. 1, 173 D.L.R. (4th) 66, [1999] 2 S.C.R. 290 (S.C.C.).

[6] Renee Pomerance, "Carved in Stone?: The New Approach to the Defence of Automatism" in 2001 Federation of Law Societies materials at c. 11.2, p. 1.

[7] *A History of the Criminal Law of England* (London: Macmillan & Co, 1883) at 108-109.

9

Mental Disorder and the Criminal Process

Dennis Theman*
(edited for the 7th edition by Joel E. Pink, Q.C.)**

Section 16 of the *Criminal Code* states:

> **16.** (1) No person is criminally responsible for an act committed or an omission made while suffering from a mental disorder that rendered the person incapable of appreciating the nature and quality of the act or omission or of knowing that it was wrong.
>
> (2) Every person is presumed not to suffer from a mental disorder so as to be exempt from criminal responsibility by virtue of subsection (1), until the contrary is proved on the balance of probabilities.
>
> (3) The burden of proof that an accused was suffering from a mental disorder so as to be exempt from criminal responsibility is on the party that raises the issue.

One of the older doctrines of the common law holds that if, because of a mental disorder, an accused person was not capable of understanding that they had committed a crime then the accused would be exempted from criminal responsibility for that offence. Therefore, if an accused person was suffering from a mental disorder at the time of the commission of the offence, provided that the disorder was such that they either could not appreciate the nature of the act which they had committed, or could not appreciate that the act was wrong, then the accused was entitled to be found "not guilty by reason of insanity". As well, if the accused was unable to stand trial due to a mental disorder (that is, they could not understand the nature of the proceedings and/or

* B.A., Dalhousie University, Halifax, Nova Scotia; LL.B., Dalhousie Law School, Halifax, Nova Scotia; formerly practised with Nova Scotia Legal Aid and Dalhousie Legal Aid Service; currently a Senior Crown Attorney with the Public Prosecution Service in Halifax, Nova Scotia, currently seconded to the Ontario A.G. prosecution services.

**B.A., Acadia University, Wolfville, Nova Scotia; LL.B., Dalhousie Law School, Halifax, Nova Scotia; practices law in Halifax, Nova Scotia.

distinction that exists between the words "appreciates" and "knows".
At pp. 134-136, he states:

> The capacity to *appreciate* the nature and quality of the act committed
> clearly imports the requirement of capacity to understand the moral signif-
> icance of the act. In *R. v. O.*, 3 *Crim. L.Q.* 151 at p. 153, (1959), McRuer,
> C.J.H.C., of Ontario charged the jury in part as follows:
>
> > ... if you find on a mere preponderance of probability, based on the
> > evidence taken as a whole ... the accused was labouring under a
> > disease of the mind to such an extent as to render her incapable of
> > foreseeing and measuring the consequences of her act or of estimat-
> > ing a right or perceiving the full force of her act, you should find her
> > not guilty on account of insanity ...

In *R. v. Borg*, [1969] 4 C.C.C. 262, [1969] S.C.R. 551, 7 C.R.N.S. 85,
the Supreme Court of Canada allowed an appeal by the Crown from the
opinion of the Alberta Supreme Court Appellate Division. The facts in
that case were that Borg had shot and killed an R.C.M.P. constable and
as well, had killed two women. He had purchased a rifle, called the police
to come to his home and upon their arrival, opened fire. His only defence
was insanity. Although the Appellate Division was divided in reversing
the conviction for capital murder, it was unanimous in accepting the legitimacy of a possible insanity verdict from the jury. The only question
which either of the opinions of that Court dealt with was the adequacy of
the Judge's charge to the jury on the issue of insanity and his explanation
of the possible ways in which the evidence might support such defence.
The majority opinion of the Supreme Court of Canada, written by Cart-
wright, J., held that the adequacy of the trial Judge's charge was irrelevant
because insanity could not be a defence on the evidence. The majority
opinion does not indicate clearly whether such was because the mental
disability was insufficient *in law* or because there was inadequate proof
that the mental disability *in fact* was operative at the time of the killing.
Either interpretation of the opinion appears possible. No legal authorities
were cited all with reference to the insanity issue in the majority opinion.
Hall, J., with Spence, J., concurring, in a dissenting opinion said at p. 282
C.C.C., pp. 103-4 C.R.N.S. of the report:

> Section 16 of the Canadian *Criminal Code* states that a man can-
> not be held to be insane unless he did not appreciate the nature and
> quality of the act he was doing. A man operating under an irresist-
> ible impulse may have *knowledge* of the nature and quality of his
> act without *appreciating* its nature and quality, a man may be aware
> of an act without foreseeing and measuring its consequences.
> (Emphasis added.)

The *Report of the Royal Commission on the Law of Insanity as a Defence in Criminal Cases* (the McRuer report on insanity, Canada: Queen's

Printer, 1956), pp. 12-3, contains the following passage which I adopt as to the meaning of the word "appreciate" in s. 16(2) of the *Code*:

> The word "appreciating" not being a word that is synonymous with "knowing", requires far-reaching legal and medical considerationwhen discussing Canadian law. It had its origin in the Stephen Draft Code. Not infrequently judicial reference is made to the New Oxford Dictionary for the definition of words used in Canadian statutes. The new Oxford Dictionary gives five different uses of the word "appreciate", depending on the context. The one application to this statute is:
>
> 2. To estimate aright, to perceive the full force of. b. esp. to be sensitive to, or sensible of, any delicate impression or distinction. "Until the truth of any thing ... be appreciated, its error, if any, cannot be detected."
>
> An examination of the civil law of England and Canada shows that there is an important difference between "know" or "knowledge" on the one hand and "appreciate" or "appreciation" on the other when used and applied to a given set of circumstances. This is best illustrated by the principles of law underlying those cases in which the maxim *volenti non fit injuria* is involved. There is a clear distinction between mere knowledge of the risk and appreciation of both the risk and the danger.
>
> Applying this law by analogy to the language of section 16 of the *Criminal Code*, it will be clear that mere knowledge of the nature and quality of the act ("Did the person know what he was doing?") is not the true test to be applied. The true test necessarily is, was the accused person at the very time of the offence—not before or after, but at the moment of the offence — by reason of disease of the mind, unable fully to appreciate not only the nature of the act but the natural consequences that would flow from it? In other words, was the accused person, by reason of disease of the mind, deprived of the mental capacity to foresee and measure the consequences of the act?

I gather from the foregoing report that really the words "appreciate" and "know" must be read in contrast and that under such section a disease of the mind which renders the accused incapable of appreciating the nature and quality of an act involves more than mere knowledge of the physical nature of the act being committed. There must be an appreciation of the factors involved in that act and a capacity to measure and foresee the consequences of the act. There must be an ability to appreciate the true significance of the conduct or as G.A. Martin (now the Honourable Mr. Justice Martin of the Appeal Division of the Supreme Court of Ontario) put it in his article "Insanity as a Defence", 8 *Crim. L.Q.* 240 at p. 244 (1964): "True knowledge of the nature and quality of the act, ... requires that mere intellectual knowledge of the physical nature of the act be fused with appropriate affect and feeling."

Further, at p. 137:

When the learned trial Judge's charge to the jury, particularly those portions quoted above, is looked at in the light of the substantive law applicable to the defence on insanity, I am, with the greatest deference, of the opinion that he erred in his directions in the following respects.

(1) That he did not adequately explain to the jury that the word "appreciate" in s. 16(2) of the *Code* is not synonymous with "know" and that it connotes more than mere knowledge of the physical nature of the act being committed. Reading the charge as a whole one is left with the distinct impression that the learned trial Judge was saying that if the appellant knew he had a gun in his hand and knew that he was discharging two bullets therefrom into the face of the deceased that he was not insane. See the broomstick, peashooter and flag emitting examples given by the trial Judge and set out in the foregoing extracts from the charge.

The classic example given by legal writers is of a mentally disordered accused who cuts a person's throat while believing (as the result of a delusion) that they are cutting a loaf of bread; or that they are aware that they are cutting a person's throat, but believe that—as with characters in a cartoon—the victim can get up and put themselves back together. If the judge or jury finds (on the balance of probabilities) that the defendant was not criminally responsible, then there are (new) provisions in the *Criminal Code* to deal with the appropriate disposition. As will be seen below, the result is no longer a potentially indefinite period of custody in a secure psychiatric facility.

FITNESS TO STAND TRIAL

If an accused person cannot participate in their trial, then it can hardly be said that a fair trial was being held. After all, if defendants cannot understand either the charges against them, or what is going on in the proceedings, then they will not be able to put forward a defence. (Indeed, their lawyers (if they have any) would not be able to discuss the case with, and receive meaningful instructions from, the defendants.) The court can order an assessment of an accused person, with respect to their fitness to stand trial, at any stage of the proceedings. This can be done on the application of either the Crown or the defence, or on the court's own motion. The fitness rule relates *only* to the ability of the defendant to understand and communicate at the time of the proceedings against them. It does not matter whether or not a defendant can recall any of the events regarding the alleged offence. Whoever raises the issue of fitness to stand trial has the burden of proving that the accused is not fit to stand trial (on the balance of probabilities). If the defendant is not represented by a lawyer, the court must order that this be done. The court can appoint counsel for a defendant.

Normally some medical evidence is presented, often in a written report (where the prosecutor and the accused agree). Just as the *Criminal Code* provides (s. 16) that everyone is presumed to be criminally responsible for their actions until the contrary is proven, so too does it state that an accused is presumed fit to stand trial until it is proven otherwise on the balance of probabilities. At this initial stage, when the fitness issue is first raised, there only needs to be *some* evidence presented for the court to seek an order to have the accused assessed for fitness to stand trial. Once that issue has been raised, if the court feels that there are reasonable grounds it can order an assessment of an accused. This assessment can be done either by remanding the defendant to a secure medical facility, or on an outpatient basis. The initial assessment period can last only five days (excluding holidays) unless both the accused and the prosecution agree. They cannot agree to a period of more than 30 days. The court has the power to extend the assessment period to a maximum of 60 days in order to complete the assessment. The court, however, cannot order that any treatment be given to the accused during such an assessment. Once the assessment has been completed, then the issue of fitness to stand trial will be determined at a hearing. It is at this point that the party who raised the fitness issue must prove that the accused is unfit to stand trial on account of a mental disorder. If the defendant is found fit to stand trial, then the proceedings must carry on as though the issue of fitness had not been dealt with.

On the other hand, if the accused is found unfit to stand trial, then a disposition hearing must be held—just as is done if the defendant is found to be not criminally responsible (see below). However, if the accused was found to be unfit to stand trial due to a mental disorder, then because the trial was either not held or not completed due to unfitness, it can be resumed if the accused should later become fit. Therefore, a court must hold an inquiry within two years to see if there is still sufficient evidence to put the defendant on trial. That is, the court must determine whether, if the accused becomes fit to stand trial, there would still enough evidence available to proceed with the trial. This inquiry must be held every two years until either the accused is found fit and a trial is held, or the accused is acquitted (due to a "want of prosecution"—i.e., not enough evidence to go to trial).

DISPOSITIONS

The biggest changes made in 1992 to the "insanity" provisions of the *Code* are in the rules regarding the disposition of those found to be either not criminally responsible or unfit to stand trial. Instead of automatically being sent to a secure psychiatric facility, there are now three options available as dispositions with respect to each outcome (i.e., not criminally responsible, or unfit to stand trial). If the accused was found to be not criminally responsible on account of a mental disorder, the three possible dispositions are:

(a) an absolute discharge (if the person is not "a significant threat to the safety of the public"); *or*
(b) a discharge subject to conditions; *or*
(c) detention in custody in a hospital, subject to conditions.

If the defendant was found to be unfit to stand trial due to a mental disorder, the three possible dispositions are:

(a) a discharge subject to conditions; *or*
(b) detention in custody in a hospital, subject to conditions; *or*
(c) a treatment order.

A treatment order disposition can only be made if it has been applied for by the prosecutor and the following conditions are met:

(a) an application must be supported by the testimony of a medical practitioner;
(b) the treatment order can only be for the purpose of rendering the accused fit to stand trial;
(c) the treatment period cannot exceed 60 days;
(d) certain types of treatment are prohibited;
(e) the court will specify the treatment to be given; and
(f) the person in charge of the hospital where the accused is to be treated must consent to the proposed treatment to be given.

These dispositions can be made either by the court or by a Review Board (of five or more members, including a psychiatrist, appointed by the provincial cabinet). The court must make the disposition if either the accused or the prosecutor request it. However, the court cannot order a person who has been found not criminally responsible to be detained (at a secure psychiatric facility) for more than 90 days. In fact, it is the Review Boards which have been given the main responsibility for deciding the appropriate disposition. Indeed, where a court has ordered an accused either to be detained, or to be discharged on conditions, following a finding of not criminally responsible, then the Review Board must review that disposition and make whatever disposition it thinks appropriate. Furthermore, to avoid the former problem of lengthy periods of custody in a secure psychiatric facility, Review Boards must now carry out an annual review of all dispositions except for absolute discharges. Very broad rights of appeal have been granted with respect to dispositions. In particular, appeals can be based upon the facts and not just upon law, as in appeals of verdicts of guilty or not guilty. A person who violates (or is about to violate) a disposition order can be arrested without a warrant by a peace officer. They are then to be brought before a Review Board, which can deal with the situation just as if they were holding a review hearing.

RECENT AMENDMENTS

In January, 2006, several changes were made to the *Criminal Code* provisions with respect to people who have either been found unfit to stand trial, or found to have been not criminally responsible on account of mental disorder:

- Review Boards can now order an assessment of the accused, as well as protecting the identity of victims and witnesses who appear at assessment hearings;
- Victims can have time to prepare victim impact statements, as well as presenting their statements orally at disposition hearings;
- Review Boards can extend the time to hold a review hearing for up to 24 months;
- The Courts can hold an inquiry and enter a stay of the proceedings when:
  — an accused person is found unfit to stand trial,
  — they are not likely ever to be found fit to stand trial, or
  — they do not pose a significant risk to the safety of the public; and
- Expanding the powers of the police regarding the arrest and re-

lease of individuals who are in violation of an assessment or disposition order.

These amendments show that there is an ongoing commitment by justice officials to review the impact and operation of the major changes, brought about in the early 1990s, respecting the difficult issues surrounding mental disorder in the Criminal Justice process.

10

Substantive Criminal Offences

*John Pearson**

BASIC PHILOSOPHY

This chapter will consider the essential elements of the offences most frequently prosecuted in adult criminal courts across Canada. These courts disposed of over 372,000 cases involving more than one million charges in 2006/2007.[1] While homicide and other sensational crimes generate intense media attention and arouse public concern, they are not the staple diet of the criminal justice system. The most frequently prosecuted *Criminal Code2* charges are offences against the administration of justice and property offences. Failure to comply with court orders and related charges constituted 24% of all cases heard in adult criminal courts in 2006/2007. Another 24% of cases involved property offences, 20% involved crimes against the person, 11% were impaired driving and other *Criminal Code* traffic crimes and 11% involved drug and other federal statute offences. All forms of sexual offences accounted for less than 2% of the caseload of adult criminal courts and homicide and attempted murder accounted for only 0.2%.[3]

The popular conception of criminal proceedings involves a dramatic trial before a jury. The reality is much different. Juries heard less than 1% of all cases in 2006/2007; judges sitting without juries heard the rest. Most cases are resolved without a trial as a result of plea negotiations ("plea bargaining"). In Ontario, for example, 75.5% of cases are resolved prior to the date set for trial and 15.8% are resolved on the day set for trial. Only 8.7% of cases proceed to trial.[4] The accused was found guilty in about two thirds (65%) of cases disposed in Canada in 2006/2007. In about one third (30%) of cases, the most serious offence was resolved by being withdrawn by the prosecution (e.g., because there was no reasonable prospect of conviction, prosecution did

* B.A., Victoria College, University of Toronto; LL.B. and LL.M., Osgoode Hall Law School of York University; Member of the Bars of Ontario and the Northwest Territories; General Counsel, Crown Law Office Criminal, Ministry of the Attorney General for Ontario. The opinions expressed in this chapter are those of the author and do not purport to represent the policy of the Ontario Ministry of the Attorney General.

was unlawfully at large.[12] An "escape" for the purposes of the offence of "escaping lawful custody" continues past the point at which a prisoner leaves prison property.[13] A court has also held that an accused who decides at the time of his release on a temporary pass not to return to the custodial institution is "unlawfully at large" from that moment.[14]

The court system would break down if large numbers of accused did not comply with their bail terms or did not appear for court when required. Consequently, significant penalties must be imposed as both specific (aimed at the offender) and general (aimed at others who might be tempted to follow the example of the offender) deterrence. The maximum penalties provided by the *Criminal Code* for administration of justice offences depend on how the prosecution elects to proceed with the case. If the prosecution concludes on the basis of the criminal record of the accused or the circumstances of the offence that the highest possible penalty should be available, the prosecution elects to proceed by indictable procedure and the maximum term of imprisonment is two years. If the prosecution wishes to avoid the added complexities of indictable procedure and elects to proceed by summary procedure, the maximum term of imprisonment is six months.

OFFENCES AGAINST PROPERTY

Introduction

Crimes against property constitute 24% of the cases heard by adult criminal courts in Canada. Protecting property rights has been a goal of the criminal law since ancient times. The nineteenth century utilitarian philosopher and law reformer Jeremy Bentham said of the Commandment, Thou shall not steal:

> Such a command, were it to rest there, could never sufficiently answer the purpose of a law. A word of so vague and unexplicit meaning can no otherwise perform this office, than by giving a general intimation of a variety of propositions, each requiring, to convey it to the apprehension, a more particular and ample assemblage of terms.[15]

Four separate parts of the *Criminal Code* are devoted to providing "a more particular and ample assemblage of terms" to define crimes in relation to property. Part IX, entitled "Offences Against Rights of Property", contains fifty-six sections and prohibits a wide range of conduct from theft and robbery to breaking and entering and forgery. Part X gathers together approximately forty additional offences of dishonesty under the title "Fraudulent Transactions Relating to Contracts and

Trade". Part XI of the *Code* prohibits "Wilful and Forbidden Acts in Respect of Certain Property", including such diverse crimes as arson, injuring cattle and keeping a cockpit. The various crimes contained in these three parts of the *Criminal Code* have historically accounted for two thirds of all criminal prosecutions. The clearance rate for property crime has always been low compared to other categories of crime.[16] Finally, Part XII.2 was recently added to the *Code* to address comprehensively the laundering of the proceeds of designated criminal activity. It prohibits transactions in relation to certain subject matter. The subject matter in question is any property or any proceeds of any property, all or part of which has been obtained or derived directly or indirectly as a result of the commission of a designated offence. The prohibited transaction is the use, transfer of possession, delivery to any person, etc., by *any* means, of the subject matter.

Theft

The most basic property crime is theft. Prior to the adoption of a *Criminal Code* in 1892,[17] Canada's theft law was based on the English common law of larceny, a law so complex and irrational that the Attorney General of Canada described it in 1878 as:

> ... [a law] of most bewildering confusion. It abounds in distinctions without real differences, and in refinements and subtleties, which I consider a reproach even to a system of judicature established in a barbarous age.[18]

The theft provisions introduced by the *Criminal Code* were designed to render the law more coherent and comprehensive. They remain the foundation of the modern crime of theft. In addition to a general theft provision, the *Criminal Code* contains some specific theft offences. Theft by a bailee of things under seizure, theft of telecommunication service, theft by a person required to account and theft by a person holding power of attorney are found in separate *Criminal Code* sections. Part IX also creates "offences resembling theft", including taking a motor vehicle without consent ("joyriding"), criminal breach of trust, fraudulently taking cattle or defacing a brand, taking possession of drift lumber and theft of a credit card.

The conduct element (*actus reus*) of theft is taking or converting to one's use, or the use of another, anything. The prohibited conduct is complete when the accused, with intent to steal, moves the subject matter of the theft. It is significant that the crime encompasses both the "taking" and "converting" of property. One essential element of common law larceny was a "taking". If the property was already in the possession of the accused, he could not "take" it. The expanded *Criminal Code* definition of theft provides that a person may commit theft by converting something obtained for some other purpose to his use.

Has a person who lawfully borrows a book from a library and then decides to keep it "converted" the book so as to be guilty of theft? The prosecution would argue that the possession of the book became unlawful when the decision was made not to return the book. The defence would argue that if there is no act of conversion, such as writing a name in the book or lending it to someone else, the *actus reus* required to establish theft is not present. It would be the position of the defence that the library has a civil cause of action against the borrower but the theft provisions of the *Criminal Code* have not been violated. Is failing to take the book back to the library by the due date an "act" of conversion? What if the person who "borrowed" the book never intended to return it?

While the concept of "property" is broadly defined in s. 2 of the *Criminal Code,* the general theft provision itself makes no specific reference to the word "property". The *Code* states that "anything, whether animate or inanimate" can be the subject matter of a theft. There are limits, however, on the scope of the term "anything". While the term includes intangible objects which are capable of being converted so as to deprive the owner of his interest, the Supreme Court of Canada held in the *Stewart* case that intangible confidential information is not included within the meaning of "anything" because it is incapable of being taken and cannot be converted in a way that deprives the owner of it.[19] Accordingly, a person who memorizes the names on a confidential list cannot be convicted of theft in relation to the information obtained.

In *Stewart*, the Court reasoned that while the information had been "taken", the document containing it remained and the information was still available to its owner. The information in the document may remain available to its owner but where the value of the information is based on its confidentiality, the lawful possessor of the information suffers a loss when deprived of the document's confidentiality. If the thief steals the document, he can be prosecuted for theft of the document but not the information on the document. It can be argued that this amounts to prosecuting the thief for stealing the wrapper but not the candy? The Supreme Court realized its decision left Canada's theft law deficient in "an information age" but concluded that legislative action rather than judicial activism was required.

Parliament has recently responded to the importance of information in modern society by enacting a *Criminal Code* section that makes it an offence, fraudulently and without colour of right, to: 1) obtain, directly or indirectly, any computer service; 2) intercept, directly or indirectly, any function of a computer system; 3) use a computer system to commit certain offences (including mischief) in relation to data or a computer system; or 4) use, possess, traffic in or permit another person to have access to a computer password that would enable a person to commit the above offences. The commission of these offences renders the accused guilty of an indictable offence and liable to imprisonment for a term not exceeding ten years, or guilty of an offence punishable on summary conviction.

The *mens rea* of theft raises some interesting issues. The physical act of taking or converting must be done fraudulently, without colour of right and with one of the intents specified in the *Criminal Code*. The word "fraudulently" implies some notion of acting intentionally and knowingly against the owner's wishes. If a person takes an umbrella out of a stand in a restaurant under the mistaken belief that the umbrella belongs to her, she has not acted fraudulently. If she takes the umbrella knowing it does not belong to her but under the mistaken belief that the restaurant provides umbrellas free of charge for the use of its customers, she acts with a "colour of right". "Colour" means an honest belief and may arise either from a mistake of law or of fact or from ignorance. Consider the situation where a restaurant patron takes an umbrella because she is opposed to the concept of property and feels an umbrella should be free for use by anyone who needs one. Her belief may be heartfelt but nonetheless she knows she is taking the property of someone else and this is against the law. The fact she is morally opposed to the law is no defence to a charge of theft.

The most frequent theft allegation is based on a taking with intent to deprive the lawful owner permanently of the property. Indeed, according to common law, larceny required intent to deprive permanently. The *Criminal Code* has a broader reach and prohibits taking or converting with intent to deprive temporarily. Suppose the accused takes an automobile from a parking lot intending to return it to the lot before the owner realizes it is missing. The accused clearly has committed a trespass, but did he have an intention to deprive the owner of the vehicle even temporarily?[20] If "intention to deprive" rests at the heart of the crime of theft, does an honest belief that the thing is of no value or use to the owner constitute a defence? Does a cook commit theft when he takes home a loaf of bread that would otherwise have been put in the garbage?[21]

The punishment that can be imposed for a theft depends on the value of the thing stolen and the manner in which the prosecutor proceeds. Theft of property of a value exceeding $5,000 is an indictable offence punishable by up to ten-years imprisonment. If the thing stolen is of a value less than $5,000, the prosecutor may proceed by indictment, in which case a custodial term of up to two years can be imposed, or by summary conviction procedure.[22]

Breaking and Entering

There are approximately 400,000 break and enters in Canada annually. More than half involve residential locations. The police only solve one in four. Property loss and damage resulting from this crime costs insurance companies an estimated $400 million annually.[23]

A break and enter occurs if a dwelling house or other premise is illegally entered with intent to commit an indictable offence.[24] The offences most often associated with break and enter are theft and mischief (vandalism). Illegal entry may be forced or unforced. Breaking down a locked door or crawling through an open window are examples of the *actus reus* of this offence. If a person enters a retail store through the public entrance during business hours for the sole purpose of hiding until after the store has closed so he can steal a large quantity of clothing, has he committed a "break"?[25]

By virtue of a *Criminal Code* provision, evidence that an accused broke and entered a place is, in the absence of any evidence to the contrary, proof the act was done with intent to commit an indictable offence in that place. Evidence of the consumption of alcohol or drugs by the accused and irrational behavior is "evidence to the contrary" precluding use of the presumption by the prosecutor and requiring her to otherwise establish the intention of the accused.[26] The *Criminal Code* also provides a statutory definition of "place", which includes an area enclosed by a permanent fence.[27]

Breaking and entering of a dwelling house is an indictable offence punishable by up to life imprisonment. An offence committed on a place other than a dwelling house can be prosecuted by indictable procedure and result in a term of imprisonment not exceeding ten years or by summary conviction procedure. What is the maximum punishment for breaking and entering a tent?[28]

False Pretences and Fraud

The *Criminal Code* creates a variety of offences relating to the obtaining of property by false pretences or by fraud. A false pretence is defined as a representation of a matter of fact, either present or past that is known by the person who makes it to be false and that is made with fraudulent intent to induce the person to whom it is made to act upon it.[29] The fundamental distinction between theft and obtaining by false pretences is that in a case of theft the lawful owner of the property does not intend to part with the property, whereas in a case of obtaining by false pretences the lawful owner's intention must be to actually part with ownership of the property.

The essence of a false pretence is that the offender has pretended that something is so when it is not. A false promise or undertaking with respect to the future does not constitute a false pretence. If a person obtains money under a contract to perform a future service that he has no intention of performing, has he made a misrepresentation with respect to a future event (a false promise) or has he misrepresented an existing fact by falsely stating a present intention to perform the contract?[30]

The definition of fraud found in the *Criminal Code* is of relatively recent origin and was primarily introduced as a means of dealing with dishonest conduct in relation to the stock market.[31] However, the charge of "criminal fraud" has grown into an "all purpose" offence for dealing with dishonest conduct. The external circumstances of the offence (*actus reus*) consist of several elements. The accused must have defrauded the public or any person, but the identity of the victim need not be ascertained. The victim must be defrauded of property, money or valuable security. While actual economic loss is not an element of the crime, the Crown must prove an actual risk of prejudice to the victim's economic interest.[32]

To make out a case of criminal fraud, the prosecution must prove that the accused engaged in "deceit, falsehood or other fraudulent means". The words "other fraudulent means" encompass all means that can properly be stigmatized as dishonest.[33] Fraudulent means are not restricted to false pretences. Consequently, a false promise can constitute part of the *actus reus* of a charge of fraud. The gist of the *actus reus* of the crime of fraud is dishonest deprivation.

The mental or fault element of fraud (the *mens rea*) is a fertile area for debate. Suppose the accused induced investors to part with their money on the representation that he would invest it in prime real estate. Instead, he used it to speculate on the stock market. He did so in the foolish, but honest, belief that he would earn a better return for the investors. The investors lose all their money when the stocks drop in value. Has a fraud been committed? Yes, the fact that the accused did not intend that anyone should lose money is irrelevant. The investors were intentionally deprived of their money by means of a dishonest representation. However, is the mental element of the offence present if the accused does not believe it is dishonest to lie to investors as long as you do not intend to cheat them out of their money? The *mens rea* for fraud requires not only that the acts of the accused be objectively dishonest, but also that the accused intend to act dishonestly.[34] Does the accused who commits acts, which he knows the general community would consider dishonest, intend to act dishonestly when his personal standard of morality is not offended by the conduct?[35]

The crimes of obtaining by false pretences and fraud are both punishable by a term of imprisonment for up to ten years when the subject matter of the offence is of a value exceeding $5,000. If the value of the subject matter is less than $5,000, both offences can be tried by indictable or by summary conviction procedure at the election of the prosecution. If the prosecutor elects indictable procedure, both offences are punishable by a maximum of two years imprisonment.

MOTOR VEHICLE OFFENCES

A Brief History of Canada's Drinking and Driving Legislation

Criminal legislation responding to the deadly mixture of alcohol and motor vehicles first appeared in Canada in 1921,[36] when it was made an offence punishable on summary conviction to drive "while intoxicated". In 1925,[37] the reach of this offence was extended by also making it a crime to have "care or control" of a motor vehicle while intoxicated. An early decision interpreting the concept of "care or control" concluded that it:

> was intended as an alternative to the driving of the car, so as, for example, to provide for the conviction of an intoxicated driver sitting in his car at rest, or an intoxicated owner driven in his car by a chauffeur obliged to obey his orders.[38]

The word "intoxicated" was not defined in the *Criminal Code* and became the subject of much judicial discussion. In response to conflicting opinions as to the evidence required to establish intoxication, the more precise offence of driving "while impaired" by alcohol or a drug was created in 1951.[39] In a further attempt to cope with the growing menace to public safety posed by drunk drivers, Parliament also introduced provisions to assist the prosecution in establishing its case. Proof that the accused occupied the driver's seat of the vehicle creates a presumption that the accused had care or control of the vehicle. The result of a chemical analysis of the blood, urine, breath or other bodily substance of the accused was also made admissible on the issue of whether the accused was intoxicated or impaired. The *Criminal Code* provided, however, that no person could be required to provide a bodily substance for analysis.

To succeed on a charge of impaired driving it is incumbent on the Crown to establish "tangible physical evidence of actual driving impairment".[40] This is not always an easy task because there is no absolute standard of impairment and evidence as to the manner of driving or the condition of the accused has to be tendered. Accordingly, Parliament provided the prosecution with further assistance by creating the additional offence of driving or having the care or control of a motor vehicle having consumed such an amount of alcohol that the proportion of alcohol in the blood of the offender exceeds 80 milligrams of alcohol per 100 millilitres of blood. This offence is often referred to as "over 80" or ".08". Since an accused cannot be legally convicted of more than one offence arising out of the same "wrongful act" or *delect*, an accused cannot be convicted of both impaired driving and "over 80" arising from the same driving conduct.

The new offence of "over 80" made it necessary to provide a method for police to determine the proportion of alcohol in a motorist's blood (the blood alcohol concentration or BAC). The introduction of a provision permitting a police officer to demand that a motorist provide a sample of breath for analysis on a breathalyzer machine, where the officer has reasonable and probable grounds to believe that the motorist is committing an impaired or "over 80" offence or has committed such an offence within the preceding two hours, was the means used to provide the police with the necessary investigative tool. Failure to comply with the officer's demand without reasonable excuse was also made a criminal offence.

Armed with these new weapons, law enforcement authorities launched a war on drinking and driving. The number of persons charged with motor vehicle offences rose steadily from 1974 to 1981. In response to public concern over this growing social, economic and safety problem, legislation was enacted in 1985 creating new offences dealing with impaired driving of a motor vehicle causing bodily harm and impaired driving causing death. Penalties were also made harsher as a further deterrent. More stringent legislation and increased enforcement efforts have had some effect—the proportion of fatally injured drivers found to have a blood alcohol concentration over the legal limit decreased from 52 per cent in 1981 to 36 per cent in 1989.[41] However, drinking and driving remains a serious problem in Canada. Impaired driving charges represent 11 % of all *Criminal Code* charges, but it has been estimated that the risk of apprehension is only one in 1,183 trips made by legally impaired drivers.[42]

Impaired Driving

While creation of the offences of impaired driving causing bodily harm and impaired driving causing death has increased, the charging options available to police—the basic offences of impaired driving and "over 80"—remain the most commonly prosecuted motor vehicle crimes. Ninety two percent of people charged with drinking and driving related offences in Canada annually are charged with either or both impaired driving and "over 80".[43]

The driver of a motor vehicle (defined in the *Criminal Code* as "a vehicle that is drawn, propelled or driven by any means other than muscular power, but does not include railway equipment") commits the offence of impaired driving by operating or having care or control of a motor vehicle while that person's ability to operate the vehicle is impaired by alcohol or a drug.[44] Bad driving is not a necessary element of the offence. The charge is directed at the ability of the accused to drive, not the manner in which the vehicle was operated. An elevated blood alcohol concentration by itself does not establish impairment. Impairment is a question of fact and non-expert opinion evidence is admissible to determine the degree of impairment.[45] The prosecution usually relies on the observations of a police officer to prove the charge. Slurred speech, blood shot eyes and poor balance are all indicia of impairment. This evidence may also be supported by evidence of the blood alcohol concentration of the accused.

The conduct requirement (*actus reus*) of the offence of impaired driving is established by proof that the ability of the accused to drive was impaired by alcohol or a drug. What must the Crown prove to satisfy the fault element (*mens rea*) of the crime? It is a fundamental principle of our criminal justice system that a person can only be held responsible for intentional conduct. Can a person who drives under the honest but erroneous belief that her ability to drive has not been impaired be convicted of impaired driving? Yes, the intentional consumption of alcohol and the intention to drive combine to form the *mens rea* of the offence. Where a person is found impaired by alcohol, a presumption arises that the condition resulted from the voluntary act of the accused in consuming alcohol or ingesting a drug. The fault element will be lacking, however, if there is a reasonable doubt as to whether the accused voluntarily consumed the alcohol or drug. The fault element will also be absent if the accused ingested a drug unaware that it might affect his ability to drive. Does it follow that *mens rea* is lacking if the accused voluntarily ingests a drug she knows might impair her ability to drive but is confident that the drug will not take effect until after she stops driving?[46]

The second major drinking and driving crime is operating or being in care or control of a motor vehicle while having a blood alcohol concentration of "over 80". The external circumstances of the offence consist of the act of driving a motor vehicle with a prohibited blood alcohol concentration. The mental element of the crime consists of the intention to drive the motor vehicle after the voluntary consumption of alcohol or a drug. It is not necessary for the prosecution to prove that when the accused drove the vehicle he knew that his blood alcohol concentration exceeded the permissible amount.[47]

To establish the blood alcohol concentration of the accused at the time of the offence, the prosecution usually relies on the results of a chemical analysis performed by means of a breathalyzer machine on at least two samples of the breath of the accused.[48] If the first of the samples was taken within two hours of the alleged time of the offence and the analysis otherwise meets requirements set out in the *Criminal Code*, its results are deemed to be, in the absence of evidence to the contrary, proof of the BAC of the accused at the time of the alleged offence.[49] The *Criminal Code* also permits the prosecution to tender evidence of the results of the analysis by way of a certificate from the breathalyzer technician, thus removing the need for the technician to appear in person to testify.

The prosecution is placed in a position to introduce breathalyzer evidence by a *Criminal Code* provision which obliges a motorist to provide breath samples where they are demanded by a police officer who believes on reasonable and probable grounds that the motorist has, within the preceding two hours, committed the offence of impaired driving.[50] Often the officer's reasonable and probable grounds are formed as a result of the motorist registering a "fail" on an approved screening device (an Alcohol Level Evaluation Roadside Tester or ALERT). A peace officer may require a motorist to submit to a test on an approved screening device where she reasonably suspects that the motorist has alcohol in his body.[51]

The breathalyzer scheme in the *Criminal Code* materially assists the prosecution in prosecuting drinking and driving offences. What would otherwise be the prosecution's obligation to establish that alcohol consumption affected the ability of the accused to drive is removed by the offence of "over 80". Motorists suspected of having alcohol in their blood are compelled to provide breath samples for roadside screening and if reasonable and probable grounds exist to believe they have committed a drinking and driving offence, they can be compelled to provide self-incriminatory evidence for chemical analysis. If the breathalyzer machine indicates a prohibited blood alcohol concentration, the onus shifts to the accused to establish that the machine is in error. Unless the accused insists on the presence of the breathalyzer technician, the prosecution's case is established through certificate evidence.

The concept of "care or control" is utilized in both the "impaired" and "over 80" offences. An accused that occupied the driver's seat of a vehicle is deemed by the *Criminal Code* to have had care or control of the vehicle unless he establishes that he did not occupy that seat for the purpose of setting the vehicle in motion.[52] This provision requires the judge to accept as proven that the accused had care or control of the vehicle by virtue of her occupancy of the driver's seat, even if the judge has a reasonable doubt about the existence of this essential element of the offence. The provision violates the presumption of innocence guaranteed by the *Charter of Rights and Freedoms* but the Supreme Court of Canada has held that the provision is a "reasonable limit" within the meaning of s.1 of the *Charter* because the objective of protecting the public against drunk drivers is sufficiently important to justify overriding a constitutionally protected right.[53]

Drinking and driving cases bring before the criminal courts individuals who pose no threat to the public except when they mix alcohol with driving. They often display personal and family circumstances conducive to sentencing leniency. Public safety demands, however, that their driving conduct be addressed by sanctions that will operate as an effective deterrent. The drinking and driving sentencing regime in the *Criminal Code* seeks to rehabilitate the offender who is amenable to curative treatment by providing that a person found guilty of impaired driving can be given a conditional discharge where medical or other evidence warrants. A prior drinking and driving record does not preclude the granting of such a discharge where the evidence establishes genuine motivation and the likelihood of rehabilitation.[54] Curative treatment provisions have not been proclaimed in force in provinces that feel curative treatment should not be available to the exclusion of punishment for the offence committed.[55]

An offender's initial conviction for the basic offence of impaired driving usually results in a fine. The *Criminal Code* provides that the fine cannot be less than $1000. In some jurisdictions, the standard fine on first conviction is higher. Imprisonment is mandatory for a second offence and the term cannot be less than fourteen days. Each subsequent offence is punishable by a term of imprisonment for not less than ninety days. If the prosecution proceeds by indictable process, the accused is liable to a maximum of five-years imprisonment. Where the offence is punishable on summary conviction, the maximum term of imprisonment is six months. A mandatory driving prohibition is an additional consequence of conviction.

Where the impaired driving has caused bodily harm to another person, the offender can be sentenced to imprisonment for up to ten years. If the offender's impaired driving caused death, life imprisonment may be imposed. Death or bodily harm have been caused by impaired driving if the driving was a real factor in bringing them about.[56] In other words, the offender's impaired condition must have been at least a contributing cause to the death or bodily harm.[57]

Dangerous Driving

Criminal negligence in the operation of a motor vehicle and dangerous driving were two separate *Criminal Code* offences until the repeal of the former in 1985. Criminal negligence in the operation of a motor vehicle would now appear to be subsumed under the general offence of criminal negligence.[58] To succeed on a charge of dangerous driving, the prosecution must prove that the accused operated a motor vehicle on a street, road, highway or other public place in a manner dangerous to the public having regard to all the circumstances, including the nature, condition and use of that place and the amount of traffic that at the time is or might reasonably be expected to be on that place.[59] The essence of the offence is the manner or character of the driving.[60]

The fault element (*mens rea*) of the crime of dangerous driving has long been a contentious issue in Canadian criminal law. Criminally negligent conduct is defined as wanton or reckless disregard for the lives or safety of others. This definition suggests that before an accused can be convicted of criminal negligence in relation to the operation of a motor vehicle the court has to be satisfied that the accused deliberately risked the likelihood that his driving would pose a danger to others.

While the issue is not entirely clear,[61] it appears the state of mind that must be proved to establish dangerous driving is objective inadvertent negligence. Accordingly, an accused who fails to consider the risk created by his driving will possess the fault element for the offence of dangerous driving if a reasonable person in the same position as the accused would have averted to the risk.[62] If the accused drives in a manner dangerous to the public because of a momentary lapse, the mental element required for a criminal conviction is not present. However, evidence of the actual mental state of the accused is not always a prerequisite to conviction. In an appropriate case evidence of a marked departure from the norm will be sufficient to establish criminal responsibility. For example, speeding through a red light and colliding with a motorcycle[63] or driving on a busy highway in an exhausted state with a blood alcohol concentration of 50 mg. will support a conviction for dangerous driving.[64]

Dangerous driving is triable by indictable procedure or by summary conviction procedure at the election of the prosecution. If the prosecution elects indictable process on a charge of dangerous driving, the maximum permissible sentence is imprisonment for a term not exceeding five years. The *Criminal Code* also provides for the offences of dangerous driving causing bodily harm, punishable by imprisonment not exceeding ten years and dangerous driving causing death, punishable by imprisonment not exceeding fourteen years.

Other Driving Offences

In addition to prohibiting certain forms of driving, the *Criminal Code* absolutely forbids driving when the driver has previously been disqualified from doing so, or when the purpose of the driving is to escape civil or criminal liability after being involved in an accident. The offence of driving while disqualified is made out when the prosecution establishes that the accused operated a motor vehicle in Canada while disqualified from driving by reason of a driving prohibition imposed under the *Criminal Code* or as a result of the operation of provincial law. The mental element of the crime is knowledge of the fact of disqualification. This is usually established by inference from proof of the external circumstances of the offence (i.e., the act of driving while under prohibition).

To succeed on a charge of failing to stop at the scene of an accident, the prosecution must show that the accused had the care, charge or control of a motor vehicle involved in an accident and failed to stop the vehicle, give his name and address and offer assistance where necessary. "Care, charge or control" is a broader concept than "care or control".

Evidence that the accused failed to comply with these requirements is presumed by the *Criminal Code* to be proof of intent to escape civil or criminal liability.

OFFENCES AGAINST THE PERSON

Introduction

A small percentage of the workload of the criminal justice system involves crimes of violence. Only about 10% of criminal incidents reported to the police annually involve violent crime.[65] Violent crimes usually involve face-to-face confrontations and the victims of such crimes are often able to identify the offender. This leads to higher clearance rates for violent as opposed to property crimes. Fifty-two percent of assaults and 78% of attempted murders result in charges. Canadian police also have a high level of success in solving homicides. In most years charges are laid with respect to 77% of all reported homicides.[66]

Violent crimes are found primarily in Part VIII of the *Criminal Code*. This Part also contains the motor vehicle offences and the breathalyzer provisions, offences against conjugal rights (bigamy and polygamy), offences against reputation (defamatory libel) and hate crimes (advocating genocide and inciting public hatred). The collection together in one part of the *Code* of such diverse crimes demonstrates the need for a fundamental reorganization of the *Code*. The second most frequent crime of violence, robbery, is not even found in this part of the *Code*. It is classified as one of the "Offences Against Rights of Property" and is contained in Part IX.

Assault

The most frequently prosecuted violent crime is assault. Non-sexual assault accounts for three quarters of all violent crimes prosecuted.[67] In addition to being a significant crime in its own right, assaultive conduct is an essential component of sexual offences and can constitute the basis for criminal responsibility with respect to homicide.

The common law drew a distinction between assault, which involved causing an apprehension of violence, and battery, which concentrated on the actual infliction of physical violence. While the *Criminal Code* recognizes the distinction between applying force to another person and causing another person, by threats, to fear violence, it uses the term "assault" to encompass both concepts. In its primary sense, an "assault" under the *Code* is the intentional application of force to the person of the victim without consent. An assault also occurs when a person attempts or threatens, by an act or gesture, to apply force to another person if the person committing the assault has, or causes the other person reasonably to believe he has the present ability to effect his purpose. A tertiary meaning for "assault" is created by the *Code* and makes it an assault to accost or impede another person or beg while openly wearing or carrying a weapon or an imitation thereof.

Although physical violence is not necessary to constitute an assault, mere words cannot amount to an assault. For an assault to take place, some threatening act or gesture must accompany the words.[68] If the foundation of the assault is an intentional application of force to the person by another, the strength of the force is immaterial. The British Columbia Court of Appeal has concluded that an accused can be convicted of assault for placing his hand for five to ten seconds on the thigh of the person seated next to him on a bus.[69]

Mens rea is an essential element of a criminal assault. Therefore a reflex action lacks the necessary intent to constitute an assault, as does an accidental touching.[70] If the intent to assault a specific person is present, but the violence is actually visited on another person, the mental element of the offence is still made out. The general intent to apply force is transferred from one person to another. So, for example, an accused committed an assault when he struck and broke a glass ornament that injured the eye of Mrs. P, even though he was seeking to strike Mrs. P's husband.[71]

For the intentional application of force on the person of another to amount to an assault, it must be without the consent of that person. A strict reading of the *Code* would suggest the absence of consent is an element that must be proved by the prosecution. The Supreme Court of Canada has decided, however, that the *Code* should be read in light of certain common law limitations on consent.[72] The common law has generated jurisprudence that illuminates the meaning of consent and places limits on the types of harmful actions to which one can validly consent. The insistence of the common law to limit the legal effectiveness of consent to a fist fight, for instance, informs the interpretation of the *Code* and vitiates consent between adults intentionally to apply force causing serious hurt or non-trivial bodily harm to each other in the course of a fist fight or a brawl. Common law restrictions on consent do not affect the validity of freely given consent to rough sporting activities carried out according to rules of the game or to medical or surgical treatment. While participating in a rough sport implies consent to some bodily contact necessarily incidental to the game, the consent does not extend to overly violent attacks or conduct which evinces a deliberate intention to inflict injury.[73]

The *Criminal Code* creates three levels of assault: common assault, assault with a weapon or causing bodily harm, and aggravated assault. Common assault can be prosecuted as an indictable offence, punishable by up to five-years imprisonment, or by summary conviction procedure. To establish that the assault caused bodily harm, the Crown must prove that the hurt or injury suffered by the victim was more than merely transient or trifling in nature.[74] Assault causing bodily harm is a crime of general, not specific, intent. The prosecution need only prove the accused intended to commit an assault. If the victim suffered bodily harm as a consequence of the assault, the crime is made out whether or not the accused intended to cause bodily harm.[75] Aggravated assault involves wounding, maiming, disfiguring or endangering the life of the victim.

Robbery

Robbery is theft accompanied by violence.[76] To obtain a conviction the prosecution must establish conduct falling into three categories. The use or threat of violence by the accused for the purpose of extorting something or to overcome resistance to a theft constitutes robbery. The infliction of personal violence at the time of, or immediately before or after, a theft also constitutes robbery. Finally, a person who commits a theft while armed with an offensive weapon or imitation thereof is guilty of robbery. The mental element of the crime requires that the Crown establish an intention to cause any of these external circumstances. Since theft is an essential element of the offence, the Crown must prove the fraudulent intent required for theft. Every one who commits robbery is guilty of an indictable offence and liable to imprisonment for life.[77] If a firearm is used in the commission of the offence, there is a minimum punishment of four years imprisonment.

Sexual Offences

Rape, as an offence, is no longer part of Canada's criminal law. It has been replaced by three offences emphasizing that sexual crimes are crimes of violence. The most basic sexual offence is sexual assault. Essentially, a sexual assault is an assault committed in circumstances of a sexual nature. The test applied to determine whether the conduct of the accused had the required sexual nature is an objective one—would the sexual context of the assault be visible to the reasonable observer?[78]

The part of the complainant's body touched, the nature of the contact, the situation in which it occurred, the words and gestures accompanying the act and all other circumstances surrounding the conduct are relevant. Intent to degrade or demean another person for sexual gratification may also be a factor in considering whether the conduct is sexual in nature.[79] The Crown is not required to prove an actual touching. A lewd suggestion accompanied by an expression of force sufficient to amount to an assault also constitutes a sexual assault.[80]

Sexual assault is a crime of general intent. This means that the prosecution need only establish that the accused knowingly committed an assault. It is not incumbent on the prosecution to establish that the accused did the act to achieve certain consequences (e.g., sexual gratification). Moreover, voluntary intoxication cannot negate general intent.[81]

Actual consent is a defence to sexual assault, unless it was obtained by threats, fraud, the exercise of authority or the victim was under the age of sixteen years (except where the accused was less than five years older than the victim and was not in a position of trust or authority with respect to the victim). An honest but mistaken belief by the accused in his victim's consent is also a defence.[82] The reasonableness of the accused's belief is merely a factor to be considered in determining the honesty of his belief.

As a matter of public policy, should an accused be exempted from criminal responsibility because he had an honest but unreasonable belief that his victim was consenting? What social value is served by absolving from criminal responsibility a man who has subjected a woman to non-consensual sexual activity because of an unreasonable belief? On the other hand, if *mens rea* is an essential component of all crimes, how can the state justify punishing a person who believes, no matter how foolishly, that he is engaging in consensual sexual activity? These questions force the criminal justice system to examine some of its basic concepts. In 1992, s. 273.2[83] was added to the *Criminal Code* to clarify the circumstances in which the common law defence of mistaken belief in consent is a defence to a charge of sexual assault. It provides that self-induced intoxication is no defence to sexual assault. It also introduces a partly objective standard in determining whether the belief of the accused in consent was honestly held by providing that mistaken belief in consent is not a defence if the accused did not take reasonable steps, in the circumstances known to the accused at the time, to ascertain that the complainant was consenting.

A sexual assault is an essential element of two other crimes: 1) sexual assault with a weapon or causing bodily harm; and 2) aggravated sexual assault. The basic offence of sexual assault can be prosecuted by indictable procedure or by summary conviction. If the prosecution elects indictable procedure, the maximum punishment for sexual assault is ten years in prison. The maximum punishment where summary conviction procedure has been utilized is eighteen months imprisonment. Sexual assault with a weapon or causing bodily harm is punishable by a term of imprisonment not exceeding fourteen years and a conviction for aggravated sexual assault results in the offender being liable to imprisonment for life. Where a firearm is used in the commission of the offence, there is a minimum punishment of imprisonment for four years.

The *Criminal Code* contains a number of special evidentiary provisions for dealing with sexual offences. Certain antiquated rules of evidence requiring the corroboration of the testimony of a complainant[84] and attaching significance to whether there was complaint about the offence at the first opportunity have been statutorily abrogated.[85] The common law proposition that a husband cannot rape his wife has also been removed from the criminal law.[86] Finally, a number of sections have been introduced to the *Code* which seek to reduce the trauma of testifying with respect to sexual offences. Save in exceptional circumstances, the complainant's prior sexual conduct is declared to be inadmissible.[87] The *Code* also permits the Crown to tender the complainant's evidence by videotape in certain cases where the complainant was under 18 years of age at the time of the alleged offence.[88]

Homicide

Homicide is the direct or indirect causing of the death of a human being. Consequently, it cannot be committed unless a human being has died and someone has caused the death. A fetus is not a "human being" for purposes of the law of homicide.[89] The requirement that the accused cause the death of the deceased is met upon proof that the act of the accused was at least a contributing cause of death.[90]

The *Criminal Code* provides that homicide is either culpable or not culpable. Homicide that is not culpable is not an offence. Accidentally causing the death of a human being by a lawful act is an example of homicide that is not culpable. Culpable homicide is divided into three categories: infanticide, manslaughter and murder. Infanticide is committed when a mother causes the death of her newly born child while not fully recovered from the effects of giving birth. The child must be under the age of one year. Infanticide is the only form of culpable ho-

of the *Food and Drugs Act*. The essential scheme of the new legislation is similar to the previous legislation. An important part of the new legislation is the schedules to the Act. Schedule I includes the most dangerous drugs, such as phencyclidine, heroin and cocaine. Schedule II lists cannabis and its derivatives. Schedule III includes drugs like amphetamines and LSD. Schedule IV includes dangerous drugs, such as barbiturates, that have therapeutic uses. Simple possession of Schedule IV drugs is not an offence.

Possession

Simple possession of any of the drugs and narcotics listed in Schedules I, II, and III of the *Controlled Drugs and Substances Act* is an offence unless the person is authorized to be in possession by the regulations to the Act. The penalty for breaching this provision depends upon the Schedule in which the substance is included. The word "possession" is not defined in the *Controlled Drugs and Substances Act* and reference must be made to the definition contained in s. 4(3) of *Criminal Code*. A person has anything in possession when he has it in his or her personal possession or knowingly has it in the possession or custody of another person or has it in any place for the use or benefit of him or herself or of another person. The *Criminal Code* also provides for "constructive possession". When one of two or more persons, with the knowledge and consent of the rest, has anything in his custody or possession, it is deemed to be in the custody and possession of each and all of them.[105] In law there is no possession of a forbidden substance without knowledge of the character of the forbidden substance.[106] Is the finding of a minute trace of a narcotic on a person sufficient to establish possession?[107]

Trafficking, Importing and Production

It is an offence to traffic in, import or produce any of the scheduled substances in the *Controlled Drugs and Substances Act* and it is an offence to be in possession of them for the purpose of trafficking. The definition of "traffic" includes "sell" and is very broad. The penalty for trafficking, importing and producing depends upon the schedule in which the substance is found. Trafficking is the act of doing one of the acts prohibited by statute. Consequently, selling a plant knowing it not to be a narcotic, but representing it to be marijuana, constitutes the offence of trafficking in a narcotic because the offender "offered" to sell a narcotic. If the accused is charged with offering to sell and deliver a narcotic to another person, the *actus reus* is the making of the offer and the *mens rea is* the intention to make the offer. The fact that the accused did not intend to deliver on his offer is irrelevant. Introducing a prospective buyer to a seller is not, in itself, trafficking since the act is not covered by any of the terms contained within the definition of trafficking. However, is the "go between" a party to the seller's trafficking by aiding and abetting the transaction?

Purchasing of a prohibited drug—by purchase alone—is not conduct that falls within the definition of trafficking. If the purchaser comes into possession of the forbidden substance he is, of course, guilty of possession. Does the purchaser also aid and abet the seller, so as to be liable as a party to the offence? An offender is a party to an offence where he does or omits to do anything for the purpose of aiding another person to commit the offence. Is the purpose of a purchaser to aid the seller in selling the drug, or is the only purpose of the purchaser to purchase the drug?[108]

Identification of the substance that is the subject matter of the prosecution is facilitated by provisions allowing for the admissibility of a certificate of a person designated as an analyst. This certificate is, in the absence of evidence to the contrary, proof of the statements contained in the certificate. Notice of the Crown's intention to rely on certificate evidence must be given to the accused before trial and, with leave of the court, the accused can require the analyst to attend trial for the purpose of cross examination.

CONCLUSION

Widespread media coverage of crime gives the impression that the crime rate is increasing in Canada. In fact, crime rates peaked in 1991 and fell throughout the rest of the 1990s, stabilizing somewhat in the early 2000s. The overall decrease was led by declines in non-violent crimes, with property crimes falling 6% and other criminal offences falling 5%. In particular, large drops were reported for break-ins (-7%), motor vehicle thefts (-7%) and thefts under $5,000 (-6%). The United States experienced a similar decrease in crime rates during these years. One explanation for the decreases may be that the majority of the male children of the "baby boomers" had passed through their most crime prone years (16 to 35 years of age) by 1991.

Even the most superficial review of the *Criminal Code* reveals pressing need for Canada to have modern criminal legislation. Our present *Criminal Code* was enacted in 1892. Its enactment constituted the culmination of an enormous amount of work consolidating and assimilating English and Canadian common and statute law. The 1892

Code provided a new country with a collected and uniform set of criminal laws. It placed Canada in the vanguard of nineteenth century criminal law reform. However, Canada's *Criminal Code* is not truly a "code" as that term is understood in Europe—it does not comprehensively and rationally set out Canada's criminal law. Despite a major revision in 1955, the *Code* remains much the same in structure, style and content as it was in 1892. It is hard to understand, procedurally deficient and includes obsolete provisions. Canada requires a new *Criminal Code*, one that reflects modern Canadian values and the principles of the *Charter of Rights and Freedoms*. Several sustained efforts to stimulate public demand for and political discussion on *Criminal Code* reform have been unsuccessful.[109] While politicians are anxious to be "tough on crime", few appear to have the appetite to tackle the laborious work required to create a modern code of Canadian criminal law.

Notes

[1] Adult Criminal Court Statistics, 2006/2007, *Juristat*, Statistics Canada, Catalogue no. 85-002-XIE, Vol. 28, No. 5, p. 1.

[2] All specific *Criminal Code* references are to R.S.C. 1985, c. C-46, as amended.

[3] Canada's homicide rate is "middle of the road" in an international context. It is 1.8 murders per 100,000 people. This is less than one-third that of the United States and Turkey and slightly lower than New Zealand. Canadians are less likely to be murdered than Scots or Finns but England, Spain, France, Italy, Germany, Poland, the Netherlands and Austria all have murder rates lower than Canada (The Lowdown on Crime in Canada, MACLEANS.CA, July 1, 2009).

[4] *Report of the Criminal Justice Review Committee*, (Toronto: Queen's Printer, 1999) at p.56.

[5] *Supra*, note 1, p. 3.

[6] *R. v. Gaudreault*, 1995 CarswellQue 102, [105 C.C.C. (3d) 270 (Que. C.A.), leave to appeal refused 108 C.C.C. (3d) vi (S.C.C.).

[7] *R. v. Stuart*, 1981 CarswellBC 695, 58 C.C.C. (2d) 203 (B.C.S.C.); followed: *R. v. Neal*, 1982 CarswellOnt 1492, 67 C.C.C. (2d) 92, 136 D.L.R. (3d) 86 (Ont. Co. Ct.).

[8] In *R. v. Custance*, (2005), 2005 CarswellMan 30, 2005 MBCA 23, 194 C.C.C. (3d) 225, [2005] 7 W.W.R. 411, 192 Man. R. (2d) 69, 340 W.A.C. 69, 28 C.R. (6th) 357 (Man. C.A.), leave to appeal refused 2005 CarswellMan 295, 2005 CarswellMan 296, 198 C.C.C. (3d) vi, 208 Man. R. (2d) 319 (note), 383 W.A.C. 319 (note), 346 N.R. 195 (note) (S.C.C.), it was held that that accused's mistaken belief that he was complying with the terms of the order was a mistake of law and no defence. The accused also failed to make out a lawful excuse by a showing of due diligence to satisfy the obligation.

[9] Toronto Star, January 6, 2004.

[10] *R. v. Ouellette*, 1978 CarswellBC 382, 39 C.C.C. (2d) 278, [1978] 2 W.W.R. 378 (B.C.C.A.).

[11] *R. v. Zajner*, 1977 CarswellOnt 655, 36 C.C.C. (2d) 417 (Ont. C.A.).

[12] *R. v. Pack*, 1972 CarswellBC 327, 10 C.C.C. (2d) 162 (B.C.C.A.) and *R. v. Piper*, 1964 CarswellMan 71, [1965] 3 C.C.C. 135, 51 D.L.R. (2d) 534 (Man. C.A.).

[13] *R. v. Stutt*, 1979 CarswellBC 810, 52 C.C.C. (2d) 53 (B.C.C.A.).

[14] *R. v. MacCaud*, 1975 CarswellOnt 1336, 22 C.C.C. (2d) 445 (Ont. H.C.).

[15] Bentham, *Morals and Legislation, Vol. 11*, p. 269.

[16] Eighty one percent of all incidents of break and enter reported in 1990 did not result in any charges being laid (Canadian Crimes Statistics, 1990, *Juristat*, Statistics Canada, (Ottawa, 1991) p. 38.

[17] S.C. 1892, c. 29.

[18] Parl. Debates, 1878, 3 Series, vol. 239, Col. 1949, quoted in *Martin's Criminal Code* (Toronto, 1955), p. 480.

[19] *R. v. Stewart*, 1988 CarswellOnt 960, 1988 CarswellOnt 110, 41 C.C.C. (3d) 481, 63 C.R. (3d) 305, 65 O.R. (2d) 637 (note), 39 B.L.R. 198, 50 D.L.R. (4th) 1, 19 C.I.P.R. 161, 21 C.P.R. (3d) 289, 28 O.A.C. 219, 85 N.R. 171, [1988] 1 S.C.R. 963 (S.C.C.).

[20] In the absence of intent to deprive, the accused cannot be convicted of theft; he or she can be convicted of the separate offence of "joyriding" found in *Criminal Code* s. 335.

[21] In *R. v. Pace*, 1964 CarswellNS 16, [1965] 3 C.C.C. 55, 50 M.P.R. 301, 48 D.L.R. (2d) 532 (N.S. C.A.), the Nova Scotia Court of Appeal held that such a taking was "fraudulent" and constituted theft.

[22] *Criminal Code*, s. 334.

[23] Statistics Canada, *Juristat, Vol. 12, No. 1* (Ottawa, 1991) p. 2.

[24] *Criminal Code*, s. 348.

[25] In *R. v. Farbridge* (1984), 1984 CarswellAlta 173, 15 C.C.C. (3d) 521, 42 C.R. (3d) 385, [1985] 2 W.W.R. 56, 34 Alta. L.R. (2d) 394, 57 A.R. 292 (Alta. C.A.), the Alberta Court of Appeal held that such conduct did not constitute "breaking" within the meaning of the *Criminal Code*.

[26] *R. v. Campbell*, 1974 CarswellOnt 1037, 17 C.C.C. (2d) 320 (Ont. C.A.).

[27] *R. v. Thibault*, 1982 CarswellNS 273, 66 C.C.C. (2d) 422, 51 N.S.R. (2d) 91, 102 A.P.R. 91 (N.S. C.A.).

[28] The answer to this question would appear to depend on the use to which the tent is being put. A tent used as a temporary residence is a "dwelling house" (see *R. v. Howe (No. 2)*, 1983 CarswellNS 313, 57 N.S.R. (2d) 325, 120 A.P.R. 325 (N.S. C.A.)) and a breaking and entering in relation to it renders the offender liable to life imprisonment.

[29] *Criminal Code*, s. 361.

[30] The leading cases on the issue are discussed in *R. v. Reid*, 1940 CarswellBC 51, 74 C.C.C. 156, 55 B.C.R. 321, [1940] 3 W.W.R. 96, [1940] 4 D.L.R. 25 (B.C. C.A.).

[31] The fraud provision found in s. 380 of the present *Criminal Code* was created in 1948. Prior to the creation of this offence, only conspiracies to defraud were criminal.

[32] *R. v. Wagman*, 1981 CarswellOnt 1174, 60 C.C.C. (2d) 23 (Ont. C.A.).

[33] *R. v. Olan*, 1978 CarswellOnt 49, 1978 CarswellOnt 593, 41 C.C.C. (2d) 145, [1978] 2 S.C.R. 1175, 86 D.L.R. (3d) 212, 21 N.R. 504, 5 C.R. (3d) 1 (S.C.C.).

[34] *R. v. Bobbie*, 1988 CarswellOnt 79, 43 C.C.C. (3d) 187, 65 C.R. (3d) 284, 29 O.A.C. 303 (Ont. C.A.).

[35] In *R. v. Lacombe*, 1990 CarswellQue 190, 60 C.C.C. (3d) 489, 37 Q.A.C. 67 (Que.

C.A.), the Court concluded that honesty is a function of community standards, not personal morality. If the accused is aware that his conduct would be considered dishonest, he possesses the *mens rea* of the offence.

[36] S.C. 1921, c. 25, s. 3.

[37] S.C. 1925, c. 38, s. 5.

[38] *R. v. Higgins* (1928), 50 C.C.C. 381 (Ont. C.A.).

[39] S.C. 1951, c. 47, s. 14.

[40] *R. v. Marks*, 1952 CarswellOnt 18, [1952] O.W.N. 608, 15 C.R. 47, 103 C.C.C. 368 (Ont. Co. Ct.).

[41] Statistics Canada, *Juristat*, Vol. II, No. 13 (Ottawa, 1991), at p. 7.

[42] C. Liban *et al.*, *Drinking—Driving Countermeasure Review: The Canadian Experience* (Toronto, Addiction Research Foundation, 1985) p. 8.

[43] *Supra*, note 41, at p. 5.

[44] *Criminal Code*, s. 253. This offence also applies to the operation of a vessel, aircraft or railway equipment.

[45] *R. v. Graat*, 1982 CarswellOnt 101, 1982 CarswellOnt 745, 2 C.C.C. (3d) 365, [1982] 2 S.C.R. 819, 18 M.V.R. 287, 31 C.R. (3d) 289, 144 D.L.R. (3d) 267, 45 N.R. 451 (S.C.C.), affirming 1980 CarswellOnt 47, 30 O.R. (2d) 247, 7 M.V.R. 163, 17 C.R. (3d) 55, 55 C.C.C. (2d) 429, 116 D.L.R. (3d) 143 (Ont. C.A.).

[46] In *R. v. Murray*, 1985 CarswellOnt 30, 22 C.C.C. (3d) 502, 36 M.V.R. 12, 12 O.A.C. 21 (Ont. C.A.) and the Ontario Court of Appeal held that the voluntary ingestion of the drug supplied the required *mens rea*. This *mens rea* was not negated by the accused's over-estimation of the time it would take the drug to take effect.

[47] *R. v. Patterson*, 1982 CarswellNS 10, 69 C.C.C. (2d) 274, 15 M.V.R. 283, 52 N.S.R. (2d) 606, 106 A.P.R. 606 (N.S. C.A.); *R. v. MacCannell*, 1980 CarswellOnt 13, 54 C.C.C. (2d) 188, 6 M.V.R. 19 (Ont. C.A.).

[48] The *Criminal Code* also permits the use of evidence of analysis performed on blood, urine or other bodily substances.

[49] *Criminal Code*, s. 258.

[50] *Criminal Code*, s. 254.

[51] *Ibid.*

[52] *Criminal Code*, s. 258.

[53] *R. v. Whyte*, 1988 CarswellBC 761, 1988 CarswellBC 290, 42 C.C.C. (3d) 97, 6 M.V.R. (2d) 138, [1988] 2 S.C.R. 3, [1988] 5 W.W.R. 26, 51 D.L.R. (4th) 481, 86 N.R. 328, 29 B.C.L.R. (2d) 273, 64 C.R. (3d) 123, 35 C.R.R. 1 (S.C.C.).

[54] *R. v. Ashberry*, 1989 CarswellOnt 73, 47 C.C.C. (3d) 138, 30 O.A.C. 376, 11 M.V.R. (2d) 1, 68 C.R. (3d) 341 (Ont. C.A.).

[55] *Criminal Code*, s. 255(5).

[56] *R. v. Ewart*, 1989 CarswellAlta 222, 53 C.C.C. (3d) 153, 100 A.R. 118, 18 M.V.R. (2d) 55 (Alta. C.A.).

[57] *R. v. Powell*, 1989 CarswellSask 14, 52 C.C.C. (3d) 403, 81 Sask. R. 301, 19 M.V.R. (2d) 36 (Sask. C.A.).

[58] *Criminal Code*, s. 219.

[59] *Criminal Code*, s. 249.

[60] *R. v. Peda*, 1969 CarswellOnt 20, [1969] 4 C.C.C. 245, [1969] S.C.R. 905, 7 C.R.N.S. 243, 6 D.L.R. (3d) 177 (S.C.C.).

[61] *R. v. Hundal*, 1993 CarswellBC 489, 1993 CarswellBC 1255, 79 C.C.C. (3d) 97, 43 M.V.R. (2d) 169, 149 N.R. 189, 14 C.R.R. (2d) 19, 22 B.C.A.C. 241, 38 W.A.C.

241, [1993] 1 S.C.R. 867, 19 C.R. (4th) 169 (S.C.C.). See D. Stuart, *Canadian Criminal Law: A Treatise* (Toronto, 1987), pp. 198 to 203.

62 *R. v. Beaudoin*, 1973 CarswellOnt 857, 12 C.C.C. (2d) 81, [1973] 3 O.R. 1 (Ont. C.A.), *R. v. F. (D.L.)*, 1989 CarswellAlta 195, 73 C.R. (3d) 391, 52 C.C.C. (3d) 357, 18 M.V.R. (2d) 62, 71 Alta. L.R. (2d) 241, 100 A.R. 122 (Alta. C.A.).

63 *R. v. Fotti*, 1978 CarswellMan 110, 45 C.C.C. (2d) 353, [1979] 1 W.W.R. 652, 1 M.V.R. 279, 2 Man. R. (2d) 182 (Man. C.A.), affirmed 1980 CarswellMan 85, 1980 CarswellMan 172, 50 C.C.C. (2d) 479, [1980] 1 S.C.R. 589, [1983] 4 W.W.R. 754, [1980] 3 W.W.R. 617, 4 M.V.R. 172, 31 N.R. 100, 2 Man. R. (2d) 180 (S.C.C.).

64 *R. v. Mason*, 1990 CarswellBC 314,, 60 C.C.C. (3d) 338 24 M.V.R. (2d) 164 (B.C. C.A.) leave to appeal refused (1990), 60 C.C.C. (3d) 338n (S.C.C.).

65 Statistics Canada, *Crime Trends in Canada, 1962 – 1990* (Ottawa, 1992).

66 Statistics Canada, *Canadian Crime Statistics, 1990* (Ottawa, 1991) p. 32.

67 *Ibid.*, p. 11.

68 *R. v. Byrne*, 1968 CarswellBC 31, [1968] 3 C.C.C. 179, 3 C.R.N.S. 190, 63 W.W.R. 385 (B.C. C.A.); *R. v. Judge* (1957), 118 C.C.C. 410 (Ont. C.A.).

69 *R. v. Burden* (1981), 1981 CarswellBC 614, 64 C.C.C. (2d) 68, [1982] 1 W.W.R. 193, 25 C.R. (3d) 283 (B.C. C.A.).

70 *R. v. Wolfe*, 1974 CarswellOnt 1066, 20 C.C.C. (2d) 382 (Ont. C.A.).

71 *R. v. Deakin*, 1974 CarswellMan 36, 16 C.C.C. (2d) 1, 26 C.R.N.S. 236, [1974] 3 W.W.R. 435 (Man. C.A.).

72 *R. v. Jobidon*, 1991 CarswellOnt 1023, 1991 CarswellOnt 110, 66 C.C.C. (3d) 454, 7 C.R. (4th) 233, 128 N.R. 321, [1991] 2 S.C.R. 714, 49 O.A.C. 83 (S.C.C.).

73 *R. v. Leclerc*, 1991 CarswellOnt 111, 67 C.C.C. (3d) 563, 7 C.R. (4th) 282, 4 O.R. (3d) 788, 50 O.A.C. 232 (Ont. C.A.).

74 *R. v. Dupperon*, 1984 CarswellSask 198, 16 C.C.C. (3d) 453, [1985] 2 W.W.R. 369, 37 Sask. R. 84, 43 C.R. (3d) 70 (Sask. C.A.).

75 *R. v. Lee*, 1988 CarswellOnt 1069, 29 O.A.C. 379 (Ont. C.A.).

76 *Criminal Code*, s. 345.

77 *Criminal Code*, s. 344.

78 *R. v. Chase*, 1987 CarswellNB 25, 1987 CarswellNB 315, 37 C.C.C. (3d) 97, 59 C.R. (3d) 193, [1987] 2 S.C.R. 293, 45 D.L.R. (4th) 98, 80 N.R. 247, 82 N.B.R. (2d) 229, 208 A.P.R. 229 (S.C.C.).

79 *R. v. Taylor*, 1985 CarswellAlta 32, 19 C.C.C. (3d) 156, 36 Alta. L.R. (2d) 275, 59 A.R. 179, 44 C.R. (3d) 263, [1985] 3 W.W.R. 415 (Alta. C.A).

80 *R. v. Ricketts*, 1985 CarswellAlta 484, 61 A.R. 175 (C.A.).

81 *R. v. Leary*, 1977 CarswellBC 314, 1977 CarswellBC 490, C.C.C. (2d) 473, [1978] 1 S.C.R. 29, 37 C.R.N.S. 60, [1977] 2 W.W.R. 628, 13 N.R. 592, 33 74 D.L.R. (3d) 103 (S.C.C.).

82 *R. v. Ewanchuk*, [1999 CarswellAlta 99, 1999 CarswellAlta 100, [1999] 1 S.C.R. 330, 131 C.C.C. (3d) 481, 235 N.R. 323, 22 C.R. (5th) 1, 169 D.L.R. (4th) 193, [1999] 6 W.W.R. 333, 232 A.R. 1, 195 W.A.C. 1, 68 Alta. L.R. (3d) 1 (S.C.C.); *R. v. Pappajohn*, 1980 CarswellBC 446, 1980 CarswellBC 546, 52 C.C.C. (2d) 481, [1980] 2 S.C.R. 120, 111 D.L.R. (3d) 1, 32 N.R. 104, [1980] 4 W.W.R. 387, 14 C.R. (3d) 243 (Eng.), 19 C.R. (3d) 97 (Fr.) (S.C.C.).

83 S.C. 1992, c. 38, s. 1

84 *Criminal Code*, s. 274.

85 *Criminal Code*, s. 275.

86 *Criminal Code*, s. 278.

87 *Criminal Code*, s. 276.

88 *Criminal Code*, s. 715.1.

89 *R. v. Sullivan*, 1991 CarswellBC 59, 1991 CarswellBC 916, 63 C.C.C. (3d) 97, 3 C.R. (4th) 277, [1991] 1 S.C.R. 489, 122 N.R. 166, 55 B.C.L.R. (2d) 1 (S.C.C.).

90 *R. v. Smithers*, 1977 CarswellOnt 25, 1977 CarswellOnt 479F, 34 C.C.C. (2d) 427, [1978] 1 S.C.R. 506, 75 D.L.R. (3d) 321, 15 N.R. 287, 40 C.R.N.S. 79 (S.C.C.).

91 *R. v. Mack*, 1975 CarswellAlta 24, 22 C.C.C. (2d) 257, [1975] 4 W.W.R. 180, 29 C.R.N.S. 270 (Alta. C.A.).

92 *Criminal Code*, s. 231(2).

93 *R. v. Smith*, 1986 CarswellNS 340, 71 N.S.R. (2d) 229, 171 A.P.R. 229 (N.S. C.A.).

94 *Criminal Code*, s. 231(4).

95 *R. v. Paré*, 1987 CarswellQue 19, 1987 CarswellQue 97, 38 C.C.C. (3d) 97, 60 C.R. (3d) 346, [1987] 2 S.C.R. 618, 45 D.L.R. (4th) 546, 80 N.R. 272, 11 Q.A.C. 1 (S.C.C.).

96 *Criminal Code*, s. 745.

97 *Criminal Code*, s. 26.

98 In *Northwest v. R.*, 1980 CarswellAlta 249, 22 A.R. 522, [1980] 5 W.W.R. 48 (Alta. C.A.), the Albert Court of Appeal held that a failure to retreat is only a factor to be considered in determining whether the accused believed on reasonable grounds that he could not otherwise preserve himself. A failure to retreat does not, in itself, remove the availability of the defence.

99 *Criminal Code*, s. 232.

100 *R. v. Wright*, 1969 CarswellSask 8, [1969] 3 C.C.C. 258, 66 W.W.R. 631, 2 D.L.R. (3d) 529, [1969] S.C.R. 335 (S.C.C.).

101 S.C. 1996, c. 19.

102 Federal drug legislation does not depend for its constitutional validity on the federal "criminal law power" of s. 91(27) of the *Constitutional Act*, 1867 but on the "peace, order anal good government" power in the opening words of s. 91.

103 Statistics Canada, *Canadian Crime Statistics, 1990* (Ottawa, 1991) p. 45.

104 *An Act to prohibit the importation, manufacture and sale of Opium for other than medicinal purposes*, S.C. 1908, c. 50.

105 *Criminal Code*, s. 4(3).

106 *R. v. Beaver*, 1957 CarswellOnt 10, 118 C.C.C. 129, [1957] S.C.R. 531, 26 C.R. 193 (S.C.C.).

107 In *R. v McBurney* (1975), 1975 CarswellBC 139, 24 C.C.C. (2d) 44, [1975] 5 W.W.R. 554 (B.C. C.A.), the British Columbia Court of Appeal held that a minute trace of narcotic is only evidence of earlier possession and does not establish present possession. The Alberta Court of Appeal reached a contrary conclusion in *R v. Quigley*, 1954 CarswellAlta 66, 111 C.C.C. 81, 20 C.R. 152, 14 W.W.R. 37 (Alta. C.A.).

108 In *R. v. Greyeyes* (1997), 1997 CarswellSask 271, 1997 CarswellSask 272, 116 C.C.C. (3d) 334, [1997] 2 S.C.R. 825, 8 C.R. (5th) 308, 214 N.R. 43, 148 D.L.R. (4th) 634, 152 Sask. R. 294, 140 W.A.C. 294, [1997] 7 W.W.R. 426 (S.C.C.), the Supreme Court of Canada held that a purchaser of a narcotic is not a trafficker, nor *per se* an aider or abettor of a trafficker.

109 Report 31, *Recodifying Criminal Law*, Law Reform Commission of Canada (Ottawa, 1997) p. 1.

11

Youth Criminal Justice Act

Robert E. Lutes, Q.C. *

INTRODUCTION

The *Youth Criminal Justice Act*[1] came into force on April 1, 2003.

A BIT OF HISTORY

The *Young Offenders Act*[2] replaced the *Juvenile Delinquents Act*[3] on April 2, 1984; an Act passed in 1908 and based on social welfare principles. The *Juvenile Deliquents Act* applied to persons over the age of 7. The social welfare policy in the *Juvenile Deliquents Act* was replaced by an offence-based approach under the *Young Offenders Act*, which called for accountability and responsibility of young persons with the requirement that they "bear responsibility" for their actions. At the same time the *Young Offenders Act* recognized that youth "should not in all instances be held accountable in the same manner or suffer the same consequences for their behaviour as adults...[4]

The *Young Offenders Act* was a controversial piece of legislation in part due to lack of information provided to the general public. In the changeover to the *Youth Criminal Justice Act*, public education will be a key component to its success.

The short history of the move from the *Young Offenders Act* to the *Youth Criminal Justice Act* is as follows:

- 1995—legislative amendments were made to the *Young Offenders Act* and at the same time the Minister of Justice for Canada asked a Standing Committee of Parliament to review the *Young Offenders Act* with a view to making recommendations for change;
- 1996—a Federal/Provincial/Territorial Task Force filed a report

---

* B.Sc., Mount Allison University, Sackville, New Brunswick; LL.B., University of New Brunswick, Fredericton, New Brunswick; LL.M., University of London, Kings College, London, England; recently retired from the Public Prosecution Service of Nova Scotia, and is presently working privately as a Facilitator and a Youth Justice Specialist.

with the Parliamentary Standing Committee with a large number of detailed recommendations for changes to the *Young Offenders Act*;

- 1997—the Standing Committee released its report setting out a number of recommendations for changes to the *Young Offenders Act*. This Report was filed with the Minister of Justice in response to the Minister's original request for the review in 1995;
- May 1998—the Minister of Justice in response to the report of the Standing Committee released a document entitled "The Strategy for The Renewal of Youth Justice";
- June 1998-April 1, 2003
  - broad consultations were held to discuss the Strategy document,
  - after extensive Parliamentary process the *Youth Criminal Justice Act* was assented to in the House of Commons February 19, 2002,
  - the date for proclamation was later set: April 1, 2003.

The *Youth Criminal Justice Act* replaces the *Young Offenders Act* and makes a number of fundamental changes to the principles, purposes, and procedures. The *Youth Criminal Justice Act* has carefully reordered and rewritten the principles that apply to young persons who come into conflict with the law.[5]

The Act, its philosophy, and its rules will be examined in this chapter in the hopes that the reader will gain new knowledge, insight, and perspective on this very topical issue.

WHAT IS THE *YOUTH CRIMINAL JUSTICE ACT*?

The *Youth Criminal Justice Act* is a federal statute that establishes the procedure to be followed when police and others in the criminal justice system take action for offences under any Act or Regulation of Parliament committed by young persons. All federal Acts and Regulations are covered by the *Youth Criminal Justice Act*; however, most cases arise as a result of offences contrary to the *Criminal Code of Canada*.[6]

The Act also provides for youth justice courts being established or designated[7] and confers jurisdiction and power upon that court to deal with young persons brought before it.[8] There are many detailed provisions to cover the various aspects of proceedings and it is not necessary to review all these in detail. Some provisions, however, will be considered later in this chapter.

WHO IS A YOUNG PERSON?

The *Youth Criminal Justice Act* applies to young persons 12 years of age and over but under 18 at the time of the commission of the offence. If an offence is committed while the person is a young person but proceedings are not taken until after the person has turned 18 and has become an adult, we still apply the provisions of the *Youth Criminal Justice Act*. Simply put, we look at the age of the person at the time of the offence.

This is the general rule; however, there are a few minor exceptions where the Act applies to persons over the age of 18. One such example is a young person who is placed on probation and violates the term of a probation order imposed under the *Youth Criminal Justice Act* after turning the age of 18. Even though the offence is created under the *Youth Criminal Justice Act*, proceedings are taken in adult court.

Under the *Juvenile Deliquents Act* the age varied across Canada, but under the *Young Offenders Act* and now the *Youth Criminal Justice Act*, age is now treated uniformly across the country (12-17, adult at 18).

PHILOSOPHY OF THE *YOUTH CRIMINAL JUSTICE ACT*

The philosophy of the *Youth Criminal Justice Act* can be seen most clearly in the sections of the Act that set out the principles.[9]

In the change over from the *Young Offenders Act* to the *Youth Criminal Justice Act*, of the objectives was to reduce the number of youth that go to court and the number of youth that are sentenced to custody. The Preamble of the *Youth Criminal Justice Act* acknowledges that "Canadian society should have a youth criminal justice system that ... reduces the over-reliance on incarceration for non-violent young persons."[10]

The *Youth Criminal Justice Act* presumes Extrajudicial Measures to be adequate for a young person when the offence is non-violent and the young person has not previously been found guilty of an offence. This presumption addresses the objective of fewer youth going to court.[11] In addition there are presumptions against a sentence to custody and statutory limitations on the imposition of a sentence to custody.[12]

The Act also recognizes that young persons have a greater dependency than adults and have a reduced level of maturity.[13] There are also a number of principles that address the needs of victims and parents.[14]

Lastly, it must be recognized that there is a broad cross-section of youth covered by the *Youth Criminal Justice Act* and that these principles need to respond to the broad variety of risks faced and offence committed by youth.

WHAT OFFENCES FALL UNDER THE *YOUTH CRIMINAL JUSTICE ACT*?

"Offence" is defined in the *Youth Criminal Justice Act* to include "an offence created by an Act of Parliament or by any regulation, rule, order, by-law or ordinance made under an Act of Parliament other than an ordinance of the Northwest Territories or a law of the Legislature of Yukon or the Legislature for Nunavut."[15]

It is true that offences under all federal statutes are caught by the *Youth Criminal Justice Act*, but in reality it is criminal offences under the *Criminal Code* that constitute the bulk of proceedings before the youth justice court. Offences under provincial and territorial laws are prosecuted under provincial or territorial procedural statutes, not the *Youth Criminal Justice Act*. Each province and territory also has the latitude of defining the age of responsibility for young persons who violate these provincial and territorial statutes, i.e., *Motor Vehicle Act* or *Liquor Control Act*. By way of example, Nova Scotia has passed a statute called the *Youth Justice Act*,[16] which applies to 12 to 17 year olds, using the same age limits as the *Youth Criminal Justice Act*.

CRIMINAL CODE

The *Criminal Code* (the "*Code*") is a federal statute that sets out offences for conduct that society has chosen to prohibit, and imposes criminal sanctions upon those who offend these rules. The *Code* sets out a comprehensive set of rules to enable the enforcement of criminal law. The *Youth Criminal Justice Act* is basically a procedural statute defining the philosophy and procedure to be followed when dealing with young persons. Rather than rewriting the provisions of the *Code* within the *Youth Criminal Justice Act*, the *Code* generally applies except where inconsistent with the *Youth Criminal Justice Act*.[17]

The general rule, therefore, is that the offences and provisions set out in the *Code* apply to offences committed by young persons, except that the *Youth Criminal Justice Act* always takes precedent when there is conflict. This statement is, as with most in law, a general statement only, and one to which there are many exceptions. To put it another way, we look first to the *Youth Criminal Justice Act* with the knowledge that the *Code* provisions apply whenever they are not inconsistent with the *Youth Criminal Justice Act*.

CANADIAN CHARTER OF RIGHTS AND FREEDOMS

In addition to all the rights of young persons set out and protected in the *Youth Criminal Justice Act* and the *Code*, there is another document of primary importance and of constitutional status: the *Canadian Charter of Rights and Freedoms.*[18]

The *Charter* came into force April 17, 1982, just two years before the *Young Offenders Act* (April 2, 1984) and provides protection of legal rights for all persons involved with the criminal justice system, both adults and young persons. The legal rights sections of the *Charter*[19] protect many aspects of our rights including the right to legal counsel, the right to be informed of that right, the right to a trial within a reasonable time, and protection from unreasonable search and seizure.

The purpose in mentioning the *Charter* is not to review these rights in any detail, but simply to make the point that young persons have all the rights and protection that adults have when criminal proceedings are initiated against them. These rights and protections have led to more formalized proceedings and more representation of young persons by legal counsel than was the case under the *Juvenile Deliquents Act.*

CASE STUDY

A Few Facts

In order to make the following review of the *Youth Criminal Justice Act* and procedures more meaningful, a hypothetical situation will be used as a reference.

Four youth, aged 11, 14, 15 and 17, were involved with the following events: the 15- and 17-year-olds left school on Friday knowing there was a large sum of money left in the safe in the principal's office and at that time decided to go back to the school that night. They told the 11- and 14-year-old that they had to return to the school to pick something up. When they arrived at the school they told the 11- and 14-year-olds to keep a lookout because they were going to break into the school. They gained access to the principal's office by breaking a window and crawling into the office. In the process of looking for the safe, the principal's office was ransacked and the exterior of the safe exposed and damaged. Coincidentally, the vice-principal returned to the school to pick up something she had forgotten and upon seeing the broken window and hearing the commotion, she went to the principal's office. The boys were surprised by seeing the vice-principal and assaulted her while trying to escape. The police were called and attended at the scene and took control of the situation. All four youth were brought into the principal's office and their parents were called. The 14-, 15-, and 17-year-old were taken back to the police station for questioning.

No Offence Committed

The 11-year-old was questioned and returned home with his parents. The age of criminal responsibility in Canada is 12 and therefore an 11-year-old cannot be held criminally responsible. The parents and the 11-year-old assured the police that nothing of this nature would happen again.

Stepping Through the Criminal Justice System

Some of the steps followed in a proceeding will now be reviewed to illustrate the workings of the criminal justice system as it applies to youth. These steps fall into two categories: Extrajudicial Measures and Court Procedures.

Extrajudicial Measures:

- offence committed;
- offence discovered/complaint;
- police intervention;
- police discretion;[20]
- Pre-Charge Screening;[21] and
- Crown Caution.[22]

Court Procedures:

- offence committed;
- offence discovered/complaint;
- police intervention;
- police discretion;[23]
- arrest and detention (note the limitations under the *Youth Criminal Justice Act*);[24]
- questioning/statement/lawyer/parent;
- Release/Appearance Notice;
- Pre-Charge Screening;[25]
- Crown Caution;[26]
- the charging process;
- Summons to Young Person/Notice to Parent;
- arraignment;
- election;[27]
- plea;

- trial;
- Pre-Sentence Report;
- hearing on adult/youth sentence if applicable;
- sentencing; and
- appeal.

Offence Committed

The offence of break and enter with intent to commit theft[28] was committed by the two young persons aged 15 and 17 upon gaining entry to the school and attempting to break into the school safe. The 14-year-old was a party to this offence through his agreement to participate and by being the lookout and yelling a warning to his friends as the vice-principal approached.

Offence Discovered/Complaint

The detection of the young persons in the commission of the offence was accidental but efficient. The criminal justice system is usually initiated by someone realizing an offence has been committed and then reporting their belief to the police, as was done in this case.

Police Intervention

Upon arriving at the school, two police officers entered the school and found the 15- and 17-year-old young persons still in the principal's office. They also found the 11- and 14-year-olds, one at the back door and the other at the window keeping a lookout, waiting for their friends and the money.

When the general public believes a criminal offence has been committed, the usual procedure is to inform the police to let them take charge of the situation and conduct an investigation.

Investigation of offences is clearly a police function and one that calls for professionally trained personnel. Not only do police have special training and expertise, but they are also vested with special powers under the *Code*. Included in these powers are the powers of arrest, detention, and search.

Police Discretion

The 11-year-old was too young to be held criminally responsible, as the *Youth Criminal Justice Act* defines "young person" to include youth aged 12 to under 18.[29] The 14-year-old was a minor participant, had no previous history of finding of guilt, but had received a police warning on a previous occasion for a shoplifting offence. The police decided to refer this young person to an Extrajudicial Sanctions program rather than initiating judicial proceedings.

Extrajudicial Measures, including Extrajudicial Sanctions, are keys to keeping young persons out of the court system. These measures are presumed to be adequate for non-violent offences and are often the most effective response to youth crime. These Measures can be used on more than one occasion.

Arrest/Detention

The 14-, 15-, and 17-year-old young persons were apprehended, detained, arrested, and taken back to the police station for questioning. It is not the usual scenario for young persons to be caught in the act or to be arrested; however, this can and does happen. Arrest of a young person is a very powerful tool in the hands of the police and illustrates quite dramatically to the young persons that they are no longer in charge of the situation. To be taken against their will to an environment over which they have no control is an effective demonstration of the power of the criminal justice system.

Much has been made of the perceived leniency of the laws that apply to youth and youth crime. The public perception is often stated in terms of the laws being powerless against youth crime. A young person, however, who has been arrested would no doubt express a different opinion. The purpose of the arrest in this situation is to end the offence while at the same time to commence the investigation. The first step in many investigations is to solicit statements from those who know something of the events before, during, and after the offence.

Questioning/Statement/Lawyer/Parent

Upon arriving at the police station, the three young persons were placed in separate rooms for questioning. The *Charter* requires the police on arrest or detention to advise the young person that he or she has the right to a lawyer and the reasons for his or her detention.[30] The *Youth Criminal Justice Act* adds the right that young persons must be advised of their right to consult with a parent, other adult or lawyer, and the right to have the person(s) consulted present. There is the additional legal requirement, imposed by case law, for the police to advise the young person of the possibility of receiving an adult sentence.[31]

The police, therefore, provided telephones to the young persons so they could call a lawyer. Parents of the young persons had already been called from the school and they came to the police station. The lawyers consulted also came to the police station. The *Youth Criminal Justice Act* provides protections for the rights of young persons and states that no statement of a young person is admissible in evidence unless: the statement is voluntary (which includes notice of the possibility of an adult sentence); the young person's rights were explained in age-appropriate language; the young person has had the opportunity to consult with counsel, a parent, or other adult; and the young person has been given a reasonable opportunity to have the person consulted present. These rights may be waived, but any waiver of rights must be videotaped, audiotaped, or given in writing or the statement will not be admitted in evidence in a court of law.[32] The *Youth Criminal Justice Act* does, however, permit a youth justice court to admit a statement if there have been technical irregularities.[33]

After consultation, the young persons chose not to give a statement.

Release/Appearance Notice

In situations where young persons have been arrested or detained, they are usually released following questioning rather than detained in a custodial facility. The interim release provisions of the *Code* apply to young persons[34] and, as with adults, the presumption at each stage of the proceeding is that the person will be released from custody. It is possible, and it does happen, that the police do not release a young person prior to the first appearance in court.

Before the *Youth Criminal Justice Act* came into effect it was determined that too many young persons in Canada were held in custody. Part of this problem stemmed from too many youths being held in custody pretrial. The *Youth Criminal Justice Act*, however, has introduced additional limitations on a young person being held in custody pretrial to address this issue.[35]

Despite these limitations, the Crown may ask for a show cause hearing before the youth justice court to show why a young person should be detained in custody pending trial or sentence. If the Crown satisfies the youth justice court that a young person should not be released from custody then the court must then inquire as to whether there is a "responsible person" to whose care a young person may be released.[36] This is an additional attempt to prevent young persons from being held in custody. If, however, the youth justice court holds that detention is appropriate and there is no responsible person to whose care the young person can be released then further detention will be ordered.

The general rule is for the police to release the young person and at that time they will serve a formal document upon a young person entitled "Appearance Notice". This document gives the young person notice of the date, time, and place where he or she must appear before the youth justice court. The young person normally signs the document to acknowledge receipt and this process initiates the formal criminal justice proceedings.

In this case, the young persons were released and issued Appearance Notices.

Pre-charge Screening

The *Youth Criminal Justice Act* makes provision for a Pre-charge Screening program being established by the Attorney General.[37] At least three provinces in Canada now have such a program in place. Generally, the program works by the police investigating offences, determining that there is sufficient information to commence a judicial proceeding and then forwarding the recommendation to lay a charge on to a Crown Attorney. The Crown would then review the file, consider the options, and in the event they agree with the police then a charge would be laid and the judicial proceeding commenced. A charge is laid by the swearing of an Information, a formal document alleging that an offence has been committed. In the other jurisdictions in Canada, where there is no Pre-charge Screening Program, the decision to charge lies with the police. There is also the possibility of the Crown making a pre- or post-charge referral to Extrajudicial Sanctions or giving a Crown Caution. (Note: procedures vary from Province to Province and Territory)

In this case, pre-charge screening was not an available option and thus was not used.

Crown Caution

The *Youth Criminal Justice Act* also makes a provision for the Attorney General to establish a program authorizing a prosecutor to administer cautions to young persons.[38] In at least two jurisdictions in Canada, the Crown has the option of giving a Crown Caution to bring a file to a conclusion without going to court. This option is not used often but is quite effective when it is used. The procedure is for the Crown to send a letter to the young person and the parents of the young person advising that the proceeding has been stopped in the hope that the young person and the parents will deal with the situation appropriately.

The Crown also gives notice that a record of the Crown Caution would be kept for future reference.

A Crown Caution was not seen as appropriate in this case.

The Charging Process

After the young persons were released the police proceeded with the rest of their investigation. In this case, the investigation included a statement from the vice-principal and principal as well as photographs of the scene. Once the investigation has been concluded and it is determined that there are reasonable grounds to believe an offence has been committed then the police must consider Extrajudicial Measures, including Extrajudicial Sanctions.[39]

In this case, the police were of the opinion that taking no further action or giving a warning or a caution would not be sufficient to hold the young persons accountable for their actions. They also considered a referral to a program or agency in the community, but a referral was not seen as an appropriate option.

In addition to these Extrajudicial Measures the police also considered a referral to an Extrajudicial Sanctions program. Both youth had a history with the police having previously received a warning and a referral to Extrajudicial Sanctions.

Because of the history with the police and the seriousness of the offence, including the assault, the decision to commence judicial proceedings was made. Proceedings are commenced by the police swearing of "Information" before a justice of the peace. This document states the names, addresses, and dates of birth of the young persons and describes the location of the offence and the offence itself. This document is then sworn before a justice of the peace, delivered to the court, and becomes a court document. This is also called "the laying of a charge".

Summons to Young Person/Notice to Parent

In the usual situation, where there has not been an Appearance Notice issued, the police would serve a document entitled "Summons to Young Person" setting out the date, time, and place for appearance before the youth justice court and compelling the appearance of the young person. One further document the police are required to serve is a "Notice to Parent"[40] to ensure that the parent(s) of the young person are aware of the fact that criminal proceedings have been initiated against their child. The date, time and place for the first court appearance are noted on the document to permit the attendance of the parent in court.

Notices to Parent were issued to parents of the two young persons.

Arraignment

In response to the "Appearance Notice" or the "Summons to Young Person" the young person will attend in youth justice court to await his or her case being called. The court will ensure that the preliminary documents are in order before reading the charge and in that regard the clerk or the Crown may be asked for the Appearance Notice or Summons to Young Person and proof of service of this document and of the Notice to Parent. The court may then confirm the age of the young person to determine whether the youth justice court has jurisdiction to conduct the proceedings. At some point either before or after these preliminaries the clerk or other court official will be asked to read the charge to the young person. The reading of the charge to the accused (young person) and the entering of a pleas constitutes the arraignment and formalizes the commencement of the criminal proceedings.

If the young person appears in court without legal counsel, the youth justice court judge may adjourn the proceeding to enable the young person to obtain legal counsel. The youth justice court has the power to order legal counsel for the young person.[41]

In this case, both young persons appeared with parents and separate legal counsel and were prepared to enter a plea.

Election

The *Charter* provides that if a person faces a term of imprisonment of five years or more then they are entitled to a trial by jury.[42] When a young person is charged with an offence for which they may be subject to an adult sentence they face the possibility of a sentence of five years or more. The young person therefore is entitled to have a trial by jury. This means that a trial judge must give the young person the option/election to choose whether they will be tried by a youth justice court judge without a jury or a court composed of a judge and jury.[43] There are detailed procedures for the election and method of trial, which in this case need not be examined in detail as they do not apply.

The rules relating to adult sentences are complex. For further information, see *A Guide to the Youth Crinimal Justice Act.*[44]

Plea

After the charge has been read the young person will then be called upon to enter a plea. Generally this involves making a plea of guilty or not guilty. If a plea of guilty is entered, the Crown will then provide the court with a statement of the facts from the Crown Sheet (a document provided to the Crown by the police) to show the court that the facts support the charge. The court, if satisfied the facts support the charge, will enter a finding of guilt and proceed to or set a date for sentencing.

If a plea of not guilty is entered, there will be a date set for trial and the young person will be released on his or her own undertaking or promise to abide by whatever conditions of release the court may set and to appear in court for their trial.

In this case, the 15-year-old pled not guilty and a trial date was set; the 17-year-old pled guilty and a pre-sentence report was requested and a date set for sentencing.

Trial

This is the part of the proceedings where the parties appear before a youth justice court judge, present evidence, and a determination of innocence or guilt is made. There are many events that can occur during a trial, but these events need not be described here as the intention is only to convey the general outline of what occurs in the court. The parties are called upon at the beginning of the trial to see if there are any preliminary motions, and in the case of the proceeding against the 15-year-old young person, a motion was made for the exclusion of witnesses. The purpose of this motion is to ensure that witnesses do not hear what each other have to say until they have given their evidence.

The Crown is then called upon to present evidence in support of the charge. In this case there were four Crown witnesses: the vice-principal who came upon the scene, the two police officers who came to the school and apprehended the young persons, and the 17-year-old young person who had already entered a plea of guilty. Each witness is sworn, promising under oath to tell the truth. The Crown then asks questions about the events of the evening at the school and at the police station. After the Crown asks questions of the witnesses (direct examination), the defence lawyer will then question each of the witnesses (cross-examination). The Crown may seek to ask further questions to clarify certain points (re-direct examination).

The evidence in this case came out much as expected with the vice-principal indicating that she heard a commotion in the school, entered the principal's office, was assaulted, called the police, and waited for their arrival. The two police officers identified the 15-year-old young person as one of the two young persons found in the principal's office, whom they arrested and took back to the police station for questioning.

The questioning was unsuccessful as no statements were made. The two young persons were released. The 17-year-old admitted involvement in the crime and identified the 15-year-old accused as his partner in this misadventure and attempt to gain access to the money in the principal's safe. The defence chose to call no evidence. An accused person is not required to say anything at any stage of the proceedings; upon arrest, on subsequent investigation, at trial, or on sentencing—this is known as "the right to remain silent".

The youth justice court judge reviewed the evidence and concluded that the Crown had proven all the elements of the offence beyond a reasonable doubt and entered a finding of guilt. The judge then ordered a pre-sentence report and set the date for sentencing.

Pre-sentence Report (PSR)

A pre-sentence report is a report prepared by a youth court worker and is provided to the Crown, the defence and the court for the purpose of the disposition hearing.[45] It is mandatory for a court to consider a PSR before imposing a custodial disposition,[46] unless the young person waives this right before the court. This is one of the many additional protections provided by the *Youth Criminal Justice Act* to a young person. In preparing a typical PSR, the worker will talk to the young offender (now that guilt has been established), the parents, victims, teachers, friends, and other persons as the youth worker deems appropriate. The purpose of the report is to give the court, the defence and the Crown some insight into the personality, attitude, educational background, and family of the young offender. The report helps to determine the appropriate sentence. If the young offender has a prior record this will usually be set out in the PSR. All parties will have a copy of the report before the sentencing hearing.

In this case, PSRs were requested by the two youth justice courts involved; one following the trial of the 15-year-old and the other following the guilty plea of the 17-year-old.

Hearing on Adult/Youth Sentence if Applicable

The Crown may seek an adult sentence for any indictable offence for which an adult is liable to imprisonment for more than two years. When the Crown does make an application for an adult sentence, a Notice to the young person is required.[47] When certain offences are committed, there is a "presumption" of an adult sentence under the provisions of the *Youth Criminal Justice Act*.[48] The presumption of an adult sentence has been challenged in the Quebec and Ontario courts both of which found that the presumption violated section 7 of the *Charter*.

The Supreme Court of Canada, in the case of *R. v. B. (D.)*,[49] settled the question of the validity of the presumption of an adult sentence and found that the presumption of an adult sentence violated s. 7 of the *Charter* and was not saved by s. 1. Hence, the presumption of an adult sentence will, through case law, no longer operate. The Crown can still make an application for an adult sentence under certain circumstances.

For further information on the question of presumptive sentences, see *A Guide to the Criminal Justice Act*.[50]

Sentences

After a "finding of guilt" the youth justice court moves to the stage of sentencing. The youth justice court listens to the representations of counsel, parents, and the young person, in addition to receiving and considering the PSR. Other evidence may be called at the option of the Crown or counsel for the young person. A Victim Impact Statement may also be considered.[51] The court must then assume the responsibility of the difficult task of deciding which option or options, from those authorized by the *Youth Criminal Justice Act*, to impose on the young person in order to accomplish the objectives of the Act.

The following is a list of the options authorized by the Act[52] and from which the youth court may choose:

(a)   reprimand;
(b)   absolute discharge;
(c)   conditional discharge;
(d)   fine;
(e)   compensation order;
(f)   restitution;
(g)   order to pay purchaser for property returned to owner;
(h)   compensation in kind or personal services;
(i)   community service order;
(j)   prohibition, seizure, or forfeiture order;
(k)   probation order (not exceeding two years);
(l)   intensive support and supervision program (if available);
(m)   attending a non-residential program (if available);
(n)   custody and supervision order;
(o)   custody and supervision order for presumptive offences;[53]
(p)   deferred custody and supervision order;
(q)   custody sentence for murder;

> (r) intensive rehabilitative custody and supervision order (pre-conditions); or
>
> (s) other reasonable and ancillary conditions.

In this case, the 17-year-old had a negative PSR, a prior youth court record for similar offences (two prior break and enters), and was seen to be the leader in the offence. The youth justice court reviewed the sentencing options and the limitations on imposing a custodial sentence[54] and chose to impose a term of four months' custody to be followed by one year of probation. The conditions attached to the probation order were the standard conditions of keeping the peace and being of good behaviour.

The 15-year-old younger offender had a positive PSR, a supportive family, and was seen to be the follower in this offence. The court emphasized rehabilitation and imposed a six-month probation order with standard conditions.

Appeal

When the Crown or the young person is not satisfied with the decision of the youth justice court judge (acquittal, finding of guilt, or sentence), there is provision for an appeal.[55] The *Youth Criminal Justice Act* sets out some of the rules that apply to appeals in youth justice cases but also adopts the general provisions in the *Code* for appeals of both summary conviction and indictable offences. (Another chapter deals in more detail with appeals.)

Many youth cases are heard each year by courts of appeal and a few young offender cases each year are heard by the highest court in the country, the Supreme Court of Canada.

In this case, the 17-year-old appealed the four-month custodial term, arguing that it was excessive. The court of appeal reviewed the limitations on custodial sentences and found that the trial court had made no error in imposing a custodial sentence considering the young person's circumstances, age, attitude, and prior record. The court of appeal did, however, vary the custodial sentence to a "deferred custody and supervision order".

ADDITIONAL POINTS OF INTEREST

Maximum Sentence

There is no issue that has gained more public attention, scrutiny, and response than the maximum sentence provisions. The general rule is that the maximum sentence is two years and an exception to this rule occurs when the offence is one for which an adult would be subject to life imprisonment under the *Code*. In those situations a young person is subject to the three-year maximum.[56] These rules apply to a single offence and there are complex provisions to enable longer terms when the sequence of offences permits the court to impose consecutive dispositions.[57]

In 1984, when the *Young Offenders Act* first came into force, the difficulty with regard to maximum penalty was that the gap between sentences for young persons and sentences for adults was too great. The maximum sentence for a young person who committed murder was three years and if a young person was subject to an adult sentence the minimum sentence was life imprisonment with no eligibility for parole for at least ten years (25 years for first degree murder).

In 1992, that gap was closed and maximum sentence for a young offender was increased for murder to five years less a day, made up of custody not to exceed three years with the balance being a placement under conditional supervision. The period of conditional supervision may become a custodial term if the circumstances merit.

In 1995, the penalties for first and second degree murder were increased to ten and seven years to be made up as follows: first degree murder—six years' custody plus four years' conditional supervision; and second degree murder—four years' custody plus three years' conditional supervision.[58] In addition to increasing the maximum penalty for young persons under the *Young Offenders Act*, there was an amendment to the *Code* to provide that the period of parole ineligibility for young persons who received an adult sentence be as follows: young persons under 16—between five and seven years; young persons 16 years or older—seven years for second degree murder and ten years for first degree murder.[59] The gap between *Young Offenders Act* dispositions and adult sentences under the *Code* for the offence of murder were closed in 1995.

The maximum sentence provisions were preserved by the *Youth Criminal Justice Act*, although the method of accessing an adult sentence has changed. Under the *Young Offenders Act* the procedure was to "transfer" a young person to ordinary court. Under the *Youth Criminal Justice Act* notice is given by the Crown that an adult sentence will be sought. The issue of adult penalties is now dealt with as a matter of sentence.

Records

The last issue to be examined is that of young offender records, a much misunderstood area of young offender law. Many people have the perception that anything to do with young offenders is secretive and that no one is permitted to disclose any information to anyone. It is also the general perception that young persons have "no record" but this is not so. The first principle to be understood is that youth justice court is an open court, open in the sense of being open to the public. This means that the general public is entitled to attend at the youth justice court and observe the proceedings unless there is a court ruling to the contrary. There are situations where the public will be excluded; however, such is also the case in adult court and is the exception to the general rule of openness.

It is true that the *Youth Criminal Justice Act* gives young persons more privacy protection than adults have in the adult system, so far as protecting identity and shortening the period that records are active. There is also the key provision in the *Youth Criminal Justice Act* to prohibit publishing the name of or any identifying information about a young person. This limitation applies to publishing or making known to the public generally information about a particular young person.[60] The names of young persons do not appear in the media due to the principle that such publication would be counter to the overall objectives of the Act. In exceptional circumstances (the young person is dangerous or assistance is needed in apprehending the young person), a peace officer may apply to the court for permission to publish the name and identity of a young person.[61]

The general rule is that once a sentence has been completed the young person is "deemed not to have been found guilty or convicted".[62] There are exceptions to this rule and the one most often used is that a court may continue to have access and make reference to a young offender's record for the purpose of release from custody or on sentencing for subsequent offences.

There is a time limit imposed even on the courts after which no reference may be made to the record of a young person,[63] for example:

- absolute discharge—1 year after the young person is found guilty;
- alternative measures—2 years after consent to participate;
- summary conviction offences—3 years after all dispositions;[64] and
- indictable offences—5 years after all dispositions.[65]

The records provisions are complex but the basic principle is to provide a balance between the need to know and the rehabilitation of young persons through protecting their identity.

FINAL POINT

The *Youth Criminal Justice Act* sets out a comprehensive scheme to deal with young persons and the reader is encouraged to examine the Act as a whole and to bear in mind that consideration of any particular section should be done in light of the overall design of young offender law. The long-standing approach of Canadian law and the law of most other countries is, and has been, to recognize that young persons are not adults and that they have special needs as a result of their age and lack of maturity. Youth however must be held responsible and accountable for their actions with rehabilitation being a focus for the response of the youth justice system.

Notes

[1] S.C. 2002, c. 1 (Assented to February 19, 2002 to come into force April 1, 2003).
[2] S.C. 1980-81-82-83, c. 110 (now cited as R.S.C. 1985, c. Y-1).
[3] R.S.C. 1970, c. J-3.
[4] *Young Offenders Act*, s. 3(1)(a.1).
[5] *Youth Criminal Justice Act*, S.C. 2002, c. 1, ss. 3, 4, 38, and 83.
[6] R.S.C. 1985, c. C-46 [hereinafter the *Code*].
[7] *Youth Criminal Justice Act*, s. 13.
[8] *Youth Criminal Justice Act*, s. 14.
[9] *Youth Criminal Justice Act*, ss. 3, 4, 38 and 83.
[10] *Youth Criminal Justice Act*, Preamble.
[11] *Youth Criminal Justice Act*, ss. 4(c) and 6.
[12] *Youth Criminal Justice Act*, s. 39.
[13] *Youth Criminal Justice Act*, para. 3(1)(b)(ii).
[14] *Youth Criminal Justice Act*, ss. 3(1)(c) and (d), 5 and 38.
[15] *Youth Criminal Justice Act*, ss. 2(1).
[16] *Youth Justice Act*, S.N.S. 2001, c. 38.
[17] *Youth Criminal Justice Act*, ss. 67(8), 67(9), 140, 141 and 142.
[18] *Canadian Charter of Rights and Freedoms*, Part I of the *Constitution Act, 1982*, being Schedule B to the Canada Act, 1982 (U.K.), 1982, c. 11 [hereinafter the *Charter*].
[19] *Charter*, ss. 7-14.
[20] *Youth Criminal Justice Act*, s. 6-10.
[21] *Youth Criminal Justice Act*, s. 23.
[22] *Youth Criminal Justice Act*, s. 8.
[23] *Supra*, note 20.
[24] *Youth Criminal Justice Act*, s. 29.

[25] *Supra*, note 21.

[26] *Supra*, note 22.

[27] *Youth Criminal Justice Act*, ss. 32(1)(c) and (d), (3) and (4), s. 67.

[28] *Criminal Code*, s. 348(1)(a).

[29] *Youth Criminal Justice Act*, s. 2.

[30] *Charter*, s. 10.

[31] *R. v. I. (L.R.)*, 1993 CarswellBC 513, 1993 CarswellBC 1273, (*sub nom.* R. v. T. (E.)) 86 C.C.C. (3d) 289, 26 C.R. (4th) 119, 37 B.C.A.C. 48, 60 W.A.C. 48, 159 N.R. 363, 109 D.L.R. (4th) 140, [1993] 4 S.C.R. 504, 19 C.R.R. (2d) 156 (S.C.C.).

[32] *Youth Criminal Justice Act*, s. 146.

[33] *Youth Criminal Justice Act*, ss. 146(5) and (6).

[34] *Youth Criminal Justice Act*, s. 33.

[35] *Youth Criminal Justice Act*, s. 29.

[36] *Youth Criminal Justice Act*, s. 31.

[37] *Youth Criminal Justice Act*, s. 23.

[38] *Youth Criminal Justice Act*, s. 8.

[39] *Youth Criminal Justice Act*, ss. 4-10.

[40] *Youth Criminal Justice Act*, s. 26.

[41] *Youth Criminal Justice Act*, ss. 25(4) and (5), 32(5).

[42] *Charter*, s. 11(f).

[43] *Youth Criminal Justice Act*, s. 67.

[44] Lee Tustin and Robert E. Lutes, *A Guide to the Youth Criminal Justice Act, 2010 Edition* (Butterworths, 2010), ss. 61-82.

[45] *Youth Criminal Justice Act*, s. 40.

[46] *Youth Criminal Justice Act*, ss. 39(6).

[47] *Youth Criminal Justice Act*, ss. 62 and 64.

[48] *Youth Criminal Justice Act*, ss. 2(1), definition of "presumptive offence".

[49] *R. v .B. (D.)*, 2008 CarswellOnt 2708, 2008 CarswellOnt 2709, 2008 SCC 25, 374 N.R. 221, 237 O.A.C. 110, 293 D.L.R. (4th) 278, [2008] 2 S.C.R. 3, 171 C.R.R. (2d) 133, 92 O.R. (3d) 399 (note), 231 C.C.C. (3d) 338, 56 C.R. (6th) 203 (S.C.C.).

[50] *Supra*, at note 44, pages 20 & 123 (ss. 2 & 61).

[51] *Youth Criminal Justice Act*, ss. 50(1).

[52] *Youth Criminal Justice Act*, ss. 42(2).

[53] *Supra*, note 48.

[54] *Supra*, note 35.

[55] *Youth Criminal Justice Act*, s. 37.

[56] *Youth Criminal Justice Act*, para. 42(2)(n).

[57] *Youth Criminal Justice Act*, ss. 42(14), (15) and (16).

[58] *Young Offenders Act*, s. 20(1)(k.1).

[59] *Criminal Code*, s. 745.1.

[60] *Youth Criminal Justice Act*, s. 110.

[61] *Youth Criminal Justice Act*, ss. 110(4) and (5).

[62] *Youth Criminal Justice Act*, s. 82.

[63] *Youth Criminal Justice Act*, ss. 119(2).

[64] The 3-year period will be extended if a subsequent offence is committed.

[65] The 5-year period will be extended if a subsequent offence is committed.

12

Courts

*Donald C. Murray**
(edited by *Shane G. Parker*)**

GENERAL

Independent and Impartial Tribunals[1]

The whole process of accusation, trial, and sentence in a criminal matter is carried out in an institutional framework which we generally describe as the courts. The court system is recognized as a distinct branch of our country's government separate from those who are elected to make laws. The courts have a government function because the courts apply and ultimately enforce (or do not enforce) the laws passed by our legislators. Indeed, in our society the concept of having different and parallel authorities making and enforcing laws is so strongly established that it is now the right of anyone in this country who is charged with an offence to be treated in accordance with principles of fundamental justice, and it rests with the courts to ensure that that occurs.

Anyone who is detained by the state is entitled to resort to the courts to have the legal validity of that detention tested. Also, anyone who is charged with an offence has the right to know, as soon as is reasonably possible, what that offence is and to have a determination made in a fair and public hearing within a reasonable time whether the offence charged against him is justified. Above all, any person charged with an offence has the right to have the determination of guilt or no guilt made by an independent and impartial tribunal. In more serious cases, a person charged with an offence has the right to a jury which acts as a fundamental part of the independent and impartial tribunal. Once such a trial has been held, so long as it determines the matters at issue between the state and the individual, the courts will not permit the issue to be determined again.

---

* B.A., Mount Allison University, Sackville, New Brunswick; LL.B., Dalhousie Law School, Halifax, Nova Scotia; practises law in Dartmouth, Nova Scotia.

**B.Sc (Hons.), University of Waterloo; MPE, University of New Brunswick; LL.B. Dalhousie Law School, Halifax Nova Scotia; currently a Crown Attorney practicing in the Province of Alberta.

Provision of the rights which have just been described requires authorities in our society that are distinct from those groups which make the laws, and distinct from those who accuse others of breaking the laws. The court system developed out of this requirement. In order to foster and maintain the confidence of all segments of society with respect to this independence and impartiality, no question of political interference can ever be permitted to sully the reputation of the courts. Independence and impartiality require more than the assumption that the decision-makers will decide the case strictly according to the law. An independent and impartial decision-maker must be recognized by the accused person, and by society generally, as a decision-maker whom none have influenced or tried to influence. This requires a social climate where anyone not involved in the actual trial and appeal processes leaves it to the courts to come to the appropriate decision, and makes no suggestion (directly or indirectly) as to what the appropriate decisions ought to be. Indeed, even after a decision is made by the courts, it is inappropriate for anyone (and particularly a legislator) to disparage the decision reached. Such statements hinder the courts in the performance of their function because, ultimately, the ability of our court system to function depends on its ability to command respect.

The courts themselves are sensitive to the need of clear impartiality in order to maintain both the reality and the appearance of independence. It is not unusual for a judge at any level of court to disqualify himself or herself from hearing a case where there has been some involvement by the judge in facts closely related to the case. This may involve something as serious as the judge's defense of the particular accused person on the particular charge before the court prior to his appointment as judge, or something less serious such as having personal knowledge of a witness where questions might arise as to the credibility of that witness. The fear is that the court might be regarded as being biased. Having a bias is having a prejudice or predisposition to be unreasonably favourable to one party rather than the other. An anticipated consistency of the court in making the same findings on the same evidence adduced by the same witnesses in two different trials is not bias.

Jurisdiction

Not every court is entitled to try a person charged with a criminal offence. Before any valid steps may be taken toward a finding of guilt or final acquittal, the charge must come before a court which has "jurisdiction". There are three kinds of authority or jurisdiction, each of which has to be present before criminal proceedings against an individual can be considered as valid. These are: (a) geographical jurisdiction[2]—the court must have authority to deal with criminal matters that arise in a certain place; (b) jurisdiction in respect of the offence[3]—the court must have authority in respect of the kind of offence that is charged; and, (c) jurisdiction over the accused person[4]—the court must have authority to deal with the person who is accused of committing a crime. Unless permitted by some special legislation, these three kinds of jurisdiction must exist before a finding of guilt or final acquittal can be made, and no agreement or consent by the accused person and the prosecution can avoid these requirements.

Historically, it was felt that "Gloucestershire men should try Gloucestershire rogues". An alleged offence should be tried in the locality where it is said to have been committed. That general rule still holds, although the *Criminal Code* does provide exceptions to give courts authority in respect of an alleged offence in the locality where the accused person is either found, arrested, or held in custody. However, that does not mean that the law enforcement authorities can simply move an accused person to a different locality, claim that he is in custody there and that the trial should proceed there. The trial will normally be held in the county where the offence has been alleged to have been committed. If there is any reason to depart from this general rule, the court's permission must be obtained to permit the trial to take place elsewhere.

The *Criminal Code* contains a number of technical provisions dealing with situations where it might be difficult to determine precisely where an offence has been committed, such as an alleged offence committed in the course of an aircraft flight, or in the delivery of a piece of mail, or on board a ship in a harbour. In cases where an offence is alleged to have been committed on or near the border of two territorial divisions, such as a county line, the *Criminal Code* applies a common sense rule that the courts of either territorial division can deal with the matter. A "territorial division", depending on the court involved, may be a province, a county, a township, city or other judicial division established by the law of the province.

The provisions of the *Criminal Code* dealing with territorial divisions and territorial jurisdiction are not merely of procedural interest. In the case of the possession of stolen goods, for example, it is possible for an individual to be convicted in one county of possessing goods stolen in that county and a neighbouring county. The value of the goods in possession might well mean the difference between being charged with a summary conviction and an indictable offence. Penalties might vary as a result.

In addition to having geographical jurisdiction, the court must have jurisdiction over the person who comes before it charged with a criminal offence. While this may not always be a problem of great concern, the law still requires that the accused person must have been found, arrested, or placed in custody within the territorial division of the court before which he appears, or that another court has ordered that the accused person be tried by the court before which he appears. In addition, all proper procedures must have been followed to summon that accused person to answer to the charge. The *Criminal Code* also provides that it will take jurisdiction over persons outside Canada who commit offences inside or outside Canada in certain circumstances. However, this is the exception rather than the rule. Special legislation is necessary to exempt persons in Canada from the regular criminal law, except where normal diplomatic immunity applies. Usually persons in the diplomatic service of another country are not subject to the laws of the host country.

A more complicated matter can be whether or not the court concerned has jurisdiction to deal in some way with the offence which has been alleged against the accused person. Other than the Supreme Court of Canada, the Federal Court, and some other courts which do not deal with truly criminal matters, courts created by the provinces deal with the criminal law of this country. Once these courts have been created by the provinces and been given authority by the provincial governments to deal with criminal matters, the federal Parliament may assign them certain powers to deal with criminal proceedings. A certain amount of co-operation is therefore required between the two levels of government in determining how criminal procedure functions with respect to the court system. It should also be understood that the need for co-operation between the two levels of government is a very practical concern; it is the provinces which determine how many judges are assigned to each particular court, though it is the federal government which appoints judges to these positions.

In determining which court may have authority to deal with an alleged criminal offence, it is necessary first to have regard to the seriousness of that offence. Generally, there is a maximum sentence for summary offences of 6 months' imprisonment and/ or a maximum fine of $2,000, unless otherwise stated. In these cases, the accused appear, plead, and are tried and sentenced by a "summary conviction court". However, there are specific exceptions, such as, sexual assault offences, which have extended the summary sentence to 18 months' imprisonment. This "summary conviction court" is the Provincial Court in a province, or in Ontario, the "Ontario Court of Justice". These courts also deal with offences against provincial statutes which are tried in accordance with the provisions of Part XXVII of the *Criminal Code*. In addition, provincial courts deal with a whole list of offences which are referred to as "absolute jurisdiction" indictable offences. Essentially these are property offences where the value of the property involved is less than $5,000, and the gaming offences of betting, book-making, and such.

Most serious criminal offences are tried by what the *Criminal Code* describes as a "superior court of criminal jurisdiction". This is the supreme court in each province (the Superior Court in Quebec, the Superior Court of Justice in Ontario, and the Queen's Bench in Alberta, Saskatchewan and Manitoba). In s. 469, the *Criminal Code* lists the offences that must be tried in these courts, which include offences against the state, such as treason and mutiny, as well as the most serious of personal offences—murder. It is important to remember that while superior courts of criminal jurisdiction must try these offences, they may also try any other indictable offence as well—even those that are in the absolute jurisdiction of a provincial court.

With respect to the rest of those offences in the *Criminal Code* which are neither summary conviction matters nor listed in ss. 469 or 553, the accused person generally has a choice as to which court will try him. In such a case, the question of which court has jurisdiction over the offence remains up in the air until such time as this "election" is made.

An accused person may choose either the summary conviction court, the superior court of criminal jurisdiction, or a third level of court between the two, described in the *Criminal Code* as a "court of criminal jurisdiction". The choice of court is made at the time the accused first appears in provincial court, and is explained to the accused person by offering him or her the opportunity to be tried before the provincial court where he is appearing, by a judge alone (court of criminal jurisdiction), or by a judge and a jury (superior court of criminal jurisdiction). A judge of a superior court of criminal jurisdiction may try a jury offence without a jury where the Crown and the accused consent (s. 473(1)).

If the accused person elects a court other than the provincial court, he or she will have the opportunity to enjoy the benefit of a preliminary inquiry before being required to stand trial. An accused person may, in some circumstances, re-elect later for a different court than that which he originally chose. However, where more than two accused persons are charged together, unless they all elect to be tried in the same court, the judge may ignore any election made for provincial court or trial before a judge without a jury. There is also provision for the Attorney General of a province to override any election made and to require that the trial be held before a judge and a jury. Once any election or directive by the Attorney General is made, the court selected gains jurisdiction to deal with the criminal offence charged against the individual and matters can proceed to a legal determination of guilt or acquittal.

Powers Generally[5]

The courts draw their powers from essentially three sources. Obviously the *Criminal Code* gives specific courts certain powers to try offences. Other matters related to the criminal law, but tangential or incidental to the ultimate finding of guilt or acquittal, are also assigned to particular courts by the *Code*. In addition to the *Criminal Code*, all of the courts can look to specific provincial or federal legislation which establishes or continues them. This legislation will indicate how the court is to function, the geographical areas over which it has authority, and the kinds of remedies which it may give. The third main source of power for courts involved in the criminal law in Canada is a common law concept called "inherent jurisdiction". As the phrase indicates, this kind of power to give remedies and deal with matters that arise during the course of criminal proceedings exists because the court exists. Inherent jurisdiction has been used to justify many things, including the right to stop criminal matters from proceeding because they are abusive, and ordering persons to clear the courtroom during a trial. Indeed, some might suggest that inherent jurisdiction is called on as a justification whenever a court wishes to do something that it feels is right, but can point to no legislative authority which says the court may do it. That may be overstating the point a little, but it is a broad enough issue that the courts of this country have generally tried to restrict any exercise of inherent jurisdiction to the superior courts of criminal jurisdiction. The justification for this is thought to be that it is the superior courts of criminal jurisdiction which are the direct descendants of the original courts of justice created in England to dispense the monarch's justice. One shorthand way of describing which courts have "inherent jurisdiction" and which courts do not has been to speak of provincial supreme courts as "superior courts", and all others below these "superior" courts as being "inferior courts". It is now considered more polite to refer to "superior courts" and "statutory courts".

Perhaps the most serious power which the courts have is the power to punish individuals for contempt. Although the matter is a high priority for law reform, at this time contempt is the only exception to the rule that no one in Canada can be convicted of a criminal offence unless that offence was enacted in statute at the time of the alleged wrongdoing. Unlike the historical power of the courts in England actually to create offences, Canadian courts have no such power except to the extent that they are reasonably free to determine what constitutes contempt. There are no minimum or maximum penalties which exist, and there is little guidance in the cases about what will constitute contemptuous behaviour either inside or outside a courtroom.

For the purposes of this chapter, emphasis will be placed on the statutory powers given to the various levels of courts. These are the powers exercised most often in the course of criminal proceedings and the ones with which the layman should be most familiar.

How Courts Relate to Each Other[6]

The courts exist in a hierarchy. Higher courts exercise authority over lower courts with respect to the right to review decisions and decide appeals from decisions. This ascending authority ensures that criminal matters are dealt with consistently and properly throughout the court system. There are two good basic reasons for this. First, it is a basic principle of law that cases that are similar or alike should be treated alike, while cases that are different should be treated differently. For example, if two different individuals are charged with murder, one in British Columbia and one in Nova Scotia, but both accused persons claim that they knew the victim had a propensity for violent and aggressive conduct which made them kill the victim before they suffered any harm, that kind of evidence should be admitted both in the British Columbia court and the Nova Scotia court. That example raises the second basic reason for the ascending authority in our court system. The criminal law is a federal law applying equally to all Canadians. The same kind of conduct should be considered criminal in Alberta as is considered criminal in Quebec. In other words, the application of the criminal law in Canada should be uniform from coast to coast.

The courts are set up so that the provincial courts lead up to the supreme court of the province, on to the provincial appeal court, and ultimately to the Supreme Court of Canada. The system thus tries to control how the criminal law is applied to accused persons. However, the courts complement this ascending authority with other rules which they have developed to promote the goal of uniformity in the criminal law. These rules are based upon the principle of *"stare decisis"*, a Latin phrase which really means nothing more than the fact that courts will try to treat like cases alike.

The issue of treating like cases alike and different cases differently depends on both the facts of a case before a court, and the authority of the court which may have decided a particular question before. The first aspect of this, the factual basis, is the ground on which a judge decides whether a case is in fact "like" another case, or whether it is distinguishable. If the case is factually different, the judge need no longer consider the other cases which are apparently similar, but, in fact, are not. When the case before a judge is factually similar, the judge has to consider whether, in conscience or law, he should make the same decision as was made in the similar case. Similar cases decided by other courts may, if they are not distinguishable, be described as of interest, persuasive, strongly persuasive, or binding. Cases which are of interest are cases from lower level courts in Commonwealth countries (which share a common approach to criminal law with Canada), cases from the United States, and sometimes lower courts in Canadian provinces other than where the matter is being decided. Judges sitting at the same level of court in the same province will find decisions of their fellow judges strongly persuasive because of a sense of "judicial comity". This avoids, at a local level, grossly apparent inconsistencies in decisions. However, no court, at any level, is bound to agree with any conclusions of law reached by another judge in the same level of court in that province. Decisions of higher courts from other provinces or countries may be considered strongly persuasive, particularly if they involve an appellate level decision, but again the lower courts in the province where the decision is being made are not required to follow that other province's appeal court, nor an appeal court in any other country.

All courts which have other courts in authority over them are bound by decisions of law made in those higher courts (that is, all courts other than the Supreme Court of Canada). Unless a significant difference can be found in the facts of the case to be decided, the earlier precedent from the higher court must be followed. The provincial appeal courts are not required to agree with each other unless there is a decision on the point from the Supreme Court of Canada. While the decisions of other courts of appeal may be persuasive, and even strongly persuasive, they are not binding. Thus, it is possible to have two or more strikingly different interpretations of the criminal law being applied in different parts of the country.

There are two ways in which different interpretations of the criminal law in different provinces can be reconciled in the court system.

First, an appeal court in one province may decide that one of its previous decisions was wrongly decided and so reverses itself on the point. Indeed, the courts will not be hesitant to do this where criminal law and the liberty of the subject is involved. The second way for uniformity to be re-established is for the Supreme Court of Canada to deal with the point in a decision. It does not particularly matter whether the Supreme Court of Canada deals with the matter as an aside which is not strictly necessary to decide the case before it, or whether the question was decided because of a question asked of the court by Parliament, or whether it decided a similar case. The Supreme Court of Canada will depart from its own previous decisions and state as authoritative a different interpretation of the law if compelling reasons exist for it to do so.

As is no doubt evident, there is a lot of room for a judge in any particular case to say whether or not he is bound to come to one decision or another. The ultimate objective of all courts is to be fair as well as appear to be fair to each person who appears before them. This is done by trying to treat cases that are the same in the same way and cases that are different differently. One could describe the presentation of a case by the prosecution and the defence as a process of demonstrating how it is the same as some, and yet different from other cases. It is ultimately up to the judge to determine which of the prosecution or the defence has satisfied him that the case is like another, or different from another, and satisfied him in a way that is persuasive that a particular authority should be followed resulting in a particular conclusion.

THE COURTS

Justices and Provincial Courts[7]

The first, or entry level, of the court system is the Provincial Court—in Quebec, the Court of Quebec; in Ontario, the Court of Justice. It is here that summary conviction and "absolute jurisdiction" offences (described in the previous section) are tried. Other indictable offences may be tried in this court if the accused person agrees or elects to be tried there. The *Criminal Code* also gives justices of the peace and provincial court judges other roles to play in the criminal justice system. For example, the *Criminal Code* authorizes justices of the peace to receive information (allegations that a criminal offence has been committed by a person), deal with the liberty of an accused person in most circumstances, and also to authorize or overrule the police with respect to the detention of property seized in the course of a criminal investigation.

The provincial court may now also grant third-party consent wiretap authorizations and issue warrants for a DNA sample.

Other than conducting trials themselves, the most important function of the provincial court judges perhaps is to hold preliminary inquiries under Part XVIII of the *Criminal Code*. A preliminary inquiry is held to determine whether there is sufficient evidence to put an accused person on trial for an offence. Sufficient reason exists where the prosecutor leads some evidence with respect to each element of the offence charged against an accused person. While it is not the duty or even the right of a justice conducting a preliminary inquiry to weigh the credibility of witnesses or the strength of the evidence on the whole of the case, which he or she must do on a trial, it is crucial for him or her to be alive to what will be required of the Crown in proving the offence charged so that someone is not put on trial and in jeopardy of a criminal punishment unnecessarily. The judicial officer conducting the preliminary inquiry may also commit an accused person to stand trial on one or more offences which were not charged against the accused person but which become apparent from the evidence led against the accused person. The preliminary inquiry, of course, does not determine any issue of guilt or no guilt. The Crown may try again before a second justice if unsuccessful the first time—or the Crown may simply decide to order the accused person to stand trial despite the finding of the preliminary inquiry.

The role of the preliminary inquiry in the criminal process only exists where an accused person chooses, or is required, to be tried in a court higher than the provincial court of a province. Recent amendments to the Criminal Code have narrowed the use of preliminary inquiries whereby the accused must now ask for one, and must narrow the issues to be heard. The changes have also allowed for the Crown to make more liberal use of hearsay and documentary evidence to expedite the inquiry. Defence counsel find it extremely useful to have this dry run to test the admissibility of certain evidence such as statements given to the police and to tie witnesses down to a specific version of events.

The most important quality of the provincial court, particularly where it is conducting a preliminary inquiry, is that it is a statutory court. As such it has only those powers given to it in a statute. Such a court has none of the "inherent jurisdiction" possessed by higher courts, and only a limited power to grant relief to an accused person other than a discharge or acquittal. For example, it is permissible for a provincial court judge to decide that a particular law is unconstitutional and will not be enforced, but when a provincial court judge is conducting a preliminary inquiry he or she cannot grant *Charter of Rights* relief to an accused person.

Courts of Criminal Jurisdiction[8]

When an accused person elects a trial by a judge alone, his trial is usually held after a preliminary inquiry. The trial court will usually be the supreme court, with the judge sitting without a jury. Historically, the "judge alone" election resulted in a trial before a distinct court part way between the provincial and supreme courts, called a county court. This intermediate level of court has been eliminated. Like the grand jury before it, the institution of a "court of criminal jurisdiction" with more expanded powers than the provincial courts, but fewer powers than the supreme (or equivalent) courts of the province, was an un- justifiable expense in today's world of easier transportation to a more restricted number of judicial centres.

Superior Courts[9]

The superior courts are the "superior courts of criminal jurisdiction" which are called the supreme, superior or Queen's Bench Court. Very briefly, these courts are superior because they can try any offence under the criminal law of Canada other than a summary conviction offence. These courts can authorize invasions of privacy by wiretap. Judges of these courts will always make themselves available to deal with ques- tions affecting the liberty of any person (whether charged or not), and in fact are the only judicial authorities who may deal with the release of an individual charged with the most serious offences such as murder, treason, and piracy. The supreme courts in each province conduct trials with and without a jury. It is also the court where summary conviction appeals may be taken. The judges who sit on the bench of the supreme court of a province are appointed by the federal government.

In addition to those powers exercised by other courts, the supreme court in each province has authority to "supervise" all courts below it. The supreme court may, by order, halt proceedings in lower courts because of a perceived abuse of procedures, or because of a lack of jurisdiction—such as failures to permit an accused person to make full answer and defence or simply because the lower court has no jurisdic- tion to proceed any further with respect to the particular criminal mat- ter. These courts may also freely exercise "inherent jurisdiction". Un- like the courts below it, a superior court of criminal jurisdiction is not restricted by any statute from doing what it feels is just and right in the circumstances of any particular case. As a result, this level of court is regarded as the most competent court to determine whether the *Charter* rights of any person have been violated. The court has every ability to give the person applying for a remedy the precise relief which appears to be just and appropriate in the circumstances.

Provincial Courts of Appeal[10]

The *Criminal Code* recognizes that the superior court of criminal jurisdiction in each province is divided into two parts—a trial division and an appeal division. The appeal bench may be called the Appeal Division or the Court of Appeal, depending upon the province involved. Courts of appeal do not hear trials of any criminal matters. Instead, they hear cases where the Crown or an accused person is aggrieved by a decision in some trial court. These appellate courts consider the correctness in law of the trial court's decision. Such appeals are heard by at least three, and perhaps five, judges. The appeal court justices are appointed by the federal government.

In most circumstances a right to appeal only exists where there is a question of law raised by the decision of the court which first heard the matter. From time to time the Crown or the accused may be upset by a decision for reasons of mixed law and fact, or simply upon an issue of fact. In these cases the party who wishes to appeal must obtain the permission or "leave" of the appeal court.

Appeals based on legal issues will be examined by the court in light of a transcript of trial evidence and any reasons for decision. There is power to hear fresh evidence, but this will not be done if, with reasonable efforts, the evidence could have been adduced at trial. Such new evidence would also have to be relevant to a decisive issue, credible, and such that if it was believed, could have affected the result. Needless to say, new evidence is permitted extremely rarely.

A court of appeal has three broad options before it in disposing of an appeal: it may dismiss the appeal, in which case the lower court decision stands; it may agree that there was a significant error in the lower court and direct a new trial; or, thirdly, it may allow the appeal and substitute the decision made in the lower court with its own decision—so long as this does not involve entering a guilty verdict where a not guilty verdict had been rendered by a jury. Among these three broad alternatives an appeal court has a number of ways of approaching a case.

It is not uncommon for a court of appeal to discover errors in law made at the trial of an accused person. Not every error will constitute a sufficient basis on which to overturn a verdict reached. The error might have been in the accused person's favour, but a conviction resulted anyway. In those circumstances, the court might decide that no substantial wrong or miscarriage of justice had occurred, that the accused person had suffered no prejudice to his position because of the error. Courts of appeal may even find this to be the case where the error was in the Crown's favour, but the evidence of guilt was so overwhelming that no other conclusion would be possible than that the accused person should be found guilty.

While appeal courts will usually strenuously avoid expressing opinions about the strength or weakness of a case, they are entitled to assess the whole of a case and determine whether the result seems unreasonable or unsupported by the evidence. In such situations the court is not considering whether the verdict is unjustified according to its own view of the facts, but whether it is unreasonable, given a rational appreciation of the facts.

Where summary conviction matters are concerned, the *Criminal Code* provides for a shortened appeal process which may be followed directly from the provincial court to the court of appeal. This, however, is only available where the appeal is on a strict question of law or jurisdiction. Unlike the usual appeal process to the county, district or supreme court, factual questions cannot be raised.

The appeal court may also be asked for its opinion on questions by the Minister of Justice for Canada whenever "he desires the assistance of that court." This may be requested where the Minister has a difficult issue to determine in his position as Minister of Justice and wishes to have some judicial assistance with respect to the matter. For example, the Minister may wish to exercise his prerogative of mercy under s. 749 of the *Criminal Code*, or wish to release an imprisoned individual because there are troubling aspects to the case despite a judicial finding of guilt. In this circumstance he may obtain the court's opinion about what to do. Is the case one where an individual should be released unconditionally, or should the accused person be provided with a new trial despite an earlier conviction? Such proceedings are extremely rare.

Supreme Court of Canada[11]

The Supreme Court of Canada is, like the provincial courts of appeal, strictly an appeals court. Nothing is heard and decided there for the first time in respect of criminal proceedings against an accused person. Instead, only those cases which involve a serious difference of legal opinion are heard, and even then, not all of these. The court comprises nine justices appointed by the federal government, with conventional recognition that three are to be from the province of Quebec, one from the Atlantic Provinces, one from Alberta, Saskatchewan and Manitoba, one from British Columbia, and three from Ontario. Subject to constitutional change, this geographical distribution of judicial positions is not legally required, but it has been followed reasonably consistently over the past number of years. The court is extremely busy. Depending upon the importance of the case, five, seven or even nine justices may sit. The court's inclination in recent years has been to emphasize the hearing of constitutional cases, particularly where such cases involve the *Canadian Charter of Rights and Freedoms.*

With respect to criminal matters, there are only two guaranteed rights of appeal to the Supreme Court of Canada. Each of these exists only with respect to indictable offences. A person whose acquittal is overturned by a court of appeal may appeal from that overturned verdict to the Supreme Court of Canada on a question of law. Unlike the ordinary appeal process to the superior court, factual questions cannot be raised.

Otherwise, an appellant (whether the accused person or the Crown) must ask the Supreme Court of Canada for leave to appeal with respect to a question of law. If there is no disagreement in the court of appeal, an appellant must apply for leave to appeal to the Supreme Court of Canada on the ground that the question is one of national importance for the administration of criminal justice in Canada. The Supreme Court of Canada can exercise a degree of control over the cases which it hears, but there are limits to which this can be carried if the court is going to maintain its authority with respect to the development of the criminal law in this country.

In dealing with an appeal, the Supreme Court of Canada may make any order that a court of appeal might have made. Thus, it may set aside a trial verdict on the ground that it is unreasonable or cannot be supported by the evidence, or overturn a decision on the basis that a wrong decision has been made on a question of law. Further, if it feels that there was a miscarriage of justice in any aspect of the case, whether or not the point was even argued before the provincial court of appeal, it may allow the appeal. Similarly, it may dismiss the appeal because there was no substantial wrong or miscarriage of justice toward the Crown or the accused despite a legal error or procedural irregularity.

Historically, a further appeal existed from the Supreme Court of Canada to the Privy Council in England, but, as the country became more independent, so did its judicial institutions and its criminal law. Earlier this century, appeals to the Privy Council in England were abolished. Since that time, Canadian criminal law has developed independently, but parallel with the criminal law of England and the other Commonwealth jurisdictions. As the court of final resort for criminal matters in Canada, the Supreme Court of Canada has gained increasing respect and done much to foster uniformity in the application of the criminal law to accused persons in this country.

Only a very small percentage of criminal cases ever get to the Supreme Court of Canada. Except for the broad directions the court can give in the few cases which come before it, much of the substance of Canadian criminal law is determined by the provincial courts of appeal, and manifested in the day to day decisions of the many provincial court judges and justices of the peace. Indeed, for most people who at some time face a criminal charge in this country, it is not the Supreme Court of Canada or even the courts of appeal which have any influence on them. The court system for them is no more than the justices of the peace and provincial court judges who apply and do most of the judging about what is and what is not criminal in this country.

Notes

[1] *Canadian Charter of Rights and Freedoms* (being Part I of the *Constitution Act, 1982* [en. by the *Canada Act 1982* (U.K.), 1982, c. 11, Sched. B]), ss. 7, 10, 11; *R. v. Vermette*, 1984 CarswellQue 27, 16 C.C.C. (3d) 532, 15 D.L.R. (4th) 218, [1984] C.A. 466, 45 C.R. (3d) 341 (Que. C.A.); *R. c. Atlantic Sugar Refineries Co.*, 1976 CarswellQue 19, (*sub nom. Ouellet (Nos. 1 & 2), Re*) 32 C.C.C. (2d) 149, (*sub nom. Ouellet, Re*) 36 C.R.N.S. 296, (*sub nom. Ouellet (No. 1 & 2), Re*) 72 D.L.R. (3d) 95, (*sub nom. Ouellet c. R.*) [1976] C.A. 788 (Que. C.A.) 32 C.C.C. (2d) 149 (Que. C.A.); *R. v. Ramsey*, 1972 CarswellNB 71, 8 C.C.C. (2d) 188, 4 N.B.R. (2d) 809 (N.B. C.A.); *R. v. Hatton*, 1978 CarswellOnt 1186, 39 C.C.C. (2d) 281 (Ont. C.A.).

[2] *Criminal Code*, R.S.C. 1985, c. C-46, ss. 2, 6-8, 470, 476-481, 531, 599, 785, 798; *R. v. Sarazin*, 1978 CarswellPEI 6, 39 C.C.C. (2d) 131, 20 Nfld. & P.E.I.R. 91, 53 A.P.R. 91, 3 C.R. (3d) 97 (P.E.I. S.C.); *R. v. Simons*, 1976 CarswellOnt 13, 30 C.C.C. (2d) 162, 34 C.R.N.S. 273 (Ont. C.A.); *R. v. Arnott*, 1970 CarswellOnt 754, 1 C.C.C. (2d) 86, [1970] 3 O.R. 618 (Ont. C.A.); *R. v. Lai*, 1985 CarswellBC 719, 24 C.C.C. (3d) 237 (B.C. C.A.); *Libman v. R.*, 1985 CarswellOnt 951, 1985 CarswellOnt 951F, 21 C.C.C. (3d) 206, 62 N.R. 161, 12 O.A.C. 33, 21 D.L.R. (4th) 174, [1985] 2 S.C.R. 178 (S.C.C.).

[3] *Constitution Act, 1867* (30 & 31 Vict.), c. 3, ss. 91(27), 92(14)-(15), 96-101; *Criminal Code*, ss. 2, 553, 785 (summary conviction court); *Criminal Code*, ss. 2, 468, 469 (superior court of criminal jurisdiction); *Criminal Code*, ss. 2, 469, 536, 554-568 (court of criminal jurisdiction).

[4] *Criminal Code*, ss. 7, 470, 477, 485, 798; *Exemption of United States Forces from Proceedings in Canadian Criminal Courts, Re*, 1943 CarswellNat 35, 80 C.C.C. 161, [1943] 4 D.L.R. 11, [1943] S.C.R. 483 (S.C.C.); *R. v. Stacey*, 1981 Car-

swellQue 245, (sub nom. *Stacey v. Montour*) 63 C.C.C. (2d) 61, [1982] 3 C.N.L.R. 158 (Que. C.A.).

[5] *R. v. Jewitt*, 1985 CarswellBC 743, 1985 CarswellBC 813, 21 C.C.C. (3d) 7, [1985] 2 S.C.R. 128, [1985] 6 W.W.R. 127, 20 D.L.R. (4th) 651, 61 N.R. 159, 47 C.R. (3d) 193 (S.C.C.); see your provincial *Judicature Act* or *Courts of Justice Act*, and compare it with the legislation establishing your provincial court.

[6] *R. v. Chaulk*, 1990 CarswellMan 385, 1990 CarswellMan 239, 62 C.C.C. (3d) 193, 2 C.R. (4th) 1, 69 Man. R. (2d) 161, [1991] 2 W.W.R. 385, 1 C.R.R. (2d) 1, 119 N.R. 161, [1990] 3 S.C.R. 1303 (S.C.C.); *R. c. Daviault*, 1994 CarswellQue 10, 1994 CarswellQue 118, 93 C.C.C. (3d) 21, 64 Q.A.C. 81, 33 C.R. (4th) 165, 24 C.R.R. (2d) 1, [1994] 3 S.C.R. 63, 173 N.R. 1, 118 D.L.R. (4th) 469 (S.C.C.); *Wolf v. R.*, 1974 CarswellAlta 98, 1974 CarswellAlta 189, 17 C.C.C. (2d) 425, 27 C.R.N.S. 150, [1975] 2 S.C.R. 107, 47 D.L.R. (3d) 741, 2 N.R. 415, [1974] 6 W.W.R. 368 (S.C.C.); *R. v. McInnis*, 1973 CarswellOnt 37, 13 C.C.C. (2d) 471, 1 O.R. (2d) 1, 23 C.R.N.S. 152 (Ont. C.A.); *R. c. Aziz*, 1981 CarswellQue 6, 1981 CarswellQue 87, 57 C.C.C. (2d) 97, [1981] 1 S.C.R. 188, 19 C.R. (3d) 26, 35 N.R. 1, 119 D.L.R. (3d) 513 (S.C.C.); *R. v. Sellars*, 1980 CarswellQue 34, 1980 CarswellQue 118, 52 C.C.C. (2d) 345, 20 C.R. (3d) 381, 110 D.L.R. (3d) 629, 32 N.R. 70, [1980] 1 S.C.R. 527 (S.C.C.); *R. v. Binus*, 1967 CarswellOnt 14, [1968] 1 C.C.C. 227, [1967] S.C.R. 594, 2 C.R.N.S. 118 (S.C.C.).

[7] *Criminal Code*, ss. 2, 490, 503, 504, 515, 535, 536, 553, 554, 798; *United States v. Sheppard*, 1976 CarswellNat 1, 1976 CarswellNat 433F, 30 C.C.C. (2d) 424, [1977] 2 S.C.R. 1067, 34 C.R.N.S. 207, 9 N.R. 215, 70 D.L.R. (3d) 136 (S.C.C.); *R. v. Marrone*, 1982 CarswellNS 174, 52 N.S.R. (2d) 311, 106 A.P.R. 311 (N.S. C.A.); *R. v. Mills*, 1986 CarswellOnt 1716, 1986 CarswellOnt 116, (*sub nom. Mills v. R.*) 26 C.C.C. (3d) 481, 16 O.A.C. 81, 52 C.R. (3d) 1, (*sub nom. Mills v. R.*) 29 D.L.R. (4th) 161, (*sub nom. Mills v. R.*) 67 N.R. 241, (*sub nom. Mills v. R.*) 21 C.R.R. 76, (*sub nom. Mills v. R.*) [1986] 1 S.C.R. 863, (*sub nom. Mills v. R.*) 58 O.R. (2d) 544 (note) (S.C.C.); *R. v. Big M Drug Mart* (1985), 1985 CarswellAlta 316, 1985 CarswellAlta 609, 18 C.C.C. (3d) 385, [1985] 1 S.C.R. 295, 18 D.L.R. (4th) 321, 58 N.R. 81, [1985] 3 W.W.R. 481, 37 Alta. L.R. (2d) 97, 60 A.R. 161, 85 C.L.L.C. 14,023, 13 C.R.R. 64 (S.C.C.).

[8] *Criminal Code*, ss. 2, 185, 469, 482, 536, 812-828; *R. v. Waugh*, 1985 CarswellNS 263, 68 N.S.R. (2d) 247, 159 A.P.R. 247, 21 C.C.C. (3d) 80 (N.S. C.A.).

[9] *Criminal Code*, ss. 2, 185, 468, 469, 522, 536, 812-828.

[10] *Criminal Code*, ss. 2, 673-687, 690, 829-839; *R. v. Palmer*, 1979 CarswellBC 533, 1979 CarswellBC 541, 50 C.C.C. (2d) 193, [1980] 1 S.C.R. 759, 30 N.R. 181, 14 C.R. (3d) 22, 17 C.R. (3d) 34 (Fr.), 106 D.L.R. (3d) 212 (S.C.C.); *R. v. Corbett*, 1973 CarswellBC 250, 1973 CarswellBC 272, 14 C.C.C. (2d) 385, 25 C.R.N.S. 296, [1975] 2 S.C.R. 275, [1974] 2 W.W.R. 524, 1 N.R. 258, 42 D.L.R. (3d) 142 (S.C.C.); *R. v. Marshall*, 1983 CarswellNS 312, 57 N.S.R. (2d) 286, 120 A.P.R. 286 (N.S. C.A.).

[11] *Criminal Code*, ss. 691-696; *Supreme Court Act*, R.S.C. 1985, c. S-26.

13

The Players of a Criminal Trial

The Honourable Judge Frank P. Hoskins*

INTRODUCTION

This chapter will attempt to provide an overview of the theoretical notions of the role of the trial judge, Crown, and defence counsel in the context of a trial in the adversarial criminal trial process. The trial judge, Crown, and defence counsel play a vital role in the conduct of a trial in the adversarial system of justice. Each player has an equally important, but distinct, function to perform in the conduct of a trial.

THE ADVERSARIAL SYSTEM OF CRIMINAL JUSTICE

The criminal trial process in Canada is based on the accusatorial or adversarial criminal justice system, which functions on the premise that every person is innocent until proven guilty beyond a reasonable doubt. The fact that a person has been charged with a particular offence means only that he or she has been accused of a crime. Such a person is presumed innocent until his or her guilt is established on relevant evidence, beyond a reasonable doubt, before an independent justice, with or without a jury. It is a principle of fundamental justice in our system that an accused is not called upon to demonstrate his or her innocence or justify his or her conduct. However, once the Crown establishes a *prima facie* case against the accused, it is up to the accused to call evidence or face conviction.

The adversarial nature of the trial process has been recognized as a principle of fundamental justice.[1] The Supreme Court of Canada recognized the constructs of the adversarial system as a fundamental part of our legal system on numerous occasions. The late Sopinka J. stated:

> The first rationale for the policy and practice referred to above is that a court's competence to resolve legal disputes is rooted in the adversary system. The requirement of an adversarial context is a fundamental tenet

* B.A., B.Ed., St. Mary's University, Halifax, Nova Scotia; LL.B., Dalhousie Law School, Halifax, Nova Scotia; Provincial Court Judge for the Province of Nova Scotia.

of our legal system and helps guarantee that issues are well and fully argued by parties who have a stake in the outcome.[2]

The Ontario Court of Appeal has also acknowledged the adversarial process as an integral part of our system of justice and described it as follows:

> Our mode of trial procedure is based upon the adversarial system in which the contestants seek to establish through relevant supporting evidence, before an impartial trier of facts, those events or happenings which form the bases of their allegations. This procedure assumes that the litigants, assisted by their counsel, will fully and diligently present all the material facts which have evidentiary value in support of their respective positions and that these disputed facts will receive from a trial Judge a dispassionate and impartial consideration in order to arrive at the truth of the matters in controversy. A trial is not intended to be a scientific exploration with the presiding Judge assuming the role of a research director; it is a forum established for the purpose of providing justice for the litigants. Undoubtedly a Court must be concerned with truth, in the sense that it accepts as true certain sworn evidence and rejects other testimony as unworthy of belief, but it cannot embark upon a quest for the "scientific" or "technological" truth when such an adventure does violence to the primary function of the Court, which has always been to do justice, according to law.[3]

The adversarial system of criminal justice has been justified over the years by many judges, lawyers, and legal commentators as capable of promoting the finest approximation of the truth.[4]

Unlike our adversarial system of criminal justice, countries in Europe employ the inquisitorial system of criminal justice, which places the obligation on the judiciary to ferret out the facts and thus ascertain the truth. The judge plays a central role in the trial process. Judges do not wait for the truth to emerge from the contentions of the opposing parties. In the inquisitorial system of criminal justice, the judge is expected to make the thorough investigations necessary to bring out the truth and prepare the case for trial.[5] It is the responsibility of the trial judge to bring out the relevant facts, not the prosecution and defence. The accused is brought before an examining judicial officer who makes an exhaustive preliminary inquiry. If the inquiry judge finds reasons to believe that the accused committed a crime, then an indictment is prepared by the prosecuting officers assigned to a particular court. After the preparation of the indictment, the accused is brought to trial. The court usually consists of three or more judges assisted by a jury. The judges take a very active part in the trial process, conducting most of the direct and cross-examinations of the witnesses.

The principal distinguishing characteristic between the adversarial and inquisitorial systems of criminal justice resides in the relative *passivity* of the judge in the adversarial system.[6] In the adversarial system of criminal justice, judges do not themselves conduct investigations into criminal cases independent of both Crown and defence, nor do they usually delegate others to do so.[7]

M. Ploscowe described the distinguishing characteristic between the adversarial and inquisitorial systems of criminal justice as follows:

> This difference in the functions of judges arises from different theories concerning the best means of separating the guilty from the innocent. In Anglo-American countries the provision of an impartial tribunal before which both sides may lay their facts is the chief means for accomplishing this purpose. In Europe, it is felt that what happens in the trial is so vitally affected by the preparation of the case in the preliminary stage that the active intervention of a judicial officer is necessary. Prosecutors tend to collect evidence indicative of guilt and to neglect facts favourable to the accused. Unless the accused is represented by counsel of equal ability to that of the prosecutor, he comes into the trial at a distinct disadvantage. The Europeans seek to maintain the balance in the trial proceedings by placing upon the judge, and not upon the parties, the primary duty of bringing out the evidence... European procedure attaches a great significance to the interrogation of the accused. Since European procedure is a judicial inquiry which should neglect no source of information on the facts surrounding the commission of a crime, the Europeans require the interrogation of the accused. He is the man who knows most about the issues, the truth or falsity of the charges. He is therefore questioned very minutely concerning them in the preliminary stage of the proceedings by the *juge d'instruction*, and again at the trial by the presiding justice. Just as in England and America, there is no legal way of compelling an accused to speak if he refuses. But in contrast to England and America, the continental countries do not warn the accused upon arrest that he has a right to maintain silence. Nor does Europe know the American rule forbidding any comment drawing unfavourable inferences from the defendant's refusal to testify. Whatever information can be obtained from the accused by rigorous questioning is admissible in a continental court.[8]

The contrast between the adversarial and inquisitorial systems of criminal justice enables one to better understand and appreciate the significance of the roles played by the participants in a criminal trial in Canada.

It is a well-established tenet in our Canadian legal system that the advocates (both Crown and defence) are expected to act as strong advocates within the adversarial process. In that regard, it is both permissible and desirable that the advocates vigorously pursue a legitimate result to the best of their ability. In the pursuit of justice, rules of just conduct that govern court practice and procedure will govern the conduct of litigation. Rules of evidence also control the court process insofar as they control the presentation of facts before the court. This vigorous pursuit of justice is a critical element of our criminal justice system as the essential purpose and feature of our adversarial system of criminal justice is to attain the truth. It should be noted, however, that judges, lawyers, and legal scholars recognize the inherent weakness of using the adversarial system of criminal justice in the search for the truth.

In the authoritative textbook entitled, *The Law of Evidence in Canada*, the esteemed authors note that:

> ... because our system is an adversarial one where fact presentation is controlled by the litigants and their counsel, this goal can be elusive in many cases. Apart from this deficiency in the framework in which the evidence is presented, the evidence itself may be inherently weak due, for example, to the imperfect recollection or perception of witnesses. In an attempt to limit these frailties, many of the rules of evidence are concerned with ensuring the reliability or accuracy of the evidence the court receives.[9]

Obviously, our adversarial system of criminal justice places a heavy burden on the players of a criminal trial. The judge, Crown, and defence must strenuously strive for perfection in performing their respective roles in the trial process.

It is a well-established principle that the adversarial system of criminal justice owes a duty of *fairness* to the players of a criminal trial within the constructs of the trial process. It is trite to say that in order to maintain the public confidence and respect in the effectiveness of the Canadian criminal justice system, the courts must ensure that trials are fair and that they appear to be fair to the informed and reasonable observer. This is the fundamental goal of the justice system in a free and democratic society. The principles of fundamental justice require that the criminal trial process be a fair one. Accordingly, each player in the trial process must ensure that there is a fair hearing.

THE ROLE OF THE JUDGE

The judiciary is perceived by some legal commentators as a third arm of government, separate from and independent of the political parties, the legislative, and the executive. Its role is to maintain the *rule of law,* to uphold the Constitution, and to administer justice, impartially, according to law.

The judiciary in Canada exercises wide powers. It enjoys judicial independence, security of tenure, and financial security. Most importantly, it enjoys the respect, and embraces the confidence of the vast majority of Canadians. Judicial independence is reinforced, not only by tenure, but also the by legal immunity from reprisals for decisions that are unpopular with the public and/or the government. To protect its impartiality, the law gives it substantial immunities from actions based on its exercise of judicial powers.[10] Judicial independence is an element of the constitutional systems of judicial impartiality.[11]

The government cannot direct judges on how to decide cases or exercise judicial discretion. Judges are not bound by policies created and employed by the government. Judges are only bound by the laws that Parliament and/or the Legislature enact.

The trust reposed in the public has been earned by the judge's ability to conduct trials fairly and impartially. Impartiality is the cornerstone of our criminal justice system and thus it is vigorously preserved by the judiciary. Judges must be sensitive to the need not only to be fair, but also to appear to all reasonable observers to be fair to all Canadians of every race, religion, nationality, and ethnic origin.[12] The courts must be held to the highest standards of impartiality. A trial will be rendered unfair if the words or actions of the presiding judge give rise to a reasonable apprehension of bias to the informed and reasonable observer.[13]

The public rightfully expects judges to undertake an open-minded, carefully considered, and dispassionately deliberate investigation of the complicated reality of each case before them.

Impartiality can be described as a state of mind in which the judge is disinterested in the outcome of the trial and is open to persuasion by the evidence and submissions of counsel. Hence there is, and must be, a presumption of impartiality of the judiciary in order to maintain the public confidence in the effectiveness of the criminal trial process.

Judges are expected to conduct themselves with integrity, impartiality, diligence, and equality. Adherence to these fundamental principles promotes public confidence in an effective criminal justice system.[14]

The traditional view of the role of the trial judge has been that of a passive participant. Lord Denning, a famous English jurist, had occasion to comment on the role of a trial judge:

> ... it is for the advocates, each in his turn, to examine the witnesses, and not for the judge to take it on himself lest by so doing he appear to favour one side or the other... The judge's part in all this is to hearken to the evidence, only himself asking questions of witnesses when it is necessary to clear up behave themselves seemly and keep to the rules laid down by law; to exclude irrelevancies and discourage repetition; to make sure by

wise intervention that he follows the points that the advocates are making and can assess their worth; and at the end to make up his mind where the truth lies. If he goes beyond this, he drops the matter of a judge and assumes the role of an advocate; and the change does not become him well.[15]

Lord Denning further stated that:

Even in England, however, a judge is not a mere umpire to answer the question 'How's that?' His object, above all, is to find out the truth, and to do justice according to law.[16]

A trial judge will rarely descend into the arena with counsel and take an active role, because he or she risks the possibility of having his or her vision clouded with the dust of the conflict.[17]

The trial judge has a wide discretion in the trial's conduct, and although he or she is always at liberty to question a witness to clarify a point or to explore an issue further, extensive interventions by a trial judge in the unfolding of the evidence are not the norm in our adversarial system. Extensive questioning by the trial judge risks producing an impression that the judge is pursuing a preconceived view of the facts.

Commenting on the right of the trial judge to question witnesses, Martin, J.A., an experienced and learned jurist, stated:

A criminal trial is, in the main, an adversarial process, not an investigation by the judge of the charge against the accused, and, accordingly, the examination and cross-examination of witnesses are primarily the responsibility of counsel. The judge, however, is not required to remain silent. He may question witnesses to clear up ambiguities, explore some matter which the answers of a witness have left vague or, indeed, he may put questions which should have been put to bring out some relevant matter, but which have been omitted. Generally speaking, the authorities recommend that questions by the judge should be put after counsel has completed his examination, and the witnesses should not be cross-examined by the judge during their examination-in-chief.[18]

It should be noted that a trial judge who endeavors to assist counsel and witnesses in the proper, complete and logical developments of all aspects of a case within the confines of the rules of evidence and the adversarial system, while maintaining complete impartiality, will advance the respect and confidence of all concerned with the effectiveness of the criminal trial process.

It is the duty of the trial judge to decide all questions of law, both substantive and procedural, which arise during the course of the proceedings. During the course of a trial, the judge may be called upon to make significant rulings that could affect the outcome of the case.

As one noted author aptly stated:

> On any average day in court a judge is routinely called on to exhibit the face of a diplomat, the wisdom of Solomon, the patience of a peace negotiator. A judge under our system doesn't have to be perfect but he or she had better come awfully close.[19]

In jury trials, the trial judge does not determine issues of fact. The trier of fact in jury trials is the jury. The jury's function is to determine from the evidence the facts to make a proper application of the law relating to those facts as explained by the trial judge. It is the exclusive responsibility of the trial judge to interpret the law and state to the jury what principles of law are applicable to the facts of the case, and such statement and exposition of the law are binding on the jury. In other words, the jury must apply the law to the facts as they find them. The jury is the trier of fact, and the trial judge is the only expert on the law with the responsibility of instructing the jury on the law.

In jury trials, the jury is entitled to accept all of the testimony of a witness, part of the testimony of a witness, or none of the testimony of a witness. If the jury accepts part of the testimony of a witness, it is not then bound to accept all of the witness testimony. If the jury rejects part of the testimony of a witness, it is not then required to reject all of the testimony of the witness. In other words, a jury, as the trier of fact, is free to accept or reject all, part, or none of the testimony of a witness. The jury's verdict must be unanimous and all jury members must be present in court when the verdict is given and either the Crown or the defence has the right to have the jury polled. If a verdict is guilty, then the trial judge must impose the appropriate punishment.

THE ROLE OF THE CROWN

In Canada, each province has an Attorney General who is the chief law officer of the Crown and a member of the Cabinet. He or she heads a ministry that exercises the authority, conferred upon the provincial government by the Constitution, over the administration of justice and the maintenance and organization of the courts.

In his or her capacity as head of the ministry, he or she is particularly associated with the Provincial Court judges who are appointed by the provincial government and who come within the administrative control of his or her ministry. In addition, the Attorney General is the prosecutor and, hence, in effect, a litigant in every criminal case except for the relatively few cases that are prosecuted by private persons.

In practice, the Attorney General acts through the numerous Crown prosecutors (Crown attorneys), who are his or her agents to prosecute criminal offences on his or her behalf. Crown attorneys in the provinces are responsible ultimately to the Attorney General, who is responsible to the legislative.

In Canada, the role of the Crown attorney is distinctly different from that of an American district attorney. The Crown attorney, unlike the local district attorney in most states, is not an elected official, but is appointed by the government. Thus, Crown attorneys do not run on law-and-order election platforms and are expected to be independent of the public pressure and pressure from the police or other law enforcement agencies.

The Crown is not an agent of the police and, unlike his or her American counterpart, does not have an investigatory staff that attends a crime scene and assists police in conducting an investigation. The Crown attorney is expected to present all relevant evidence, which sheds light upon the offence of which the accused is charged, to the trier of fact (trial judge or the jury).

The role of the Crown attorney was eloquently summarized by the Supreme Court of Canada in 1955:

> It cannot be over-emphasized that the purpose of criminal prosecution is not to obtain a conviction; it is to lay before a jury what the Crown considers to be credible evidence relevant to what is alleged to be a crime. Counsel have a duty to see that all available legal proof of the facts is presented: it should be done firmly and pressed to its legitimate strength, but it must also be done fairly. The role of prosecutor excludes any notion of winning or losing; his function is a matter of public duty than which in civil life there can be none charged with greater personal responsibility. It is to be efficiently performed with an ingrained sense of the dignity, the seriousness and the justness of judicial proceedings.[20]

The adversarial criminal justice system does not create a contest between the Crown attorney and the accused, who may be represented by counsel, as the Crown attorney has a dual responsibility—that of producing the evidence of the accused's guilt and seeing that justice is done through a fair trial on its merits.

The Crown has resources far greater than those available to an accused. Availability of police for investigation, for example, allows the Crown attorney to find witnesses and evidence from many sources not available to the accused. The Crown attorney must exercise discretion fairly and dispassionately in commencing a criminal prosecution. This discretion must be insulated from political and public pressures. Even the most horrendous crimes committed by notorious offenders must be carefully and thoroughly analyzed to ascertain that the essential elements of a criminal prosecution are present. There must be a "realistic prospect of conviction," which is supported by credible and admissible evidence, to warrant a prosecution. The Crown attorney cannot react to pressures and initiate a prosecution when, in his or her opinion, the evidence is incomplete or insufficient, as it would be a dereliction of duty to do otherwise. It is not the role of the Crown attorney to commence a prosecution in hope of obtaining a conviction or merely to satisfy public opinion.

The Crown attorney's duty to the court is to present evidence fairly and objectively. He or she must weigh the evidence and should never be less than objective in its presentation or in his or her submissions to the court. It is a well-recognized principle that the personal views of a prosecutor should never be expressed, as they have no part in the prosecutorial process.

The Crown attorney plays a very responsible and respected role in the conduct of criminal trials. The Crown attorney exercises a public function involving much discretion and power, and must act fairly and dispassionately with an ingrained sense of dignity.

Generally, a Crown attorney's discretion is exercised without reference to fixed objective standards. It includes discretion in the choice of charge, pre-trial disclosure of information to the defence, whether to proceed summarily or by indictment, preferring indictments, and relaying charges in certain circumstances.

THE ROLE OF THE DEFENCE COUNSEL

The theoretical notion of the role of defence counsel in the adversarial criminal trial process is to "represent his or her client resolutely, honourably and within the limits of the law."[21] A defence counsel must also "ask every question, raise every issue and advance every argument, however distasteful, that the advocate reasonably thinks will help the client's case."[22] Or, to phrase it another way, the role of defence counsel is to protect the interests of his or her client. There are, nonetheless, several limits on the extent to which he or she may do so.

It should be noted that the defence counsel is not the alter ego of his or her client. The function of defence counsel is to provide professional assistance and advice. Defence counsel must, accordingly, exercise his or her professional skill and judgment in the conduct of the case and not allow him- or herself to be a mere mouthpiece for the client. It is, of course, fundamental to his or her role that defence counsel should, while acting with proper courtesy to the court, fearlessly uphold the client's interests without regard to any unpleasant consequence to him- or herself or to any other person.[23]

Lord Reid, a learned English jurist, described the theoretical notion of the role of defence counsel in the adversarial criminal trial process as follows:

> Every counsel has a duty to his client fearlessly to raise every issue, advance every argument and ask every question, however distasteful, which he thinks will help his client's case. But, as an officer of the court concerned in the administration of justice, he has an overriding duty to the court, to the standards of his profession, and to the public, which may and often does lead to a conflict with his client's wishes or with what the client thinks are his personal interests. Counsel must not mislead the court, he must not lend himself to casting aspersions on the other party or witnesses for which there is no sufficient basis in the information in his possession, he must not withhold authorities or documents which may tell against his clients but which the law or the standards of his profession require him to produce. And by so acting he may well incur the displeasure or worse of his client so that if the case is lost, his client would or might seek legal redress if that were open to him.[24]

Indeed, defence counsel are necessary for the proper functioning of the adversary process. As previously mentioned, the adversarial trial process is an attempt by two contestants with differing views to persuade a trial judge. Without the presence of defence counsel, there would be no adversary for the Crown. Hence, it is the function of the defence counsel to fearlessly raise every question and advance every argument that he or she believes will advance the client's case. Defence counsel, however, in executing his or her professional duties on behalf of the client, cannot or should not become judgmental of the client's alleged misconduct. Defence counsel must not usurp the function of the judge and/or jury.

It is the defence counsel's responsibility, not the client's, to decide what witnesses to call, whether a witness should be cross-examined, and if so how it should be done. There is at least one decision that only the client can make and that is the decision as to whether to plead guilty or not guilty.[25]

It should also be noted that even if the client admits his or her guilt to defence counsel, it does not preclude defence counsel from forcing the Crown to prove each and every essential element of the offence charged. There are, however, ethical restrictions on defence counsel with respect to the manner in which he or she is entitled to conduct the defence for the client.[26] Notwithstanding the right of an accused to require the Crown to prove his or her guilt beyond a reasonable doubt, defence counsel is under a duty, after making a thorough and exhaustive investigation of the case, to advise the client as to what the probable outcome of the case is likely to be. It is the duty of defence counsel to clearly, in language the client understands, explain the various options that are available and the consequences of each choice. Defence counsel should never advise or permit a client to plead guilty until defence counsel has completed a thorough and exhaustive investigation of the facts and the relevant law. Defence counsel must be satisfied that the Crown has sufficient evidence on each and every essential element of the charge that supports a *prima facie* case against his or her client. Indeed, defence counsel must be satisfied that his or her client possessed the requisite *mens rea* and completed the *actus reus* of the offence (charge) before advising the client how to plead to the charge. Although defence counsel is free to advise his or her client in strong terms as to the plea that should be entered, the ultimate choice is that of the client and it must be a free and informed choice.

Defence counsel must take his or her instructions from the client. However, defence counsel is not bound to follow instructions that are unreasonable and, in proper cases, is entitled to refuse to act for a client who rejects his or her advice or where there is a breach of trust in the client-solicitor relationship.[27]

Furthermore, defence counsel cannot promote his or her client's interests by introducing false evidence or making misleading statements, as that would pervert justice. This does not mean, however, that defence counsel has any duty to assist the Crown in discovering or presenting evidence that could incriminate his or her client. Thus, the defence counsel role is not to assist in the search for the truth, but to verify the results of the search conducted by the Crown. In essence, the role of defence counsel could be likened to marking mathematics exams—he or she checks the calculations to make sure that they are correct. He or she then points out to the trier of fact (judge or jury) any computations that do not add up and mentions any factors that were left out of the math by the Crown.

As well, the defence counsel must refrain from asserting his or her own personal views on the merits of the case. He or she is to be involved in the case only professionally, not personally. It is his or her job to present the evidence of others to the court and to argue about the legal significance of that evidence, but he or she cannot him- or herself give evidence.

The defence counsel is constrained by a duty of honesty. As stated, the defence counsel cannot knowingly present false or misleading evidence. If the client admits elements of the offence (charge) to his or her defence counsel, then defence counsel is precluded from setting up an affirmative defence that is inconsistent with those admissions. Defence counsel, however, can still test the strength of the Crown's case and raise any technical or procedural deficiencies as a defence. Thus, the role of the defence counsel can be seen as a shepherd of the criminal trial process itself. He or she is there to ensure that, if the accused is convicted, it was done according to the proper procedure and as a result of sufficient, convincing, and admissible evidence. He or she is there only to force the Crown to play by the rules. He or she is not there to cheat in order to obtain an acquittal for the client.

All law societies in Canada have approved a code of conduct for its members regardless whether one is a Crown Attorney (prosecutor) or defence counsel.

Notes

[1] *R. v. Swain*, 1991 CarswellOnt 1016, 1991 CarswellOnt 93, 63 C.C.C. (3d) 481, 5 C.R. (4th) 253, 125 N.R. 1, 3 C.R.R. (2d) 1, 47 O.A.C. 81, [1991] 1 S.C.R. 933, 4 O.R. (3d) 383, 83 D.L.R. (4th) 193 (S.C.C.).

[2] *Borowski v. Canada (Attorney General)*, 1989 CarswellSask 241, 1989 Carswell-Sask 465, 47 C.C.C. (3d) 1, [1989] 3 W.W.R. 97, [1989] 1 S.C.R. 342, 57 D.L.R. (4th) 231, 92 N.R. 110, 75 Sask. R. 82, 33 C.P.C. (2d) 105, 38 C.R.R. 232 (S.C.C.), at p. 13 [C.C.C.].

[3] *Phillips v. Ford Motor Co. of Canada* (1971), 1971 CarswellOnt 657, 18 D.L.R. (3d) 641, [1971] 2 O.R. 637 (Ont. C.A.) at p. 661 [D.L.R.].

[4] Don Stuart, *Learning Canadian Criminal Procedure*, 5th ed. (Toronto: Carswell, 1998) at 473.

[5] M. Ploscowe, *The Development of Present Day Criminal Procedures in Europe and America* (1934-35) 48 *Harv. L. Rev.* 433-37.

[6] *Ibid.*

[7] *Ibid.*

[8] *Ibid.*

[9] John Sopinka, Sydney N. Lederman, and Alan W. Bryant, *The Law of Evidence in Canada*, 1st ed. (Markham: Butterworths, 1992).

[10] *R. v. S. (R.D.)*, 1997 CarswellNS 301, 1997 CarswellNS 302, [1997] 3 S.C.R. 484, 10 C.R. (5th) 1, 118 C.C.C. (3d) 353, 161 N.S.R. (2d) 241, 477 A.P.R. 241, 151 D.L.R. (4th) 193, 218 N.R. 1, 1 Admin. L.R. (3d) 74 (S.C.C.).

[11] *Ibid.*

[12] *Ibid.*

13 *Ibid.*

14 See the Honourable Richard J. Scott's—Chief Justice, Manitoba Court of Appeal—article entitled, "Judicial Ethics" (National Criminal Law Program, University of British Columbia, July 1998) at section 7.1.

15 *Jones v. National Coal Board,* [1957] 2 Q.B. 55, [1957] 2 All E.R. 155 (Eng. C.A.), at p. 64 [Q.B.].

16 *Ibid,* at p. 63 [Q.B.].

17 *Yuill v. Yuill,* [1945] 1 All E.R. 183, [1945] P. 15 (Eng. C.A.), at p. 189 [All E.R.].

18 *R. v. Valley,* 1986 CarswellOnt 822, 26 C.C.C. (3d) 207, 13 O.A.C. 89 (C.A.), at p. 230 [C.C.C.], leave to appeal refused (1986), 26 C.C.C. (3d) 207 (note) (S.C.C.).

19 Jack Batten, *Judges* (MacMillan of Canada, 1986).

20 *R. v. Boucher,* 1954 CarswellQue 14, (*sub nom. Boucher v. R.*) 110 C.C.C. 263, (*sub nom. Boucher v. R.*) 20 C.R. 1, (*sub nom. Boucher v. R.*) [1955] S.C.R. 16 (S.C.C.), at p. 270 [C.C.C.].

21 See *Nova Scotia Legal Ethics and Professional Handbook* (Nova Scotia Barristers' Society, 1990), at c. 10.

22 *Ibid.*

23 Arthur G. Martin, "The Role and Responsibility of the Defence Advocate" (1969-70) 12 Crim. L.Q. 376.

24 *Rondel v. Worsley* (1967), [1969] 1 A.C. 191, [1967] 3 All E.R. 993, [1967] 3 W.L.R. 1666, 111 Sol. Jo. 927 (U.K. H.L.), at p. 227-28 [A.C.].

25 *Nova Scotia Legal Ethics and Professional Handbook, supra,* note 21

26 *Ibid.*

27 *Ibid.*

14

Trial Procedure

The Honourable Judge Brian D. Williston*

INFORMATION AND INDICTMENT[1]

Information

Both summary and indictable charges may be commenced by the laying of an information.[2] By definition, the information is a written complaint upon oath by a person stating that he or she has reasonable and probable grounds to believe that a person has committed an offence.[3] The information must be sworn before a justice of the peace who has no right to refuse to accept it, provided it complies with the formality requirements as set out in the *Criminal Code*.[4] In effect, the informant swearing out the information is stating in writing, under oath, that he or she believes that certain facts alleged to constitute an offence are true.

In practice, the usual informant who swears out an information in a criminal proceeding is a police officer. However, any citizen has the right to lay an information on any charge provided he or she meets certain formalities as set out in the *Criminal Code*.

Limitation by Time

One restriction on the laying of a criminal charge is the limitation period which accompanies specific offences. At common law (since a criminal trial was always initiated in the name of His Majesty and because it was presumed that the King could do no wrong), the laying of such charges was not restricted by time periods.[5] Although this common law principle is still in effect today, it has been modified and is now subject to a few statutory exceptions.

Generally, there is no time limit for the laying of an information charging an indictable *Criminal Code* offence, but there are exceptions for some indictable offences. For example, a charge for treason must

---

* B.A., St. Francis Xavier University, Antigonish, Nova Scotia; LL.B., Dalhousie Law School, Halifax, Nova Scotia; Provincial Court Judge for the Province of Nova Scotia.

be sworn within three years from the time it was committed.[6] In respect of summary conviction offences, or hybrid offences where the Crown wishes to proceed summarily, an information must be sworn out not later than six months after the subject matter of the proceedings arose unless the prosecution and defendant agree.[7] Prior to the recent amendment that now allows the charge to proceed summarily with consent, the prosecution often elected to proceed by indictment in hybrid offences where more than six months had passed before the laying of the information.

Formalities of Information

Before the justice of the peace hears the oath or affirmation on the taking of the information, he or she must be satisfied that the information is in the appropriate form,[8] and that it contains at least the following:

(a)   name, address and occupation of informant;
(b)   the date and place of the laying of the information;
(c)   the name of the accused and address (if known); and
(d)   a statement of the offence alleged, including the date of commission (the date of the offence is not restricted to a particular day, but may cover a time period), place of the offence (must be within the jurisdiction of the court that will subsequently hear the case), the substance of the offence, the name of the statute violated, and, though not mandatory, the section of the statute which has been violated.

If the person laying the charge refuses to take the solemn oath as to its truth, a solemn affirmation by that person affirming the truth of the allegations is sufficient.[9]

Ordinarily, where the information meets the time limit requirements and the formalities set out above, the justice has no discretion to reject the information. However, the consent of the Attorney General of Canada or the Attorney General of a province is required before some certain specific charges may be laid.[10]

Since an information is a "charging document," its primary purpose is to describe the offence alleged with such particularity as will inform an accused of the specific act or omission for which he is called upon to answer. Unless the charge is murder, the information may charge more than one individual and may contain more than one charge (called a "count"). Murder must not be joined with any other charge, other than charges arising from the same transaction as the murder charge, unless the accused consents.[11] Furthermore, since summary conviction offences cannot be tried together with indictable offences, they should not appear on the same information.

A justice, having accepted the information, has an inherent discretion to decide whether or not to issue process (a summons or warrant) requiring the accused to appear in a court to answer the charge. The justice is not required to issue process unless he or she is satisfied that there is evidence capable of belief to support the charge. For instance, the justice might refuse to issue process if, after hearing the complainant and other witnesses, the conclusion is reached that the charge is in effect, an abuse of the administration of justice. Where the justice is of the belief that a case has been made out for compelling the accused to attend before a justice in the same territorial division to answer to the charge, a summons may be issue to the accused to appear in court.[12] (The summons process will be discussed in the next section.)

In some instances, the justice may have reasonable and probable grounds to believe that it would be *in the public interest* to issue a warrant for the arrest of the accused.[13] An example of such a situation would be a case where the justice has information which indicates that the accused has no intention to appear in court and is in the process of making plans to leave the jurisdiction. However, it would only be in the most exceptional circumstances that a justice would issue a warrant for the arrest of an accused after an information has been laid.

Indictment

An indictment is also a charging document. However, in contrast to an information, an indictment is an unsworn document prepared by an Attorney General or his agent, or by a person who has the consent of the Attorney General.[14] The indictment is the document that commences proceedings in the Supreme Court where criminal trials are heard only in the case of indictable offences. As in the case of the information, the indictment, although unsworn, is a written accusation of a specific offence.[15]

Where the accused elects trial before any court other than a provincial court judge, an indictment is substituted for the information upon committal for trial. With the exception of an indictment charging the offence of murder,[16] the indictment may contain any number of charges or counts.[17] It may also contain charges founded on facts disclosed by the evidence at the preliminary inquiry, in addition to, or in substitution for, any charge for which the accused was committed for trial.[18] In the case of an indictment charging murder, unless the accused consents to the joinder of other counts, only counts that arise out of the same transaction as the murder count may be joined in the indictment.

SUMMONS AND SUBPOENA

Two of the most common methods of compelling an individual's attendance in court are by summons or subpoena.

Summons

A summons is a court order directed to an accused requiring his attendance at a specified time and place to answer to the charge as set out in the summons.[19] It may be issued by a justice after an information has been sworn alleging that the accused committed an offence.[20]

Under new changes to the *Criminal Code*, a justice who receives information from a private citizen alleging an offence is no longer automatically permitted to issue a summons or warrant to compel the appearance of the accused. Instead, the justice must refer the matter to a Provincial Court judge or in Quebec, a judge of the Court of Quebec, or to a designated justice, to consider whether to compel the appearance of the accused. The judge or designated justice may issue a summons or warrant only after being satisfied that the Attorney General has received a copy of the information and notice of the hearing. At the hearing, the justice must consider the allegations and evidence in deciding whether to issue the summons or warrant.[21]

The summons must be personally served on the person to whom it is directed by a peace officer,[22] unless he is unable to personally serve the document. In such a case, the peace officer may serve it on a person who appears to be at least 16 years of age and is residing at the accused's usual or last residence.[23]

The summons may be served upon an accused by a peace officer anywhere in Canada[24] and may be executed on any day including Sundays and statutory holidays.[25] Proof of service of the summons may be given by the peace officer either in his testimony before the court or by his sworn affidavit.[26] If the accused fails to attend court as required by the summons, the justice or judge may issue a warrant to cause the accused to be arrested and brought before that court.[27]

Subpoena

A subpoena, which literally means "under penalty of the court" is a court order directed to a person who is likely to give material evidence at trial requiring his attendance in court at a specified time and date.[28] It must be served on the witness in the same manner as a summons is served on an accused person.[29] The subpoena may also specify that the witness is not only required to attend court, but ordered as well to bring any documents in his or her possession or control.[30] This is known as a *subpoena duces tecum.*

After the subpoena has been served on a person, that witness is under court order to attend and remain until the completion of the proceeding or trial unless excused by the trial judge.[31] If any person fails to attend or remain in court following service of a subpoena, the judge or justice may issue a warrant for that person's arrest.[32] The judge or justice before whom a witness is brought pursuant to a warrant of arrest may order detention in custody[33] or release on a recognizance to appear and give evidence when required.

ARRAIGNMENT

The arraignment of an accused consists of calling the accused "to the bar" of the court to plead to the charge against him or her. It is an established practice which serves not only to make the accused aware of the charge he or she is called upon to answer, but also to identify the accused to the public.[34]

An accused is usually arraigned on the charge or charges in the information on his or her first appearance in court. The judge or the clerk of the court calls the accused by name and, on his or her appearance before the court, reads the charge contained in the information. If the alleged offence is a summary offence, or an indictable offence within the absolute jurisdiction of the provincial court judge or if the accused that is charged with an indictable offence elects to be tried by that court, the accused will be asked how he or she wishes to plead to the charge. In cases where the accused elects to be tried in Supreme Court by a judge or jury, he or she will be re-arraigned before that court provided that the accused is committed to stand trial. A preliminary inquiry (which was discussed in Chapter 12) may be held by the justice prior to the arraignment in Supreme Court at the request of either the Crown or the accused.

PLEA

After the arraignment or reading of the charge, the accused is called upon to "plead" to the charge or charges in the information or indictment. In this way, the accused person is able to state his position to the court.

An accused who is called upon to plead may plead guilty or not guilty, or enter one of the special pleas of *autrefois acquit* (that he has already been indicted, tried and acquitted for the same alleged offence), *autrefois convict* (that he has been formerly convicted of the same crime) or pardon.[35] If an accused refuses to plead, a not guilty plea is entered by the court.[36]

In early days, at common law, a person could not be tried until he entered a plea to the charges against him. If he refused to plead, the court would order that heavy weights of iron be placed on his chest and deny him food until he either agreed to plead or died. It is said that many deliberately chose to die rather than take the chance of being convicted as a felon and therefore have their lands taken away from them by the Crown.[37]

Where an accused pleads guilty, whether to the offence charged or with the consent of the Crown to an included offence, the trial judge may, in his or her discretion, accept the plea. Where the facts do not appear to support the charge, or where the accused makes a further statement which casts doubt on the acceptability of the plea, the judge may enter a not guilty plea and proceed to hold a trial. Recent amendments to the *Criminal Code* now require that the court may only accept a plea of guilty if it is satisfied that he or she is voluntarily admitting to the essential elements of the offence along with the accused's clear understanding that the court is not bound by any agreement between the accused and the prosecutor.[38]

The special pleas of *autrefois acquit, autrefois convict* and pardon are set out in the *Criminal Code*.[39] The first two pleas are based on one of the basic principles of criminal law: that no person is to be placed in jeopardy twice for the same or substantially the same matter. Thus, if he is charged again, he can plead his former conviction or acquittal as a complete defence to the second charge. In determining whether the special pleas of *autrefois acquit* or *autrefois convict* should succeed, the judge must decide whether there was a previous final acquittal or conviction on a charge which is substantially the same as the present one on the same factual transaction.[40] In the case of a plea of pardon as a bar to the prosecution of an offence, the judge would determine whether the accused had been previously granted a royal pardon either by the Cabinet or by Parliament for the same offence arising from the same set of facts.

PRESENCE OF THE ACCUSED

Pursuant to new amendments to the *Criminal Code*, the accused need not be personally present but may instead appear and enter a plea via closed circuit television by video and audio link as long as the parties can see each other and communicate simultaneously.[41]

Furthermore, the requirement that an accused be present for the whole of the trial has now been changed to allow that person to appoint counsel to represent him or her in routine court appearances even for indictable offences. However, the accused must be personally present for jury selection, *habeas corpus* applications, or when evidence is being taken.[42]

Notes

[1] For a detailed discussion of the trial process, see E.G. Ewaschuk, *Criminal Pleadings and Practice in Canada*, 2nd ed. (Aurora: Canada Law Book, 1987), and R.E. Salhany, *Canadian Criminal Procedure*, 6th ed. (Aurora: Canada Law Book, 1994).

[2] *Criminal Code*, R.S.C. 1985, c. C-46, ss. 504, 788(1).

[3] *Ibid.*

[4] See *Casey v. Automobiles Renault Canada Ltd.*, 1963 CarswellNS 35, [1964] 3 C.C.C. 208, 49 M.P.R. 154, 46 D.L.R. (2d) 665 (N.S. C.A.), at p. 222 [C.C.C.], *per* MacDonald J.

[5] Salhany, *supra*, note 1, at p. 10.

[6] *Criminal Code*, subs. 48(1).

[7] *Criminal Code*, subs. 786(2).

[8] *Criminal Code*, Form 2.

[9] *Canada Evidence Act*, R.S.C. 1985, c. C-5, ss. 14 and 15 stipulates the procedure for affirmation. See also *R. v. Walsh* (1978), 1978 CarswellOnt 1228, 45 C.C.C. (2d) 199 (Ont. C.A.).

[10] Examples of sections of the *Criminal Code* which require the consent of the Attorney General before commencing proceedings are s. 174(3) for the offence of nudity in a public place, and s. 136(3) for the offence of giving contradictory evidence in a judicial proceeding.

[11] *Criminal Code*, s. 589.

[12] *Criminal Code*, subs. 507(1)(*b*).

[13] *Criminal Code*, subs. 507(4).

[14] *Criminal Code*, ss. 566, 575, 577; Forms 3 and 4.

[15] See *R. v. Perrigo*, 1972 CarswellOnt 40, 10 C.C.C. (2d) 336, 20 C.R.N.S. 245 (Ont. Dist. Ct.) at 340 [C.C.C].

[16] *Criminal Code*, s. 589.

[17] *Criminal Code*, subs. 591(1).

[18] *Criminal Code*, subs. 574(1).

[19] *Criminal Code*, subs. 507(1)(*b*).

[20] *Criminal Code*, subs. 507(1).

[21] *Criminal Code*, s. 507.1.

[22] *Criminal Code*, subs. 509(2).

[23] *Criminal Code*, subs. 509(2).

[24] *Criminal Code*, s. 703.1.

[25] *Criminal Code*, s. 20.

[26] *Criminal Code*, subs. 509(3).

[27] *Criminal Code*, subs. 512(1), (2).

[28] *Criminal Code*, subs. 700(1).

[29] *Criminal Code*, subs. 701(1).

[30] *Criminal Code*, subs. 700(1).

[31] *Criminal Code*, subs. 700(2).

[32] *Criminal Code*, s. 705.

[33] *Criminal Code*, s. 706. The maximum period of detention is 30 days whereupon the prisoner must be brought before a superior court judge for review of the detention order; the total period of detention is not allowed to exceed 90 days—see also *Criminal Code*, s. 707.

[34] See J.F. Archbold, *Criminal Pleading, Evidence and Practice*, 40th ed., S. Mitchell and J.H. Buzzard, eds. (London: Sweet and Maxwell Ltd., 1979), at p. 214.

[35] *Criminal Code*, ss. 606(1) and 607(1).

[36] *Criminal Code*, subs. 606(2).

[37] See Salhany, *supra*, note 1, at 132-33.

[38] *Criminal Code*, subs. 606(1.1).

[39] *Criminal Code*, s. 607.

[40] *Criminal Code*, ss. 609 and 610; see also *R. v. Wright*, 1963 CarswellOnt 8, [1963] S.C.R. 539, [1963] 3 C.C.C. 201, 40 C.R. 261, 40 D.L.R. (2d) 563 (S.C.C.).

[41] *Criminal Code*, ss. 606(5) and 650.11.

[42] *Criminal Code*, s. 650.01.

15

The Adversary System of Justice

*The Honourable Judge John D. Embree**
(edited for 7th edition by *Joel E. Pink, Q.C.*)***

Other chapters in this book deal with "the players" in a criminal trial, the nature of our adversary system, and some basic principles of law that apply to the trial of a criminal charge. All of that will assist you in understanding the trial process, as discussed in this chapter. Once the accused is before the proper court,[1] has been arraigned, and has entered a plea of not guilty, the trial is ready to begin.

In general, there are three parts to a criminal trial, which we will call: (1) the case for the Crown; (2) the case for the defence; and (3) the court's decision or verdict. The largest portion of most criminal trials consists of the testimony of witnesses called by the Crown or defence. This chapter examines the trial process with emphasis on the method utilized to present evidence to the court through the testimony of the witnesses for each side.

THE CASE FOR THE CROWN

Where an accused is being tried by a court composed of a judge and jury, the usual first step is an opening address to the jury by the Crown Attorney. This address is to familiarize the jury with the facts of the offence alleged against the accused and usually entails a brief summary of the evidence that the Crown expects each of its witnesses to give. This gives the jury members some insight into how the case will proceed and allows them to grasp the significance of each witness's testimony in the larger scenario. After this introduction to the Crown's case, the Crown Attorney will then begin presenting evidence.

In trials where no jury is involved and the presiding judge will rule upon the accused's guilt or innocence, it is not normal procedure to

* B.A., Dalhousie University, Halifax, Nova Scotia; LL.B., Dalhousie Law School, Halifax, Nova Scotia; Judge of the Provincial Court, Province of Nova Scotia.
**B.A., Acadia University, Wolfville, Nova Scotia; LL.B., Dalhousie Law School, Halifax, Nova Scotia; practices law in Halifax, Nova Scotia.

have an opening address. Rather, the Crown will immediately commence presenting its evidence against the accused to the court.

Certain legal guidelines exist for the Crown's presentation of evidence. For example, the Crown has a general duty to call all material witnesses to the criminal actions alleged against the accused, regardless of whether their testimony is consistent with the accused's guilt or not. Likewise, the Crown has a duty not to hold back evidence that would assist an accused. However, the Crown has a wide discretion in determining what witnesses are material and there is certainly no duty on the Crown to call a witness whose credibility is questionable.[2]

Other guidelines to which the Crown must adhere concern the admissibility of evidence. Only certain types of evidence can be considered by a court and this is dealt with, in part, in Chapter 16, "Basic Principles of Evidence". As long as the Crown Attorney stays within the boundaries of these legal guidelines, he or she has the ultimate control over the Crown's presentation of the case. The Crown Attorney must always be mindful of the essential ingredients of the offence charged, because the Crown has the obligation to provide sufficient proof of each ingredient. For example, the case for the Crown must disclose when and where the alleged offence occurred (within certain parameters), the identity of any victim, and the identity of the accused as the perpetrator. All of these can be established by the various forms of evidence discussed in Chapter 16, "Basic Principles of Evidence".

All the evidence presented at a trial, including the testimony of any witnesses called, must be in the presence of the accused, since any accused has the right to be present during the whole of his or her trial.[3] The accused may, in certain circumstances, be available by electronic means where his or her physical presence is not practicable.[4] Except in special circumstances,[5] the public is entitled to attend any trial, as the proceedings against the accused must be held in open court. In addition to a court's limited power to exclude the public in certain cases, the court also has the authority to order that the identity of a victim in a sexual assault or gross indecency case not be published in any newspaper or broadcast on radio or television.[6]

While members of the public are free to attend most trials, a witness at that trial may not get the same opportunity. The Crown or defence can ask the court to exclude any witnesses until each is called upon to testify. While a trial judge has a discretion when deciding whether to grant such an application, it is normal for such a request to be granted. One of the usual reasons for the Crown or defence to make such a request is to ensure that several witnesses to the same event do not have their recollections influenced by hearing the descriptions given in the preceding testimony. Therefore, it is not uncommon for witnesses in a criminal trial to find themselves excluded from the courtroom, at least until their role as a witness is concluded.

When a witness is called to testify in a criminal trial, the usual procedure is for the witness to come forward and take an oath to tell the truth.[7] Once this is done, the witness occupies a position (either sitting or standing) in a "witness box" or "witness stand", which each person will occupy, in turn, when testifying.

The process of questioning the witness is now ready to begin. This process is called examination. There are various forms of examination depending on who is asking the questions. The party who calls the witness has the first opportunity to examine him or her and this is called direct examination or examination-in-chief. In the case for the Crown, when the Crown Attorney concludes his or her direct examination, then counsel for the accused is permitted to question the witness. This is called cross-examination. When cross-examination has ended, the Crown enjoys a limited right of redirect examination. A trial judge also has a certain latitude, either during or at the end of counsel's questions, to put his or her own questions to the witness. Each stage in the examination of a witness has its own legal requirements and restrictions. We will now consider the rules applicable to the proper questioning of a witness at each stage.

DIRECT EXAMINATION

In the case for the Crown, the witnesses for the Crown will be questioned first by the Crown Attorney in direct examination. The object of this is to obtain relevant information from the witness about the offence charged and/or the accused's involvement in it. With some exceptions,[8] witnesses can only testify (and hence can only be asked questions) about what they have perceived with their own senses. What did they hear? What did they see? The testimony given must be within the personal knowledge of the witness.

Any exhibits that the Crown wishes to place before the court will usually be introduced during direct examination of a witness who had contact with the item or can explain its significance.

The way questions are phrased on direct examination is restricted. There is a general prohibition against leading questions. A leading question is one that suggests the answer to the witness. Take, for example, the case of a witness who was called to testify that he observed A strike B with a club. That witness should not be asked "Did you see A walk up to B and strike him with a club?" Rather, the more appropriate question, after establishing the relevant time and place, would be "What did you see?"

The traditional explanation for this rule against leading questions is that such inquiries promote giving responses that are the most favourable to the party calling the witness. Such questions may also discourage a witness from giving an answer in his or her own words that he or she may consider to be more full and complete. (After all, part of a witness' oath stipulates that he or she tell "... the whole truth...")

However, the rule against leading questions does have certain exceptions. In practice, leading questions are objectionable only when they relate to the proof of issues material to the case. Therefore, it is permissible, and even preferable, for counsel to ask leading questions regarding subjects that are not in dispute or are merely introductory in nature.

In the case for the Crown, the Crown Attorney will continue to ask questions of each witness on direct examination until all the necessary information has been provided. The principal restrictions are that the questions must relate to matters relevant to the alleged offence and they must be put in the proper manner.

Sometimes it will be necessary for the Crown Attorney to do more than just ask proper questions to obtain the whole story from a witness. For instance, a witness may forget certain facts surrounding a particular incident or he or she may be unwilling to divulge those facts.

When a witness has difficulty remembering the circumstances of a particular occurrence, the witness may be asked questions designed to direct his or her mind to certain events (provided that the questions do not suggest the answer). Should this prove ineffective in assisting the witness' recollection, then certain materials can be provided to the witness to refresh his or her memory. For example, if the witness wrote down details of an event when those details were still fresh in her mind, the witness may be shown that earlier writing to refresh her memory. A slightly more involved procedure is also available, whereby a witness is shown written notes to assist him in giving testimony when he has no recollection at all of the events about which he is being questioned.

If a witness is being uncooperative on direct examination, the *Canada Evidence Act*[9] provides certain options that can be employed by the questioning lawyer. During the case for the Crown, the Crown Attorney can apply to the court for a declaration that a witness is adverse if that witness seems unfavourable by taking positions in his or her testimony that are contrary to the position advanced by the Crown.[10] If the court agrees that the witness is adverse, the Crown is then permitted to contradict that witness by other evidence or may seek to establish that the witness, at some other time, made a statement inconsistent with his or her testimony.[11] These provisions regarding adverse witnesses are an exception to the normal rule that the party calling a witness is not permitted to cast doubt upon the credibility of that witness.

Another related general rule of trial procedure is that the party calling a witness cannot cross-examine the witness. However, the court can allow the Crown or defence to cross-examine one of its witnesses if that witness, earlier, made a written statement that is inconsistent with the witness's testimony. This can be done even if the witness has not been shown to be adverse.[12]

CROSS-EXAMINATION

Upon the conclusion of the Crown's direct examination of a witness, the defence then has the right to ask questions of the witness in cross-examination. Cross-examination provides the defence with an opportunity to weaken or overcome any aspect of the witness's direct examination that favours the Crown. It also allows the defence to bring forward other information that may be beneficial.

The range and form of questioning on cross-examination is much broader than on direct. For instance, the restriction against asking leading questions does not apply. Therefore, questions asked by the defence may, and often do, suggest the answers sought. The scope of the permissible subject matter is also extended. Cross-examination is not limited to the subjects raised in the witness's direct examination. Defence counsel is free to ask anything about issues relevant to the alleged offence. This includes the witness's credibility and reliability. In general, credibility is a combination of all the factors that can make the witness believable. The strength of the witness's senses and memory are usually key factors. Does the witness have good eyesight or hearing and did he or she have a good opportunity to see or hear what the witness says he or she did? Is the witness intelligent? How long has it been since the date in question and why does the witness remember the relevant events? Such questioning is designed to cast doubt upon the correctness of any related statements made by the witness. (Can he or she be mistaken, confused, or perhaps overlooking something?)

Another key factor under the general umbrella of credibility is a witness's predisposition for being, or desiring to be, truthful. This is referred to as credit. Topics relevant to credit could, for example, include bad character (low reputation in the community or previous convictions)[13] and bias against the accused or toward the Crown.

The *Canada Evidence Act* allows for cross-examination of a witness on any previous statements made in writing by him or her;[14] if these are inconsistent, this also goes to credit.

Where two or more accused are jointly charged, the right of cross-examination arises equally to all of them and each defence counsel may cross-examine every Crown witness, if desired.

REDIRECT EXAMINATION

After a Crown witness has undergone cross-examination, the Crown has a limited right of redirect examination. This allows the Crown Attorney to question the witness on subjects or explanations that arose initially on cross-examination. Therefore, a judge will usually not permit the Crown to raise new matters on redirect examination or return to subjects already touched upon in direct examination unless it is felt that the failure to ask these questions earlier was an inadvertent omission by counsel. If new matters are raised on redirect examination, the court may permit additional cross-examination by the defence. When putting questions on redirect examination, however, the Crown Attorney is bound by the same rules that govern questioning in direct examination.

The case for the Crown proceeds in this fashion, witness after witness, until the Crown has presented all the evidence, including exhibits, that it wishes to present. Then the Crown will formally close its case.

THE CASE FOR THE DEFENCE

An accused in a criminal trial is entitled "to make full answer and defence personally or by counsel."[15] This permits the accused to utilize all legal means to answer the charge against him or her. The right to make full answer and defence allows the accused to call witnesses and to testify him- or herself, if the accused chooses.[16]

The right to make full answer and defence exists to protect an accused. However, the best interests of an accused in any particular case may dictate that no defence evidence of any kind is put forward. The Crown always carries the final burden of proof and the accused is always presumed innocent.[17]

Where the accused is being tried by a judge and jury, the defence has the opportunity at the start of its case (the same as the Crown does) to address the jury and briefly outline the evidence to be called. Counsel for the accused will then call the desired witnesses and the same process will ensue as occurred during the case for the Crown, with the roles reversed. Counsel for the accused will conduct direct examination followed by cross-examination of that witness by the Crown Attorney. Redirect examination, if any, then occurs.

This process continues for all defence witnesses, including the accused, if he or she testifies. The accused is not required to testify, and a court cannot interpret this as going to show guilt. However, certain restrictions on cross-examining the accused exist that do not apply to any other witnesses. For example, the Crown cannot question an accused so as to put his or her bad character in issue unless, on direct examination, he or she claimed to be a person of good character, in one or more respects.

An accused may be cross-examined as to any previous convictions.[18] The accused may make application to exclude evidence of his or her criminal record from being the subject of cross-examination.[19] The existence of any criminal record can be considered by a judge or jury in weighing the trustworthiness of the accused as a witness. However, such evidence cannot be used as a basis for concluding that, because he or she has committed other offences, the accused committed the offence with which he or she is charged. Thus, cross-examination suggesting that result is not proper. Any misdeeds or questionable actions committed by an accused in the past and which have not resulted in convictions are not normally allowable subjects for cross-examination, because such information is primarily evidence of bad character and can serve to prejudice an accused in the mind of a judge or juror.[20]

The conduct of the case for the defence is, within legal limits, the prerogative of the defence. Witnesses can be called in any order, and the accused, if called, can occupy any position in that order. While the defence is usually aware of the witnesses to be called by the Crown, and their purported testimony, the Crown is often not aware of what, if any, witnesses may be called by the defence. The exception to this might include where the defence is relying on an alibi witness and there is a general obligation to notify the Crown Attorney of this.

Once the defence has tendered all the witnesses and exhibits that it wishes, the case for the defence is then closed.

PRESENTATION OF FURTHER EVIDENCE

If relevant evidence has been presented during the case for the defence that the Crown could not have reasonably foreseen when it was presenting its own case, then the Crown may be permitted to call rebuttal evidence. Such evidence must serve to contradict or refute some portion of the defence evidence, but it cannot constitute a repetition of earlier Crown evidence. Evidence that was relevant while the Crown's case was proceeding, but which was not called by the Crown, cannot subsequently form proper rebuttal evidence. However, if the evidence has only become relevant as a result of testimony or exhibits tendered by the defence, then it may constitute legitimate rebuttal.

Since credibility is a relevant factor when cross-examining witnesses, questions may be asked about matters that do not relate to the commission of the offence charged. However, the Crown is usually not permitted to call additional evidence to rebut the responses given to such questions because these may be considered collateral matters and not the proper subject of rebuttal evidence.[21]

The questioning of witnesses called on rebuttal follows the same direct examination, cross-examination, and redirect examination format that applies to any other witness.

At any time during the presentation of testimony in a criminal trial, the presiding judge has the right to ask questions of a witness. Usually such questions are designed to clarify matters that may be unclear in the judge's mind. Both the Crown Attorney and defence counsel are entitled to pursue their direct and cross-examinations with only minimal interference from the bench (assuming these examinations are carried out properly). In asking questions, a judge must act very carefully since he or she may not yet have heard all the circumstances of the case and an inappropriate question or a question put at an inappropriate time can interfere with the presentation of evidence by one side or the other.

A judge must not only be unbiased, but must also appear to be unbiased. Therefore it is inappropriate for a judge to appear to favour one party through any questioning of witnesses. However, situations may arise where the interests of justice require certain information to come out and the trial judge has the power to make the necessary inquiries.

VERDICT

Once the Crown and defence have both closed their cases and any rebuttal evidence is heard, both sides make their closing arguments.[22] If the trial is before a judge and jury, closing remarks will be made to the jury, followed by the trial judge's address on the relevant legal principles the jury must apply. (If the trial is before a judge alone, this last stage is eliminated and counsel address their arguments to the bench.)

In arriving at a verdict, a judge or jury must determine what the facts are in the particular case. This involves an assessment of which testimony is believable and which may not be. Every offence has certain necessary legal components and the judge or jury must consider the facts in light of these and determine whether the accused has been proven guilty beyond a reasonable doubt.[23]

If the Crown has satisfied the onus upon it, the judge's or jury's verdict will be "guilty as charged". The verdict will be "not guilty" if a reasonable doubt exists about the accused's guilt, either because of the sufficiency of the evidence or because of a legal defence that entitles the accused to an acquittal.

In addition to the options of guilty or not guilty, some criminal charges carry within them lesser offences for which an accused may be convicted if the Crown has established all of their essential elements but not all the ingredients of the more serious charge.[24]

Where the evidence does not disclose the commission of the offence charged, but does establish an attempt to commit that offence, then the accused may be convicted of attempting to commit the offence.[25]

In a trial by judge and jury, the jury will retire to a separate room to deliberate on the evidence and the trial judge's directions. The court will then adjourn until the jury has reached its verdict.[26] When court resumes and the jury verdict is made known, no reasons for that verdict are given.

When the trial is before a judge alone, it is not necessary for the judge to render his or her verdict immediately. The judgment can be reserved and given at a later date.[27] When the verdict is delivered, it is normal for the trial judge to give reasons for his or her decision.

If the verdict is not guilty, then the accused is discharged and the proceedings terminate. If the accused is convicted of the full offence or some lesser offence, the court is then required to consider an appropriate sentence. This process is dealt with in Chapter 19, "Sentencing Powers and Principles".

Notes

[1] What constitutes a proper court in each case is discussed in Chapter 4, "Classification of Criminal Offences"; Chapter 12, "Courts"; and Chapter 18, "The Jury Trial".

[2] Two Supreme Court of Canada decisions that discuss the Crown's responsibility in this regard are: *R. v. Lemay*, 1951 CarswellBC 4, 14 C.R. 89, 102 C.C.C. 1, [1952] 1 S.C.R. 232 (S.C.C.); and *R. v. Wu*, 1934 CarswellBC 102, 62 C.C.C. 90, [1934] 4 D.L.R. 459, [1934] S.C.R. 609 (S.C.C.).

[3] *Criminal Code*, R.S.C. 1985, c. C-46, subs. 650(1).

[4] *Criminal Code*, subs. 650(1.1) and (1.2).

[5] Subsection 486(1) of the *Criminal Code* requires that all proceedings against an accused be held in open court except where the presiding judge "is of the opinion that it is in the interest of public morals, the maintenance of order or the proper administration of justice, or that it is necessary to prevent injury to International relations or National Defence or National Security, to exclude all or any members of the public from the court room for all or part of the proceedings..."

[6] *Criminal Code*, subs. 486(3).

[7] Certain exceptions to this process exist that permit a witness to take an affirmation rather than an oath. In some circumstances, such as where child witnesses are concerned, it may be necessary for the witness to give unsworn testimony. See *Canada Evidence Act*, R.S.C. 1985, c. C-5, ss. 13, 14, 15, 16.

[8] See Chapter 16, "Basic Principles of Evidence".

[9] R.S.C. 1985, c. C-5.

[10] See two cases decided by the Ontario Court of Appeal, namely *Hanes v. Wawanesa Mutual Insurance Co.*, 1961 CarswellOnt 116, [1963] 1 C.C.C. 176, 28 D.L.R. (2d) 386, [1961] O.R. 495 (Ont. C.A.), reversed 1963 CarswellOnt 61, [1963] 1 C.C.C. 321, 36 D.L.R. (2d) 718, [1963] S.C.R. 154 (S.C.C.); and *R. v. Cassibo*, 1982 CarswellOnt 850, 70 C.C.C. (2d) 498, 39 O.R. (2d) 288 (Ont. CA.).

[11] *Canada Evidence Act*, subs. 9(1).

[12] *Canada Evidence Act*, subs. 9(2).

[13] *Canada Evidence Act*, s. 12.

[14] *Canada Evidence Act*, s. 10.

[15] *Criminal Code*, subs. 650(3).

[16] The accused always has a choice about whether or not to testify. The Crown cannot compel him or her to be a witness.

[17] See Chapter 3, "Basic Principles of Criminal Law". It may be that the Crown has the benefit of certain presumptions or provisions that place some onus on the accused. These need to be considered when deciding whether or not to call defence evidence.

[18] *Canada Evidence Act*, s. 12.

[19] *R. v. Corbett*, 1988 CarswellBC 756, 1988 CarswellBC 252, 41 C.C.C. (3d) 385, 64 C.R. (3d) 1, [1988] 1 S.C.R. 670, [1988] 4 W.W.R. 481, 85 N.R. 81, 28 B.C.L.R. (2d) 145, 34 C.R.R. 54 (S.C.C.).

[20] Similar fact evidence is an exception. A court can permit cross-examination of an accused concerning possible prior improper conduct if the conduct is sufficiently similar to be relevant on the issue of whether this accused committed the criminal act with which he or she is currently charged.

[21] The prohibition against rebutting collateral matters does have certain exceptions. The Crown would be permitted to prove the accused has a criminal record if the accused denied it. If the Crown could establish that the accused had previously made a statement that contradicts his or her present testimony, such evidence could constitute proper rebuttal. If the defence has put the good character of the accused in issue during its case, the Crown is also entitled to rebut that.

[22] The order in which closing arguments are made depends on whether or not the accused has called evidence. By virtue of subs. 651(3) of the *Criminal Code*, counsel for the accused is entitled to address the court last if no defence witnesses have been called. Otherwise, the Crown Attorney is entitled to address the court last.

[23] In doing that, the judge or jury will consider the relevant aspects discussed in Chap-

ter 16, "Basic Principles of Evidence", and Chapter 8, "Guilty in Fact—Not Guilty
  in Law".
24 *Criminal Code*, s. 662.
25 *Criminal Code*, s. 660.
26 Any jury verdict must be unanimous. If the jury members cannot all agree, after fair
  and complete deliberation, then a new trial will be held.
27 *Criminal Code*, subs. 645(4).

16

The Basic Principles of Evidence

The Honourable Judge Brian D. Williston*

As described in Chapter 15, our system of justice in Canada is an "adversarial system" in which a party presents the evidence to support his or her version of the facts and the judge acts as an impartial arbiter to hear and determine the issues. Furthermore, the judge, in his or her discretion, determines whether the evidence sought to be introduced is admissible. The common law attaches great importance, particularly in criminal cases, to the use or purpose for which evidence may be considered. Therefore, to ensure that an accused person receives a fair trial, rules of evidence have been developed over the years to assist judges in their determination of what evidence will be allowed in a criminal trial.

DIRECT AND CIRCUMSTANTIAL EVIDENCE

In a criminal trial, evidence may be adduced which is either direct evidence, or circumstantial evidence, or a combination of both.

Direct evidence is evidence that applies directly to the essential facts which the Crown must prove in order to establish the guilt of the accused. If a witness gives evidence that he saw A shoot B, this is direct evidence that A shot B.

Circumstantial evidence is evidence of a fact or facts which, taken together, are of such a nature that the guilt of an accused may be inferred.[1] If a witness gives evidence that he found a gun in A's possession, and it is proven that a bullet removed from B's body had been fired from that same gun, this is circumstantial evidence which may lead to the inference that A shot B.

Both direct evidence and circumstantial evidence are equally admissible in a criminal trial to prove the guilt of an accused person.[2] However, because of the inherent danger of drawing an incorrect inference from circumstantial evidence, the law directs that certain guidelines must be followed. The law is clear that an accused must not be

* B.A., St. Francis Xavier University, Antigonish, Nova Scotia; LL.B., Dalhousie Law School, Halifax, Nova Scotia; Provincial Court Judge for the Province of Nova Scotia.

convicted on circumstantial evidence alone unless that evidence leads to the conclusion that the accused is guilty of the offence charged and is inconsistent with any other rational conclusion.[3]

The reason for this rule is readily apparent. A person should not be convicted of a crime on a mere guess or suspicion. Therefore, the judge or jury trying the case must be very careful in drawing an inference of guilt from circumstantial evidence. Former Chief Justice McRuer of the Supreme Court of Canada summed up the reason for the special treatment given to circumstantial evidence in this way:

> The rule makes it clear that the case is to be decided on the facts, that is, the facts proved in evidence, and the conclusions alternative to the guilt of the accused must be rational conclusions based on inferences drawn from proven facts. No conclusion can be a rational conclusion that is not founded on evidence. Such a conclusion would be a speculative, imaginative conclusion, not a rational one.[4]

RELEVANCY

For evidence to be admissible in a criminal trial, it must first and foremost be relevant to the case. All evidence which is irrelevant is therefore inadmissible. This however, was not always so. At one time, substitutes such as trial by ordeal or battle or by oath, where the function of swearers was not to present evidence but simply to swear for or against the accused, were the means by which guilt or innocence was proven.

Under our present rule of law, the guilt or innocence of an accused is determined in a criminal trial in which only evidence relevant to that determination is allowed. It is the duty of the trial judge to ensure that the evidence which is presented is relevant to the issue of whether the accused is guilty of the offence with which he is charged.

A leading judicial pronouncement on relevancy was made by Mr. Justice Dickson of the Supreme Court of Canada in his decision in *Graat v. R.*:[5]

> Admissibility is determined, first, by asking whether the evidence sought to be admitted is relevant. This is a matter of applying logic and experience to the circumstances of the particular case. The question which must then be asked is whether, though probative, the evidence must be excluded by a clear ground of policy or of law.

Since relevancy is simply defined as whatever is logically probative or whatever accords with common sense, it is in the discretion of the trier of fact in the case to determine whether the evidence is relevant or not.[6]

In some cases, counsel for the Crown or the defence may introduce evidence which does not appear relevant in the first instance, with the expectation that further evidence will unfold which will establish the relevancy of the earlier evidence. In such a case, the judge may allow the evidence to be presented as being "tentatively relevant" until further evidence establishes the relevancy of the earlier evidence.[7]

HEARSAY AND BASIC EXCEPTIONS

The rule against hearsay is one of the most misunderstood and misapplied rules of evidence.[8] Objections to what counsel refer to as "hearsay" cause vigorous debate during criminal trials.

Hearsay is commonly understood as a statement of fact made by a person who did not personally witness the fact, but was told about it by someone else. The hearsay rule was developed because our "adversarial system" depends on the right of counsel to cross-examine the witnesses produced by his opponent and thereby test their credibility.

If the reporting of a fact during a trial were to be given, not by the person who had first-hand knowledge, but through the testimony of another person repeating that person's description, the opposing counsel would be denied the opportunity of exposing imperfections in the absent person's perception, memory and sincerity. The reliability of the statement can only be tested if the person is in the courtroom and subject to cross-examination and under oath.

Of course, the factors which might render an out-of-court statement by an unreliable person should only be of concern when that statement is tendered for the purpose of establishing the truth of the matter stated. If witness A recounts under oath what citizen B told him, this may or may not be hearsay evidence, depending on the questioner's intention. The clearest explanation of the rule is without doubt that of the House of Lords in *Subramaniam v. Public Prosecutor*:[9]

> Evidence of a statement made to a witness by a person who is not himself called as a witness may or may not be hearsay. It is hearsay and inadmissible when the object of the evidence is to establish the truth of what is contained in the statement. It is not hearsay and is admissible when it is proposed to establish by the evidence, not the truth of the statement, but the fact that it was made.

Where a witness testifies as to what another person told him or her and that testimony is offered merely to prove the fact that it was said, rather than its truth, that evidence would not be excluded by the trial judge. The remarks so reported by the witness would not constitute evidence that what was said was true; only one thing would be established: that the remarks were, in fact, made. The remarks might serve to indicate the state of mind of the person who originally made them or might assist the trier of fact in understanding the witness' subsequent attitude or actions.[10]

From this analysis of the basis for the hearsay rule, one might conclude that all out-of-court statements will be excluded from evidence if offered to the court for the purpose of establishing the truth of the matter stated. However, the rule against hearsay is not an absolute one and many exceptions have become well established in law.

Basic Exceptions to the Hearsay Rule

The purpose of the hearsay rule is to ensure the trustworthiness and accuracy of evidence by subjecting the person who made the out-of-court statement to cross-examination in court. Many of the exceptions to the hearsay rule can be explained on the basis that although the adversary is denied the right to cross-examine the person who made the remarks, the out-of-court statement was made under conditions which promote sincerity and accurateness to such a degree that the statement should be received in evidence.

The most common exceptions to the hearsay rule are the following:

1. *Dying Declarations.* The circumstances under which the declaration is made are so solemn that there is a degree of trustworthiness attached, even though the declarant is not available for cross-examination. In criminal cases such declarations are only admissible providing the offence charged is murder, manslaughter or criminal negligence causing death. Furthermore, the declarant must have had a settled expectation of death and the statement must be one relating to the cause of death.[11]

2. *Out-of-Court Statement by Accused.* Subject to being tested as to voluntariness, such statements may be admitted as evidence of declarations made against penal interest.[12] (See below, Confessions, Statements and Admissions, for a more detailed discussion of these statements.)

3. *Statements in Performance of Duty by a Deceased Person.* If a person now deceased had made records in the course of business which he was required to make and had no personal interest in the matter, those records might be admitted as evidence. Their accuracy and sincerity could be reasonably

expected where the deceased was under an obligation to faithfully discharge his duties at the time of making the record.[13]

4. *Public Documents.* The law places a great deal of confidence in public officers who are expected and trusted to perform their duties with such accuracy and sincerity that their records may be allowed in evidence at the discretion of the trial judge.[14]

5. *Statutory Exceptions.* The *Canada Evidence Act* allows the introduction of government records, business documents, and records kept by financial institutions provided that certain formalities are met without requiring the attendance in court of the person who made the record or document.[15]

In a series of decisions, notably *R. v. Khan*,[16] *R. v. Smith*,[17] and *R. v. B. (K.G.)*,[18] the Supreme Court of Canada has now recognized a further conceptual framework of hearsay exceptions. In *Smith*, Chief Justice Lamer makes a number of observations relating to the admission of hearsay evidence when he states:

> The decision of this court in *Khan*, therefore, should be understood as the triumph of a principled analysis over a set of ossified judicially created categories.
>
> . . .
>
> What is important, in my view, is the departure signaled by *Khan* from a view of hearsay characterized by a general prohibition on the reception of such evidence, subject to a limited number of defined categorical exceptions, and a movement toward an approach governed by the principles which underlie the rule and its exceptions alike.[19]

As to the issue of *reliability and necessity* set out in the *R. v. Khan* decision, the Chief Justice went on to say:

> The criterion of "reliability" — or, in Wigmore's terminology, the circumstantial guarantee of trustworthiness — is a function of the circumstances under which the statement in question was made.
>
> If a statement sought to be adduced by way of hearsay evidence is made under circumstances which substantially negate the possibility that the declarant was untruthful or mistaken, the hearsay evidence may be said to be "reliable", *i.e.*, a circumstantial guarantee of trustworthiness is established. The evidence of the infant complainant in *Khan* was found to be reliable on this basis.[20]

Later Chief Justice Lamer added:

> hearsay evidence of statements made by persons who are not available to give evidence at trial ought generally to be admissible, where the circumstances under which the statements were made satisfy the criteria of necessity and reliability set out in *Khan*, and subject to the residual discretion of the trial judge to exclude the evidence when its probative value is slight and undue prejudice might result to the accused.[21]

OPINIONS

Witnesses testifying in a criminal trial are usually confined to giving evidence of facts which are founded on personal observation and are not allowed to give evidence by way of opinion.[22] The opinion rule shares common roots with the rule against hearsay. A witness whose testimony was not based on facts which were personally observed would only be guessing or speculating about the facts of the case.[23]

Opinion Evidence from Lay Persons

The modern opinion rule does allow persons who qualify as "experts" to testify concerning their opinions about knowledge within their areas of expertise. The courts have relaxed the rule somewhat even for the ordinary lay witness in certain areas of evidence. The lay person will be allowed to give opinion evidence on personal observation regarding:[24]

(a) identity of persons or things;
(b) handwriting;
(c) mental or physical condition;
(d) intoxication;
(e) value;
(f) speed.[25]

Opinion Evidence from the Expert Witness

The "expert" witness may be allowed to give opinion evidence where he or she possesses special knowledge greater than the jury that will assist them in their deliberations.[26] Before a witness is allowed to give an expert opinion, the court must be satisfied that the witness has special knowledge or skill relating to the matter on which his opinion is being sought.[27] The witness need not have taken a recognized course of study to be so qualified. It is sufficient, if by training and practice, he has acquired a good knowledge of the subject of which he is testifying and has the practical ability to use his judgment in that regard.[28]

Before a witness can be presented to the jury as an expert, the court must hear evidence concerning that person's qualifications.[29] The procedure followed in determining whether a person will be permitted to give expert opinion involves an examination of the witness on the witness stand. Counsel presenting the witness adduces evidence in two stages: (a) an outline of the field in which the witness is sought to be qualified, and (b) evidence from the witness as to his special knowledge and practical application of that knowledge. Usually included in such an examination is the number of times that the witness has been qualified previously as an expert in the various courts. Of course, the opposing counsel has the right to cross-examine the witness respecting his so-called qualifications in the area which is the subject matter of the inquiry. In all cases an expert opinion may not be given unless the witness is shown to have such skill, experience or knowledge in his particular field as to make it appear that his opinion would rest on a substantial foundation and would tend to assist the trier of the facts in the search for the truth.

No matter how well qualified the expert witness may be, this, in itself, is not enough to enable that person to express an opinion in a criminal trial. There must also be a factual basis for the opinion, and the jury should be aware of the facts upon which the opinion is predicated in order that they may properly evaluate it.[30]

The expert witness must base his or her opinion on facts established by the evidence. The facts may be presented in two ways: (a) the expert may furnish the basic evidence if he or she has personal knowledge, or (b) the facts may be presented by other witnesses. In the latter case, the facts already in evidence from other witnesses would be incorporated into a hypothetical question and presented to the expert as his basic premise. The opinion elicited on hypothetical facts would, of course, be based on the assumption that the other witnesses' testimony is true.

The question as to whether the facts upon which expert testimony is based are true rests entirely with the judge or jury trying the case. Furthermore, although the trier of fact is required to consider any expert testimony presented during the trial, he is not bound to accept it and may follow his own opinion as to what weight, if any, he will give to that evidence.[31]

Recent changes to the *Criminal Code* now provide that a party who intends to have an expert witness testify must give notice of that intention to the other party at least 30 days before the trial begins or within any other period of time set down by the judge. The notice must include the name of the witness and his or her qualifications. If the witness is being called by the prosecution, a copy of the expert's report must also be provided. If there is no report, a summary of the expert's opinion must be provided to the defence.[32]

CONFESSIONS, STATEMENTS AND ADMISSIONS

Statements made out-of-court by an accused are technically a form of "hearsay" evidence when introduced by the Crown in a criminal trial. However, such statements are one of the exceptions to the general ban on hearsay evidence as statements against interest made by a party-litigant.[33]

A statement or confession may be oral or written. A statement that is made by an accused person to someone in authority (*e.g.*, a police officer) is often the most critical evidence in a criminal trial. An out-of-court statement by an accused is often the link which enables the Crown to establish an otherwise weak case beyond a reasonable doubt.

The Voluntariness Rule

For the accused person's out-of-court statement to a person in authority to be admissible as evidence against the accused, the Crown must demonstrate beyond a reasonable doubt that it was free and voluntary. This requirement of voluntariness has a long-standing tradition in English common law. In Canada, the leading statement which has been accepted as the rule governing the admissibility of such statements was the opinion given by Lord Sumner of the Privy Council in the 1914 case of *Ibrahim v. R.* and reaffirmed more recently in the year 2000 in the Supreme Court of Canada's decision in *R. v. Oickle*:[34]

> It has long been established as a positive rule of English criminal law, that no statement by an accused is admissible in evidence against him unless it is shewn by the prosecution to have been a voluntary statement, in the sense that it has not been obtained from him either by fear of prejudice or hope of advantage exercised or held out by a person in authority. The principle is as old as Lord Hale.

Confessions which are forced from an accused by violence or threats of violence or induced by promises of special treatment are not admissible as evidence. Rejection of the evidence must follow if the words or acts of a person in authority might reasonably be believed to have induced the accused to make a statement under the apprehension of harm or advantage. The theory for the rejection of such confessions is that if they are made under such conditions, they are untrustworthy.

The *Voir Dire*

The question of whether a statement made by an accused is admissible is determined by the presiding judge during a process known as a *voir dire*.[35] The *voir dire* is a hearing which is held during the course of the trial to determine the admissibility of evidence such as a statement of the accused. If the trial is one which is being held before a jury, the members of the jury are excluded from the courtroom until the judge makes a decision regarding the admissibility of the evidence which is being tested during the *voir dire*.

The admissibility of the accused's statement is dependent on the prosecution's proof of voluntariness during the *voir dire*. All the surrounding circumstances concerning the taking of the statement must be investigated by the court before a confession can be ruled voluntary. In assessing the circumstances in which the statement was made, the judge may consider, for example, whether the customary police warning was given, whether promises or threats were made by word or conduct, whether the detention of the accused was of undue duration and whether there has been a violation of the accused's fundamental rights under the *Charter of Rights*.

Inculpable and Exculpable Statements

The guidelines governing the admissibility of confessions apply to both inculpatory (incriminating) and exculpatory (tending not to incriminate) statements.[36] The reason for this non-distinction is that statements which were exculpatory at the time they were made may become inculpatory at the trial. For example, when an accused is arrested for a sexual assault, he may state that has never seen the complainant before and does not know her. This is an exculpatory statement. During the trial, there may be overwhelming evidence from exhibits or from eye witnesses which firmly establish that the accused had been with the complainant. Realizing that the statement cannot stand, the accused testifies that he met the complainant that day but did not sexually assault her. The "exculpatory" statement becomes important now and may be considered as incriminating evidence against the accused.

Persons in Authority

In order for the voluntariness rule to be applied to a statement, it is first of all necessary that it be made to a person in authority, such as a police officer.[37] Statements made by an accused to persons other than "persons in authority" are admissible without proof of voluntariness. The courts have considered as persons in authority anyone whom the accused might reasonably believe to be in a position to affect the course of a prosecution against him.[38] The test as to who is considered a person in authority is therefore a subjective one. In addition to police officers, the accused's employer, school principal, private detectives, insurance adjusters and victims of the crime are examples of persons who have been held to be persons in authority. If in making the statement the accused is unaware that he is making it to a person in authority, such as an undercover police officer, the voluntariness rule does not apply.[39] However, there are other considerations discussed below which may still render such a statement inadmissible as evidence.

Additional Considerations

Judgments from our highest court have extended the rules governing the admissibility of statements by an accused. The Supreme Court of Canada has held that a free and voluntary statement might still be excluded from a trial if the person making the statement was in such a condition that his statements could not be considered "the utterances of an operating mind."[40] In a further decision of that court, it was held that if a person was so incapacitated (such as by drunkenness) that he was not aware of what he was saying and, due to that condition, was not aware of the consequences of making the statement, the statement should not be admissible as evidence despite its "voluntariness".[41]

Therefore, in ascertaining whether the prosecution has discharged its burden of proving that the confession is legally admissible, the judge must examine all the circumstances in which the out-of-court statement has been obtained. In addition to requiring that the prosecution prove that no person in authority made any promises or threats, the judge must be satisfied beyond a reasonable doubt that there was not any atmosphere of oppression created, and that the confession constitutes the statement of a person in full command of his intellectual faculties.

The Supreme Court of Canada held that a person detained by the state in the course of the criminal process has the absolute right to choose whether to speak with the police or remain silent.[42] The court held that the scope of that right must extend to exclude statements obtained by police "tricks" which deprive suspects of the ability to freely exercise this choice. In that court case the accused had been arrested by the police for an armed robbery. After consulting with his lawyer, the accused indicated to the investigating police officers that he did not wish to give them a statement. He was then placed in a jail cell with an undercover police officer who tricked him into giving damaging information. The Supreme Court held that the police had overstepped the fine line between their duty to investigate crime and the right of an accused to remain silent. By their charade the police had induced the accused to unwittingly give them a statement although he had earlier declined to speak to them. Accordingly, the statement was ruled inadmissible.

TYPES OF WITNESSES

An important feature of criminal trials in Canada as well as other common law countries is the right to call witnesses who are likely to give material evidence concerning the case.

There are many types of witnesses in a criminal trial. The various types of witnesses include sworn and unsworn witnesses, children, spouses, accomplices, the accused, lay and expert witnesses.[43]

Sworn and Unsworn Witnesses

Formerly, at common law, a witness was not permitted to give evidence unless it was under oath.[44] By definition an oath was a statement by a person that he would tell the truth and an appeal to God to witness the truth of his testimony. The courts were concerned with binding the conscience of the witness and an oath was considered essential for that purpose. Today, however, everyone is presumed to be competent to testify either under oath,[45] by solemn affirmation[46] or, in the case of persons under 14 years of age, on a promise to tell the truth.[47]

Child Witnesses

Recent changes to the *Canada Evidence Act* have enacted a presumption that a witness under the age of 14 years has the capacity to testify.[48] This change also directs that a witness under 14 years of age not take an oath or solemn declaration and that such evidence be received if the witness is able to understand and respond to questions and promises to tell the truth.

If a party challenges the capacity of the proposed child witness to understand and respond to questions, that party has the burden of satisfying the court that there is an issue to be tried. If the court is satisfied that there is an issue to be tried, the Judge will conduct an inquiry to determine the child's ability to understand and respond to questions. During the process of making that determination, no question may be asked of the child as to his understanding of the nature of the promise to tell the truth.

If the evidence of the child witness is received by the court, it has the same effect as if taken under oath.

Witness Whose Capacity is in Question

If a party challenges the mental capacity of a witness of 14 years of age or older to testify, and satisfies the court that there is an issue to be tried, the court must conduct an inquiry to detemine whether that person understands the nature of an oath or solemn affirmation and whether the person is able to communicate the evidence.[49] If the court determines that the witness does not understand the nature of an oath or solemn declaration but is able to communicate the evidence, the witness may testify on a promise to tell the truth. However, the witness shall not testify of the court finds that the witness neither understands the nature of an oath or solemn declaration and is unable to communicate the evidence.

Persons with Disabilities

Recent amendments to the *Canada Evidence Act* state that if a witness has difficulty communicating to the court by reason of a physical disability, the judge may order that the person be permitted to give evidence by any means that enables the evidence to be intelligible. Furthermore, if a witness with a mental disorder who has the required capacity to give evidence but has difficulty communicating to the court due to a disability, the judge may permit the witness to give the evidence by any means that allows the evidence to be intelligible. Before making this decision, the court may hold an inquiry to determine if the means by which the witness may be permitted to give evidence is necessary and reliable.[50]

The new amendments also make it clear that a witness may give evidence on the identity of an accused whom the witness is able to identify visually or in any other sensory manner.[51]

Spouses

A spouse (the wife or husband of the accused) is not a competent or compellable witness for the prosecution except in specific cases allowed at common law and by the *Canada Evidence Act*.[52]

At one time under the common law a spouse was not competent to give evidence either for or against the other except in cases of offences against the person or liberty of the other.[53] This common law position was changed by legislation which allows the spouse to be a competent witness for the defence in all cases.

Further statutory enactments expanded the common law exemptions wherein a spouse is declared not only competent but compellable as a witness for the prosecution against the accused.[54] Therefore, the present law in Canada allows a wife or husband to be compelled to testify as a witness where the alleged offence comes within one of the exceptions enumerated in the *Canada Evidence Act*. Prosecutors are now permitted to call the spouses as witnesses in such cases as alleged child abuse and sexual assault.

Accomplices and Co-accused

A co-accused jointly charged with an accused cannot be called by the prosecution as a witness in the trial.[55] However, this rule only applies when the accused persons are tried together. When the accused persons are tried separately, each co-accused may be compelled by the prosecution to give evidence against the other.[56] Similarly, an accomplice, if not charged, is a competent and compellable witness for the prosecution against the accused.

Accused as Witness

In common law, an accused person was not considered a competent witness and therefore was not allowed to give evidence during his trial.[57] Legislation has removed the common law disqualification of an accused's evidence and gives a person charged with an offence the right to testify on his own behalf during the trial.[58] However, the accused may not be compelled by the prosecution to give evidence and the failure to testify even on his or her own behalf cannot be referred to during any proceeding.

Lay Witness

The lay witness or ordinary witness may testify concerning facts which he personally observed or experienced. The lay witness may also be permitted to give "opinion evidence" on facts which were observed or experienced by him and that opinion is of a type that persons without special training in such matters are qualified to make on the basis of their everyday knowledge or experience. For example, the non-expert lay witness may be allowed to give opinion evidence on the identification of handwriting, persons and things, apparent age, the physical and mental state of a person, intoxication, the condition of things, certain questions of value and estimates of speed and distance. (For more background in this area, see OPINIONS above.)

Expert Witness

If a person is accepted by the court as an "expert witness," that person may be allowed to give opinion evidence where he possesses special knowledge or skill relating to the matter on which the opinion is being sought. (For a more detailed discussion of the expert witness, see OPINIONS above.)

EXHIBITS

Exhibits are documents or materials which are produced and introduced to a court during a trial. They are used as proof of facts which form the subject matter of the trial. In practice, before an exhibit is referred to in a criminal trial, it is marked by the clerk of the court for identification in the court proceeding. The general rules governing the admissibility of evidence also apply to exhibits. If an exhibit produced by a litigant in a trial offends any of the exclusionary rules of evidence, it will be excluded by the trial judge just as any other type of inadmissible evidence.

The proof of continuity or the "chain of possession" of an exhibit is a very important factor when an exhibit is being tendered during a trial as evidence. Evidence must be heard which will serve to identify the exhibit and relate it to the subject matter of the proceeding. However, even though in some cases the party tendering the exhibit is unable to prove an unbroken chain of possession prior to its introduction in court, the exhibit may still be admissible as evidence provided it does not offend other exclusionary rules.[59] Failure to prove continuity of the exhibit is nevertheless an important consideration which can have a devastating effect on the weight that the judge or jury may give to that piece of evidence.

The "best evidence rule" applies to exhibits as well. Unless allowed by statute or unless there are exceptional circumstances, the court may accept only an original and not a copy as an exhibit. However, unless barred by a specific statute, where a litigant can account for the absence of original evidence, then, in the absence of bad faith or fraud, secondary evidence of that material may be admissible.[60]

Where an exhibit (such as photographs of the deceased in a murder trial) might have an inflammatory effect, it will nevertheless be admitted into evidence unless it is of minimal probative value in comparison to its prejudicial effect.[61]

CREDIBILITY

A very important element in the testimony of every witness is that person's credibility.[62] It is credibility which determines whether a person's testimony will be accepted or rejected by the trier of fact in a criminal case.

The role of the judge or jury hearing the case is to weigh and assess the evidence carefully as it unfolds. In order to gauge the witnesses' credibility, the trier of the facts must consider a number of factors.

In *R. v. White*, Mr. Justice Estey of the Supreme Court of Canada expressed his views with regard to instructions that should be given to juries by trial judges concerning the credibility of witnesses:

> The issue of credibility is one of fact and cannot be determined by following a set of rules that it is suggested have the force of law and, in so far as the language of Mr. Justice Beck may be so construed, it cannot be supported upon the authorities. Anglin J. (later Chief Justice) in speaking of credibility stated: "By that I understand not merely the appreciation of the witnesses' desire to be truthful but also of their opportunities of knowledge and powers of observation, judgment and memory — in a word, the trustworthiness of their testimony, which may have depended very largely on their demeanour in the witness box and their manner in giving evidence": *Raymond v. Bosanquet Tp.*, (1919), 50 D.L.R. 560 at p. 566, 59 S.C.R. 452 at p. 460.

> The foregoing is a general statement and does not purport to be exhaustive. Eminent Judges have from time to time indicated certain guides that have been of the greatest assistance but so far as I have been able to find there has never been an effort made to indicate all the possible factors that might enter into the determination. It is a matter in which so many human characteristics, both the strong and the weak, must be taken into consideration. The general integrity and intelligence of the witness, his

> power to observe, his capacity to remember and his accuracy in statement are important. It is also important to determine whether he is honestly endeavouring to tell the truth, whether he is sincere and frank or whether he is biased, reticent and evasive. All these questions and others may be answered from the observation of the witness' general conduct and demeanour in determining the question of credibility.[63]

The trier of fact in a criminal case may believe all the evidence, a part of the evidence, or none of the evidence given by a witness. Some of the factors which are considered in weighing the evidence and judging credibility are the following:

1. The interest the witness has in the outcome of the case; whether the witness is biased and in such circumstances is giving a prejudiced account.
2. Whether the witness has been discussing the case with others and has gradually built up an account of what he or she believes is true but is more the result of rationalizing what took place, rather than what the witness personally observed.
3. The attitude of the witness when testifying: whether the witness answers frankly or gives the impression that he or she is hesitant and attempting to conceal information.
4. Whether there are any discrepancies between what the witness states in court and what he or she may have said at an earlier time.
5. Whether there are any discrepancies between what the witness stated during direct examination and what that same witness said during cross-examination.
6. Whether the testimony given by the witness is confirmed or contradicted by the testimony of other witnesses or evidence.

The foregoing propositions are only a guide and are by no means a complete set of questions for use in assessing the credibility of a witness. In fact, there are no fixed rules for the assessment of evidence. It is left to the common sense, reason, and experience of the jury or judge trying the case to make the final determination of what weight, if any, will be placed on a particular piece of testimony or exhibit introduced during the trial.

CHARACTER EVIDENCE

The character of an accused person is a factor which may be considered by the judge or jury trying a criminal case to determine the guilt or innocence of an accused.

In law, as in life, evidence of character is divided into two categories, good and bad. The admissibility of evidence of bad character is treated very differently from that of good character.

In presenting its case, the prosecution is not entitled to adduce evidence of bad character to show that the accused is by reputation likely to have committed the offence charged. The classic statement made by a court in dealing with evidence of bad character was in the case of *Makin v. New South Wales (A.G.):*[64]

> It is undoubtedly not competent for the prosecution to adduce evidence tending to show that the accused has been guilty of criminal acts other than those covered by the indictment, for the purpose of leading to the conclusion that the accused is a *person likely from his criminal conduct or character* to have committed the offence for which he is being tried.

The reason for this rule is, of course, very evident. If the Crown were allowed to adduce evidence of bad character in advancing its case against an accused, the judge or jury hearing the case might simply convict on the basis that "bad people commit crimes" regardless of the weight of the evidence.

On the other hand, our rules of evidence allow evidence of good character to be presented by the defence to show that the accused is not the kind of person likely to have committed the offence charged. When evidence of good character is adduced by the defence, it must be considered by the trier of the case unless it is rebutted by the Crown.

The defence may place the character of the accused in issue in a number of ways. First, the accused may testify as to his own character. The defence may also cross-examine the Crown witnesses in order to bring out evidence of the accused's good character. And finally, witnesses may be called by the defence regarding the reputation of the accused.

Evidence of good character is restricted to evidence of general reputation as opposed to particular acts and personal opinions. This principle was explained by Lord Justice Cockburn in *R. v. Rowton:*[65]

> I find it uniformly laid down in the books of authority that the evidence to character must be evidence to general character in the sense of reputation; that evidence of particular facts although they might go far more strongly

than the evidence of general reputation to establish that the disposition and tendency of the man's mind was such as to render him incapable of the act with which he stands charged, must be put out of consideration altogether.

Once evidence of good character has been adduced by the defence, it is open for the Crown to call rebuttal evidence to establish that the accused's reputation is bad as opposed to good. The prosecution may rebut evidence of good character by (1) calling witnesses and (2) by proof of previous convictions. When the prosecution introduces rebuttal evidence by calling witnesses, the evidence is limited to that of general reputation rather than personal opinion or particular acts of the accused. In addition, the *Criminal Code* of Canada[66] allows the Crown to adduce evidence of the accused's conviction for any previous offence where the accused has introduced evidence of good character.

Notes

[1] For an in-depth discussion of circumstantial evidence, see P.K. McWilliams, *Canadian Criminal Evidence*, 3d ed. (Aurora: Canada Law Book, 1991) ch. 5.

[2] In *Truscott, Re*, 1967 CarswellOnt 64, (*sub nom. R. v. Truscott*) [1967] 2 C.C.C. 285, (*sub nom. R. v. Truscott*) 1 C.R.N.S. 1, (*sub nom. R. v. Truscott*) 62 D.L.R. (2d) 545, [1967] S.C.R. 309 (S.C.C.), at 360 [C.C.C.], Hall J., referring to the probative value of circumstantial evidence, stated:

> The case against Truscott was predominantly but not exclusively one of circumstantial evidence. I recognize fully that guilt can be brought home to an accused by circumstantial evidence; that there are cases where the circumstances can be said to point inexorably to guilt more reliably than direct evidence; that direct evidence is subject to the everyday hazards of imperfect recognition or of imperfect memory or both. The circumstantial evidence case is built piece by piece until the final evidentiary structure completely entraps the prisoner in a situation from which he cannot escape. There may be missing from that structure a piece here and there and certain imperfections may be discernible, but the entrapping mesh taken as a whole must be continuous and consistent. The law does not require that the guilt of an accused be established to a demonstration but is satisfied when the evidence presented to the jury points conclusively to the accused as the perpetrator of the crime and excludes any reasonable hypothesis of innocence. The rules of evidence apply with equal force to proof by circumstantial evidence as to proof by direct evidence. The evidence in both instances must be equally credible, admissible and relevant.

[3] *R. v. McIver*, 1964 CarswellOnt 181, [1965] 1 C.C.C. 210, [1965] 1 O.R. 306, (Ont. H.C.), affirmed 1965 CarswellOnt 5, [1965] 4 C.C.C. 182, [1965] 2 O.R. 475, 45 C.R. 401 (Ont. C.A.), which was affirmed 1966 CarswellOnt 7, [1966] S.C.R. 254, [1966] 2 C.C.C. 289, 48 C.R. 4 (S.C.C.).

4   *Ibid.*, at 214 [C.C.C.].
5   *R. v. Graat*, 1982 CarswellOnt 101, 1982 CarswellOnt 745, 2 C.C.C. (3d) 365, [1982] 2 S.C.R. 819, 18 M.V.R. 287, 31 C.R. (3d) 289, 144 D.L.R. (3d) 267, 45 N.R. 451 (S.C.C.), at 378 [C.C.C.].
6   McWilliams, *Canadian Criminal Evidence, supra*, note 1, 3:10900.
7   See *R. v. Piton* (1943), 80 C.C.C. 72, [1943] 4 D.L.R. 51 (Ont. C.A.), at 77 [C.C.C.].
8   For further extensive discussion on hearsay, see McWilliams, *Canadian Criminal Evidence, supra*, note 1, ch. 8 and Sir Rupert Cross, *On Evidence*, 5th ed. (London: Butterworths, 1979).
9   *Subramaniam v. Public Prosecutor*, [1956] 1 W.L.R. 965, 100 S.J. 566 (Malaysia P.C.), at 970 [W.L.R.].
10 See *R. v. Abbey*, 1982 CarswellBC 230, 1982 CarswellBC 740, 68 C.C.C. (2d) 394, [1982] 2 S.C.R. 24, 138 D.L.R. (3d) 202, 43 N.R. 30, 39 B.C.L.R. 201, 29 C.R. (3d) 193, [1983] 1 W.W.R. 251 (S.C.C.); and *R. v. Wildman* (1981), 1981 CarswellOnt 1164, 60 C.C.C. (2d) 289, 5 O.A.C. 268, 55 N.R. 54 (Ont. C.A.), at 298 [C.C.C.].
11 See *R. v. Laurin (No. 4)* (1902), 6 C.C.C. 104 (Que. K.B.); *R. v. McIntosh*, 1937 CarswellBC 87, 69 C.C.C. 106, [1938] 1 W.W.R. 211 (B.C. C.A.); *R. v. Garlow*, 1976 CarswellOnt 943, 31 C.C.C. (2d) 163 (Ont. H.C.); *R. v. Mulligan*, 1973 CarswellOnt 27, 23 C.R.N.S. 1 (Ont. S.C.), affirmed on other grounds 1974 CarswellOnt 11, 26 C.R.N.S. 179, 18 C.C.C. (2d) 270 (Ont. C.A.), affirmed 1976 CarswellOnt 411, 1976 CarswellOnt 411F, 28 C.C.C. (2d) 266, [1977] 1 S.C.R. 612, 9 N.R. 27, 66 D.L.R. (3d) 627 (S.C.C.); *R. v. Buck*, 1940 CarswellOnt 32, 74 C.C.C. 314, [1940] O.R. 444, [1941] 1 D.L.R. 302, [1940] O.W.N. 473 (Ont. C.A.); *Bernard-Chapdelaine v. R.*, 1934 CarswellQue 49, 63 C.C.C. 5, [1935] S.C.R. 53, [1935] 2 D.L.R. 132 (S.C.C.); *R. v. Dingham*, 1978 CarswellBC 257, 4 C.R. (3d) 193 (B.C. S.C.); and *R. v. Jurtyn*, 1958 CarswellOnt 24, 121 C.C.C. 403, 28 C.R. 295, [1958] O.W.N. 355 (Ont. C.A.).
12 See *R. v. O'Brien*, 1977 CarswellBC 403, 1977 CarswellBC 494, 35 C.C.C. (2d) 209, [1978] 1 S.C.R. 591, [1977] 5 W.W.R. 400, 38 C.R.N.S. 325, 16 N.R. 271, 76 D.L.R. (3d) 513 (S.C.C.).
13 See *Myers v. Director of Public Prosecutions*, [1964] 2 All E.R. 881, 48 Cr. App. R. 348, [1965] A.C. 1001, [1964] 3 W.L.R. 145 (U.K. H.L.).
14 See *R. v. Finestone*, 1953 CarswellQue 9, 107 C.C.C. 93, 17 C.R. 211, [1953] 2 S.C.R. 107 (S.C.C.).
15 See *Canada Evidence Act*, R.S.C. 1985, c. C-5, ss. 25, 26, 29, 30, 31.
16 See *R. v. Khan*, 1990 CarswellOnt 108, 1990 CarswellOnt 1001, 59 C.C.C. (3d) 92, 113 N.R. 53, 79 C.R. (3d) 1, 41 O.A.C. 353, [1990] 2 S.C.R. 531 (S.C.C.).
17 See *R. v. Smith*, 1992 CarswellOnt 997, 1992 CarswellOnt 103, 75 C.C.C. (3d) 257, 139 N.R. 323, 94 D.L.R. (4th) 590, 15 C.R. (4th) 133, [1992] 2 S.C.R. 915, 55 O.A.C. 321 (S.C.C.).
18 See *R. v. B. (K.G.)*, 1993 CarswellOnt 76, 1993 CarswellOnt 975, 79 C.C.C. (3d) 257, 19 C.R. (4th) 1, [1993] 1 S.C.R. 740, 61 O.A.C. 1, 148 N.R. 241 (S.C.C.).
19 *Supra*, note 17, at 269 [C.C.C.].
20 *Ibid.*, at 270 [C.C.C.].
21 *Ibid.*, at 273 [C.C.C.].
22 7 J. Wigmore, *Evidence*, s. 1917 (Chadbourn rev. 1978).
23 General discussions of opinion and expert evidence can be found, in A. Maloney

and P.V. Tomlinson, "Opinion Evidence," in *Studies in Canadian Criminal Evidence*, R.E. Salhany and R.J. Carter eds. (Toronto: Butterworths, 1972), at 219.

[24] For an excellent synopsis of the modern opinion rule together with supporting case citations, see McWilliams, *Canadian Criminal Evidence, supra*, note 1, ch. 9.

[25] In *R. v. Graat, supra*, note 5, at 378 [C.C.C.], Dickson J. stated:

> The subjects upon which the non-expert witness is allowed to give opinion evidence is a lengthy one. The list mentioned in *Sherrard v. Jacob, supra*, is by no means exhaustive: (1) the identification of handwriting, persons and things; (2) apparent age; (3) the bodily plight or condition of a person, including death and illness; (4) the emotional state of a person— *e.g.* whether distressed, angry, aggressive, affectionate or depressed; (5) the condition of things—*e.g.* worn, shabby, used or new; (6) certain questions of value; and (7) estimates of speed and distance.

[26] 7 J. Wigmore, *Evidence*, s. 1923 (Chadbourn rev. 1978); and *R. v. Fisher*, 1961 CarswellOnt 14, 130 C.C.C. 1, [1961] S.C.R. 535, 35 C.R. 107 (S.C.C.).

[27] *Rice v. Sockett*, 1912 CarswellOnt 673, 8 D.L.R. 84, 23 O.W.R. 602, 27 O.L.R. 410 (Ont. C.A.); *R. v. Dugandzic*, 1981 CarswellOnt 1107, 57 C.C.C. (2d) 517 (Ont. C.A.); *R. v. Bunniss*, 1964 CarswellBC 184, [1965] 3 C.C.C. 236, 44 C.R. 262, 50 W.W.R. 422 (B.C. Co. Ct.).

[28] For example, in *R. v. Dugandzic, supra*, note 27, the Ontario Court of Appeal held that a member of the R.C.M.P. Customs and Excise Section who, although he did not possess a chemistry degree, had taken training courses and had been involved in a number of investigations pertaining to illegal possession of stills, was permitted to give his opinion as to the identification of the apparatus found in the accused's possession.

[29] See *R. v. Blunden* (1977), 1977 CarswellNS 4, 40 C.C.C. (2d) 492, 2 C.R. (3d) 301 (N.S. Co. Ct.); also *R. v. Marks* (1952), 1952 CarswellOnt 18, 103 C.C.C. 368, [1952] O.W.N. 608, 15 C.R. 47 (Ont. Co. Ct.); *Baker v. Hutchinson* (1976), 1976 CarswellOnt 306, 13 O.R. (2d) 591, 1 C.P.C. 291 (Ont. C.A.).

[30] See *R. v. Neil*, 1957 CarswellAlta 1, 119 C.C.C. 1, [1957] S.C.R. 685, 26 C.R. 281, 11 D.L.R. (2d) 545 (S.C.C.); and *R. v. Arbuckle*, 1966 CarswellBC 130, [1967] 2 C.C.C. 32, 50 C.R. 45, 57 W.W.R. 656 (B.C. S.C.), reversed 1967 CarswellBC 39, [1967] 3 C.C.C. 380, 1 C.R.N.S. 318, 59 W.W.R. 605, 5 R.F.L. Rep. 487 (B.C. C.A.).

[31] *R. v. Ortt*, 1968 CarswellOnt 140, [1968] 4 C.C.C. 92, [1968] 2 O.R. 307, 10 Crim. L.Q. 456 (Ont. C.A.).

[32] *Criminal Code*, s. 657.3.

[33] For a more comprehensive discussion of out-of-court statements by an accused, see McWilliams, *Canadian Criminal Evidence, supra*, note 1, Pt. IV, at 415-538; and Kaufman, *The Admissibility of Confessions*, 3rd ed. (Toronto: Carswell, 1979), Supplement (1986).

[34] *Ibrahim v. R.*, [1914] A.C. 599, [1914-15] All E.R. Rep. 874, 24 Cox C.C. 174 (Hong Kong P.C.), at 609-610 [A.C.]; *R. v. Oickle*, 2000 CarswellNS 257, 2000 CarswellNS 258, 2000 SCC 38, 147 C.C.C. (3d) 321, 36 C.R. (5th) 129, 190 D.L.R. (4th) 257, 259 N.R. 227, [2000] 2 S.C.R. 3, 187 N.S.R. (2d) 201, 585 A.P.R. 201 (S.C.C.).

[35] For a general discussion of the procedure on the *voir dire* regarding admissibility of

statements, see *Erven v. R.*, 1978 CarswellNS 22, 1978 CarswellNS 108, [1979] 1 S.C.R. 926, 25 N.R. 49, 6 C.R. (3d) 97, 30 N.S.R. (2d) 89, 49 A.P.R. 89, 44 C.C.C. (2d) 76, 92 D.L.R. (3d) 507 (S.C.C.).

[36] *R. v. Piche*, 1970 CarswellMan 62, 1970 CarswellMan 81, [1971] S.C.R. 23, 74 W.W.R. 674, 12 C.R.N.S. 222, 11 D.L.R. (3d) 700, [1970] 4 C.C.C. 27 (S.C.C.).

[37] See Cross *On Evidence, supra,* note 8, at 541; and *R. v. Parnerkar (No. 2),* 1974 CarswellSask 67, 17 C.C.C. (2d) 11, [1974] 5 W.W.R. 1013 (Sask. C.A.), at 126 [C.C.C.].

[38] *R. v. Pettipiece*, 1972 CarswellBC 148, 7 C.C.C. (2d) 133, 18 C.R.N.S. 236, [1972] 5 W.W.R. 129 (B.C. C.A.).

[39] *R. v. Rothman*, 1981 CarswellOnt 43, 1981 CarswellOnt 93, [1981] 1 S.C.R. 640, 20 C.R. (3d) 97, 121 D.L.R. (3d) 578, 35 N.R. 485, 59 C.C.C. (2d) 30 (S.C.C.).

[40] See *R. v. Ward*, 1979 CarswellAlta 192, 1979 CarswellAlta 164, [1979] 2 S.C.R. 30, 7 C.R. (3d) 153 (Eng.), 10 C.R. (3d) 289 (Fr.), 25 N.R. 514, 14 A.R. 412, [1979] 2 W.W.R. 193, 44 C.C.C. (2d) 498, 94 D.L.R. (3d) 18 (S.C.C.); and *R. v. Horvath*, 1979 CarswellBC 667, 1979 CarswellBC 758, [1979] 2 S.C.R. 376, 44 C.C.C. (2d) 385, [1979] 3 W.W.R. 1, 93 D.L.R. (3d) 1, 7 C.R. (3d) 97, 25 N.R. 537, 11 C.R. (3d) 206. In *Horvath*, the traditional voluntariness rule was expanded (or, more properly, recognized as not having been exhaustively defined in *Ibrahim*) to prohibit the admission into evidence of statements obtained from an accused as the result of his involuntary hypnosis by a person in authority (in this case an R.C.M.P. officer). For further discussion of the matter see A.G. Henderson "Mental Incapacity and the Admissibility of Statements" (1980), 23 Crim. L.Q. 62.

[41] *R. v. Clarkson*, 1986 CarswellNB 14, 1986 CarswellNB 104, 50 C.R. (3d) 289, [1986] 1 S.C.R. 383, 26 D.L.R. (4th) 493, 66 N.R. 114, 69 N.B.R. (2d) 40, 25 C.C.C. (3d) 207, 19 C.R.R. 209, 177 A.P.R. 40 (S.C.C.). This case deals with the admissibility of statements made by an accused. At trial, after a *voir dire*, the trial judge had held that he was not satisfied that the accused had sufficiently recovered from her high degree of intoxication for her to comprehend what she was doing when she made the statement nor for her to comprehend the consequences of making the statement. The majority of the New Brunswick Court of Appeal concluded that the trial judge had erred in law in his decision. On a further appeal by the accused to the Supreme Court of Canada, the appeal was allowed and the verdict of acquittal was restored.

[42] *R. v. Hebert*, 1990 CarswellYukon 4, 1990 CarswellYukon 7, 57 C.C.C. (3d) 1, 47 B.C.L.R. (2d) 1, [1990] 2 S.C.R. 151, 77 C.R. (3d) 145, [1990] 5 W.W.R. 1, 110 N.R. 1, 49 C.R.R. 114 (S.C.C.).

[43] For a detailed and comprehensive report on witnesses, see P.K. McWilliams, *Canadian Criminal Evidence*, 2d ed. (Aurora: Canada Law Book, 1984) ch. 34.

[44] *R. v. Brasier* (1779), 168 E.R. 202, 1 Leach 199.

[45] *Canada Evidence Act*, s. 13.

[46] *Ibid.*, s. 14.

[47] *Ibid.*, s. 16.1

[48] *Ibid.*

[49] *Ibid.*, s. 16.

[50] *Ibid.*, s. 6.

[51] *Ibid.*, s. 6.1.

of the interceptions and to report to Parliament about the use of the section.

Bill C-47 represents extensive updating of the legislative provisions dealing with the interception of private communications and the ability of investigative departments to obtain data and records related to, and which arise from, using technology to communicate and/or accessing computer databanks. The Bill is the culmination of the "Lawful Access Initiative"[7] publicly launched in 2002. Its purpose is to ensure that communication service providers have the technical capacity to provide lawful access to police agencies of communication data and to amend the *Code* and other acts of Parliament, such as the *Canadian Security Intelligence Service Act* and *Competition Act* to allow Canadian laws to keep pace with the ever evolving technology. Amendments to the *Code*, for example, reflect efforts to modernize procedural law, concepts and language and establish new investigative techniques with appropriate judicial authorization, all to capture technological advances. Balancing the competing interests of investigative capabilities and privacy rights provides the contextual framework for any such legislative initiatives.[8]

Part VI of the *Code*, entitled "Invasion of Privacy" (ss. 183 to 196), contains the main provisions concerning "wiretap law". These sections deal primarily with the requirements and procedure for the interception of private communications and radio based telephone communications (cellular telephones). The *Code* also provides a statutory scheme for other forms of electronic surveillance—that is, the interception and monitoring of activities other than private communications. These are contained in Part XV of the *Code* and set out the requirements for the issuing of a search warrant for video surveillance, (s. 487.01), tracking devices (s. 492.1) and telephone number recorder devices (s. 492.2).

CRIMINAL CODE PROVISIONS—PART VI AND PART XV

Part VI — Invasion of Privacy

Communications and Privacy Considerations

The introductory provision (s. 183) defines concepts that establish, in part, the framework for determining whether a communication is private and interception of those communications requires adherence to the *Code* provisions:

> "private communication" means any oral communications, or any telecommunication, that is made by an originator who is in Canada or is intended by the originator to be received by a person who is in Canada

and that is made under circumstances in which it is reasonable for the originator to expect that it will not be intercepted by any person other than the person intended by the originator to receive it, and includes any radio-based telephone communication that is treated electronically or otherwise for the purpose of preventing intelligible reception by any person other than the person intended by the originator to receive it;

. . .

"intercept" includes listen to, record or acquire a communication or acquire the substance, meaning or purport thereof.

Other concepts, which will be referred to, are defined as follows:

"electro-magnetic, acoustic, mechanical or other device" and means any device or apparatus that is used or is capable of being used to intercept a private communication, but does not include a hearing aid used to correct subnormal hearing of the user to not better than normal hearing;

. . .

"type of communication" means private communication and/or radio based telephone communications;

. . .

"agent of the state" means a peace officer; and a person acting under the authority of, or in cooperation with a peace officer.

"Communications" have been interpreted to mean the passing of thoughts, ideas, words or information from one person to another—that is, the exchange of information between persons. While a person may begin the communication process by dialing a number, a communication occurs when the originator is in a position to deliver a message or information.[9] A communication, however, only becomes private if there is a reasonable belief or expectation that the communication will not be listened to or recorded through artificial means by anyone and in particular law enforcement authorities or someone acting on their behalf.

The expectation that a conversation will not be intercepted must be both objectively and subjectively considered to be reasonable in the circumstances. This means that not only must the party to the communication believe it to be private (subjective) but there must be a societal recognition that, in the circumstances under consideration, there is a legitimate expectation of privacy (objective). The existence of an expectation of privacy has been the subject of judicial interpretation.

Whenever agents of the state use a form of electronic surveillance to gather evidence consisting of communications or activities in circumstances where an expectation of privacy exists, the reasonableness of doing so is subject to *Charter* scrutiny. Specifically, the use of electronic surveillance is reviewed by the courts in the context of s. 8 of the *Charter*—the right to be secure against unreasonable search or seizure. Each case is determined on the facts peculiar to it or common to other decided cases. In *R. v. Wong*,[10] Chief Justice Lamer, on behalf of the Supreme Court of Canada, made this observation:

> I agree with my colleague that unauthorized surreptitious electronic surveillance may, in certain circumstances, violate an individual's rights under s. 8. I agree that such surveillance will violate s. 8 where the target of the surveillance has a reasonable expectation of privacy. However, in my view, the consideration of whether an individual has a reasonable expectation of privacy can only be decided within the particular factual context of the surveillance, not by reference to a general notion of privacy in a free and democratic society which an individual enjoys at all times. A person has the right, under s. 8 to be free from unauthorized surreptitious electronic surveillance where that person has a reasonable expectation that the agents of the state will not be watching or recording private activity nor monitoring or recording private conversations. Whether such an expectation is reasonable will depend on the particular circumstances; a person does not necessarily enjoy this right in all circumstances.

The application of s. 8 of the *Charter* to police activities is considered at a later point.

In *R. v. Tam*,[11] the Court ruled that telephone calls made by kidnappers to the victim's father were not private communications in that the kidnappers "had to know" that the communications would not be kept private. As well, given that the interception or recordings were not made by the police or anyone acting on their behalf, compliance with Part VI of the *Code* was not required. Similarly, telephone calls placed to a police station switchboard[12] and police broadcasts over mobile police radios and intercepted by a scanner[13] were found not to be private communications.

In some circumstances, telephone communications made by inmates within a prison facility were not considered to be private communications. This determination was made after findings of fact, which included that inmates were advised personally that communications may be monitored and the taping was done for purposes of security within the institution and not during the course of investigating offences. This position has, however, been the subject of contrary views even in situations when a notice was posted warning of communication monitoring. Although attracting a lessened expectation of privacy, wholesale or universal intercepting of inmates' communications has been found to contravene the *Charter*.[14]

Transmissions over a voice or message pager where a message can be overheard or listened to by persons other than the recipient of the message have, as well, been found not to be private communications.[15] Similarly, in circumstances where a police officer answered a telephone during the course of searching a residence, the communication did not attract an expectation of privacy. The action of the police officer was found not to constitute an illegal interception.[16]

In order to keep pace with technology and with *Charter* considerations, the definition of a private communication was expanded to include radio-based telephone communications to capture cellular telephones that have been treated electronically or scrambled. Clearly, persons who communicate by way of such a telephone have a reasonable expectation of privacy. Cellular telephones, which are not electronically treated, can be intercepted by anyone with a scanner and consequently communications over such telephones are not private within the meaning of the *Code*. Although cellular telephones without a scrambling device can be intercepted by anyone, the 1993 amendments to the *Code* (subs. 184.5(2)) appear to require that "agents of the state" who want to intercept those types of communications must have an authorization to do so unless the interception occurs in relation to s. 184.1 or s. 184.4.

The legislation, however, protects such "untreated" telephones by making it an offence to intercept communications maliciously or for gain (subs. 184.5(1)) and, without consent, wilfully to use or disclose such communications or to disclose their existence (subs. 193.1(1)). These sections recognize, however, exceptions to the disclosure liability in situations, for example, where disclosure is necessary in the interests of justice for a law enforcement investigation, prosecution of criminal offences or in proceedings where evidence is given under oath (subs. 193.1(2), (3)). A conviction under s. 184.5 or s. 193.1 of the *Code* may, in addition to any other punishment, result in being required to pay punitive damages to the victim of up to $5,000.

The wilful interception of private communications, except in certain circumstances, is an offence which does not require an ulterior motive such as gain (s. 184 of the *Code*). Other offences, which relate to the interception of private communications, are ss. 191 and 342.1. Section 191, again with exceptions, makes illegal possessing, selling or purchasing devices or components designed primary for the inter-

quirements of s. 184.1 do not apply to the provisions of s. 184.4. There must, however, be reasonable belief as to:

(a) the urgency so that an authorization could not be obtained with reasonable diligence;

(b) the immediate necessity to prevent an unlawful act that would cause serious harm to a person or property; and

(c) either the originator or intended recipient is the person likely to cause or be the victim of the harm.

In the event of subsequent court proceedings, the circumstances surrounding the interceptions are questions of fact to be decided at trial.

Given that these powers can be exercised without a prior independent judicial review, the circumstances and procedures for intercepting such communications are subject to scrutiny as has occurred in the context of s. 184.4 (discussed above in the introduction). While the provisions are generally self-explanatory, two concepts arise which have been considered by the courts in other contexts, those being reasonable grounds or belief and consent, which have been discussed. The concept of reasonable grounds or belief is a requirement common to all provisions that deal with wiretap or interception powers and is discussed in more detail below.

Sections 184.2, 185, 188

Sections 184.2, 185 and 188 are referred to as judicially authorized interceptions. Prior to intercepting communications, a judge must approve the request or application. The level of court to which the application is made, the person designated or recognized in law as having the authority to apply for the interceptions and the particulars necessary for each application are set out in the provisions. Section 184.2 differs from ss. 184 and 186 in that a judicial authorization under that provision may be granted for the investigation of any offence under the *Code* or a federal statute and is not restricted to those listed in s. 183. As well, no special designation by the person who makes the application to the judge is required. Further, s. 184.2 does not require that other investigative means or techniques have been tried and failed or unlikely to proceed. The provision has been found not to contravene s. 8 of the *Charter*, unreasonable search and seizure.[19]

Section 184.2 is a "consent interception" and the requirements are as follows:

(a)   an application to a Provincial Court or Superior Court Judge by a peace officer or public officer appointed, designated to administer, or enforce federal or provincial law;

(b)   consent by the originator or intended receiver of the communication to the interception;

(c)   reasonable grounds that an offence under the *Criminal Code* or other federal statute has been or will be committed;

(d)   the particulars of the offence;

(e)   the period of time of the authorization requested (not to exceed 60 days unless renewed);

(f)   the particulars of any other authorization under this section or s. 186 that was granted;

(g)   the type of communications to be intercepted (e.g., private and/or radio-based telephone communications);

(h)   the identity of persons, if known, and a general description of the places (if possible) to be intercepted; and

(i)   a general description of the manner of interception—that is, the type of device (e.g., electrical, acoustic) that may be used to do the interceptions.

A judge may then grant the authorization if satisfied that there are reasonable grounds to believe the appropriate offence has been or will be committed, there is consent, and reasonable grounds exist to believe that information about the offence will be obtained through interception. This *Code* provision encompasses the same concept of consent as discussed above. The form of the judge's order or authorization is set out in subs. 184.2(4) and generally parallels the procedural contents of the application, such as, the offences, type of communications, identity of persons if known and a general description of places. The judge may also order terms and conditions that are considered necessary in the public interest. These are referred to as "minimization" clauses, which impose restrictions, for example, on how, when or where persons may be intercepted.

This is the only provision, however, that permits an application to be made by telephone or other forms of telecommunication (e.g., fax machines, electronic mail). The information provided to the judge must be on oath, either orally or in written form. The authority is set out in s. 184.3 and arises when it is impractical to appear personally in the circumstances. The judge, who is satisfied on the facts as to that impracticability, must make a record (in writing or otherwise) of the application and place the record of the application and the authorization in a sealed package. The judge is required to provide a copy of the authorization to the applicant if the application was transmitted to the judge in writing or direct the applicant create a facsimile copy if the application was made by a means other than in writing. Authorizations that are given in this manner are only valid for 36 hours.

The other two forms of applications for judicial authorizations are contained in ss. 185 and 188.

Section 185 applications are made:

(a) by an agent who has been personally designated by the federal Minister of Public Safety and Emergency Preparedness or the Attorney General of a province;

(b) to a judge of a superior court;

(c) with a sworn affidavit setting out the reasonable grounds as to the offences which will, are, or have been committed; and

(d) setting out:
- the type of private communications proposed to be intercepted (e.g., private and/or radio-based telephone communications),
- the names, addresses, and occupations, if known, of all persons whose private communications will assist the investigation,
- a general description of the nature and location of places to be intercepted;
- a general description of the manner of interceptions (e.g., electro, mechanical, acoustic, or other device as defined in s. 183),
- the details of whether other applications have been made and withdrawn or not granted,
- the time period of the authorization, and
- other investigative procedures that have been tried and failed or why they would unlikely succeed or where urgency makes it impractical to use other procedures.

The affidavits seeking an order to intercept private communications must contain full, frank and fair disclosure of the reasonable grounds relevant to the offences under investigation and the persons whose communications may be intercepted and places where interceptions may occur. It is not necessary to disclose all incriminating information as to a person's involvement in the offences that is known to the police or each and every investigative step taken to date.[20]

Intercepting private communications need not be an investigative tool of last resort—that is, there is nothing else left that could be done—it has to be more than just a helpful or useful technique in the investigation. The authorization may be granted when "no other reasonable alternative method of investigation" is available and intercepting private communications becomes an investigative necessity. The law requires that investigative agencies specifically address the need for electronic surveillance in the context of the particular investigations.[21] For this reason, the nature, progress and difficulties encountered in the investigation are generally set out for the judge. Other investigative techniques commonly used prior to seeking an authorization may include surveillance, undercover peace officers, informants, and, search warrants. Further, an authorization to intercept private communications can be obtained and employed together with other investigative techniques (e.g., police agents, undercover officers). The police are entitled, in a *bona fide* investigation, to fully investigate offences and the persons believed to be involved.[22]

The investigative necessity for intercepting the private communications of each person under investigation is not required to be demonstrated, in every circumstance, but is in relation to the investigation as a whole.[23] As well, the fact that authorities have enough information to justify a charge is not a bar to continuing the investigation by way of interception when proper grounds are shown. The investigative authority is entitled to press forward and uncover the full extent of the offence(s) alleged.[24]

Persons who are "known" to the police and whose communications will assist in the particular investigation must be disclosed to the judge.[25] While they may not necessarily be named as persons who will be the main objects of the interceptions (targets), their identities (if known) must be disclosed. Failure to do so may result in their communications being ruled inadmissible into evidence.

An intention to intercept at known places (e.g., residences) must also be disclosed. A general description of a place is permitted under s. 185(1)(e) if that is the only information reasonably available at the time of the application. Automobiles are considered places for the purposes of intercepting communications.[26] During the course of intercepting communications, authorities may develop reasonable grounds to believe that the "targets" or named persons are going to, using, about to go to or use telephones, locations, or other forms of communications. Interception can occur at those places which were previously unknown or unidentifiable to the authorities under a clause in the authorization commonly called "resort to" places, locations or telecommunications. "Resort to" simply means to "go" and does not require proof of frequent attendance. These interceptions have been found to be valid as it is reasonable to recognize that a "target" or named person may hold conversations in several different places. Subsequent requests for authorizations to intercept communications must, however, include the "resorted to" location as a named place if there is an intention to continue intercepting communications at that location.[27] The concept of a "resort to" location has been found not to extend to an interview room at a police station so as to allow an interception of communications between a detained person and his parents.[28]

The interception of "unknown" persons is permitted under what is commonly referred to as a "basket clause". The authorization grants authority to intercept unknown and unidentified persons either in conversation with targets or when in a "known" place or on a named telephone.[29] In order to implement an authorization, a peace officer may enter onto property or into a place so as to install listening devices.[30]

When an authorization to intercept communications is given pursuant to an application under s. 185, it is commonly referred to as a conventional authorization. It is the usual or customary means of applying for and receiving authority to intercept communications.

Section 186

A judge who approves an application under s. 185 or s. 188 is guided by the dictates of s. 186, which states in part:

> **186 (1)** An authorization under this section may be given if the judge to whom the application is made is satisfied
>> (a) that it would be in the best interests of the administration of justice to do so; and
>> (b) that other investigative procedures have been tried and have failed, other investigative procedures are unlikely to succeed or the urgency of the matter is such that it would be impractical to carry out the investigation of the offence using only other investigative procedures.
>
> **(2)** No authorization may be given to intercept a private communication at the office or residence of a solicitor, or at any other place ordinarily used by a solicitor and by other solicitors for the purpose of consultation with clients, unless the judge to whom the application is made is satisfied that there are reasonable grounds to believe that the solicitor, any other solicitor practicing with him, any person employed by him or any other such

solicitor or a member of the solicitor's household has been or is about to become a party to an offence.

(3) Where an authorization is given in relation to the interception of private communications at a place described in subsection (2), the judge by whom the authorization is given shall include therein such terms and conditions, as he considers advisable to protect privileged communications between solicitors and clients.

(4) An authorization shall
> (a) state the offence in respect of which private communications may be intercepted;
> (b) state the type of private communication that may be intercepted;
> (c) state the identity of the persons, if known, whose private communications are to be intercepted, generally describe the place at which private communications may be intercepted, if a general description of that place can be given, and generally describe the manner of interception that may be used;
> (d) contain such terms and conditions as the judge considers advisable in the public interest; and
> (e) be valid for the period, not exceeding sixty days, set out therein.

. . .

A judge, when deciding whether or not to grant an order or authorization to intercept private communications, must conclude that the investigative necessity requirement has been met. As well, the judge must be satisfied that:

(a) a specific crime has been or is being committed;
(b) the interception will afford evidence of the crime.

This determination is made on the whole of the information or material placed before the judge.[31] Strict adherence to the form of the authorization is essential. Failure to set out any of those requirements may result in the authorization being found at later proceedings to be an unreasonable search or seizure.

Although special provisions exist regarding intercepting solicitor-client communications, a judge is not required or obligated by the provisions of the *Code*, specifically to impose terms protecting such communications.[32] Generally, authorizations to intercept solicitors occur in exceptional circumstances where the lawyer is believed to be involved or about to become a party in the offence.[33] The protection for lawyers extends to persons or solicitors employed by or with them. Without express authorization under subs. 186(2), interceptions at places ordinarily used for business by solicitors would be unlawful.

Interceptions may be made at places named or "targets" (persons) named in the authorization even when conversations are to a solicitor, and the solicitor is talking on his/her office phone. Care must be taken to distinguish between issues of lawfulness of the interceptions and privilege. The fact that the interception of communications by solicitors is authorized and lawful does not dissolve the privilege if the communication was *bona fide* that is, not for a criminal purpose.

Subsection 189(6) recognizes that intercepted communications that are privileged are inadmissible without the consent of the privilege holder. Admissibility into evidence of lawfully intercepted communications ultimately turns on a court determining whether or not they are privileged communications and the reasonableness of the police action in intercepting such communications. Privileged solicitor-client communications are only admissible under stringent conditions and only when the innocence of the accused is at stake. Enforcement agencies must take reasonable steps to prevent inadvertent interception of privileged communications and must establish monitoring and review systems for such communications as required by law.[34]

The concept of privilege also arises in the course of intercepting communications between legally recognized spouses. The law is divided on the use in on-going investigations to which such lawfully intercepted communications can be put. While interception of communications can occur between spouses, some courts have concluded that the content of those communications can form the basis of reasonable grounds in continuing to investigate offences (i.e., in subsequent requests for an authorization or a search warrant). Other courts take a different view of such subsequent use, based upon the wording of subs. 189(6).[35]

Authorizations granted under ss. 184.2, 184.3, 186 and 188 can be carried out anywhere in Canada. If, however, execution of the authorization requires entry into or upon property of any person outside the province from where the authorization was granted, then a judge of the other province must confirm or endorse the original authorization. If, during the course of carrying out the authorization in another province or territory, police officers require the assistance of persons outside the province or territory, and this was not provided for in the original authorization, a judge of another province may order that assistance be given (s. 188.1). This occurs, for example, when the assistance of an out of province communications company is needed to make the technical connection or "hookup" between the telephone or other forms of telecommunication equipment to be intercepted and the police agency's equipment which will intercept the communications.

Authorizations that are granted, with or without conditions, or refused pursuant to ss. 185 and 188 are the subject of a mandatory annual report prepared by the office of the Minister of Public Safety and Emergency Preparedness and the Attorney General of each province. As well, persons who were the "object of interceptions"—that is, those who were named as principal "targets" in an authorization—and whose communications were actually intercepted must receive written notification. The notification must be made within 90 days of the termination of the interceptions or upon an application for a delay of notification for a term fixed by a judge but not to exceed three years, from the last date within which the authorization was valid. Delay of notification may occur when the investigation is continuing or a new investigation begins. The court (not necessarily the specific judge), which granted the authorization, must also be provided with a certificate of notification. There is no requirement that the notice of interception contain any details or the contents of the authorization.[36] Failure to provide this notice does not render the interceptions inadmissible into evidence at subsequent proceedings when they would be otherwise admissible.[37]

Section 188

Applications made under s. 188 are for emergency authorizations. With some modifications they adopt the requirements of s. 185. While a written affidavit is not required, all oral information supplied in support of the application must be on oath[38] and by the peace officer specifically designated to make the application.[39] The application is made when the urgency of a situation requires interceptions to begin before a conventional authorization could be reasonably obtained. Judges who grant these authorizations are specifically designated to do so. These emergency authorizations are only valid for 36 hours.

Renewals

A conventional authorization granted pursuant to s. 186 is valid for a period of 60 days. Renewals may be granted for subsequent periods of time up to sixty days. These renewals of the earlier or original authorization only extend the period of time or dates when interceptions are permitted. A renewal authorization does not permit new persons or new places to be intercepted. Renewals must be granted prior to the expiration of the preceding authorization. Renewal applications are granted pursuant to subs. 186(6) and (7) of the *Code*.

When additional and/or different persons are to be intercepted, new places are named or the outstanding authorization has lapsed, a new application must be made and a new authorization granted pursuant to s. 186.[40]

Criminal Organizations

In 1997 and 2001, the *Code* was amended to include provisions intended to address the investigation and prosecution of persons involved in activities relating to criminal organizations.[41] Section 2 of the *Code* defines, through s. 467.1(1), a "criminal organization" as three or more persons whose primary activity relates to committing serious offences (with a penalty of more than five years) which, if committed, would directly or indirectly, result in a material benefit by the group or one of its members.

The provisions attempt to address a national problem of organized criminals and gangs engaged in a variety of destructive activities.

Part VI of the *Code* was modified to reflect the particular requirements of criminal organization investigations. Accommodation for these types of investigations was made recognizing, in part, that such investigations may extend for long periods of time. Section 186.1 of the *Code* was added allowing for an authorization to intercept private communications for up to one year, rather than the 60 days permitted in ss. 184.2(4)(e) and 186(4)(e). Further, subs. 186(1.1) eliminates the investigative necessity requirement under s. 186. The elimination of that legislative requirement has been found not to contravene *Charter* rights. Various courts have had divided opinion on the constitutionality of the criminal organization provisions.[42] An in-depth discussion of the criminal organization provision is not undertaken. The reader should be alert to the existence of these provisions

Terrorism and Terrorist Activities

In 2001 and 2002, legislative provisions were enacted to respond to the realities of terrorism and related activities. Section 2 of the *Code* now includes definitions of "terrorism offence", "terrorist group" and "terrorist activities" through the operation of ss. 83.01 to 83.23 of Part II.1. Those sections contain detailed definitions, investigative tools, and provisions for the detention, arrest, release, prosecution and sentencing of persons allegedly engaged in such activities. Part VI of the *Code* was amended to include the terrorism related offences. Such offences, now listed in s. 183, may be investigated through the use of Part VI authorizations. As with investigations related to criminal organizations, law enforcement agencies can apply to intercept communications for up to one year and without the need to satisfy the investigative necessity requirements, pursuant to subs. 186(1.1) and s. 186.1.

Some of the provisions were time limited and ceased to apply as of March 2007. Bill C-19 was introduced in 2009 to re-enact those provisions. As with the discussion of criminal organizations, this overview is not intended to be exhaustive. Readers should review the provisions to determine their intent and applicability to particular circumstances.

Introduction of the Communications in Court

Proof Required by the Crown

In certain circumstances, intercepted private communications can be entered as evidence. The Crown, however, must give reasonable notice of its intention to do so to all of the persons charged, even if they are not a party to the communication, and provide a transcript or statement containing full particulars of the intercepted communications sought to be tendered. Providing a copy of the tape recording itself instead of a transcript is sufficient to comply with subs. 189(5) of the Code.[43] Reasonable notice means sufficient time to prepare for the proceedings in which the interceptions will be tendered. The accused or counsel acting on those instructions can waive proof of notice. A notice given prior to a preliminary inquiry hearing is valid for all subsequent proceedings.[44]

The Crown is not permitted, even if notice is given, to tender into evidence communications between legally recognized spouses (not common law) when they are the only parties to the communications. These communications are considered, in law, privileged and inadmissible. There is Canadian authority for the proposition that divorce, prior to trial, dissolves the spousal privilege and subs. 189(6) does not apply. The intercepted communications were accepted into evidence, subject to the requirements of subs. 186(5).[45] In Canada, the only other privileged communications are solicitor-client when made for the purpose of giving advice, receiving or carrying out instructions. Such communications may extend, depending upon the circumstances, to third parties acting as agents of the solicitor. Communications made for a criminal purpose are not protected. Solicitor-client privilege, interception of solicitors' communications and admissibility issues are discussed above in more detail.

During the course of a prosecution using intercepted communications as evidence, the Crown must prove voice identification and the integrity and continuity of the tapes or compact discs used to record the communications. Voice identification is a question of fact and does not require an expert to testify as to who the parties are to a communication.[46] Integrity means that the equipment used to record the communications was working properly and recording of the communication has not been changed or altered. Continuity means the chain of actual control or custody over the tapes/discs to be tendered. The Crown need not call every witness who handled the tapes/discs, however briefly, but, as stated, must satisfy the Court that the original recordings have not been tampered with or altered.

Challenging the Intercepted Communications by the Defence

Prior to enactment of the *Charter*, an accused person could only have access to the materials put before the authorizing judge if, among other things, fraud, willful non-disclosure or misleading disclosure could be demonstrated. It is now recognized in case law and by statute (s. 187) that there is entitlement to full disclosure of the materials, subject to editing, in order to make full answer and defence.[47] An application can be made to a judge for the sealed packets to be opened and materials released. Materials may be edited only if the release of the information would be prejudicial to the public interest which includes editing to prevent the following:

(a) identification of confidential informers;
(b) compromise of ongoing investigations;
(c) disclosure of particular investigative techniques so as to endanger persons and prejudice future investigations; and
(d) prejudice interests of innocent third parties.

The trial judge may order additional disclosure if a judicial summary of the deleted material is not sufficient for full answer and defence.[48]

As stated above, whenever a police activity invades a reasonable expectation of privacy then the activity is a "search". The interception of private communications is considered, therefore, to be a search and seizure under s. 8 of the *Charter*. When deciding whether a particular investigative technique offends s. 8 of the *Charter*, courts evaluate the technology used according to its current capability and not in the context of future evolution of that technology.[49] Challenging the admissibility of evidence obtained from interceptions is subject to subs. 24(2) of the *Charter*. Sections 8 and 24 of the *Charter* state:

> **8** — Everyone has the right to be secure against unreasonable search or seizure.
>
> . . .
>
> **24 (1)** — Anyone whose rights or freedoms, as guaranteed by this *Charter*, have been infringed or denied may apply to a court of competent jurisdiction to obtain such remedy as the court considers appropriate and just in the circumstances.
>
> **(2)** — Where, in proceedings under subsection (1), a court concludes that evidence was obtained in a manner that infringed or denied any rights or freedoms guaranteed by this *Charter*, the evidence shall be excluded if it is established that, having regard to all the circumstances, the admission of it in the proceedings would bring the administration of justice into disrepute.

The pre-1993 statutory provision (now s. 186 of the *Code*), which required judicial authorization to intercept private communications, has been found to conform to minimum constitutional requirements demanded by s. 8 of the *Charter*.[50]

A challenge to the constitutionality of a particular provision of the *Code* or to the admissibility of evidence obtained as a result of a search or seizure is made to the trial judge, usually in the form of a pre-trial motion.[51] The making of such motions is governed by certain procedural requirements (e.g., notice of the motion and the showing of a factual or evidentiary basis for the motion) so as to avoid what the courts refer to as "fishing expeditions".[52] A *Charter* motion challenging intercepted communications as evidence cannot be made during a preliminary inquiry because such challenges can only be made to the trial judge.[53]

In circumstances where there is no judicial order or authorization permitting the search for or seizure of evidence, there is a presumption of unreasonableness under s. 8 of the *Charter*. The burden is on the Crown to demonstrate, on a balance of probabilities—that is, more probable than not—that the search or seizure was reasonable. A search is reasonable if authorized by law, the law itself is reasonable and the manner of carrying out the search is reasonable.[54]

The 1993 provisions opened the possibility of a constitutional challenge particularly to the provisions that do not require prior judicial approval to carry out interceptions (e.g., ss. 184.1 and 184.2). It should be noted, however, that the Supreme Court of Canada in *Hunter et al v. Southam Inc.*[55] found that it might not be reasonable in every instance to insist on prior authorization in order to sanction governmental intrusion upon a person's expectation of privacy. The justification for a "warrantless" search can arise in "exigent" circumstances. These are circumstances where it is impractical (e.g.. a crime is in progress) to obtain prior approval or urgency. The absence of prior judicial authorization does not necessarily make electronic surveillance unlawful but runs the risk of being found unreasonable in a given fact situation.

Section 8 *Charter* challenges are made on the basis that the evidence was obtained contrary to the provisions of the *Code* or the judicial order allowing a search and seizure or that during the search or seizure, the manner in which it was conducted was unreasonable. For example, in s. 184.1 the absence of reasonable grounds to believe a risk of bodily harm would make the "search or seizure" of intercepts unreasonable. Even if there were reasonable grounds, intercepting the communications of everyone who lived in the neighbourhood where the risk arose would be unreasonable as the manner of carrying out the interception would be too invasive or intrusive.

In circumstances where a judicial authorization exists (e.g., ss. 186 or 188), the burden, or onus is on the accused person to show, on a balance of probabilities, that the evidence was obtained in a manner that infringed or denied a particular *Charter* right. Section 8 of the *Charter* is the most commonly used provision to challenge the tendering into evidence of intercepted communications. The first issue that arises is whether an accused has "standing" to seek *Charter* relief from the trial judge. If the Crown objects to the standing of an accused person to bring a *Charter* challenge, the accused person has the onus of demonstrating that a personal privacy right or interest has been allegedly breached.[56]

The Basis of a Section 8 Charter Challenge

Numerous challenges have been made to intercepted communications being tendered into evidence at criminal proceedings. The basis for most objections to the admissibility of this evidence is s. 8 and subs. 24(2) of the *Charter*.

A common objection relates to an allegation that "minimization" clauses should have been provided for or were ignored by the police. It is unreasonable to have clauses in an authorization, which would in effect permit the interception of anyone, anywhere in Canada. The authorization, or in the absence of an authorization, the conduct of the police must be such as to minimize wide spread invasive interception of communications.[57] To avoid this, interception occurs with respect to either named or known persons or named/known places or telephones. As stated previously, interceptions of 'unknown' persons are permissible if they are in conversation with a named person or the conversation occurs at a known or named telephone or place. Consideration of whether or not minimization is necessary has been discussed in *R. v. Garofoli* as follows:

> In my view, while a requirement of live monitoring or visual confirmation would generally be appropriate when telephone calls are proposed to be intercepted at public pay telephones, the same considerations do not apply with respect to the private residence of a person named in an authorization unless there are special circumstances calling for live monitoring. It must be remembered that constant live monitoring of a private residence can also constitute a serious invasion of privacy.
>
> The presence of special circumstances must be determined on the basis of what will enable the police to obtain the evidence with a minimum invasion of privacy. Thus, if the information in the possession of the police indicates that the subject visits the premises only occasionally and for a short duration, this should be reflected in the extent of the electronic surveillance. It may require live monitoring to determine the presence of the target, and indeed may be a term in the authorization. Wholesale interception of all communication in and out of the residence in these circumstances will run the risk of being found to be an unreasonable search and seizure. On the other hand, if the target is an occupant and is usually present, other considerations will apply. Such information may be lacking initially, but will often be available after a period of electronic surveillance pursuant to a valid authorization. On renewal, or application for a new authorization, this information must be utilized to minimize the invasion of privacy.[58]

The manner in which the interceptions are carried out, therefore, may attract a *Charter* review at trial.

Another common challenge to evidence involving intercepted communications is whether reasonable grounds existed to believe an offence is being or has been committed or that the communications of persons intercepted would assist the investigation. Reasonable grounds or belief has been interpreted to mean reasonable probability (more probable than not) rather than proof beyond a reasonable doubt or a *prima facie* case. A *prima facie* case means a case sufficient on its face, being supported by at least the requisite minimum evidence, one that usually prevails in the absence of evidence to the contrary.[59]

Reasonable grounds must be more than suspicion, "mere rumor or gossip" and cannot take the form of "bold conclusory" statements.[60]

An example of that kind of statement would be, "John Doe is a thief, everyone knows that and he has stolen goods in his house."

Reasonable grounds to believe that an offence is being or has been committed may consist of a number of different types or sources of information which, when taken together, form the basis of the belief. Such information may come from surveillance of suspects, past related criminal record or association to others engaged in criminal behavior, investigative techniques such as undercover operations, being the subject of previous investigations, searches of residences and/or places of employment and informants or persons who pass on information (tips) to police agencies whether or not for reward. Reasonable grounds of belief can include hearsay statements but the degree of hearsay information (e.g., first- or second-hand information) should be identified.[61]

When assessing the reliability of informant statements or tips, judges consider "the totality of the circumstances" and look at a variety of factors including:

(a)   the degree of detail of the "tip";
(b)   the informer's source of knowledge;
(c)   indicia of the informer's reliability such as past performance or confirmation from other investigative sources.

When challenging intercepted communications on the basis of informant reliability, the accused cannot embark on a fishing expedition of all the materials in the possession of the police. The right to full answer and defence is the right to disclosure of material that was considered by the judge who authorized the interceptions.[62]

Charter motions challenging the admissibility of intercepted communications frequently involve a request by the accused person or their counsel to cross-examine the affiant or peace officer(s) that possessed the alleged grounds for the application. The trial judge does not automatically grant the right to cross-examination. A basis for the cross-examination is necessary and that may be done by demonstrating that the cross examination will provide evidence showing that conditions in the authorization or statutory pre-conditions in the *Code* were not complied with—that is, the existence of reasonable grounds or other investigative techniques tried and failed or unlikely to succeed.[63] On appeal, deference is shown to a trial judge's refusal to permit cross examination unless the judge failed to exercise discretion properly or the accused can show that the cross examination would have materially modified the basis upon which the authorization was granted.[64]

A person whose conversations were intercepted and who can demonstrate they were "known" to the police but not disclosed to the authorizing judge may also apply to have communications ruled inadmissible pursuant to subs. 24(2) of the *Charter*. As stated, "known" does not merely mean that the police were aware of their existence or even their involvement in criminal behaviour; "known" means that there are reasonable grounds to believe their conversations will assist in the investigation because of their involvement in the offences under investigation or because of their association with persons under investigation.[65]

Another avenue of attack is with respect to "investigative necessity". As discussed above, while interception need not be a technique of "last resort",[66] information must be placed before the authorizing judge that shows other investigative techniques have been tried and failed or unlikely to succeed. Failure to do so will result in a finding that the intercepted communications were obtained in breach of s. 8 *Charter* rights.

The standard for reviewing an authorization is often called the "no evidence" test. The order or authorization should not be set aside unless on the whole of the evidence or material there is or remains after a challenge to it no basis upon which the authorization could have been granted. A trial or reviewing judge cannot simply substitute their view for that of the authorizing judge, even if, in the circumstances, they would not have granted the order or authorization.[67]

Even the existence of false or misleading information in the grounds of the affidavit that was before the authorizing judge, does not lead automatically to the authorization being set aside. The judge reviewing an affidavit, for example, will strike out portions of the affidavit found to be improper. The decision on whether the authorization could have been granted is based then on what information is left.[68] "Full, fair and frank disclosure" must be the prevailing theme in seeking such authorizations and "boiler plating" is not permitted. While an affiant can use precedents to assist in drafting the affidavit in support of an application for an authorization, consideration must be given to whether the precedents apply in the context of the particular investigation.[69]

Admissibility of Evidence — Section 24 of the Charter

When a judge finds a s. 8 *Charter* breach, the accused must then demonstrate, on a balance of probabilities, that in all of the circumstances, admitting the evidence that was the subject of a *Charter* breach would bring the administration of justice into disrepute. In *R. v. Grant*,[70] the Supreme Court of Canada revised the approach to the admissibility of evidence under s. 24(2) of the *Charter*.

> A review of the authorities suggests that whether the admission of evidence obtained in breach of the *Charter* would bring the administration of justice into disrepute engages three avenues of inquiry, each rooted in the public interests engaged by s. 24(2), viewed in the long term, forward-looking and societal perspective. When faced with an application for exclusion under s. 24(2), a court must assess and balance the effect of admitting the evidence on society's confidence in the justice system having regard to: (1) the seriousness of the *Charter*-infringing state conduct (admission may send the message the justice system condones serious state misconduct), (2) the impact of the breach on the *Charter*-protected interests of the accused (admission may send the message that individual rights count for little), and (3) society's interests in the adjudication of the case on its merits. The court's role on a s. 24(2) application is to balance the assessments under each of these lines of inquiry to determine whether, considering all the circumstances, admission of the evidence would bring the administration of justice into disrepute. These concerns, while not precisely tracking the categories of considerations set out in *Collins*, capture the factors relevant to the s. 24(2) determination as enunciated in *Collins* and subsequent jurisprudence.

The task for the courts remains one of achieving a balance between individuals and societal interests with a view to determining whether the administration of justice would be brought into disrepute by the admission of evidence.

The evidence sought to be excluded, as stated, could be the intercepted private communications, and/or data/records created by or from the use of communication devices, or in the case of other forms of electronic surveillance (e.g., videos), the activities of the accused.

Private communications that have been intercepted under Part VI of the *Code* authorizations are considered by the courts to be "real evidence" (tangible)—that is, evidence that existed regardless of a breach by the police of a *Charter* right. The conversations or activities would have existed whether or not the authorities intercepted them. This factor would be considered under the impact analysis—that is, the nature of the intrusion on the *Charter*-protected interests. Real evidence is different than evidence which the accused was conscripted to create (e.g., confessions, participation in a police lineup). Conscripted evidence would not have existed but for the participation of the accused in constructing the evidence and usually involves police compulsion or enticement in creating the evidence. Admissibility determinations are made, however, on a case-by-case basis. Intercepted communications and related data/records are considered to be real evidence and, as such, generally reliable, an important factor in the subs. 24(2) analysis. Absent fraud, material misleading or non-disclosure in obtaining the authorization or unreasonable conduct by authorities in the carrying out of the terms of the authorization, intercepted communications will be ruled admissible under subs. 24(2).[71]

Part XV—Special Procedure and Powers

Other Forms of Electronic Surveillance

The *Code* makes provision for three other forms of electronic surveillance.

Video Surveillance

Section 487.01 reads as follows:

> **487.01 (1) Information for general warrant** — A provincial court judge, a judge of a superior court of criminal jurisdiction or a judge as defined in section 552 may issue a warrant in writing authorizing a peace officer to, subject to this section, use any device or investigative technique or procedure or do any thing described in the warrant that would, if not authorized, constitute an unreasonable search or seizure in respect of a person or a person's property if
>
> (a) the judge is satisfied by information on oath in writing that there are reasonable grounds to believe that an offence against this or any other Act of Parliament has been or will be committed and that information concerning the offence will be obtained through the use of the technique, procedure or device or the doing of the thing;
> (b) the judge is satisfied that it is in the best interest of the administration of justice to issue the warrant; and
> (c) there is no other provision in this or any other Act of Parliament that would provide for a warrant, authorization or order permitting the technique, procedure or device to be used or the thing to be done.
>
> **(2) Limitation** — Nothing in subsection (1) shall be construed as to permit interference with the bodily integrity of any person.
>
> **(3) Search or seizure to be reasonable** — A warrant issued under subsection (1) shall contain such terms and conditions as the judge considers advisable to ensure that any search or seizure authorized by the warrant is reasonable in the circumstances.
>
> **(4) Video surveillance** — A warrant issued under subsection (1) that authorizes a peace officer to observe, by means of a television camera or

other similar electronic device, any person who is engaged in activity in circumstances in which the person has a reasonable expectation of privacy shall contain such terms and conditions as the judge considers advisable to ensure that the privacy of the person or of any other person is respected as much as possible.

(5) Other provisions to apply — The definition "offence" in section 183 and sections 183.1, 184.2, 184.3 and 185 to 188.2 ... 190, 193 and 194 to 196 apply, with such modifications as the circumstances require, to a warrant referred to in subsection (4) as though references in those provisions to interceptions of private communications were read as references to observations by peace officers by means of television cameras or similar electronic devices of activities in circumstances in which persons had reasonable expectations of privacy.

(6) Provisions to apply — Subsections 487(2) and (4) apply, with such modifications as the circumstances require, to a warrant issued under subsection (1).

The requirements of previously discussed sections of the *Code* are incorporated into this section. The same considerations as to ss. 8 and 24 of the *Charter* apply. The operative or determinative factor is the reasonable expectation of privacy. Activities conducted in a public place or where there is public access would not enjoy this protection. Subject to comments already set out, video warrants can be executed anywhere in Canada.

This section was introduced as a result of the decision of the Supreme Court of Canada in *R. v. Wong*.[72] Police officers had videotaped persons gambling in a hotel room. The Court concluded that:

(i)   unauthorized video surveillance is a "search" and offends a reasonable expectation of privacy protected, in those circumstances, by s. 8; and

(ii) a reasonable expectation of privacy does not depend upon whether a person is engaged in illegal activities at the time of the "search".

The evidence of the video surveillance was, however, admitted into evidence under subs. 24(2) of the *Charter*. The Court concluded that the police officers had acted in good faith, had reasonable belief that an offence had been committed and were operating on the state of the law as it existed at the time they conducted their investigation.

Tracking Devices

Section 492.1 states:

492.1 (1) Information for tracking warrant — A justice who is satisfied by information on oath in writing that there are reasonable grounds to suspect that an offence under this or any other Act of Parliament has been or will be committed and that information that is relevant to the commission of the offence, including the whereabouts of any person, can be obtained through the use of a tracking device, may at any time issue a warrant authorizing a peace officer or a public officer who has been appointed or designated to administer or enforce a federal or provincial law and whose duties include the enforcement of this Act or any other Act of Parliament and who is names in the warrant

    (a) to install, maintain and remove a tracking device in or on any thing, including a thing carried, used or worn by any person; and

    (b) to monitor, or to have monitored, a tracking device installed in or on any thing.

(2) Time limit for warrant — A warrant issued under subsection (1) is valid for the period, not exceeding sixty days, mentioned in it.

(3) Further warrants — A justice may issue further warrants under this section.

(4) Definition of "tracking device" — For the purposes of this section, "tracking device" means any device that, when installed in or on any thing, may be used to help ascertain, by electronic or other means, the location of any thing or person.

The inclusion of the tracking device provisions is a response to the Supreme Court's decision in *R. v. Wise*.[73] The Court concluded that a "beeper" or tracking device installed on a motor vehicle and monitored was an invasion of a reasonable expectation of privacy. Absent prior authorization, the search was *prima facie* unreasonable and in violation of s. 8.

The Court also decided that there is a lesser privacy interest in a motor vehicle and the evidence obtained was "real" evidence. There was no police compulsion or enticement for the accused to create the evidence—that is, enter or drive his car. The evidence was admitted pursuant to subs. 24(2) of the *Charter*.

The test for authorities to meet when applying to obtain a tracking device from a judge is "reasonable grounds to suspect" and is a lower threshold than "reasonable grounds to believe". This may be, in part, due to the type of information that is obtained from the device. Merely tracking the location, without more, of an automobile or a vessel for example is not as intrusive as recording a person's activities or their words. As well, given that the devices usually attach to mobile units which may be in use in public areas, there is a lesser expectation of privacy in those circumstances than would exist in one's home.

Dial or Digital Number Recorder

Section 492.2 of the *Code* states:

> **492.2 (1) Information re number recorder** — A justice who is satisfied by information on oath in writing that there are reasonable grounds to suspect that an offence under this or any other Act of Parliament has been or will be committed and that information that would assist in the investigation of that offence could be obtained through the use of a number recorder, may at any time issue a warrant authorizing a peace officer or a public officer who has been appointed or designated to administer or enforce a federal or provincial law and whose duties include the enforcement of this Act or any other Act of Parliament and who is names in the warrant
>
> > (a) to install, maintain and remove a number recorder in relation to any telephone or telephone line; and
> >
> > (b) to monitor, or to have monitored, the number recorder.
>
> **(2) Order re telephone records** — When the circumstances referred to in subsection (1) exist, a justice may order that any person or body that lawfully possesses records of telephone calls originated from, or received or intended to be received at, any telephone give the records, or a copy of the records, to a person named in the order.
>
> **(3) Other provisions to apply** — Subsections 492.1(2) and (3) apply to warrants and orders issued under this section, with such modifications as the circumstances require.
>
> **(4) Definition of "number recorder"** — For the purposes of this section, "number recorder" means any device that can be used to record or identify the telephone number or location of the telephone from which a telephone call originates, or at which it is received or is intended to be received.

A digital number recorder is intended to record the date, time, and duration of telephone calls, the telephone number being called from and the number being called. Conflicting court decisions exist about whether the standard of reasonable grounds to "suspect" is constitutionally deficient. Some courts have concluded that the expectation of privacy requires authorities to possess more than suspicion when applying for this order.[74] This judicial concern has arisen because of the amount and type of information that a number recorder can potentially capture, in addition to telephone numbers called or telephone numbers received or intended to be received. These devices also capture the use of cell phones within a local area and other types of transmission data such as location of the phone, and numbers dialed or received.

In *R. v. Harris*,[75] the Court concluded that subs. 492.2(2) allowed for the seizure of cell phone records to trace the geographic location of such cell phones. In *R. v. Mahmood*,[76] the Court determined that there is a reasonable expectation of privacy in cell phone data recorded by transmission towers such that it attracts a s. 8 *Charter* protection against unreasonable search and seizure. Further, the Court balanced the privacy interests at stake in the context of the investigation and concluded that the "sheer scope and unbridled breadth" of the data collected from thousands of cell phone users, including Mr. Mahmood, within a particular area and time frame militated against admitting evidence under subs. 24(2) of the *Charter*.

New Communications Technology

With changing technology persons can now communicate through means not envisioned even five years ago. Persons engaged in criminal activities, facilitate or actually carry out criminal conduct by using communication devices that operate through traditional telecommunications systems (telephone lines), as well as through wireless technology. Computers and related communication devices (e.g., Blackberries™ cellular telephones) have electronic mail, voice, visual, text messaging, or fax capabilities. An authorization that is granted pursuant to s. 186 of the *Code* can be broad enough to include authority to intercept communications when made over such technologies during the course of an investigation. Transmission data related to communications, location of cell phones, numbers dialed or received and subscriber information can be obtained through judicially authorized warrants or orders (e.g., s. 492.2).

Persons who communicate through such means have a reasonable expectation of privacy. Agents of the state cannot intercept such communications unless prior judicial authorization is obtained. As communication technology advances and becomes mainstream, police agencies will face new challenges investigating offences being committed through the use of such technology. For example, unlike oral conversations in which the parties to the communication can usually be identified, many electronic means of communicating now allow relative anonymity. As well, the type of investigative tools differ depending upon the nature of the technology being used to conduct or facilitate criminal offences, the information sought to be captured and whether investigators intend to capture private communications in real time (e.g., electronic messaging as it is happening) or seeking access to stored electronic messages

In *R. v. Giles* and in *R. v. Weir*,[77] the Courts considered the seizure of e-mail messages by the police in the course of investigations. In *Giles*, encrypted messages were seized from the memory chip of a BlackBerry during a search incident to an arrest; in *Weir*, a search warrant (under s. 487 of the *Code*) was used to seize e-mail materials from the Internet service provider. Although in neither case were the messages seized through an authorization to intercept private communications, the seizures were found to be reasonable and, in the circumstances, not a breach of a *Charter* right. In both cases, the messages existed in a stored state and as such the seizures were not considered to be interceptions of private communications.

The rapid development of new forms of technology will create considerable challenges in the future. Law enforcement agencies will need the investigative tools capable of uncovering criminal activity being conducted through new and sophisticated means of communicating such as those that are web-based. Novel legal issues will arise when information captured by police agencies from intercepting communications made over these technologies result in prosecutions and the information is to be tendered as evidence

Communication service providers are an essential avenue for investigating agencies seeking lawful access to technical and subscriber information and communications passing through their systems.

Legislation will need to balance the competing demands between personal privacy interests and the public interest in detecting serious criminal offences. Inevitably, the courts will be called upon to examine and reconcile the parameters of these legitimate and competing interests. It is in this context that the 'Lawful Access Initiative' evolved and Bill C-47 has been introduced in Parliament.[78]

Notes

[1] S.C. 1973-74, c. 50, as amended.

[2] R.S.C. 1970, c. C-34, as amended. All Criminal Code references are to R.S.C. 1985, c. C-46.

[3] S.C. 1993, c. 40, as amended.

[4] S.C. 1997, c. 23, as amended; S.C. 1999, c. 5, as amended; S.C. 2001, c. 32 as amended; S.C. 2001, c. 41, as amended; S.C. 2002, c. 22, as amended; S.C. 2004, c.12, c. 15, as amended; S.C. 2005 c. 10, as amended; S.C.2008, c. 6, as amended.

5 Bill C-31: Omnibus Bill; May 2009 (1st Reading); Bill C-47: *Technical Assistance for Law Enforcement in the 21st Century Act;* July 2009 (2nd Reading).

6 *R. v. Riley,* 2008 CarswellOnt 4332, [2008] O.J. No. 2887, 234 C.C.C. (3d) 181, 60 C.R. (6th) 105, 174 C.R.R. (2d) 250 (Ont. S.C. J.); *R. v. Tse,* 2008 CarswellBC 1948, [2008] B.C.J. No. 1767, 180 C.R.R. 24, 2008 BCSC 211, 235 C.C.C. (3d) 161 (B.C. S.C.); *R. v. Six Accused Persons,* 2008 CarswellBC 334, 2008 BCSC 212, 2008] B.C.J. No. 293, 166 C.R.R. (2d) 304, 231 C.C.C. (3d) 237 (S.C.).

7 Lawful Access Initiative—summary report and consultation paper available at http://www.canada.justice.gc.ca/en/cons/la-al.

8 *R. v. Chehil,* 2009 CarswellNS 602, 248 C.C.C. (3d) 370, 71 C.R. (6th) 55, 284 N.S.R. (2d) 130, 901 A.P.R. 130, 2009 NSCA 111 (N.S. C.A.); *R. v. Patrick,* 2009 CarswellAlta 481, 2009 CarswellAlta 482, 2009 SCC 17, 242 C.C.C. (3d) 158, 304 D.L.R. (4th) 260, 4 Alta. L.R. (5th) 1, 387 N.R. 44, 454 A.R. 1, [2009] 1 S.C.R. 579, [2009] 5 W.W.R. 387, 64 C.R. (6th) 1 (S.C.C.); *R. v. Cuttell,* 2009 CarswellOnt 5896, 247 C.C.C. (3d) 424, 2009 ONCJ 471 (Onr. C.J.).

9 *R. v. Fegan,* 1993 CarswellOnt 92, 21 C.R. (4th) 65, 13 O.R. (3d) 88, 80 C.C.C. (3d) 356, 62 O.A.C. 146, 14 C.R.R. (2d) 250 (Ont. C.A.).

10 *R. v. Wong,* 1990 CarswellOnt 58, 1990 CarswellOnt 1008, 60 C.C.C. (3d) 460, 1 C.R. (4th) 1, 120 N.R. 34, [1990] 3 S.C.R. 36, 2 C.R.R. (2d) 277, 45 O.A.C. 250 (S.C.C.).

11 *R. v. Tam ,* 1993 CarswellBC 1142, 80 C.C.C. (3d) 476 (B.C.S.C.).

12 *R. v. Monachan,* 1981 CarswellOnt 57, 60 C.C.C. (2d) 286, 22 C.R. (3d) 1 (Ont. C.A.); aff'd 1985 CarswellOnt 949, 1985 CarswellOnt 949F, 16 C.C.C. (3d) 576, [1985] 1 S.C.R. 176, 57 N.R. 76 (S.C.C.).

13 *R. v. Comeau,* 1984 CarswellNB 14, 52 N.B.R. (2d) 168, 137 A.P.R. 168, 37 C.R. (3d) 286, 11 C.C.C. (3d) 61 (N.B. C.A.).

14 *R. v. M. (M.L.),* 2005 CarswellBC 1010, 2005 BCSC 385, *(sub nom. R. v. McIsaac)* [2005] B.C.J. No. 946, 29 C.R. (6th) 274 (B.C. S.C.); *R. v. S. (D.J),* 2002 CarswellBC 1246, 2002 BCSC 614 (B.C. S.C.); *R. v. Olson,* 1993 CarswellBC 856, 37 B.C.A.C. 155, 60 W.A.C. 155 (B.C. C.A.); contra: *R. v. Williamson,* 1998 CarswellAlta 235, 123 C.C.C. (3d) 540, 52 C.R.R. (2d) 277, *(sub nom. R. v. Feist)* 218 A.R. 332 (Alta.Q.B.); *R. v. Rodney,* 1991 CarswellBC 423, 65 C.C.C. (3d) 304, 5 C.R. (4th) 393 (B.C. C.A.).

15 *R. v. Lubovac,* 1989 CarswellAlta 791, 52 C.C.C. (3d) 551, 101 A.R. 119 (Alta. C.A.); *R. v. Nin,* 1985 CarswellQue 278, 34 C.C.C. (3d) 89 (Que. C.S.P.).

16 *R. v. Singh,* 1998 CarswellBC 1535, 127 C.C.C. (3d) 429, 110 B.C.A.C. 198, 178 W.A.C. 198 (B.C.C.A.); *R. v. Williams,* 2009 CarswellBC 1970, 2009 BCCA 284, 246 C.C.C. (3d) 443, 273 B.C.A.C. 86, 461 W.A.C. 86 (B.C. C.A.).

17 *R. v. Commisso,* 1983 CarswellBC 694, 1983 CarswellBC 729, 7 C.C.C. (3d) 1, [1983] 2 S.C.R. 121, 1 D.L.R. (4th) 577, 49 N.R. 26, [1984] 1 W.W.R. 673, 36 C.R. (3d) 105 (S.C.C); *R. v. Chesson,* 1988 CarswellAlta 550, 1988 CarswellAlta 144, 43 C.C.C. (3d) 353, [1988] 6 W.W.R. 193, [1988] 2 S.C.R. 148, 87 N.R. 115, 61 Alta. L.R. (2d) 289, 90 A.R. 347, 65 C.R. (3d) 193 (S.C.C.).

18 R.S.C. 1985, c. C-23.

19 *R. c. Bordage,* 2000 CarswellQue 1225, 146 C.C.C. (3d) 549 (Que. C.A.); *R. v. Pritchard,* 2002 CarswellBC 3577, 2002 BCSC 470 (B.C. S.C.).

20 *R. v. Mapara,* 2003 CarswellBC 450, 2003 BCCA 131, [2003] 13 B.C.J. No. 452, 179 B.C.A.C. 92, 295 W.A.C. 92, 180 C.C.C. (3d) 184 (B.C. C.A.); aff'd 2005

CarswellBC 963, 2005 CarswellBC 964, 2005 SCC 23, [2005] 1 S.C.R. 358, 40 B.C.L.R. (4th) 203, 332 N.R. 244, 211 B.C.A.C. 1, 349 W.A.C. 1, [2005] 6 W.W.R. 203, 195 C.C.C. (3d) 225, 251 D.L.R. (4th) 385, 28 C.R. (6th) 1 (S.C.C.); *R. v. Chow*, 2005 CarswellBC 961, 2005 CarswellBC 962, 2005 SCC 24, [2005] 1 S.C.R. 384, 332 N.R. 275, 211 B.C.A.C. 31, 349 W.A.C. 31, 195 C.C.C. (3d) 246, 251 D.L.R. (4th) 406, 28 C.R. (6th) 21 (S.C.C.); *R. v. Araujo*, 2000 CarswellBC 2438, 2000 CarswellBC 2440, 2000 SCC 65, 149 C.C.C. (3d) 449, 2000] 2 S.C.R. 992, 79 C.R.R. (2d) 1, 38 C.R. (5th) 307, 193 D.L.R. (4th) 440, 143 B.C.A.C. 257, 235 W.A.C. 257, 262 N.R. 346 (S.C.C.); *R. v. Schreinert*, 2002 CarswellOnt 1688, 165 C.C.C. (3d) 295, 159 O.A.C. 174 (Ont.C.A.); *R. v. Moore*, 1993 Carswell-BC 496, 81 C.C.C. (3d) 161, 21 C.R. (4th) 387, 27 B.C.A.C. 253, 45 W.A.C. 253 (B.C.C.A.); aff'd 1995 CarswellBC 68, 1995 CarswellBC 637, 95 C.C.C. (3d) 288, 38 C.R. (4th) 44, [1995] 1 S.C.R. 756, 179 N.R. 313, 60 B.C.A.C. 161, 99 W.A.C. 161 (S.C.C.).

[21] *R. v. Wasfi*, 2006 CarswellBC 267, 2006 BCCA 55, 206 C.C.C. (3d) 203, 222 B.C.A.C. 130, 368 W.A.C. 130 (B.C. C.A.); *R. v. Paulson*, 1995 CarswellBC 2520, 97 C.C.C. (3d) 344, 57 B.C.A.C. 217, 94 W.A.C. 217 (B.C.C.A.); *R. v. Smyk*, 1993 CarswellMan 147, 86 C.C.C. (3d) 63, [1994] 1 W.W.R. 513, 88 Man. R. (2d) 303, 51 W.A.C. 303 (Man. C.A.); *R. v. Hiscock*, 1992 CarswellQue 207, 72 C.C.C. (3d) 303, 46 Q.A.C. 263, [1992] R.J.Q. 895 (Que. C.A.); *R. v. Araujo, supra*, note 20.

[22] *R. v. Cheung*, 1997 CarswellBC 2241, 119 C.C.C. (3d) 507, 97 B.C.A.C. 161, 157 W.A.C. 161 (B.C.C.A.); leave to appeal refused [1997] S.C.C.A. No. 596, 227 N.R. 291 (note), 122 C.C.C. (3d) vi, 119 B.C.A.C. 320 (note), 194 W.A.C. 320 (note), 1998] 1 S.C.R. vii (S.C.C.); *R. v. Wasfi, supra*, note 21.

[23] *R. v. Pham*, 2002 CarswellBC 762, 2002 BCCA 247, 165 C.C.C. (3d) 97, 167 B.C.A.C. 66, 274 W.A.C. 66 (C.A.); *R. v. Tahirkheli* (1998), 1998 CarswellOnt 3963, 130 C.C.C. (3d) 19, 113 O.A.C. 322 (Ont. C.A.); *R. v. Wasfi, supra*, note 21.

[24] *R. v. Rosebush*, 1992 CarswellAlta 792, 77 C.C.C. (3d) 241, 131 A.R. 282, 25 W.A.C. 282 (Alta. C.A.), leave to appeal refused 78 C.C.C. (3d) vi (note) (S.C.C.). reconsideration refused 80 C.C.C. (3d) vi (note), [1993] 2 S.C.R. x (note) (S.C.C.); *R. v. Morrison*, 1989 CarswellOnt 106, 50 C.C.C. (3d) 353, 34 O.A.C. 50, 72 C.R. (3d) 332 (Ont. C.A.).

[25] *R. v. Adams*, [2006] B.C J. No. 533 (B.C. S.C.); *R. v. Nugent*, 2005 CarswellOnt 218, 193 C.C.C. (3d) 191, 127 C.R.R. (2d) 120 (Ont. C.A.); *R. v. Mooring*, 2003 CarswellBC 664, 2003 BCCA 199, [2002] B.C.J. No. 682, 181 B.C.A.C. 63, 298 W.A.C. 63, 174 C.C.C. (3d) 51, 13 C.R. (6th) 283 (C.A.); *R. v. Chesson, supra*, note 17; *R. v. Chow, supra*, note 20; *R. v. Schreinert, supra*, note 20.

[26] *R. v. Papalia* (1988), 1988 CarswellOnt 963, 1988 CarswellOnt 76, 43 C.C.C. (3d) 129, 65 C.R. (3d) 226, [1988] 2 S.C.R. 137, 87 N.R. 25, 29 O.A.C. 149, 66 O.R. (2d) 64 (note) (S.C.C.).

[27] *R. v. Vrany*, 1979 CarswellOnt 922, 46 C.C.C. (2d) 14 (Ont. C.A.); *R. v. Moore, supra*, note 20.

[28] *R. v. Mojtahedpour*, 2003 CarswellBC 33, 2003 BCCA 22, [2003] B.C.J. No.48, 171 C.C.C. (3d) 428, 104 C.R.R. (2d) 107, 178 B.C.A.C. 47, 292 W.A.C. 47 (B.C.C.A.).

[29] *R. v. Thompson*, 1990 CarswellBC 218, 1990 CarswellBC 760, 80 C.R. (3d) 129, [1990] 6 W.W.R. 481, [1990] 2 S.C.R. 1111, 49 B.C.L.R. (2d) 321, 50 C.R.R. 1,

114 N.R. 1, 73 D.L.R. (4th) 596, 59 C.C.C. (3d) 225 (S.C.C.); *R. v. Mooring, supra*, note 25; *R. v. Chow, supra*, note 20; *R. v. Nugent, supra*, note 25.

[30] *R. v. Lyons*, 1984 CarswellBC 776, 1984 CarswellBC 826, 15 C.C.C. (3d) 417, [1984] 2 S.C.R. 633, [1985] 2 W.W.R. 1, 14 D.L.R. (4th) 482, 56 N.R. 6, 43 C.R. (3d) 97, 58 A.R. 2 (S.C.C.); *R. v. Chesson*, supra, note 17.

[31] *R. v. Garofoli*, 1990 CarswellOnt 119, 1990 CarswellOnt 1006, 80 C.R. (3d) 317, [1990] 2 S.C.R. 1421, 116 N.R. 241, 43 O.A.C. 1, 36 Q.A.C. 161, 60 C.C.C. (3d) 161, 50 C.R.R. 206 (S.C.C.); *R. v. Sanelli*, 1990 CarswellOnt 77, 1990 CarswellOnt 986, 74 C.R. (3d) 281, 103 N.R. 86, 37 O.A.C. 322, *(sub nom. R. v. Duarte)* 53 C.C.C. (3d) 1, *(sub nom. R. v. Duarte)* 65 D.L.R. (4th) 240, *(sub nom. R. v. Duarte)* [1990] 1 S.C.R. 30, *(sub nom. R. v. Duarte)* 45 C.R.R. 278, *(sub nom. R. v. Duarte)* 71 O.R. (2d) 575 (S.C.C.).

[32] *R. v. Paterson*, 1985 CarswellOnt 79, 18 C.C.C. (3d) 137, 7 O.A.C. 105, 44 C.R. (3d) 150 (Ont. C.A.); *R. v. Chambers*, 1983 CarswellBC 537, 9 C.C.C. (3d) 132, 37 C.R. (3d) 128 (B.C.C.A.).

[33] *R. v. Doiron*, 2007 CarswellNB 249, 2007 CarswellNB 250, 2007 NBCA 41, 221 C.C.C. (3d) 97, 315 N.B.R. (2d) 205, 158 C.R.R. (2d) 299, 815 A.P.R. 205 (N.B.C.A.); leave to appeal refused 2007 CarswellNB 586, 2007 CarswellNB 587, [2007] S.C.C.A. No. 413, 383 N.R. 393 (note), 333 N.B.R. (2d) 429 (note), 855 A.P.R. 342 (note) (S.C.C.); *R. v. Desjardins*, 1990 CarswellNfld 77, 61 C.C.C. (3d) 376, 88 Nfld. & P.E.I.R. 143, 274 A.P.R. 143 (Nfld. S.C.).

[34] *R. v. Doiron, supra*, note 33; *Maranda c. Québec (Juge de la Cour du Québec)*, 2003 CarswellQue 2477, 2003 CarswellQue 2478, 2003 SCC 67, 178 C.C.C. (3d) 321, 15 C.R. (6th) 1, 113 C.R.R. (2d) 76, *(sub nom. Maranda v. Richer)* [2003] 3 S.C.R. 193, *(sub nom. Maranda v. Richer)* 232 D.L.R. (4th) 14, *(sub nom. Maranda v. Leblanc)* 311 N.R. 357; *R. v. Lavallee, Rackel & Heintz*, 2002 CarswellAlta 1818, 2002 CarswellAlta 1819, 2002 SCC 61, 216 D.L.R. (4th) 257, 4 Alta. L.R. (4th) 1, [2002] 11 W.W.R. 191, 2002 D.T.C. 7267 (Eng.), 2002 D.T.C. 7287 (Fr.), 3 C.R. (6th) 209, [2002] 4 C.T.C. 143, 312 A.R. 201, 281 W.A.C. 201, *(sub nom. Lavallee, Rackel & Heintz v. Canada (Attorney General))* 167 C.C.C. (3d) 1, *(sub nom. Lavallee, Rackel & Heintz v. Canada (Attorney General))* 164 O.A.C. 280, *(sub nom. Lavallee, Rackel & Heintz v. Canada (Attorney General))* 96 C.R.R. (2d) 189, *(sub nom. Lavallee, Rackel & Heintz v. Canada (Attorney General))* [2002] 3 S.C.R. 209, *(sub nom. Lavallee, Rackel & Heintz v. Canada (Attorney General))* 292 N.R. 296, *(sub nom. Lavallee, Rackel & Heintz v. Canada (Attorney General))* 217 Nfld. & P.E.I.R. 183, *(sub nom. Lavallee, Rackel & Heintz v. Canada (Attorney General))* 651 A.P.R. 183 (S.C.C.); *R. c. Robillard*, 2000 CarswellQue 2576, 151 C.C.C. (3d) 296, [2001] R.J.Q. 1, 39 C.R. (5th) 189 (Que.C.A.); *R. v. McClure*, 2001 CarswellOnt 496, 2001 CarswellOnt 497, 151 C.C.C. (3d) 321, 40 C.R. (5th) 1, 195 D.L.R. (4th) 513, 142 O.A.C. 201, 80 C.R.R. (2d) 217, 2001 SCC 14, [2001] 1 S.C.R. 445, 266 N.R. 275 (S.C.C.).

[35] *R. v. Lee*, [2001] No. CC010051 (B.C.S.C.); *R. v. Do*, 2000 CarswellYukon 129, 2000 YTTC 52, [2000] Y.J. No. 140 (Y.T. Terr. Ct.); *R. v. Heyden*, [1998] O.J. No. 1385 (G.D.).

[36] *R. v. Zaduk*, 1979 CarswellOnt 1454, 46 C.C.C. (2d) 327, 24 O.R. (2d) 362, 98 D.L.R. (3d) 133 (Ont. C.A.).

[37] *R. v. Welsh (No. 6)*, 1977 CarswellOnt 775, 32 C.C.C. (2d) 363, 74 D.L.R. (3d) 748, 15 O.R. (2d) 1 (Ont. C.A.).

38 *R. v. Galbraith*, 1989 CarswellAlta 74, 49 C.C.C. (3d) 178, 66 Alta. L.R. (2d) 387, 70 C.R. (3d) 392, 98 A.R. 241, 41 C.R.R. 142 (Alta. C.A.).

39 *R. v. Myers*, 1993 CarswellNS 382, 126 N.S.R. (2d) 237, 352 A.P.R. 237 (N.S. S.C.).

40 *R. v. Nicolucci*, 1989 CarswellQue 231, 53 C.C.C. (3d) 546, 29 Q.A.C. 174, [1990] R.J.Q. 296 (Que. C.A.); *R. v. Thompson, supra*, note 29.

41 S.C. 1997, c. 23, as amended; S.C. 2001, c. 32, as amended.

42 *R. v. Lindsay*, 2009 CarswellOnt 3687, 2009 ONCA 532, 68 C.R. (6th) 279, 245 C.C.C. (3d) 301, 251 O.A.C. 1, 97 O.R. (3d) 567 (Ont. C.A.); *R. v. Terezakis*, 2007 CarswellBC 1669, 2007 BCCA 384, 223 C.C.C. (3d) 344, 245 B.C.A.C. 74, 405 W.A.C. 74, 51 C.R. (6th) 165 (B.C. C.A.); *R. v. Doiron, supra*, note 33; *R. v. Doucet*, 2003 CarswellQue 2854, 18 C.R. (6th) 103 (Que. S.C.); *R. v. Pangman*, 2000 CarswellMan 332, 2000 MBQB 85, 76 C.R.R. (2d) 77, [2000] 8 W.W.R. 536, 147 Man. R. (2d) 93 (Man.Q.B).

43 *R. v. Dass*, 1977 CarswellMan 126, 39 C.C.C. (2d) 465, [1978] 3 W.W.R. 762, 3 C.R. (3d) 193 (Man.Q.B.).

44 *R. v. Welsh (No. 6)*, *supra*, note 37.

45 *R. v. Lloyd*, 1981 CarswellBC 633, 1981 CarswellBC 404, 64 C.C.C. (2d) 169, [1981] 2 S.C.R. 645, 31 C.R. (3d) 157, 35 B.C.L.R. 145, 131 D.L.R. (3d) 112, 39 N.R. 474 (S.C.C.); *R. v. Rendon*, [1997] O.J. No. 5505 (Ont. Gen. Div.).

46 *R. v. Williams*, 1995 CarswellOnt 118, 40 C.R. (4th) 181, 23 O.R. (3d) 122, 80 O.A.C. 119, 98 C.C.C. (3d) 160 (Ont. C.A.).

47 *R. v. Dersch*, 1990 CarswellBC 1478, 1990 CarswellBC 1479, 43 O.A.C. 256, 77 D.L.R. (4th) 473, 50 C.R.R. 272, 36 Q.A.C. 258, 51 B.C.L.R. (2d) 145, 116 N.R. 340, 80 C.R. (3d) 299, *(sub nom. Dersch v. Canada (Attorney General))* 60 C.C.C. (3d) 132, *(sub nom. Dersch v. Canada (Attorney General))* [1991] 1 W.W.R. 231, *(sub nom. Dersch v. Canada (Attorney General))* [1990] 2 S.C.R. 1505 (S.C.C.).

48 *R. v. Laws*, 1998 CarswellOnt 3509, 18 C.R. (5th) 257, 128 C.C.C. (3d) 516, 165 D.L.R. (4th) 301, 41 O.R. (3d) 499, 56 C.R.R. (2d) 1, 112 O.A.C. 353 (Ont. C.A.); *R. v. Garofoli, supra*, note 31.

49 *R. v. M. (A.)*, 2008 CarswellOnt 2257, 2008 CarswellOnt 2258, 2008 SCC 19, 230 C.C.C. (3d) 377, 55 C.R. (6th) 314, 236 O.A.C. 267, 293 D.L.R. (4th) 187, 92 O.R. (3d) 398 (note), 373 N.R. 198, [2008] 1 S.C.R. 569 (S.C.C.); *R. v. Tessling*, 2004 CarswellOnt 4351, 2004 CarswellOnt 4352, 2004 SCC 67, [2004] 3 S.C.R. 432, 326 N.R. 228 (Eng.), 326 N.R. 228 (Fr.), 192 O.A.C. 168, 189 C.C.C. (3d) 129, 244 D.L.R. (4th) 541, 75 O.R. (3d) 480 (note), 23 C.R. (6th) 207, 123 C.R.R. (2d) 257 (S.C.C.); *R. v. Chehil, supra*, note 8; *R. v. Wise*, 1992 CarswellOnt 982, 1992 CarswellOnt 71, [1992] 1 S.C.R. 527, 11 C.R. (4th) 253, 8 C.R.R. (2d) 53, 51 O.A.C. 351, 133 N.R. 161, 70 C.C.C. (3d) 193 (S.C.C.); *R. v. Thompson, supra*, note 29; *R. v. Sanelli* (sub nom. *R. v. Duarte*), *supra*, note 31.

50 *R. v. Finlay*, 1985 CarswellOnt 123, 23 C.C.C. (3d) 48, 52 O.R. (2d) 632, 23 D.L.R. (4th) 532, 11 O.A.C. 279, 48 C.R. (3d) 341, 18 C.R.R. 132 (Ont. C.A.); *R. v. Sanelli* (sub nom. *R. v. Duarte*), *supra*, note 31.

51 *R. v. Durette*, 1992 CarswellOnt 955, 72 C.C.C. (3d) 421, 54 O.A.C. 81, 9 O.R. (3d) 557 (Ont. C.A.), reversed 1994 CarswellOnt 54, 1994 CarswellOnt 1152, 88 C.C.C. (3d) 1, 163 N.R. 321, 70 O.A.C. 1, [1994] 1 S.C.R. 469, 28 C.R. (4th) 1 (S.C.C.); *R. v. DeSousa*, 1992 CarswellOnt 100, 1992 CarswellOnt 1006F, 76 C.C.C. (3d) 124, 15 C.R. (4th) 66, [1992] 2 S.C.R. 944, 11 C.R.R. (2d) 193, 9 O.R. (3d) 544 (note),

142 N.R. 1, 95 D.L.R. (4th) 595, 56 O.A.C. 109 (S.C.C.); *R. v. Garofoli, supra*, note 31.

[52] *R. v. Lising*, 2005 CarswellBC 2691, 2005 CarswellBC 2692, 2005 SCC 66, 217 B.C.A.C. 65, [2005] 3 S.C.R. 343, 49 B.C.L.R. (4th) 33, [2006] 4 W.W.R. 403, 358 W.A.C. 65, 241 N.R. 147, 33 C.R. (6th) 241, 201 C.C.C. (3d) 449, (*sub nom. R. v. Pires*) 259 D.L.R. (4th) 441, (*sub nom. R. v. Pires*) 136 C.R.R. (2d) 85 (S.C.C.); *R. v. Benoit*, 1999 CarswellNfld 66, [1999] N.J. No. 77, 134 C.C.C. (3d) 203, 173 Nfld. & P.E.I.R. 183, 530 A.P.R. 183, 172 D.L.R. (4th) 115 (Nfld. C.A.); *R. v. Dwernychuk*, 1992 CarswellAlta 263, 77 C.C.C. (3d) 385, 42 M.V.R. (2d) 237, 135 A.R. 31, 33 W.A.C. 31, 12 C.R.R. (2d) 175 (Alta. C.A.); *R. v. Loveman*, 1992 CarswellOnt 80, 71 C.C.C. (3d) 123, 12 C.R. (4th) 167, 8 C.R.R. (2d) 294, 52 O.A.C. 94, 8 O.R. (3d) 51 (Ont. C.A.); *R. v. Kutynec*, 1992 CarswellOnt 79, 70 C.C.C. (3d) 289, 12 C.R. (4th) 152, 7 O.R. (3d) 277, 52 O.A.C. 59, 8 C.R.R. (2d) 300 (Ont. C.A.).

[53] *R. v. C. (P.R.)*, 1997 CarswellPEI 21, 150 Nfld. & P.E.I.R. 327, 470 A.P.R. 327; leave to appeal refused (sub nom. *R. v. Hahn)*, [1998] S.C.C.A. No. 269 (S.C.C.).

[54] *R. v. Collins*, 1987 CarswellBC 94, 1987 CarswellBC 699, 33 C.C.C. (3d) 1, [1987] 3 W.W.R. 699, [1987] 1 S.C.R. 265, 38 D.L.R. (4th) 508, 74 N.R. 276, 13 B.C.L.R. (2d) 1, 56 C.R. (3d) 193, 28 C.R.R. 122 (S.C.C.).

[55] *Canada (Director of Investigation & Research, Combines Investigation Branch) v. Southam Inc.*, 1984 CarswellAlta 121, 1984 CarswellAlta 415, 33 Alta. L.R. (2d) 193, 27 B.L.R. 297, 41 C.R. (3d) 97, 84 D.T.C. 6467, (*sub nom. Hunter v. Southam Inc.*) 14 C.C.C. (3d) 97, (*sub nom. Hunter v. Southam Inc.*) 11 D.L.R. (4th) 641, (*sub nom. Hunter v. Southam Inc.*) 55 A.R. 291, (*sub nom. Director of Investigations & Research Combines Investigation Branch v. Southam Inc.*) [1984] 6 W.W.R. 577, (*sub nom. Hunter v. Southam Inc.*) [1984] 2 S.C.R. 145, (*sub nom. Hunter v. Southam Inc.*) 55 N.R. 241, (*sub nom. Hunter v. Southam Inc.*) 2 C.P.R. (3d) 1, (*sub nom. Hunter v. Southam Inc.*) 9 C.R.R. 355 (S.C.C.); *R. v. Patrick, supra*, note 8.

[56] *R. v. M. (A.), supra*, note 49; *R. v. Tessling, supra*, note 49; *R. v. Lam*, 2004 CarswellAlta 111, 2004 ABQB 78, 351 A.R. 332, 37 Alta. L.R. (4th) 141 (Alta. Q.B.); *R. v. Belnavis*, 1997 CarswellOnt 2926, 1997 CarswellOnt 2927, 118 C.C.C. (3d) 405, 151 D.L.R. (4th) 443, 103 O.A.C. 81, 10 C.R. (5th) 65, 29 M.V.R. (3d) 1, 216 N.R. 161, 34 O.R. (3d) 806 (headnote only), [1997] 3 S.C.R. 341, 46 C.R.R. (2d) 272 (S.C.C.); *R. v. Edwards*, 1996 CarswellOnt 1916, 1996 CarswellOnt 2126, 104 C.C.C. (3d) 136, 45 C.R. (4th) 307, 192 N.R. 81, 26 O.R. (3d) 736, 132 D.L.R. (4th) 31, 33 C.R.R. (2d) 226, 88 O.A.C. 321, [1996] 1 S.C.R. 128 (S.C.C.); *R. v. Shayesteh*, 1996 CarswellOnt 4226, 111 C.C.C. (3d) 225, 94 O.A.C. 81, 31 O.R. (3d) 161 (Ont. C.A.).

[57] *R. v. Chan*, 2001 CarswellBC 1766, 2001 BCSC 831, [2001] B.C.J. No. 1686 (B.C. S.C.); *R. v. Thompson, supra*, note 29; *R. v. Mapara, supra*, note 20; *R. v. Chow, supra*, note 20.

[58] *R. v. Garofoli, supra*, note 31, at paras. 121-122.

[59] Canadian Law Dictionary, J. Yogis, Q.C., 1983.

[60] *R. v. Debot*, 1989 CarswellOnt 111, 1989 CarswellOnt 966, 52 C.C.C. (3d) 193, 73 C.R. (3d) 129, [1989] 2 S.C.R. 1140, 102 N.R. 161, 37 O.A.C. 1, 45 C.R.R. 49 (S.C.C.).

61 *R. v. Debot, supra,* note 60; *R. v. Troncoso,* 1994 CarswellBC 1036, *(sub nom. R. v. Madrid)* 48 B.C.A.C. 271, *(sub nom. R. v. Madrid)* 78 W.A.C. 271 (B.C.C.A.).

62 *R. v. Araujo, supra,* note 20; *R. c. Bordage, supra,* note 19; *R. v. Barzal,* 1993 CarswellBC 1154, 84 C.C.C. (3d) 289, 33 B.C.A.C. 161, 54 W.A.C. 161 (B.C. C.A.).

63 *R. v. Araujo, supra,* note 20.

64 *R. v. Lising, supra,* note 52; *R. v. Camara,* 2005 CarswellBC 3083, 2005 BCCA 639, 219 B.C.A.C. 306, 361 W.A.C. 306 (B.C. C.A.); *R. v. Garofoli, supra,* note 31.

65 *R. v. Chesson, supra,* note 17; *R. v. Mooring, supra,* note 25; *R. v. Mapara, supra,* note 20; *R. v. Chow, supra,* note 20; *R. v. Chan, supra,* note 57.

66 *R. v. Araujo, supra,* note 20.

67 *Canada (Procureur général) c. Bisson,* 1994 CarswellQue 126, 1994 CarswellQue 126F, 94 C.C.C. (3d) 94, 65 Q.A.C. 241, [1994] 3 S.C.R. 1097, 173 N.R. 237 (S.C.C.); *R. v. Araujo, supra,* note 20; *R. v. Garofoli, supra,* note 31; *R. v. Lising, supra,* note 52.

68 *Canada c. Bisson, supra,* note 67; *R. v. Lising, supra,* note 52.

69 *R. v. Chan, supra,* note 57; *R. v. Araujo, supra,* note 20.

70 *R. v. Grant,* 2009 CarswellOnt 4104, 2009 CarswellOnt 4105, 2009 SCC 32, 245 C.C.C. (3d) 1, 66 C.R. (6th) 1, 253 O.A.C. 124, 82 M.V.R. (5th) 1, [2009] 2 S.C.R. 353, 391 N.R. 1, 309 D.L.R. (4th) 1 (S.C.C.). See also *R. v. Harrison,* 2009 CarswellOnt 4108, 2009 CarswellOnt 4109, 2009 SCC 34, 245 C.C.C. (3d) 86, 66 C.R. (6th) 105, 253 O.A.C. 358, [2009] 2 S.C.R. 494, 97 O.R. (3d) 560 (note), 391 N.R. 147, 309 D.L.R. (4th) 87 (S.C.C.); *R. v. Buhay,* 2003 CarswellMan 230, 2003 CarswellMan 231, 2003 SCC 30, [2003] 1 S.C.R. 631, 10 C.R. (6th) 205, 107 C.R.R. (2d) 240, [2004] 4 W.W.R. 1, 225 D.L.R. (4th) 624, 174 C.C.C. (3d) 97, 305 N.R. 158, 177 Man. R. (2d) 72, 304 W.A.C. 72 (S.C.C.); *R. v. Collins, supra,* note 54.

71 *R. v. Fliss,* 2002 CarswellBC 191, 2002 CarswellBC 192, 161 C.C.C. (3d) 225, 49 C.R. (5th) 395, 163 B.C.A.C. 1, 267 W.A.C. 1, [2002] 1 S.C.R. 535, 2002 SCC 16, 99 B.C.L.R. (3d) 1, 283 N.R. 120, [2002] 4 W.W.R. 395, 209 D.L.R. (4th) 347, 91 C.R.R. (2d) 189 (S.C.C.); *R. v. Rendon,* 1999 CarswellQue 3021, 140 C.C.C. (3d) 12, 33 C.R. (5th) 311 (Que.C.A.); affirmed 2001 CarswellQue 982, 2001 CarswellQue 983, *(sub nom. R. c. Denton)* 2001 SCC 34, *(sub nom. R. v. Denton)* 270 N.R. 201, *(sub nom. R. v. Peters)* 156 C.C.C. (3d) 222, *(sub nom. R. v. Peters)* [2001] 1 S.C.R. 997 (S.C.C.); *R. v. Mooring, supra,* note 25; *R. v. Nugent, supra,* note 25.

72 *R. v. Wong,* supra note 10. See also *R. v. Brown,* 2008 CarswellAlta 523, 2008 CarswellAlta 524, 2008 SCC 18, [2008] 6 W.W.R. 17, 55 C.R. (6th) 240, 87 Alta. L.R. (4th) 1, *(sub nom. R. v. Kang-Brown)* 293 D.L.R. (4th) 99, *(sub nom. R v. Kang-Brown)* 230 C.C.C. (3d) 289, *(sub nom. R. v. Kang-Brown)* [2008] 1 S.C.R. 456, *(sub nom. R v. Kang-Brown (G.))* 373 N.R. 67, *(sub nom. R. v. Kang-Brown)* 432 A.R. 1, *(sub nom. R. v. Kang-Brown)* 424 W.A.C. 1 (S.C.C.); *R. v. M. (A.), supra,* note 49; R. v. Tessling, supra, note 49.

73 *R. v. Wise, supra,* note 49. See also *R. v. Brown, supra,* note 72; *R. v. M. (A.), supra,* note 49; *R. v. Tessling, supra,* note 49.

74 *R. v. Cody,* 2007 CarswellQue 8780, 2007 QCCA 1276, 51 C.R. (6th) 1, 228 C.C.C. (3d) 331, [2007] R.J.Q. 2381 (Que. C.A.); *R. v. Nguyen,* 2004 CarswellBC 280, 2004 BCSC 77, [2004] B.C.J. No. 248, 20 C.R. (6th) 135 (B.C. S.C.); *R. v. Cody* (sub nom. *R. v. Whitman-Langille*), 2004 CarswellQue 12058, [2004] Q.J. No.

14164 (Que. S.C.); conviction affirmed on different issue (sub nom. *R. v. Langille*) 2007 CarswellQue 297, 2007 QCCA 74; *R. v. Fegan*, supra, note 9.

[75] *R. v. Griffin*, 2008 CarswellQue 3430, 2008 QCCA 825, 58 C.R. (6th) 86, 2008 QCCA 824, (*sub nom. R. v. Harris*) 237 C.C.C. (3d) 374 (Que. C.A.), reversed on different issue 2009 CarswellQue 5997, 2009 CarswellQue 5998, 2009 SCC 28, [2008] S.C.C.A. No. 235, 67 C.R. (6th) 1, 388 N.R. 334, 307 D.L.R. (4th) 577, 244 C.C.C. (3d) 289 (S.C.C.).

[76] *R. v. Mahmood*, 2008 CarswellOnt 5907, 236 C.C.C. (3d) 3, [2008] O.J. No. 3922 (Ont. S.C.J.), application to reconsider 2009 CarswellOnt 4520, [2009] O.J. No. 3192 (Ont. S.C.J.).

[77] *R. v. Giles*, 2007 CarswellBC 3299, 2007 BCSC 1147 (B.C. S.C.); *R. v. Weir*, 2001 CarswellAlta 1069, 2001 ABCA 181, 156 C.C.C. (3d) 188, 85 C.R.R. (2d) 369, 95 Alta. L.R. (3d) 225, [2001] 11 W.W.R. 85, 281 A.R. 333, 248 W.A.C. 333 (Alta.C.A.); applied in *R. v.Budd*, 2004 CarswellOnt 3483, [2004] O.J. No. 3519 (Ont. S.C.J.).

[78] Lawful Access Initiative, *supra*, note 7; Bill C-47, *supra*, note 5.

18

The Jury Trial

Donald C. Murray, Q.C. *
(edited for the 7th edition by Joel E. Pink, Q.C.) **

INTRODUCTION

Why We Have Juries

As the previous chapters of this book have indicated, a criminal trial is a contest between the state and an individual against whom there is allegation of anti-social behaviour. The trial of the accused person is the necessary step required of the state to prove its allegation of crime beyond a reasonable doubt before society gains the right to punish the accused. The court decides whether the allegations against the accused person have been proved, and whether, in law, those allegations constitute an offence entitling the state to exact some punishment.

Our society has rejected the notion that the guilt of a person can only be determined by persons trained in the law (such as lawyers and judges). Instead, in many cases our system of justice permits the common sense of legally untrained persons to make these decisions. The jury represents the community where the alleged offence occurred, as well as society generally. In this way, it is the community that determines the existence or absence of any right of the state to impose punishment on an individual member of society. In theory at least, the jury is the safety valve on the state's power over individual freedom. The jury introduces both the appearance and reality of fairness because it is independent from the state, the accused person, and the institutional legal system.

What Juries Do

This discussion of what juries do at a trial relates to what is known as a "petit" (pronounced "petty") jury. There used to be provision in

---

* B.A., Mount Allison University, Sackville,NewBrunswick; LL.B., Dalhousie Law School, Halifax, Nova Scotia; practises law in Dartmouth, Nova Scotia.

**B .A., Acadia University, Wolfville, Nova Scotia; LL.B., Dalhousie Law School, Halifax, Nova Scotia; practices law in Halifax, Nova Scotia.

the *Criminal Code* for what was known as a "grand jury", but this kind of jury has been abolished in Canada. It was called "grand" because it originally consisted of 24 jurors, twice the number of the usual petit jury. The numbers were gradually reduced so that by the time the grand jury system was abolished, there could be fewer grand jurors sitting in respect of a case than would sit on an actual trial.

Historically, in England, the grand jury performed various community functions, the most important of these being the determination of whether persons should stand trial for particular offences. The grand jury could not only find that an individual should stand trial on an indictment prepared by the Crown, but could also, by a process called "presentment", determine that someone should stand trial because of the jurors' own knowledge of what might have occurred in the community. No charge needed to be laid by the Crown. However, for the most part, the grand jury system was often referred to as "the great bulwark of civil liberty". It could prevent persons being called on to answer publicly for alleged crimes without there being reasonable grounds for the accusation of crime, a decision now left to police officers and prosecutors. It will remain an unanswered question whether this efficiency outweighs the community value obtained by having the grand jury involved in decisions about which criminal accusations now proceed to take up the valuable time of our courts.

Essentially, the role of the jury in a criminal trial is to find facts. The jury decides what and who is to be believed. Even though a jury may believe that the case put forward against an accused person is probably true, the jurors should not make a finding of guilt against the accused person unless they decide that there is no reasonable doubt about the matter. Neither a judge nor a lawyer in a jury trial is able to say "This is a fact", because it is only the jury that will make that decision. It is up to the jurors to decide, from their own inner senses of what is believable and what credit is to be given to certain pieces of evidence, whether the state has shown beyond all reasonable doubt that what it says happened did happen, and that those acts constituted what the law says is a crime.

A jury's main job, then, is to determine whether or not the accused person at trial is guilty or not guilty. In some circumstances a jury can go further than this. For example, it is always open to jurors to recommend mercy towards the accused person when, in their opinion, the circumstances warrant it. This might occur where the offence involved a technical breach of the law, or where there was some circumstance which, while not being legally relevant, somehow reduced the anti-social nature of the crime. While such a recommendation was more common many years ago, the power to make it still exists. Indeed, it is assumed that juries will sometimes express sympathy for the position of an accused person by either rendering a not guilty verdict entirely or by convicting the accused person of some less serious offence than the one with which he was initially charged.

Similarly, in some cases a jury may express its disapproval and shock at an offence. The *Criminal Code* recognizes this in the case of a charge of murder. Where a person is found guilty of having intentionally killed another person, but without having planned and deliberated over that killing, that person is sentenced to imprisonment for life. The convicted person will, in the normal course, be eligible for parole after serving 10 years of his sentence. However, the jury which comes to this verdict of guilt is required to consider whether the period of the convicted person's eligibility for parole should be increased beyond the 10 years. Each juror may recommend any number of years above 10 to a maximum of 25 years. While this is only a recommendation which the judge will consider in sentencing an accused person, it demonstrates how the jury is permitted to express the sense of community outrage created by the offence proven against the accused person.

Finally, jurors are given authority to hear and determine applications for reduction in parole eligibility in some cases. These types of cases arise where an individual has been sentenced to life imprisonment and his or her eligibility for parole is greater than 15 years. At or after the 15 years, the convicted person may apply to a jury to have parole eligibility reduced to 15 years, or such greater number of years as the jury thinks fit. Essentially the only decision for any jury called to decide such a case is whether the person applying is fit to be a candidate for parole. Whether the person actually gets parole or not remains a decision of the National Parole Board.

How Jurors Do Their Job

As a jury will be deciding the facts of a criminal case, its first task will be to listen, see, and appreciate the evidence. Although the practice can vary from judge to judge and jurisdiction to jurisdiction, jurors are normally entitled to take notes of the proceedings. Indeed, in trials which will deal with lengthy and complex issues, the court may supply the jury with notebooks and writing instruments for the purpose. While jurors should confine their note-taking to matters which they feel may turn out to be especially important (so that they can properly listen to and observe the witnesses), note-taking is not restricted. A juror may take such notes as he, in his own fashion, finds useful. The principle under which note-taking is permitted is the same as that which applies to various other aspects of criminal justice in this country. Anything will be done which assists the decision-maker in dealing with evidence reasonably, intelligently and expeditiously.

When counsel and the judge have completed their questioning of any witness, a juror may be permitted to ask questions of that witness. This is, however, up to the judge, who may prefer to ask any questions himself so as to prevent the witness giving inadmissible evidence.

In some cases it is helpful to have the jury see the actual scene of the alleged crime. This will be done where it will assist the jury to better appreciate the oral testimony given by the witnesses and where it is not possible to recreate the scene adequately through photographs or other media of communication such as film or videotape. The *Criminal Code* requires that when a view is in the interests of justice, a view can be taken under controlled conditions of any place, thing or person. Communication by the jury with any such person has to be prevented. The judge must attend, as well as the accused, though an accused person can be excused. Whether or not a view will be permitted is up to the judge, and where he feels that nothing would be gained, it may be refused, even though the jury requested it.

Historically, when a jury was hearing a case it was necessary to keep the jurors together and not permit them to separate during court adjournments. This, however, was quite burdensome on jurors, and the *Criminal Code* now permits the judge to allow the members of the jury to separate at any time before they retire to consider the verdict. Thus, during the course of a trial, it is possible for jurors to live at home and attend to necessary affairs during adjournments so long as they do not discuss the case with anyone. The fear is that jurors may be influenced (despite their oath) by such discussions and by media reports about the case. Where (for reasons of the jury's own protection or for other cause) the judge decides that permission to separate cannot be given, the jury is kept under the charge of constables who are to ensure that the jurors communicate only with each other or the judge. The extreme hardship that this can cause is evident in the fact that the jurors must do everything together—take meals together, sleep overnight in the same hotel, and, if the judge permits it, go to church or the movies together. Every telephone call, haircut, and even every trip to confession, has to be hedged with precautions so that the jury's verdict cannot be suspected of being influenced.

Removing the jury from outside influence lies at the very foundation of the confidence of the public in the system of trial by jury. Nothing should take place, or seem to take place, which could weaken this respect for the jury in the public mind. Should doubt be cast on whether this objective is still being achieved (despite a judge's orders about separating), the judge may order the jury to be "sequestered", or he may feel it necessary to discharge the jury and put the accused's trial off for a period of time. If, despite a serious breach of the judicial directions, the judge does not discharge the jury, it may well lead to the accused obtaining a new trial upon appeal.

Throughout the trial a jury that is permitted to separate is usually provided with light refreshments in the jury room. When they are together and considering their verdict, the jurors are entitled to suitable and sufficient refreshment, food and lodging. This is so the jurors can concentrate on the case put before them in a calm and relaxed manner. Obviously a jury should not be kept for a lengthy period of time without refreshment, but the jury does not have any right to demand when it shall eat, drink, and deliberate, nor what it shall eat or drink. If refreshment is not provided and a jury is forced to deliberate for a lengthy period of time, and if it can reasonably be supposed that the lack of refreshment influenced the verdict which was ultimately given, this may nullify any verdict reached.

Jurors are paid for their work. The amounts which they are paid are not substantial, but such payment recognizes that jurors are performing an important function or service on behalf of society. Many large employers now simply continue an employee's regular daily wages when that employee is called on to perform jury duty. However, it must be recognized that not everyone summoned for jury duty enjoys this employment benefit. This can lead to substantial financial hardship for a person who serves as a juror during a lengthy trial. The possibility exists that this might prevent jurors from giving due consideration to either the Crown or defence evidence because of preoccupation with their own worries. It would be improper for the Crown to pay any special compensation, just as it would be improper for the accused to reimburse jurors for financial losses. This is a weakness of a system which does not provide full financial compensation to jurors. Jury duty remains an obligation of citizenship which may cost a citizen some financial loss to discharge.

Once all the evidence has been heard and the addresses of counsel and the judge have been given, the jurors retire by themselves to consider their verdict. They are protected in their jury room by a sworn constable or constables who remain outside the door of the jury room. This permits the jury to deliberate with complete frankness under the

direction of an elected foreman and with no chance of outside interference. Obviously then, jurors are not permitted to deliberate in open
court. In order to arrive at a verdict it may be necessary to untangle the
truth from conflicting, incomplete, distorted or deliberately falsified accounts of what happened. This can be extremely difficult intellectually
and emotionally and take a long period of time. The secrecy of the jury
room precludes any investigation into the methods by which, or the efficiency with which, jurors discharge this task. The motives for which
the verdict was reached, or the beliefs which led up to it, are not to be
disclosed at all. This rule applies whether or not the deliberations eventually end in a verdict.

Above all, juries are entitled to take their time with their decisions.
Juries are entitled to assume that they will be properly accommodated
if they need to continue their deliberations beyond the first day. Jurors
are also entitled to assume that they will not be required to perform their
functions to the point of exhaustion. The law is looking for a verdict
which is the result of the effective consideration of the issues, free of
pressure. If the appearance of such pressure exists the verdict may be
regarded as unsafe or unsatisfactory and a new trial may be required.
Therefore, it is usually improper for a judge to permit a jury to deliberate late into the evening, particularly where the jury has already been
considering the matter for a substantial period of time. Justice cannot
be seen to be done where a jury is required to decide an issue involving
a person's liberty in haste and under pressure to reach a conclusion.

It is not unusual for a jury, having heard the instructions of the
judge with respect to the applicable law, to decide that it needs to hear
the evidence on a particular point again. While juries are not encouraged to re-hear evidence, if they make a request to do so they should
not be refused or discouraged. Indeed, if transcripts of evidence are
available and asked for, these should be given to the jury. So long as the
jury's request is reasonable, every effort should be made to assist and
make deliberations easier. If the jury merely wants to clarify its recollection with respect to one particular aspect of the case, only portions
of the evidence need to be read back or replayed for it. For example,
if the crucial issue in a case is identification and the jury wishes to be
reminded about what a particular witness said on that point, any direct
examination and cross-examination on the point should be read back.
The total evidence of that witness does not need to be read back, nor
other points which might be considered important as reflecting upon the
credibility of the answers which that witness gave. However, the jury
should remember that its task is to decide the case on the whole of the

evidence and not simply upon a few questions and answers from particular witnesses. Of course, the jury may re-hear the entire evidence of a witness or witnesses if it wishes. Similarly, and this is particularly so in long and complex trials with more than one accused person, the jury may rehear a summary of the judge's address where the theory of the defence is summarized. However, the theory of the Crown should also be summarized again so that no imbalance is created.

By assessing the believability of witness testimony and considering other evidence seen and heard, the jury decides what is or is not a fact in a case. Once the facts of a case have been found, in order to reach a verdict, the jury must analyze them according to the instructions of law given to them by the judge. This is not an easy task and, after retiring to deliberate, it is quite common for juries to request clarification of the law from the judge. Questions are asked by means of written notes to the judge from the jury foreman. The judge is then under an obligation to advise counsel for both the Crown and defence of the question, to read the question in open court in the presence of the accused person and the jury, and then to answer it. The answer may in fact be no answer—the judge may be forced to say that the question relates to something which is irrelevant and of no concern to the jury, or that it relates to a matter of fact for the jury to decide by themselves. The jury then retires again and continues its deliberations.

Finally, the jury comes to the end of its deliberations. Deliberations may end in agreement or in disagreement. In order to render a verdict the jurors must be unanimous. This means that unanimity is required for both a verdict of guilt and a verdict of not guilty. Should the jury be unable to agree on a verdict it is called a "hung jury", and at some point in the future the accused person will have to undergo a new trial with a new jury. If the jurors do agree on a verdict the jury foreman writes the verdict on the back of the indictment. In most cases, this completes the task of the jurors and they are thanked and discharged. Depending on the need for jurors for other cases, jurors who have tried one case may be excused from having to try any other at that court sitting.

PICKING A JURY

When Juries are Used

For the most serious offences, where the punishment is five or more years' imprisonment, an accused person has a constitutional right to the benefit of a jury trial. The *Criminal Code* gives an accused person this right whenever he is charged with an indictable offence, subject to some limited exceptions which are set out in s. 553 of the *Criminal Code*. The accused person usually has the choice or opportunity to have a jury trial, though he need not take advantage of that opportunity. In cases where guilt or innocence may be determined on a technical legal issue, the accused person may elect to be tried by a judge alone.

Up until recently there were some offences which were required to be tried by a judge with a jury, such as treason, mutiny, sedition, piracy and murder. These offences will be tried by a jury unless the accused person and the Crown Attorney consent to the trial being held before a judge of a superior court of criminal jurisdiction alone.

The Attorney General, through a Crown Attorney, may require a jury trial in any case through the direct indictment procedure of the *Criminal Code*. These rights and opportunities for a jury are seen as procedural in nature and so the provisions of the *Criminal Code* govern and a provincial Jury Act cannot diminish these rights in any way.

Who May Sit on a Jury

The *Criminal Code* allows any person to sit on a jury who is qualified to be a juror according to the law of the province where the trial is to take place. The only stipulation required by the *Criminal Code* is that no person be disqualified, exempted or excused from serving as a juror on the basis of sex. The provincial juror qualifications are found in provincial statutes commonly called *The Jury Act* or *The Juries Act*. In Canada, these Acts generally require only that a potential juror be a Canadian citizen, a resident in the province (some require residency for one year), and at least the age of majority (provincial voting age of 18 or 19). Even if someone is sworn as a juror who is not qualified in these basic ways to sit on a jury, the *Criminal Code* provides that the verdict of such a jury is still good.

Who May Not Sit on a Jury

Each of the provincial Jury Acts disqualifies or exempts various classes of people from jury service. These exemptions are generally designed to enhance the appearance of the jury as a body of citizens independent from the state which, after all, is the prosecuting authority. In addition to all representatives of Her Majesty the Queen, such as the Lieutenant Governor of each province, elected federal and provincial politicians are uniformly ineligible for jury service. In most cases the officers of Parliament and the legislatures are also ineligible. Federally and provincially appointed judges are ineligible, and some provinces go so far as to disqualify justices of the peace and coroners as well. Barristers and solicitors are uniformly disqualified, and in some provinces this extends to anyone with legal training who intends to practice law. Usually other officers employed in the court system are disqualified as well.

As police officers are often central to any criminal prosecution, they are almost always precluded from being part of a jury. While some provinces go so far as to disqualify anyone who comes within the definition of "peace officer" in the *Criminal Code*, thereby including mayors, sheriffs, prison employees, and such, other provinces such as Nova Scotia only disqualify full-time police officers. It is also common now for provinces to provide in their jury legislation that employees of the provincial Attorney General's Department or the federal Departments of Justice and the Solicitor General not be permitted to sit on a jury. While this last disqualification may eliminate from jury service many people who really have nothing to do with law enforcement or prosecution, the appearance on a jury of an employee of a prosecutorial arm of government detracts from the appearance of independence which a jury requires.

Beyond the exemptions referred to above, other disqualifications exist in each province which suggests that even though jury service is important, it is not as important as some other services performed in society. For example, a few provinces still exempt medical practitioners, and still fewer exempt dental practitioners and veterinarians. Some exempt members of the Canadian Forces who are on active service and a very few still disqualify clergymen or ministers of a religion. New Brunswick, with its large forest industry, specifically exempts firefighters from jury duty.

Historically there was no question that even though a person might be disqualified by position from jury duty, that person's spouse remained eligible. The more common approach now of the provincial Acts is to disqualify the spouse as well of persons disqualified by their occupation or office.

Persons with a criminal record are not disqualified from serving on juries. Each province appears to have slightly different rules and only a few have taken the step to disqualify prisoners. The most common provision provides that a person is ineligible who is charged with or has been convicted within the past five years of an offence which could result in a fine of $1,000 or one year's imprisonment or more, and who has not been pardoned.

The Jury Acts also have provisions to give some assurance that any jury selected will be capable of dealing with the task of appreciating the evidence and coming to a decision about it. Blindness is commonly a ground of exemption. More important, mental or physical disabilities which seriously impair the individual's ability to function as a juror, or which would be incompatible with the juror's duties, provide further bases of exemption. Also, all of the Jury Acts provide for the exemption of an individual from jury duty on the basis of age. Some simply state that those over the age of 69 years are disqualified. Others exempt such individuals from jury duty unless they indicate that they still wish to be available. Still others allow an individual to apply to be removed from consideration for jury duty upon reaching a certain age.

Another important consideration for jurors in this bilingual country is whether or not the juror would be competent in the language of trial. There was always provision in the *Criminal Code* for mixed juries in Quebec. Most of the provincial Jury Acts now provide that if the juror is not competent in the language which will be used at trial then he may be exempted from jury duty. In addition, the *Criminal Code* permits any juror to be challenged who does not speak the official language of Canada that is the language of the accused or in which he can best give testimony, and where a juror does not speak either of Canada's official languages. However, that provision of the *Criminal Code* is only in force in a few provinces.

Finally, it is recognized that jury duty can be a hardship on some individuals and the Jury Acts provide for applications to be made either to the presiding judge or to the Sheriff to be excused for reasons of hardship, religious objection, or, in some provinces, because of illness of the potential juror or of someone to whom the potential juror is responsible for giving care. In addition, most provinces exempt persons who have been called on for jury duty for the next two or three years. The Nova Scotia Act limits the obligation of jury service to one family member per session, and where the juror is an employee of someone who employs fewer than 15 people, again only one employee per session of the court.

How the Jury Panel is Selected

Each province determines who is to be on the jury list in a different way. For example, in Nova Scotia, a jury committee develops a list of names picked at random from the most recent election rolls in each county. In Newfoundland, the list is made up from an enumeration of qualified persons who reside within 25 miles of the court location. Provinces such as New Brunswick and Saskatchewan use records which exist for medical care purposes, while other provinces simply permit the Sheriff to make up a jury list from election rolls, assessment rolls, and other public documents as might be convenient.

The jury list or "panel" is usually developed by the Sheriff of the county in which the court will sit. The names included in the panel are, in most cases, kept secret until shortly before the beginning of the court session in which the trial is to be held. Outside of statute, an accused person has no right to a copy of the jury panel. The *Criminal Code* itself only allows an accused person a copy of the panel of jurors where the offence involves treason or high treason.

The Sheriff summons the jurors named on the jury list for a particular court session to appear on the first day of that session. Attendance is taken and the Sheriff is usually asked to explain or investigate any absences. At that time either the Crown or an accused person may challenge the jury panel, on the basis that the list was developed as a result of partiality, fraud or wilful misconduct on the part of the Sheriff or other officer by whom the panel was returned. A challenge to the panel is limited to those grounds.

Without evidence of some kind of wrongdoing on the part of the Sheriff, it is not open to challenge the jury list on the basis that it does not adequately represent the different races or ethnic groups within society. In any event, that would be difficult for a Sheriff to determine by a mere perusal of names on other kinds of lists. However, if the type of lists referred to in making up the jury list systemically or practically exclude specific, identifiable groups there may be a challengeable problem. It is not appropriate to simply top up a randomly selected list with a group of specifically selected persons from an identifiable but systemically excluded group. Dealing with this issue in the next several years will call for considerable ingenuity. Where the objective is sexual equality on the jury panel this may be the kind of thing that the Sheriff may more properly be able to arrange. In at least one case, this has led to the selection of a new panel.

The purposes of the jurors' selection procedures are essentially threefold. First, to distribute the burden of jury service equally between all who are liable to it; second, to develop useful lists for the use by the courts of jurors who are likely to attend when called upon; and third, to prevent the selection of particular individuals for any jury (commonly called "packing"). Thus, if the responsible officials have essentially met these objectives, even though there might be some minor defects in their approach, the panel will stand as valid.

If a challenge to the panel is to be successful, it must be demonstrated that there is some danger in proceeding with the panel which has been summoned. It is not enough to say that too few have been summoned and the number of choices of potential jurors thus limited. Nor is it a proper objection to say that too many have been summoned so that the Crown may more easily control who eventually sits on the jury.

Jurors selected from the panel will become judges of the court for the duration of that trial and must be treated as such. Therefore, it is improper for anyone to attempt a survey of the panel with respect to possible reactions to the issues expected to arise at trial. It is regarded as an interference with the administration of justice. Again the governing principle is that even a suspicion of some improper interference with the course of justice requires that steps be taken to correct that impression. Justice should not only be done, but manifestly and undoubtedly be seen to be done. If the jury panel has been interfered with in any way the Sheriff may be required to summon a new panel.

Once the jury panel has been summoned and is present in court, it is then available for counsel to select jurors to serve on petit juries which will try the various charges set down for trial at that court session. In larger centers this may mean that one or more trials are proceeding while another is beginning. The petit jury selected for a particular trial need only be selected from those qualified jurors who are present in the courtroom where the selection is taking place. The other members of the jury panel who are absent from the courtroom, engaged in service on another trial, are simply unavailable for selection to that particular petit jury for that particular trial. If not selected to sit on any petit jury, a member of the panel is required to continue in attendance at the court according to the direction of the presiding judge until the court session is complete. As indicated earlier, depending on the length of any particular trial and the number of trials set down for that particular court session, it may be that a juror who is selected to serve on one trial will be excused from attendance as a member of the panel for the balance of the court session. However, this remains at the discretion of the judge.

How the Jury is Selected

The point of the exercise in selecting a criminal jury is to find 12 people who will fairly and impartially try the case which will be presented. While the practice varies from province to province, and even perhaps within provinces, the jury is chosen as the result of a random selection of cards from a box where all the cards of all potential jurors in attendance have been shaken together. The potential jurors whose names are called step forward to the jury box and then are called again so that the second stage of the selection process can begin.

This second stage involves any peremptory challenge or challenge for cause which the Crown or defence may wish to make. It was also at this stage that a juror might have been "stood aside" (i.e., put aside provisionally) by the Crown Attorney if he had not otherwise been challenged. This is now a judicial function, exercised much less frequently than it ever was by the Crown. If the potential juror is neither challenged nor stood aside, he is then sworn and becomes a member of the petit jury for the particular trial concerned. This process is continued until 12 jurors are sworn. So long as the Crown and accused person have the opportunity to make any necessary challenges or requests to stand aside, and the order of selection of jurors is at random, the jury can probably be said to be legally empanelled.

It is becoming increasingly common, particularly for the defence counsel, to desire to question prospective jurors for the purpose of being able to make intelligent judgments as to whether or not to make a challenge. The law is reasonably well established that neither defence counsel nor the Crown Attorney has any general right to question a prospective juror. This puts the character of the prospective juror in issue and subjects him to embarrassment in the presence of the other members of the jury panel. Also, it appears to waste the court's time without apparent reason except in the hope that counsel may stumble upon some justifiable ground of challenge.

There is some merit in the fact that jury selection cannot be meaningful if nothing of substance is known about the individual who is a potential juror. Some provinces therefore require by statute that the age, occupation and residence of the prospective juror appear on the jury list. In other provinces the prospective juror discloses this information at the time that he is called forward in court. In some centers it has become the practice for jury panel members to fill out a court-supervised questionnaire concerning their age, occupation, family situation, and so forth. Also, the presiding judge may make it a practice to question the panel itself, to ensure that those present are eligible to sit on a jury and to determine whether or not they might have been affected by any pre-trial publicity. If the presiding judge does decide to question the panel, or to hear claims for exemption, it will be necessary for the questions and answers to be stated out loud in the hearing of the accused so that the accused person can know that no question of partiality is being raised which he or his counsel may wish to deal with.

Depending upon the nature of the case, counsel at a trial may be permitted to ask certain questions of prospective jurors. While it remains a matter in the discretion of the trial judge, counsel have been permitted to ask questions on a number of subjects, including whether police officers (by virtue of their status) may be automatically more credible to the jurors, whether media reports have been read and led to the formation of any opinions about the group with whom the accused were clearly associated, and whether the juror (having heard an outline of the Crown's case) could render a verdict without bias or prejudice against the accused person. This type of question is designed to determine, before the trial even begins, whether the prospective juror is biased in favour of either the Crown or the defence.

Most other questions will not be permitted unless there is some factual basis for suspecting bias on the part of a particular juror. For example, any racial prejudice harboured by a juror has been rejected as a permissible subject of questioning, as have views as to the offence of rape, and whether family members or close friends had been subjected to criminal activities of similar kind as alleged against the accused person. Questions as to how the juror might react to a disagreement with other members of the jury are not appropriate either. Questions that imply that the juror may not comply with his oath are not permissible.

In the process of jury selection there is no guarantee that jurors will have any particular attributes. The system takes 12 people from the street, with their virtues and their blemishes. The expectation exists that the blemishes of one will be more than compensated for by the virtues of the others. It is generally thought and hoped that jurors today are intelligent people, well able to put from their minds something heard elsewhere and able to disregard their own prejudices in following the instructions of the trial judge. Indeed, it is often remarked that an accused person is entitled to an impartial jury, not a sympathetic one.

The *Criminal Code* permits the Crown and the accused any number of challenges to be made for cause. However, the causes which may be the basis for challenge are strictly limited. Essentially these are that the juror's name is not included in the panel, that the juror is biased, that he is an alien, that he is physically unable to perform the duties of a juror properly, that he has been convicted of an offence for which he was sentenced to death or to a term of imprisonment exceeding 12 months, or, in those jurisdictions where it applies, that he is incapable in the appropriate language. The court may require that such challenges be in writing so that the juror subject to the challenge is not embarrassed by the statement of challenge in open court.

A challenge for cause can only be made after an individual juror has been called forward as a prospective petit juror and before he is sworn as a petit juror. Any other time is either too soon or too late. If it has not been put into writing, the reason for the challenge should be stated by counsel. The judge may, in his discretion, require some evidence of these grounds. If the other party (Crown or defence) admits the challenge which is made, the juror will not be sworn. If the challenge is not admitted, the opposite party may argue that no sufficient reason exists in law for such a challenge. Once the judge is satisfied that there is some foundation to the challenge and it is proper in law, a trial of the truth of the challenge must be held. For this purpose two "triers" are called forward and sworn to decide the matter. These "triers" may be anyone who happens to be present in the courtroom and need not have been part of the jury panel. Once their function has been explained to them, the trial of the challenge may proceed.

The party making the challenge may call the proposed juror as a witness, as well as any other evidence necessary to establish the challenge. This should not take long and any questioning should be succinct, relevant and fair. The other party may also question any witnesses called and introduce other evidence. If the judge permits it, counsel may address brief argument to the triers, followed by the judge giving the triers a short direction as to the question which they are to answer. The jurors decide this question on the basis of whether or not the challenge is probably true. If they are unable to agree, two other persons are to be sworn to determine the issue. If the challenge is indeed true, then the prospective juror is not sworn. As will be indicated later, if the ground of challenge is not proved to have been true the juror may be sworn, challenged peremptorily or stood aside. Challenges for cause are reasonably rare. However, they are not precluded simply because the judge has properly asked certain questions of the jury panel which are designed to weed out cases of obvious bias.

The fundamental objective of permitting challenges for cause is, as with many other procedural safeguards in the criminal justice system, designed to ensure that an accused person has a fair trial, or to avoid situations where it is unlikely that the accused will have a fair trial. The most commonly used ground of challenge is that the juror is biased, because "the causes of favour are infinite". They will involve being related to a witness or other participant at the trial, being associated through employment or socially with a participant in the trial, and perhaps having retired from an occupation which would render the person otherwise exempt—such as a retired policeman. Merely knowing a witness or other participant in the trial will not provide a basis for a good challenge for cause on the basis of partiality. Rarely will a potential juror say that he is prejudiced against an accused person, but it sometimes happens. Simply having prior knowledge of the case through media reports may not be a good reason of challenge either—even when those media reports included reporting about a previous conviction subsequently overturned on appeal. In such cases, the nature of the media reports and what they contained would have to be considered. If they had referred to evidence which would not be admissible at the new trial, or if they were sensational without reason, then these media reports might afford a good ground of challenge for cause if they had affected the prospective juror's outlook on the case. Ultimately, it comes to a question of whether, in all the circumstances disclosed, it is likely or unlikely that the prospective juror could fairly try the case.

Finally, it is not sufficient in law to make out a challenge for cause on the basis that a prospective juror sat on the petit jury dealing with the same case, but that for some reason or other the trial was not completed. However, where the previous jury reached the state of deliberating, it would be improper to allow the new jury to contain members of the previous jury—even though that previous jury may not have come to any conclusion as a result of its deliberations. At the same time, if different accused persons are involved, there is nothing to prevent a juror from serving on two petit juries at one session of the court for trials which deal with the same offence.

In addition to the right of both Crown and an accused to challenge any number of prospective jurors for cause, the Crown and the defence are each entitled to challenge prospective jurors by what are called peremptory challenges. A peremptory challenge is a challenge made without any reason having been disclosed. After an unsuccessful challenge for cause, either the defence or the Crown may then make use of one of their peremptory challenges. Counsel's right to exercise the peremptory challenge is purely subjective. The fact that a juror is objectively impartial does not mean that he is believed to be impartial by the accused person or by the Crown. Thus, a peremptory challenge is entirely discretionary and not subject to any conditions except number. No embarrassment is intended to the prospective juror who is challenged peremptorily—it may simply be that one of the counsel involved feels that another prospective juror may be called whom he believes will better understand the case to be put forward.

The number of peremptory challenges available to an accused person will vary depending upon the seriousness of the offence with which he is charged. For example, an accused person who is charged with high treason or first degree murder is entitled to 20 peremptory challenges. If he may be sentenced to more than five years' imprisonment for some other offence, he is entitled to challenge 12 jurors peremptorily. Otherwise, an accused person is entitled to challenge four jurors in this way. The Crown is also entitled to challenge an equal number of jurors peremptorily.

Where accused persons are charged jointly and the Crown wishes to try them together, each of them still has the same number of peremptory challenges as if he were being tried alone. However, where an accused person faces more than one charge at the same trial he is limited in his peremptory challenges to the largest number allowed in respect of any single count. The Crown is similarly limited. The Crown and defence alternate in indicating whether or not each is content with a prospective juror or exercising a challenge with respect to them. Once a peremptory challenge has been made, it cannot be withdrawn.

As the reader might expect, by the time the accused person and the Crown have exercised rights to challenge peremptorily and for cause, it sometimes occurs that 12 jurors are not sworn by the time the jury panel has been exhausted. In this circumstance the Crown may request the court to order the Sheriff or other officer to summon as many persons as might be needed to provide a full jury. The persons summoned need not be qualified in the same way as the members of the jury panel, and may be summoned "by word of mouth"—in effect, pulled right off the street. These individuals become part of the general panel for the purposes of the particular trial, and the same proceedings are taken with respect to calling, challenging and directing them to stand by as was the case for the regular members of the panel. Before these "talesmen" can be summoned, it is necessary that the jury panel be truly exhausted. Talesmen should not be sought if another petit jury from the same panel has completed its deliberations and become available during the course of the jury selection process in the trial concerned. This prevents any unqualified person from being given the role of juror in a trial unless absolutely necessary.

Once the twelfth juror has been sworn, the criminal trial of the accused person is ready to begin.

Getting Off the Jury

When an individual has been sworn in as a juror, it is a rare circumstance that permits him to get off the jury. Whether there is sufficient cause in any case is up to the presiding judge. Unless some severe disruption of the trial is apparent, or something to suggest that the jury will not be impartial if the discharge is not granted, a request to be discharged will not be lightly granted. Indeed, the only cause for which permission of the presiding judge is not required is death. The trial may continue so long as there are at least 10 jury members.

The kind of illness which will justify the discharge of a juror is illness of a nature where the juror should not continue to act. Thus, if a juror has to be hospitalized it may be enough to secure his discharge. However, if the hospital stay is to be a short one and the jury is not prevented from separating during adjournment, a judge might decide, in his discretion, to await the juror's recovery. If the illness has occurred before the accused is arraigned and put in charge of the jury, then the full jury complement could be empanelled prior to the formal commencement of the trial.

As indicated, whether other circumstances will justify the discharge of a juror will depend on the discretion of the trial judge. This should be done in cases of apparent bias—for example where through some error a person with a close personal connection to the victim has been sworn as a jury member, or where a juror has been summoned to give evidence on behalf of the prosecution in a similar case and had dealings with the same police officers involved in both cases. To merely have a juror smile at an accused person may be enough to cast sufficient doubt on that juror's impartiality to justify that juror being discharged. Obviously this may require questioning a juror more extensively than might otherwise be permitted in borderline cases.

A juror should not have any contact with counsel during the conduct of the case, no matter how innocent. Nor should a juror have contact outside of the actual trial process with the accused or with any witnesses.

If any issue arises as to the truth or appropriateness of the cause for discharging a juror, it appears that some questioning by the judge (with other questioning by counsel) should be permitted. Once the decision has been made to discharge a juror, some greater explanation than reading of the *Criminal Code* provision which permits it should be given. This prevents the remaining jurors from speculating as to why one of their number is no longer with them. Speculation could work to the prejudice of an accused person. Sometimes, of course, there is the risk that an explanation will increase the chances of an unfair trial for both the accused and the Crown. If that kind of harm is significant then it may well be appropriate for the jury to be discharged entirely because their independence has been poisoned beyond cure.

OTHER THINGS ABOUT JURIES

Protecting Jurors

During the course of trial, and primarily while deliberating, jurors are not entitled to communicate with anyone about the case. While deliberating, or while sequestered, a juror may not communicate with anyone other than another juror or the Sheriff's officer who is in charge of the jury. At the same time, publication restrictions exist on the media to prevent jurors from hearing about things going on in the courtroom when they are not present. It is an offence to attempt to influence, or to agree to be influenced, in respect to jury duty.

As to what goes on in the jury room itself, none of this may be disclosed unless it relates to an offence of obstruction of justice. There are several reasons for this. Above all, a juror should be entitled to be completely frank with respect to his views of the case when among the other jury members. Perpetual secrecy of what is said in the jury room assists in fostering this kind of frankness. Another reason for the rule against the disclosure of jury proceedings is that individual jurors may from time to time wish to avoid responsibility for the consequences of their findings and say later that they disagreed with the jury's ultimate conclusion. The courts are steadfast in their refusal to listen to such claims. If there is any misconduct to be complained of it must come from the officer who had charge of the jury or from some other person who actually witnessed the misconduct. This means that few jury verdicts could be overturned. Deliberations are conducted entirely in private. Even if a case of misconduct could be established, the court might still refuse to consider what transpired in the jury room, because an allegation of impropriety could properly be met only by calling members of the jury—and that would be precluded by the *Criminal Code*. If the courts permitted this kind of challenge to verdicts too readily, it might encourage interested parties to attempt to ascertain particulars of the jury's deliberations by whatever means human ingenuity could devise. That is regarded in Canada as contrary to public policy and a great danger both to the jury system and to the public's confidence in that system.

Taking the Case Away from a Jury

The *Criminal Code* allows a trial judge to discharge the jury entirely and direct the accused to be tried with a new jury if something has happened in the course of trial—either in the courtroom or outside—which might lead to a miscarriage of justice. The most common case of a trial being brought to an abrupt stop by the jury being discharged occurs where there has been some apparent interference with the jury which compromises its independence. The judge must decide whether he considers this apparent compromise to be serious enough to lead to a possible miscarriage of justice.

The presence of the Sheriff or Sheriff's officer in the jury room for some period of time during deliberations will not automatically lead to discharging the jury before it comes to a verdict. At the same time, there is no justification for counsel ever to enter the jury room during a jury's deliberations. The publication by a newspaper of a statement by an accused person which has been ruled inadmissible in evidence is also the kind of thing which will justify a judge discharging a jury—especially where it is known that the newspaper accounts have been provided to the jury.

There may be other causes to discharge a jury, such as long adjournments between the hearing of witnesses. The judge has to be convinced that the minds of the jurors will be prejudicially affected by what has occurred and that a fair trial is no longer possible. This can be a difficult decision, particularly where each side has gone to considerable expense of time, money, and effort in preparing to proceed with the trial.

The third basis for taking the case away from a properly constituted jury is strictly a legal one. It flows from the fact that at a jury trial the judge remains the judge of the law. It is the responsibility of the judge to determine at the end of the Crown's case, on motion of the defence, whether or not there is any evidence on each essential element of the charge against the accused person. This has nothing to do with the weight or quality of the evidence. For example, a crime requires a criminal. Unless the accused is identified as a participant in the crime charged before the court, then an essential ingredient of the Crown's proof is absent. When such cases arise, the judge has the responsibility to direct the jury to retire to its jury room and then to return with a verdict of not guilty on the charge which the judge indicates. It is not open to the jury at this point to disagree with the judge's direction. That can be corrected on appeal, if there has been an error.

Dealing with Jury Decisions

Once the evidence has been heard, the addresses of counsel given, and instructions of the judge made, the length of the rest of the trial really sits within the control of the jury itself. Deliberations may take some time or they may be over very quickly. The judge, and sometimes counsel, will try to simplify the issues for the jury, but this can do little to shorten matters if the jury contains members with strongly opposing

122, 15 O.R. (3d) 324 (Ont. C.A.), leave to appeal refused (1994), 87 C.C.C. (3d) vi (S.C.C.).

Challenging the Panel

Criminal Code, ss. 629, 630.

R. v. Catizone, 1972 CarswellOnt 52, 23 C.R.N.S. 44 (Ont. Co. Ct.).

R. v. LaForte, 1975 CarswellMan 142, 25 C.C.C. (2d) 75, 62 D.L.R. (3d) 86 (Man. C.A.).

R. v. Hutchison, 1975 CarswellNB 113, 11 N.B.R. (2d) 327, 26 C.C.C. (2d) 423 (N.B. C.A.), affirmed 1976 CarswellNB 27, 1976 CarswellNB 27F, (sub nom. *R. v. Ambrose*) [1977] 2 S.C.R. 717, (sub nom. *R. v. Ambrose*) 30 C.C.C. (2d) 97, (sub nom. *R. v. Ambrose*) 14 N.B.R. (2d) 452, (sub nom. *R. v. Ambrose*) 9 N.R. 431, (sub nom. *R. v. Ambrose*) 69 D.L.R. (3d) 673 (S.C.C.).

R. v. Morrow (1914), 24 C.C.C. 310, (Que. K.B.).

R. v. Butler, 1984 CarswellBC 526, 63 C.C.C. (3d) 243, 3 C.R. (4th) 174, [1985] 2 C.N.L.R. 107 (B.C. C.A.).

R. v. Comeau, 1973 CarswellNS 21, 14 C.C.C. (2d) 472, 28 C.R.N.S. 285, 6 N.S.R. (2d) 238 (N.S. C.A.).

R. v. Caldough, 1961 CarswellBC 133, 131 C.C.C. 336, 36 C.R. 248, 36 W.W.R. 426 (B.C. S.C.).

How the Jury is Selected

Criminal Code; ss. 631, 643.

R. v. Punch, 1985 CarswellNWT 53, 22 C.C.C. (3d) 289, [1986] 1 W.W.R. 592, 48 C.R. (3d) 374, 18 C.R.R. 74, [1986] 2 C.N.L.R. 114, [1985] N.W.T.R. 373 (N.W.T. S.C.).

R. v. Harri (1922), 38 C.C.C. 234 (Ont. S.C.).

R. v. Palomba (No. 1), 1975 CarswellQue 10, 32 C.R.N.S. 31, [1975] Que. C.A. 340, 24 C.C.C. (2d) 19 (Que. C.A.), at p. 48 [C.R.N.S.].

General Questioning

R. v. Bryant, 1980 CarswellOnt 1414, 54 C.C.C. (2d) 54 (Ont. H.C.).

R. v. McAuslane , 1973 CarswellOnt 29, 23 C.R.N.S. 6 (Ont. Co. Ct.).

R. v. Sophonow, 1984 CarswellMan 347, 12 C.C.C. (3d) 272, 29 Man. R. (2d) 1, 11 D.L.R. (4th) 24 (Man. C.A.), affirmed 1984 CarswellMan 285, 1984 CarswellMan 285F, [1984] 2 S.C.R. 524, 11 C.R.R. 183, 15 D.L.R. (4th) 480, 57 N.R. 13, 17 C.C.C. (3d) 128, 31 Man. R. (2d) 8 (S.C.C.).

Challenges for Cause

Criminal Code, ss. 638-640.

R. v. Pilgar, 1912 CarswellOnt 631, 20 C.C.C. 507, 23 O.W.R. 433, 8 D.L.R. 830, 27 O.L.R. 337 (Ont. C.A.).

R. v. Hubbert, 1977 CarswellOnt 464, 1977 CarswellOnt 16, 33 C.C.C. (2d) 207, [1977] 2 S.C.R. 267, 15 O.R. (2d) 324, 38 C.R.N.S. 381, 15 N.R. 139 (S.C.C.), affirming 1975 CarswellOnt 32, 29 C.C.C. (2d) 279, 11 O.R. (2d) 464, 31 C.R.N.S. 27 (Ont. C.A.).

Hamilton, J.F., "Challenging for Cause", (1977), 39 C.R.N.S. 58.

R. v. Barrow, 1984 CarswellNS 237, 14 C.C.C. (3d) 470, 65 N.S.R. (2d) 1, 147 A.P.R. 1 (N.S. C.A.), reversed 1987 CarswellNS 42, 1987 CarswellNS 344, [1987] 2 S.C.R. 694, 38 C.C.C. (3d) 193, 87 N.S.R. (2d) 271, 222 A.P.R. 271, 81 N.R. 321, 61 C.R. (3d) 305, (sub nom. *Barrow v. R.*) 45 D.L.R. (4th) 487 (S.C.C.).

R. v. Rowbotham, 1988 CarswellOnt 58, 41 C.C.C. (3d) 1, 63 C.R. (3d) 113, 25 O.A.C. 321, 35 C.R.R. 207 (Ont. C.A.).

Peremptory Challenges

Criminal Code, ss. 633-636.

Cloutier v. R., 1979 CarswellQue 15, 1979 CarswellQue 164, 48 C.C.C. (2d) 1, [1979] 2 S.C.R. 709, 12 C.R. (3d) 10, 28 N.R. 1, 99 D.L.R. (3d) 577 (S.C.C.).

R. v. Taillon, 1960 CarswellSask 22, 127 C.C.C. 275, 33 C.R. 245, 32 W.W.R. 91 (Sask. C.A.).

R. v. Lalonde, 1898 CarswellQue 64, 2 C.C.C. 188, 7 Que. Q.B. 201 (Que. Q.B.).

Talesman

Criminal Code, s. 642.

R. v. James, 1968 CarswellBC 97, [1969] 1 C.C.C. 278, 64 W.W.R. 659 (B.C. C.A.).

Discharge of Jurors

Criminal Code, s. 644.

Vescio v. R., 1948 CarswellMan 1, 6 C.R. 433, 92 C.C.C. 161, [1949] 1 D.L.R. 720, [1949] S.C.R. 139 (S.C.C.).

R. v. Basarabas, 1982 CarswellBC 674, 1982 CarswellBC 745, 2 C.C.C. (3d) 257, [1982] 2 S.C.R. 730, 46 N.R. 69, [1983] 4 W.W.R. 289, 31 C.R. (3d) 193, 144 D.L.R. (3d) 115 (S.C.C.).

R. v. Holcomb, 1973 CarswellNB 108, 15 C.C.C. (2d) 239, 6 N.B.R. (2d) 858, [1973] S.C.R. vi (S.C.C.), affirming 1973 CarswellNB 71, 12 C.C.C. (2d) 417, 6 N.B.R. (2d) 485 (N.B. C.A.).

R. v. MacKay, 1980 CarswellBC 564, 53 C.C.C. (2d) 366, [1980] 6 W.W.R. 108 (B.C. C.A.).

OTHER THINGS ABOUT JURIES

Protecting Jurors

Criminal Code; ss. 139, 647-649.

Martin, J.C., "Secrecy of Jury Deliberations" (1958-59), 1 Crim. L.Q. 187.

R. v. Perras (No. 2), 1974 CarswellSask 69 18 C.C.C. (2d) 47, [1974] 5 W.W.R. 187,, 48 D.L.R. (3d) 145 (Sask. C.A.).

R. v. Zacharias, 1987 CarswellBC 369, 39 C.C.C. (3d) 280, 19 B.C.L.R. (2d) 379 (B.C. C.A.).

Taking the Case Away

Criminal Code, s. 647.

R. v. Gilson, 1965 CarswellOnt 13, [1965] 4 C.C.C. 61, [1965] 2 O.R. 505, 46 C.R. 368, 51 D.L.R. (2d) 289 (Ont. C.A.).

R. v. Mercier, 1973 CarswellQue 193, 12 C.C.C. (2d) 377, [1975] C.A. 51 (Que. C.A.).

R. v. Dorion, 1953 CarswellMan 9, 17 C.R. 352, 10 W.W.R. (N.S.) 379, 61 Man. R. 336 (Man. Q.B.).

R. v. Mezzo, 1986 CarswellMan 327, 1986 CarswellMan 40, (sub nom. *Mezzo v. R.*) 52 C.R. (3d) 113, 30 D.L.R. (4th) 161, 68 N.R. 1, [1986] 4 W.W.R. 577, 43 Man. R. (2d) 161, (sub nom. *Mezzo v. R.*) [1986] 1 S.C.R. 802, (sub nom. *Mezzo v. R.*) 27 C.C.C. (3d) 97 (S.C.C.).

Exhorting the Jury

R. v. Isaac, 1979 CarswellYukon 4, 48 C.C.C. (2d) 481 (Y.T. C.A.).

Hung Jury

Criminal Code, s. 653.

R. v. Gaffin (1904), 8 C.C.C. 194 (N.S. S.C.).

R. v. Dyson, 1971 CarswellOnt 273, 5 C.C.C. (2d) 401, [1972] 1 O.R. 744 (Ont. H.C.).

Questioning and Polling the Jury

R. v. Logan, 1944 CarswellBC 66, 82 C.C.C. 234, 60 B.C.R. 473, [1944] 3 W.W.R. 299, [1944] 4 D.L.R. 287 (B.C. C.A.).

R. v. Edmonstone, 1907 CarswellOnt 201, 13 C.C.C. 125, 10 O.W.R. 581, 15 O.L.R. 325 (Ont. C.A.).

R. v. Tuckey, 1985 CarswellOnt 100, 9 O.A.C. 218, 20 C.C.C. (3d) 502, 46 C.R. (3d) 97 (Ont. C.A.).

R. v. Bryan, 1970 CarswellBC 214, 1 C.C.C. (2d) 342, 75 W.W.R. 507, 12 C.R.N.S. 298 (B.C. C.A.).

Overturning Jury Decisions

Criminal Code, s. 686.

R. v. Corbett, 1973 CarswellBC 250, 1973 CarswellBC 272, 14 C.C.C. (2d) 385, 25 C.R.N.S. 296, [1975] 2 S.C.R. 275, [1974] 2 W.W.R. 524, 1 N.R. 258, 42 D.L.R. (3d) 142 (S.C.C.).

R. v. J., 1929 CarswellMan 22, 52 C.C.C. 7, [1929] 1 W.W.R. 625, 38 Man. R. 144 (Man. C.A.).

A Juror's Obligations

R. v. MacLean, 1906 CarswellNS 184, 11 C.C.C. 283, 1 E.L.R. 334, 39 N.S.R. 147 (N.S. S.C.).

R. v. Morgentaler, 1985 CarswellOnt 114, 48 C.R. (3d) 1, 22 C.C.C. (3d) 353, 11 O.A.C. 81, 52 O.R. (2d) 353, 22 D.L.R. (4th) 641, 17 C.R.R. 223 (Ont. C.A.), reversed 1988 CarswellOnt 45, 1988 CarswellOnt 954, 37 C.C.C. (3d) 449, 44 D.L.R. (4th) 385, 26 O.A.C. 1, 62 C.R. (3d) 1, 31 C.R.R. 1, 82 N.R. 1, (sub nom. *R. v. Morgentaler (No. 2)*) [1988] 1 S.C.R. 30, 63 O.R. (2d) 281 (note) (S.C.C.).

Deschambault v. R., 1985 CarswellQue 20, 49 C.R. (3d) 151 (Que. C.A.), leave to appeal to allowed (1987), 54 C.R. (3d) xxvii (S.C.C.).

19

Sentencing Powers and Principles

*Kenneth W.F. Fiske, Q.C.**
*(edited for the 7th edition by Joel E. Pink, Q.C.)***

INTRODUCTION

> Sentencing is of course an inexact science involving a blend of many factors with aims that often conflict and competing interests that not always can be harmonized.

This chapter is not an attempt to provide a comprehensive review of the law of sentencing in Canada. It is meant to introduce the lay person to sentencing by discussing certain important features of law. As this chapter deals solely with sentencing, no effort is made to acquaint the reader with the effect of parole upon sentences of imprisonment.

The reader is asked to recall at the conclusion of this chapter the following factual situation. The reader should formulate a sentence which in his mind is appropriate in all the circumstances, and then compare it with that arrived at by the Court of Appeal which is revealed at the end of the chapter.

The accused is 25 years of age, married, and the father of two children. His family had recently moved to another province, and the accused remained in Nova Scotia to arrange for the transfer of the family's belongings. Early one morning, the accused broke into a dwelling occupied by an elderly widow who lived alone. He grabbed the victim from behind in an upstairs hallway. He felt her breasts and attempted sexual intercourse. The victim's pleas that he desist eventually succeeded. After remaining in the house for a lengthy period of time, the accused left. The victim suffered bruises to her arms, but no permanent physical injury. However, the incident had a traumatic effect upon her and she is now afraid to live alone for fear of being attacked again. The accused was charged with breaking and entering a dwelling and

---

* LL.B., Dalhousie University, Halifax, Nova Scotia; Chief Crown Attorney (Appeals),Nova Scotia Public Prosecution Office.
**B.A., Acadia University, Wolfville, Nova Scotia; LL.B., Dalhousie Law School, Halifax, Nova Scotia; practices law in Halifax, Nova Scotia.

committing the indictable offence of sexual assault, contrary to section 348(1)(b) of the *Criminal Code* of Canada.

He pleaded guilty to the charge. The pre-sentence report from the adult probation officer submitted to the sentencing judge was generally favourable. The accused stated he was intoxicated at the time of the offence and has now joined Alcoholics Anonymous. He has a prior criminal record consisting of two convictions for break, enter and theft, one in 1977 and the other in 1985. The accused was on probation at the time of the offence.

GENERAL PRINCIPLES OF SENTENCING—PRIOR TO THE PASSAGE OF SECTION 718 OF THE *CRIMINAL CODE* OF CANADA

The paramount concern of a trial judge in sentencing an offender is the protection of the public. This does not mean that in every case the public is best protected from criminal conduct by the imprisonment, for long periods of time, of those convicted of criminal offences. General principles have been developed by courts of appeal which provide a measure of guidance to trial judges in imposing sentences designed to protect the public. In no other area of law is the statement "each case depends upon its own merits" more relevant than in the sentencing process.

Based on the particular circumstances of a case, the trial judge may determine that the public's protection is best achieved by imposing a sentence which produces a deterrent effect. Deterrence in the abstract obviously includes an element of fear. Such a sentence seeks to restrain or discourage repetition of the criminal conduct by punitive measures. In sentencing, the element of deterrence can be applied either generally or in the specific. A sentence reflecting general deterrence is directed, not at the offender, but at those in the community who might consider committing the same or a similar offence and, in this way, serves as a warning to the community at large. On the other hand, a sentence reflecting specific (individual) deterrence is aimed at dissuading the offender before the court from future criminal behaviour. A trial judge may impose a sentence which reflects both the general and specific aspects of the element of deterrence. A deterrent sentence usually means a term of imprisonment.

A sentencing judge may determine that the interests of the general public are best served by a sentence designed to promote the reformation and rehabilitation of the convicted person. The consequences to an offender of such a sentence are not as harsh or severe as those of a deterrent sentence. It provides an incentive to the individual to distance himself from criminal behaviour. The rationale behind a sentence of this nature is that leniency of treatment will likely encourage the offender to return to a law-abiding course in life. A youthful first offender is a much likelier candidate for a rehabilitative sentence than is an older, repeat offender.

A sentencing judge may reject both extremes and decide that the protection of the public can be achieved by blending deterrence and rehabilitation in sentencing the offender. For example, the judge may order a term of imprisonment as a deterrent effect, and direct that upon release the individual abide by the conditions of a probation order, in order to facilitate the rehabilitation of the offender.

Generally speaking, sentencing lies in the discretion of the court that convicts a person of a criminal offence (subs. 718.3(1) and (2)). It should be remembered that judges, in sentencing persons convicted of crimes, will always be guided by the principle "justice must always be tempered with mercy". Retribution in the sense of revenge has no place in modern sentencing law.

GENERAL PRINCIPLES OF SENTENCING AS SET OUT IN SECTION 718 OF THE *CRIMINAL CODE* OF CANADA

On September 3, 1996, the *Criminal Code* was amended, and the following inserted:

> **718.** The fundamental purpose of sentencing is to contribute, along with crime prevention initiatives, to respect for the law and the maintenance of a just, peaceful and safe society by imposing just sanctions that have one or more of the following objectives:
>> (a) to denounce unlawful conduct;
>> (b) to deter the offender and other persons from committing offences;
>> (c) to separate offenders from society, where necessary;
>> (d) to assist in rehabilitating offenders;
>> (e) to provide reparations for harm done to victims or to the community; and
>> (f) to promote a sense of responsibility in offenders, and acknowledgment of the harm done to victims and to the community.
>> 1995, c. 22, s. 6.

> **718.1** A sentence must be proportionate to the gravity of the offence and the degree of responsibility of the offender.

> **718.2** A court that imposes a sentence shall also take into consideration the following principles:

(a) a sentence should be increased or reduced to account for any relevant aggravating or mitigating circumstances relating to the offence or the offender, and, without limiting the generality of the foregoing,

(i) evidence that the offence was motivated by bias, prejudice or hate based on race, national or ethnic origin, language, colour, religion, sex, age, mental or physical disability, sexual orientation, or any other similar factor,

(ii) evidence that the offender, in committing the offence, abused the offender's spouse or common-law partner or child,

(iii) evidence that the offender, in committing the offence, abused a position of trust or authority in relation to the victim,

(iv) evidence that the offence was committed for the benefit of, at the direction of or in association with a criminal organization, or

(v) evidence that the offence was a terrorism offence shall be deemed to be aggravating circumstances;

(b) a sentence should be similar to sentences imposed on similar offenders for similar offences committed in similar circumstances;

(c) where consecutive sentences are imposed, the combined sentence should not be unduly long or harsh;

principle of totality

(d) an offender should not be deprived of liberty, if less restrictive sanctions may be appropriate in the circumstances; and

(e) all available sanctions other than imprisonment that are reasonable in the circumstances should be considered for all offenders, with particular attention to the circumstances of aboriginal offenders.

1995, c. 22, s. 6; 1997, c. 23, s. 17;
2000, c. 12, s. 95(c); 2001, c. 41, s. 20.

718.3 (1) Where an enactment prescribes different degrees or kinds of punishment in respect of an offence, the punishment to be imposed is, subject to the limitations prescribed in the enactment, in the discretion of the court that convicts a person who commits the offence.

(2) Where an enactment prescribes a punishment in respect of an offence, the punishment to be imposed is, subject to the limitations prescribed in the enactment, in the discretion of the court that convicts a person who commits the offence, but no punishment is a minimum punishment unless it is declared to be a minimum punishment.

(3) Where an accused is convicted of an offence punishable with both fine and imprisonment and a term of imprisonment in default of payment of the fine is not specified in the enactment that prescribes the punishment to be imposed, the imprisonment that may be imposed in default of pay-

ment shall not exceed the term imprisonment that is prescribed in respect of the offence.

(4) The court or youth justice court that sentences an accused may direct that the terms of imprisonment that are imposed by the court or the youth justice court or that result from the operation of subsection 734(4) or 743.5(1) or (2) shall be served consecutively, when

(a) the accused is sentenced while under sentence for an offence, and a term of imprisonment, whether in default of payment of a fine or otherwise, is imposed;

(b) the accused is found guilty or convicted of an offence punishable with both a fine and imprisonment and both are imposed;

(c) the accused is found guilty or convicted of more than one offence, and

(i) more than one fine is imposed,

(ii) terms of imprisonment for the respective offences are imposed, or

(iii) a term of imprisonment is imposed in respect of one offence and a fine is imposed in respect of another offence; or

(d) subsection 743.5(1) or (2) applies.

1995, c. 22, s. 6; 1997, c. 18, ss. 106, 141;
1999, c. 5, s. 30; 2002, c. 1, s. 182

After an offender has been found guilty, the *Criminal Code* provides that as soon as practicable, the court shall conduct proceedings to determine the appropriate sentence to be imposed. If he or she is a first- or second-time offender, the court may request a report to be prepared by a probation officer. This is known as a pre-sentence report. A pre-sentence report contains such things as age, maturity, character, behaviour, attitude and willingness to make amends, history of previous dispositions, history of any alternative measures used to deal with the offender, and any other useful material that will assist a sentencing judge.

RELEVANT FACTORS IN SENTENCING—PRIOR TO THE PASSAGE OF SECTION 718 OF THE *CRIMINAL CODE* OF CANADA

The number of factors which a trial judge may consider in sentencing a person convicted of a criminal offence is almost infinite in number. However, a number of important factors have emerged out of the case law on sentencing. These include the nature of the offence committed, the facts surrounding the commission of the offence, the age and circumstances of the offender, and the presence of a criminal record.

The sentencing judge will first look at the nature of the offence committed. The relative gravity or seriousness of a particular offence can be found in the very words of the statute creating it. Generally speaking, indictable offences are more serious in nature than offences punishable by summary conviction. Secondly, the maximum penalty prescribed for an offence gives an indication of how seriously the lawmakers regard the offence. The offence of causing a disturbance by shouting is summary conviction in nature and carries with it a maximum penalty of six months in jail. On the other hand, kidnapping is an indictable offence and a person convicted of this crime is liable to be imprisoned for life. A number of offences are "dual character" in nature—that is, the Crown has the option of proceeding against the accused by either indictment or summary conviction. In terms of degree of gravity of such offences, it can be said they fall into the middle ground between summary conviction and indictable offences.

The age of the offender is an important factor in sentencing. Hand-in-hand with the age of the offender is the existence of a record or prior criminal conviction. For instance, a youthful or elderly first offender can generally expect some measure of leniency in sentencing as opposed to a repeat offender. More will be said of criminal records later.

The character, personality and lifestyle of an offender are considered prior to the imposition of sentence. The pre-sentence report is a useful vehicle for placing this information before the sentencing judge. The standard features of such a report include the age, marital status, and education of the offender. The offender's family background and present living conditions are explored, and in the case of a youthful offender, the attitude of his parents. The report chronicles the offender's employment history and notes any particular trades or skills he possesses. A brief medical and psychological profile of the offender is included, and any behavioural or personality traits discerned by the author of the report (usually a probation officer) in his interviews with the offender are documented. If the reporter has had the opportunity to discuss the offender with a number of individuals, including police officers, relatives and employers, he will indicate in the report the attitudes of this group toward the offender. Finally, the reporter will provide the sources of his information.

The circumstances surrounding the commission of the offence are, of course, a material consideration in sentencing. An incident of "shoplifting" may not be regarded as seriously as the theft of a great deal of money by an employee of a bank. In considering the facts of an offence, judges are attentive to the manner in which the offence was committed, the degree of planning and deliberation (premeditation) that preceded the offence, the use of violence, the employment of offensive weapons, and the use of threats of bodily harm or death to facilitate the commission of the offence. The duration of an offence may be a significant circumstance. Crimes of violence are viewed seriously by the courts and deterrent sentences are consistently imposed for such offences. In particular, those violent offences which can be described as crimes of "stark horror" attract severe punishment to reflect the community's denunciation of them.

In certain cases, the age and condition of the victim of the crime are important considerations. The courts have declared that, by reason of their vulnerability to criminal behaviour, young children and the elderly, the handicapped and the infirm are all deserving of special protection through the sentencing process.

The existence of a criminal record may have a dramatic effect upon sentence. A short record of minor criminal offences or a record that is "stale" may be given little weight in sentencing. An offender who has accumulated a small number of criminal convictions may still be susceptible to the remedial effects of a rehabilitative sentence. A record disclosing a gap of a long period of time between the present offence and the last offence listed on the record is an indication that the offender has at least attempted rehabilitation and reform by avoiding criminal behaviour.

However, a lengthy record of criminal convictions or a record of offences similar to or the same as the offence for which sentence is to be imposed may have a direct bearing on the sentence handed down by the judge. An offender who accumulates a lengthy record by consistently committing one criminal offence after another can be fairly described as one who has dedicated his life to crime and for which the hope of eventual rehabilitation is a lost cause. The fact that an offender committed the offence for which he is being sentenced while on probation, parole or bail for a previous offence, is one which may weigh heavily against him.

The foregoing are the major factors relevant to sentencing. There are a number of other circumstances which a judge may also take into consideration in reaching his decision.

A plea of guilty is a mitigating circumstance which the judge may take into account. The rationale for this proposition is that such a plea saves the community the expense of a trial.

Where two or more individuals took part in the commission of an offence, the degree of active participation of each is considered. Furthermore, the excessive leniency toward one of the offenders by one judge does not bind a different judge sentencing another of the offenders to impose a likewise lenient sentence. However, all things being equal between the offenders, the judge sentencing the second offender should be mindful of the penalty imposed on the first so that a disparity between the sentences does not become evident.

A genuine expression of remorse for his criminal conduct by the offender is a factor which weighs in his favour. The lack of remorse on the part of an offender has the opposite effect. In cases where the victim of an offence incurs expense due to damaged or stolen property or injury, voluntary restitution by the offender is looked upon favourably by a sentencing judge.

The prevalence of a particular type of offence in the community may be detrimental to the interests of an offender, should he face sentencing for that offence. As an example, an offender convicted of the offence of breaking and entering a dwelling may be subject to a penalty stiffer than the norm if the judge is satisfied the incidence of this offence in the community is on the rise.

A word on drunkenness is appropriate at this time. Although a state of intoxication may be relevant and sometimes crucial to the issue of the intent of an accused to commit a criminal offence, it cannot be used by the offender as an excuse for his behaviour at the sentencing stage. Courts have consistently declared that the fact an offender was under the influence of alcohol or drugs at the time of the commission of the offence cannot be used in mitigation of sentence.

Evidence of the good character of an offender is, of course, a relevant consideration in sentencing, except in certain offences. Good character will not assist an offender if the offence involved a breach of a position of trust held by the offender. This holds true for both business and personal relationships. An employee of a commercial enterprise, a lawyer or a financial advisor who use their positions of trust to enrich themselves by illegal means cannot point to evidence of good character as a factor worthy of consideration in their favour.

A parent or relative of a young child, or a person who stands *in loco parentis* to a young child, and who sexually abuses the child, will be dealt with severely because of the position of trust occupied in relation to the child. The rationale for this approach is that the commission of the offence was facilitated because of the position of authority held by the offender over the child. Courts have consistently viewed the sexual abuse of a child by an adult as an offence which must be strongly deterred in order to reflect society's repudiation of this repugnant crime. The involvement of a breach of trust in the commission of this offence serves to aggravate an already serious situation. However, judges should not allow pure emotion caused by moral indignation to result in overly severe sentences for this offence.

In certain cases, the psychological profile of an offender may constitute an important consideration in sentencing. The report of a psychologist or a psychiatrist is important in this regard. If indications are the offender labours under a psychological handicap requiring treatment, the judge, in imposing sentence, may recommend to the penal authorities that such treatment be arranged or provided in the institution. The mental deficiency of an offender is a mitigating factor a judge should consider in sentencing.

Victims of crime will also have a say in the sentencing process. Victim impact statements will be filed with the court and copies will be given to the accused. The weight given to the victim impact statement will vary from case to case.

The *Criminal Code* gives the trial judge discretion not to impose a jail sentence. If the sentence is not a minimum term of imprisonment and is less than two years and the trial judge is satisfied that the accused is not a danger to the safety of the community, he or she may order that the term of imprisonment be served in the community rather than in a jail. Section 742.1 states:

> Where a person is convicted of an offence, except an offence that is punishable by a minimum term or imprisonment, and the court
>> (a) imposes a sentence of imprisonment of less than two years, and
>> (b) is satisfied that serving the sentence in the community would not endanger the safety of the community and would be consistent with the fundamental purpose and principles of sentencing set out in sections 718 to 718.2,
>
> the court may, for the purposes of supervising the offender's behaviour in the community, order that the offender serve the sentence in the community, subject to the offender's complying with the conditions of a conditional sentence order made under section 742.3.
>
> 1995, c. 22, s. 6; 1997, c. 18, s. 107.1.

The provisions of s. 742.1 are such a new concept that I think it is important for you to understand how the court should apply this section in imposing a conditional sentence. In the case of *R. v. Parker*,[1] the 21-year-old accused was convicted of two counts of dangerous driving causing death and two counts of dangerous driving causing bodily harm. The accused drove his high-performance motor vehicle in an erratic manner on a busy street. Not an experienced driver, he exceeded the speed limit. While attempting to pass another vehicle, the accused lost control, went over the curb and hit four teenagers sitting on a church lawn—two died. The other two were seriously injured and suffered permanent emotional scarring. Alcohol was not a contributing factor and there was no related criminal record. The accused was remorseful and accepted responsibility. There was a positive pre-sentence report. The accused had a dysfunctional home life and had children he supported. The sentence of two years less a day, two years probation, and ten years driving prohibition was appropriate.

The trial judge exercised his discretion under s. 742.1 of the *Criminal Code* and ordered that the accused serve his sentence in the community with strict conditions, including house arrest for the full period, and 240 hours of community service, which included speaking to young persons to convey the message that this type of tragedy could happen to them. In upholding the decision of the trial judge, Justice Bateman of the Nova Scotia Court of Appeal states:

> The conditional sentencing provision has understandably stirred some judicial debate. One area of focus has been the requirement that the judge be satisfied that "serving the sentence in the community would not endanger the community." The issue is whether this precondition to imposing a conditional sentence should be interpreted so as to include considerations of general deterrence and denunciation, or restricted to factors specific to the offender. As Finlayson, J.A., wrote in *R. v. Pierce*, [1997] O.J. No. 715 (Q.L.) at para. 32 [reported 114 C.C.C. (3d) 23 at p. 34]:
>
> > Another significant difference of opinion is with respect to what Parliament meant by the phrase "endanger the safety of the community." Counsel for the appellant interprets this as meaning that if the particular accused does not pose a threat to the safety of the community in the sense of re-offending, the accused's serving of the sentence in the community would not "endanger the safety of the community." All previous concerns about the fundamental purpose of sentencing codified in s. 718 would be of diminished importance. In contrast, the Crown submits that "safety of the community" means more than the risk posed by the individual accused re-offending but encompasses the need for general deterrence.
>
> I agree with the conclusion of Rosenberg, J.A., in *Wismayer, supra*, that "endanger the community" is to be restricted to factors particular to the offender and does not include matters of general deterrence and denunciation.
>
> In *Pierce, supra*, Finlayson, J.A., said in this regard at paragraph 45 [at pp. 38-39]:
>
> > A resolution of this difference of opinion as to the meaning of com-

munity safety might at first blush appear to be central to the development of a methodology of imposing conditional sentences. However, *if the narrower interpretation of community safety is simply regarded as the sine qua non to the exercise of a discretion to permit the sentence to be served in the community, I have little difficulty with it.* In the final analysis, the discretion must be exercised in accordance with recognized sentencing principles. This takes us back to the concerns of specific and general deterrence expressed by the Crown including s. 718.2. [Emphasis added.]

General deterrence and denunciation, along with all other sentencing objectives, remain factors in the judge's ultimate exercise of discretion, once the offender meets the preconditions set out in s. 742.1. In exercising that discretion the judge considers again the objectives and purpose of sentencing as mandated in s. 718. In other words, those objectives guide the judge in determining, not only the length of the custodial term, but, ultimately, whether a conditional sentence is ordered.

I acknowledge that it may seem an academic exercise whether general deterrence and denunciation are considered at the precondition stage, within the definition of "endanger the community," or thereafter. In my view, however, it is logical that they be weighed in conjunction with all of the other sentencing objectives, once the preconditions are met, so as to preclude undue emphasis on these two factors in comparison to all others.

The cases which advocate the broader interpretation of "endanger the community," with respect, in my view, arose in response to the position of some of the courts that first struggled to interpret these amendments and concluded that, once an offender met the preconditions, the court was obliged to impose a conditional sentence (see, for example in *R. v. Scidmore*, [1996] O.J. No. 4446 (Q.L.) [reported 112 C.C.C. (3d) 28] (Ont. C.A.)). It was, therefore, important to interpret "endanger the community" in the broadest possible fashion. If accepting, as do I, that a discretion remains in the sentencing judge whether to impose a conditional sentence, although the preconditions in s. 742.1 are satisfied, and that the exercise of discretion requires the judge to revisit the objectives and purpose of sentencing, it is unnecessary to resort to the broad definition, because general deterrence and denunciation are considered, along with all other objectives in the final exercise of discretion. To consider general deterrence and denunciation in the context of "endanger the community" and again in the final exercise of discretion would result in an overemphasis upon those two objectives, in comparison to all others.

It is important to emphasize that a conditional sentence is only considered where the judge has decided that no disposition other than incarceration is a fit sentence. Without doubt this creates a conundrum which is resolved only when one remembers that the conditional sentence is a form of incarceration, albeit served in the community.

In this regard, I find the remarks of Twaddle, J.A. in *R. v. Arsiuta*, [1997] M.J. No. 89 (Q.L.) (Man. C.A.) [reported 114 C.C.C. (3d) 286 at p. 287] germane:

> In this regard "conditional sentence" is a bit of a misnomer. It is not a new form of sentence, but rather a new way in which a prison sentence can be served. A judge must first impose a prison term—using all the sentencing principles to arrive at one of the right length—and then, if the sentence is for a term of less than two years and the judge is satisfied that the serving of the sentence in the community will not endanger the community's safety, the judge may direct that it be served there subject to strict conditions.

Once the judge has determined that a custodial sentence is warranted and the preconditions are met, the judge is then to consider whether the objectives sought through incarceration in an institution can be adequately addressed by some form of control within the community.

If a trial judge orders this, he or she is then obliged to have the accused enter into a conditional sentence order (s. 742.3) which requires the accused to do the following:

(a) keep the peace and be of good behaviour;

(b) appear before the court when required to do so by the court;

(c) report to a supervisor;

(d) remain within the jurisdiction of the court unless written permission to go outside the jurisdiction is obtained from the court or the supervisor;

(e) notify the court or the supervisor in advance o any change of name or address, and promptly notify the court or the supervisor of any change of employment occupation.

In addition, one or more of the following conditions may be included in the Order:

(f) to abstain from the consumption of alcohol or intoxicating substances;

(g) abstain from owning or possessing or carrying a weapon

(h) provide for the support or care of dependants;

(i) perform up to 240 hours of community service over a period not exceeding 18 months;

(j) attend treatment programs provided by the province; and

(k) comply with any other reasonable condition.

If an accused person who is on a conditional sentence order violates it, another hearing will be held and, if satisfied on the balance of probabilities that the offender has without reasonable excuse breached a condition of a conditional sentence order, the court may:

(a) take no action;
(b) change the optional conditions;
(c) suspend the conditional sentence and direct the offender serve in custody a portion of the unexpired sentence; or
(d) terminate the conditional sentence altogether and direct the offender be committed to custody until expiration of his sentence (subs. 742.6(9)).

There are provisions that allow police officers to enroll an accused person in authorized programs as designated by the Lieutenant Governor in Council of a province, in which the accused will partake in community service and, if successfully completed, the charge against him or her will be withdrawn. If the accused is able to partake in alternative measures and successfully completes it, he or she will be spared going through the court process and will avoid the resulting criminal conviction and/or criminal record.

It is evident that there are some very interesting and new provisions that serve to protect the public, involve the victim and which may be in the best interest of the offender.

TYPES OF SENTENCES

When the subject of punishment for criminal offences is raised, people tend to think of it in terms of imprisonment. However, imprisonment is but one form of punishment that may be ordered as a consequence of a conviction for a criminal offence.

Imprisonment is, of course, physical confinement and restraint of an offender within a penal institution for the duration of the term of the sentence, subject to early release on parole. A term of imprisonment of two years or more must be served in federal penitentiary (*Criminal Code*, s. 743.1). On the other hand, an offender sentenced to imprisonment for less than two years serves it in a provincial correctional facility. The maximum term of imprisonment that can be served in a provincial institution is two years less one day.

Generally speaking, a sentence commences when it is imposed (s. 719). An exception is the intermittent sentence (s. 732). This type of sentence permits the offender to serve his sentence of imprisonment at intermittent times (for example, on weekends). A sentence of imprisonment can be made intermittent only if it does not exceed 90 days in length. The offender is subject to a probation order at all times when he is not in actual confinement in jail. Part of a day served in an institution counts as one full day in reduction of the intermittent sentence. For example, an individual ordered to serve a sentence intermittently on weekends from Friday evening to Monday morning is deemed to have served four days in jail each weekend.

The *Code* provides (s. 731) that, upon conditions set out in a probation order, a judge may choose to suspend the passing of sentence altogether and order the offender released from custody. A suspended sentence is not available in respect of offences committed for which a minimum punishment is prescribed. Should the offender breach any of the conditions of the probation order during its term, he is liable to be returned to court to be sentenced for the offence for which sentence was originally suspended. He is also subject to additional penalties for breaching the probation order.

Probation cannot be ordered as a sentence by itself. It must be combined with either a fine or a term of imprisonment not exceeding two years (s. 731). Note that probation cannot be ordered in addition to both a fine and imprisonment. The term of any probation order cannot exceed three years (s. 732.2). A court cannot order one probation order to be served consecutive to another (that is, one after the other).

Section 732.1 provides for the form and content of a probation order. Certain conditions are mandatory in every probation order. The *Code* lists a number of optional conditions and grants to the court making the order the power to impose other reasonable conditions.

A probation order comes into force on the date it is made, except in the case where the offender is sentenced to imprisonment, in which case the order becomes effective upon the expiration of that part of the sentence. The conditions and term of a probation order may be subsequently changed by the court (s. 732.2). In addition, a probation order made in one province may be transferred to another (s. 733). Although the subject of some debate, it appears a judge may order that an offender serve a period of probation following the expiration of an intermittent sentence.

Another familiar type of sentence is the fine (s. 734). The word "fine" is defined (s. 716) to include "a pecuniary penalty or other sum of money, but does not include restitution." In the case of an indictable offence for which the maximum punishment does not exceed five years, the offender may be either fined in lieu of any other prescribed punishment or he may be fined in addition to that punishment. However, if the offence is one for which a minimum term of imprisonment is provided, the offender cannot be fined in lieu of the term of imprisonment. An individual convicted of an indictable offence punishable by imprisonment for more than five years may be fined in addition to, but not in lieu of, the other punishment prescribed. In the case of a summary conviction offence, and unless otherwise provided, an individual is liable to a fine in addition to or in lieu of any other punishment that may be imposed.

In sentencing an offender to payment of a fine following conviction for a criminal offence, a judge may direct that a term of imprisonment in default of payment of the fine be imposed. A corporation convicted of either an indictable or summary conviction offence is subject, of course, to a fine only (s. 735).

A novel form of sentencing is the absolute and conditional discharge (s. 730). A discharge is not available to a corporation. To qualify for a discharge, an offender cannot have committed an offence for which a minimum punishment is prescribed, or an offence the maximum penalty for which is imprisonment for 14 years or more. The judge must be satisfied that a discharge order is in the best interests of the accused and not contrary to the public interest. If an accused is discharged either absolutely or conditionally, he does not stand convicted of the offence in respect of which the order is made. However, the accused may appeal against the finding of guilt as if it were a conviction, and the Crown may appeal against the decision not to convict the accused as if it were an acquittal. A number of cases have set out the criteria which a court should consider when determining whether to discharge an accused.

If an accused who has been discharged on conditions prescribed in a probation order and, while bound by the probation order, commits an offence, including the offence of breach of probation (s. 734), the court that ordered the conditional discharge may revoke the discharge, convict the accused of the offence to which the discharge relates and impose the appropriate sentence as if a conviction had been entered at the time of the discharge. The court may also exercise the powers granted by subs. 732.2(5).

A special form of punishment is the indeterminate sentence which may be imposed upon an accused who has been found by the court to be a dangerous offender under Part XXIV of the *Code*. An accused must be convicted of a "serious personal injury offence" as defined by s. 752 in order to be sentenced as a dangerous offender. Other mandatory criteria to support the finding of an accused as a dangerous offender are set out in s. 753. Although an accused has been declared a dangerous offender, it does not mean that an indeterminate sentence must then be imposed. The judge may either sentence him to a federal penitentiary for an indeterminate period of time in place of any other sentence that may be imposed for the offence, or the judge may, having declared the accused a dangerous offender, sentence him to a definite term of imprisonment within the limits prescribed for the particular offence of which he was convicted.

A person declared a dangerous offender under Part XXIV of the *Code* and sentenced to an indeterminate period of imprisonment is eligible for parole after serving three years of the sentence. The Parole Board must consider the dangerous offender for parole at this time, and every two years thereafter if parole is not granted (s. 761).

A person may also be determined to be a long-term offender under Part XXIV. If this finding is made, the judge must impose a minimum sentence of two years in prison, to be followed by a period of community supervision, which can be a maximum of ten years in length.

Another special form of sentence concerns the eligibility for parole of an individual who has been convicted of second degree murder under subs. 235(1). An offender convicted of this offence must be sentenced to imprisonment for life. Section 745.4 provides that the trial judge, in imposing sentence, must determine the period of imprisonment the offender will serve before being eligible for parole, which cannot be less than 10 years. Having regard to certain factors enumerated in s. 745.4, the judge may, in his or her discretion, substitute for the 10-year minimum a term of imprisonment greater than 10 but not more than 25 years which the offender will serve before being eligible for parole.

In cases where a jury has convicted the accused of second degree murder, the presiding judge must ask them for a recommendation respecting the number of years the accused will serve before being eligible for parole (s. 745.2). The jury need not make a recommendation and the presiding judge, although required to consider it, is not bound by the jury's recommendation if one is made.

For the purposes of appeals against sentence in proceedings by indictment, a number of declarations and orders made under the *Code* are deemed to be part and parcel of the sentencing process. One such order is that relating to parole eligibility following conviction for second degree murder.

A trial judge who convicts a person of impaired driving (s. 253(a)), driving with an excessive blood/alcohol concentration (s. 253(b)), or refusing or failing to comply with an A.L.E.R.T. or breathalyzer demand

(s. 254), must make an order against the offender under s. 259 prohibiting that person from operating a motor vehicle for a period of time, the limits of which are set out in the subsection and depend upon whether it is a first, second or subsequent offence.

Other dispositions include mandatory and discretionary prohibition orders respecting the possession of firearms, ammunition and explosive substances (subs. 100(1) and (2)); orders for punitive damages resulting from the unlawful use of wiretaps (subs. 194(1)); forfeiture orders respecting things seized under valid search warrants (subs. 199(3)); restitution or forfeiture orders dealing with property obtained by the commission of criminal offences (s. 491.1); and orders for compensation for loss of property as a result of criminal offences (ss. 738, 739). At first glance, such dispositions may not be considered elements of the range of sentences open to a court in exacting punishment for criminal behavior. However, they are as much a part of the process of sentencing as imprisonment, fines, and probation. As noted, some of the orders described fall within the discretion of the judge to impose, while others are mandatory and must be made in addition to the other punishment prescribed for the offence.

QUANTUM OF SENTENCE

The offence of arson is created by s. 433, which provides a maximum penalty upon conviction of imprisonment for 14 years. This is typical of the vast majority of indictable criminal offences created by the *Code* and other federal penal statutes in that only the maximum, and not a minimum, punishment is provided for commission of the offence. On the other hand, many of the provisions creating summary conviction criminal offences make no reference to the punishment to which an offender is liable upon conviction. There are, in both cases, a few exceptions (i.e., life imprisonment for murder).

In terms of maximum punishment, an indictable offence will fall into one of five categories: imprisonment for two years, five years, 10 years, 14 years, or life. If no punishment is provided for a particular indictable offence, then the maximum penalty will be imprisonment for five years (s. 743). Unless otherwise provided in the section creating a specific offence, an individual convicted of a summary conviction offence is liable to be imprisoned for a maximum term of six months and fined up to $2,000 (subs. 787(1)). The maximum fine payable by a corporation convicted of a summary conviction offence is, unless otherwise specifically provided, $25,000 (s. 735(b)).

In the case of an indictable offence, the amount of a fine lies in the discretion of the court. Unless a specific amount is otherwise provided, there is no cap on the amount of a fine that may be levied in respect of an indictable offence.

Anyone attending sentencing proceedings will invariably hear the judge and counsel from time to time refer to the "range" of sentence applicable to the particular offence. This simply means that out of a number of cases decided by courts of appeal on sentences for a particular offence, a discernible scale of sentence for the offence has emerged. Many times counsel will speak in terms of the low end, median, and high end of the applicable "range". An example will serve to illustrate this point. The maximum penalty that can be imposed for the offence of manslaughter is imprisonment for life (s. 236). In Nova Scotia, there is a wide range of sentence that may be considered for this offence. Sentences for manslaughter run from a "low" of suspended sentence and probation, to a "median" of four to 10 years' imprisonment, and to a "high" of imprisonment for 20 years. The closer the circumstances of a particular case approach the commission of a murder, the more likely sentences for manslaughter will fall within the median of high end of the range. For instance, in the case of *R. v. Julian*,[2] a sentence of 20 years' imprisonment was upheld on appeal for an offender convicted of manslaughter who, intoxicated and in a fit of rage, set fire to a dwelling that resulted in the deaths of three small children. On the other hand, in the case of *R. v. Cormier*,[3] a suspended sentence and probation was upheld on appeal in respect of a woman who had stabbed her husband to death after a domestic dispute during which the husband had physically abused her, which unfortunately had not been an uncommon occurrence.

This does not mean that maximum punishments for criminal offences have, in the development of an applicable range of sentence, been judicially scrapped. However, the maximum penalty for an offence is usually reserved for the most incorrigible offender who has committed the offence in the most aggravating of circumstances. In short, it is the "worst offender" in the "worst case" that receives the maximum punishment.

A range of sentence cannot be found for every criminal offence. The more often sentence appeals for a particular offence are determined by a court of appeal, the more likely an applicable range of sentence will emerge. A range of sentence exists for such crimes as break and enter, robbery, manslaughter, and possession of stolen property, but not for such "rare" offences as dueling, piratical acts (mutiny), and defacing coinage. The object of a range of sentence for an offence is to ensure "uniformity" of sentence. Similar offenders committing the same offence in similar circumstances should receive approximately the same punishment.

Another phrase heard from time to time in courtrooms during sentencing is "totality of sentence". Where the offender is being sentenced for a number of criminal offences, or is being sentenced for an offence that he committed while on parole, and therefore already under sentence for a previous offence, the judge, in imposing sentence, must consider the "principle of totality".

Let us assume an accused is charged with six counts of breaking and entering a dwelling house, and four counts of possession of stolen property. He pleads guilty to all 10 charges at the same time, and now faces sentence. Taking the offences in isolation, the judge is of the opinion that one year in prison is a fit sentence for each. However, if such a sentence is imposed with respect to each charge and the sentences ordered served consecutively (one after the other); a total term of imprisonment of 10 years would result. A judge must ask himself whether the total term of incarceration exacts a burden of sentence too onerous for the offender to bear. The judge decides that a global sentence of three years' imprisonment for all 10 offences is appropriate in this case. To achieve this end, the total sentence is apportioned among the 10 offences. For the sake of example, the offender is sentenced to serve four months for each of the break and enter offences, and three months for each of the charges of possession of stolen property.

Courts should avoid the application of what is known as the "cookie-cutter" approach to sentencing offenders. Simply put, judges should avoid rigidity in sentencing. Punishment should not be exacted primarily on the basis of the nature of the offence committed, with little or no regard to other relevant factors. A judge may decide that, regardless of other circumstances, the minimum sentence he will impose for the offence of manslaughter is at least 10 years' imprisonment. Rigidity in sentencing may also take the following form. A judge may take the view that imprisonment is the only effective sentence for the offence of theft, irrespective of what was stolen, by whom, and in what circumstances. Courts of appeal consistently frown upon any rigid approach to sentencing.

Recently, some appellate courts in Canada have approved, for certain offences, the application of a "tariff" of sentence. A specific sentence is declared a "benchmark" or starting point in determining the sentence ultimately to be imposed. The sentencing judge adjusts the tariff sentence upward or downward to take into account the circumstances of the particular offence and the offender before the court.

One cannot leave the subject of quantum of sentence without considering the subject of concurrent and consecutive sentences. A concurrent sentence is one that is served at the same time as another sentence. As already noted, a consecutive sentence is one that is served after the expiration of another sentence. To repeat what has already been stated, a sentence generally commences when it is imposed (s. 719). However, when an offender is sentenced at the same time for two or more offences, or is sentenced for an offence while already serving a sentence for a previous offence, the judge may direct that the sentences be served consecutively, that is, one after the other (subs. 718.3(4)). If the judge fails to expressly direct that two or more sentences be served consecutively, they will be deemed to be concurrent sentences.

An example is useful. Where an offender is sentenced to imprisonment for one year for each of three offences, and the judge has directed that the sentences be concurrent, the net effect is that the offender will serve one year in prison. On the other hand, if the judge has directed the three sentences be served consecutively, then the offender will serve a term of imprisonment of three years. The totality principle has already been discussed—it has been called the "twin" of consecutive sentences.

A sentencing judge does not possess an unfettered discretion in deciding whether two or more sentences will be served concurrently or consecutively. If the offences were the result of "one simple criminal enterprise", then generally concurrent sentences should be imposed. On the other hand, when the offences are separated by time and place, consecutive sentences are appropriate.

In determining the punishment to be imposed for a criminal offence, a judge may consider time spent by an offender in pre-trial custody (subs. 719(3)). In most jurisdictions, it is accepted practice to give two days' credit for every one day served.

A sentencing judge cannot take into consideration when an offender may be eligible for parole when imposing a sentence of imprisonment. Subject to the provisions of the *Criminal Code* dealing with parole eligibility in cases of murder, a sentencing judge cannot intrude upon the functions of the Parole Board.

APPEALS

Indictable Offences

An offender (subs. 675(1)(b)) and the Crown (subs. 676(1)(d)) enjoy the same right of appeal under the *Criminal Code* against the sentence imposed by a trial judge upon conviction in proceedings by indictment. The definition section in Part XXI (s. 673) is important: it defines the court to which the appeal is taken, describes an "indictment" to include an information charging an indictable offence (in cases where the proceedings were conducted before a provincial court judge), and provides an expanded definition of "sentence" to include certain declarations, orders and dispositions made under various sections of the *Code*.

It is the nature of the proceedings that determines the forum of the appeal, not the nature of the conviction. A person charged with and convicted of an indictable offence appeals against sentence to the court of appeal. Similarly, a person charged with an indictable offence, but convicted of an included offence which is summary conviction in nature, appeals against sentence to the court of appeal under Part XXI of the *Code*.

An appeal against sentence is not an appeal as of right. The appellant can only appeal sentence with the leave (or permission) of the court of appeal or a judge of that court. Therefore, in theory at least, it appears reasonable to assume that an application for leave to appeal against sentence is a proceeding separate and distinct from the actual sentence appeal before the court of appeal. In practice, this is not the case. In Nova Scotia, the application for leave to appeal and the merits of the appeal are heard and determined together by the court. The appeal is argued before the Court of Appeal as if leave to appeal had already been granted.

There are three exceptions to this general rule. When an offender appeals sentence only, and applies for bail pending the hearing of the appeal under s. 679, it is a condition precedent to bail that the appellant convince the judge (of the court of appeal hearing the bail application) that the sentence appeal has merit and that leave to appeal against sentence should be granted. Secondly, in cases of second degree murder, an offender (subs. 675(2)) or the Crown (subs. 676(4)) may appeal to the court of appeal an order made under s. 745.4 respecting the term of imprisonment the offender must serve before being eligible for parole. The third exception deals with dangerous offenders and long-term offenders under Part XXIV of the *Code*. A person found to be a dangerous offender and sentenced to detention in a penitentiary for an indeterminate period may appeal to the court of appeal against that sentence (subs. 759(1)).

A sentence appeal to the court of appeal is argued at a hearing in open court on either a transcript of the sentencing in the lower court or a statement of facts agreed to by both counsel. In Nova Scotia, the majority of sentence appeals are argued on the transcript. The rules of court provide that copies of relevant documents, such as the information or indictment, the extract of a criminal record, the pre-sentence report or psychological assessment, must be placed before the court of appeal so that the court will have all relevant material in order to consider the merits of the case. The court of appeal must consider the fitness of the sentence under review, and may either vary the sentence within the limits prescribed for the offence or dismiss the appeal (s. 687). The rules of court may make provision for the trial judge to submit to the court of appeal a report of the sentencing (s. 682). In Nova Scotia, such a report is mandatory by virtue of the criminal appeal rules.

On the sentence appeal, the court of appeal may consider certain matters, documents or reports that were not before the sentencing judge (s. 687). From time to time the court of appeal is asked to receive and consider a post-sentence report dealing with the conduct of the offender since the passing of sentence. Courts of appeal have developed certain general principles applicable to the exercise of the powers of the court under s. 687 on sentence appeals.

The court of appeal will not vary a sentence under review merely because the judges of the court are of the opinion that they would have imposed a different sentence had they been sitting as trial judges. Similarly, the court of appeal will not vary a sentence solely for the reason the sentence strikes the members of the court, upon initial consideration, as being overly lenient or excessively harsh, as the case may be. However, the court will vary a sentence under appeal if it is satisfied the sentencing judge made a mistake in applying the recognized principles of sentencing to the particular case. The court of appeal will also vary a sentence in a case where it is of the view that the sentence is clearly inadequate or excessive, as the case may be, having considered the nature of the offence committed, the facts surrounding the commission of the offence, and the circumstances of the particular offender, including the presence of any record of previous criminal convictions. Examples illustrating the two situations in which a sentence will be varied are in order.

The accused is 18 years of age, and attending his final year of school. His future plans include attendance at university. He pleaded guilty to the theft of store merchandise valued at less than $5,000 (shop-lifting), his first criminal offence. The stolen goods were recovered and the accused has expressed regret for his behavior. He has never present-ed a disciplinary problem either at home or at school. The trial judge expressed the view that specific deterrence was of primary importance in this case and proceeded to impose a sentence of imprisonment. The sentence reflects an error in principle. The accused is a youthful first offender and, in all the circumstances, should have received a sentence that reflected his prospects for rehabilitation.

The accused is convicted after trial on a charge of robbery with violence. He assaulted an elderly man and robbed him of his wallet con-taining cash, none of which was recovered. The accused is in his late twenties and has committed other crimes of violence. At the time the crime was committed, he was on parole for a previous offence. He has shown no remorse for his behavior. The trial judge, declaring the need for deterrence, sentenced the accused to three months in jail. Based on the serious nature of the offence committed, the use of violence against an elderly victim, and the accused's lengthy criminal record, the sen-tence is manifestly inadequate and a term of imprisonment in a federal penitentiary should have been imposed.

Summary Conviction Offences

Under s. 813, both an offender and the Crown may appeal against a sentence in summary conviction proceedings. In this case, the appeal is made to the appeal court as defined in s. 812. Leave to appeal sen-tence is not required. (Section 785 contains relevant definitions.) On an appeal, the court must consider the fitness of the sentence imposed, and may either vary the sentence within the limits prescribed for the of-fence, or may dismiss the appeal (subs. 822(6)). The appeal is based on the record of the trial court, save in exceptional circumstances when a hearing *de novo* is ordered by the appeal court under subs. 822(4).

Theoretically, an offender or the Crown may further appeal against sentence from the appeal court to the court of appeal, under s. 839. However, such an appeal can only be taken on a question of law alone. Courts of appeal have historically regarded an appeal against quantum of sentence as one that does not raise a question of law alone.

An offender or the Crown may wish to appeal sentence from the tri-al court directly to the court of appeal. This can be done under the pro-cedure of summary appeal (s. 830), but the appeal is restricted to ques-tions of law or jurisdiction. For example, a judge convicts an accused of a summary conviction offence and sentences him to three months in jail, a fine of $500, and probation for two years. This "illegal" sentence may be corrected by the court of appeal on summary appeal. Note that in this hypothetical case, no issue of quantum of sentence is involved.

Appeals in General

From time to time the question is asked whether a court hearing a sentence appeal may vary the sentence contrary to the wishes of the party who initiated the appeal. Can the court of appeal increase a sentence where it is the offender who has appealed? The court can do so, provided the Crown has given notice of its intention to seek an increased penalty. The practice is that the court of appeal will not vary a sentence contrary to the relief sought by the appellant unless the opposing party has cross-appealed against the sentence.

The Supreme Court of Canada has held that it has jurisdiction to hear an appeal involving sentence in proceedings by indictment, not under s. 691 or s. 693 of the *Code*, but under subs. 41(1) of the *Supreme Court Act*. The majority of the Supreme Court of Canada has held that, in theory, it has the power to deal with an appeal involving the "fitness" of a sentence, but, in practice, the court will be very reluctant to do so. However, the Supreme Court of Canada will consider sentence appeals that raise important questions of law. In the case referred to, the court considered, in the case of a guilty plea, the standard of proof required of any facts alleged by the Crown in aggravation of sentence and disputed by the accused.

CONCLUSION

Names of cases are not important in considering the appropriate sentence; what is important are the principles applied, the application of the law, and the range of sentence imposed. In the case referred to in the Introduction, the trial judge sentenced the accused to imprisonment for three years. On appeal by the Crown, this sentence was varied to six years' imprisonment. The Court of Appeal decided the sentence imposed did not give proper consideration to the element of deterrence, and was inadequate in its denunciation of the offender's conduct. The offender was on probation at the time of the offence, and had a prior record of convictions for the offence of breaking and entering.

Notes

[1] *R. v. Parker*, 1997 CarswellNS 203, 116 C.C.C. (3d) 236. 194, 29 M.V.R. (3d) 298, 159 N.S.R. (2d) 166, 468 A.P.R. 166 (N.S. C.A.).

[2] *R. v. Julian*, 1973 CarswellNS 14, 6 N.S.R. (2d) 504, 24 C.R.N.S. 289 (N.S. C.A.).

[3] *R. v. Cormier*, 1974 CarswellNS 166, 9 N.S.R. (2d) 687, 22 C.C.C. (2d) 235 (N.S. C.A.).

20

The Appeal Process

Kenneth W.F. Fiske, Q.C. *

INTRODUCTION

The purpose of this chapter is to acquaint the student with the appeal process in criminal proceedings. It is a general overview and no attempt is made to discuss every *Criminal Code* section or rule of court respecting appeals. The chapter is intended to inform the student of those appeal provisions most commonly used and the practice and procedure of appeals to such an extent that if the student were to attend the hearing of an appeal he or she would come away with an understanding and appreciation of what transpired in the appeal courtroom.

GENERAL

The curtain has come down on the trial. The accused has been convicted of a criminal offence and sentenced for it, or he has been found not guilty of the charge against him. In either case, there exists the prospect of an appeal to a higher court. The route the appeal takes and the parameters of the appeal depend on the nature of the charge against the accused. If the charge was indictable in nature or one on which the Crown chose to proceed by indictment (in the case of a Crown option or "hybrid" offence), the appeal is made under the provisions of Part XXI of the *Criminal Code* to the court of appeal for the province or territory as defined in s. 2 of the *Code*. On the other hand, if the accused was charged with a summary offence or an offence on which the Crown elected to proceed by summary conviction, the appeal is made to the "appeal court" defined in s. 812 of the *Criminal Code* following the appeal provisions of Part XXVII. It is the nature of the proceedings (indictable or summary conviction) and not the nature of the conviction which determines those provisions of the *Criminal Code* applicable to the appeal.

An appeal in any proceedings is a creature of statute, that is, there

---

* LL.B., Dalhousie University, Halifax, Nova Scotia; Chief Crown Attorney (Appeals), Nova Scotia Public Prosecution Service.

can be no appeal to a higher court of law unless legislation (such as the *Criminal Code*) specifically provides for it.

INDICTABLE OFFENCES

The Appeal

A person convicted of an indictable offence may appeal to the court of appeal from either the conviction or the sentence or both. An offender may appeal from conviction "as of right" on any ground that involves a question of law. Furthermore, an offender may appeal the conviction, with the leave (or permission) of the court of appeal or a judge of the court, on grounds involving questions of mixed law and fact or fact alone. The offender may also appeal, with leave of the court of appeal or a judge, from the sentence imposed following the conviction. An offender's rights of appeal from conviction and sentence are described in s. 675 of the *Criminal Code*. An appeal from conviction and/or sentence in respect of a summary conviction offence can be heard by a court of appeal under s. 675, but the appeal must be joined with an appeal of an indictable offence.

Under s. 676 of the *Code*, the Attorney General of the province or territory may appeal from a verdict of acquittal entered by the trial court. The Attorney General may also appeal, with the leave of the court or a judge, from a sentence imposed on an offender. The Attorney General can also appeal, under s. 676, an acquittal or a sentence in respect of a summary conviction case, but such an appeal must be joined with an appeal from acquittal or sentence of an indictable offence. There is an important distinction between an offender's right of appeal in relation to a conviction and the Attorney General's right of appeal from a verdict of acquittal. The Attorney General's appeal against an acquittal is strictly confined to grounds involving a question of law.

A brief explanation of "leave to appeal" is appropriate. In theory, an application for leave to appeal is a proceeding separate from an appeal. The requirement for leave to appeal means the party proposing to appeal must convince the court of appeal or a judge of the court that the appeal should be heard by the court. The party seeking leave to appeal is not obliged to satisfy the court the appeal will be successful, but must show the proposed appeal does have some merit. Put another way, the party seeking leave must satisfy the court or the judge that the appeal, if heard, would not be a waste of the court's time.

What is a question of law? This issue continues to vex judges and lawyers alike. The line separating questions of law from questions of fact or mixed law and fact is not always clear. However, a number of issues have been defined as constituting questions of law. The interpretation of statutory provisions, a trial judge's explanation of the law to a jury, the admissibility of evidence, and the issue whether an individual's rights under the *Canadian Charter of Rights and Freedoms* have been infringed are considered questions of law. It has often been said that whether there is any evidence to support a verdict is a question of law, but that the sufficiency of evidence supporting a verdict is a question of fact. Generally speaking, a finding in respect of credibility of witnesses by the trier of fact (a judge or a jury) is a question of fact.

As already mentioned, the Crown is restricted to a question of law alone in an appeal from acquittal. An offender, on the other hand, may appeal a conviction on the ground that the guilty verdict is unreasonable (see subpara. 686(1)(a)(i) *Criminal Code*). Prior to the year 2000, the preponderance of judicial opinion was that the Crown could not appeal an acquittal on the ground the verdict was perverse (unreasonable) as such a determination necessarily involved questions of mixed fact and law or fact alone. However, the Supreme Court of Canada ruled that the issue whether a verdict is unreasonable constitutes a question of law. Is it now open to the Crown to appeal an acquittal on the ground the verdict is unreasonable? The answer is no, because the Supreme Court declared that, for policy reasons, the Crown should not be allowed to appeal an acquittal based on the reasonableness of the verdict.[1]

Special Provisions

When the *Criminal Code* speaks of a "sentence", the tendency is to regard it as involving a term of imprisonment. However, a sentence may include an order for a payment of a fine, or fine or imprisonment coupled with probation, or a suspended sentence. Under what is called the "expanded" definition of sentence in s. 673, a sentence for the purposes of appeal may also include, among other dispositions, a weapons prohibition order under s. 109 or s. 110, a driving prohibition order under s. 259, a probation order under s. 731, and a conditional sentence order under s. 742.1 (although technically a conditional sentence is a sentence of imprisonment).

An offender against whom a parole eligibility order has been made can appeal that order to the court of appeal under s. 743.6 (in cases of certain designated offences) or s. 745.4 (in cases of second-degree murder). Section 675(2) provides that an offender convicted of second-degree murder may appeal as of right from the parole eligibility order made against him or her, provided the number of years the offender must serve in prison before being eligible for parole exceeds ten. Under subs. 676(4), the Attorney General may appeal from a parole eligibility order in murder cases provided the number of years of imprisonment the offender must serve is fewer than 25. The Attorney General can also appeal the refusal to make a parole eligibility order in respect of other offences (see subs. 676(5) of the *Code*).

The *Criminal Code* also provides for appeals in cases of verdicts based on mental disorder. An offender found unfit to stand trial may appeal against that verdict to the court of appeal and an offender found not criminally responsible on account of mental disorder may also appeal to the court of appeal from that special verdict. The Attorney General may appeal to the court of appeal, on a question of law only, a verdict that an accused is unfit to stand trial or a special verdict that the offender is not criminally responsible on account of mental disorder.

Notice of the Appeal

The party instituting appeal proceedings is called an appellant.[2] An appellant proposing to appeal is required by s. 678 of the *Criminal Code* to give notice of the appeal to the court within the period of time prescribed by the rules of court. The judges of a court of appeal have the power to make rules of court under s. 482. The manner in which the appeal is made is also directed by the rules. For instance, in Nova Scotia, Rule 91 of the *Civil Procedure Rules* provides that an offender must give notice of an appeal within 25 days of the sentence, whether the appeal is from conviction or sentence or both conviction and sentence. The court of appeal or a judge of the court may at any time extend the time for giving notice of an appeal.

The rules respecting notice of an appeal by the Attorney General may vary from province to province. In Nova Scotia, an offender must file notice of the appeal with the registrar of the Court of Appeal and, at the same time, send a copy of the notice to the Attorney General. On the other hand, the Attorney General, to effectively appeal a verdict of acquittal or a sentence, must within 25 days of the acquittal or sentence, as the case may be, file notice of the appeal with the registrar, serve a copy of the notice personally on the respondent, and thereafter file with the registrar proof (usually a certificate of service signed by a police officer) the notice of appeal has been served on the respondent. By virtue of s. 678.1 of the *Criminal Code*, the Attorney General may apply to a judge of the court of appeal for an order directing substitutional service of the notice of appeal on another person in circumstances where the accused cannot be found after reasonable efforts have been made to serve him or her with the notice.

In Nova Scotia, as in other provinces, the form of the notice of appeal is prescribed by the rules of court. It is a document which contains information essential to give notice to the opposing party of the proceedings under appeal and the case which must be met. The appellant must clearly state in the notice what he or she proposes to appeal. An offender must indicate whether he or she intends to appeal conviction or sentence or both. The Attorney General, on the other hand, must state whether he appeals from an acquittal or a sentence. The notice must include a statement of the grounds (or reasons) for the appeal, followed by a statement of the decision and order that the party wishes the Court of Appeal to make at the conclusion of the appeal. For example, if the appeal is from conviction the offender will state in his notice that the Court of Appeal should allow his appeal, quash the conviction entered at trial, and either enter an acquittal or order that a new trial should be held.

Release from Custody

Many years ago, an offender sentenced to imprisonment following conviction and who appealed the conviction or sentence remained in prison until the appeal was determined. The *Criminal Code* made no provision for bail pending appeal. Such is not the case today.

An offender sentenced to imprisonment and who appeals from conviction or sentence or both is entitled under s. 679 to make application for release from custody pending the determination of the appeal. An application for bail pending appeal is heard and determined by a judge of the court of appeal. The grounds for release and the conditions of bail are specified in the section. If an offender seeks to be released from custody pending an appeal from sentence only, he or she must first obtain, from the judge hearing the application, leave to appeal the sentence before the bail application can be considered.

The decision of a judge to release an offender from custody or deny the application for bail may be reviewed by the court under s. 680. Such a review by the court of appeal (or, with the consent of the parties, a single judge of the court) will only be conducted if so directed by the chief justice or acting chief justice of the court.

Evidence on Appeal

Under s. 683 of the *Criminal Code* the court of appeal has the power to hear new or "fresh" evidence on an appeal. Most appeals are based on the record of the proceedings in the trial court. However, in appeals from conviction, a court of appeal may hear a motion by the appellant to present fresh evidence to the court. The party offering the fresh evidence will be permitted to present it to the court upon meeting certain criteria. New evidence will generally not be admitted by the court of appeal if, by due diligence, it could have been presented at the trial. The fresh evidence must be relevant in the sense that it can be shown to bear on a decisive or potentially decisive issue in the case. The evidence offered must be credible. The evidence must be such that, if it is believed, it could have affected the verdict at trial.

In a case where the appeal includes an application to adduce fresh evidence, the motion to present the new evidence is heard first. If the motion to adduce fresh evidence is not dismissed by the court of appeal, judgment will be reserved and the other grounds of appeal, if any, will then be heard by the court. The court of appeal will consider the question of the fresh evidence in light of the whole of the case and if the court is satisfied the fresh evidence should be admitted it will allow the appeal and either enter a verdict of acquittal or return the proceedings to the lower court for another trial.

In sentence appeals, s. 687 of the *Code* grants to a court of appeal a broad discretion to admit on appeal material that was either unavailable or not presented at the sentencing hearing.

Powers of the Court of Appeal

The powers of a court of appeal in respect of appeals from conviction, acquittal and sentence are found in ss. 686 and 687 of the *Criminal Code*. A thorough knowledge of these sections is required to fully appreciate the extent of the powers of a court of appeal in relation to an appeal and the implications of the decisions of the court. Simply put, the court of appeal will either allow or dismiss an appeal.

Conviction or Acquittal

An appeal from conviction will be allowed if the court of appeal is of the opinion the verdict at trial should be set aside on the ground that it is unreasonable or cannot be supported by the evidence. The court will allow the appeal if it is shown the trial court made a wrong decision on a question of law. The court of appeal will also allow an appeal from conviction on any ground in a case where the court is satisfied a miscarriage of justice has occurred. Obviously the court of appeal will dismiss the appeal if it is not decided in favour of the appellant on any of the three grounds mentioned. The court may also affirm a conviction even though a procedural irregularity occurred at the trial.

One particular ground for dismissing an appeal from conviction has been the subject of comment by courts over the years. The court of appeal may dismiss an appeal, notwithstanding it is of the opinion the trial court made a wrong decision on a question of law, if the court concludes the error resulted in no substantial wrong or miscarriage of justice. In other words, an offender is not guaranteed success on his appeal from conviction if he or she demonstrates the trial court made an error by, for example, admitting certain evidence which should not in law have been introduced. If the Attorney General is able to satisfy the court of appeal the verdict would necessarily have been the same even though the error was made, then the appeal will be dismissed.

Where a court of appeal allows an appeal from conviction, it must quash the conviction and either direct a verdict of acquittal or order another trial. Where the Crown is successful on an appeal from acquittal the court of appeal must set aside the verdict and either order a new trial or enter a verdict of guilty. If the court enters a conviction it must either pass sentence or direct the trial court to do so. However, where the Attorney General's appeal involves a jury verdict and the court of appeal concludes the appeal should be allowed, the court can only direct a new trial.

Before leaving the subject of the powers of a court of appeal in relation to an appeal by the Attorney General from a verdict of acquittal, it is important to note the following point. Just as an offender is not guaranteed automatic success on his or her appeal from conviction by demonstrating the trial court committed an error in law in reaching its decision, the Attorney General likewise is not guaranteed success in similar circumstances. Even though the court of appeal is satisfied the trial court committed an error in law in reaching its verdict of acquittal, the court will grant relied only in those cases in which it is satisfied the error had a direct bearing on the verdict. In other words, the Attorney General must persuade the court the verdict would not necessarily have been the same if the error in law had not been made.[3]

Sentence

On an appeal from sentence, the court of appeal must consider the fitness of the sentence imposed by the trial court, unless the sentence under appeal is one which is fixed by law. For example, an offender convicted of second degree murder and sentenced to life imprisonment cannot appeal a parole eligibility order which requires him to serve ten years of his sentence before being eligible for parole as such an order is the minimum fixed by s. 745(c) of the *Criminal Code*. In considering the fitness of the sentence under appeal, the court of appeal may receive any evidence it considers relevant to the issue of sentence—see s. 687.

On a sentence appeal, the court of appeal may allow the appeal and vary the sentence (that is, increase the sentence or lower it) within the limits prescribed for the offence of which the offender was convicted, or the court may simply dismiss the appeal. In order to succeed in an appeal from sentence, the appellant must convince the court of appeal that the sentence under review is "clearly unreasonable" or, put another way, "demonstrably unfit". This non-interventionist standard of appellate review has been endorsed by the Supreme Court of Canada.[4]

Miscellaneous Powers

The court of appeal has the power in its discretion to suspend, until the determination of the appeal, the payment of any fine or victim fine surcharge, any forfeiture or restitution order, and a probation order (subs. 683(5)). Likewise, under s. 261, the court may suspend the operation of any driving prohibition order made by the trial court under s. 259.

Under s. 684, a court of appeal or a judge of the court may assign counsel to act on behalf of an accused person who is a party to an appeal where it appears desirable in the interests of justice to do so and if the accused does not have the means to obtain legal assistance. Where counsel is assigned under this provision and legal aid is not granted to the accused, his legal fees must be paid by the Attorney General.

A court of appeal has no power to award costs to a party on an appeal or on any proceedings preliminary or incidental to an appeal (subs. 683(3)). For example, if an offender is successful on his appeal from conviction he cannot recover his legal costs incurred as a result of the appeal.

Attendance at Appeal

As a general rule, an appellant who is in custody is entitled to be present at the hearing of the appeal if he or she so desires (s. 688). For instance, an appellant who is a prisoner of a penal institution and who wishes to argue his or her own appeal before the court of appeal must be brought from the institution to court for the hearing of the appeal. It is the obligation of the Attorney General to make the arrangements to have the prisoner present at the hearing. However, an appellant in custody and represented by counsel does not enjoy the same privilege. The effect of subs. 688(2) of the *Criminal Code* is to deny a prisoner represented by counsel the opportunity of attending the hearing of the appeal unless otherwise provided by rules of court or unless a judge of the court allows the prisoner to be present.

A prisoner-appellant may either argue his or her appeal orally before the court of appeal or, in lieu of personal appearance, argument on the appeal may be presented in writing.

SUMMARY CONVICTION OFFENCES

The Appeal

Under s. 813 of the *Criminal Code*, a person convicted of a summary conviction offence may appeal to the summary conviction appeal court (in Nova Scotia, a judge of the Supreme Court) from either conviction or sentence or both, without the leave of the appeal court. Similarly, the Attorney General may appeal from an acquittal or sentence in summary conviction proceedings to the appeal court without leave. In either case, the appeal can be made on any ground, be it law, mixed law and fact or fact alone. However, it is important to note that when the Attorney General seeks to appeal from an acquittal on factual issues, the appeal can only be made on the basis that the verdict is unreasonable or one which cannot be supported by the evidence.[5]

An appellant must give notice of the appeal in such manner and within such period of time as directed by the rules of court (s. 815). The appeal court has the power to extend the time for bringing an appeal. In Nova Scotia, Rule 63 of the *Civil Procedure Rules* governs summary conviction appeals. The time limit for giving notice of an appeal, by the offendor or the Attorney General, is the same as that provided in Rule 91.

Section 816 of the *Criminal Code* is the authority for the release of an appellant from custody pending the determination of the summary conviction appeal.

Under s. 821, once a notice of appeal has been given in accordance with the rules of court, the clerk of the appeal court must notify the trial court of the appeal and that court must then transmit all documents and other material in its possession in connection with the proceedings under appeal to the appeal court.

Although there are important distinctions between appeals in indictable and summary conviction proceedings, there are also many similarities. By virtue of subs. 822(1), the provisions of ss. 683 to 689 in relation to appeals in indictable offences (with a few exceptions) apply, with all necessary modifications, to summary conviction appeals.

Prior to 1977, all summary conviction appeals were conducted in the form of a trial *de novo*. In other words, the appeal was actually a new trial, this time before a judge of the appeal court. Today the overwhelming majority of summary conviction appeals are decided by the appeal court based on the record of the trial proceedings. However, trials *de novo* as summary conviction appeals to the appeal court are allowed by subs. 822(4) of the *Criminal Code*. Such an appeal will be permitted because of the poor condition of the record of the trial court or for any other reason the appeal court, on the application of the appellant, is satisfied the interests of justice would be better served by hearing and determining the appeal by holding a new trial. Trials *de novo* in the appeal court are now the exception rather than the rule.

Unlike appeals in indictable offences, s. 826 provides that an appeal court may make an order as to costs which it considers just and reasonable.

There is another form of summary conviction appeal, and that is found under s. 830 of the *Criminal Code*. The appeal is made, without leave, to the "appeal court" as referred to in s. 829. The appeal, however, is confined to a question of law or an issue dealing with the jurisdiction of the trial court. Factual issues cannot form the basis for the appeal. The appeal is based on a transcript of the trial proceedings unless the appellant files with the court of appeal a statement of facts which has been agreed to in writing by the respondent. In Nova Scotia, the majority of such appeals are based on the record of the trial proceedings and not a statement of facts. The section further provides that an appeal under s. 830 must be made in the manner and within the period of time directed by any rules of court.

According to s. 836 of the *Code*, an appellant who appeals under s. 830 and whose appeal is dismissed cannot then institute appeal proceedings under s. 813 to the summary conviction appeal court in the same proceedings. The appellant does not get two kicks at the same can.

To the Court of Appeal

If an appeal is taken to the summary conviction appeal court under s. 813 or s. 830 of the *Criminal Code*, the decision of the appeal court is subject to a further appeal to the court of appeal as defined in s. 673.

Such an appeal can only be made with the leave of the court of appeal or a judge of the court and solely on a question of law (s. 839). By virtue of subs. 839(2), the provisions of ss. 673 to 689, with necessary modifications as required by the circumstances, apply to an appeal to the court of appeal under s. 839. As in appeals under ss. 813 and 830, a court of appeal hearing a summary conviction appeal under s. 839 may make an order for costs on the appeal. In practice in Nova Scotia, however, such orders are rare and when made not overly generous.

PROCEDURE ON APPEALS

In the Court of Appeal

The practice and procedure of criminal appeals are to a large extent governed by the respective rules of court which vary from jurisdiction to jurisdiction. For obvious reasons, the writer has chosen to expound on appeal practice and procedure from a Nova Scotia perspective.

At the time a notice of appeal is filed in the office of the registrar of the Court of Appeal, the appellant must make arrangements for the preparation of the trial transcript. As previously mentioned, an appeal is based on the record of the trial proceedings. The appellant is responsible for putting together the appeal book. The appeal book is a bound volume the length of which varies from case to case. In the case of an appeal from conviction, it will include copies of the notice of appeal, the information (and indictment if the trial was heard in Supreme Court), any exhibits of a documentary nature entered at the trial (such as written statements and diagrams), and a transcript of the proceedings at trial. The transcript usually comprises an index of the witnesses called at the trial, a numerical listing of all exhibits entered into evidence, the testimony of the witnesses, the arguments of counsel, and the decision of the trial judge. In the case of a jury trial, a transcript of the trial judge's charge or instructions to the jury and the verdict of the jury will replace a transcript of the trial judge's decision in a non-jury case. Furthermore, in a jury case, the rules of court require the appeal book contain the trial judge's certificate that the charge to the jury as reproduced in the transcript is accurate, although this is no longer a statutory requirement as subs. 682(3) of the *Criminal Code* was repealed in 1997.

In the case of an appeal from sentence, the appeal book will contain copies of the notice of appeal, the information (and in applicable cases the indictment), the presentence report presented to the trial court, the offender's criminal record (if any), other material (medical reports, letters, etc.) submitted to the court prior to sentencing, the warrant of committal, any probation or other order made as a result of the sentencing, and a transcript of the sentencing proceedings. The transcript will include any evidence called at the sentencing hearing, the submissions of counsel on sentencing, and the trial judge's decision.

In a summary conviction appeal to the court of appeal under s. 839 of the *Criminal Code*, an appeal book will contain, in addition to the entire trial record, copies of the notice of appeal to the Supreme Court, the appeal court's decision, and any order made by that court.

In Nova Scotia, in lengthy cases, judges of the Court of Appeal encourage counsel to agree on exclusion from the appeal book those portions of a trial transcript which do not have any bearing on the grounds for the appeal.

Counsel for the parties assemble in chambers to set dates for the filing of the respective written arguments (called factums) and the hearing of the appeal. The "setting down" hearing, as it is called, can be held before the appeal book is filed, but in such a case the appellant must beforehand file with the court a certificate stating when the appeal book will be available. A single judge of the Court of Appeal presides in chambers. The chambers judge will review the court's docket and assign a date and time for the hearing of the appeal after ascertaining from counsel the nature of the appeal and the probable length of the hearing. The "setting down" can also be conducted by teleconference (telephone) chambers if the parties so wish. The chambers judge and counsel are brought together by telephone conference call.

The rules of court provide for both appellant and respondent to file with the Court of Appeal and serve on the opposing party a factum containing the party's written arguments on the appeal. The factum consists of a brief overview (or summary) of the appeal, a statement of the facts of the case, a list of the grounds or issues in the appeal, the arguments in support of the parties position in the appeal, the party's submission on the standard of appellate review of each issue, and a statement of the decision the party contends the court should make. At the conclusion of each factum is a list of the authorities (cases and other materials) and statutory provisions referred to in the factum. Each party to an appeal must also file with the Court of Appeal a book of authorities containing copies of those cases referred to in its factum, although the rules of court encourage the parties to file a joint book of authorities.

In prisoner appeals, the rules of court provide that the Attorney General must prepare the appeal book. A prisoner is not obligated to file a factum but may do so if he or she wishes.

The appeal culminates in the actual hearing itself. In most cases a panel of three judges of the Court of Appeal will sit to hear an appeal. In a rare instance (as in an important constitutional case) a panel of five judges of the court will sit. The members of the panel and the counsel present will each have copies of the appeal book and the factums. The appellant will address the court first, and then the respondent will follow. The court will usually ask questions aimed at clarifying the positions of the parties in relation to the issues. After the respondent has completed its submission, the appellant is entitled to a short reply to the respondent's arguments. At the conclusion of the hearing, the court will either deliver its judgment from the bench (*i.e.*, immediately), or it will reserve its judgment for delivery to the parties at a later date.

As previously discussed, an offender may appeal from conviction on certain grounds with leave of the court or a judge of the court, and that both an offender and the Attorney General may appeal from sentence with leave of the court or a judge. With one exception, however, there is no separate hearing of applications for leave to appeal. At the hearing of the appeal, an application for leave to appeal is argued as if leave had been granted. In its judgment the court will either grant or refuse leave to appeal. If leave is granted, the court will then proceed to dispose of the appeal.

Reference has already been made to the exception to this rule. An offender who appeals from sentence and makes application for release from custody pending the appeal must first obtain leave to appeal the sentence from a judge of the court before an application for bail will be heard.

In the Summary Conviction Appeal Court

In a notice of appeal filed in the appeal court, the appellant must include notice of a motion to be made to a judge of the court for an order setting a date, time and place for the hearing of the appeal and dates for the filing of the appellant's and respondent's briefs (written submissions) and any reply briefs. The requirements for obtaining the transcript and filing the appeal book are the same as in appeals to the Court of Appeal.

The procedure at the actual hearing of the appeal closely resembles that followed in the Court of Appeal.

APPEALS TO SUPREME COURT OF CANADA

Indictable Offences—Conviction and Acquittal

Under s. 691 of the *Criminal Code* an offender convicted of an indictable offence and whose conviction is affirmed by the court of appeal may appeal to the Supreme Court of Canada on a question of law on which a judge of the court of appeal has dissented (that is, the judge has disagreed with the opinion of the other judges of the court on a particular issue) or on any question of law with the leave of the Supreme Court. A person acquitted of an indictable offence other than on the basis of mental disorder and whose acquittal is reversed by the court of appeal may appeal to the Supreme Court on a question of law on which an appeal court judge has dissented or in the case where the court of appeal has entered a guilty verdict, and in all other cases on any question of law with the leave of the Supreme Court.

By virtue of s. 693, the Attorney General may appeal to the Supreme Court on any question of law on which a judge of the court of appeal has dissented or on any question of law with the leave of the Supreme Court, in cases where the court of appeal has set aside a conviction pursuant to an offender's appeal under s. 675 or has dismissed an appeal taken by the Attorney General against a verdict of acquittal under s. 676.

A person who has been found not criminally responsible on account of mental disorder and whose verdict is affirmed on that ground by the court of appeal or against whom a verdict of guilty has been entered by the court of appeal may appeal to the Supreme Court of Canada. Similarly, a person found unfit to stand trial and who has seen that verdict affirmed by the court of appeal may also appeal to the Supreme Court. Such appeals are restricted to a question of law on which a judge of the court of appeal has dissented or on a question of law if leave to appeal is granted by the Supreme Court.

In the Supreme Court of Canada, an application for leave to appeal is a separate proceeding from an appeal. A panel of three judges of the court decides each application for leave to appeal. Most applications for leave to appeal are decided on the basis of the written submissions of the parties. If the court refuses leave to appeal, that brings the case to an end. If leave is granted, the appeal itself is heard by a panel of five, seven or nine judges of the court at a later date. The practice and procedure on applications for leave to appeal and appeals to the Supreme Court of Canada are governed by the *Supreme Court Act*, R.S.C. 1985, c. S-26, and the rules of the court.

Sentence and Summary Conviction Offences

The *Criminal Code* makes no provision for an appeal or application for leave to appeal to the Supreme Court of Canada in relation to a sentence for an indictable offence or a verdict or sentence in summary conviction proceedings. However, subs. 40(1) of the *Supreme Court Act* does provide for an application for leave to appeal to the Supreme Court in these instances. Generally speaking, the court will grant leave to appeal in respect of a summary conviction matter or a sentence for an indictable offence if the person applying for leave to appeal convinces the court that the issue raised in the case is one of national importance. The court is usually persuaded to grant leave to appeal if the applicant can point to judgments of different courts of appeal which have reached the opposite conclusion on the point of law in issue. Although the Supreme Court has held[6] that it does have jurisdiction to consider the fitness of a sentence, for policy reasons it will not do so. The court will hear an appeal in a sentence case if the judgment of the court of appeal raises an important issue of law respecting sentencing.[7]

DANGEROUS OFFENDERS

Part XXIV of the *Criminal Code* deals with special classes of offenders—the dangerous offender and the long-term offender. A person found to be a dangerous offender under s. 753 of the *Code* must be sentenced by the court making that finding to an indeterminate period of detention in a penitentiary. A person found to be a long-term offender under s. 753.1 must be sentenced to imprisonment for a minimum of two years and upon release to mandatory supervision in the community for up to ten years (described as long-term supervision).

Within Part XXIV it is s. 759 that provides for appeals to the court of appeal. A person found to be a dangerous offender may appeal that finding. A person found to be a long-term offender may appeal that designation or appeal the length of the period of long-term supervision ordered. The Attorney General may appeal from the dismissal of an application made under either s. 753 or s. 753.1 or appeal the length of the period of supervision ordered in respect of a person found to be a long-term offender. Not unlike appeals under ss. 675 and 676 of the *Code*, the scope of appeals under Part XXIV differs as between an offender and the Attorney General. The former may be based on any issue of law or fact or mixed law and fact, while by contrast the latter are confined to an issue of law.

The appeal provisions in respect of indictable offences (Part XXI) apply to appeals under s. 759 of the *Criminal Code* with all necessary modifications.

EXTRAORDINARY REMEDIES

Any discussion of appeals in criminal cases would not be complete without some reference to appeals in applications to a court (in Nova Scotia, the Supreme Court) for remedies in the nature of *certiorari, habeas corpus, mandamus*, and prohibition. The initial application to the Supreme Court for relief afforded by one of these special procedures is not an appeal. However, Part XXVI of the *Criminal Code* provides for an appeal from the decision of a court allowing or refusing an application for one of the extraordinary remedies (also called prerogative writs). In these cases, the appeal is taken to the court of appeal as defined in s. 2.

Generally speaking, the extraordinary remedies are available to correct jurisdictional errors committed by a lower court. The remedy of *certiorari* is available to an accused to test the validity of the order committing him or her to stand trial after a preliminary inquiry, and the Attorney General may utilize this remedy if an accused is discharged following a preliminary inquiry. An offender who disputes his or her continued detention in custody may test the authority of the detention by way of an application for an order in the nature of *habeas corpus*. The remedy of *mandamus* is sought if the party seeking that remedy contends the lower court should have done something in the proceedings which it was bound by law to do. Prohibition is available to a party who argues the lower court should be prohibited from proceeding with a particular case. The practice and procedure in respect of applications for the extraordinary remedies are largely governed by the common law, supplemented by the provisions of Part XXVI of the *Criminal Code* and the rules of court. In Nova Scotia, in criminal proceedings, Rule 64 of the *Civil Procedure Rules* applies to extraordinary remedies. Section 784 of the *Criminal Code* gives the court of appeal the authority to hear an appeal in applications for relief by way of extraordinary remedy. In Nova Scotia, such appeals are not common.

MISCELLANEOUS APPEAL PROVISIONS

The reader should be aware of some recent (and not so recent) amendments to the *Criminal Code* that have created rights of appeal in certain situations. For instance, s. 676.1 of the *Code* may be used to appeal to the court of appeal an order for costs made by a trial court.

Depending on the offence committed, a trial court can order an offender to provide certain bodily substances (e.g., blood) for forensic DNA testing. By virtue of s. 487.054 of the *Code*, a party against whom a DNA order has been made can appeal to the summary conviction appeal court (in summary proceedings) or the court of appeal (in indictable proceedings) and ask the court to set aside the order, and the Attorney General can appeal the refusal of a trial judge to order the taking of a bodily substance for forensic DNA testing. Similarly, s. 490.014 provides for an appeal, by either the Attorney General or an offender, from proceedings in the trial court for an order under the *Sex Offender Information Registration Act*.

It is not only decisions and verdicts of trial courts that can be appealed. Under s. 672.72 of the *Criminal Code*, the decision of a Review Board established under Part XX.1 (Mental Disorder) is subject to appeal to the court of appeal.

ATTORNEY GENERAL OF CANADA

In most provinces and territories, criminal proceedings under select federal statutes (e.g., the *Controlled Drugs and Substances Act*) are conducted by the Attorney General of Canada through the Public Prosecution Service of Canada. The Attorney General of Canada has the same rights of appeal as the Attorney General of a province or territory in both indictable and summary conviction proceedings (ss. 696, 813, 830(4) and 839(5) of the *Criminal Code*).

PROVINCIAL STATUTORY OFFENCES

Offences under provincial statutes are summary conviction in nature. In Nova Scotia,[8] the summary conviction appeal provisions of Part XXVII of the *Criminal Code* apply in respect of provincial regulatory offences (sometimes referred to as quasi-criminal offences).

Notes

[1] *R. v. Biniaris* (2000), 143 C.C.C. (3d) 1, 2000 CarswellBC 753, 2000 CarswellBC 754, 134 B.C.A.C. 161, 219 W.A.C. 161, 32 C.R. (5th) 1, 2000 SCC 15, 184 D.L.R. (4th) 193, [2000] 1 S.C.R. 381, 252 N.R. 204 (S.C.C.).

[2] The "respondent" is the person opposing or responding to the appeal made by the appellant.

[3] *R. v. Vézeau* (1976), 28 C.C.C. (2d) 81, 1976 CarswellQue 43F, 1975 CarswellQue 19, [1977] 2 S.C.R. 277, 34 C.R.N.S. 309, 8 N.R. 235, 66 D.L.R. (3d) 418 (S.C.C.); and *R. v. Morin* (1988), 44 C.C.C. (3d) 193, 1988 CarswellOnt 82, 1988 Carswel-

lOnt 967, 66 C.R. (3d) 1, [1988] 2 S.C.R. 345, 88 N.R. 161, 30 O.A.C. 81 (S.C.C.). For the practical application of this rule, reference should be made to *R. v. Bedgood* (1990), 60 C.C.C. (3d) 92 (N.S. C.A.).

4 *R. v. Shropshire* (1995), 102 C.C.C. (3d) 193, 1995 CarswellBC 906, 1995 CarswellBC 1149, 43 C.R. (4th) 269, 188 N.R. 284, 129 D.L.R. (4th) 657, 65 B.C.A.C. 37, 106 W.A.C. 37, [1995] 4 S.C.R. 227 (S.C.C.); *R. v. M. (C.A.)* (1996), 105 C.C.C. (3d) 327, 1996 CarswellBC 1000, 1996 CarswellBC 1000F, 46 C.R. (4th) 269, 194 N.R. 321, 105 C.C.C. (3d) 327, 73 B.C.A.C. 81, 120 W.A.C. 81, [1996] 1 S.C.R. 500 (S.C.C.).

5 *R. v. Gillis* (1981), 60 C.C.C. (2d) 169, 1980 CarswellNS 179, 45 N.S.R. (2d) 137, 86 A.P.R. 137 (N.S. C.A.).

6 *R. v. M. (C.A.), supra*, note 4.

7 For example, see *R. v. Proulx* (2000), 140 C.C.C. (3d) 449, 2000 CarswellMan 32, 2000 CarswellMan 33, 2000 SCC 5, [2000] 4 W.W.R. 21, 49 M.V.R. (3d) 163, 30 C.R. (5th) 1, 182 D.L.R. (4th) 1, 249 N.R. 201, [2000] 1 S.C.R. 61, 142 Man. R. (2d) 161, 212 W.A.C. 161 (S.C.C.).

8 *Summary Proceedings Act*, R.S.N.S. 1989, c. 450, s. 7(1).

21

Search and Seizure

The Honourable Justice Frank P. Hoskins P.C.J. *
and
Shane G. Parker **

INTRODUCTION

The criminal law is constantly evolving in society's effort to strike a balance between individual liberties and law enforcement objectives. Protecting society as a whole and protecting individual rights are important and thus any conflict between them must be resolved in a manner compatible with human dignity. The *Canadian Charter of Rights and Freedoms*[1] has had a great impact upon the development of appropriate legal standards for determining the balancing point between individual and state interests. With the advent of the *Charter*, the law of *search and seizure* has created a voluminous and evolving body of jurisprudence. For that reason, this chapter is not meant to be an exhaustive review of the law, but rather a general overview, for anything more than that would clearly exceed its scope and purpose.

CANADIAN CHARTER OF RIGHTS AND FREEDOMS

Protection against Unreasonable Search and Seizure

The supreme law of Canada is the *Constitution of Canada*. It includes the *Charter*, which *guarantees the rights and freedoms set out in it subject only to such reasonable limits prescribed by law as can be demonstrably justified in a free and democratic society.* Our rights and freedoms in Canada are not absolute; they are guaranteed only to such reasonable limits as can be demonstrably justified in our society. Hence, courts are mindful of that in their deliberation of search and seizure issues. The Supreme Court of Canada views the *Charter* as a

---

* B.A., B.Ed., St. Mary's University, Halifax, Nova Scotia; LL.B., Dalhousie Law School, Halifax, Nova Scotia; Judge of the Provincial Court of Nova Scotia.
**B.Sc. (Hons.), University of Waterloo; MPE, University of New Brunswick; LL.B., Dalhousie Law School, Halifax, Nova Scotia; currently Special Prosecutor-Organized Crime with Alberta Justice.

purposive document: its purpose is to guarantee and protect, within the limits of reason, the enjoyment of the rights and freedoms it enshrines. It is intended to constrain government action that is inconsistent with those rights and freedoms.[2]

Prior to the *Charter*'s proclamation in 1982, Canadian citizens had little protection against unreasonable search and seizure. Apart from technical arguments regarding the validity of the search warrant or the manner with which it was executed, citizens had little with which to argue against unreasonable search and seizure. Indeed, in most cases, evidence illegally obtained as a result of an illegal search or seizure was ruled admissible.[3] The admission of such evidence relevant to an issue before the court and of substantial probative value was considered to operate unfortunately for the accused, but not unfairly.[4] It was only the admission of evidence gravely prejudicial to the accused, the admissibility of which was tenuous and whose probative value in relation to an issue before the court was trifling and could operate unfairly, which could be excluded. In other words, judicial discretion to exclude relevant evidence was limited to evidence obtained unlawfully and whose prejudicial effect outweighed its probative value.[5]

With the advent of the *Charter*, Canadian citizens enjoy a new substantive right that protects them against an unreasonable search or seizure. The combined effect of ss. 8 and 24 of the *Charter* provides protection against unreasonable search or seizure that did not exist prior to the *Charter*'s proclamation. Sections 8 and 24 of the *Charter* state:

8. Everyone has the right to be secure against unreasonable search or seizure.

24. (1) Anyone whose rights or freedoms, as guaranteed by this *Charter*, have been infringed or denied may apply to a court of competent jurisdiction to obtain such remedy as the court considers appropriate and just in the circumstances.

(2) Where, in proceedings under subsection (1), a court concludes that evidence was obtained in a manner that infringed or denied any rights or freedoms guaranteed by this *Charter*, the evidence shall be excluded if it is established that, having regard to all the circumstances, the admission of it in the proceedings would bring the administration of justice into disrepute.

Section 8 of the *Charter* guarantees a broad and general right to be secure from unreasonable search or seizure. The guarantee of security from unreasonable search and seizure only protects a *reasonable expec-*

tation of privacy. The Supreme Court of Canada, in limiting the term *reasonable*, implied that:

> an assessment must be made as to whether in a particular situation the public's interest in being left alone by government must give way to the government's interest in intruding on the individual's privacy in order to advance its goals, notably those of law enforcement.[6]

The need for privacy will vary with the nature of the matter sought to be protected, the circumstances in which and the place where state intrusion occurs, and the purposes of the intrusion.[7] Justice Binnie, in *R. v. Tessling*,[8] summed up the balance between people demanding privacy but insisting on safety. His Lordship explained that there exists various privacy interests, including personal, territorial and informational privacy. The more intrusive the state conduct into traditional sanctuaries of life like the home, intimate details of lifestyle and choices, or termed biographical core of information, or deep bodily integrity the more recognized those privacy interests are to trump state interest.

A reasonable expectation of privacy is to be determined in light of the totality of the circumstances. The factors to be considered in assessing the circumstances may include the accused's presence at the time of the search, possession or control of the property or place searched, ownership of the property or place, historical use of the property or item, ability to regulate access, existence of a subjective expectation of privacy, and the objective reasonableness of the expectation.[9]

The following is a summary of the principles pertaining to the nature of s. 8 of the *Charter*:

1. A claim for relief under subs. 24(2) [of the *Charter*] can only be made by the person whose *Charter* rights have been infringed.
2. Like all *Charter* rights, s. 8 is a personal right. It protects people and not places.
3. The right to challenge the legality of a search depends upon the accused establishing that his or her personal rights to privacy have been violated.
4. As a general rule, two distinct inquiries must be made in relation to s. 8. First, has the accused a reasonable expectation of privacy? Second, if he has such an expectation, was the search conducted by the police reasonably?
5. A reasonable expectation of privacy is to be determined on the basis of the totality of the circumstances.

6. The factors to be considered in assessing the totality of the circumstances may include, but are not restricted to, the following:
   (i) presence at the time of the search;
   (ii) possession or control of the property or place searched;
   (iii) ownership of the property or place;
   (iv) historical use of the property or item;
   (v) the ability to regulate access, including the right to admit or exclude others from the place;
   (vi) the existence of a subjective expectation of privacy; and
   (vii) the objective reasonableness of the expectation.
7. If an accused person establishes a reasonable expectation of privacy, the inquiry must proceed to the second stage to determine whether the search was conducted in a reasonable manner.[10]

The operative word in s. 8 of the *Charter* is *unreasonable*, which means that "*a search or seizure will be reasonable if it is authorized by law, if the law itself is reasonable and if the manner in which the search or seizure was carried out is reasonable.*"[11] Thus, an accused may be able to challenge the constitutionality of a search or seizure in any of the three broad areas:

1. Was the search or seizure authorized by law?
2. Can the law authorizing the search or seizure withstand constitutional scrutiny under the *Charter*? or
3. Was the search or seizure conducted by the peace officer executed in a reasonable manner?

It should be noted that Parliament has chosen to use the word *or* rather than *and*, which means that a search is distinctive from a seizure.

It is clear that the *onus* is on the accused to establish on a *balance of probabilities* that the admission of evidence as a result of a *Charter* violation could bring the administration of justice into *disrepute*.[12] There is no automatic exclusion of evidence obtained in a manner that infringes *Charter* rights.

In 2009, the Supreme Court of Canada changed the test under section 24(2) that had been applied for approximately 22 years. There are three sets of factors that must be taken into account in determining whether the evidence should *not* be admitted pursuant to subs. 24(2) of the *Charter*:

1.   **The seriousness of the breach**—The concern is to preserve the public confidence in the rule of law and its process. Inadvertent or minor breaches minimally undermine public confidence, while deliberate or reckless breaches risk bringing disrepute;

2.   **The impact of the breach on Charter interests**—This may range from fleeting and technical to profoundly intrusive; and

3.   **Society's interest in adjudication on the merits**—The issue is whether the truth seeking function of a criminal trial and seeing offenders dealt with according to law is better served by the inclusion or exclusion of the evidence. The court should consider the reliability of the evidence and the importance of the evidence to the Crown's case[13]

This categorization of relevant factors is merely a guideline that courts consider.

COMMON LAW

Search or Seizure Without Warrant

In Canada, there are only two possible sources of legal authority for a search or seizure: the common law and statute law. The *Charter* is not itself a source of any such authority.[14] A search or seizure without prior authorization is *prima facie* unreasonable.[15] In other words, a search or seizure will be *reasonable* if it is pursuant to a warrant that has been properly issued by a judicial officer, on *reasonable and probable grounds*, founded by evidence on oath. However, the prosecution can justify a warrantless search or seizure as being reasonable once it establishes that the warrantless search or seizure was authorized by the application of the *common law*. Under the *common law*, a search or seizure is reasonable only if it is *an incident to a lawful arrest*, or is conducted under the authority of the *plain view doctrine*, or where there has been *informed consent*, or where there are *exigent circumstances* where a situation of urgency exists, or it is otherwise impractical to obtain prior authorization to obtain a warrant.

Search or Seizure Incidental to Arrest

A peace officer (or a citizen) has the authority at common law to search a person incident to a lawful arrest.[16] The right to search incident to an arrest derives from the fact of arrest or detention of the person and thus a search or seizure may be conducted before or after the arrest.[17] The Supreme Court of Canada has stated that the exercise of this power is not unlimited and consideration must be given to the following underlying interests:

1. This power does not impose a duty. The police have some discretion in conducting the search. Where they are satisfied that the law can be effectively and safely applied without a search, the police may see fit not to conduct a search. They must be in a position to assess the circumstances of each case so as to determine whether a search meets the underlying objectives.

2. The search must be for a valid objective in pursuit of the ends of criminal justice, such as the discovery of an object that may be a threat to the safety of the police, the accused or the public, or that may facilitate escape or act as evidence against the accused. The purpose of the search must be not unrelated to the objectives of the proper administration of justice, which would be the case, for example, if the purpose of the search was to intimidate, ridicule or pressure the accused in order to obtain admissions.

3. The search must not be conducted in an abusive fashion and, in particular, the use of physical or psychological constraint should be proportionate to the objectives sought and the other circumstances of the situation.[18]

These broad propositions help define the scope of the common law power of search incidental to an arrest. These propositions are to be construed in a restrictive manner.[19] There are no readily ascertainable limits on the scope of the common law power of search incidental to arrest and it is, therefore, the court's responsibility to set boundaries that allow the state to pursue its legitimate interest, while vigorously protecting the individual's right to privacy. The scope of the search incident to arrest can refer to many different aspects of the search. It can refer to the items seized during the search and/ or the place to be searched. Indeed, the scope of the search incident to arrest does not extend to the collection of the bodily substances[20] or to the search of impounded motor vehicles. Scope can also refer to the temporal limits on the power of search.

The authority of the search does not arise as a result of a reduced expectation of privacy of the arrested person. Rather, it arises out of the need for the law enforcement authorities to gain control of things or information that outweighs the individual's interest in privacy. In other words, the search is only justifiable if the purpose of the search is related to the purpose of the arrest.

A search that does not meet the above-noted objectives could be characterized as unreasonable *and thus in breach of s. 8 of the Charter.*

The right of the police to enter a private dwelling to effect an arrest without a warrant exists only where there are *exigent circumstances* that make it impracticable to obtain a warrant. A peace officer is permitted to enter a private dwelling, by force if necessary, to prevent the commission of an offence that would cause immediate and serious injury to any person, or to prevent destruction of evidence, or to arrest someone in the act of hot pursuit, if the officer believes on reasonable grounds that the person is in the dwelling house, and the conditions for obtaining a warrant exist.[21]

Strip-searches

In appropriate searches incidental to arrest, or under certain situations governed by government rule such as prisons and border crossings, a strip search may be permissible. A *strip-search* is defined as removing or rearranging some or all of a person's clothing to permit a visual inspection of a person's private areas or undergarments.[22] The Supreme Court of Canada reaffirmed the notion that strip-searches are inherently humiliating and degrading for detainees regardless of the manner in which they are carried out.[23] Thus, the Supreme Court imposed stringent requirements upon the police that must be satisfied before and during the search. Unlike a *frisk* or a *pat-down* search, which only requires the existence of the requisite reasonable grounds for an arrest to be constitutionally valid, a *strip-search* requires *additional grounds* as a prerequisite for the arrest to be constitutionally valid. The additional grounds must be directly related to the purpose of the strip-search. As stated, a search is only justifiable if the purpose of the search is related to the purpose of the arrest.[24] Thus, there must be a *valid purpose*, which could include any of the following purposes:

(i) to discover weapons;

    (ii)   to ensure the safety of the police, the detainee and other persons;

   (iii) to discover evidence related to the reason for the arrest; or

   (iv) to preserve or prevent the disposal of evidence by the detainee.[25]

The Supreme Court of Canada recognized the importance of preventing unjustified strip-searches before they occur. Iacobucci and Arbour JJ., writing for the majority, observed:

> The importance of preventing unjustified searches before they occur is particularly acute in the context of strip searches, which involve a significant and very direct interference with personal privacy. Furthermore, strip searches can be humiliating, embarrassing and degrading for those who are subject to them, and any *post facto* remedies for unjustified strip searches cannot erase the arrestee's experience of being strip searched. Thus, the need to prevent unjustified searches before they occur is more acute in the case of strip searches than it is in the context of less intrusive personal searches, such as pat or frisk searches. As was pointed out in *Flintoff, supra*, at p. 257, "[s]trip-searching is one of the most intrusive manners of searching, and also one of the most extreme exercises of police power".[26]

The Supreme Court of Canada also recommended the following questions as a framework for the police in deciding how best to conduct a strip-search incident to arrest in compliance with the *Charter*:

1.   Can the strip search be conducted at the police station and, if not, why not?

2.   Will the strip search be conducted in a manner that ensures that health and safety of all involved?

3.   Will the strip search be authorized by a police officer acting in a supervisory capacity?

4.   Has it been ensured that the police officer(s) carrying out the strip search are of the same gender as the individual being searched?

5.   Will the number of police officers involved in the search be no more than is reasonably necessary in the circumstances?

6.   What is the minimum of force necessary to conduct the strip search?

7.   Will the strip search be carried out in a private area such that no one other than the individuals engaged in the search can observe the search?

8. Will the strip search be conducted as quickly as possible and in a way that ensures that the person is not completely undressed at any one time?

9. Will the strip search involve only a visual inspection of the arrestee's genital and anal areas without any physical contact?

10. If the visual inspection reveals the presence of a weapon or evidence in a body cavity (not including the mouth), will the detainee be given the option of removing the object himself or of having the object removed by a trained medical professional?

11. Will a proper record be kept of the reasons for and the manner in which the strip search was conducted?[27]

Strip-searches should be conducted at the police station *unless* there are exigent circumstances that require the detainee to be searched before he or she is transported to the police station. Such exigent circumstances will only be established where the police have reasonable grounds to believe that it is necessary to conduct the search in the field rather than at the police station.[28]

Searches of Motor Vehicles

Furthermore, the outer limits of the common law power of warrantless search incident to a lawful arrest extends to include a motor vehicle in which the driver, or passenger, is the suspect and who emerged at, or shortly before, arrest.[29] The temporal factual foundation seems to be the salient factor in motor vehicle cases where a peace officer is conducting a search or seizure incident to an arrest. In other words, the searches are only justifiable if the purpose of the search is related to the purpose of the arrest. The courts are reluctant to set a strict limit on the amount of time that can elapse between the time of the search and the time of arrest.[30] Therefore, there must be a reasonable explanation for any delay.

The minimum requirements for a warrantless search or seizure of a motor vehicle are as follows:

(1) that the vehicle be stopped or the occupants be detained lawfully;

(2) that the officer conducting the search have reasonable and probable grounds to believe that an offence has been, is being, or is about to be committed and that a search will disclose evidence relevant to that offence;

(3) that exigent circumstances, such as imminent loss, removal,

or destruction of the evidence, make it not feasible to obtain a warrant;
(4)   that the scope of the search itself bears a reasonable relationship to the offence suspected and the evidence sought.[31]

Generally, a search does not have to be contemporaneous with the arrest. There may be exigent circumstances that force the peace officer to delay the search and seizure; for example, waiting for a peace officer of the same sex to arrive and conduct the search.[32]

It is difficult to articulate what the limitations are in respect to the scope of the common law incident to a lawful arrest. At best, the courts are guided by the above-noted underlying interests and will be mindful that "the greater the intrusion, the greater must be the justification and the greater the constitutional protection."[33]

Search incident to investigative detention

In 2004 the Supreme Court of Canada reaffirmed that it is constitutionally permissible for a peace officer to conduct a lawful search or seizure of a detainee in the context of an *investigative detention* in which there are *insufficient* grounds to make an arrest, but there are *reasonable grounds to suspect* (or *articulable cause*) that the detainee is implicated in the activity under investigation.[34] In other words, there is common law police power to detain a person in the course of a police investigation where there is a *constellation of objectively discernible facts* which give the detaining officer *reasonable cause to suspect* that the detainee is criminally implicated in the activity under investigation.[35] However, the scope of such a search incidental to an investigative detention is limited to one reasonably designed to locate weapons. The officer must have reasonable grounds to believe that his or her safety or the safety of others is at risk.[36] The officer is only permitted to engage in a protective par-down search of the detained individual.[37] Moreover, a search arising from an investigative detention should be brief in duration and does not impose an obligation on the detained individual to answer questions posed by the police officer.[38] The reasonableness of the search will be considered on the *totality of the circumstances*.

Five years later the Supreme Court of Canada revisited the definition of "detention" and whether a person must be informed of the right to counsel. In *R. v. Grant* and in the companion case of *R. v. Suberu*,[39] the Court said that detention refers to the suspension of a person's section 9 and 10 rights under the *Charter* and occurs when there is a significant physical or psychological restraint. Psychological restraint is when there is a legal obligation to comply with the officer's demand, or a reasonable person would conclude from the state conduct that the person had no choice but to comply. The Court recognized the need for law enforcement to question people and that if police are generally investigating a crime the person is not "detained". However, one of the demarcations of detention is when the police turn to specifically focusing on that person. The Court gave further considerations that would guide the analysis. In *Seberu* the Court held that a person must be given there section 10 rights upon detention.

Plain View Doctrine

A warrantless search or seizure will be authorized at *common law* by the application of the *plain view doctrine*. This doctrine has been recognized and applied in Canada, England, and the United States. The doctrine seems to have been drawn from American jurisprudence.

The plain view doctrine holds that objects falling in plain view of a peace officer, who has the right to be in a position to have that view, are subject to seizure without a warrant and may be introduced into evidence.[40]

The essence of this doctrine is the right of the officer to be in a position to have a plain view. The courts have held that:

> What is central to the application of the "plain view" doctrine is that the police officer had a prior justification for the intrusion into the place where the "plain view" seizure occurred. Thus the foundation for a lawful seizure on the basis of the "plain view" doctrine is lawful presence in the premises where the property is found in "plain view".[41]

The preconditions for the application of the plain view doctrine are as follows:

1. the police officer must lawfully make an "initial intrusion" or otherwise properly be in a position from which he can view a particular area.
2. the officer must discover incriminating evidence "inadvertently", which is to say, he may not "know in advance the location of [certain] evidence and intend to seize it," relying on the plain view doctrine only as a pretext.
3. it must be "immediately apparent" to the police that the items they observe may be evidence of a crime, contraband, or otherwise, subject to seizure.[42]

These requirements having been met, when peace officers lawfully engaged in an activity in a particular area perceive a suspicious object, they may seize it immediately.[43]

Police do have authority under s. 489 of the *Criminal Code* for a codified version of the plain view doctrine while they are executing a search warrant. This will be discussed later in the chapter.

Consent Searches or Seizures

A peace officer is permitted in law to conduct a warrantless search or seizure of a person, place, or thing where he or she has the *informed consent* to do so by that person. However, the prosecution must demonstrate to the court that that person purporting to consent to a warrantless search or seizure relinquished his or her constitutional rights and freedoms with full knowledge and appreciation of the consequences of waiving those rights and freedoms in order for the search or seizure to be reasonable and thus constitutional.[44]

The preconditions to a valid consent to an otherwise unauthorized search or seizure are as follows:

(i) there was a consent, express or implied;

(ii) the giver of the consent had the authority to give the consent in question;

(iii) the consent was voluntary in the sense that that word is used in *Goldman*, supra, and was not the product of police oppression, coercion or other external conduct which negated the freedom to choose whether or not to allow the police to pursue the course of conduct requested;

(iv) the giver of the consent was aware of the nature of the police conduct to which he or she was being asked to consent;

(v) the giver of the consent was aware of his or her right to refuse to permit the police to engage in the conduct requested; and

(vi) the giver of the consent was aware of the potential consequences of giving the consent.[45]

As is evident from these preconditions, there are certain underlying values that give meaning to the concept of consent. The courts are mindful of these underlying values when they are called upon to balance the competing interest of individual rights with that of effective crime prevention and control.

Third-party Consent

It is possible for the police to obtain consent from a third party who is not the suspect, provided that the third party has a legally meaningful consent to give.[46] Searches performed on the strength of third party consent can be problematic for the Crown; particularly in those circumstances where the central issue of the case turns on the legality of the ability of the third party to provide consent. For this reason, the police are usually advised to obtain a warrant. Moreover, with a warrant the police do not have to be concerned with the *withdrawal of consent* during the search.

School Searches

The student's *reasonable expectation of privacy* in the school environment is significantly diminished as it is assumed that the student realizes that teachers and other school officials are required at times to conduct searches to ensure a safe environment and to maintain order and discipline in the school.[47] To require a warrant or other prior judicial authorization for a search would be impracticable and unworkable in the school environment.[48] Thus, a warrantless search is not *prima facie* unreasonable, but rather permissible in the school environment. The courts take a more lenient and flexible approach in respect to searches conducted by teachers and school officials than would be applied to searches conducted by the police. Recently, the Supreme Court of Canada affirmed that there should be a modified standard for reasonable searches of students on school property conducted by teachers or school officials within their scope of responsibility and authority to maintain order, discipline and safety within the school.[49] Cory J., writing for the majority of the Supreme Court, stated:

> A search by school officials of a student under their authority may be undertaken if there are reasonable grounds to believe that a school rule has been or is being violated, and that evidence of the violation will be found in the location or on the person of the student searched. Searches undertaken in situations where the health and safety of the students is involved may well require different considerations. All the circumstances surrounding a search must be taken into account in determining if the search is reasonable.
>
> ... Ordinarily, school authorities will be in the best position to evaluate the information they receive...
>
> ... The reasonable grounds may be based upon information received from

just one student whom the school authority considers credible, or may be based upon information from more than one student or from observations of teachers or principals, or from a combination of these pieces of information which considered together the relevant authority believes to be credible.[50]

This standard, however, will not apply to any actions taken that are beyond the scope of the authority of the teachers or school officials. Nor will it apply to situations in which the teachers or school officials are acting as *agents* of the police. In other words, the teachers or school officials would not have conducted the search of the student, but for the involvement of the police.[51]

The police have greater limitations than school staff in schools. Schools are not a *Charter*-free zone. In 2008, the Court was faced with an appeal whereby police used sniffer dogs looking for drugs based on the Principal's long standing invitation to search for drugs. While students were in class, backpacks lined the gym wall and the dog sniffed out drugs. One bag was singled out and was searched by the officer who found illegal drugs. The Court held in a narrow majority that the police do have a common law power to search using drug dogs, but the use of sniffer dogs must be done on a *Charter* compliant standard of reasonable suspicion. There was no suspicion in this case, so the illegal drugs were ruled inadmissible and the student was acquitted.

At the same time the Court was considering drug dogs at schools, they also answered the use of drug dogs at bus stations. In *R. v. Brown*,[52] the Court held that travelers have privacy interests that still require the police to have reasonable suspicion before they have the dogs sniff the luggage of random passengers. This case was more controversial since the Alberta Court of Appeal had held that travelers did not have a reasonable expectation of privacy in the type of information (the smell of narcotics) the dogs sensed.

Exigent Circumstances

As previously mentioned, there may be exigent circumstances where an unauthorized (warrantless) search or seizure is reasonable and in accordance with s. 8 of the *Charter*. For example, a peace officer may enter a private dwelling, by force if necessary, to prevent the commission of an offence, or to prevent the destruction of evidence, or to arrest someone in hot pursuit, where there are exigent circumstances that make it impracticable to obtain prior authorization for a warrant.[53] Similarly, firefighters have been held to be entitled to enter private premises where a fire is occurring to extinguish it in their effort to protect life and property.[54]

Indeed, there are cases where the justification for a warrantless search or seizure is found in the exigent circumstances involving motor vehicles, vessels, or other movable places that may move away quickly and thus make it impossible to obtain prior judicial authorization for a warrant.[55] These kinds of circumstances are usually associated with drug cases. Legal arguments usually focus on the *reasonableness* of the search or seizure and on subs. 24(2) of the *Charter*, whether the admission of the evidence could bring the administration of justice into disrepute.

Investigative Road Blocks

Consider that police receive a 911 call that a crime has been committed, like a robbery, and the police set up a road block to catch the fleeing culprits. Do the police have the authority to stop individuals looking for the culprits? The Quebec Court of Appeal and the Supreme Court of Canada have held that, under common law, the police have had such an authority as an extension of their need to protect the public and investigate crime.[56]

The situation in *Clayton* was different from the relatively sterile facts in *Murray*. In *Murray* there had been a bank robbery and the police checked all vehicles leaving the community using the few bridges. In *Clayton* there had been a 911 call late at night from outside a strip club in Toronto that said, four to ten "black guys" were in the parking lot and were flashing glocks with clips (loaded semi-automatic handguns). The caller described four vehicles. Four minutes later police arrived to the "gun call". Immediately a call one of the cars fitting the description given by the caller tried to exit the parking lot. The police stopped the car and told the driver they were investigating a gun complaint. The driver reluctantly got out of the car and put his hands on the roof as directed. Meanwhile the passenger dealt with the other officer. He was evasive, looking straight ahead and wearing gloves, on a warm evening. The passenger, Clayton, got out but prevented the officer from looking in the car. The officer tried to move Clayton to the side, and Clayton shoved the officer and fled. Other officers chased Clayton, tackled him and found a loaded handgun when they searched him. The driver, Farmer, was also placed under arrest and search incidental to arrest located a loaded handgun.

The Court held that police do have a common law power to detain people in a blockade if it is no more intrusive than is reasonable to address the risk. The Court stressed the need to assess the circumstances in totality like the seriousness of the charge, information known by the police at the time and how tailored the police responded given the geography and time. The Court held that the police acted reasonable.

Abandonment

The doctrine of abandonment is premised on the notion that the owner has relinquished his or her *reasonable expectation of privacy* (privacy interest) in relation to the discarded material. Indeed, when a person deliberately discards or abandons his or her trash, it is logical to include that the person no longer gas a subjective expectancy of privacy concerning it. In fact, there is no reasonable expectation of privacy in relation to information that may be obtained from the trash which has been abandoned by a householder to the municipal garbage disposal system.[57] Therefore, the collection of discarded material by the police is *not* considered to be a *seizure*. Another illustration of this doctrine would include a person discarding a cigarette-butt or soiled tissue containing DNA.

Garbage Grabs

Does a person have an expectation of privacy in their garbage?

In *R. v. Patrick*,[58] police had suspicions that Patrick was operating an ecstasy lab in his home in Calgary. In order to gain grounds to obtain a warrant to enter his home, and to confirm or refute their suspicions, six times the police took Patrick's garbage which was placed inside the garbage cans in a cut out in the fence facing the back lane. The bags were on Patrick's property, but the public could access them. The information the police obtained from the garbage did allow the police to have sufficient information to get a search warrant. Upon search of the home, police did find the makings of a drug lab. The Court did find that it was a form of abandonment, but factually dependant on the placement of the garbage (i.e., if the garbage was next to the door, but not set out for pick up, there would be an expectation of privacy) and the Court was concerned with the sensitive and personal type of information that people could access about lifestyle and choices.

ABANDONMENT

Search or Seizure with Warrant

The prevention of unjustified searches or seizures can only be accomplished by a system of *prior judicial authorization* where feasible. A requirement of prior authorization to validate intrusions by the state upon individuals' expectations of privacy serves as a procedural safeguard against unjustified intrusions by the state and creates a mechanism that provides an opportunity for an entirely neutral and impartial judicial officer, before the search or seizure, to assess the competing interests between the state and the individual. Thus, individuals' expectations of privacy will be breached only where the appropriate standard has been met, and the interests of the state are thus demonstrably superior.[59]

There are numerous federal and provincial statutes that confer the power of search and seizure. Each legislation authorizing searches or seizures is usually drafted to accommodate the individual purposes and circumstances governed by that particular statute and, accordingly, the search and seizure provisions vary considerably from one to the other.[60] However, s. 487 of the *Criminal Code* authorizes the issuance of a search warrant in respect to all *federal* statutes.[61]

For our purposes, there are too many federal and provincial statutes that confer the power of search and seizure to examine; therefore, we will examine the most important general sources of the statutory powers.

Search Warrant Defined

There is no statutory definition of a *search warrant*, perhaps because it is self-defining. The Supreme Court of Canada has provided a definition of the term as follows:

> A search warrant may be broadly defined as an order issued by a justice under statutory powers, authorizing a named person to enter a specified place to search for and seize specified property which will afford evidence of the actual or intended commission of a crime. A warrant may be issued upon a sworn Information and proof of reasonable grounds for its issuance. The property seized must be carried before the justice who issued the warrant to be dealt with by him according to law.[62]

The Supreme Court also commented on the role of the *search warrant* in the administration of justice:

> Search warrants are part of the investigative pre-trial process of the criminal law, often employed early in the investigation and before the identity of all of the suspects is known. Parliament, in furtherance of the public interest in effective investigation and prosecution of crime, and through the enactment of s. 443 of the *Code*, has legalized what would otherwise be an illegal entry of premises and illegal seizure of property...[63]

The general source of statutory powers of search and seizure is found in s. 487 of the *Criminal Code*, which authorizes a judicial officer to issue a search warrant provided certain specific conditions are met. Section 487 provides:

487. (1) Information for search warrant — A justice who is satisfied by Information on oath in Form 1 that there are reasonable grounds to believe that there is in a building, receptacle or place

> (a) anything on or in respect of which any offence against this Act or any other Act of Parliament has been or is suspected to have been committed,
>
> (b) anything that there are reasonable grounds to believe will afford evidence with respect to the commission of an offence, or will reveal the whereabouts of a person who is believed to have committed an offence, against this Act or any other Act of Parliament, or
>
> (c) anything that there are reasonable grounds to believe is intended to be used for the purpose of committing any offence against the person for which a person may be arrested without warrant, or
>
> (c.1) any offence-related property,

may at any time issue a warrant authorizing a peace officer or a public officer who has been appointed or designated to administer or enforce a federal or provincial law and whose duties include the enforcement of this Act or any other Act of Parliament and who is named in the warrant

> (d) to search the building, receptacle or place for any such thing and to seize it, and
>
> (e) subject to any other Act of Parliament, to, as soon as practicable, bring the thing seized before, or make a report in respect thereof to, the justice or some other justice for the same territorial division in accordance with section 489.1.

(2) Endorsement of search warrant — Where the building, receptacle, or place in which anything mentioned in subsection (1) is believed to be is in any other territorial division, the justice may issue his warrant in like form modified according to the circumstances, and the warrant may be executed in the other territorial division after it has been endorsed, in Form 28, by a justice having jurisdiction in that territorial division.

(2.1) Operation of computer system and copying equipment — A person authorized under this section to search a computer system in a building or place for data may

> (a) use or cause to be used any computer system at the building or

place to search any data contained in or available to the computer system;

(b) reproduce or cause to be reproduced any data in the form of a print-out or other intelligible output;

(c) seize the print-out or other output for examination or copying; and

(d) use or cause to be used any copying equipment at the place to make copies of the data.

(2.2) Duty of person in possession or control — Every person who is in possession or control of any building or place in respect of which a search is carried out under this section shall, on presentation of the warrant, permit the person carrying out the search

(a) to use or cause to be used any computer system at the building or place in order to search any data contained in or available to the computer system for data that the person is authorized by this section to search for;

(b) to obtain a hard copy of the data and to seize it; and

(c) to use or cause to be used any copying equipment at the place to make copies of the data.

(3) Form — A search warrant issued under this section may be in the form set out as Form 5 in Part XXVIII, varied to suit the case.

(4) Effect of endorsement — An endorsement that is made on a warrant as provided for in subsection (2) is sufficient authority to the peace officers or public officers to whom it was originally directed, and to all peace officers within the jurisdiction of the justice by whom it is endorsed, to execute the warrant and to deal with the things seized in accordance with section 489.1 or as otherwise provided by law.

As noted above, in s. 487, the following conditions must be met before a judicial officer can issue a search warrant:

1. the judicial officer (the justice) must be satisfied by Information on oath in Form 1 that reasonable and probable grounds exist to believe (a), (b) or (c);

2. the person requesting the warrant must identify him- or herself;

3. the thing or things to be searched for must be adequately described;

4. the offence with respect to which the warrant is required must be named; and

5. the address or location of the place for search must be specified.

These condition precedents prevent the authorities from engaging in speculative fishing expeditions in the vague hope that they will find something that might support a charge. The public's protection is safe-guarded by the screening process envisioned by s. 487. This initial ju-dicial screening process provides a fundamental safeguard of the rights of all citizens and thereby is an integral part of the principles of funda-mental justice. Therefore, bypassing this process is contrary to ss. 7 and 9 of the *Charter*.

Section 487 has been held to meet the *constitutional standard of reasonableness* in accordance with s. 8 of the *Charter*.[64]

Information Upon Oath

Section 487 prescribes that the justice must be presented with an *In-formation* upon oath in Form 1 before he or she can issue a warrant. The peace officer presenting the justice with an *Information* upon oath is not at liberty to swear the *Information* in a perfunctory manner with reck-less disregard as to the truth of his or her assertion. To do so is clearly an affront to the courts and is at variance with the right of the citizen to be left alone by the authorities. The officer must be satisfied that he or she can personally swear to the truth of the *Information* according to its terms, by having either personal knowledge or information and belief (upon reasonable and probable grounds). The British Columbia Supreme Court stated:

> taking an oath embraces more than the mechanical act of taking the Bible or raising one's hand to affirm. There must also be a conscious acknowl-edgment that one has taken the oath or obligation to speak the truth and to be responsible for the consequences of perjury. These are very important matters, and I refuse to say anything that would detract or water down the absolute necessity for complying with the minimum requirements of the law before entering into the homes and bedrooms of peaceful citizens at night.[65]

Thus, mere convenience to the peace officer, suspicion, or a genuine desire to maintain the law for the protection of the general public will not be sufficient reason for the peace officer not to be open and honest in his or her application to the justice.

Reasonable and Probable Grounds

Beyond the oath or affirmation of the applicant lies the requirement for the basis upon which the justice may exercise his or her judicial discretion with respect to the warrant's issue. What is the standard the justice must use in deciding whether or not he or she is satisfied that reasonable and probable grounds exist?

First, the justice must believe on reasonable and probable grounds that an offence against the *Criminal Code* or any other Federal Act has been or is suspected to have been committed. Having been satisfied of that, the justice must go on to the second stage and determine if there are reasonable and probable grounds to believe a search will afford evidence with respect to the commission of the offence, or anything that is intended to be used for the purpose of committing an offence, at the place to be searched. There must be a factual basis connecting the articles specified in the warrant with the alleged offence and with the location of the search. Moreover, the peace officer is only permitted to search for those articles specified in the warrant and in those locations specified in the warrant.[66]

It is important to note that the peace officer must not only state his or her belief in having reasonable and probable grounds, but must also set out those grounds for the belief in order for the justice to have jurisdiction to exercise his or her judicial powers. It is not acceptable for the peace officer to merely state his or her conclusions.

The applicant must also state whether his or her grounds are based on personal knowledge or information and belief (hearsay knowledge). Often, peace officers rely on information received by others. These other persons may have knowledge obtained from others as well. With respect to hearsay knowledge, the officer must specify the source of his or her knowledge. If the officer is relying on confidential sources, then the officer does not have to disclose the name of his or her police informer; only the means of the informer's knowledge, the reliability of the informer on previous occasions, and any corroborating evidence of the informer's information.[67] Public policy dictates that the confidential source (usually police informers) must be protected. Without this immunity, few, if any, informers would assist the police.

If the justice is not satisfied that there is sufficient information to exercise his or her judicial discretion, then a warrant will not be issued. The justice can identify to the applicant the deficiencies in the *Information* to obtain the warrant, but cannot participate in remedying the *Information*. The justice is only permitted to reconsider the application to obtain the warrant after the deficiencies have been remedied. This reconsideration is considered a new process or application and may be heard by the same justice who denied it earlier or by another justice.[68]

Forms of Warrant

The form of a search warrant issued pursuant to s. 487 must be in Form 5, which is a prescribed form located in the forms section of the *Criminal Code*. This form may be varied to suit the case. In addition to setting out the above-noted condition precedents of s. 487, Form 5 also specifies the time when it can be executed. Any warrant issued under s. 487 must be executed by day unless the justice, by the warrant, specifically authorizes execution of it by night (s. 499). During the day is defined as being between 6:00 a.m. and 9:00 p.m. The warrant should also indicate the period within which the search must be executed.

As a general rule, the articles to be seized under a search warrant must contain a sufficient description in the warrant so that the peace officer to whom it is directed will know exactly what to look for and preclude fishing expeditions.[69] In James A. Fontana's authoritative textbook entitled *The Law of Search and Seizure in Canada*, a number of principles regarding descriptions have been extracted from case law and include the following:

1. The description should be as specific as possible and both the Information and the warrant should contain as much detail with respect to the identity of the goods or individual items as available to the informant.

2. Where the goods are identifiable only by class or type, and where the subject may possess many goods of that class or type, they should be further identified by time period or as relating to a certain transaction or by other additional delineating factors.

3. The officer should know, with some degree of specification, what he is looking for when executing the warrant.

4. The officer should know not only the fact that the goods are believed to be present on the premises, but what those goods are, if the Information has been properly prepared. In other words, while the officer may be there under power of the warrant to determine *whether* the goods are present, the officer is not there to determine *what* those goods are.

5. The description of the goods should be such that the executing officer merely locates, identifies and removes the goods; the officer is not there to pick and choose or select, at his or her discretion, things which the officer feels may be of assistance. For this reason broad, general descriptions appear to give to the officer the discretion which is not contemplated.[70]

The person executing the warrant is limited to seizing only those articles described in the warrant. The individual may seize, in addition to the articles specified in the warrant, anything that they believe on *reasonable grounds* has been obtained by or has been used in the commission of an offence.[71] Further, only the person to whom the warrant is directed is authorized to conduct the search and seize the named articles. There does not, however, appear to be any prohibition against others, such as owners of stolen property or experts who are more qualified in identifying the articles, from accompanying the peace officer.

Seizure of Thing Not Specified

Section 489 of the *Criminal Code* provides that in certain circumstances a peace officer executing a warrant or otherwise acting in the execution of his duty may have occasion to seize items that either have not been named in a warrant or have come into his or her view by virtue of being lawfully present in a place pursuant to a warrant or otherwise in the execution of the officer's duty. Things may be seized in these situations if they fall into one or more of three categories. They will be anything that the peace officer believes on *reasonable grounds*:

(a) has been obtained by the commission of an offence against this or any other Act of Parliament;

(b) has been used in the commission of an offence against this or any other Act of Parliament; or

(c) will afford evidence in respect of an offence against this or any other Act of Parliament.

Third-Party Assistance Orders

Section 487.02 of the *Criminal Code* provides that the issuing judge may order any person to provide assistance, where the person's assistance may reasonably be considered to be required to give effect to the warrant. The nature of that assistance will depend upon what may be reasonably considered to be required to give effect to the warrant.

Telewarrants

The telewarrant provisions of the *Criminal Code*, ss. 256 and 487.1, provide a self-contained code regarding the issuance and execution of telewarrants. These provisions were enacted to allow peace officers to obtain a search warrant by way of telephone or other means of telecommunication. These telewarrant provisions set out special circumstances of urgency where it would be impractical for a peace officer to appear in person before a justice to obtain an ordinary warrant.

Unlike ordinary search warrants, the telewarrant may be issued only in respect of indictable offences that have been committed, and can be issued only by a justice designated for that purpose by the chief judge of the provincial court having jurisdiction. Further, telewarrants may be issued upon the *Information* of peace officers only.

The *Information* submitted by telephone or other telecommunication must be on oath and recorded *verbatim* by the justice who shall, *as soon as practicable*, cause a certified record to be filed with the clerk of the court for the territorial division in which the warrant is intended for execution.

In subs. 487.1(4), the *Information* on oath submitted by telephone, or other means of telecommunication, must include:

> (a) a statement of the circumstances that make it impracticable for the peace officer to appear personally before a justice;
> (b) a statement of the indictable offence alleged, the place or premise to be searched and the items alleged to be liable to seizure;
> (c) a statement of the peace officer's grounds for believing that items liable to seizure in respect of the offence alleged will be found in the place or premises to be searched; and
> (d) a statement as to any prior application for a warrant under this section or any other search warrant, in respect of the same matter, of which the peace officer has knowledge.

As per subs. 487.1(5), the justice will consider all of the above-noted information and may only issue a telewarrant if satisfied that the *Information*:

> (a) is in respect of an indictable offence and conforms to the requirements of subsection (4);
> (b) discloses reasonable grounds for dispensing with an information presented personally and in writing; and
> (c) discloses reasonable grounds, in accordance with subsection 256(1) or paragraph 487(1)(a), (b) or (c), as the case may be, for the issuance of a warrant in respect to an indictable offence.

Blood Sample Telewarrant

Section 256 authorizes the issuance and execution of a warrant to take *blood*. Under this section, the *Information* on oath submitted by telephone or other telecommunication must include a statement setting out the alleged offence and identifying the person whose blood samples it is proposed to take. The justice must be satisfied on the basis of the

Information that there are reasonable grounds to believe that the following conditions have been met:

> (a) the person has, within the preceding four hours, committed, as a result of the consumption of alcohol, an [impaired driving offence (s. 253)] and the person was involved in an accident resulting in the death of another person or in bodily harm to himself or herself or to any other person, and
> (b) a qualified medical practitioner is of the opinion that
>> (i) by reason of any physical or mental condition of the person that resulted from the consumption of alcohol or a drug, the accident or any other occurrence related to or resulting from the accident, the person is unable to consent to the taking of samples of his or her blood, and
>> (ii) the taking of samples of blood from the person would not endanger the life or health of the person.

The justice may issue a warrant authorizing a peace officer to require a qualified medical practitioner to take, or to cause to be taken by a qualified technician under the direction of a qualified medical practitioner, such samples of the suspect's blood as, in the person's opinion taking the samples, are necessary to enable a proper alcohol content analysis to be made. Unlike general telewarrants, a justice does *not* have to be designated for the issuance of a specific blood telewarrant. It should be noted that a telewarrant, either a general telewarrant pursuant to s. 487.1, or a specific blood telewarrant pursuant to s. 256 issued by a justice, has the same legal effect as an ordinary search warrant issued pursuant to s. 487.

Execution of Warrants

As stated above, a search warrant must be executed by day unless it expressly authorizes execution by night, and a search warrant must be executed within a reasonable time period, if the time is not specified, after it has been issued.[72] Where a search warrant is executed after its specified time limitation, the warrant will be quashed or its execution may be held to be unreasonable and thus contrary to s. 8 of the *Charter*.[73] A search warrant may be executed on a Sunday or on a statutory holiday. The person to whom the search warrant is directed is authorized to conduct the search and seize the specified articles named in the warrant. Where a search warrant is to be executed by peace officers, it need not be addressed to a specific or named peace officer.

The issuing justice of the search warrant has the discretion to impose *reasonable conditions* as to its execution in order to minimize the degree of intrusion by the executors of the warrant.[74]

It is the duty of everyone who executes a search warrant to have it in their possession for inspection, where it is feasible to do so, and to produce it when requested to do so and to allow the owner or occupant a reasonable amount of time to examine the document (subs. 29(1)). Further, the executor of the search warrant must, except where exigent circumstances exist, identify him- or herself as a peace officer and state the purpose for which entry is demanded. This is not required if entry is necessary to prevent the destruction of evidence. In the case of dwellings, the executor of the warrant must exercise more circumspection in the manner of the warrant's execution. Generally speaking, a peace officer in execution of a search warrant is not entitled to forcibly enter a temporarily unoccupied dwelling unless exigent circumstances exist. If the dwelling to be searched is unoccupied at the time of the search, the executor of the warrant should leave a copy of the warrant in a prominent place within the dwelling. If the person in charge of the premises refuses to permit entry, the executor of the warrant is entitled to use reasonable force to gain entry into the dwelling (subs. 25(1)).

The Supreme Court of Canada's comments are instructive:

> An unexpected intrusion of a man's property can give rise to violent incidents. It is in the interests of the personal safety of the householder and the police as well as respect for the privacy of the individual that the law requires, prior to entrance for search or arrest, that a police officer identify himself and request admittance. No precise form of words is necessary. In *Semayne's Case* it was said that he should "signify the cause of his coming, and to make request to open doors" ... The traditional demand was "Open in the name of the King." In the ordinary case police officers, before forcing entry, should give: (i) notice of presence by knocking or ringing the doorbell; (ii) notice of authority, by identifying themselves as law enforcement officers; and (iii) notice of purpose, by stating a lawful reason for entry. Minimally they should request admission and have admission denied although it is recognized there will be occasions on which, for example, to save someone within the premises from death or injury or to prevent destruction of evidence or if in hot pursuit, notice may not be required.[75]

The executor of the search warrant has no legal authority to search anyone whom he or she finds in the dwelling during the search. The right to search someone has only been recognized as an incident of arrest. However, a peace officer is entitled to control the premises if he or she has reason to believe that such detention is a necessary part of the search authorized; for instance, for the safety of the persons executing the warrant or to prevent the possible destruction of evidence.[76]

A search warrant may be executed only in the territorial division in which the justice of the peace who issued it has jurisdiction. However, a search warrant issued in one province can be executed in another province where a justice in the province of execution endorses the warrant (subs. 487(2)).

Administrative and/or Regulatory Searches

In the context of investigations of regulatory offences, the issue that often arises is to what extent the Charter applies to the regulatory investigators conducting searches and seizures.

The law is clear that where the investigation has a predominantly penal purpose, the use of the investigatory tools of regulatory authorities is *limited*. In other words, the regulatory investigators are entitled to rely upon all of the powers of search and seizure which emanate from the authorizing statute, as long as the investigation does not become *criminal* in nature. When the purpose of the investigation *changes* from a regulatory offence investigation to a *criminal offence investigation*, the investigation must comply with all of the standards mandated by the *Charter*, including the protection against unreasonable search and seizure.

Right To Enter Private Dwellings To Make Arrest

Prior to May 22, 1997, the law permitted the police to enter and arrest a person in a dwelling without having met the above preconditions. On May 22, 1997, the Supreme Court of Canada released a ruling that had a profound impact upon on the law governing arrests of persons in dwellings.[77] The Court held that the privacy interest outweighs the law enforcement interest and, thus, warrantless entry into dwellings is prohibited unless exigent circumstances exist. The initial impact of the Supreme Court's judgment was widespread and profound, as the police were forced to change entrenched police practice.[78] It was unclear as to how compliance with the Supreme Court's judgment was going to be achieved because of the lack of statutory authority.[79] Parliament responded by amending the *Criminal Code*. On December 18, 1997, ss. 529 to 529.5 of the *Criminal Code* came into force. These provisions authorize justices of the peace to issue warrants permitting the entry of dwellings for purposes of arrest. The justice must be satisfied that there are reasonable grounds for the arrest and reasonable grounds to believe the person will be found at the named location, before giving the police the authority to enter. Section 529.3(1) provides that an officer may enter a dwelling for the purposes of arrest without warrant, if there are reasonable grounds to believe that the person is present in the dwelling and the conditions for obtaining a warrant exist, but by reason of exigent circumstances it would be impracticable to obtain a warrant. Also, as earlier mentioned, an exception that authorizes warrantless entry of dwellings is the doctrine of "hot or fresh" pursuit. In cases of "hot pursuit", society's interest in effective law enforcement takes precedence over the privacy interest and the police are permitted to enter a dwelling to make an arrest without warrant.[80] "Hot" or "fresh" pursuit (pursuit is continuous pursuit), conducted with reasonable diligence so that pursuit and capture, along with the commission of the offence, may be considered as forming part of a single transaction.[81]

The common law provides the authority for the police to enter a dwelling, over the objection of the tenant, in order to investigate a "911" telephone call that was disconnected before contact could be made with the caller. The entry into the dwelling without warrant was justified on the basis of the common law duties of the police to protect life, prevent death, and prevent serious injury.[82]

It should be noted that, after making a lawful arrest, a peace officer is permitted to extend the search to the premises, or to the immediate surroundings where the arrest was effected and which is under the control of the person arrested.[83] The peace officer is entitled to control the premises so as to avoid a potentially dangerous situation. During this period the peace officer need not permit a detained person the opportunity to call a lawyer.[84]

A search warrant authorizes the search of premises or property specified in the warrant. Hence, a search warrant does not authorize the search of persons found in specified premises or property in the absence of statutory authority to do so, or in the absence of a search incidental to an arrest.[85]

Border Searches

Other legislation also speaks to the state's ability to subject people to searches. One example is the *Corrections Act* and another is the *Customs Act*. Even though Parliament has given the power to officers to conduct searches in these settings, the *Charter* standard must still be applied. Individuals may challenge the legislation to question if the statute is *Charter* complaint with s. 8.

The Supreme Court of Canada has held that the reasonableness of border searches within the meaning of s. 8 of the *Charter* must be treated differently from searches occurring in other circumstances. The Supreme Court observed:

the degree of personal privacy reasonably expected at customs is lower than in most other situations. People do not expect to be able to cross international borders free from scrutiny. It is commonly accepted that sovereign states have the right to control both who and what enter their boundaries. For the general welfare of the nation, the state is expected to perform this role... travellers seeking to cross national boundaries fully expect to be subject to a screening process. This process will typically require the production of proper identification and travel documentation and involve a search process beginning with completion of a declaration of all goods being brought into the country. Physical searches of luggage and of the person are accepted aspects of the search process where there are grounds for suspecting that a person has made a false declaration and is transporting prohibited goods.[86]

Moreover, the Supreme Court expressed the view that:

routine questioning by customs officers, searches of luggage, frisk or pat searches, and the requirement to remove in private such articles of clothing as will permit investigation of suspicious bodily bulges, permitted under ss. 143 and 144 of the *Customs Act*, are not unreasonable within the meaning of s. 8.[87]

General Investigative Search Warrant

Since Confederation, Parliament has increasingly expanded provisions under various statutes for issuing search warrants. With the advent of the *Charter*, developments in law and technology, and the evolution of investigative techniques, Parliament has had to amend the *search and seizure* provisions of the *Criminal Code*. Within the last decade, Parliament, prompted by the Supreme Court of Canada pronouncements,[88] developed a much more elaborate legislative regime regarding search and seizure.

In August 1993, s. 487.01 of the *Criminal Code* was proclaimed authorizing the issuance of a warrant that allows a peace officer to use *any device, investigative technique or procedure, including video surveillance*, which would otherwise constitute an unreasonable search or seizure, contrary to s. 8 of the *Charter*.

This section authorizes a provincial court judge or a Supreme Court judge the power to issue a *general investigative warrant*.[89] A justice of the peace is *not* authorized to issue a *general investigative warrant*. In addition, unlike the *ordinary search warrant* (s. 487), a *general investigative warrant* (s. 487.01) can only be issued to a *peace officer* as defined in s. 2 of the *Criminal Code*.

General investigative warrants were introduced to provide the means for the police to obtain prior judicial authorization for a broad range of investigative techniques and procedures to gather information concerning an offence under investigation. It is a very powerful tool available to law enforcement officers.

In subs. 487.01(1), the following preconditions must be met before an issuing judge can issue a *general investigative warrant*:

> (a) . . . there are *reasonable grounds* to believe that an offence against [the *Criminal Code* or any other [federal] Act. . . *has been committed or will be* committed and that information *concerning the offence will be* obtained through the use of the technique, procedure or device or the doing of the thing;
>
> (b) . . it is in the *best interests of the administration of justice* to issue the warrant; and
>
> (c) there is *no other* provision in [the *Criminal Code* or any other [federal] Act ... that would provide for a warrant, authorization or order permitting the technique, procedure or device to be used or the thing to be done. [Emphasis added.]

Presumably, it was Parliament's intent that both the law enforcement agencies and the authorizing judicial authorities should be appropriately circumspect in considering whether or not the more intrusive *general investigative warrant* is reasonable in the circumstances.[90]

There are several significant distinctions between the *general investigative warrant* and the *ordinary warrant*, the result of which has provided law enforcement agencies with broad and sweeping powers to engage in highly intrusive investigative techniques and/ or procedures.[91] In the seminal case of *R. v. Noseworthy*, the Ontario Court of Appeal observed:

> (a) The power to issue warrants under the section is limited to provincial court judges and superior court judges. It is not extended to justices of the peace;
>
> (b) An issuing judge is not bound by the strictures of other warrant provisions, but rather is governed by the "best interests of the administration of justice".
>
> (c) Whereas s. 487 is limited to searching a building, receptacle or a place for a specified thing and to brining that thing or reporting with respect to it to the court, s. 487.02 authorizes a court to issue a warrant to "use any devise or investigative technique or procedure or do anything described in the [page 380] warrant." Thus, s. 487.01 is both more specific and more general than s. 487.
>
> (d) This section authorizes warrants relating to offences not yet committed.
>
> (e) Apart from its location in proximity to "devise or investigative technique or procedure", there is nothing in the context to suggest that "any thing" should be read *ejudem generis*. More specifically, "any thing" is

not modified by the word "similar" or the phrase "of the same nature" or anything resembling them.

(f) Unlike s. 487, s. 487.01(3) and (4) provide that the judge may make the issuance of the warrant conditional upon such terms and conditions as she or he considers advisable.

(g) Section 487.01 does not provide simply for seizing things which are evidence, contraband or instrumentalities, but rather it provides for the doing of any thing which will yield information concerning an offence, thus paralleling the breadth of the informational privacy interests protected by s. 8 of the *Charter*. See *R. v. Plant*, [1993] 3 S.C.R. 282 at 296-297.[92]

The scope of the *general investigative warrant* is what clearly distinguishes it from the *ordinary warrant*. Thus, the following distinguishing features must be considered in order to appreciate its breadth.

Jurisdiction to Authorize

As stated above, unlike an *ordinary warrant*, the *general investigative warrant* must be authorized by a provincial court judge or a superior court of criminal jurisdiction or a judge as defined in s. 522 of the *Criminal Code*. A justice of the peace is not authorized to issue a *general investigative warrant*.[93] Thus, it is arguable that Parliament's intent was to ensure that the complexity of the multitude of factual and legal aspects of the general investigative warrant would necessitate careful and thorough judicial scrutiny.[94]

The Person to Whom it Shall Be Issued and Where it Can Be Executed

Unlike an *ordinary warrant*, the *general investigative warrant* can only be issued to a *peace officer*, as defined in s. 2 of the *Criminal Code*. Therefore, the peace officer will, undoubtedly, in certain circumstances, have to apply for an *assistance order* as in accordance with s. 487.02 of the *Criminal Code*. *As with ordinary search warrants*, the *general investigative warrant* can be executed in another territorial division. However, if the warrant is to be executed in another territorial division and the warrant requires entry into private property or requires an assistance order, then the warrant must be confirmed by a judge in that territorial division. Also, s. 487.03 provides that a warrant may be confirmed where it is executed in another territorial division. Such confirmation is in addition to the backing procedure set out in subs. 487(2), which is applicable to a *general investigative warrant*.[95]

To Use Any Device, Technique, Procedure or Do Anything

As suggested above, Parliamentarians could not envision every conceivable type of investigative activity that would be captured by the *general investigative warrant* regime. Accordingly, the phrase *"use any device or investigative technique or procedure or do any thing"* has been interpreted very broadly by the Ontario Court of Appeal in *R. v. Noseworthy*,[96] wherein the Court defined the words *"any thing"* very widely. In that case, the motion judge had interpreted the words "'any thing' as being qualified by the preceding specific enumeration of 'device' and 'investigative technique or procedure', . . ." The judge went on to state, "the words 'or do anything' in subs. 487.01(1) ought to be read *ejusdem generis* with the words 'device' and 'investigative technique or procedure' and not as having an independent significance on their own." The Court of Appeal ruled that the motion judge erred in interpreting the section so narrowly and held that, because of the safeguards that had been included in the *general investigative warrant* legislation, as well as the fact that there was nothing in the context of the phrase "any thing" to suggest that it should be read *ejusdem generis* with "device" or "investigative technique or procedure".

The Search or Seizure of Information as Opposed to Evidence

The *general investigative warrant* contemplates the search or seizure of *Information* concerning an offence under investigation, unlike the *ordinary warrant*, which *limits* the search or seizure to *evidence of the offence* that exists in a building, receptacle *or place. The import of the word "information"* permits the search or seizure of *intangibles* and suggests that the *Information* may or may not itself ultimately be evidence,[97] "thus paralleling the breadth of the informational privacy interest protected by s. 8 of the *Charter*."[98]

Information Concerning the Offence as Opposed to Evidence of an Offence

The use of the words *"concerning the offence"* reflects Parliament's intent to broaden the power of law enforcement agencies' investigative ability. Thus, the search or seizure is broadened to include anything concerning the offence. Unlike the *ordinary warrant* which restricts the investigative ability of law enforcement agencies to search for or seize tangibles that *will afford evidence* in respect to the commission of an offence, which could include information seized that has no evidentiary value, but may be used to further other investigative avenues.

In *R. v. Brand*,[99] police obtained a general warrant to covertly investigate drug related activity on property owned by Ford. In accordance with the warrant police found a marihuana grow operation. This information was later used in a CDSA warrant. The accused was convicted and appealed for two reasons: First, the general warrant used the phrase, "information or evidence that would assist in the investigation could be obtained through general warrant"; and secondly there were grounds to use either a 487 or CDSA warrant and thus violating the provision that 'no other provision or act of parliament. The Court held that real issue is whether there existed reasonable grounds to believe that the execution of a general warrant was likely to yield information concerning the offence under investigation. More will be said about the use of other warrants.

Anticipatory Searches

The *ordinary warrant* restricts the search or seizure to an offence *that has been committed*, whereas, the *general investigative warrant* also authorizes the search of an offence *that has not yet been committed*: an anticipated offence.[100]

In a Building, Receptacle or Place

The *ordinary warrant* contemplates a search of or seizure from a *building, receptacle or place*. The *general investigative warrant* does not have this restriction. The *general investigative warrant* contemplates the use of an investigative technique, procedure or device or the doing of the thing, which would otherwise violate s. 8 of the *Charter*.

In the Best Interest of the Administration of Justice

Unlike an *ordinary warrant*, the *general investigative warrant* requires the issuing judge to consider whether or not it is *in the best interest of the administration of justice* to issue the warrant. Arguably, this additional requirement was included as a safeguard to necessitate careful and thorough judicial scrutiny.

Mr. Justice Casey Hill has suggested several factors that ought to be considered in determining whether or not the issuing of the warrant is *in the best interest of the administration of justice*. He stated:

> These words are identical to the wording in section 186(1)(a) of the *Code*, relating to the issuance of an authorization of Part VI of the *Code*, and accordingly, reference to the jurisprudential and textual authorities inter-

preting that provision may be helpful. Although there is no crystallized inventory of factors to be considered, certainly some or all of the following ought to be considered in determining whether the interests of law enforcement in securing the evidence by the proposed means outweighs the intrusion on the subject *of* the search; the seriousness of the offence under investigation, the nature of the intrusion, the nature of the information sought to be searched for/ seized, the significance of the information to the investigation, the availability of alternative measures to secure the information, the duration and location of the search, etc.[101]

Chief Justice McLachlin and Justice Charon, in *R. v. Grant,*[102] stated:

> The term "administration of justice" is often used to indicate the processes by which those who break the law are investigated, charged and tried. *More broadly, however, the term embraces maintaining the rule of law and upholding Charter rights in the justice system as a whole.*
> [Emphasis added.]

In other words, the best interest of the administration of justice refers to the balancing of the state's interest in investigating crime and protecting individual *Charter* rights.

Limiting Interference with Bodily Integrity

Parliament has expressly limited the scope of the *general investigative warrant* as it relates to the *interference with the bodily integrity of any person.*[103] Within the context of the *general investigative warrant* there are numerous decisions that have considered the scope of this limiting prohibition.[104] Many of these decisions pre-date the enactment of the DNA legislation and thus turn on the meaning of the expression *interference with the bodily integrity of any person* in the context *of* a search or seizure for the purpose of conducting DNA analysis. Hence, these decisions have become moot. However, in cases where the *general investigative warrant* contemplates a search or seizure that does not include a seizure for the purposes of DNA analysis, the issues surrounding the scope of the expression *interference with the bodily integrity* of any person is a live issue. As noted by one legal commentator:

> The different ways in which the expression has been used in the cases are not necessarily determinative of a reading of s. 487.01(3); the scope of this limiting section will only be determined as cases dealing with the expression in this *context* begin to be litigated. Some initial views can be attempted, however. It seems clear that the notion of bodily integrity includes the preservation of the completeness of the subject's physical being. This would, therefore, prohibit any investigative technique that

sought to gather *living cells* which remained attached to the person. If this view is correct, then warrants to pluck hair (scalp or body), take blood, or scraped skin samples are not authorized. Other activity which merely "harvest" dead or expelled matter might, however, be legal. This would include harvests of dead cells in saliva, urine and fecal matter, and perhaps hair combs.

The other aspect of "bodily integrity" that seems clear in quality (if not degree) is the notion that no physical harm be occasioned in the execution of the warrant. Thus, while surgery to remove a bullet from a suspect would not "seize" any living tissue, it would necessitate an interference with the physical body of the suspect. Quaere whether this provision could be used for non-intrusive medical techniques, for example x-rays or ultrasounds to gather information about a non-cooperative victim or from a target?[105]

Terms and Conditions

The *general investigative warrant* mandates the imposition of *terms and condition* as the issuing judge considers advisable to ensure that any search or seizure is reasonable in the circumstances. It would seem that Parliament included a provision for terms and conditions, which has been used in similarly intrusive provisions of the *Criminal Code* such as Impression warrants, DNA warrants, and *Part VI applications. There is no such provision in the legislated regime governing the ordinary warrant.* Obviously, the nature of the terms and conditions imposed will vary depending on the nature of the investigation as well as the degree of intrusion upon the privacy interest of those affected. The terms and conditions will likely increase proportionally to the degree of invasion into the subject's privacy.

The lack of terms became an issue in the trial decision of *R. v Knight.*[106] The trial judge, in reviewing the defence challenge to general warrant, held that the police should have had conditions imposed and, as a result, the warrant violated the protection of life, liberty and the security of the person. The RCMP, under the authority of a general warrant, staged a theft of drugs that Knight was transporting on the ferry in order to stimulate conversations of the suspects, which they were intercepting. The trial judge said that Knight's safety was jeopardized since those working with Knight may have blamed him for the loss and seriously harmed him for losing their valuable stash of drugs. The reasoning went that the police should have anticipated this and conditions should have been drafted to protect Knights' section 7 rights.

The Newfoundland Court of Appeal reversed the trial judge's decision and upheld the issuing of the general warrant. It was noted the issuing justice would have considered that the police had wiretap in place and were constantly surveilling Knight and he was not in increased risk of harm. The case does raise the question of what limits "any technique" will be applied by the courts.

No Other Provision in *Criminal Code* or Any Other Act of Parliament

The *general investigative warrant* provisions impose an obligation upon law enforcement agencies to exhaust all other federally legislated options before contemplating a *general investigative warrant*.

Although, in *R. v. Brand* and *R. v. Ha*,[107] both the B.C. and Ontario Courts of Appeal accepted that even though police may have grounds to get a 487 warrant or other warrants, does not mean they are precluded from using a general warrant. Both cases saw the police use a general warrant to repeatedly and covertly enter a premises. The police had grounds to get other types of warrants, but desired to continue their investigations without the suspects knowing the police were investigating them. Both Courts held that they were not going to limit the police and second guess their decisions to continue the investigations. Ultimately the issuing justice must consider whether the general warrant is in the best interest of the administration of justice.

The procedure to obtain a *general investigative warrant* is commenced by an *Information* on oath in writing submitted to a provincial or Supreme Court justice. There is no prescribed form for the *Information* or warrant, as there is in respect to the *ordinary warrant* (s. 487). Thus, it is not uncommon for the authorities to adapt the s. 487 documents (Forms 1 and 5) accordingly.

The *general investigative warrant* permits police officers to employ various creative investigative techniques where the only limiting factors, other than bodily integrity and administration of justice concerns, are the energy and imagination of the investigator. For example, the following are some of investigative techniques and/ or procedures that have been utilized under the authority of a *general investigative warrant*:

- perimeter searches of private property;
- Multiple covert entries;
- Staging a theft;
- crime scene examinations;
- temporarily taking vehicles for forensic examination or to install tracking devices;
- marking property for tracing;

- police surveillance or observation post on private property;
- requiring a person to provide handwriting samples;
- Westcan observations from an aircraft;
- anticipatory search warrants;
- installing a default program into a computer to disable it so that the computer is brought in for servicing, etc.;
- substituting legal substances while seizing illegal substance;
- introducing an undercover officer as an inmate into jail if fictitious documentation is required;
- simulating the commission of crime by law enforcers; and
- creating diversions to enable wiretap installations or other searches to take place.[108]

The above-noted examples are not in any way meant to be an exhaustive list, but rather a sampling of the type of activity that may be authorized by a *general investigative warrant*.

As stated, the *general investigative warrant* may be issued to search or seize an article from a person or to view a person and may also be issued in respect to *intangible* property.

It is important to note that subs. 487.01(2) states that nothing in the above-noted subsection shall be construed as to permit interference with the *bodily integrity* of any person. Further, subs. 487.01(3) permits inclusion of *terms and conditions* considered advisable to ensure the reasonableness of any search or seizure conducted. Also, it is important to note that specific provisions are made in subs. 487.01(4) and (5) for *video surveillance warrants*. They authorize a peace officer to observe, by means of a television camera or other similar electronic device, any person engaged in an activity in circumstances in which the person has a reasonable expectation of privacy. Section 487.01 appears to be *very broad in its scope* and thus is undoubtedly of great benefit to police investigators.

While persons other than peace officers are empowered by this section to make such seizures, it will only be *peace officers* who will be executing *general investigative warrants*.

Video Surveillance Warrant

A *general investigative warrant*, which authorizes a peace officer to observe by means of a television camera or other similar electronic device, requires the issuing judge to impose terms and conditions to protect the privacy of the targeted person and others as the judge may deem advisable.[109] It is of significance to note that a general *investiga-*

tive warrant that authorizes video surveillance must satisfy the threshold requirements of the provisions of Part VI of the *Criminal Code*. Unlike the other *general investigative warrants* that can be obtained for any *federal* offences, this special type of a *general investigative warrant* can only be obtained for the *designated offences* enumerated in s. 183 of the *Criminal Code*. Further, if *audio* surveillance is being sought, then an authorization pursuant to Part VI of the *Criminal Code* is required.[110]

General Investigative Telewarrants

The *general investigative warrant* regime provides that, where a peace officer believes that it would be impracticable to appear personally before a judge to make an application for a *general investigative warrant*, a warrant may be issued on an information, submitted by telephone or other means of telecommunication, and, for that purpose, s. 487.1 of the *Criminal Code* applies to the warrant, with such modifications as the circumstances may require.

Section 487.1 of the *Criminal Code* sets out the requirements for a telewarrant to be issued. This section details a number of procedural conditions that must be fulfilled to comply with the telewarrant section. Telewarrants are available in cases where a peace officer believes an *indictable offence* has been committed and appearing personally for an application for a warrant would be impracticable. For *ordinary warrants* the information may be received by a justice who has been especially appointed by the chief of the provincial court judge having jurisdiction over the matter.

Obviously, subs. 487.01(7) would require that *general investigative telewarrants* could only be entertained by a provincial court or superior court judge. Arguably, while subs. 487.1(1) pertains to general warrants for offences that have been committed, subs. 487.01(7) would allow that a *general investigative telewarrant* to be obtained for offences that have not yet been committed in keeping with the purpose of the *general investigative warrant* provisions. Clearly, further modifications would have to be made to conform to the prerequisites of a *general investigative warrant*. A judge would also have to be satisfied that an information submitted by telephone or other means of telecommunication is in respect to an *indictable offence* and conforms to the procedural requirements (as modified) of what should be in the application set out in subs. 487.1(4). Lastly, the issuing judge must be satisfied that the information provided disclosed reasonable grounds for dispensing with the information being presented personally and in writing and further discloses all the prerequisites for the issuance of a *general investigative warrant*.

Restitution of Property or Report by Peace Officer

The *Criminal Code* provisions related to returning property seized during the execution of a *general investigative warrant*, as well as the *reporting obligation* of the executing peace officer, are contained in s. 489.1. Where a peace officer has seized anything under a *general investigative warrant* or otherwise in the execution of a *general investigative warrant*, the peace officer shall, as soon as is practicable, deal with the property in one of the ways listed in the section applicable to the circumstances. Whether or not the property is detained, a report to the issuing judge or one of the same jurisdiction in the prescribed form must be made.[111] There is an ongoing issue as to whether or not this section is applicable in circumstances where the thing seized is not *a tangible or physical* item, such as a seizure of *Information* or the making of *observations*. However, with respect to the seizures of tangible or physical items this section is clearly applicable.

Detention Orders

The procedures and time limits for detaining items seized pursuant to a *general investigative warrant*, or while in the execution of a *general investigative warrant*, are set out in s. 490 of the *Criminal Code*. Original detention periods may be *extended* if the peace officer makes application for the continued detention where the thing seized *might be reasonably required* for the purposes of any investigation, or a preliminary hearing, trial, or other proceeding, and that it is in the interest of justice to do so.

Sealing Orders

The sealing provisions of the *Criminal Code* take on special significance in cases of *general investigative warrants*. Because these warrants are issued at various stages in an investigation, there are many situations when publicly disclosing the information used to obtain a *general investigative warrant* or divulging the use of any device or investigative technique or procedure would impede the investigation.

Subsection 487.3(1) provides that a judge issuing any warrant including a *general investigative warrant* may, on application made at the time of issuing the warrant, or at any time thereafter, make an order prohibiting access to, and the disclosure of any information relating to, the warrant or authorization on the ground that:

> (a) the ends of justice would be subverted by the disclosure for one of the reasons referred to in subsection (2) or the information might be used for an improper purpose; and
> (b) the ground referred to in paragraph (*a*) outweighs in importance the access to the information.

Subsection 487.3(2) of the *Criminal Code* enumerates the reasons that a judge may choose to seal the warrant information:
For the purposes of paragraph (1)(*a*), an order may be made under subsection (1) on the ground that the ends of justice would be subverted by the disclosure

> (a) if disclosure of the information would
>> (i) compromise the identity of a confidential informant,
>> (ii) compromise the nature and extent of an ongoing investigation,
>> (iii) endanger a person engaged in particular intelligence-gathering techniques and thereby prejudice future investigations in which similar techniques would be used, or
>> (iv) prejudice the interests of an innocent person; and
> (b) for any other sufficient reason.

Subsection 487.3(3) establishes the procedure for sealing the packet and outlines what the packet should contain. Pursuant to subs. 487.3(4), an application may be made to terminate or vary the conditions of a sealing order to a judge who would have jurisdiction to hear any proceeding arising out of the investigation.

The Supreme Court of Canada reaffirmed that there must be a presumption of openness rather than secrecy to legal proceedings. The Supreme Court held that, to obtain a sealing order, a party seeking to limit public access to legal proceedings must rely on more than a generalized assertion that publicity could compromise investigative efficacy. The party (usually the Crown) must, at the very least, allege a *serious* and *specific risk* to the integrity of the criminal investigation. In other words, it is no longer enough for the Crown to rely on a generalized assertion of possible disadvantage to an ongoing investigation. The Crown must demonstrate that, absent a sealing order, there is a serious risk to the integrity of the criminal investigation.[112]

Impression Warrants

Many of the identification techniques which once had been authorized under the *general investigative warrant* provisions are now captured by impression warrants pursuant to s. 487.092. Thus, it is appropriate at this juncture to examine the relevant provisions.

Section 487.092 of the *Criminal Code* authorizes a peace officer, or anyone acting under the peace officer's direction, to obtain any handprint, fingerprint, footprint, foot impression, teeth impression, or other print or impression, of the body or any part of the body in respect of a person. The justice must be satisfied by Information on oath in writing:

> (a) ... that there are reasonable grounds to believe that a [federal] offence ... has been committed and that information concerning the offence will be obtained by the print or impression; and
> (b) that it is in the best interest of the administration of justice to issue the warrant.

This section also requires the issuing justice to impose terms and conditions to ensure that any search or seizure authorized by the warrant is reasonable in the circumstances.

DNA Warrant

The DNA warrant scheme, contained in ss. 487.04 to 487.09 of the *Criminal Code*, was enacted in 1995 by Bill C-104, *An Act to amend the Criminal Code and Young Offenders Act (forensic DNA analysis)*, S.C. 1995, c. 27.

Prior to the proclamation of Bill C-104, the police had no authority to seize biological specimens from a suspect's body in the absence of the suspect's consent. As the first cases involving DNA evidence were working their way through the criminal justice system, it became apparent that there was a void in the law. At issue was the manner in which the DNA evidence was gathered. The police relied upon either the suspect's consent or their common law power to search (incident to an arrest) for authority to seize bodily substances.[113] The enactment of s. 487.01 (*general investigative warrant*) of the *Criminal Code* in 1993 did not resolve the issue.[114]

In 1994, the Supreme Court of Canada rendered its judgment in *R. v. Borden*,[115] wherein the Court acknowledged the lack of either a statutory or common law authority (in the absence of informed consent) to forcibly search for, and seize, biological specimens from a suspect's body.

As the case law evolved, it became apparent that it was necessary for Parliament to create a statutory warrant procedure for the seizure of certain bodily substances for the purposes of DNA analysis. Thus, the purpose of the enactment of Bill C-104 was to clarify the state of the law as to the circumstances and the manner in which the police could forcibly search for, and seize, biological specimens for the purposes of DNA analysis.[116] In the context of the Supreme Court of Canada's pronouncement that there has to be clear rules guiding—not prohibiting—police conduct in the sensitive areas where law enforcement objectives and privacy interests interplay, Bill C-104 was drafted to respect constitutional requirements pertaining to the powers of search and seizure of the police. The drafters of the legislation had the benefit of looking at the comparative experience in other countries with a view to examining and selecting the best of their statutory regimes. Moreover, in 1994, the Department of Justice had issued a consultation paper identifying issues and seeking comment to which a number of responses were received.[117] The response to the consultation paper showed that Canadians supported the creation of a mechanism that would allow the police to seize samples of biological substances from suspects for the purposes of DNA analysis and for the establishment of a DNA data bank.

The DNA warrant scheme of ss. 487.04 to 487.09 of the *Criminal Code*, enacted by Bill C-104, has withstood constitutional scrutiny.[118] It has been held that the scheme ensures that the suspect has the benefit of all of the traditional safeguards inherent in the prior judicial authorization model. In addition to these traditional safeguards, the DNA warrant scheme offers several additional protections.

In *Stillman*, Corey J. specifically contemplated, in *obiter dicta*, that the DNA warrant scheme would meet all constitutional requirements. His Lordship stated:

> In my view, police actions taken without consent or authority which intrude upon an individual's body in more than a minimal fashion violate s.7 of the *Charter* in a manner that would as a general rule tend to affect the fairness of the trial. Those opposed to this position may argue that it leads to a requirement that the state will have to justify legislation permitting bodily intrusion. Yet, I do not find that to be an unduly onerous requirement when dealing with bodily intrusions. Although the issue was not raised it would seem that the recent provisions of the *Code* permitting DNA testing might well meet all constitutional requirements. The procedure is judicially supervised, it must be based on reasonable and probable grounds and the authorizing judge must be satisfied that it is minimally intrusive. It cannot be forgotten that the testing can establish innocence as readily as guilt as the Guy-Paul Morin case so vividly demonstrates. It

seems to me that the requirement of justification is a reasonable safeguard which is necessary to control police powers to intrude upon the body. This is the approach I would favour.[119]

The DNA warrant scheme has been recognized as a tremendous benefit to the criminal justice system. It not only serves to assist law enforcement agencies in identifying persons who have committed crimes, but also serves to exclude persons who may be wrongly accused of committing crimes.[120]

When Bill C-104 was introduced to Parliament, both the Minister of Justice and the Solicitor General of Canada announced that legislation providing for a *National DNA Data Bank* would be addressed in a second legislative initiative.

National DNA Data Bank

In 1996 the Solicitor General launched the federal government's consultations on the second phase of its DNA initiative by releasing a consultation paper entitled "Establishing a National DNA Data Bank".[121] This was followed up by meetings in each province and territory between federal officials (Solicitor General, Royal Canadian Mounted Police, Department of Justice, and Correctional Services Canada) and provincial and territorial government officials, police services and their associations, corrections officials, victims groups, privacy officials, civil liberties, the legal community, national voluntary organizations, women's organizations, and medical and forensic science associations. The consultations concluded at the end of April 1996 and the results were later published.

Accordingly, on September 29, 1998, the House of Commons passed Bill C-3, S.C. 1998, c. 37, *An Act respecting DNA identification and to make consequential amendments to the Criminal Code and other acts* (short title: the *DNA Identification Act*).

In 1999, a DNA working group, composed of federal, provincial, and territorial prosecutors, recommended some practical changes to the *Criminal Code* provisions that had been enacted as part of the *DNA Identification Act* that would help make the legislation more effective. The federal government moved to implement these recommendations in Bill S-10 (*An Act to amend the National Defence Act, the DNA Identification Act and the Criminal Code*). The *DNA Identification Act* and the *Act to Amend the National Defence Act, the DNA Identification Act and the Criminal Code* were proclaimed on June 30, 2000. This legislation governs creating and operating the *National DNA Data Bank*, which is administered by the Commissioner of the RCMP and housed at the RCMP headquarters in Ottawa, Ontario. The data bank consists of DNA profiles contained in the *Convicted Offenders Index* and the *Crime Scene Index*.

The *Crime Scene Index* contains DNA profiles obtained from unsolved crime scenes. The *Convicted Offenders Index* contains the profiles of offenders convicted of certain designated offences. The data bank compares samples of DNA collected from crime scenes and/ or from offenders convicted of designated offences. Whenever a new DNA profile is added to the DNA data bank, the sample is cross-referenced with DNA profiles in the *Crime Scene Index* and the *Convicted Offenders Index*. If a match is found, contact is then made with investigators.

The DNA data bank is a powerful investigative tool and is of invaluable assistance in detecting and prosecuting certain designated offences. This legislation is an important government initiative with a laudable objective "of fostering effective crime control, protecting the innocent, enforcing society's criminal laws and substantially improving the search for the truth in the criminal trial process."[122]

The anticipated benefits of the *DNA data bank*, without limiting the foregoing, will include the following:

- exonerate the innocent;
- identify suspects sooner and thus enable the police to apprehend the suspect sooner and possibly prevent the commission of future acts of misconduct;
- link crime scenes where no suspect has been identified;
- eliminate suspects where there is no match between the crime scene and the data bank;
- determine whether or not a serial offender is involved;
- assist the police with matters committed by the same person in different jurisdictions; and
- act as a general deterrent.

In Canada, the *DNA data bank*, as of February 2, 2001, has already proven to be an extremely valuable public safety tool, linking several crime scenes and convicted offenders in its first seven months of operation. There are already 1,183 crime scene samples and 2,282 convicted offender samples in the data bank.[123]

Like Canada, other countries have embraced the notion that the *DNA data bank* has proven to be of invaluable assistance in pursuing the ends of criminal justice, such as discovering evidence that might either incriminate or establish the innocence of a person. For instance, the *DNA data bank* for England and Wales became operational in 1995 and is presently the largest in the world with almost 700,000 profiles. The samples in that data bank originate from persons arrested for certain offences, voluntary submissions, and samples obtained during "sweeps" (wherein all persons in the vicinity of a crime are tested). There were matches involving 100 cases in the first six months and in an 18-month period, it identified 46 murder, 175 rape and more than 19,000 burglary suspects. The number of matches grows as the number of samples in the data bank increases and it now averages 300/ 500 hits per week and has solved more than 51,000 crimes.[124]

In the United States, all 50 states have legislation to allow for *DNA data banks* and they have the option of participating in the American DNA Data Bank (CODIS). Within minutes of the American DNA Data Bank being operational, a rape and attempted murder in Wisconsin was matched to an offender. The number of matches grows as the number of samples in the CODIS Data Bank increases and, as of March 23, 2000, over 1,100 investigations have been assisted.[125]

In interpreting any section of the *Criminal Code*, or indeed of any statute, it is always crucial to begin by considering the section itself and the rationale underlying it. This accords with the contextual approach that has been adopted and applied in many of the Supreme Court of Canada's decisions. It follows that a proper understanding of the provision must begin with an examination of all relevant and admissible indicators of legislative meaning in an attempt to discern the sections purpose. The *DNA Identification Act* contains both a statement of purpose and a statement of principles that will, hopefully, provide the courts with an indication of the intent behind the legislation and, indeed, assist the court in its assessment of the constitutionality of measures chosen by Parliament to address certain issues.

Parliament has outlined its purpose in creating this new *DNA data bank* legislation in s. 3 of the Act:

> The purpose of this *Act* is to establish a national DNA data bank to help law enforcement agencies identify persons alleged to have committed designated offences, including those committed before the coming into force of this *Act*.

Furthermore, the principles guiding the legislation have been enumerated in s. 4 of the Act:

> It is recognized and declared that:

> (a) the protection of society and the administration of justice are well served by the early detection, arrest and conviction of offenders, which can be facilitated by the use of a DNA profiles;
> (b) the DNA profiles, as well as samples of bodily substances from which the profiles are derived, may be used only for law enforcement purposes in accordance with this *Act*, and not for any unauthorized purpose; and
> (c) to protect the privacy of individuals with respect to personal information about themselves, safeguards must be placed on
>> (i) the use and communication of, and access to, DNA profiles and other information contained in the national DNA data bank; and
>> (ii) the use of, and access to, bodily substances that are transmitted to the Commissioner for the purposes of this *Act*.

Section 4 of the Act clearly acknowledges and reinforces the importance of protecting the privacy of individuals in respect of the collection, use, and retention of DNA profiles, samples, and/ or any information in respect to a DNA profile. Access to information derived from a DNA profile, sample, or any information with respect to a DNA profile, is strictly limited to those responsible for the operation of the data bank. Any misuse or abuse of this information is a criminal offence, which may be prosecuted by indictment.

Young offenders are treated the same as adult offenders for the purposes of inclusion in the DNA data bank, and their DNA profile will be governed by the same rules of access for as long as it is retained in the DNA data bank. However, periods of retention for their profiles and samples parallel provisions for young offender's police records as contained in the *Youth Criminal Justice Act*.[126]

It is of significance that any and all orders made under the *DNA data bank* legislation are subject to judicial discretion. Under the legislation, the court can include any terms and conditions that they consider advisable to ensure that taking the samples is reasonable in the circumstances. Thus, the court has the opportunity to add further safeguards, if necessary.

The Privacy Commissioner provides independent oversight of the operation and ensures compliance with the *Privacy Act*.[127] Section 37 of the *Privacy Act* authorizes the Privacy Commissioner to carry out investigations in respect of personal information under the control of federal government institutions to ensure compliance with the provisions of the *Privacy Act*. The DNA data bank is subject to audit by the Privacy Commissioner.

Arguably, the new *DNA data bank* legislation improves on the

DNA warrant scheme contained in ss. 487.04 to 487.09 of the *Criminal Code*. The new *DNA data bank* legislation is less intrusive and requires, as a precondition, a conviction for a designated offence before application and, therefore, meets the reasonableness standard in striking a just and appropriate balance between individual and societal interests.

Forensic DNA typing evidence has been instrumental in securing convictions in many offences against the person, from assault to murder. It has also been instrumental in eliminating suspects and has led to the exoneration and release of previously convicted persons. Forensic DNA typing is conducted in many countries, including the United States, Great Britain, France, Germany, Australia, and New Zealand.

With the evolutionary advances in DNA technology, very little genetic material is required for DNA analysis. The provisions contained in s. 487.05 provide for the seizure of certain kinds of bodily substances for DNA analysis. For instance, hair plucked from any part of the body, epithelial cells, or a few drops of blood obtained by pricking the skin with a simple lancer will suffice for purposes of analysis.

DNA Warrant Conditions

The following preconditions must be met before a provincial court judge can issue a warrant to a peace officer or another person acting under the direction of a peace officer to obtain a bodily substance by means of special investigative procedures for DNA analysis. According to subs. 487.05(1), he/she must be satisfied by written *Information* on oath that there are reasonable grounds to believe:

(a) that a designated offence has been committed;
(b) that a bodily substance has been found
    (i) at the place where the offence was committed,
    (ii) on or within the body of the victim of the offence,
    (iii) on anything worn or carried by the victim at the time when the offence was committed, or
    (iv) on or within the body of any person or thing or at any place associated with the commission of the offence;
(c) that the suspect was a party to the designated offence;
(d) that forensic DNA analysis of a bodily substance from the suspect will provide evidence of whether the bodily substance, as referred to in paragraph (2) was from that person; and
(e) that it is in the best interests of the administration of justice to issue the warrant.

It is important to note that the provincial court judge, in considering whether to issue the warrant, must have regard to all the relevant matters (as per subs. 487.05(2)), including:

> (a) the nature of the designated offence and the circumstances of its commission, and
> (b) whether there is
>> (i) a peace officer or another person who is able, by virtue of training or experience, to obtain a bodily substances from the person, by means of the investigative procedures described in subsection 487.06(1) ...

The warrant authorizes only three investigative procedures for the collection of bodily substances from a suspect by means of (as per subs. 487.06(1)):

> (a) the plucking of individual hairs from the person, including the root sheath;
> (b) the taking of buccal swabs by swabbing the lips, tongue and inside cheeks of the mouth to collect epithelial cells; or
> (c) the taking of blood by pricking the skin surface with a sterile lancet.

Execution of the DNA Warrant

The peace officer, or another person acting under the direction of the officer executing the DNA warrant, must ensure that the privacy of the suspect is respected in a manner which is reasonable in the circumstances (subs. 487.07(3)). The provincial court judge has the discretion to include terms and conditions in the warrant to ensure that the seizure of the bodily substance is carried out in a reasonable manner (subs. 487.06(2)).

Before executing a DNA warrant, the police officer must inform the suspect of the following (as per subs. 487.07(1)):

> (a) the contents of the warrant;
> (b) the nature of the investigative procedure by means of which a bodily substance is to be obtained from that person;
> (c) the purpose of obtaining a bodily substance from that person;
> (d) the possibility that the results of forensic DNA analysis may be used in evidence;
> (e) the authority of the peace officer and any other person under the direction of the peace officer to use as much force as is necessary for the purpose of executing the warrant; and
> (f) in the case of a young person, the rights of the young person under subsection (4).

Further, a person against whom a warrant is executed must be informed that he or she (as per subs. 487.07(2)):

> (a) may be detained for the purpose of executing the warrant for a period that is reasonable in the circumstances for the purpose of obtaining a bodily substance from the person; and
> (b) may be required by the peace officer who executes the warrant to accompany the peace officer.

It is important to note that a young person against whom a warrant is executed has, in addition to any other rights arising from his or her detention under the DNA warrant, the following rights (as per subs. 487.07(4)):

> (a) the right to a reasonable opportunity to consult with, and
> (b) the right to have the warrant executed in the presence of counsel and a parent or, in the absence of a parent, an adult relative or, in the absence of a parent and an adult relative, any other appropriate adult chosen by the young person.

If a young person wishes to waive these above-noted additional rights, then they must do so in one of the following ways (as per subs. 487.07(5)):

1. by a recording on audiotape or videotape or otherwise of his or her desire to waive the additonal rights; or
2. provide a written statement signed by the young person that he or she has been informed of the right being waived.

It should be noted that a peace officer is entitled to use as much force as is necessary to execute the warrant (para. 487.07(1)(e)).

Limitations on Use of Bodily Substances

There are provisions in s. 487 that limit the use that can be made of the bodily substances and the results of the forensic DNA analysis. The bodily substances and the results of the forensic DNA analysis can only be used in the course of investigating the designated offences or in judicial proceedings for such offences (subs. 487.08(1) and (2)). In addition, subs. 487.08(3) provides a criminal offence for persons who contravene this limitation.

Destruction of Bodily Substances

Subsection 487.09(1) provides that a bodily substance that is obtained from a suspect in the execution of a warrant and the results of forensic DNA analysis must be destroyed forthwith after any of the following occurrences:

> (a) the results of that analysis establish that the bodily substance referred to in paragraph 487.05(1)(b) was not from that person;
> (b) the person is finally acquitted of the designated offence and any other offence in respect of the same transaction; or
> (c) the expiration of one year after
>> (i) the person is discharged after a preliminary inquiry into the designated offence or any other offence in respect of the same transaction,
>> (ii) the dismissal, for any reason other than acquittal, or the withdrawal of any information charging the person with the designated offence or any other offence in respect of the same transaction, or
>> (iii) any proceeding against the person for the offence or any other offence in respect of the same transaction is stayed . . .
>
> unless during that year a new Information is laid or an indictment is preferred charging the [suspect] with the designated offence or any other offence in respect of the same transaction or the proceeding is recommenced.

Notwithstanding the above, the judge has the discretion to order that a bodily substance that is obtained from a person and the results of forensic DNA analysis not be destroyed during any period that the judge considers appropriate, if the judge is satisfied that the bodily substance, or its results, might reasonably be required in an investigation or prosecution of the accused (suspect) for another designated offence or of another person for the designated offence or any other offence in respect of the same transaction (subs. 487.09(1)). It should also be noted that a DNA warrant can be used in the investigation of any of the designated offences committed prior to the coming into force of the enactment.

At the same time Parliament passed the DNA warrant regime, they also granted courts the power to authorize police to take the bodily impressions of a person if the police had reasonable grounds to do so.

Search of Lawyers' Offices

There has been an observable trend in Canada and the United States toward more aggressive investigatory methods, which include issuing warrants to search law offices for evidence of crime.[128] Thus, the courts have expressed serious concerns about the dangers of law office searches in light of solicitor-client privilege and have urged Parliament to create protective measures.[129] Accordingly, the issuing Justice is obligated to protect solicitor-client privilege through the application of the following principles that are related to the issuance of search warrants:

- No search warrant can be issued with regard to documents that are known to be protected by solicitor-client privilege.
- Before searching a law office, the investigative authorities must satisfy the issuing justice that there exists no other reasonable alternative to the search.
- When allowing a law office to be searched, the issuing justice must be rigorously demanding so as to afford maximum protection of solicitor-client confidentiality.
- Except when the warrant specifically authorizes the immediate examination, copying and seizure of an identified document, all documents in possession of a lawyer must be sealed before being examined or removed from the lawyer's possession.
- Every effort must be made to contact the lawyer and the client at the time of the search warrant's execution. Where the lawyer or the client cannot be contacted, a representative of the Bar should be allowed to oversee the sealing and seizing of documents.
- The investigative officer executing the warrant should report to the justice of the peace the efforts made to contact all potential privilege holders, who should then be given a reasonable opportunity to assert a claim of privilege and, if that claim is contested, to have the issues judicially decided.
- If notifying potential privilege holders is not possible, the lawyer who had custody of the documents seized, or another lawyer appointed either by the Law Society or by the court, should examine the documents to determine whether a claim of privilege should be asserted, and should be given a reasonable opportunity to do so.
- The Attorney General may make submissions on the issue of privilege, but should not be permitted to inspect the documents beforehand. The prosecuting authority can only inspect the documents if and when it is determined by a judge that the documents are not privileged.
- Where sealed documents are found not to be privileged, they may be used in the normal course of the investigation.
- Where documents are found to be privileged, they are to be re-

turned immediately to the holder of the privilege, or to a person designated by the court.[130]

Production Orders

In 2004 Parliament enacted new Criminal Code provisions which create new investigative powers. Sections 487.011 to 487.017 create two new avenues for law enforcement officers to obtain prior judicial authorization to gather information and/ or evidence. These new provisions create a *Production Order*, which is an order that a judge can make compelling a person who is *not* under investigation to produce documents or data relevant to the commission of a crime. Failure to comply with a production order is an offence punishable by a fine or imprisonment of not more than six months, or both. In 2009 Parliament had first reading of an Act to amend Production orders which would expand police use of this form of judicial authorization, especially in relation to electronic information like internet accounts and IP address holders. Production Orders may see expansion from Parliament.

Detention of Seized Items

Subsection 489.1(1)(a) imposes a duty upon a peace officer to return, *as soon as practicable*, seized articles to the person lawfully entitled to its possession where the officer is satisfied:

> (i) that there is no dispute as to who is lawfully entitled to possession of the thing seized, and
> (ii) that the continued detention of the thing seized is not required for the purposes of any investigation or a preliminary inquiry, trial or other proceeding ...

The peace officer must obtain a receipt for any articles returned and file a report to the justice who issued the warrant or some other justice for the same territorial division who has jurisdiction. Where the peace officer is not satisfied that either of the above conditions are met, the peace officer must bring the seized articles to a justice having jurisdiction or report to the justice that the articles seized are being detained to be dealt with by the justice as in accordance with subs. 490(1). Where a person other than a peace officer has seized anything under a warrant, that person shall, as soon as practicable, bring the thing seized before a justice. Articles seized by non-peace officers may not be summarily returned.

Subsection 490(1) provides that a justice must return the articles seized to the person lawfully entitled to their possession *unless* the Crown satisfies the justice that detaining the articles is required for the purposes of any investigation or a preliminary inquiry, trial or other proceeding. If the justice is satisfied that the articles seized are required for the purposes of any investigation or a preliminary inquiry, trial, or other proceeding, the justice must order the detention of the seized articles, making sure that the seized articles are properly preserved until the conclusion of the investigation or legal proceedings.

This power should not confused with certain provincial legislation which allows provinces to seize proceeds or instruments of crime termed civil forfeiture even if there is no criminal conviction. The civil forfeiture proceedings use the balance of probabilities and not proof beyond reasonable doubt.

Specific Powers of Search and Seizure

In addition to the general powers of search and seizure prescribed in the *Criminal Code*, the *Criminal Code* also contains specific powers of search and seizure in relation to certain offences, which include the following:

- s. 117.04—Weapons, Firearms, Ammunition or Explosive Substance;
- s. 164—Crime Comics, Obscene Publications, or Child Pornography;
- subs. 199(1)—Gaming and Betting, Pool-Selling, Book-making, Lotteries, Keeping Common Bawdy-Houses;
- s. 320—Hate Propaganda;
- s. 395—Valuable Minerals; and
- s. 462.32—Proceeds of Crime.
- s. 492.1—tracking warrant
- s. 492.2—number recorder warrant (phone records)

Search and Seizure in Drug Offences

The primary source of search and seizure power in respect to offences involving drugs is the *Controlled Drugs and Substances Act*,[131] which creates a scheme for regulating certain dangerous drugs and narcotics, known as *controlled substances*.

The provisions of the *Controlled Drugs and Substances Act* which deal with search and seizure are as follows:

11. (1) A justice who, on *ex parte* application, is satisfied by information on oath that there are reasonable grounds to believe that

  (a) a controlled substance or precursor in respect of which this Act has been contravened,

  (b) any thing in which a controlled substance or precursor referred to in paragraph (a) is contained or concealed,

  (c) offence-related property, or

  (d) any thing that will afford evidence in respect of an offence under this Act

is in a place may, at any time, issue a warrant authorizing a peace officer, at any time, to search the place for any such controlled substance, precursor, property or thing and to seize it.

(2) For the purposes of subsection (1), an information may be submitted by telephone or other means of telecommunication in accordance with section 487.1 of the *Criminal Code*, with such modifications as the circumstances require.

(3) A justice may, where a place referred to in subsection (1) is in a province other than that in which the justice has jurisdiction, issue the warrant referred to in that subsection and the warrant may be executed in the other province after it has been endorsed by a justice having jurisdiction in that other province.

(4) An endorsement that is made on a warrant as provided for in subsection (3) is sufficient authority to any peace officer to whom it was originally directed and to all peace officers within the jurisdiction of the justice by whom it is endorsed to execute the warrant and to deal with the things seized in accordance with the law.

(5) Where a peace officer who executes a warrant issued under subsection (1) has reasonable grounds to believe that any person found in the place set out in the warrant has on their person any controlled substance, precursor, property or thing set out in the warrant, the peace officer may search the person for the controlled substance, precursor, property or thing and seize it.

(6) A peace officer who executes a warrant issued under subsection (1) may seize, in addition to the things mentioned in the warrant,

  (a) any controlled substance or precursor in respect of which the peace officer believes on reasonable grounds that this Act has been contravened;

  (b) any thing that the peace officer believes on reasonable grounds to contain or conceal a controlled substance or precursor referred to in paragraph (a);

  (c) any thing that the peace officer believes on reasonable grounds is offence-related property; or

(d) any thing that the peace officer believes on reasonable grounds will afford evidence in respect of an offence under this Act.

(7) A peace officer may exercise any of the powers described in subsection (1), (5) or (6) without a warrant if the conditions for obtaining a warrant exist but by reason of exigent circumstances it would be impracticable to obtain one.

(8) A peace officer who executes a warrant issued under subsection (1) or exercises powers under subsection (5) or (7) may seize, in addition to the things mentioned in the warrant and in subsection (6), any thing that the peace officer believes on reasonable grounds has been obtained by or used in the commission of an offence or that will afford evidence in respect of an offence.

12. For the purpose of exercising any of the powers described in section 11, a peace officer may
      (a) enlist such assistance as the officer deems necessary; and
      (b) use as much force as is necessary in the circumstances.

Section 487, conventional *Criminal Code* warrants, can also be used for any drug search. However, as can be seen, the above-noted provisions of the *Controlled Drugs and Substances Act* provides broader powers of search and seizure to peace officers than those contained in s. 487 of the *Criminal Code* in at least four ways. First, s. 12 of the *Controlled Drugs and Substances Act* authorizes the use of as much force as is necessary in the circumstances in executing a warrant; s. 487 of the *Criminal Code* does not have any such provision. Second, a *Controlled Drugs and Substances Act* may authorize a peace officer to search *any time.* There is no need to justify night entry as there is for a *Criminal Code* warrant. Third, a peace officer executing a search warrant under the *Controlled Drugs and Substances Act* may search any person found in the place he or she is searching. A peace officer executing a *Criminal Code* search warrant may only keep persons present under reasonable surveillance. Fourth, in executing a *Controlled Drugs and Substances Act* search warrant, a peace officer is permitted to enlist such assistance as he or she deems necessary. The *Criminal Code* warrant requires civilians assisting to be named.

It should be noted that much of what has been discussed above regarding the law surrounding search and seizure is also applicable to the *Controlled Drugs and Substance Act.*

Notes

[1] Part I of the *Constitutional Act*, 1982, being Schedule B to the Canada Act, 1982 (U.K.). c. 11 (hereinafter the *Charter*).

[2] *Canada (Director of Investigation & Research, Combines Investigation Branch) v. Southam Inc.*, 1984 CarswellAlta 121, 1984 CarswellAlta 415, 33 Alta. L.R. (2d) 193, 27 B.L.R. 297, 41 C.R. (3d) 97, 84 D.T.C. 6467, (sub nom. *Hunter v. Southam Inc.*) 14 C.C.C. (3d) 97, (sub nom. *Hunter v. Southam Inc.*) 11 D.L.R. (4th) 641, (sub nom. *Hunter v. Southam Inc.*) 55 A.R. 291, (sub nom. *Director of Investigations & Research Combines Investigation Branch v. Southam Inc.*) [1984] 6 W.W.R. 577, (sub nom. *Hunter v. Southam Inc.*) [1984] 2 S.C.R. 145, (sub nom. *Hunter v. Southam Inc.*) 55 N.R. 241, (sub nom. *Hunter v. Southam Inc.*) 2 C.P.R. (3d) 1, (sub nom. *Hunter v. Southam Inc.*) 9 C.R.R. 355 (S.C.C.), at 106 [C.C.C.].

[3] *R. v. Wray*, 1970 CarswellOnt 22, 1970 CarswellOnt 207F, [1971] S.C.R. 272, [1970] 4 C.C.C. 1, 11 C.R.N.S. 235, 11 D.L.R. (3d) 673 (S.C.C.).

[4] *Ibid.*

[5] *Ibid.*

[6] *Canada (Director of Investigation & Research, Combines Investigation Branch) v. Southam Inc., supra*, note 2, at 108 [C.C.C.].

[7] *R. v. Colarusso*, 1994 CarswellOnt 50, 1994 CarswellOnt 1149, 87 C.C.C. (3d) 193, 49 M.V.R. (2d) 161, 69 O.A.C. 81, 110 D.L.R. (4th) 297, 19 C.R.R. (2d) 193, 162 N.R. 321, 26 C.R. (4th) 289, [1994] 1 S.C.R. 20 (S.C.C.), at 215 [C.C.C.].

[8] *R. v. Tessling*, 2004 CarswellOnt 4351, 2004 CarswellOnt 4352, REJB 2004-72161, 326 N.R. 228 (Eng.), 326 N.R. 228 (Fr.), 192 O.A.C. 168, [2004] 3 S.C.R. 432, 2004 SCC 67, 189 C.C.C. (3d) 129, 244 D.L.R. (4th) 541, 75 O.R. (3d) 480 (note), 23 C.R. (6th) 207, 123 C.R.R. (2d) 257 (S.C.C.).

[9] *R. v. Edwards*, 1996 CarswellOnt 1916, 1996 CarswellOnt 2126, 104 C.C.C. (3d) 136, 45 C.R. (4th) 307, 192 N.R. 81, 26 O.R. (3d) 736, 132 D.L.R. (4th) 31, 33 C.R.R. (2d) 226, 88 O.A.C. 321, [1996] 1 S.C.R. 128 (S.C.C.), at 150 [C.C.C.].

[10] *R. v. Collins*, 1987 CarswellBC 94, 1987 CarswellBC 699, 3 C.C.C. (3d) 1, 56 C.R. (3d) 193, [1987] 3 W.W.R. 699, [1987] 1 S.C.R. 265, 38 D.L.R. (4th) 508, 74 N.R. 276, 13 B.C.L.R. (2d) 1, 328 C.R.R. 122 (S.C.C.), at 14 [C.C.C.].

[11] *Ibid.*

[12] *Ibid.*

[13] *R. v. Grant*, 2009 CarswellOnt 4104, 2009 CarswellOnt 4105, 2009 SCC 32, 245 C.C.C. (3d) 1, 66 C.R. (6th) 1, 253 O.A.C. 124, 82 M.V.R. (5th) 1, [2009] 2 S.C.R. 353, 391 N.R. 1, 309 D.L.R. (4th) 1 (S.C.C.).

[14] *Canada (Director of Investigation & Research, Combines Investigation Branch) v. Southam Inc., supra*, note 2.

[15] *Canada (Director of Investigation & Research, Combines Investigation Branch) v. Southam Inc., supra*, note 2.

[16] *Cloutier c. Langlois*, 1990 CarswellQue 8, 1990 CarswellQue 110, 53 C.C.C. (3d) 257, 74 C.R. (3d) 316, [1990] 1 S.C.R. 158, 105 N.R. 241, 46 C.R.R. 37, 30 Q.A.C. 241 (S.C.C.).

[17] *R. v. Debot*, 1989 CarswellOnt 111, 1989 CarswellOnt 966, 52 C.C.C. (3d) 193, 73 C.R. (3d) 129, [1989] 2 S.C.R. 1140, 102 N.R. 161, 37 O.A.C. 1, 45 C.R.R. 49 (S.C.C.).

[18] *Cloutier c. Langlois, supra*, note 16, at 278 [C.C.C.].

[19] *R. v. Caslake*, 1998 CarswellMan 1, 1998 CarswellMan 2, 121 C.C.C. (3d) 97, 13

C.R. (5th) 1, 48 C.R.R. (2d) 189, [1998] 1 S.C.R. 51, 123 Man. R. (2d) 208, 159 W.A.C. 208, [1999] 4 W.W.R. 303, 155 D.L.R. (4th) 19, 221 N.R. 281 (S.C.C.), at 115 [C.C.C.].

20 *R. v. Stillman*, 1997 CarswellNB 107, 1997 CarswellNB 108, 113 C.C.C. (3d) 321, [1997] 1 S.C.R. 607, 42 C.R.R. (2d) 189, 144 D.L.R. (4th) 193, 5 C.R. (5th) 1, 185 N.B.R. (2d) 1, 472 A.P.R. 1, 209 N.R. 81 (S.C.C.).

21 *R. v. Feeney*, 1997 CarswellBC 1015, 1997 CarswellBC 1016, 115 C.C.C. (3d) 129, 7 C.R. (5th) 101, 212 N.R. 83, [1997] 2 S.C.R. 13, [1997] 6 W.W.R. 634, 146 D.L.R. (4th) 609, 91 B.C.A.C. 1, 148 W.A.C. 1, 44 C.R.R. (2d) 1 (S.C.C.), reconsideration granted 1997 CarswellBC 3179, 1997 CarswellBC 3180, [1997] 2 S.C.R. 117 (S.C.C.).

22 *R. v. Golden*, 2001 CarswellOnt 4301, 2001 CarswellOnt 4253, 2001 SCC 83, 207 D.L.R. (4th) 18, 159 C.C.C. (3d) 449, 47 C.R. (5th) 1, 279 N.R. 1, [2001] 3 S.C.R. 679, 153 O.A.C. 201, 89 C.R.R. (2d) 271 (S.C.C.).

23 *Ibid.*, at 490 [C.C.C.].

24 *R. v. Caslake, supra*, note 19, at para. 17

25 *Canada (Director of Investigation & Research, Combines Investigation Branch) v. Southam Inc., supra*, note 2.

26 *R. v. Golden, supra*, note 22, at para. 89.

27 *Ibid.*.

28 *Ibid.*, at para. 102.

29 *R. v. D. (I.D.)*, 1987 CarswellSask 394, 38 C.C.C. (3d) 289, 61 C.R. (3d) 292, [1988] 1 W.W.R. 673, 60 Sask. R. 72, 33 C.R.R. 348 (C.A.).

30 *Ibid.*

31 *Ibid.*, at para. 37.

32 *R. v. Guberman*, 1985 CarswellMan 226, 23 C.C.C. (3d) 406, [1986] 2 W.W.R. 356, 37 Man. R. (2d) 219 (Man. C.A.).

33 *R. v. Simmons*, 1988 CarswellOnt 91, 1988 CarswellOnt 968, [1988] 2 S.C.R. 495, 45 C.C.C. (3d) 296, 66 C.R. (3d) 297, 67 O.R. (2d) 63, 18 C.E.R. 227, 55 D.L.R. (4th) 673, 89 N.R. 1, 30 O.A.C. 241, 38 C.R.R. 252, 2 T.C.T. 4102 (S.C.C.), at para. 31.

34 *R. v. Mann*, 2004 CarswellMan 303, 2004 CarswellMan 304, 2004 SCC 52, 185 C.C.C. (3d) 308, 21 C.R. (6th) 1, 241 D.L.R. (4th) 214, 122 C.R.R. (2d) 189, 324 N.R. 215, [2004] 3 S.C.R. 59, [2004] 11 W.W.R. 601, 187 Man. R. (2d) 1, 330 W.A.C. 1 (S.C.C.).

35 *R. v. Ferris*, 1998 CarswellBC 1300, 126 C.C.C. (3d) 298, 16 C.R. (5th) 287, 54 C.R.R. (2d) 62, 162 D.L.R. (4th) 87, 50 B.C.L.R. (3d) 109, [1998] 9 W.W.R. 14, 108 B.C.A.C. 244, 176 W.A.C. 244 (C.A.), leave to appeal refused (1998), 129 C.C.C. (3d) vi (S.C.C.).

36 *R. v. Mann, supra*, note 34, at para. 45.

37 *Ibid.*, at para. 45.

38 *Ibid.*

39 *R. v. Suberu*, 2009 CarswellOnt 4106, 2009 CarswellOnt 4107, 2009 SCC 33, 245 C.C.C. (3d) 112, 66 C.R. (6th) 127, 390 N.R. 303, 97 O.R. (3d) 480 (note), [2009] 2 S.C.R. 460, 309 D.L.R. (4th) 114, 252 O.A.C. 340 (S.C.C.).

40 See Black's Law Dictionary, 5th ed. (West: St. Paul, Minn., 1979), at 1036.

41 *R. v. Nielson*, 1988 CarswellSask 304, 39 C.R.R. 147, (sub nom. *R. v. Nielsen*) 43

C.C.C. (3d) 548, (sub nom. *R. v. Nielsen*) 66 Sask. R. 293, (sub nom. *R. v. Nielsen*) [1988] 6 W.W.R. 1 (Sask. C.A.).

[42] *R. v. Sanchez-Ruiz*, 1991 CarswellNB 20, 121 N.B.R. (2d) 106, 304 A.P.R. 106, (sub nom. *R. v. Ruiz*) 68 C.C.C. (3d) 500, (sub nom. *R. v. Ruiz*) 10 C.R. (4th) 34 (N.B. C.A.), at 509 [C.C.C.], affirmed 1993 CarswellNB 6, 1993 CarswellNB 153, 25 C.R. (4th) 407, 139 N.B.R. (2d) 241, 357 A.P.R. 241, 158 N.R. 315, (sub nom. *R. v. Ruiz*) [1993] 3 S.C.R. 649 (S.C.C.).

[43] *Ibid.*

[44] *R. v. Dyment*, CarswellPEI 7, 1988 CarswellPEI 73, 45 C.C.C. (3d) 244, 66 C.R. (3d) 348, 10 M.V.R. (2d) 1, 89 N.R. 249, [1988] 2 S.C.R. 417, 73 Nfld. & P.E.I.R. 13, 229 A.P.R. 13, 55 D.L.R. (4th) 503, 38 C.R.R. 301 (S.C.C.).

[45] *R. v. Wills*, 1992 CarswellOnt 77, 70 C.C.C. (3d) 529, 12 C.R. (4th) 58, 34 M.V.R. (2d) 296, 9 C.R.R. (2d) 360, 7 O.R. (3d) 337, 52 O.A.C. 321 (C.A.), at para. 69.

[46] *R. v. Kenny*, 1992 CarswellOnt 73, 11 C.R. (4th) 325, (sub nom. *R. v. Mercer*) 70 C.C.C. (3d) 180, (sub nom. *R. v. Mercer*) 52 O.A.C. 70, (sub nom. *R. v. Mercer*) 7 O.R. (3d) 9 (Ont. C.A.), leave to appeal refused (1992), (sub nom. *R. v. Mercer*) 74 C.C.C. (3d) vi (S.C.C.).

[47] *R. v. M. (M.R.)*, 1998 CarswellNS 346, 1998 CarswellNS 347, 129 C.C.C. (3d) 361, 20 C.R. (5th) 197, 171 N.S.R. (2d) 125, 519 A.P.R. 125, [1998] 3 S.C.R. 393, 57 C.R.R. (2d) 189, 5 B.H.R.C. 474, 233 N.R. 1, 166 D.L.R. (4th) 261 (S.C.C.).

[48] *Ibid.*

[49] *Ibid.*

[50] *Ibid.*, at paras. 48-50.

[51] *Ibid.*

[52] *R. v. Brown*, 2008 CarswellAlta 523, 2008 CarswellAlta 524, 2008 SCC 18, [2008] 6 W.W.R. 17, 55 C.R. (6th) 240, 87 Alta. L.R. (4th) 1, (sub nom. *R v. Kang-Brown*) 230 C.C.C. (3d) 289, (sub nom. *R. v. Kang-Brown*) 293 D.L.R. (4th) 99, (sub nom. *R. v. Kang-Brown*) [2008] 1 S.C.R. 456, (sub nom. *R v. Kang-Brown (G.)*) 373 N.R. 67, (sub nom. *R. v. Kang-Brown*) 432 A.R. 1, (sub nom. *R. v. Kang-Brown*) 424 W.A.C. 1 (S.C.C.).

[53] *R. v. Feeney*, supra, note 21.

[54] *R. v. Grenkow*, 1994 CarswellNS 284, 95 C.C.C. (3d) 255, 136 N.S.R. (2d) 264, 388 A.P.R. 264 (N.S. C.A.), leave to appeal refused (1995), 97 C.C.C. (3d) vi (note) (S.C.C.).

[55] *R. v. McComber*, 1988 CarswellOnt 87, 4 C.C.C. (3d) 241, 66 C.R. (3d) 142, 29 O.A.C. 311, 49 M.V.R. (2d) 97 (Ont. C.A.).

[56] *R. c. Murray*, 1999 CarswellQue 1048, 136 C.C.C. (3d) 197, 1 M.V.R. (4th) 24, 32 C.R. (5th) 253 (Que. C.A.); *R. v. Clayton*, 2007 CarswellOnt 4268, 2007 CarswellOnt 4269, 2007 SCC 32, 220 C.C.C. (3d) 449, 364 N.R. 199, 281 D.L.R. (4th) 1, 47 C.R. (6th) 219, 158 C.R.R. (2d) 81, 227 O.A.C. 314, [2007] 2 S.C.R. 725 (S.C.C.).

[57] *R. v. Krist*, 1995 CarswellBC 650, 100 C.C.C. (3d) 58, 42 C.R. (4th) 159, 62 B.C.A.C. 133, 103 W.A.C. 133, 31 C.R.R. (2d) 3511 (B.C. C.A.).

[58] *R. v. Patrick*, 2009 CarswellAlta 481, 2009 CarswellAlta 482, 2009 SCC 17, 242 C.C.C. (3d) 158, 304 D.L.R. (4th) 260, 4 Alta. L.R. (5th) 1, 387 N.R. 44, 454 A.R. 1, [2009] 1 S.C.R. 579, [2009] 5 W.W.R. 387, 64 C.R. (6th) 1 (S.C.C.).

[59] *Canada (Director of Investigation & Research, Combines Investigation Branch) v. Southam Inc.*, supra, note 2.

[60] J.A. Fontana, *The Law of Search and Seizure in Canada*, 3rd ed. (Markham: Butterworths, 1992).

[61] *Criminal Law Amendment Act*, S.C. 1985, c. 19, s. 69.

[62] *MacIntyre v. Nova Scotia (Attorney General)*, (1982 CarswellNS 21, 1982 CarswellNS 110, 26 C.R. (3d) 193, [1982] 1 S.C.R. 175, 49 N.S.R. (2d) 609, 40 N.R. 181, 96 A.P.R. 609, 132 D.L.R. (3d) 385, (sub nom. *Nova Scotia (Attorney General) v. MacIntyre*) 65 C.C.C. (2d) 129 (S.C.C.), at 141 [C.C.C.].

[63] *Ibid.*

[64] *Canada (Director of Investigation & Research, Combines Investigation Branch) v. Southam Inc., supra*, note 2.

[65] *Sieger v. Barker*, 1982 CarswellBC 37, 27 C.R. (3d) 91, 34 B.C.L.R. 354, (sub nom. *Sieger v. R.*) 65 C.C.C. (2d) 449 (B.C. S.C.), at 452 [C.C.C.].

[66] *R. v. Carroll*, 1989 CarswellNS 429, 88 N.S.R. (2d) 165, 47 C.C.C. (3d) 263, 42 C.R.R. 339, 225 A.P.R. 165 (N.S. C.A.).

[67] *R. v. Church of Scientology*, 1985 CarswellOnt 1652, 21 C.C.C. (3d) 147, 15 C.R.R. 23 (Ont. H.C.), affirmed, 1987 CarswellOnt 1401, (sub nom. *Church of Scientology v. R. (No. 6)*) 31 C.C.C. (3d) 449, 30 C.R.R. 238, 18 O.A.C. 321 (Ont. C.A.), leave to appeal refused [1987] 1 S.C.R. vii.

[68] *R. v. Haley*, 1995 CarswellNS 135, 142 N.S.R. (2d) 107, 407 A.P.R. 107 (N.S. C.A.).

[69] *R. v. Yorke*, 1992 CarswellNS 433, 77 C.C.C. (3d) 529, 115 N.S.R. (2d) 426, 314 A.P.R. 426 (C.A.), affirmed 1993 CarswellNS 440, 1993 CarswellNS 273, 84 C.C.C. (3d) 286 (note), [1993] 3 S.C.R. 647, 158 N.R. 396, 125 N.S.R. (2d) 238, 349 A.P.R. 238 (S.C.C.).

[70] *Supra*, note 60, at 85.

[71] *Criminal Code*, s. 489.

[72] *R. v. Coull*, 1986 CarswellBC 681, 33 C.C.C. (3d) 186 (B.C. C.A.).

[73] *R. v. Jamieson*, 1989 CarswellNS 293, 48 C.C.C. (3d) 287, 90 N.S.R. (2d) 164, 230 A.P.R. 164 (N.S. C.A.).

[74] *Baron v. R.*, 1993 CarswellNat 845, 1993 CarswellNat 1375, EYB 1993-67286, [1993] S.C.J. No. 6, 18 C.R. (4th) 374, 93 D.T.C. 5018, (sub nom. *Baron v. Canada*) [1993] 1 S.C.R. 416, (sub nom. *Baron v. Canada*) [1993] 1 C.T.C. 111, (sub nom. *Baron v. Canada*) 78 C.C.C. (3d) 510, (sub nom. *Baron v. Canada*) 13 C.R.R. (2d) 65, (sub nom. *Baron v. Minister of National Revenue*) 146 N.R. 270, (sub nom. *Baron v. Canada*) 99 D.L.R. (4th) 350 (S.C.C.).

[75] *Eccles v. Bourque*, 1974 CarswellBC 414, 1974 CarswellBC 354, 19 C.C.C. (2d) 129, 27 C.R.N.S. 325, [1975] 2 S.C.R. 739, [1975] 1 W.W.R. 609, 50 D.L.R. (3d) 753, 3 N.R. 259 (S.C.C.), at para. 9.

[76] *Levitz v. Ryan*, 1972 CarswellOnt 915, 9 C.C.C. (2d) 182, [1972] 3 O.R. 783, 29 D.L.R. (3d) 519 (Ont. C.A.).

[77] See: Renee M. Pomerance's article entitled "Entry and Arrest in Dwelling Houses" (1998), 13 C.R. (5th) 84.

[78] *Ibid.*

[79] *Ibid.*

[80] *R. v. Feeney, supra*, note 21.

[81] *R. v. Macooh*, 1993 CarswellAlta 411, 1993 CarswellAlta 563, 82 C.C.C. (3d) 481, 22 C.R. (4th) 70, 16 C.R.R. (2d) 1, 105 D.L.R. (4th) 96, 141 A.R. 321, 46 W.A.C. 321, [1993] 2 S.C.R. 802, 155 N.R. 44 (S.C.C.).

82 *R. v. Godoy*, 1998 CarswellOnt 5223, 1998 CarswellOnt 5224, 131 C.C.C. (3d) 129, 21 C.R. (5th) 205, 235 N.R. 134, 117 O.A.C. 127, 168 D.L.R. (4th) 257, [1999] 1 S.C.R. 311 (S.C.C.).

83 *R. v. Rao*, 1984 CarswellOnt 53, 12 C.C.C. (3d) 97, 40 C.R. (3d) 1, 46 O.R. (2d) 80, 9 D.L.R. (4th) 542, 4 O.A.C. 162, 10 C.R.R. 275 (C.A.), leave to appeal refused (1984), 40 C.R. (3d) xxvi (S.C.C.).

84 *R. v. Mutch*, 1986 CarswellSask 413, 26 C.C.C. (3d) 477, 47 Sask. R. 122, 22 C.R.R. 310 (Q.B.).

85 *Ibid.*

86 *R. v. Simmons, supra*, note 33, at para. 52.

87 *Ibid.*, at para. 53.

88 *R. v. Wong*, 1990 CarswellOnt 58, 1990 CarswellOnt 1008, 60 C.C.C. (3d) 460, 1 C.R. (4th) 1, 120 N.R. 34, [1990] 3 S.C.R. 36, 2 C.R.R. (2d) 277, 45 O.A.C. 250 (S.C.C.).

89 For the purposes of this chapter and for the sake of clarity, the s. 487.01 warrant will be referred to hereinafter as a *general investigative warrant*; whereas the s. 487 warrant will be referred to hereinafter as an *ordinary warrant*.

90 See F.P. Hoskins and M.A. Murphy, *General Investigation Warrants*, prepared for the OCAA Search and Seizure Course, London, Ontario (August 2002).

91 *R. v. Kuitenen*, 2001 CarswellBC 1582, 2001 BCSC 677, 45 C.R. (5th) 131, 85 C.R.R. (2d) 95 (S.C.), at para. 20.

92 *R. v. Noseworthy*, 1997 CarswellOnt 1712, 116 C.C.C. (3d) 376, 43 C.R.R. (2d) 313, 100 O.A.C. 76, 33 O.R. (3d) 641 (Ont. C.A.), at para. 11.

93 *R. v. Soldat*, 1995 CarswellNWT 29, [1995] N.W.T.R. 349 (N.W.T. S.C.).

94 *Saskatchewan v. Silver Lake Farms Inc.*, 2000 CarswellSask 61, 2000 SKCA 11, (sub nom. *R. v. Silver Lake Farms Inc.*) [2000] S.J. No. 54 (Sask. C.A.), wherein Halderman J. stated, at para. 9 that:

> Because of these more complex factual and legal aspects of the General Warrant, Parliament apparently concluded that only Provincial Court or Superior Court Judges would have jurisdiction to authorize General Warrants and DNA warrants.

95 *Criminal Code*, s. 487.01.

96 See *R. v. Noseworthy, supra*, note 92. In this case, the police sought and obtained a *general investigative warrant* to seize items that at the time of issuance were in police possession. The items in question had been seized under the authority of an *ordinary warrant*. Because of shortcomings in the issuance and execution of the first warrant, the Crown had agreed to have the warrant quashed but applied to retain some of the items seized. The judge denied the request for retention because of the defects in the original warrant. A different police officer applied for a *general investigative warrant* to re-seize the items at the time they were to be returned to the accused later the same day. The application was made before a new judge. The officer appropriately indicated in his *information to obtain* the history of the matter, further information from his investigation of the accused, as well as the belief that no other federal authority existed for this type of re-seizure.

97 See The Honourable Mr. Justice Casey Hill, *The General Investigative Search Warrant*, prepared for the National Criminal Law Program, 1995, St. John's, Newfoundland, section 1.8.

98 *Eccles v. Bourque, supra*, note 75, at 380 [C.C.C.]; wherein the Court refers to *R.*

v. *Plant*, 1993 CarswellAlta 94, 1993 CarswellAlta 566, [1993] 3 S.C.R. 281, 24 C.R. (4th) 47, 157 N.R. 321, [1993] 8 W.W.R. 287, 145 A.R. 104, 55 W.A.C. 104, 17 C.R.R. (2d) 297, 12 Alta. L.R. (3d) 305, 84 C.C.C. (3d) 203 (S.C.C.), at 296-97 [S.C.R.].

99 *R. v. Brand*, 2008 CarswellBC 384, 2008 BCCA 94, 229 C.C.C. (3d) 443, 56 C.R. (6th) 39, (sub nom. *R. v. Ford*) 252 B.C.A.C. 108, (sub nom. *R. v. Ford*) 422 W.A.C. 108, (sub nom. *R. v. Ford*) 167 C.R.R. (2d) 139 (B.C. C.A.).

100 *R. v. Noseworthy, supra*, note 92.

101 *Supra*, note 97, at 7.

102 *R. v. Grant, supra*, note 13, at para 67.

103 *Criminal Code*, subs. 487.01(2).

104 See for instance: *R. v. Beamish*, 1996 CarswellPEI 88, 144 Nfld. & P.E.I.R. 338, 451 A.P.R. 338 (P.E.I. T.D.); *R. v. Hutchinson*, 1995 CarswellOnt 1267, 98 C.C.C. (3d) 221 (Ont. Gen. Div.); *R. v. McDowell*, 1995 CarswellAlta 166, 29 Alta. L.R. (3d) 235, [1995] 7 W.W.R. 603, 171 A.R. 67 (Alta. Q.B.); *R. v. Nguyen*, 1995 CarswellOnt 3182 (Ont. Gen. Div.); and *R. v. Greffe*, 1990 CarswellAlta 42, 1990 CarswellAlta 651, 55 C.C.C. (3d) 161, 75 C.R. (3d) 257, [1990] 3 W.W.R. 577, 107 A.R. 1, [1990] 1 S.C.R. 755, 107 N.R. 1, 73 Alta. L.R. (2d) 97, 46 C.R.R. 1 (S.C.C.).

105 Hutchison & Bury, *Search and Seizure Law in Canada* (Carswell: Toronto, 1962) at 16-40.1.

106 *R. v. Knight*, 2006 CarswellNfld 317, 2006 NLTD 186, 149 C.R.R. (2d) 189, 48 C.R. (6th) 94, 262 Nfld. & P.E.I.R. 20, 794 A.P.R. 20 (N.L. T.D.), reversed 2008 CarswellNfld 342, 2008 NLCA 67, 241 C.C.C. (3d) 353, 62 C.R. (6th) 328, 281 Nfld. & P.E.I.R. 269, 863 A.P.R. 269 (N.L. C.A.).

107 *R. v. Brand, supra*, note 99; R. v. Ha, 2009 CarswellOnt 2197, 2009 ONCA 340, 245 C.C.C. (3d) 546, 65 C.R. (6th) 24, 249 O.A.C. 43, 96 O.R. (3d) 751 (Ont. C.A.).

108 *Supra*, note 97.

109 *Criminal Code*, subs. 487.01(4). (This provision is a direct response to the issue raised in *R. v. Wong, supra*, note 88.)

110 These comments are predicated on circumstances wherein a *reasonable expectation of privacy* exists.

111 The report is submitted to the issuing judge or a judge of the same jurisdiction, not a justice of the peace.

112 *Toronto Star Newspapers Ltd. v. Ontario*, 2005 CarswellOnt 2613, 2005 Carswel-lOnt 2614, 2005 SCC 41[2005] 2 S.C.R. 188, 253 D.L.R. (4th) 577, 29 C.R. (6th) 251, 197 C.C.C. (3d) 1, 132 C.R.R. (2d) 178, 76 O.R. (3d) 320 (note), (sub nom. *R. v. Toronto Star Newspapers Ltd.*) 335 N.R. 201, (sub nom. *R. v. Toronto Star Newspapers Ltd.*) 200 O.A.C. 348 (S.C.C.).

113 *R. v. Stillman, supra*, note 20, wherein it was concluded that there was no such power at common law to seize bodily substances incident to an arrest. Also, note that in s. 487 of the *Criminal Code* R.S.C. 1985, c. C-46, authority is only provided to "search of a place for a thing".

114 There is a division of authority as to whether or not the police could use a general warrant (subs. 487.01) to seize biological samples directly from a suspect's person, given the limitation of subs. 487.01(1) that such a warrant was not to be permitted to

interfere with bodily integrity: see *R. v. Beamish, supra*, note 104; *R. v. Hutchinson, supra*, note 104.

[115] *R. v. Borden*, 1994 CarswellNS 26, 1994 CarswellNS 437, 92 C.C.C. (3d) 404, 33 C.R. (4th) 147, 24 C.R.R. (2d) 51, [1994] 3 S.C.R. 145, 171 N.R. 1, 119 D.L.R. (4th) 74, 134 N.S.R. (2d) 321, 383 A.P.R. 321 (S.C.C.).

[116] *R. v. Stillman, supra*, note 20, at 376 [C.C.C.].

[117] See the consultation paper that preceded the enactment of Bill C-104, entitled "Obtaining and Banking DNA Forensic Evidence" (Department of Justice, September 20, 1994).

[118] *R. v. Stillman, supra*, note 20, at 357 [C.C.C.]; *F. (S.) v. Canada (Attorney General)*, 2000 CarswellOnt 60, 32 C.R. (5th) 79, (sub nom. *R. v. F. (S.)*) 141 C.C.C. (3d) 225, (sub nom. *R. v. F. (S.)*) 70 C.R.R. (2d) 41, (sub nom. *R. v. F. (S.)*) 182 D.L.R. (4th) 336, (sub nom. *S.F. v. Canada (Attorney General)*) 128 O.A.C. 329 (Ont. C.A.); *R. v. Dwyer*, 2000 CarswellOnt 4791, [2000] O.J. No. 4683 (C.J.); and *R. v. Feeney*, 1999 CarswellBC 622, 23 C.R. (5th) 74, [1999] B.C.J. No. 688 (S.C.), at 12 [B.C.J.].

[119] *R. v. Stillman, supra*, note 20, at 357 [C.C.C.].

[120] See *R. v. Feeney, supra*, note 118, at 12 [B.C.J.].

[121] See *Establishing a National DNA Data Bank, Summary of Consultations* (Department of Solicitor General in 1997). This document provides a complete list of the organizations represented at DNA Consultation Sessions. The main issues identified in the consultation paper were: (1) the scope of DNA data bank—whose DNA should be banked; (2) when should bodily substances be collected; (3) who should collect bodily substances from convicted offenders; (4) should bodily substances, as well as DNA data, be retained in a data bank; and (5) how would a national DNA data bank be funded?

[122] *F. (S.) v. Canada (Attorney General), supra*, note 118, at 301 [C.C.C.].

[123] See the Solicitor General of Canada, Hon. Lawrence MacCaulay's comments at www.sgc.gc.ca.

[124] See R. Willing, "Fear Keeps Up as DNA Science Speeds Forward" *USA Today* (29 March 2000).

[125] See statement for the record of Dr. Dwight E. Adams, Deputy Assistant Director, Forensic Analysis Branch, FBI on "Forensic DNA Analysis" before the subcommittee on the Crime of the House Judiciary Committee, Washington, D.C. (March 23, 2000) (www.fbi.gov./ pressm/ congress/ congressoo/ dadams.htm).

[126] S.C. 2002, c. 1, as amended.

[127] R.S.C. 1985, c. P-21.

[128] *R. v. Lavallee, Rackel & Heintz*, 2002 CarswellAlta 1818, 2002 CarswellAlta 1819, 2002 SCC 61, 3 C.R. (6th) 209, 4 Alta. L.R. (4th) 1, 216 D.L.R. (4th) 257, 2002 D.T.C. 7267 (Eng.), 2002 D.T.C. 7287 (Fr.), [2002] 4 C.T.C. 143, [2002] 11 W.W.R. 191, 312 A.R. 201, 281 W.A.C. 201, (sub nom. *Lavallee, Rackel & Heintz v. Canada (Attorney General)*) 167 C.C.C. (3d) 1, (sub nom. *Lavallee, Rackel & Heintz v. Canada (Attorney General)*) 164 O.A.C. 280, (sub nom. *Lavallee, Rackel & Heintz v. Canada (Attorney General)*) 96 C.R.R. (2d) 189, (sub nom. *Lavallee, Rackel & Heintz v. Canada (Attorney General)*) [2002] 3 S.C.R. 209, (sub nom. *Lavallee, Rackel & Heintz v. Canada (Attorney General)*) 292 N.R. 296, (sub nom. *Lavallee, Rackel & Heintz v. Canada (Attorney General)*) 217 Nfld. & P.E.I.R. 183,

(sub nom. *Lavallee, Rackel & Heintz v. Canada (Attorney General)*) 651 A.P.R. 183 (S.C.C.), at 15 [C.C.C.].

[129] *Ibid.*

[130] *Ibid.*

[131] S.C. 1996, c. 19.

22

Proceeds of Crime and Money Laundering

*David Schermbrucker**

PROCEEDS OF CRIME

Introduction: the Controversial Case of Luis Pinto

In 1983, Luis Pinto was arrested in the United States on a charge of trafficking in cocaine. As part of a plea bargain to reduce his jail sentence, Pinto disclosed to the police that he had an account at a Montreal branch of the Royal Bank of Canada holding some $400,000, which Pinto said was his profit from previous drug deals. The American authorities notified the RCMP, who then obtained a search warrant to seize the funds.

The Quebec courts, however, quashed the search warrant, ruling that although the funds were indisputably illegal drug profits, money in a bank account is not a "thing" that can be seized under a search warrant because a bank account balance is really just a debt owed by the bank to the customer.[1] There was no other means to seize the funds so Luis Pinto got to keep his drug profits. Needless to say, this prompted disbelief and outrage within the law enforcement community: how could an admitted drug dealer get to keep his profits of crime simply because the Canadian criminal law had no tools to confiscate them?

Concern at the International Leve and Canada's Response

Coincidentally, in the mid-1980s, global crime became recognized as a serious problem for the international community. Global crime was destabilizing the economies and political structures of some nations; it was promoting violence, piracy and exploitation, and the results were being felt especially in the poorer nations. Policing was becoming harder as criminals were operating across international borders. In particu-

---

* Counsel, Department of Justice (Canada), Federal Prosecution Service, Halifax Integrated Proceeds of Crime Unit.

lar, the international drug trade was singled out as a threat that needed to be addressed by all nations. On December 20, 1988, Canada became a signatory to what is commonly known as the "Vienna Convention", more formally called the *United Nations Convention against Illicit Traffic in Narcotic Drugs and Psychotropic Substances*,[2] which came into force in November 1990. The Vienna Convention obliged Canada to take steps against international drug dealing, and in particular to create laws to confiscate drug profits and prohibit money laundering.[3]

This led to the present regime of "proceeds of crime" and "anti-money laundering" measures in federal Canadian statutes, including some new approaches to pre-existing laws. These measures include:

- Part XII.2 of the *Criminal Code*[4] is a comprehensive package dealing with the offence of "money laundering"—s. 462.31—as well as the pre-trial seizure or restraint of property alleged to proceeds of crime, and some investigative tools such as a "tax information" order under s. 462.48. The federal and most provincial prosecution services have dedicated units set up to work under Part XII.2, targeting major criminal profiteers and organized crime; the federal teams are known as Integrated Proceeds of Crime or "IPOC" Units; the provincial teams as Provincial Proceeds of Crime or "PPOC" Units; their respective mandates depend on federal vs. provincial jurisdiction, which is discussed below.
- The offence of "possession of proceeds of crime" is found in s. 354 of the *Criminal Code*, which deals with possession of any property obtained or derived from the commission of an indictable offence, and which originally dealt with stolen property. But enterprise criminals such as drug dealers can be and frequently are charged with "possession of proceeds of crime" under this offence-creating section, if the police have evidence that the alleged drug dealer's assets (houses, cash, fancy cars, etc.) must have been purchased from drug profits.
- There are "offence related property" measures in the *Code* and in the *Controlled Drugs and Substances Act* (known as the "CDSA") dealing with seizure, restraint and forfeiture of the instruments of crime such as marihuana grow houses, drug trafficking paraphernalia, and so on. Although not dealing with "proceeds of crime" *per se*, these measures often intersect with true proceeds of crime laws.
- There is also the regime in *Code*, s. 490 which deals with the

disposition of seized exhibits. Subsection 490(9) is sometimes used to forfeit property which is criminally tainted.

- Various parts of the *Proceeds of Crime (Money Laundering) and Terrorist Financing Act* are relevant—e.g., by creating obligations on the part of certain businesses such as banks and real estate agents to disclose suspicious transactions to the authorities, and by enacting measures to disrupt funding to terrorist organizations.

The Philosophy Behind Seizing and Forfeiting Proceeds of Crime

The main objective of Canada's proceeds of crime provisions is, quite simply, to deprive enterprising criminals of the profits of their crimes. It was always possible to prosecute a major level drug dealer or other money-making criminal, and if convicted the offender might well receive a lengthy jail sentence. But historically, as the Pinto case demonstrated, the fruits of crime were beyond the reach of the criminal law. Our law-makers believed that as a matter of criminal law policy this needed correction and, as we have seen, this became a matter of international treaty obligation. Furthermore, it was felt that many enterprising criminals were not deterred by the prospect of even a lengthy jail sentence if caught: if they could do the time, they would do the crime; but if their criminal profits could be taken away, maybe they would think twice about committing the crime in the first place.

Justice Doherty put it this way in *R. v. Wilson*:

> The purpose of Pt. XII.2 [of the Code] is clear. It is intended to give effect to the age old adage that crime does not pay. It is now recognized that some crime is big business, and that massive profits, both direct and indirect, can be made from criminal activity. Pt. XII.2 is a response to that realization and provides a comprehensive scheme whereby those direct and indirect profits may be located, seized and eventually forfeited to the Crown.[5]

In *R. v. Rosenblum*, the British Columbia Court of Appeal said:

> [20] Part XII.2 is entitled "Proceeds of Crime". The objective of Part XII.2 is to deal with economically motivated crime, emulating the focus of federal legislation in the United States known as the Racketeering Influenced and Corrupt Organizations Statute ("RICO"). A major feature of RICO is the mandatory forfeiture of assets acquired in violation of that act.

> [21] In Canada, it was felt that economically motivated crime was inadequately treated in the existing provisions of the Criminal Code which

dealt with the knowing possession of stolen property, or with offences rooted in fraud. The result was Bill C-61 which, when enacted and given Royal Assent, came into force on 1 January 1989.[6]

See also *Québec (Procureure générale) c. Laroche*, where the Supreme Court of Canada said, per Lebel J.:

[25] The legislative objective of Part XII.2 plainly goes beyond mere punishment of crime: an analysis of the provisions of that Part shows that Parliament intended to neutralize criminal organizations by taking the proceeds of their illegal activities away from them. Part XII.2 intends to give effect to the old adage that crime does not pay... As German, *supra*, has observed, Part XII.2 organizes the fight against organized crime around a strategy that focuses on the proceeds of crime, as opposed to the offender. As well, the effectiveness of that struggle depends largely on the speed with which proceeds of crime can be identified, located, seized and ultimately forfeited. For that reason, Part XII.2 provides for new enforcement techniques that enable the police to freeze or immobilize the property of criminal organizations regardless of whose possession it may be in, even before charges are laid.[7]

Canada's Reliance on the Criminal Law Burden of Proof— "Beyond a Reasonable Doubt"

Perhaps the most important feature of Canada's proceeds of crime laws is that, with the few exceptions discussed below, it is conviction-based. Forfeiture of the proceeds of crime is structured as a sentencing measure directed against the person who has been found guilty of the crime which generated the proceeds in question. Put another way, in general the offender must be charged and found guilty by a judge or jury of an underlying offence ("predicate offence"), before the alleged proceeds of his or her crime can be forfeited by the judge imposing sentence. If the offender is found not guilty of the offence, the judge has no authority to order the proceeds to be forfeited.

Even those criminal measures which allow for forfeiture outside of the criminal trial process—for example *Code*, subs. 490(9) forfeiture dealing with seized exhibits, or the residual forfeiture provisions in s. 462.38 dealing with property belonging to an accused person who has died or absconded—require the Crown to prove that the property in question is proceeds of crime *beyond a reasonable doubt*, which is the same burden of proof as would be required to obtain a conviction at trial.

This focus on the criminal trial process, and the government's burden of proving criminal taint beyond a reasonable doubt, distinguishes

Canada's proceeds of crime laws from other regimes. In the United States, for example, under the federal "RICO" statute mentioned in *Rosenblum*,[8] or the more recent federal *Civil Asset Forfeiture Reform Act* ("CAFRA")[9] which replaced RICO in 2000, there is a system of administrative forfeiture of proceeds of crime—*i.e.* forfeiture without conviction. Under such regimes, the police are authorized by law to seize suspected proceeds of crime and forfeit them directly; typically the alleged offenders have to take the initiative to try to get the assets back by applying through the courts.

The important difference between criminal forfeiture, as we have in Canada, and civil or administrative forfeiture, as in the United States, is that Canada has chosen to subordinate our criminal proceeds of crime laws to the presumption of innocence. Generally speaking, in Canada, we do not forfeit property alleged to be proceeds of crime unless and until the government has proven beyond a reasonable doubt that the property in question is indeed derived from crime.

Proceeds of Crime—The Definition

For the purposes of seizing and forfeiting criminal profits, the following definition of "proceeds of crime" is provided by the *Code*:

462.3 (1) Definitions—In this part,

. . .

"proceeds of crime" means any property, benefit or advantage, within or outside Canada, obtained or derived directly or indirectly as a result of
 (a) the commission in Canada of a designated offence, or
 (b) an act or omission anywhere that, if it had occurred in Canada, would have constituted a designated offence.

Note that the property must be the proceeds of a "designated offence". This is also defined in subs. 462.3(1) as follows:

"designated offence" means
 (a) an indictable offence under this or any other Act of Parliament, other than an indictable offence prescribed by regulation, or
 (b) a conspiracy or an attempt to commit, being an accessory after the fact in relation to, or any counselling in relation to, an offence referred to in paragraph (a).

What Parliament has done here is, first, to restrict "predicate offences" for proceeds of crime to indictable offences and, second, to allow Parliament to exempt certain indictable offences from the regime by regulation.

Indictable offences are generally more serious than summary conviction offences, and restricting "proceeds of crime" to the fruits of indictable offences is clearly intended to limit the reach of Part XII.2 of the *Code* to relatively serious crimes. Some examples of indictable offences that might generate profits are: drug trafficking, extortion, robbery, fraud, living off the avails of prostitution (or "pimping") and corruption. (It is convenient now to mention that as a matter of prosecutorial jurisdiction as between the provincial and the federal prosecution services, where the predicate offence falls under the *Code*, the provincial Crown generally has authority; where the predicate offence falls under another federal criminal statute, such as the *Controlled Drugs and Substances Act*, the federal Crown has authority. Predictably, this federal-provincial distinction is not quite so simple in practice.)

The clause in para. 462.3(1)(a) of the *Code* that defines a designated offence as being "other than an indictable offence prescribed by regulation" allows the federal government to exempt offences from the *Code*'s proceeds of crime provisions simply by passing a regulation. Instead of going through the more complicated and lengthier Parliamentary procedures to amend the *Code* itself, regulations are normally passed by Governor-in-Council, in effect a formal meeting of the government's senior ministers, and are put in force by publication in the *Canada Gazette*, Parliament's official newspaper. At present a dozen or so such offences are exempt—e.g., offences against the *Income Tax Act* and the *Copyright Act*. As explained in the text accompanying the pertinent regulation presently in force:

> These offences are regarded as inappropriate for inclusion in the *Criminal Code* proceeds of crime scheme for a number of reasons. In some cases, the proceeds derived from the commission of the excluded offence are subject to particular procedures contained in the statute in which that offence is found. For example, offences under the *Income Tax Act, Excise Act*, and *Excise Tax Act*, are being excluded because those statutes already provide for comprehensive and specifically designed rules and penalties for dealing with tax evasion and for recovering any unpaid tax. Under the *Copyright Act* any benefit obtained by the commission of a copyright offence should be returned to the authors whose copyright has been breached, rather than being forfeited to the Crown as proceeds of crime.[10]

We are left, then, with the idea that any indictable offence, other than one excluded by regulation, can be a "predicate offence", and the profits of that offence are susceptible to Canada's criminal proceeds of crime laws. In practice, this usually means profitable crimes such as drug trafficking and related activity—e.g., marihuana grow operations, prostitution, extortion, and so on. Again, the jurisdictional question of whether the proceedings to seize, restrain or forfeit the proceeds of crime will be handled by a federal or provincial prosecution service depends on which of the two would be expected to prosecute the offender: provincial Crowns in *Code* offences; federal Crowns in other federal offences.

Seizure and Restraint of Proceeds of Crime

The Canadian public likely believes that when the police bust a drug dealer, or other criminal profiteer, they can simply seize and immediately forfeit his or her proceeds of crime. This perception is no doubt fuelled by television shows based partly on the American experience, as well as by press conferences arranged by the police when they do a major bust and display for the TV cameras piles of cash and luxury items seized from the accused. The reality is quite different.

As stated above, the eventual forfeiture of an offender's proceeds of crime in Canada is generally a sentencing measure, based on conviction for a predicate offence. There are measures for pre-trial seizure of proceeds of crime, but they are not as "quick and dirty" as Canadians might think. In fact, they can be quite complicated and drawn out. This is most of all because the police generally need prior judicial authorization to seize or restrain suspected proceeds of crime; the police cannot just go out and seize proceeds of crime on their own.

Under ss. 462.32 and 462.33 of the *Code*, counsel for the Attorney General (again, a federal or provincial Crown, depending on which branch has carriage of the case) can apply to a judge of the superior court for a Special Warrant or Restraint Order. A Special Warrant authorizes the seizure of property that can be moved, such as jewellery or a vehicle; a Restraint Order authorizes the restraint of immoveable assets such as real estate or a bank account balance.

Both ss. 462.32 (Special Warrant) and 462.33 (Restraint Order) of the *Code* contemplate that the prosecutor will apply in writing to a judge of the superior court without giving notice ("*ex parte*"), on the theory that if notice of the application was given to the suspect there is a risk that the suspect would quickly take steps to conceal or convert the suspected proceeds of crime and place them beyond reach of the authorities. The objective of a Restraint Order or Special Warrant under Part XII.2 is simple: to preserve the property for possible forfeiture by preventing the owner or others from selling, moving or encumbering the property. The *Code* therefore authorizes these steps to be taken *ex parte*.

The application for restraint or seizure of proceeds of crime must be supported by an affidavit setting out the offence under investigation, a description of the property alleged to be proceeds of crime, the person believed to be in possession of the property, and (most importantly) the grounds upon which the property may be subject to forfeiture as proceeds of crime. This last criterion—grounds that the property is forfeitable—is discussed below.

As well, the Attorney General (usually represented by a senior prosecution official) must provide the judge to whom the application for restraint or seizure is made with a written undertaking "with respect to the payment of damages or costs, or both", in relation to the issuance and execution of the order or warrant. This is intended to provide some guarantee that if the alleged offender or other affected person turns out to have been unfairly prejudiced by the seizure or restraint, he or she will be compensated.

It is significant that these applications are made to the superior court (usually called the province's Supreme Court or Court of Queen's Bench). The superior courts have inherent jurisdiction and so are familiar with property rights, and their processes are usually more formal than in the provincial courts.

If the superior court judge grants the application, ordinarily the resulting Restraint Order or Special Warrant will be served upon any affected persons (the suspect or accused, as well as anyone else with an interest in the property such as a registered owner or lien holder), and will be registered on the local land titles registry system or personal property security registry as the case may be. These steps would put all affected parties on notice of the Order or Warrant, and prevent third parties from (un)wittingly purchasing a property or granting a collateral mortgage on a property that has been, in fact, restrained or seized.

Restraint Orders and Special Warrants normally expire after six months, pursuant to s. 462.35 of the *Code*, unless criminal charges are laid for a predicate offence in respect of which the property may be forfeited. The prosecutor can apply for an extension of the 6 month limit, but must show some justification—e.g. the investigation is ongoing and the police are not ready to lay criminal charges. This often happens in complicated proceeds of crime investigations. The judge considering an application for an extension will likely want some explanation of why further time is needed: see, for example, *R. v. Dixon*.[11] The law appears to be that affected persons (usually the accused, but also anyone with an interest in the property) should be given notice of an application to extend a Restraint Order or Special Warrant, and an opportunity to oppose it in court. Of course by now those affected parties will be aware of the Restraint Order or Special Warrant—their assets have been seized or restrained—and there is no need now to proceed in secrecy, or *ex parte*.

Administratively, the Seized Property Management Directorate ("SPMD"), which is a branch of the Ministry of Public Works and Government Services (Canada), is authorized and mandated by statute to safeguard property seized and restrained under these provisions, pending any further court Order to either forfeit or return the property. Ordinarily a Management Order will be obtained from the court (and this is typically included in the body of the Restraint Order or Special Warrant), which will specify SPMD's obligations and responsibilities. SPMD is also statutorily authorized to sell or otherwise dispose of property that has been forfeited as "proceeds of crime", usually by public auction or sealed tender. The net proceeds of sale are deposited to the Consolidated Revenue Fund, which is the federal government's general "bank account".

The Crown has no authority to sell seized or restrained property until it is ordered forfeited, unless the owner agrees. This is because until there is a conviction and a trial judge orders forfeiture as part of sentencing, the accused is presumed to be innocent and the property is only alleged to be proceeds of crime ("may be subject to forfeiture"). However, subs. 462.331(3) of the *Code* allows for interim sale of the property where it is "perishable or rapidly depreciating", and also permits a court to authorize the property's destruction (on notice to the owner) where the property has "little or no value". These cases will likely be very rare, since most property seized or restrained as proceeds of crime is in the form of valuable assets—real estate, cash, gold or other valuables, bank accounts, and so on—and not perishable or valueless goods. In some situations, such as where the real estate market is slipping and the defendant's trial is a long time off, or where the defendant owes substantial loan payments on a vehicle that has been seized, the defendant may choose to agree to an interlocutory sale with the proceeds of sale to be deposited to an interest-bearing account pending forfeiture or return as the case may be, at the conclusion of the criminal charges.

In the case of money in a bank account it is likely that a Restraint Order would simply direct the bank to freeze the account or a specified sum in the account. In other cases, such as a dwelling house, the Restraint Order might allow the owners or occupiers to continue to possess and enjoy the property, subject perhaps to conditions requiring them to maintain the property in good repair, to continue to make mortgage or insurance payments, and so on. A Restraint Order will be subject to any reasonable conditions that a judge thinks appropriate.

Movable property subject to a Special Warrant, such as a vehicle, would probably be seized and kept in a safe place by the SPMD, which is under a duty to take reasonable care to ensure that the property is preserved until it is either forfeited or returned. A report must be made to the court when a Special Warrant is executed and frequently a report is also made once a Restraint Order is served and registered. These reports are intended to keep the Courts informed about the status of assets seized or restrained under judicial authorization, so that ultimately police and prosecutors are accountable to the courts for their handling of seized or restrained assets at all stages of the investigation and prosecution.

The "Theory of Forfeiture"

As mentioned above, one of the very important aspects of an *ex parte* application for a Restraint Order or Special Warrant for suspected proceeds of crime is that the issuing judge must be satisfied that there are reasonable grounds to believe that the property in question "may be subject to forfeiture". This entails a demonstration, in the affidavit supporting material and perhaps reflected in the submissions of Crown counsel at the time of the application, of the Crown's "theory of forfeiture". This does not require proof of the defendant's guilt, or proof that the property is in fact proceeds of crime—indeed such proof is usually not possible since in all likelihood the police investigation is still in its early stages, and any inquiries made to this point are done on the assumption that the suspected offender should not be made aware he or she is under investigation, lest he or she hide or dispose of the proceeds of crime in question. All that is required in the application material is evidence upon which the judge can conclude that the property "may be subject to forfeiture".

The party bringing an *ex parte* application (in this case the Crown prosecutor) has a well-recognized duty to be fair and frank with the court, so as not to take advantage of an affected person who has no knowledge of the application. Along with the evidence showing why the property sought to be seized or restrained is forfeitable as proceeds of crime, the issuing judge must also be advised of any evidence pointing the other way. In *R. v. Seman*,[12] for example, the judge reviewing a Restraint Order found that the Crown had not made full disclosure of relevant circumstances to the issuing judge; he therefore revoked the Restraint Order, and ordered the Crown to pay damages and costs.

Release of Seized or Restrained Funds for Legal Fees, Business or Living Expenses, or Bail

Where property alleged to be proceeds of crime has been seized or restrained under ss. 462.32 or 462.33, and prior to any forfeiture application, any person with an interest in the property may apply to the superior court for release of all or part of the property for the purpose of:

(i) meeting the reasonable living expenses of the person who was in possession of the property at the time the warrant was executed or the order was made or any person, who, in the opinion of the judge, has a valid interest in the property and of the dependents of that person;

(ii) meeting the reasonable business and legal expenses of a person referred to in subparagraph (i), or

(iii) permitting the use of the property in order to enter into a recognizance [of bail].[13]

This situation usually arises when the police and prosecutors have seized or restrained assets of significant value, and the accused or the suspect (if charges have not yet been laid) wants access to the assets in order to pay business, living or legal expenses. The superior court judge is clearly given authority to order the Crown to make seized or restrained assets available to the applicant for those purposes. Before making such an order, the judge must be satisfied that the applicant "has no other assets or means available" for these purposes[14] and that nobody else is lawfully entitled to the property instead. Ordinarily the applicant, who is the property-owner and usually, but not always, the accused, will need to produce evidence that he has no substitute assets and therefore needs access to the property in question for the stated purpose(s). Crown counsel may cross-examine the applicant as to his assets, but not as to the source of funds since that could result in the applicant incriminating himself on charges pending.[15]

This ability to release seized or restrained property prior to trial, for the purpose of living expenses, business costs, legal fees, and bail, is an explicit recognition of the fact that although the property in question is potentially subject to forfeiture as proceeds of crime, the accused is nevertheless presumed to be innocent, and fairness requires that the accused and any other affected persons should be able to seek relief from seizure or restraint of the property for legitimate purposes. As stated by Doherty J.A. in *R. v. Wilson*:

When a person applies for release of property under s. 462.34 there has not been any finding that the property is in fact the proceeds of crime.

> There has only been a finding, following an ex-parte hearing, that there are reasonable grounds to believe that the property is the proceeds of crime. It may well turn out that the person from whom the property was seized is entitled to the possession of that property. Nor, when an application for release of funds is made, has there been any finding that the person who seeks the release of those funds has committed any crime. Furthermore, when a person applies for release of property under s. 462.34, he or she will be facing proceedings in which the assistance of counsel is needed. That need has a constitutional underpinning, and must be given due weight.[16]

There have been many cases in which access to seized or restrained property has been granted under s. 462.34. The vast majority of these have been in order to pay legal fees. Frequently the need for legal fees relates to charges in respect of which the property was seized or restrained, but not always, and the *Code* does not so specify. In one case, $275,000 in seized property was ordered released to the accused under this provision so he could pay for legal expenses for an unrelated murder charge.

Substantive Review of Restraint Orders and Special Warrants

Canadian criminal law generally holds that a ruling by a court in criminal proceedings is not subject to review or appeal unless there is a statutory right to such review or appeal.

The *Code* does not explicitly allow an appeal of the correctness of a judge's decision to grant a Restraint Order or Special Warrant under Part XII.2. However, s. 462.34, which allows for such Orders and Warrants to be varied so that property can be released for business, living, or legal expenses, has been interpreted by the Supreme Court of Canada as implicitly allowing for substantive review, on the grounds that Restraint Orders and Special Warrants implicate the constitutional right to be secure from unreasonable seizure (*Charter*, s. 8), and that:

> it would be difficult to do justice to the party affected by a restraint order or warrant of seizure if the reviewing judge were not permitted to consider the merits of the decision to make the order or issue the warrant. In fact, this is the only procedure available for challenging those decisions, with the exception of the admittedly rare remedy of a direct appeal to the Supreme Court of Canada. The broad reach of those measures may also have a serious effect on an individual's personal situation or economic interests, or even, in some instances, the survival of a business. Given that Parliament has chosen to circumscribe the remedies of the parties affected in this way, the scope of those remedies should be interpreted in such a way as to preserve their effectiveness and usefulness.[17]

In short, any person who wishes to challenge the restraint or seizure of his or her property may apply to the superior court. This ability to review a Restraint Order or Special Search Warrant, in the absence of any *Code* provisions allowing for review, is consistent with Parliament having given the power to issue those Orders or Warrants to the superior courts, which (as noted above) have inherent jurisdiction and therefore can control their own processes including reviewing their own orders.

Forfeiture of Proceeds of Crime

As previously mentioned, forfeiture is generally a sentencing function. There are two parallel provisions for forfeiture at the sentencing hearing.

First, subs. 462.37(1) of the *Code* provides:

> **462.37 (1) Order of forfeiture of property on conviction**—... where an offender is convicted ... of a designated offence and the court imposing sentence on the offender, on application of the Attorney General, is satisfied, on a balance of probabilities, that any property is proceeds of crime and that the designated offence was committed in relation to that property, the court shall order that the property be forfeited to Her Majesty to be disposed of as the Attorney General directs or otherwise dealt with in accordance with the law.

Note once again the reference to a "designated offence" and to "proceeds of crime". The property in question must not only be "proceeds of crime" as discussed above, but it must have some connection to the designated offence of which the offender has been convicted. The Crown prosecutor must prove these criteria "on a balance of probabilities" in order to obtain forfeiture of the property. Although in criminal law the Crown usually has the onus of proof "beyond a reasonable doubt", the lesser onus here is appropriate because the offender has already been convicted of the designated offence in a criminal trial where the onus is proof beyond a reasonable doubt.

The simplest case to which subs. 462.37(1) might apply is a case where the defendant is convicted of "possession of property obtained by crime" contrary to s. 354 of the *Code*. Consider a drug dealer convicted of possession of $100,000 cash, which the Crown has proven came from previous drug deals.[18] In such a case, the property itself would be forfeitable because the offence of possession of property obtained by crime was clearly committed "in relation to that property". The property might be cash from previous drug sales, the profits of a fraud scam, or an asset purchased with the fruits of past crimes. In the original example of Luis Pinto, subs. 462.37(1) would apply if Pinto was convicted under s. 354 of the *Criminal Code* of possession of property (the $400,000) knowing it was proceeds of an indictable offence (trafficking in cocaine). It has been held that the Crown need not prove the specific crimes from which the proceeds were derived or obtained.[19]

Another typical scenario is where the defendant has been convicted of a profitable crime (such as drug trafficking) and the Crown seeks forfeiture of the known profits of that crime without also seeking a conviction for "possession of proceeds of crime". Here, the property sought to be forfeited is directly connected to the crime of which the offender has been convicted, and the fact the offender was not charged with or convicted of the separate offence of "possession of proceeds of crime" under s. 354 of the *Code* does not interfere with the forfeiture of those proceeds of crime. For example, in *R. v. Warwaruk*,[20] the accused was convicted of gaming house offences in connection with the operation of an illegal casino and a large sum of money was established to be the accused's profits from that casino. Although there was no charge of possession of proceeds of crime, the accused's profits were ordered forfeited under subs. 462.37(1) by the judge imposing sentence on the theory that the gaming house offence was committed "in relation to" the profits.

Where the judge finds that the property in question is proceeds of crime under subs. 462.37(1), the judge "shall" order forfeiture. There is no discretion. However, there is relief from forfeiture for innocent third parties (as discussed below).

As to the second forfeiture provision, subs. 462.37(2) allows the sentencing judge to order forfeiture of property other than property in respect of which the designated offence was committed:

> **462.37 (2) Proceeds of crime derived from other offences**—Where the evidence does not establish to the satisfaction of the court that the designated offence of which the offender is convicted ... was committed in relation to property in respect of which an order of forfeiture would otherwise be made under subsection (1) but the court is satisfied, beyond a reasonable doubt, that that property is proceeds of crime, the court may make an order of forfeiture under subsection (1) in relation to that property.

Under this clause, a sentencing judge can forfeit any property, even if it is not directly connected to the offence for which the defendant is being sentenced, upon proof beyond a reasonable doubt that the property is proceeds of crime. On this theory, the sentencing court's jurisdiction is not restricted to proceeds of the very crime before the court but may include proceeds of any other crime, assuming the Crown can prove this beyond a reasonable doubt. As was stated by Fish J.A. (as he then was) in *R. c. Lore*:

> Reading ss. 462.37(1) and (2) in context, it seems to me that the former applies to property obtained by the offender in committing the offence for which the offender is convicted, while the latter relates to property obtained by the offender through the commission of other crimes. Any apparent ambiguity in the English version of the provisions vanishes, I believe, in the light of the French version.[21]

As wide as this second ground for forfeiture seems to be, the Crown's decision to seek forfeiture of the proceeds of crimes unrelated to the crime for which the defendant is being sentenced must not work an unfairness or be abusive. For instance, if a defendant was prosecuted for trafficking in a small amount of a controlled substance such as cannabis resin (hashish), it would likely be improper for the Crown at the sentencing for that offence to seek forfeiture of the defendant's house on the ground it was purchased with drug profits from a previous large cocaine deal. One possible rule of thumb for invoking the secondary forfeiture power under subs. 462.37(2) is that the property sought to be forfeited must have had some connection to the offence for which the defendant was convicted, such that evidence about that property would have been relevant at the trial.

This secondary forfeiture provision was considered in *R. v. Hape*.[22] Larry Hape was convicted of laundering money in the 1990s and, at sentencing, the Crown sought forfeiture of $3 million which was alleged to be the proceeds of prior drug trafficking offences in the 1980s. The trial judge refused to forfeit the $3 million, on the grounds that:

> [23] Parliament did not contemplate freestanding forfeiture applications directed toward any "proceeds of crime" whatsoever, but intended that a forfeiture application be directed toward proceeds of crime that bore some nexus to the crime for which the offender was convicted.

The Ontario Court of Appeal agreed, saying:

> [41] The Crown's submission that it can introduce entirely new allegations, unrelated to those advanced at trial, as part of a forfeiture hearing during the sentencing proceedings raises serious constitutional problems. The forfeiture provisions cannot be read so as to allow the Crown to circumvent the comprehensive process complete with constitutional protections, associated with the charging and prosecuting of criminal allegations. The section does not contemplate the forfeiture of property that was not the subject matter of the criminal allegation made at trial.

That being said, in 2005 Parliament enacted Bill C-53, proclaimed in force November 25, 2005, which provides that in the case of an offender convicted of a "criminal organization offence" under the *Code* or an offence under ss. 5, 6 or 7 of the *CDSA* (trafficking, importing or producing drugs or substances), the sentencing judge is obliged to forfeit any property of the offender identified by the Crown if the judge is satisfied that:

> (*a*) within 10 years before the proceedings were commenced in respect of the offence for which the offender is being sentenced, the offender engaged in a pattern of criminal activity for the purpose of directly or indirectly receiving a material benefit, including a financial benefit; or
> (*b*) the income of the offender from sources unrelated to designated offences cannot reasonably account for the value of all the property of the offender.[23]

In this scenario, the property in question could be totally unrelated to the offence of which the accused has been convicted. The accused does have the opportunity to prove that the property in question is not the proceeds of crime and should thus not be forfeited, but the onus is upon him, not the prosecution. This new provision has still not been tested by the courts.

It should be noted that property that is the proceeds of crime may be forfeited whether or not the Crown has seized or restrained it, whether or not its location is known, and whether or not it has been converted into another form. These circumstances may make it difficult to carry out a forfeiture order but they are not a legal bar to forfeiture.

Fine In Lieu of Forfeiture

In some situations where the property cannot be ordered forfeited for practical reasons, a fine in lieu of forfeiture "may" be made by the sentencing judge against the accused: *Code*, subs. 462.37(3). This is a discretionary power, as indicated by the use of the word "may", and the *Code* does not indicate what factors the court should take into account in deciding whether to order a fine in lieu of forfeiture.

As a general rule discretionary powers are exercised "judicially"—i.e., by reliance upon principle and not whimsy. A judge deciding whether to order a fine in lieu of forfeiture of property that has gone missing might look to the extent to which the defendant connived in the property's disappearance, whether the offender is still benefiting from the property at the time of sentencing, the value of the property in relation to the seriousness of the offence(s) before the court, how much jail time in default the defendant will have to serve if the fine goes unpaid, and so on. One factor that previously was considered relevant is the ability of the offender to pay a fine; however, this was recently addressed by statutory amendment: subs. 734(2) of the *Code* now says that although an offender's ability to pay a fine is critical to most criminal cases, this factor is not applicable to imposing a fine in lieu of forfeiture.

This provision was before the Newfoundland and Labrador Court of Appeal in the case of *R. v. Appleby*.[24] There, the police had seized some $700,000 cash hidden beneath the poured cement floor of a garage, and wiretap evidence established that it was the proceeds of drug trafficking. The accused applied for the release of some of that seized cash to fund his defence to the drug trafficking charges under s. 462.34. (The accused had been denied legal aid, largely because of this substantial cash seizure, with the legal aid commission taking the position that he could apply for access to some of the cash instead of funding his criminal defence through legal aid). In due course the superior court ordered some $330,000 to be released to fund the accused's legal defence. Eventually, the accused was convicted, and at sentencing the remaining $370,000 was ordered forfeited. The Crown applied for a $330,000 fine in lieu of forfeiture on the ground that this money, having been paid out for legal expenses, was proceeds of crime no longer available for forfeiture. The sentencing judge declined to order the fine, and the Newfoundland and Labrador Court of Appeal dismissed the Crown's appeal from that discretionary ruling. The Crown applied for leave to appeal to the Supreme Court of Canada, but the Supreme Court refused leave to hear the appeal.

Relief from Forfeiture

The *Criminal Code* expressly recognizes that forfeiture orders might work an unjust hardship on innocent third parties. Before a forfeiture order can be made, the judge must require that "any person who, in the opinion of the court, appears to have a valid interest in the property" be given notice of the forfeiture application (*Code*, subs. 462.41(1)). Further, the judge may refuse to forfeit any property and instead order it to be returned to a third party, where the judge is satisfied that the third party is lawfully entitled to the property and is innocent of any complicity in the underlying offences (*Code*, s. 462.41(3)). These remedies operate prior to any order of forfeiture being made.

Once a forfeiture order has been made, s. 462.42 allows anyone— other than a person charged with an underlying designated offence in relation to the property, or a person who appears to have connived in a transfer of the property to avoid forfeiture—to apply within 30 days of the forfeiture order to a judge of the superior court, for a declaration that their interest in the property is exempt from the forfeiture order in question.

The person claiming relief must appear not to be complicit in the offence underlying the forfeiture order. For example, in *R. v. Brooks*,[25] the police stopped a Lincoln Town Car stopped near Maple Creek, Saskatchewan. They found eleven kilograms of cannabis marihuana were in the trunk. The registered owner of the Lincoln, Marcelle Brooks, was a passenger in the front seat. Brooks was initially charged, along with the driver of the car, with possession of the cannabis for the purposes of trafficking. Brooks was acquitted based on a lack of proof of knowledge, but the driver was convicted. The Crown applied for forfeiture of the Lincoln. Ms. Brooks applied for relief from forfeiture, saying that since she had been found not guilty of the offence in question, and since the vehicle was registered to her, it should be exempt from forfeiture. The Court of Queen's Bench, however, held that despite her acquittal, Brooks was not "apparently innocent of any complicity" in the offence in question, and her application for relief was therefore dismissed.

In *R. v. Tatarchuk*,[26] the accused was convicted of defrauding Carl Rosenstock of approximately $125,000. Rosenstock had, prior to the criminal trial, obtained a judgment against Tatarchuk in civil court. Rosenstock then found out that the defendant had a sum of money on deposit in an account at First Marathon Securities under the alias John Anderson, and he served a garnishment against that account. Then, at the sentencing of Tatarchuk on the fraud charges before Judge Dimos, the Crown sought and obtained forfeiture of the First Marathon account under Part XII.2 of the *Code*, on the theory that the funds were "proceeds of crime" derived from the fraud in question. Rosenstock, the victim of the fraud, then sought relief from forfeiture under this section of the *Code* and the Court granted it, saying, at para. 17:

> [Rosenstock] is one of the victims of a series of crimes committed by Tatarchuk and is innocent of any complicity in or collusion in relation to these crimes. Judge Dimos, in making the order of forfeiture, decided that the funds held by Marathon were the proceeds of these crimes. Payment of proceeds of crime to one of the victims of the crimes cannot in any fashion be seen as benefiting the wrongdoer.

An example of unsuccessful relief from forfeiture is *R. v. Wilson*.[27] Here, the police had seized approximately $25,000 during a search of the residence of the accused Garth and Joyce Hibbert, who were charged with drug offences. The Hibberts were unable to continue to pay their lawyers' fees and accordingly decided to assign their interest in the seized $25,000 to their lawyers (including lawyer Wilson). However, this assignment was not disclosed until after the charges against Joyce Hibbert had been withdrawn by the Crown, Garth Hibbert had pleaded guilty and had been sentenced, and the $25,000 had been ordered forfeited as "proceeds of crime". Then, lawyer Wilson applied for relief from forfeiture of the $25,000, arguing that the money had been assigned to him and he was entitled to relief from forfeiture. This claim was dismissed on the ground that the lawyer's assignment could not take precedence over the forfeiture order, particularly since the judge who made the forfeiture order was unaware of the assignment. The Court of Appeal upheld that decision, motivated in part by the fact that the monies assigned to the lawyer for legal fees had already been forfeited as proceeds of crime, and that therefore the defendants had no assignable interest in the money. The lawyer Wilson might have been better off to seek access to the seized money under s. 462.34, as discussed above.

In Rem Forfeiture

As mentioned above, there are some exceptions to the general rule that forfeiture of proceeds of crime in Canada is conviction-based. First, where charges have been laid and the accused absconds or unfortunately dies before the criminal trial is completed, the court can forfeit property upon proof beyond a reasonable doubt that it is proceeds of crime. Second, quite apart from criminal charges, the court can forfeit property where it is illegal for anyone to possess it. This is called *in rem* forfeiture since the proceedings are against the property (*rem* means "thing" in Latin) as opposed to proceedings against a person (*in personam* forfeiture, as for example, under s. 462.37)

Deceased or Absconding Accused

In the first category, subs. 462.38(2) of the *Code* provides that where, upon an application for forfeiture, a judge finds that:

> (a) any property is, beyond a reasonable doubt, proceeds of crime,
> (b) proceedings in respect of a designated offence committed in relation to that property were commenced, and
> (c) the accused charged with the offence referred to in paragraph (*b*) has died or absconded,
>
> order that the property be forfeited to Her Majesty to be disposed of as

the Attorney General directs or otherwise dealt with in accordance with the law.

In *R. v. Clymore*,[28] the accused and his father drove to Kelowna, BC, from the United States with over $1 million (US) in a suitcase. Over a few days they attempted, with some success, to purchase Treasury Bills using false names. This attracted police attention and the Clymores were arrested for "personation". Several hundred thousand dollars in US currency was found in their car. This led to "money laundering" charges, but the Clymores slipped across the border to the United States again and, upon a Crown application to forfeit the money under s. 462.38, the judge found that the defendants had absconded, that the $1 million was proceeds of crime although the Crown was not able to specify the exact crime, and ordered it forfeited. Interestingly, Clymore the son surfaced some years later after having been arrested in the United States, and wanted to reopen the forfeiture hearing, but the BC Court of Appeal refused.

In *R. v. Marriott*,[29] a home belonging to the accused and his spouse was restrained under s. 462.33 as being purchased and financed with drug profits. The accused were charged but, before the trial could commence, they were murdered. The Court held that there was no requirement for a criminal "proceeds of crime" conviction respecting the property in question, and forfeited the property upon being satisfied beyond a reasonable doubt that the purchase price and the mortgage payments were made with drug profits.

It is worth emphasizing that, in an application under s. 462.38, the Crown must prove that the property is proceeds of crime "beyond a reasonable doubt". This is undoubtedly because the defendant(s), having died or absconded, do not stand trial at which this standard of proof would have to be met by the Crown.

Section 490(9)

The second category of *in rem* forfeiture is under subs. 490(9) of the *Code*. Section 490 authorizes the provincial courts (whose justices also issue search warrants) to supervise all property seized by the police during a criminal investigation. The court can order that seized property be held for further investigation, or as evidence in a pending criminal proceeding. Where charges are not laid, ordinarily the property must be returned to its rightful owner. However, in some cases where charges are not laid, or are laid and discontinued, the Crown may allege that the property is inherently illegal to possess (it is proceeds of crime), that the person from whom it was seized is therefore not entitled to have it back, and that the property should be forfeited to the Crown.

Subsection 490(9) of the *Code* reads:

> **490 (9) Disposal of things seized**—Subject to this or any other Act of Parliament, if
>> (a) a judge . . . or
>> (b) a justice . . .
>
> is satisfied that the periods of detention . . . in respect of anything seized have expired and proceedings have not been instituted in which the thing detained may be required . . . he shall
>> (c) if possession of it by the person from whom it was seized is lawful, order it to be returned to that person; or
>> (d) if possession of it by the person from whom it was seized is unlawful and the lawful owner or person who is lawfully entitled to its possession is known order it to be returned to the lawful owner . . .
>
> and *may, if possession of it by the person from whom it was seized is unlawful,* or if it was seized when it was not in the possession of any person, and the lawful owner or person who is lawfully entitled to its possession is not known, *order it to be forfeited to Her Majesty,* to be disposed of as the Attorney General directs, or otherwise dealt with in accordance with the law.
>
> [Emphasis added to denote the route to forfeiture.]

This provision has been "on the books" for some 50 years or more, and was originally intended to deal with property that was inherently contraband (e.g., drugs), stolen property that could not be traced back to its rightful owner, or other seized goods that ought not to be returned to the person from whom they were seized. Forfeiture of property under subs. 490(9) does not involve a criminal trial or a criminal conviction, yet once again the Crown must prove beyond a reasonable doubt that the property is tainted by criminality.

In *R. v. Daley*,[30] for instance, the respondent Daley purchased a standby air ticket at the Calgary Airport for a flight to Montreal, paying $460 cash, all in $20 bills. Upon being questioned by a suspicious police officer, Daley provided a false name and false identification. A search revealed $13,000 in cash knotted up in a pair of jeans in Daley's luggage, $3,600 cash in his pocket (for a total of $16,600), and additional false identification. Daley said the money was his savings from years of hard work, and that he intended to use it to open a barber shop. Subsequent inquiries showed that Daley had reported minimal income to the tax authorities over the past few years. Further, a debt sheet consistent with cocaine trafficking was also found in Daley's personal effects.

The Crown was not able to prosecute Daley for a specific criminal offence in relation to the cash in question, but brought an application for forfeiture under subs. 490(9). After litigation on the question whether Daley's *Charter* rights had been breached by his detention and search, the Alberta Court of Appeal concluded that in all the circumstances the money in question was clearly proceeds of crime, and ordered it forfeited under subs. 490(9).

Another example is *Ryan v. Canada (Attorney General)*,[31] in which the police stopped a pickup truck for speeding. Upon searching the vehicle for open liquor, the arresting officer found $25,000 in cash in a concealed compartment under the rear seat. The money was seized and detained pending further investigation. The Crown was not able to prosecute Daley or his passengers for any specific crime, but applied to forfeit the $25,000 under subs. 490(9) on the theory that it was proceeds of drug trafficking and therefore the occupants of the pickup truck could not lawfully possess it. Since there was no direct evidence of any actual drug deal, the Crown relied on circumstantial evidence, including the manner in which the currency was bundled, its location in the vehicle, and expert evidence as to the nature of the drug trade and how cash is used and transported for the purposes of drug deals. The Court concluded that the Crown had proven beyond a reasonable doubt that the money was the proceeds of crime, that it was therefore unlawful for the vehicle's occupants to possess it, and accordingly ordered the money forfeited.

By contrast, in *R. v. Sendji & Bafoly*,[32] the respondents were stopped at airport security en route from Halifax to Montreal. Sendji was found to have a brick-sized stack of $20 bills, covered in tin foil, in his underwear. Additional money was found in the respondents' shoes and luggage. In all, $109,000 in cash was seized. Some of it had red stains on it, and there were also pieces of paper the same size as the bank notes, some with crude copies of the serial numbers. Charges of "possession of proceeds of crime" and "counterfeiting" were laid but later discontinued, and the Crown sought forfeiture under subs. 490(9) instead. At the hearing the respondents testified, and explained that they were originally from Cameroon, that cash was the standard manner of banking in their family, that the red marks on the banknotes were from a ritualistic "purification" of the money with iodine in substitution for goat's blood, and that they were carrying the $109,000 to Halifax to purchase cars for resale. Although the Crown called evidence to show that the money was likely being used in a "black money scam", the judge was not satisfied that the Crown had proven this beyond a reasonable doubt, and ordered the money returned. On appeal, this was affirmed.

It is important to note that the courts have consistently held that although the Crown does not have to obtain a conviction for a specific crime in order to apply for forfeiture under subs. 490(9), nevertheless the Crown must prove beyond a reasonable doubt that the property in question is derived from crime or otherwise inherently illegal to possess. A reasonable doubt as to taint will result in the property not being forfeited.

Finally, subs. 490(9) gives a statutory right of appeal to any person who "feels aggrieved" by a forfeiture order or restoration order under subs. 490(9).

A Note about "Offence-Related Property"

Related to proceeds of crime is the doctrine of "offence-related property". Property used in any manner in the commission of a specified offence is defined as "offence-related property", and in practice refers to equipment and buildings used for the production of cannabis marihuana, vehicles routinely used to transport drugs for the purposes of trafficking, fortified clubhouses alleged to be used for criminal offences by outlaw motorcycle gangs, and other property that is used for the purpose of the commission of specified offences. Although not necessarily derived from crime as are proceeds of crime, offence-related property is treated in similar fashion by the criminal law: it can be seized, restrained, and forfeited upon conviction.[33]

Civil Forfeiture of the Proceeds of Crime

In the 1990s, the provinces, beginning with Ontario and Alberta, began to create provincial laws to restrain and forfeit proceeds of crime and offence-related property. By the mid-2000s these statutes were common and included:

- British Columbia: *Civil Forfeiture Act*
- Alberta: *Victims Restitution and Compensation Payment Act*
- Saskatchewan: *Seizure of Criminal Property Act*
- Manitoba: *Criminal Property Forfeiture Act*
- Ontario: *Remedies for Organized Crime and Other Unlawful Activities Act*
- Nova Scotia: *Civil Forfeiture Act*

These laws, however, faced an enormous hurdle: under the constitution, the federal Parliament has exclusive jurisdiction over all matters relating to criminal law. While the provinces have authority to legislate over property and civil rights, and while this is the basis upon which the provincial law-makers purported to pass these laws, one could be forgiven for wondering if in truth these laws were criminal in nature and therefore beyond the authority of the provincial legislatures. The Supreme Court recently determined this.

In 2003, Robin Chatterjee was driving his car just north of Toronto when the police pulled him over because he was missing a front license plate. They found that he was in breach of his probation—he was supposed to be living in Ottawa, while by his own admission he was actually living in Thornhill, some 400 kilometres away—and arrested him. A search of his car incident to arrest turned up $29,000 cash and some grow equipment (a lamp and a fan) that reeked of marihuana. But no marihuana was found and Chatterjee was not charged with any drug or proceeds of crime offence. The Ontario Crown applied to forfeit the $29,000 under the civil forfeiture statute. Chatterjee argued that the statute—known as the *Civil Remedies Act, 2001*—encroached on federal criminal law jurisdiction and was unconstitutional.

Eleven interveners—including most of the provincial Attorneys General, and criminal defence associations—joined in the case before the Supreme Court of Canada. In the end, the Supreme Court sided with the provincial governments and found the statute to be valid provincial law. Justice Binnie summarized the Court's reasoning thus:

> [3] ...The *CRA* was enacted to deter crime and to compensate its victims. The former purpose is broad enough that both the federal government (in relation to criminal law) and the provincial governments (in relation to property and civil rights) can validly pursue it. The latter purpose falls squarely within provincial competence. Crime imposes substantial costs on provincial treasuries. Those costs impact many provincial interests, including health, policing resources, community stability and family welfare. It would be out of step with modern realities to conclude that a province must shoulder the costs to the community of criminal behaviour but cannot use deterrence to suppress it.

> [4] Moreover, the *CRA* [*Civil Remedies Act*] method of attack on crime is to authorize *in rem* forfeiture of its proceeds and differs from both the traditional criminal law which ordinarily couples a prohibition with a penalty (see *Reference re Firearms Act (Canada)*, 2000 SCC 31, [2000] 1 S.C.R. 783) and criminal procedure which in general refers to the means by which an allegation of a particular criminal offence is proven against a particular offender. The appellant's answer, however, is that the effect of

the *CRA in rem* remedy just adds to the penalties available in the criminal process, and as such the *CRA* invalidly interferes with the sentencing regime established by Parliament. It is true that forfeiture may have *de facto* punitive effects in some cases, but its dominant purpose is to make crime in general unprofitable, to capture resources tainted by crime so as to make them unavailable to fund future crime and to help compensate private individuals and public institutions for the costs of past crime. These are valid provincial objects. There is no operational conflict between the forfeiture provisions of the *Criminal Code*, R.S.C. 1985, c. C-46, and the *CRA*. It cannot reasonably be said that the *CRA* amounts to colourable criminal legislation. Accordingly, I would dismiss the appeal.[34]

MONEY LAUNDERING

The term "money laundering" refers to activity undertaken by criminal profiteers (usually drug dealers) and their assistants to take criminal profits and conceal or convert them into some other form. The offence of money laundering under s. 462.31 of the *Code* indicates the breadth of activity intended to be caught by the section:

> **462.31 (1) Laundering proceeds of crime**—Every one commits an offence who uses, transfers the possession of, send or delivers to any person or place, transports, transmits, alters, disposes of or otherwise deals with, in any manner and by any means, any property or any proceeds of any property with intent to conceal or convert that property or those proceeds, knowing or believing that all or a part of that property or of those proceeds was obtained or derived directly or indirectly as a result of
> > (a) the commission in Canada of a designated offence; or
> > (b) an act or omission anywhere that, if it had occurred in Canada, would have constituted a designated offence.
>
> **(2) Punishment**—Every one who commits an offence under subsection (1)
> > (a) is guilty of an indictable offence and liable to imprisonment for a term not exceeding ten years; or
> > (b) is guilty of an offence punishable on summary conviction.
>
> **(3) Exception**—A peace officer or a person acting under the direction of a peace officer is not guilty of an offence under subsection (1) if the peace officer or person does any of the things mentioned in that subsection for the purposes of an investigation or otherwise in the execution of the peace officer's duties.

This provision covers all profitable crimes—fraud, robbery, etc.—but by far the main focus of interdiction is in respect of drug dealing, so that is the focus here.

The Problem with Cash

Cash is a major headache for drug dealers. Drug users purchasing cannabis, ecstasy, cocaine, and the like for personal use invariably pay with cash, and invariably with $20 bills. Cash is anonymous, untraceable, and it doesn't "bounce". Drug users and sellers like cash for all of these reasons. But at some point the flow of cash becomes a problem.

From the street user upwards, to the street dealer, to the middle retailer, and to the wholesale supplier, the amount of cash involved grows and multiplies. One kilogram of cocaine on the Canadian wholesale market may cost $40,000 (depending on the region and other circumstances). If, as is common, this is paid in $20 bills that have trickled up from the consumers, and each banknote weighs about a gram, the wholesale drug dealer now has two kilograms of cash. (Apparently high-level drug traffickers frequently weigh rather than count their money!)

It was precisely because international drug traffickers and money launderers use cash that the Canadian Mint stopped production of the pink $1,000 bill in May 2000; one $1,000 bill would equal fifty $20 bills.

Such a large sum of cash is not just bulky; it attracts attention. A drug dealer purchasing a car or home entertainment centre or an air ticket with a stack of bills runs the risk of being noticed and singled out, attracting the attention of law enforcement. Further, it is impractical to simply walk into the bank and deposit $40,000 in cash into an account. Banks and other financial institutions have always been encouraged by the law enforcement community to report suspicious cash transactions to the police. Section 462.47 of the *Code* specifically confers lawful justification on anyone who discloses to the police "any facts on the basis of which that person reasonably suspects that any property is proceeds of crime or that any person has committed or is about to commit a designated offence." (Indeed, as discussed below, financial institutions are now legally obliged to report certain transactions to FINTRAC as well.)

Finally, the drug dealer must try to distance himself from the source of the funds, to avoid being tied to drug dealing.

Money laundering is, quite simply, the process of concealing and converting cash for all of these reasons. Here are some typical methods of money laundering that have turned up in real cases.

In "smurfing", a drug dealer takes a large sum of cash (e.g., $40,000) and either personally or with the assistance of others goes to a series of banks and deposits it in smaller increments (e.g., ten transactions of

$4,000), hoping to avoid scrutiny because of the smaller multiple transactions.

"Fronting" is a term used to describe the use of an apparently legitimate business to funnel cash into the banks. For example, a restaurant's daily cash receipts would be boosted with drug money, and all of the cash is then commingled and deposited. The bank thinks the restaurant is doing well, nothing seems suspicious, and the only downside for the drug dealer is that he or she will owe taxes on the money. Other businesses frequently used for fronting include used-car dealerships and convenience stores, but any business that would ordinarily have cash-paying customers is suitable.

Another common method is "false gambling", in which a drug dealer takes a large sum of cash to the casino or racetrack, and gambles with it. The odds are pretty good that over a period of steady gambling the drug dealer will win back a substantial portion of the original cash, but now he has casino or racetrack winnings—often paid out by cheque—instead of drug money. A variation on this method is to over-purchase a winning lottery ticket; i.e., to offer a lottery winner $15,000 cash for a winning lottery ticket worth a prize of $10,000, and once again the drug dealer has lottery winnings instead of drug money, albeit at a discount

Although there are not yet any publicly documented cases, the potential to use a "White Label Automated Teller Machine" to launder drug money is interesting. Anyone can lease or buy a non-bank or "white label" ATM from a number of (legitimate) companies, which also provide a hook-up to the familiar inter-branch banking system (e.g., Interac). A criminal organization could simply place a white label ATM in a bar, a train station, or some other innocuous high-volume location, and regularly fill the ATM with $20 bills from the drug trade. Every time a customer withdraws cash from the ATM, his or her bank account is debited and the organization's account is credited through Interac. Bill by bill, hundreds of thousands of dollars in drug money could be laundered in this way. Obviously the companies that operate "white label" ATM bank machines are perfectly legitimate, upstanding corporate citizens, and in no way implicated in the money laundering scenario described here. As with many techniques for money laundering, drug dealers and other criminal profiteers do frequently take advantage of honest law-abiding people and businesses.

One long-standing avenue for money laundering is the use of "offshore banking", where financial institutions operating in foreign jurisdictions offer a variety of services not available domestically. Again, these are by and large legitimate financial institutions, however, money launderers can take advantage of some of the services offered. Such services include anonymous banking, which allows a customer to take cash to the bank or an affiliate of the bank, and deposit it into an account anonymously. The account may be in the depositor's name, another person's name, or a fictitious name—all that matters is that someone (often under a pseudonym) has authority to transfer the money to another bank. Frequently the money will be transferred several times, heavily insulating the drug dealer from police scrutiny and distancing him from the original cash.

Recently anonymous debit cards have become a popular offering of offshore financial institutions. Customers can go on-line and obtain a debit card that will work in any ATM anywhere in the world. The debit card has no name on it, can be "juiced up" by depositing cash at any bank, and can be mailed or given to someone else (e.g., in payment of a drug debt) and all the person needs is a PIN in order to get cash from any ATM in the world. This and other "offshore banking" services no doubt have legitimate purposes; the only point here made is that they can be exploited by persons interested in concealing and converting illegal proceeds of crime.

Money Laundering—The Offence

Returning to the offence of money laundering, as defined above, it has the following elements:

(1) an act of laundering which, as indicated in the section, can be virtually any action taken in order to "conceal" or "convert" the property in question;
(2) the intention to "conceal" or "convert" which, as well, is rather broad; and
(3) the knowledge *or belief* that the property has been obtained or derived from a designated offence.

Two points are worth exploring a bit further. First, the statutory term "conceal or convert" has been interpreted as follows by Laskin, J.A., of the Ontario Court of Appeal, in *R. v. Tejani*, at para. 28:[35]

> [28] The words "conceal" and "convert" are not synonymous. Conceal does mean to hide. But convert has a broader meaning; it means to change or transform. By using the broader word "convert", Parliament no doubt recognized that a good deal of money laundering is effected by simple currency exchanges, by simple conversions from Canadian to U.S. dollars. In other words, although the purpose of laundering money is to dis-

guise the source of the funds, this disguising is often accomplished by a mere currency exchange. To prohibit money laundering by simple currency exchanges, Parliament used the word "convert".

Second, s. 461.31 provides that the defendant is guilty where he or she conceals or converts the property "knowing or believing" that it is proceeds of crime. This is to be compared to the offence of possession of proceeds of crime, discussed above, where the defendant must know that the property is proceeds of crime, and mere belief is insufficient.

Belief that the money is derived from crime, as a basis for liability for money laundering, was added following the case of *United States v. Dynar*.[36] Arye Dynar jumped at the chance to launder large quantities of drug money from American drug dealers, in exchange for a percentage. In fact, the supposed American drug dealers were undercover police agents, and the money was police money. At that time, the laundering provisions made it an offence to launder property "knowing that . . . it was obtained or derived directly or indirectly" from one of the designated offences. Dynar argued that he could not be convicted of the offence of laundering since, although he *believed* the money was drug money, logically he could not be said to *know* that it was drug money, since in fact it was not.

The Courts eventually found that Dynar could be found guilty of attempting to launder drug money—incidentally resolving several law school textbook questions about knowledge *versus* belief, and impossible attempts—and the primary issue was cleared up when Parliament amended the statute to insert the words "or believing" into the offence of money laundering.

Finally, the wording of subs. 462.31(3) should be noted. This provision exempts from criminal liability any peace officer or person acting under the peace officer's direction, who commits what would otherwise be an act of money laundering, where this is done "for the purposes of an investigation or otherwise in the execution of the peace officer's duties." This exemption enables an undercover police officer or police agent to handle drug money without committing a crime, making it possible for the police to lawfully engage in undercover operations, "reverse stings", and other methods used to target money launderers.

FINTRAC

Largely in response to the problem posed by international money laundering, the "Financial Action Task Force on Money Laundering" (commonly known as FATF) was established at a G-7 summit in Paris in 1989:

> The Task Force was given the responsibility of examining money launder-ing techniques and trends, reviewing the action which had already been taken at a national or international level, and setting out the measures that still needed to be taken to combat money laundering. In April 1990, less than one year after its creation, the FATF issued a report containing a set of Forty Recommendations, which provide a comprehensive blueprint of the action needed to fight against money laundering.

> During 1991 and 1992, the FATF expanded its membership from the original total of 16 to 28 members. Since that early period, the FATF has continued to examine the methods used to launder criminal proceeds and has completed two rounds of mutual evaluations of its member coun-tries and jurisdictions. FATF has updated the Forty Recommendations to reflect the changes which have occurred in money laundering and has sought to encourage other countries around the world to adopt anti-money laundering measures.[37]

In 1991, Canada's *Proceeds of Crime (Money Laundering) Act* was proclaimed, establishing record-keeping obligations on the part of fi-nancial institutions in order to make it easier for law enforcement to investigate and prosecute money laundering offences. This first step has since been greatly expanded and the present *Proceeds of Crime (Money Laundering) and Terrorist Financing Act*[38] goes a lot further than the 1991 legislation.

However in 1996, FATF reported that Canada (among other na-tions) was not yet in compliance with all of FATF's Forty Recommen-dations, and over the next few years a mutual evaluation of Canada's performance *vis-à-vis* anti-money laundering measure was carried out. By May 1999, legislation to establish the Financial Transactions and Reports Analysis Centre of Canada (FINTRAC) was tabled in Parlia-ment. Following the terrorist attacks on the World Trade Towers in New York on September 11, 2001, additional measures were passed to cover the recording and reporting of financial transactions of not just money laundering activity, but also terrorist financing.

This leads us to the present FINTRAC regime, and measures de-signed to uncover money laundering and terrorist financing activity, and to share certain information with law enforcement agencies.

FINTRAC is a civilian (non-police) agency operating under the au-thority of the Ministry of Finance (Canada). The Centre receives reports from persons, businesses, and other entities obliged to keep records and make reports of certain transactions, analyzes the reports, and compiles information databases in an attempt to combat money laundering and terrorist financing. Those required to keep records of financial transactions and make reports to FINTRAC include banks, credit unions, real estate brokers, casinos, accountants—essentially everyone who is either in the money business, or who might conduct large money transactions in the course of their ordinary business. The records that must be kept include all sorts of details, *e.g.*, who the customer is, the nature and amount of the transaction, any account numbers involved, and so forth. Reports required to be made to FINTRAC concern suspicious transactions and large cash transactions, and must include sufficient detail to enable FINTRAC to identify the nature and purpose of the transaction in question and the persons involved. FINTRAC expects reports to be made electronically, which is cheaper and quicker than a paper report, and allows the data to be stored and analyzed more efficiently. Significantly, it is an offence for a business or entity that is required to make a report to FINTRAC on a suspicious transaction or large cash transaction to "tip off" the customer that the report has been made.

In the original version of the PCMLFTA, lawyers were included in the list of entities required to keep records and make reports to FINTRAC. However, court challenges, based on the argument that requiring lawyers to report on their clients would infringe solicitor-client privilege, were successful[39] and lawyers were officially taken off the list on March 24, 2003.

Clearly a large number of innocent transactions will be caught in the net described above, and FINTRAC's job is essentially to sort out the very small number of suspect transactions from the whole. If it appears that there are reasonable grounds to believe that information about a transaction would assist in a money laundering or terrorist financing investigation, FINTRAC is allowed to share certain information with law enforcement officials about the transaction and let them carry out their own investigation.

Finally, FINTRAC has counterparts in many other countries who may share information with each other—FinCen in the United States, AUSTRAC in Australia, and NCIS in the United Kingdom. Thus on the domestic front as well as internationally, FINTRAC is set up to detect money laundering and terrorist financing activities by enlisting the assistance of businesses and other persons dealing in money with their customers, and to share information with its counterparts in the international arena and domestic law enforcement authorities

458 / From Crime to Punishment

A Note on Terrorist Financing

In early 2002, Bill C-36 came into force in Canada. This Bill was a cohesive package of amendments to the *Criminal Code* and to other laws, as a direct response to the increasing global threat of terrorism in general and to the attacks on the World Trade Centre in New York on September 11, 2001, in particular.

Under this anti-terrorism legislation, it is possible to seize, freeze, and forfeit property owned by, used by, or intended for use by a terrorist or terrorism group (*Code*, ss. 83.13, 83.14). Further, it is now a criminal offence for anyone to deal directly or indirectly with any property, or enter into or facilitate any transaction respecting any property, owned or controlled by a terrorist or terrorist group (s. 83.08).

While it might seem a bit feeble to try to combat terrorism by going after terrorists' property, in fact there is a very practical and useful aspect to these provisions. The Governor in Council (federal Cabinet) has authority to identify terrorists and terrorism groups by putting them on a list that is then published in the Canada Gazette. This listing is based on information supplied by the Solicitor General. Once a group is listed this way, they are literally defined to be a terrorist group (*Code*, subs. 83.05(6), defining "terrorist group"). As mentioned above, it is a criminal offence for anyone—a bank, a credit card company, a lumber-yard—to do business with a terrorist group. Thus anyone put on the list in this fashion will be unable to withdraw money from the bank, make a mortgage or credit card payment, or do any of the hundreds of things ordinary citizens do every day. In effect, the freezing measures are designed to put terrorists literally out of business.

Finally, it is important to note that anyone who is listed as a terrorist group can apply to the courts for a judicial review (*Code*, subs. 83.05(6)). This supervision of government by the courts is, of course, not just confined to terrorism. As has been shown above, our judges play a key role in implementing the proceeds of crime and money laundering provisions as well. Indeed, it is one of the cornerstones of our democracy that the ultimate decision-making authority in our criminal law rests with the judiciary.

Notes

[1] *Québec (Attorney General) v. Royal Bank*, 1983 CarswellQue 31, (sub nom. *Royal Bank c. Bourque*) 38 C.R. (3d) 363 (Que. S.C.), affirmed 1985 CarswellQue 9, 18 C.C.C. (3d) 98, 44 C.R. (3d) 387 (Que. C.A.).

2 Cited as E/ Conf. 82/ 15 (1988), the text of the convention can be found at: http:// www.unodc. org/pdf/convention_1988_en.pdf.

3 For a good account of the legislative history, see: German, *Proceeds of Crime* (Toronto: Carswell, looseleaf) at 2.1-3.2; MacFarlane, Frater & Proulx, *Drug Offences in Canada*, 3d ed. (Aurora: Canada Law Book, looseleaf) at 11.20 - 11.135.

4 *Criminal Code* of Canada, R.S.C. 1985, c. C-46, as amended [hereinafter the *Code*].

5 *R. v. Wilson*, 1993 CarswellOnt 129, 25 C.R. (4th) 239, (sub nom. *Wilson v. Canada*) 86 C.C.C. (3d) 464, (sub nom. *Wilson v. R.*) 15 O.R. (3d) 645, (sub nom. *Wilson v. R.*) 66 O.A.C. 219 (C.A.), at para. 11.

6 *R. v. Rosenblum*, 130 C.C.C. (3d) 481, 1998 CarswellBC 2803, 116 B.C.A.C. 98, 190 W.A.C. 98, 167 D.L.R. (4th) 639 (C.A.), at paras. 20, 21.

7 *Québec (Procureure générale) c. Laroche*, 2002 CarswellQue 2413, 2002 CarswellQue 2414, 6 C.R. (6th) 272, [2002] 3 S.C.R. 708, 219 D.L.R. (4th) 723, 295 N.R. 291, 169 C.C.C. (3d) 97, 99 C.R.R. (2d) 252 (S.C.C.), at para. 25.

8 *R. v. Rosenblum, supra*, note 6.

9 *Civil Asset Forfeiture Reform Act*, Pub.L. No. 106-185, 115 Stat. 202 (2000); see U.S. Code, Title 18, Part I, Chapter 46, §981.

10 *Regulations Excluding Certain Indictable Offences from the Definition of "Designated Offence"* SOR/2002-63, January 31, 2002: http://canadagazette.gc.ca/partII/2002/20020213/ html/sor63-e.html

11 *R. v. Dixon*, 2002 CarswellOnt 728 (Ont. S.C.J.).

12 *R. v. Seman*, 1994 CarswellMan 245, 93 Man. R. (2d) 151 (Man. Q.B.).

13 *Code*, para. 462.34(4)(c).

14 See *R. v. Wilson*, 2001 CarswellNS 295, 2001 NSSC 129, 196 N.S.R. (2d) 272, 613 A.P.R. 272 (N. S.C.); and *R. v. Innocente*, 2001 CarswellNS 389, 2001 NSSC 138, 198 N.S.R. (2d) 77, 621 A.P.R. 77 (N.S. S.C.).

15 See *Morra v. R.*, 1992 CarswellOnt 119, 17 C.R. (4th) 325, (sub nom. *R. v. Morra*) 77 C.C.C. (3d) 380, (sub nom. *R. v. Morra*) 11 C.R.R. (2d) 379 (Ont. Gen. Div.); *Terezakis v. British Columbia (Department of Justice)*, 1999 CarswellBC 2742 (B.C. S.C.); and *R. v. Trang*, 2001 CarswellAlta 1413, 2001 ABQB 919, 88 C.R.R. (2d) 134, 161 C.C.C. (3d) 210, 300 A.R. 112 (Alta. Q.B.).

16 *R. v. Wilson, supra*, note 5, at para. 46.

17 *Québec (Procureure générale) c. Laroche, supra*, note 7, *per* Lebel J. at para. 70.

18 See, for example, *R. v. Hutt*, 1994 CarswellOnt 2368 (Ont. Gen. Div.).

19 See *R. v. Tortone*, 1993 CarswellOnt 114, 1993 CarswellOnt 986, 23 C.R. (4th) 83, 84 C.C.C. (3d) 15, 15 O.R. (3d) 64 (note), [1993] 2 S.C.R. 973, 65 O.A.C. 81, 156 N.R. 241 (S.C.C.).

20 *R. v. Warwaruk*, 2000 CarswellMan 23, [2000] M.J. No. 25, 143 Man. R. (2d) 315 (Man. Q.B.), reversed on other grounds 2002 CarswellMan 354, 2002 MBCA 100, [2002] M.J. No. 320, 166 Man. R. (2d) 135, 278 W.A.C. 135, [2002] 11 W.W.R. 48, 169 C.C.C. (3d) 76 (Man. C.A.).

21 *R. c. Lore*, 1997 CarswellQue 315, 7 C.R. (5th) 190, 116 C.C.C. (3d) 255, [1997] R.J.Q. 1561 (C.A.), leave to appeal refused (1999), (sub nom. *R. v. Lore*) 239 N.R. 398 (note) (S.C.C.); see also *Québec (Procureure générale) c. Laroche, supra*, note 7, *per* Lebel J. at para. 36.

22 *R. v. Hape*, 2002 CarswellOnt 4295 (Ont. S.C.J.), affirmed 2005 CarswellOnt 3298, 201 O.A.C. 126 (Ont. C.A.), affirmed 2007 CarswellOnt 3563, 2007 CarswellOnt

3564, 2007 SCC 26, 47 C.R. (6th) 96, 363 N.R. 1, 227 O.A.C. 191, 160 C.R.R. (2d) 1, [2007] 2 S.C.R. 292, 220 C.C.C. (3d) 161, 280 D.L.R. (4th) 385 (S.C.C.).

23 *Code*, s. 462.37(2.01).

24 *R. v. Appleby*, 2007 CarswellNfld 304, [2007] N.J. No. 200, 2007 NLTD 109, 268 Nfld. & P.E.I.R. 75, 813 A.P.R. 75 (N.L. T.D.), affirmed 2009 CarswellNfld 23, 2009 NLCA 6 , 242 C.C.C. (3d) 229, 282 Nfld. & P.E.I.R. 134, 868 A.P.R. 134 (N.L. C.A.), leave to appeal refused 2009 CarswellNfld 282, 2009 CarswellNfld 283 (S.C.C.).

25 *R. v. Brooks*, 2000 CarswellSask 660, 2000 SKQB 515, [2001] 3 W.W.R. 532, 198 Sask. R. 63 (Sask. Q.B.).

26 *R. v. Tatarchuk*, 1992 CarswellAlta 125, 4 Alta. L.R. (3d) 300, [1993] 1 W.W.R. 349, 133 A.R. 6 (Alta. Q.B.).

27 *R. v. Wilson, supra*, note 5.

28 *R. v. Clymore*, 1992 CarswellBC 1097, 74 C.C.C. (3d) 217 (B.C. S.C.).

29 *R. v. Marriott*, 2001 CarswellNS 172, 2001 NSCA 84, 42 C.R. (5th) 339, 194 N.S.R. (2d) 64, 606 A.P.R. 64, (sub nom. *Stone Estate, Re*) 155 C.C.C. (3d) 168 (C.A.).

30 *R. v. Daley*, 2001 CarswellAlta 874, 2001 ABCA 155, 94 Alta. L.R. (3d) 238, 44 C.R. (5th) 26, 85 C.R.R. (2d) 215, [2001] 9 W.W.R. 16, 156 C.C.C. (3d) 225, 281 A.R. 262, 248 W.A.C. 262 (Alta. C.A.).

31 *Ryan v. Canada (Attorney General)*, 2002 CarswellNS 213, 2002 NSSC 143 (N.S. S.C.).

32 *R. v. Sendji & Bafoly*, (June 29, 2001) (N.S. Prov.Ct.), affirmed (January 4, 2002) Court file S.H. No. 172950 (N.S. S.C.) (unreported).

33 For a discussion of what to do with a marihuana grow operation being run in a house that is also occupied by innocent others see the Supreme Court of Canada's judgments in *R. v. Craig*, 2009 CarswellBC 1357, 2009 CarswellBC 1358, 2009 SCC 23, 244 C.C.C. (3d) 1, 388 N.R. 254, 306 D.L.R. (4th) 577, 66 C.R. (6th) 201, 271 B.C.A.C. 1, 458 W.A.C. 1; *R. v. Nguyen*, 2009 CarswellBC 1359, 2009 CarswellBC 1360, 2009 SCC 25, 66 C.R. (6th) 231, 244 C.C.C. (3d) 48, 388 N.R. 329, 306 D.L.R. (4th) 624, 271 B.C.A.C. 67, 458 W.A.C. 67; and *R. c. Ouellette*, 2009 CarswellQue 4982, 2009 CarswellQue 4983, 2009 SCC 24, 66 C.R. (6th) 235, 244 C.C.C. (3d) 42, 388 N.R. 320, 306 D.L.R. (4th) 618; the Court approved "partial forfeiture" in certain cases.

34 *Chatterjee v. Ontario (Attorney General)*, 2009 CarswellOnt 1949, 2009 CarswellOnt 1950, 2009 SCC 19, 242 C.C.C. (3d) 129, 65 C.R. (6th) 1, 387 N.R. 206, 304 D.L.R. (4th) 513, 249 O.A.C. 355, 97 O.R. (3d) 399 (note), [2009] 1 S.C.R. 624 (S.C.C.).

35 *R. v. Tejani*, 1999 CarswellOnt 2707, 27 C.R. (5th) 351, 138 C.C.C. (3d) 366, 123 O.A.C. 329 (Ont.C.A.), leave to appeal refused 2000 CarswellOnt 917, 2000 CarswellOnt 918, [1999] S.C.C.A. No. 509, 253 N.R. 397 (note), 42 C.C.C. (3d) vi, 134 O.A.C. 199 (note) (S.C.C.).

36 *United States v. Dynar*, 1997 CarswellOnt 1981, 1997 CarswellOnt 1982, 8 C.R. (5th) 79, 44 C.R.R. (2d) 189, [1997] 2 S.C.R. 462, 213 N.R. 321, 115 C.C.C. (3d) 481, 147 D.L.R. (4th) 399, 33 O.R. (3d) 478 (headnote only), 101 O.A.C. 321 (S.C.C.).

37 http://www1.oecd.org/fatf/AboutFATF_en.htm#What%20is.

38 S.C. 2000, c. 17, known awkwardly as the PCMLTFA.

[39] *Law Society (British Columbia) v. Canada (Attorney General)*, 2002 CarswellBC 160, 2002 BCCA 49, [2002] B.C.J. No. 130, 98 B.C.L.R. (3d) 310, 160 C.C.C. (3d) 378, 207 D.L.R. (4th) 736, [2002] 3 W.W.R. 483 (B.C. C.A.), leave to appeal allowed 2002 CarswellBC 899, 2002 CarswellBC 900, [2002] S.C.C.A. No. 52, 292 N.R. 397 (note), 173 B.C.A.C. 320 (note), 283 W.A.C. 320 (note) (S.C.C.); *Federation of Law Societies of Canada v. Canada (Attorney General)*, 2002 CarswellNS 293, 2002 NSSC 95, [2002] N.S.J. No. 199, 203 N.S.R. (2d) 53, 635 A.P.R. 53, 20 C.P.C. (5th) 188 (N.S. S.C.).

23

Canadian Charter of Rights and Freedoms

Mark Heerema*

INTRODUCTION

No review of criminal law in Canada would be complete without mention of the *Canadian Charter of Rights and Freedoms* (the "*Charter*"). The *Charter* is a constitutionally-entrenched bill of rights containing a wide-range of rights and freedoms that affect all Canadians such as the freedom of religion, the freedom of expression, the freedom of association, mobility rights, the right to be free from unreasonable search and seizure, and the presumption of innocence.

It is difficult to overstate the degree to which the *Charter* has impacted the political and legal landscape in Canada. In less than 30 years, many highly-charged and highly-controversial issues have in some way been scrutinized for compliance with the *Charter*, a sample of which includes anti-abortion laws, anti-marihuana laws, the definition of marriage, the collection of DNA, the use of corporal punishment, the legality of strip searches, the use of police informants, and the use of the death penalty in other countries. In tackling these issues and others, courts in Canada, lead by the Supreme Court of Canada, have actively protected the rights offered to Canadians in the *Charter*.

We are in the midst of the *Charter* era. A time in Canadian jurisprudence defined by the impact of *Charter* rights and freedoms. It is arguable that criminal law, more than any other area of law, has been most directly impacted by the *Charter*. While not only are the provisions of the *Criminal Code* subject to *Charter* review, all actions of law enforcement must comply with the *Charter*. Put somewhat differently, the laws of the state and the actions of the state must satisfy the *Charter*.

Please note that the full text of the *Charter* has been set out in Appendix "A" to this chapter.

---

* B.A., University of Alberta, Camrose, Alberta; LL.B., Dalhousie Law School, Halifax, Nova Scotia; LL.M., University of Cambridge, Cambridge, England; Crown Attorney, Special Prosecutions Section, Nova Scotia Public Prosecution Service, Halifax, Nova Scotia.

THE CHARTER: A PART OF CANADA'S CONSTITUTION

The *Charter* became part of the Constitution of Canada on April 17, 1982, as it was formally enacted as Part I of the *Constitution Act, 1982*. Section 52 of the *Constitution Act, 1982*, states as follows:

> The Constitution of Canada is the supreme law of Canada, and any law that is inconsistent with the provisions of the Constitution is, to the extent of the inconsistency, of no force or effect.

It is the supremacy of the Constitution of Canada which has truly cemented the rights and freedoms protected by the *Charter*. Before reviewing specific *Charter* rights and freedoms relevant to criminal law, it is useful to first gain some appreciation of constitutional law in Canada.

The Intersection of Criminal Law and Constitutional Law Prior to the Enactment of the Charter

Since Confederation in 1867, the federal and provincial governments have been subject to the Constitution of Canada. Prior to the *Constitution Act, 1982*, the Constitution was known as the *British North America Act, 1867,* which contained the original Act of the British Parliament of 1867, as well as, all subsequent amendments.

At a general level, the *British North America Act, 1867* concerns itself with matters of polity; that is, outlining how Canada is organized as a federal state. Accordingly, one of the most important functions of the *British North America Act, 1867* is to delineate the distribution of powers between the federal and provincial governments.

Under the *British North America Act, 1867*, jurisdiction over the criminal justice system is shared between the federal government and provincial governments.

Subsection 91(27) of the *British North America Act, 1867* provides the federal government with power over

> The Criminal Law, except the Constitution of Courts of Criminal Jurisdiction, but including the Procedure in Criminal Matters

This federal power has been interpreted to bestow upon the federal government the exclusive right to define and create criminal offences. Pursuant to subs. 92(14), provinces are given power over,

> The Administration of Justice in the Province, including the Constitution, Maintenance, and Organization of Provincial Courts, both of Civil and of

Criminal Jurisdiction, and including Procedure in Civil Matters in those Courts.

In interpreting and enforcing this aspect of Canada's Constitution, courts have been required to adjudicate disputes where it is alleged that either the federal government, or a provincial government, has overstepped their powers under the *British North America Act, 1867*. The 1976 decision of the Supreme Court of Canada involving Dr. Henry Morgentaler is an excellent example of the Court's role in this regard.[1]

Dr. Morgentaler is an extremely prolific and controversial doctor who operated abortion clinics at a time when abortions were prohibited (with exceptions) by the *Criminal Code*. In 1976, Dr. Morgentaler brought an appeal to the Supreme Court of Canada stating that the general prohibition against abortions in the *Criminal Code* was unconstitutional on the basis that it exceeded the power of the federal government under s. 91 of the *British North America Act, 1867*. The Supreme Court of Canada decided that the anti-abortion offence was constitutional as it was aimed at criminal law matters and, accordingly, was within the legislative competency of the federal government pursuant to subs. 91(27).

Today, the 1976 decision in *Morgentaler* stands as an excellent example of how constitutional and criminal law intersected prior to the *Charter*. If the court was satisfied that the legislative body was within their jurisdiction pursuant to the heads of powers listed in ss. 91 or 92, the constitutionality of the law was preserved, no matter how the court felt the law impacted "rights" or "freedoms"recognized by statute or common-law. In 1977, just prior to the enactment of the *Charter*, the Supreme Court of Canada succinctly captured this reality:

> The Courts will not question the wisdom of enactments ... but it is the high duty of this Court to insure that the Legislatures do not transgress the limits of their constitutional mandate and engage in the illegal exercise of power.[2]

This changed with the enactment of the *Charter*.

The Intersection of Criminal Law and Consitutional Law After the Enactment of the Charter

The enactment of the *Charter* into the Constitution of Canada has provided courts with a new ability to review laws. No longer restricted simply to matters of legislative competence, the Constitution now contains a set of substantive rights and freedoms for courts to scrutinize laws and actions of the state.

Thus, two main constitutional questions can now be raised: first, does the legislative body have the jurisdiction to pass the law; and, second, does the law comply with the provisions of the *Charter*?

Initially, it was unclear how courts would respond to their newfound powers under the *Charter*. Would the *Charter* remain a mere reflection of hopes and dreams, yet contain nothing which the courts would be willing to enforce? For some, the prospect of courts striking down laws with respect to the *Charter* was offensive to notions of democracy. Others felt that courts were obligated to honour the intention of the *Charter*, a hard-fought document reflecting a proper exercise of the democratic process.

These questions and speculations were soon laid to rest by the Supreme Court of Canada. In their early judgments on the *Charter*, the Court quickly embraced their role as guardians of the Constitution. The *Charter* was interpreted to be a purposive document, a "living tree" that would be interpreted in a manner which permitted its growth and adjustment over time.[3] In an early decision in *Hunter* v. *Southam*,[4] the Court stated as follows, at para. 16:

> The task of expounding a constitution is crucially different from that of construing a statute. A statute defines present rights and obligations. It is easily enacted and as easily repealed. A constitution, by contrast, is drafted with an eye to the future. Its function is to provide a continuing framework for the legitimate exercise of governmental power and, when joined by a *Bill* or a *Charter of Rights*, for the unremitting protection of individual rights and liberties. Once enacted, its provisions cannot easily be repealed or amended. It must, therefore, be capable of growth and development over time to meet new social, political and historical realities often unimagined by its framers. The judiciary is the guardian of the constitution and must, in interpreting its provisions, bear these considerations in mind.

The early enthusiasm for applying the *Charter* by courts has not waned or dissipated. Directly or indirectly, the *Charter* has been pivotal in shaping and developing many areas of law in Canada, not just criminal law.

Before addressing specific rights and freedoms, let us return to Dr. Morgentaler. As noted above, in 1976 the Supreme Court of Canada upheld the anti-abortion provisions of the *Criminal Code* as being within the legislative competence of Parliament pursuant to subs. 91(27) of the *British North America Act, 1867*. Following the enactment of the *Charter*, Morgentaler launched a new challenge against the same provisions of the *Criminal Code*, this time claiming that the law offended s. 7 of the *Charter* as being contrary to the "security of the person".[5]

In a 5-2 decision, the Supreme Court of Canada agreed with Dr. Morgentaler. While affirming that the prohibition against abortion was within the scope of the federal government's criminal law power under s. 91 of the *British North America Act, 1867*, the Supreme Court of Canada found that the abortion provisions violated s. 7 of the *Charter*, and that the violation could not be saved under s. 1.

This latter *Morgentaler* decision poignantly demonstrates the new *Charter* era. It is no longer sufficient for Parliament or legislatures to stay simply within their respective legislative powers, now they must also ensure that the laws they enact do not violate the *Charter*. In this way, the *Charter* represents a new dimension of the intersection between constitutional and criminal law.

THE CHARTER AND CRIMINAL LAW

General

In beginning to think about criminal law in Canada, or any country for that matter, it is useful to view it as an attempt to find a mediated balance between two very strong interests. The first interest is law enforcement and protection. Clearly the state has an interest in eradicating crime, protecting its citizens, and punishing those who violate society's "rules". Yet, we know that if this was the only interest to protect, our society would look and feel very different: cameras on every street corner, the submission of DNA-profiles at birth, direct monitoring of all communications by the state, etc. This does not reflect modern society. There is an equally strong interest that individuals have to live their lives in a private manner without continual state-interference and intrusion. A natural and healthy tension exists between these conflicting interests which criminal law must address. In Canada, the *Charter* has been instrumental in effecting this balance:

> It is a deeply ingrained value in our democratic system that the ends do not justify the means. In particular, evidence or convictions may, at times, be obtained at too high a price. This proposition explains why as a society we insist on respect for individual rights and procedural guarantees in the criminal justice system. All of these values are reflected in specific provisions of the *Charter* such as the right to counsel, the right to remain silent, the presumption of innocence and in the global concept of fundamental justice. Obviously, many of the rights in ss. 7 and 14 of the *Charter* relate to norms for the proper conduct of criminal investigations and trials, and the courts are called on to ensure that these standards are observed. The

principles expressed in the *Charter* obviously do not emerge in a legal, social, or philosophical vacuum. With respect to criminal law in particular, the courts have, throughout the development of the common law and in the interpretation of statutes, consistently sought to ensure that the balance of power between the individual accused and the state was such that the interests and legitimate expectations of both would be recognized and protected.[6]

The *Charter* provides many relevant rights and freedoms to individuals who find themselves in the criminal justice system. It is important to note that the *Charter* did not invent these rights. Many, if not all of them, existed in some form in Canadian law prior to 1982. Nevertheless, it is the status of these rights that has changed with the enactment of the *Charter*. Now constitutionally-protected, these rights cannot be violated by the state, except for in a manner which is in compliance with the *Charter*.

Given the scope of this chapter, not all of the rights and freedoms contained in the *Charter* will be explored; however, what follows is a short summary with case examples of the key rights and freedoms pertaining to criminal law.

THE CHARTER

Section 1—The *Canadian Charter of Rights and Freedoms* guarantees the rights and freedoms set out in it subject only to such reasonable limits prescribed by law as can be demonstrably justified in a free and democratic society

The *Charter* begins by answering a difficult question: are *Charter* rights and freedoms absolute, and if not, how can they be limited? Section 1 clarifies that while the rights and freedoms contained in the *Charter* are guaranteed, they are not absolute. *Charter* rights and freedoms are subject only to such reasonable limits prescribed by law as can be demonstrably justified in a free and democratic society.

In *R. v. Oakes*,[7] the Supreme Court of Canada outlined a two-part test to determine the existence of a reasonable limit—now commonly referred to as the "*Oakes* test". A limitation on a *Charter* right will only be permitted where: (a) the limitation relates to a pressing and substantial objective, and (b) the means used to accomplish the objective are proportional; that being, the limitation is: (i) rationally connected to the objective; (ii) minimally impairing; and (iii) the deleterious effects do not outweigh the importance of the objective.

In *Charter* parlance, courts often refer to a violation of the *Charter* as being "saved by s. 1", which acknowledges that while a *Charter* right may have been violated, the limitation on the right is justified given our free and democratic society.

In *R. v. Butler*,[8] the accused was the owner of a store which sold pornographic materials. Following the execution of a search warrant by police, Butler was charged with a number of offences including possession and distribution of obscene materials. These offences relied on the definition of "obscene" contained in subs. 163(8) of the *Criminal Code* which holds that a publication shall be deemed to be obscene where "a dominant characteristic of which is the undue exploitation of sex, or of sex and any one or more of the following subjects, namely, crime, horror, cruelty and violence".

Butler argued that the definition of obscenity in the *Criminal Code* impermissibly violated the right to freedom of expression contained in s. 2(b) of the *Charter*. While the Supreme Court of Canada agreed that s. 2(b) was violated, they held that the prohibition against "obscene" material captured by this section (which they interpreted to be sexual activities paired with violence, dehumanizing, or degrading treatment) served a pressing and substantial objective aimed at preserving equality and to prevent harm to females. Thus, while subs. 163(8) of the *Criminal Code* was found to violate s. 2(b) of the *Charter*, it was upheld as a reasonable limitation under s. 1.

Section 7—Everyone has the right to life, liberty and security of the person and the right not to be deprived thereof except in accordance with the principles of fundamental justice.

Sections 7 to 14 of the *Charter* contain what are known as "Legal Rights". It is fitting that s. 7 begins this group of rights as it is an extremely robust right which has the potential to capture a plethora of state law and state action. It has been stated that s. 7 is a right of general application, such that the remaining Legal Rights in ss. 8 to 14 are best viewed as specific examples of deprivations of life, liberty and security of the person that are not in accordance with the principles of fundamental justice.[9]

Analytically, it is useful to break s. 7 down into two distinct components.

First, the right contained in s. 7 is triggered where there is a deprivation of "life, liberty and security of the person". Life, liberty and security of the person have been interpreted to be disjunctive, such that an applicant need only show that one of the three qualities is being deprived by the state. The interests protected in this section are intended to address fundamental and core life choices and not pure economic interests. Some examples of deprivations include: being in custody,[10] corporal punishment,[11] the requirement to be fingerprinted[12] and serious state-imposed psychological stress.[13]

If s. 7 is triggered, the second-prong of the analysis is determining whether the deprivation is in accordance with a principle of fundamental justice. The Supreme Court of Canada has held that principles of fundamental justice are found in the basic tenets and principles of our legal system. To qualify as a "principle of fundamental justice", the principle must: (a) be considered a legal principle; (b) enjoy sufficient consensus that it is vital to our notions of justice; and (c) be capable of precise articulation.[14] Examples of principles of fundamental justice include: that youths be entitled to a presumption of diminished moral responsibility;[15] that criminal offences which could result in custodial sentence have *mens rea* as an element of the offence;[16] that laws not be vague;[17] and the right to silence.[18]

The right within s. 7 is internally qualified; only violations that are *not* in accordance with a principle of fundamental justice will be considered breaches of s. 7. Given this internal qualification, if a s. 7 violation is found, only in very exceptional circumstances is it possible for the violation to be "saved by s. 1".[19]

In *R. v. Martineau*,[20] Martineau and an accomplice set out to commit a robbery; during the course of the robbery, however, his accomplice unexpectedly killed both victims. Martineau was convicted of murder on the basis of the "constructive murder" provisions in the *Criminal Code*, which hold that if death occurs during the commission of certain offences, it will automatically be deemed to be murder.

On appeal, the Supreme Court of Canada struck down the constructive murder provisions of the *Criminal Code*, on the basis of s. 7. In reaching their decision, the Court concluded, at para. 13, that it was "a principle of fundamental justice that a conviction for murder cannot rest on anything less than proof beyond a reasonable doubt of subjective foresight of death." As Martineau did not foresee death as a possibility, his murder conviction was a violation of s. 7 and was not saved by s. 1.

Section 8—Everyone has the right to be secure against unreasonable search or seizure

At its core, s. 8 of the *Charter* addresses a narrow issue: when must the public's interest in being left alone by government give way to "the government's interest in intruding on the individual's privacy in order to advance its goals, notably those of law enforcement"?[21]

In finding this balance, the Supreme Court of Canada has held that s. 8 is only engaged where an individual has a reasonable expectation of privacy.[22] The existence of a reasonable expectation of privacy is a contextual inquiry based on the totality of the circumstances.[23] A reasonable expectation of privacy does not simply accord with a desire for privacy as, for instance, many individuals who commit criminal offences may *desire* privacy, but that does not mean that it is reasonable for them to *expect* privacy. Determining whether a reasonable expectation of privacy exists is a judgment made from the perspective of the reasonable and informed person "who is concerned about the long-term consequences of government action for the protection of privacy."[24]

Many decisions have focused on whether, in a particular situation, an individual possesses a reasonable expectation of privacy. Notable findings include: individuals in their home, or on their property, have a heightened expectation privacy;[25] mere guests in a residence typically do not have a reasonable expectation of privacy;[26] guests of a hotel room typically have a reasonable expectation of privacy;[27] people have a reasonable expectation of privacy in information about their biographical core which they would wish to keep secret;[28] people have a reasonable expectation of privacy in their DNA;[29] people have a reduced expectation of privacy over business records;[30] people have a reduced expectation of privacy at border crossings;[31] and students have a reduced expectation of privacy at schools.[32]

Where an individual has a reasonable expectation of privacy, s. 8 has been interpreted to require that searches or seizures only occur after they have been judicially authorized. The concern noted by the courts is that the protections offered by s. 8 will be rendered meaningless unless judicial *pre*authorization, as opposed to *post*authorization, is the norm. The standard is that a search or seizure should only occur after a search warrant is issued by a judicial official who has been satisfied as to the existence of reasonable and probable grounds to believe that an offence was committed, and further, that evidence of that offence exists in the place that is to be searched.

When searches are conducted without a warrant they will be presumed to be unreasonable, and hence, in violation of s. 8. Nevertheless, the presumption of an "unreasonable" search or seizure may be rebutted where it can be demonstrated that (a) the search or seizure was authorized by law; (b) the law itself is reasonable; and (c) the manner in which the search was carried out was also reasonable.[33]

The law has recognized numerous categories of valid warrantless searches, including, search incident to arrest,[34] search incident to detention,[35] searches at international borders,[36] and consent searches.[37]

In *R. v. Golden*,[38] the police entered a restaurant and arrested Golden in relation to alleged drug offences. Following a pat-down search, the officers failed to find any drugs or weapons on Golden, at which point, they decided to conduct a strip-search. The strip-search involved Golden being forced to bend over a table in the restaurant with his pants down. At trial, Golden claimed that the search was a violation of his s. 8 right. The Supreme Court of Canada agreed with Golden claiming that, while s. 8 does permit certain exceptions to warrantless searches, s. 8 requires that a strip-search incident to arrest can only be done where there are reasonable and probable grounds justifying the strip-search, relating to (a) discovering weapons; (b) ensuring the safety of officers and others; or (c) to prevent the disposal of evidence. The Supreme Court of Canada added a further caveat holding that strip-searches should only occur at a police station, absent the existence of exigent circumstances.

Section 9—Everyone has the right not to be arbitrarily detained or imprisoned

In the course of executing their duties, police officers routinely interact with individuals. Such dealings can range from a quick hello to a lengthy interrogation. In interpreting s. 9 of the *Charter*, perhaps the most difficult question faced by courts is determining when on this vast spectrum of civilian-police interactions should an individual be considered "detained".

The Supreme Court of Canada has held that an individual is detained when they are, by physical or psychological compulsion, obligated to comply with the demands of the authorities, or form a reasonable belief that they are under the state's control and unable to simply leave or walk away.[39] The determination of when an individual is detained is a fact-based inquiry, based on all the circumstances.

Section 9 protects people from being *arbitrarily* detained or imprisoned. While courts have struggled to define this imprecise term, generally a person will be arbitrarily detained unless there is a reasoned foundation apparent on the facts that would justify their detention.[40]

Perhaps the most common example of arbitrary detention is where police randomly stop motor vehicles to investigate potential motor vehicle infractions. In a trilogy of cases, the Supreme Court of Canada stated that while these detentions are certainly arbitrary, the violations were nevertheless saved under s. 1 of the *Charter* as a pressing and substantial objective related to the safety of individuals on the roadway.[41]

In *R. v. Mann*,[42] police officers were patrolling an area in Winnipeg, Manitoba, looking for a suspect in relation to a recent break and enter. As they were patrolling, they spotted Mann, who they felt fit the description of the suspect. They approached Mann and engaged him in a pat-down search, which resulted in their finding drugs. One of the questions the Supreme Court of Canada addressed in its decision was whether the police officers had the ability to engage in an "investigative" detention of Mann as it was clear that the police, at the time, did not have sufficient grounds to arrest Mann. The Supreme Court of Canada held that police have the right to engage in an "investigative detention" where there exists reasonable grounds to suspect in all the circumstances that the individual is connected to a particular crime. Further, the Court held that in conducting an investigative detention the police may engage in a pat-down search if there exists grounds to believe that it is necessary for officer safety.

Section 10—Everyone has the right on arrest or detention
  (a) to be informed promptly of the reasons therefor;
  (b) to retain and instruct counsel without delay and to be informed of that right; and
  (c) to have the validity of the detention determined by way of habeas corpus and to be released if the detention is not lawful.

Pursuant to s. 10(a) of the *Charter*, upon detention or arrest, police must inform the individual of the reasons. In interpreting this right, courts have held that precise or formulaic language is not required. Rather, the nature of the inquiry will focus on whether the detainee is given an explanation sufficient to enable them to understand the reason for their detention and, further, to allow them to consider whether they should consult counsel.[43]

The right contained in s. 10(b) of the *Charter* places a number of distinct obligations upon the police. First they must, as the section states, advise a detained or arrested person of their right to retain and instruct counsel without delay. Once the individual has been advised, police must provide them with a reasonable opportunity to exercise this right. If a detainee expresses a desire to retain counsel, the police must refrain from attempting to elicit further information from the detainee until they have exercised their right.[44] The obligation to cease attempting to elicit information from a detainee will end if that individual is not diligent in pursuing counsel.[45]

The Supreme Court of Canada has held that a detained individual can only meaningfully retain and instruct counsel if they know the jeopardy they are facing. Accordingly, if a major shift in the investigation occurs, such that individual may be facing additional or more serious charges, the individual should be so advised and re-advised of their right to retain and instruct counsel.[46]

In *R. v. Evans*,[47] police interviewed a youth of "subnormal mental capacity" in relation to potential drug offences. At the outset of their interview, Evans was advised of his right to retain and instruct counsel and when asked if he understood, he replied no. The police did not seek to clarify this with Evans, but proceeded to interview him. During the course of the interview it became apparent that Evans may have committed two murders. At no point did the police re-advise Evans of his right to retain and instruct counsel, but rather continued in their interrogation.

On appeal, the Supreme Court of Canada found two violations of s. 10 of the *Charter*. First, the Court found that the police failed to comply with Evans' s. 10(b) right by not explaining to Evans what his right to retain and instruct counsel meant when he stated he did not understand this right, especially as police were aware of Evans' limited mental capacity. Second, the Court found that the police also breached s. 10(b) when they failed to re-advise Evans of his right to retain counsel after their interrogation and investigation began to focus on two potential murders.

Section 11—Any person charged with an offence has the right
(a) to be informed without unreasonable delay of the specific offence;
(b) to be tried within a reasonable time;
(c) not to be compelled to be a witness in proceedings against that person in respect of the offence;
(d) to be presumed innocent until proven guilty according to law in a fair and public hearing by an independent and impartial tribunal;
(e) not to be denied reasonable bail without just cause;
(f) except in the case of an offence under military law tried before a military tribunal, to the benefit of trial by jury where the maximum punishment for the offence is imprisonment for five years or a more severe punishment;
(g) not to be found guilty on account of any act or omission unless, at the time of the act or omission, it constituted an offence under Canadian or international law or was criminal according to the general principles of law recognized by the

community of nations;
(h) if finally acquitted of the offence, not to be tried for it again
and, if finally found guilty and punished for the offence, not to
be tried or punished for it again; and
(i) if found guilty of the offence and if the punishment for the
offence has been varied between the time of commission and the
time of sentencing, to the benefit of the lesser punishment

Section 11 of the *Charter* contains nine separate principles which govern the criminal trial process in Canada. While each of the nine paragraphs are important in their own way, summarized below are two rights of particular importance.

Section 11(b): The Right to be Tried Within a Reasonable Time.

For most, being charged with a criminal offence is an extremely stressful and frightening experience. In addition to prolonging this type of stress, the Supreme Court of Canada has noted that the right to be tried within a reasonable time contained within s. 10(b) of the *Charter* protects an accused person's liberty interests (in relation to bail) and further protects their ability to make full answer and defence as the passage of time can often prejudice the ability of an accused person to lead certain evidence or effectively cross-examine witnesses.[48] Yet, it is not only the accused person who claims an interest in a quick trial, the community and society in general have an interest in seeing matters dealt with effectively and efficiently by courts.[49]

It is not possible to quantify a time-range which would constitute an "unreasonable" delay in all cases. While courts will use some basic guidelines, all delays must be considered in light of a variety of factors including, the complexity of the case; the reason for adjournments, if any; any waivers given; the conduct of the accused; and the conduct of the Crown.[50]

In *R. v. Finta*,[51] the accused was a commander with the Hungarian military during the Second World War. It was alleged that the accused actively took part in the deportation of Jews to concentration camps. The accused was charged with a number of offences related to these activities in Canada nearly 45 years after they were alleged to have occurred. One of the main issues on appeal was whether the delay in having charges laid against the accused violated his s. 11(b) right. In rejecting this ground of appeal, the Supreme Court of Canada held that pre-charge delay is not protected under s. 11(b). Section 11(b) only protects against delays which occur following the laying of charges.

Section 11(d): Presumption of Innocence

The presumption of innocence is a hallowed and often-celebrated legal doctrine dating much farther back than the enactment of the *Charter*. Nevertheless, its inclusion in the *Charter* has constitutionally affirmed that the onus is on the Crown to prove each element of an offence beyond a reasonable doubt. If a law requires an accused person to prove or disprove anything, to the extent that if he or she fails they may be convicted despite the possibility of a reasonable doubt existing, s. 11(d) will be found to have been breached.[52]

An interesting issue is whether requiring an accused person to lead evidence supporting a potential defence is contrary to the presumption of innocence. After all, if the defence in fact exists and the accused fails to lead evidence supporting it, they may be convicted despite the possibility of a reasonable doubt existing. The Supreme Court of Canada has clarified that where a potential defence exists, an accused person does bear the burden of adducing sufficient evidence to give rise to an "air of reality" to the defence, at which point, the onus shifts to the Crown to rebut the defence. This requirement on the accused has been found not to violate the presumption of innocence.[53]

In *R. v. Chaulk*,[54] Chaulk and an associate broke into a home where they stabbed and bludgeoned the occupant to death. At trial, Chaulk attempted to raise questions relating to the status of his mental-health. Following conviction, Chaulk appealed and, in so doing, challenged subs. 16(4) of the *Criminal Code*, which held that an accused person is sane unless they prove otherwise. The majority of the Supreme Court of Canada agreed with Chaulk that this provision violated the presumption of innocence. The Court held that if Chaulk failed to overcome the presumption, he could be convicted despite the existence of a reasonable doubt regarding his sanity. This was held to violate the presumption of innocence which is intended to protect an accused person from facing a conviction where a reasonable doubt may exist.

Section 24 (1)—Anyone whose rights or freedoms, as guaranteed by this Charter, have been infringed or denied may apply to a court of competent jurisdiction to obtain such remedy as the court considers appropriate and just in the circumstances

(2)—Where, in proceedings under subsection (1), a court concludes that evidence was obtained in a manner that infringed or denied any rights or freedoms guaranteed by this Charter, the

evidence shall be excluded if it is established that, having regard to all the circumstances, the admission of it in the proceedings would bring the administration of justice into disrepute

From the perspective of an accused person facing the prospect of a conviction, perhaps the single most important question is what will happen if the court finds that his or her *Charter* rights were violated? After all, what practical value is a *Charter* right if there is no remedy for a violation?

Prior to the enactment of the *Charter*, courts were reluctant to grant remedies where they found that the rights of an accused person were violated. *R. v. Wray*[55] is a case indicative of this pre-*Charter* reality. Wray was charged with murder and was subject to extensive interrogation while in police custody. During the course of his interrogation he was kept from contacting a lawyer. Eventually, Wray led the officers to the murder weapon. In hearing the appeal, the Supreme Court of Canada held that while the police had acted improperly in denying counsel to the accused, there was no basis in law to exclude the evidence of the gun.

The inclusion of s. 24 in the *Charter* has produced a dramatic change in how courts approach evidence obtained at the expense of an accused person's rights. While a variety of *Charter* remedies have been recognized by courts, perhaps the two most important remedies with respect to criminal law are a stay of proceedings and the exclusion of evidence.

Stay of Proceedings

A stay of proceedings is the ultimate remedy in criminal law. It causes an immediate and final halt to the proceedings against an accused person. It has been described by the courts as the remedy of last resort, such that it can only be used where no other remedy would be fair in the circumstances and only in the clearest of circumstances.[56]

The Supreme Court of Canada has outlined a two-part test in determining whether a stay is an appropriate remedy. First, it must be considered whether the prejudice caused by the abuse in question will be manifested, perpetuated or aggravated through the conduct of the trial or by its outcome. Second, there must be no other remedy reasonably capable of removing that prejudice.

In *R. v. Carosella*,[57] the complainant attended a sexual assault crisis centre and during the course of a lengthy interview at the centre, detailed how she was sexually assaulted by the accused, a former teacher of hers. The interviewer made detailed notes. Following the interview, the complainant spoke with police and charges were subsequently laid against the accused. As per their policy, the centre shredded all notes of the interview. At trial, the accused argued that the loss of this evidence breached his right to disclosure and to make full answer and defence. For example, the accused noted that he would not be able to cross-examine the complainant on any potential inconsistencies between her testimony at trial and her previous account of the events given at the centre. The Supreme Court of Canada agreed, citing that the accused's s. 7 rights had been violated. In considering an appropriate remedy, the majority of the Supreme Court of Canada held that a stay of proceedings was the only remedy in the circumstances, as to allow the trial would unduly perpetuate the prejudice to the accused that resulted from the breach of his *Charter* rights.

Subsection 24(2): Exclusion of Evidence

The power of the court to exclude evidence pursuant to subs. 24(2) is the most common *Charter* remedy used in criminal law. Nevertheless, courts continue to struggle to define the circumstances under which this remedy should apply. Determining when tainted evidence would bring the "administration of justice into disrepute" is an inherently problematic task given the broad and imprecise wording of the test.[58]

Until recently, the Supreme Court of Canada relied upon an analytical framework developed in *R. v. Collins* and refined in *R. v. Stillman*. The analysis relied upon three distinct inquiries: (1) whether the evidence will undermine the fairness of the trial by effectively conscripting the accused against himself or herself; (2) the seriousness of the *Charter* breach; and (3) the effect of excluding the evidence on the long-term repute of the administration of justice.

The perceived difficulty with the *Collins/Stillman* analysis was that courts were blindly developing presumptions: if evidence was "conscriptive" and otherwise non-discoverable (i.e., evidence that the accused had to actively participate to create—for example, a confession) it would be excluded, whereas, if the evidence was "non-conscriptive" real evidence (i.e., evidence that existed absent the *Charter* breach—for example, a weapon), it would be admitted.

In 2009, in a trilogy of cases, the Supreme Court of Canada unveiled a new approach to determining when evidence obtained as a result of a violation of the *Charter* should be admitted or excluded under subs. 24(2). In addressing an application under s. 24, courts must now assess: (1) the seriousness of the *Charter*-infringing state conduct; (2)

the impact of the breach on the *Charter*-protected interests of the accused; and, (3) society's interest in the adjudication of the case on its merits.

Whether this new approach overcomes the concerns which lead the Court to look for a new approach is difficult to say. Nevertheless, it is certain that no matter what analytical framework is used, the decision to admit or exclude tainted evidence will continue to pose a very difficult question for courts given the consequences of such a decision.

In *R. v. Harrison*,[59] a police officer on patrol in Ontario activated his emergency lights after spotting a vehicle missing its front license plate. The officer soon realized that the vehicle was registered in Alberta, and thus was exempt from having a front license plate. Despite this, the officer decided to proceed with a traffic stop. Harrison, who was driving the vehicle, was questioned by the officer and subsequently arrested for driving with a suspended license. After arresting Harrison, the officer proceeded to search the entire vehicle and found a box which contained 35 kg of cocaine. Harrison was charged with possession of cocaine for the purposes of trafficking.

The Supreme Court of Canada, agreeing with the lower courts, held that the vehicle stop and subsequent search of the vehicle breached ss. 8 and 9 of the *Charter*. The main issue on appeal was whether the evidence of the cocaine should be excluded pursuant to subs. 24(2). The Supreme Court of Canada found the police misconduct to be serious, which produced a significant incursion on Harrison's *Charter* rights. While acknowledging the inherent reliability of the evidence, the Court nevertheless decided that condoning the actions of the police officer in this case by allowing the admission of the evidence would not enhance the long-term repute of the administration of justice and, accordingly, found the evidence to be inadmissible.

CONCLUSION

The foregoing review has provided only a snap-shot of key sections of the *Charter* that pertain to criminal law. However, even this basic review should provide some insight into how powerful these rights and freedoms are. Powerful, not simply for the mere text of the sections, but powerful because these rights and freedoms are constitutionally-protected and guarded by a judiciary willing to provide Canadians with the protections offered by them.

Notes

1. *R. v. Morgentaler (No. 5)*, 1975 CarswellQue 3, 1975 CarswellQue 31F, [1976] 1 S.C.R. 616, 30 C.R.N.S. 209, 4 N.R. 277, 20 C.C.C. (2d) 449, 53 D.L.R. (3d) 161 (S.C.C.).

2. *Amax Potash Ltd. v. Saskatchewan,* 1976 CarswellSask 76, 1976 CarswellSask 115, [1977] 2 S.C.R. 576, [1976] 6 W.W.R. 61, 11 N.R. 222, 71 D.L.R. (3d) 1 (S.C.C.), at 590 [S.C.R.].

3. *Reference re s. 94(2) of the Motor Vehicle Act (British Columbia),* 1985 Carswell-BC 398, 1985 CarswellBC 816, [1985] 2 S.C.R. 486, 24 D.L.R. (4th) 536, 63 N.R. 266, 69 B.C.L.R. 145, 23 C.C.C. (3d) 289, 18 C.R.R. 30, 36 M.V.R. 240, [1986] 1 W.W.R. 481, 48 C.R. (3d) 289 (S.C.C.) [hereinafter referred to as"*BC Motor Vehicle*"].

4. *Canada (Director of Investigation & Research, Combines Investigation Branch) v. Southam Inc.,* 1984 CarswellAlta 121, 1984 CarswellAlta 415, 33 Alta. L.R. (2d) 193, 27 B.L.R. 297, 41 C.R. (3d) 97, 84 D.T.C. 6467, (sub nom. *Hunter v. Southam Inc.*) 11 D.L.R. (4th) 641, (sub nom. *Hunter v. Southam Inc.*) 55 A.R. 291, (sub nom. *Hunter v. Southam Inc.*) 14 C.C.C. (3d) 97, (sub nom. *Director of Investigations & Research Combines Investigation Branch v. Southam Inc.*) [1984] 6 W.W.R. 577, (sub nom. *Hunter v. Southam Inc.*) [1984] 2 S.C.R. 145, (sub nom. *Hunter v. Southam Inc.*) 55 N.R. 241, (sub nom. *Hunter v. Southam Inc.*) 2 C.P.R. (3d) 1, (sub nom. *Hunter v. Southam Inc.*) 9 C.R.R. 355 (S.C.C.) [hereinafter referred to as "*Hunter v. Southam*"].

5. *R. v. Morgentaler,* 1988 CarswellOnt 954, [1988] S.C.J. No. 1, 1988 CarswellOnt 45, 44 D.L.R. (4th) 385, 26 O.A.C. 1, 37 C.C.C. (3d) 449, 62 C.R. (3d) 1, 31 C.R.R. 1, 82 N.R. 1, 63 O.R. (2d) 281 (note), (sub nom. *R. v. Morgentaler (No. 2)*) [1988] 1 S.C.R. 30 (S.C.C.).

6. *R. v. Mack,* 1988 CarswellBC 701, 1988 CarswellBC 767, [1988] 2 S.C.R. 903, [1989] 1 W.W.R. 577, 90 N.R. 173, 67 C.R. (3d) 1, 37 C.R.R. 277, 44 C.C.C. (3d) 513 (S.C.C.), at 938-939 [S.C.R.].

7. *R. v. Oakes,* 1986 CarswellOnt 95, 1986 CarswellOnt 1001, [1986] 1 S.C.R. 103, 26 D.L.R. (4th) 200, 65 N.R. 87, 14 O.A.C. 335, 24 C.C.C. (3d) 321, 50 C.R. (3d) 1, 19 C.R.R. 308, 53 O.R. (2d) 719 (S.C.C.).

8. *R. v. Butler,* 1992 CarswellMan 100, 1992 CarswellMan 220, [1992] 1 S.C.R. 452, [1992] 2 W.W.R. 577, 11 C.R. (4th) 137, 70 C.C.C. (3d) 129, 134 N.R. 81, 8 C.R.R. (2d) 1, 89 D.L.R. (4th) 449, 78 Man. R. (2d) 1, 16 W.A.C. 1 (S.C.C.).

9. *BC Motor Vehicle, supra,* note 3, at para. 63.

10. *Ibid.*

11. *Canadian Foundation for Children, Youth & the Law v. Canada (Attorney General),* 2004 CarswellOnt 252, 2004 CarswellOnt 253, 2004 SCC 4, 315 N.R. 201, 115 C.R.R. (2d) 88, 16 C.R. (6th) 203, 46 R.F.L. (5th) 1, 234 D.L.R. (4th) 257, 180 C.C.C. (3d) 353, 183 O.A.C. 1, 70 O.R. (3d) 94 (note), (sub nom. *Canadian Foundation for Children v. Canada*) [2004] 1 S.C.R. 76 (S.C.C.) [hereinafter referred to as "*CFY*"].

12. *R. v. Beare,* 1987 CarswellSask 674, 1987 CarswellSask 675, [1988] 2 S.C.R. 387, [1989] 1 W.W.R. 97, 55 D.L.R. (4th) 481, 88 N.R. 205, 71 Sask. R. 1, 45 C.C.C. (3d) 57, 66 C.R. (3d) 97, 36 C.R.R. 90 (S.C.C.).

13. *Morgentaler, supra,* note 5.

14. *CFY, supra,* note 11.

[15] *R. v. B. (D.)*, 2008 CarswellOnt 2708, 2008 CarswellOnt 2709, 2008 SCC 25, [2008] 2 S.C.R. 3, 374 N.R. 221, 237 O.A.C. 110, 293 D.L.R. (4th) 278, 171 C.R.R. (2d) 133, 92 O.R. (3d) 399 (note), 231 C.C.C. (3d) 338, 56 C.R. (6th) 203 (S.C.C.).

[16] *BC Motor Vehicle, supra*, note 3.

[17] *Canada v. Pharmaceutical Society (Nova Scotia)*, 1992 CarswellNS 15, 1992 CarswellNS 353, 15 C.R. (4th) 1, (sub nom. *R. v. Nova Scotia Pharmaceutical Society*) [1992] 2 S.C.R. 606, (sub nom. *R. v. Nova Scotia Pharmaceutical Society*) 93 D.L.R. (4th) 36, (sub nom. *R. v. Nova Scotia Pharmaceutical Society*) 43 C.P.R. (3d) 1, (sub nom. *R. v. Nova Scotia Pharmaceutical Society*) 74 C.C.C. (3d) 289, (sub nom. *R. v. Nova Scotia Pharmaceutical Society*) 10 C.R.R. (2d) 34, (sub nom. *R. v. Nova Scotia Pharmaceutical Society (No. 2)*) 139 N.R. 241, (sub nom. *R. v. Nova Scotia Pharmaceutical Society (No. 2)*) 114 N.S.R. (2d) 91, 313 A.P.R. 91 (S.C.C.).

[18] *R. v. Hebert*, 1990 CarswellYukon 4, 1990 CarswellYukon 7, [1990] 2 S.C.R. 151, 47 B.C.L.R. (2d) 1, 77 C.R. (3d) 145, [1990] 5 W.W.R. 1, 57 C.C.C. (3d) 1, 110 N.R. 1, 49 C.R.R. 114 (S.C.C.).

[19] *R. v. Ruzic*, 2001 CarswellOnt 1238, 2001 CarswellOnt 1239, 2001 SCC 24, [2001] 1 S.C.R. 687, 268 N.R. 1, 145 O.A.C. 235, 82 C.R.R. (2d) 1, 41 C.R. (5th) 1, 153 C.C.C. (3d) 1, 197 D.L.R. (4th) 577 (S.C.C.), at para. 92.

[20] *R. v. Martineau*, 1990 CarswellAlta 143, 1990 CarswellAlta 657, [1990] 2 S.C.R. 633, [1990] 6 W.W.R. 97, 112 N.R. 83, 58 C.C.C. (3d) 353, 76 Alta. L.R. (2d) 1, 79 C.R. (3d) 129, 50 C.R.R. 110, 109 A.R. 321 (S.C.C.).

[21] *Hunter v. Southam, supra*, note 4, at p. 159-160 [S.C.R.].

[22] *Hunter v. Southam, supra*, note 4.

[23] *R. v. Edwards,* 1996 CarswellOnt 1916, 1996 CarswellOnt 2126, [1996] 1 S.C.R. 128, 45 C.R. (4th) 307, 192 N.R. 81, 26 O.R. (3d) 736, 104 C.C.C. (3d) 136, 132 D.L.R. (4th) 31, 33 C.R.R. (2d) 226, 88 O.A.C. 321 (S.C.C.).

[24] *R. v. Patrick*, 2009 CarswellAlta 481, 2009 CarswellAlta 482, 2009 SCC 17, [2009] 1 S.C.R. 579, 242 C.C.C. (3d) 158, 304 D.L.R. (4th) 260, 4 Alta. L.R. (5th) 1, 387 N.R. 44, 454 A.R. 1, [2009] 5 W.W.R. 387, 64 C.R. (6th) 1 (S.C.C.), at para. 14.

[25] *R. v. Silveira*, 1995 CarswellOnt 21, 1995 CarswellOnt 525, [1995] 2 S.C.R. 297, 38 C.R. (4th) 330, 23 O.R. (3d) 256 (note), 97 C.C.C. (3d) 450, 124 D.L.R. (4th) 193, 181 N.R. 161, 28 C.R.R. (2d) 189, 81 O.A.C. 161 (S.C.C.), at para. 140; *R. v. Feeney*, 1997 CarswellBC 1015, 1997 CarswellBC 1016, [1997] 2 S.C.R. 13, 212 N.R. 83, 7 C.R. (5th) 101, [1997] 6 W.W.R. 634, 115 C.C.C. (3d) 129, 146 D.L.R. (4th) 609, 91 B.C.A.C. 1, 148 W.A.C. 1, 44 C.R.R. (2d) 1 (S.C.C.), at para. 43.

[26] *R. v. Edwards, supra*, note 23.

[27] *R. v. Wong*, 1990 CarswellOnt 58, 1990 CarswellOnt 1008, [1990] 3 S.C.R. 36, 1 C.R. (4th) 1, 120 N.R. 34, 60 C.C.C. (3d) 460, 2 C.R.R. (2d) 277, 45 O.A.C. 250 (S.C.C.).

[28] *R. v. Plant*, 1993 CarswellAlta 94, 1993 CarswellAlta 566, [1993] 3 S.C.R. 281, 157 N.R. 321, [1993] 8 W.W.R. 287, 145 A.R. 104, 55 W.A.C. 104, 17 C.R.R. (2d) 297, 12 Alta. L.R. (3d) 305, 84 C.C.C. (3d) 203, 24 C.R. (4th) 47 (S.C.C.).

[29] *R. v. B. (S.A.)*, 2003 CarswellAlta 1525, 2003 CarswellAlta 1526, 2003 SCC 60, [2003] 2 S.C.R. 678, 178 C.C.C. (3d) 193, 311 N.R. 1, 231 D.L.R. (4th) 602, 21 Alta. L.R. (4th) 207, 339 A.R. 1, 312 W.A.C. 1, [2004] 2 W.W.R. 199, 112 C.R.R. (2d) 155, 14 C.R. (6th) 205 (S.C.C.).

[30] *R. v. Jarvis*, 2002 CarswellAlta 1440, 2002 CarswellAlta 1441, 2002 SCC 73,

[2002] 3 S.C.R. 757, 317 A.R. 1, 284 W.A.C. 1, 6 C.R. (6th) 23, 2002 D.T.C. 7547, [2003] 1 C.T.C. 135, 101 C.R.R. (2d) 35, [2003] 3 W.W.R. 197, 8 Alta. L.R. (4th) 1, 219 D.L.R. (4th) 233, 169 C.C.C. (3d) 1, 295 N.R. 201 (S.C.C.).

31 *R. v. Simmons*, 1988 CarswellOnt 91, 1988 CarswellOnt 968, [1988] 2 S.C.R. 495, 67 O.R. (2d) 63, 66 C.R. (3d) 297, 55 D.L.R. (4th) 673, 89 N.R. 1, 30 O.A.C. 241, 45 C.C.C. (3d) 296, 38 C.R.R. 252, (sub nom. *Simmons v. R.*) 18 C.E.R. 227, (sub nom. *Simmons v. R.*) 2 T.C.T. 4102 (S.C.C.).

32 *R. v. M. (M.R.)*, 1998 CarswellNS 346, 1998 CarswellNS 347, [1998] 3 S.C.R. 393, 171 N.S.R. (2d) 125, 519 A.P.R. 125, 57 C.R.R. (2d) 189, 5 B.H.R.C. 474, 233 N.R. 1, 166 D.L.R. (4th) 261, 20 C.R. (5th) 197, 129 C.C.C. (3d) 361 (S.C.C.).

33 *R. v. Collins*, 1987 CarswellBC 94, 1987 CarswellBC 699, [1987] 1 S.C.R. 265, [1987] 3 W.W.R. 699, 74 N.R. 276, 13 B.C.L.R. (2d) 1, 33 C.C.C. (3d) 1, 56 C.R. (3d) 193, 28 C.R.R. 122, (sub nom. *Collins v. R.*) 38 D.L.R. (4th) 508 (S.C.C.).

34 *R. v. Caslake*, 1998 CarswellMan 1, 1998 CarswellMan 2, [1998] 1 S.C.R. 51, 48 C.R.R. (2d) 189, 123 Man. R. (2d) 208, 159 W.A.C. 208, [1999] 4 W.W.R. 303, 121 C.C.C. (3d) 97, 155 D.L.R. (4th) 19, 221 N.R. 281, 13 C.R. (5th) 1 (S.C.C.).

35 *R. v. Mann*, 2004 CarswellMan 303, 2004 CarswellMan 304, 2004 SCC 52, [2004] 3 S.C.R. 59, 21 C.R. (6th) 1, 241 D.L.R. (4th) 214, 185 C.C.C. (3d) 308, 122 C.R.R. (2d) 189, 324 N.R. 215, [2004] 11 W.W.R. 601, 187 Man. R. (2d) 1, 330 W.A.C. 1 (S.C.C.).

36 *R. v. Simmons, supra*, note 31.

37 *R v. Wills*, 1992 CarswellOnt 77, 70 C.C.C. (3d) 529, 34 M.V.R. (2d) 296, 9 C.R.R. (2d) 360, 12 C.R. (4th) 58, 7 O.R. (3d) 337, 52 O.A.C. 321 (Ont.C.A.).

38 *R. v. Golden*, 2001 CarswellOnt 4253, 2001 CarswellOnt 4301, 2001 SCC 83, [2001] 3 S.C.R. 679, 207 D.L.R. (4th) 18, 279 N.R. 1, 47 C.R. (5th) 1, 159 C.C.C. (3d) 449, 153 O.A.C. 201, 89 C.R.R. (2d) 271 (S.C.C.).

39 *R. v. Grant*, 2009 CarswellOnt 4104, 2009 CarswellOnt 41052, 2009 SCC 32, [2009] 2 S.C.R. 353, 253 82 M.V.R. (5th) 1, 245 C.C.C. (3d) 1, 66 C.R. (6th) 1, 391 N.R. 1, 309 D.L.R. (4th) 1, O.A.C. 124 (S.C.C.).

40 *R. v. Iron*, 1987 CarswellSask 316, 33 C.C.C. (3d) 157, 45 M.V.R. 287, 27 C.R.R. 243, 55 C.R. (3d) 289, [1987] 3 W.W.R. 97, 53 Sask. R. 241 (Sask. C.A.), at 177 [C.C.C.].

41 *R. v. Hufsky*, 1988 CarswellOnt 54, 1988 CarswellOnt 956, [1988] 1 S.C.R. 621, 4 M.V.R. (2d) 170, 84 N.R. 365, 27 O.A.C. 103, 40 C.C.C. (3d) 398, 63 C.R. (3d) 14, 32 C.R.R. 193 (S.C.C.); *R. v. Dedman*, 1985 CarswellOnt 103, 1985 CarswellOnt 942, 34 M.V.R. 1, 11 O.A.C. 241, 20 D.L.R. (4th) 321, 60 N.R. 34, (sub nom. *Dedman v. R.*) [1985] 2 S.C.R. 2, (sub nom. *Dedman v. R.*) 46 C.R. (3d) 193, (sub nom. *Dedman v. R.*) 20 C.C.C. (3d) 97 (S.C.C.); and *R. v. Ladouceur*, 1990 CarswellOnt 96, 1990 CarswellOnt 997, [1990] 1 S.C.R. 1257, 21 M.V.R. (2d) 165, 40 O.A.C. 1, 48 C.R.R. 112, 108 N.R. 171, 56 C.C.C. (3d) 22, 77 C.R. (3d) 110, 73 O.R. (2d) 736 (note) (S.C.C.).

42 *R. v. Mann, supra*, note 35.

43 *R. v. Evans*, 1991 CarswellBC 417, 1991 CarswellBC 918, [1991] 1 S.C.R. 869, 4 C.R. (4th) 144, 63 C.C.C. (3d) 289, 124 N.R. 278, 3 C.R.R. (2d) 315 (S.C.C.).

44 *R. v. Manninen*, 1987 CarswellOnt 967, 1987 CarswellOnt 99, [1987] 1 S.C.R. 1233, 76 N.R. 198, 38 C.R.R. 37, 58 C.R. (3d) 97, 21 O.A.C. 192, 34 C.C.C. (3d) 385, 41 D.L.R. (4th) 301, 61 O.R. (2d) 736 (note) (S.C.C.).

45 *R. v. Tremblay*, 1987 CarswellOnt 111, 1987 CarswellOnt 972, [1987] 2 S.C.R.

435, 45 D.L.R. (4th) 445, 79 N.R. 153, 25 O.A.C. 93, 37 C.C.C. (3d) 565, 60 C.R. (3d) 59, 32 C.R.R. 381, 2 M.V.R. (2d) 289 (S.C.C.).

[46] *R. v. Evans, supra,* note 43.

[47] *Ibid.*

[48] *R. v. Godin,* 2009 CarswellOnt 3100, 2009 CarswellOnt 3101, 2009 SCC 26, 67 C.R. (6th) 95, 389 N.R. 1, 245 C.C.C. (3d) 271, [2009] 2 S.C.R. 3, 309 D.L.R. (4th) 149, 252 O.A.C. 377 (S.C.C.), at para.30.

[49] *R. v. Askov,* 1990 CarswellOnt 111, 1990 CarswellOnt 1005, [1990] 2 S.C.R. 1199, 79 C.R. (3d) 273, 59 C.C.C. (3d) 449, 49 C.R.R. 1, 74 D.L.R. (4th) 355, 75 O.R. (2d) 673, 113 N.R. 241, 42 O.A.C. 81 (S.C.C.).

[50] *R. v. Morin,* 1992 CarswellOnt 984, 1992 CarswellOnt 75, [1992] 1 S.C.R. 771, 12 C.R. (4th) 1, 71 C.C.C. (3d) 1, 134 N.R. 321, 8 C.R.R. (2d) 193, 53 O.A.C. 241 (S.C.C.).

[51] *R. v. Finta,* 1994 CarswellOnt 61, 1994 CarswellOnt 1154, [1993] 1 S.C.R. 1138, 61 O.A.C. 321, 150 N.R. 370, 28 C.R. (4th) 265, [1994] 1 S.C.R. 701, 20 C.R.R. (2d) 1, 70 O.A.C. 241, 88 C.C.C. (3d) 417, 112 D.L.R. (4th) 513, 165 N.R. 1 (S.C.C.).

[52] *R v. Whyte,* 1988 CarswellBC 761, 1988 CarswellBC 290, [1988] 2 S.C.R. 3, 6 M.V.R. (2d) 138, [1988] 5 W.W.R. 26, 51 D.L.R. (4th) 481, 86 N.R. 328, 29 B.C.L.R. (2d) 273, 42 C.C.C. (3d) 97, 64 C.R. (3d) 123, 35 C.R.R. 1 (S.C.C.).

[53] *R. v. Osolin,* 1993 CarswellBC 512, 1993 CarswellBC 1274, [1993] 4 S.C.R. 595, 109 D.L.R. (4th) 478, 19 C.R.R. (2d) 93, 26 C.R. (4th) 1, 38 B.C.A.C. 81, 62 W.A.C. 81, 86 C.C.C. (3d) 481, 162 N.R. 1 (S.C.C.).

[54] *R. v. Chaulk,* 1990 CarswellMan 239, 1990 CarswellMan 385, [1990] 3 S.C.R. 1303, 2 C.R. (4th) 1, 62 C.C.C. (3d) 193, 69 Man. R. (2d) 161, [1991] 2 W.W.R. 385, 1 C.R.R. (2d) 1, 119 N.R. 161 (S.C.C.).

[55] *R. v. Wray,* 1970 CarswellOnt 22, 1970 CarswellOnt 207F, [1971] S.C.R. 272, 11 C.R.N.S. 235, [1970] 4 C.C.C. 1, 11 D.L.R. (3d) 673 (S.C.C.).

[56] *R. c. Taillefer,* 2003 CarswellQue 2765, 2003 CarswellQue 2766, 2003 SCC 70, [2003] 3 S.C.R. 307, 114 C.R.R. (2d) 60, 179 C.C.C. (3d) 353, 233 D.L.R. (4th) 227, 313 N.R. 1, 17 C.R. (6th) 57 (S.C.C.).

[57] *R. v. Carosella,* 1997 CarswellOnt 85, 1997 CarswellOnt 86, [1997] 1 S.C.R. 80, 2 B.H.R.C. 23, 112 C.C.C. (3d) 289, 98 O.A.C. 81, 4 C.R. (5th) 139, 142 D.L.R. (4th) 595, 207 N.R. 321, 41 C.R.R. (2d) 189, 31 O.R. (3d) 575 (headnote only) (S.C.C.).

[58] *R. v. Grant, supra,* note 39.

[59] *R. v. Harrison,* 2009 CarswellOnt 4108, 2009 CarswellOnt 4109, 2009 SCC 34105, [2009] 2 S.C.R. 494, 253 O.A.C. 358, 245 C.C.C. (3d) 86, 66 C.R. (6th) , 97 O.R. (3d) 560 (note), 391 N.R. 147, 309 D.L.R. (4th) 87 (S.C.C.).

APPENDIX

CONSTITUTION ACT, 1982
R.S.C. 1985, Appendix II, No.44
En. Canada Act 1982 (U.K.), c. 11

SCHEDULE B

CANADIAN CHARTER OF RIGHTS AND FREEDOMS

PART I

CANADIAN CHARTER OF RIGHTS AND FREEDONS

Whereas Canada is founded upon principles that recognize the supremacy of God and the rule of law:

Guarentee of Rights and Freedoms

Rights and freedoms in Canada 1. The Canadian Charter of Rights and Freedoms guarantees the rights and freedoms set out in it subject only to such reasonable limits prescribed by law as can be demonstrably justified in a free and democratic society.

Fundamental Freedoms

Fundamental freedoms 2. Everyone has the following fundamental freedoms:
(a) freedom of conscience and religion;
(b) freedom of thought, belief, opinion and expression, including freedom of the press and other media of communication;
(c) freedom of peaceful assembly; and
(d) freedom of association.

Democratic Rights

Democratic rights of citizens 3. Every citizen of Canada has the right to vote in an election of members of the House of Commons or of a legislative assembly and to be qualified for membership therein.

Maximum duration of legislative bodies

4. (1) No House of Commons and no legislative assembly shall continue for longer than five years from the date fixed for the return of the writs of a general election of its members.

Continuation in special circumstances

(2) In time of real or apprehended war, invasion or insurrection, a House of Commons may be continued by Parliament and a legislative assembly may be continued by the legislature beyond five years if such continuation is not opposed by the votes of more than one-third of the members of the House of Commons or the legislative assembly, as the case may be.

Annual sitting of legislative bodies

5. There shall be a sitting of Parliament and of each legislature at least once every twelve months.

Mobility Rights

Mobility of citizens

6. (1) Every citizen of Canada has the right to enter, remain in and leave Canada.

Rights to move and gain livelihood

(2) Every citizen of Canada and every person who has the status of a permanent resident of Canada has the right
(a) to move to and take up residence in any province; and
(b) to pursue the gaining of a livelihood in any province.

Limitation

(3) The rights specified in subsection (2) are subject to
(a) any laws or practices of general application in force in a province other than those that discriminate among persons primarily on the basis of province of present or previous residence; and
(b) any laws providing for reasonable residency requirements as a qualification for the receipt of publicly provided social services.

Affirmative action programs

(4) Subsections (2) and (3) do not preclude any law, program or activity that has as its object the amelioration in a province of conditions of individuals in that province who are socially or economically disadvantaged if the rate of employment in that province is below the rate of employment in Canada.

Legal Rights

Life, liberty and security of person

7. Everyone has the right to life, liberty and security of the person and the right not to be deprived thereof except in accordance with the principles of fundamental justice.

Search or seizure

8. Everyone has the right to be secure against unreasonable search or seizure.

Detention or imprisonment

9. Everyone has the right not to be arbitrarily detained or imprisoned.

Arrest or detention

10. Everyone has the right on arrest or detention

(a) to be informed promptly of the reasons therefor;

(b) to retain and instruct counsel without delay and to be informed of that right; and

(c) to have the validity of the detention determined by way of habeas corpus and to be released if the detention is not lawful.

Proceedings in criminal and penal matters

11. Any person charged with an offence has the right

(a) to be informed without unreasonable delay of the specific offence;

(b) to be tried within a reasonable time;

(c) not to be compelled to be a witness in proceedings against that person in respect of the offence;

(d) to be presumed innocent until proven guilty according to law in a fair and public hearing by an independent and impartial tribunal;

(e) not to be denied reasonable bail without just cause;

(f) except in the case of an offence under military law tried before a military tribunal, to the benefit of trial by jury where the maximum punishment for the offence is imprisonment for five years or a more severe punishment;

(g) not to be found guilty on account of any act or omission unless, at the time of the act or omission, it constituted an offence under Canadian or international law or was criminal according to the general principles of law recognized by the community of nations;

(h) if finally acquitted of the offence, not to be tried for it again and, if finally found guilty and punished for the offence, not to be tried or punished for it again; and

(i) if found guilty of the offence and if the punishment for the offence has been varied between the time of commission and the time of sentencing, to the benefit of the lesser punishment.

Treatment or punishment

12. Everyone has the right not to be subjected to any cruel and unusual treatment or punishment.

Self-crimination

13. A witness who testifies in any proceedings has the right not to have any incriminating evidence so given used to incriminate that witness in any other proceedings, except in a prosecution for perjury or for the giving of contradictory evidence.

Interpreter 14. A party or witness in any proceedings who does not understand or speak the language in which the proceedings are conducted or who is deaf has the right to the assistance of an interpreter.

Equality Rights

Equality before and under law and equal protection and benefit of law 15. (1) Every individual is equal before and under the law and has the right to the equal protection and equal benefit of the law without discrimination and, in particular, without discrimination based on race, national or ethnic origin, colour, religion, sex, age or mental or physical disability.

Affirmative action programs (2) Subsection (1) does not preclude any law, program or activity that has as its object the amelioration of conditions of disadvantaged individuals or groups including those that are disadvantaged because of race, national or ethnic origin, colour, religion, sex, age or mental or physical disability.

Official Languages of Canada

Official languages of Canada 16. (1) English and French are the official languages of Canada and have equality of status and equal rights and privileges as to their use in all institutions of the Parliament and government of Canada.

Official languages of New Brunswick (2) English and French are the official languages of New Brunswick and have equality of status and equal rights and privileges as to their use in all institutions of the legislature and government of New Brunswick.

Advancement of status and use (3) Nothing in this Charter limits the authority of Parliament or a legislature to advance the equality of status or use of English and French.

English and French linguistic communities in New Brunswick 16..1 (1) The English linguistic community and the French linguistic community in New Brunswick have equality of status and equal rights and privileges, including the right to distinct educational institutions and such distinct cultural institutions as are necessary for the preservation and promotion of those communities.

Role of the legislature and government of New Brunswick (2) The role of the legislature and government of New Brunswick to preserve and promote the status, rights and privileges referred to in subsection (1) is affirmed.

Proceedings of Parliament

17. (1) Everyone has the right to use English or French in any debates and other proceedings of Parliament.

Proceedings of New Brunswick legislature

(2) Everyone has the right to use English or French in any debates and other proceedings of the legislature of New Brunswick.

Parliamentary statutes and records

18. (1) The statutes, records and journals of Parliament shall be printed and published in English and French and both language versions are equally authoritative.

New Brunswick statutes and records

(2) The statutes, records and journals of the legislature of New Brunswick shall be prin-ted and published in English and French and both language versions are equally authoritative.

Proceedings in courts established by Parliament

19. (1) Either English or French may be used by any person in, or in any pleading in or process issuing from, any court established by Parliament.

Proceedings in New Brunswick courts

(2) Either English or French may be used by any person in, or in any pleading in or process issuing from, any court of New Brunswick.

Communications by public with federal institutions

20. (1) Any member of the public in Canada has the right to communicate with, and to receive available services from, any head or central office of an institution of the Parliament or government of Canada in English or French, and has the same right with respect to any other office of any such institution where
    (a) there is a significant demand for communications with and services from that office in such language; or
    (b) due to the nature of the office, it is reasonable that communications with and services from that office be available in both English and French.

Communications by public with New Brunswick institutions

(2) Any member of the public in New Brunswick has the right to communicate with, and to receive available services from, any office of an institution of the legislature or government of New Brunswick in English or French.

Continuation of existing constitutional provisions

21. Nothing in sections 16 to 20 abrogates or derogates from any right, privilege or obligation with respect to the English and French languages, or either of them, that exists or is continued by virtue of any other provision of the Constitution of Canada.

Rights and privileges preserved

22. Nothing in sections 16 to 20 abrogates or derogates from any legal or customary right or privilege acquired or enjoyed either before or after the coming into force of this Charter with respect to any language that is not English or French.

Minority Language Educational Rights

Language of instruction

23. (1) Citizens of Canada

    (a) whose first language learned and still understood is that of the English or French linguistic minority population of the province in which they reside, or

    (b) who have received their primary school instruction in Canada in English or French and reside in a province where the language in which they received that instruction is the language of the English or French linguistic minority population of the province,

have the right to have their children receive primary and secondary school instruction in that language in that province.

Continuity of language instruction

(2) Citizens of Canada of whom any child has received or is receiving primary or secondary school instruction in English or French in Canada, have the right to have all their children receive primary and secondary school instruction in the same language.

Application where numbers warrant

(3) The right of citizens of Canada under subsections (1) and (2) to have their children receive primary and secondary school instruction in the language of the English or French linguistic minority population of a province

    (a) applies wherever in the province the number of children of citizens who have such a right is sufficient to warrant the provision to them out of public funds of minority language instruction; and

    (b) includes, where the number of those children so warrants, the right to have them receive that instruction in minority language educational facilities provided out of public funds.

Enforcement

Enforcement of guaranteed rights and freedoms

24. (1) Anyone whose rights or freedoms, as guaranteed by this Charter, have been infringed or denied may apply to a court of competent jurisdiction to obtain such remedy as the court considers appropriate and just in the circumstances.

Exclusion of evidence bringing administration of justice into disrepute

(2) Where, in proceedings under subsection (1), a court concludes that evidence was obtained in a manner that infringed or denied any rights or freedoms guaranteed by this Charter, the evidence shall be excluded if it is established that, having regard to all the circumstances, the admission of it in the proceedings would bring the administration of justice into disrepute.

General

Aboriginal rights and freedoms not affected by Charter

25. The guarantee in this Charter of certain rights and freedoms shall not be construed so as to abrogate or derogate from any aboriginal, treaty or other rights or freedoms that pertain to the aboriginal peoples of Canada including
(a) any rights or freedoms that have been recognized by the Royal Proclamation of October 7, 1763; and
(b) any rights or freedoms that now exist by way of land claims agreements or may be so acquired.

Other rights and freedoms not affected by Charter

26. The guarantee in this Charter of certain rights and freedoms shall not be construed as denying the existence of any other rights or freedoms that exist in Canada.

Multicultural heritage

27. This Charter shall be interpreted in a manner consistent with the preservation and enhancement of the multicultural heritage of Canadians.

Rights guaranteed equally to both sexes

28. Notwithstanding anything in this Charter, the rights and freedoms referred to in it are guaranteed equally to male and female persons.

Rights respecting certain schools preserved

29. Nothing in this Charter abrogates or derogates from any rights or privileges guaranteed by or under the Constitution of Canada in respect of denominational, separate or dissentient schools.

Application to territories and territorial authorities

30. A reference in this Charter to a province or to the legislative assembly or legislature of a province shall be deemed to include a reference to the Yukon Territory and the Northwest Territories, or to the appropriate legislative authority thereof, as the case may be.

Legislative powers not extended

31. Nothing in this Charter extends the legislative powers of any body or authority.

Application of Charter

Application of Charter

32. (1) This Charter applies
(a) to the Parliament and government of Canada in respect of all matters within the authority of Parliament including all matters relating to the Yukon Territory and Northwest Territories; and
(b) to the legislature and government of each province in respect of all matters within the authority of the legislature of each province.

Exception

(2) Notwithstanding subsection (1), section 15 shall not have effect until three years after this section comes into force.

Exception where express declaration

33. (1) Parliament or the legislature of a province may expressly declare in an Act of Parliament or of the legislature, as the case may be, that the Act or a provision thereof shall operate notwithstanding a provision included in section 2 or sections 7 to 15 of this Charter.

Operation of exception

(2) An Act or a provision of an Act in respect of which a declaration made under this section is in effect shall have such operation as it would have but for the provision of this Charter referred to in the declaration.

Five year limitation

(3) A declaration made under subsection (1) shall cease to have effect five years after it comes into force or on such earlier date as may be specified in the declaration.

Re-enactment

(4) Parliament or the legislature of a province may re-enact a declaration made under subsection (1).

Five year limitation

(5) Subsection (3) applies in respect of a re-enactment made under subsection (4).

Citation

Citation

34. This Part may be cited as the *Canadian Charter of Rights and Freedoms*.

24

Solicitor/Client Privilege

*Shane G. Parker**

An integral part of the adversary system is to safeguard what a client confidentially tells his or her lawyer in their professional capacity. For effective representation, and appropriate legal advice, an honest, full, and frank discussion between the lawyer and client must exist and be encouraged. Essentially, for a lawyer to advocate a position, that lawyer must know all the circumstances, including the illegal and embarrassing points, regarding the client's position and why the position is being taken.

Solicitor-client privilege is the oldest of all privileges with roots in the 16th century. The basis was the oath and honour as a solicitor, professional man, and as a gentleman to keep his client's secret.[1] Through the 18th century, the rationale and the focus became more on the rights of the client and to protect the client rather than protecting the lawyer's honour. Mr. Justice Cory, in *Smith v. Jones*,[2] states:

> The solicitor-client privilege has long been regarded as fundamentally important to our judicial system. Well over a century ago in *Anderson v. Bank of British Columbia* ..., the importance of the rule was recognized:
>
>> The object and meaning of the rule is this; that as, by reason of the complexity and difficulty of our law, litigation can only be properly conducted by professional men, it is absolutely necessary that a man, in order to prosecute his rights or to defend himself from an improper claim, should have recourse to the assistance of professional lawyers, ... to use a vulgar phrase, that he should be able to make a clean breast of it to the gentleman whom he consults with a view to the prosecution of his claim, or the substantiating of his defence ... that he should be able to place unrestricted and unbounded confidence in the professional agent, and that the communications he so makes to him should be kept secret, unless with his consent (for it is his privilege, and not the privilege of the confidential agent), that he should be enabled properly to conduct his litigation.

---

* B.Sc. (Hons), University of Waterloo; M.P.E., University of New Brunswick; LL.B. Dalhousie Law School, Special Prosecutor Organized Crime, Alberta Justice.

Solicitor-client privilege is one of the highest privileges recognized by courts, even more so than medical/ psychiatric, religious, or marital privileges. The Supreme Court of Canada, in *R. v. Lavallee, Rackel & Heintz*,[3] affirms and strengthens the proposition that was repeated in *Descôteaux*.[4] Arbour, J. for the majority in *Lavallee* stated:

> It is critical to emphasize here that all information protected by the solicitor-client privilege is out of reach for the state. It cannot be forcibly discovered or disclosed and it is inadmissible in court. It is the privilege of the client and the lawyer acts as a gatekeeper, ethically bound to protect the privileged information that belongs to his or her client. Therefore, any privileged information acquired by the state without the consent of the privilege holder is information that the state is not entitled to as a rule of fundamental justice.[5]

Despite its importance, solicitor-client privilege is not absolute. It is subject to certain exceptions. In *Smith v. Jones*, Cory, J. examined whether the privilege should be displaced in the interest of protecting the safety of the public:

> Just as no right is absolute so too the privilege, even that between solicitor and client, is subject to clearly defined exceptions. The decision to exclude evidence that would be both relevant and of substantial probative value because it is protected by the solicitor-client privilege represents a policy decision. It is based upon the importance to our legal system in general of the solicitor-client privilege. In certain circumstances, however, other societal values must prevail.[6]

However, solicitor-client privilege must be as close to absolute as possible to ensure public confidence and retain relevance. As such, it will only yield in certain clearly defined circumstances, and does not involve a balancing of interests on a case by case basis. The majority in *R. v. Lavallee, Rackel & Heintz*, after quoting with approval Cory's comments, added:

> Indeed, solicitor-client privilege must remain as close to absolute as possible if it is to retain relevance. Accordingly, this Court is compelled in my view to adopt stringent norms to ensure its protection.[7]

The Supreme Court of Canada on several occasions has clearly indicated the importance and the magnitude of solicitor-client privilege. It could even be said that solicitor-client privilege is almost a kin to *Charter* right for a person who is a client and often is an accused.

WHAT ATTRACTS PRIVILEGE?

For solicitor-client communications to attract privilege, the following must occur:

(1) the communication is for legal advice (not friendly or financial advice);

(2) it relates to the specific legal purpose and basis for the relationship; and

(3) it is made in confidence (without the presence of a third party, for example).

Once those three criteria are met, the confidence is permanently maintained.

There is a distinction between professional confidentiality (all that is said) and solicitor-client privilege. Not all communications that are confidential are also privileged. Confidentiality is a substantive rule whereas a privilege is a bar to admissibility of the evidence.[8] It bears repeating that there are limits to the rule. The *Lavallee* decision is an illustration of the point. In *Lavallee*, s. 488.1 of the *Criminal Code* was struck down. Section 488.1 of the *Criminal Code* was a provision that governed how search warrants were to be executed at a lawyer's office (where privileged documents abound!). The Supreme Court of Canada found that s. 488.1 of the *Code* was unconstitutional as it did not adequately protect that fundamental right of justice of solicitor-client privilege. While search warrants can still be used in a lawyer's office, there must be more safeguards to protect the client's privilege on a case-by-case basis than those in that provision of the *Code*. The court could not allow law offices to be havens of crime and sanctuaries for rogues of society. While it was important to protect solicitor-client privilege, there was a limit how far the court would go with balancing the community or the public's right to justice.

WHEN DOES PRIVILEGE COMMENCE?

Privilege commences when, according to *Descôteaux c. Mierzwinski*,[9] the communication to a legal advisor is:

1. made to the advisor or his/her assistants in their professional capacity; and

2. given in order to establish the existence of a valid claim or eligibility to retain the lawyer's services.

The privilege continues through the stages of obtaining, formulating, or giving legal advice.[10]

Privilege can be waived. It is only the client who can waive or disclose confidential information. The lawyer is ethically and duty bound not to reveal confidential communications (see Provincial Code/Barristers' Society Ethics). The lawyer cannot be compelled to disclose the information.

Privilege is both an evidentiary and substantive rule of law. *Lavallee* re-iterated that the rule is about fundamental justice (i.e., a substantive rule), and in terms of inadmissibility is also an evidentiary rule as well.

EXCEPTIONS TO THE RULE

There are exceptions to the rule. For instance, if the communication is in furtherance of a crime, it loses privilege. This is the case where the communication is a crime itself, like a client uttering death threats towards a witness. Also no privilege attaches where it was made to obtain advice to facilitate the commission of a crime; for instance, if a bad guy asks his lawyer, "Where is the best place to move money of a crime to avoid detection?" In other words, "How do you launder money?" This is an example of advice sought to facilitate the commission of a crime. This communication is not privileged.

One such example is *R. v. Dorion*.[11] Eric Dorion, a lawyer in New Brunswick, was convicted of obstructing justice and sentenced to four and a half years in jail. The story starts with a fire at a Moncton pub. It was alleged that one of the owners hired an arsonist named Lefebvre. After being arrested Lefebvre co-operated with the police. As time unfolded and, after entering his guilty plea and into an agreement with the Crown, Lefebvre told police that Dorion offered him money to change his guilty plea and to refuse to testify for the Crown. Lefebvre next agreed to wear a body pack to have his conversations with Dorion recorded. However, unknown to Lefebvre, the police were intercepting all of his conversations as the police did not fully trust him. Through time the police also intercepted the communications between Dorion and the bar co-owner, who was Dorion's client. By the second trial, Lefebvre was uncooperative with the Crown and claimed the conversations at the jail were privileged. The Court ruled that the communications involving Dorion were furthering a criminal offence and were admissible. Privilege was pierced. There was an issue with how the police tried to separate out privileged calls from those violating the protection, but noted the distinction between protecting the privilege and prohibiting/precluding all the communications with a lawyer. Privilege is not absolute.

Public safety is another exception. In *Smith v. Jones*, the Court states a three-part test. Public safety is invoked when:

1. there is a clear risk to an identifiable person or group;
2. the risk is of serious bodily harm or death; and
3. the danger is imminent.

A further exception includes, when innocence is at stake such as when there is a genuine risk of a wrongful conviction.[12]

Privilege does not attach when the client raises an allegation of lawyer misconduct. In this situation, the lawyer is allowed to defend him- or herself from the allegation raised by the client.

Finally, when Crown counsel provides advice to the police but the legality of the police procedure is in question, privilege is lost. Privilege is held by police force,[13] but like other forms of privilege has limits. Communications between the Crown and police are ordinarily confidential and are protected in the same way as solicitor-client privilege would be in the course of, for instance, an accused and defence counsel.

CONTRAST TO OTHER PRIVILEGES

There exist other forms of privilege. One other privilege is for those who give information to law enforcement on a confidential basis. A person may give information to the police by way of special programs like CrimeStoppers, or by having a relationship with particular police officer. The term used to describe the person who is giving information is as a "confidential informant". The Supreme Court of Canada has recognized on numerous times the extreme value this source of information is to law enforcement and the grave risk to the personal safety of those who supply the information. It is a special privilege that is greater than certain Charter rights such as access to disclosure. It is elevated status so as to continue the flow of information and to ensure the safety of the informant by keeping his/her identity, or information that may tend to identify the person, confidential.[14]

Informant privilege, like solicitor client privilege is a *class* privilege. It applies simply by establishing that the informer is present. A court does not have any discretion with regard to privilege and is under a duty to protect the informer's identity. It is an absolute rule with one very narrow and difficult exception: the innocence of the accused is truly at stake, whereby only the informer could establish the accused is innocent at trial.[15] Otherwise, the privilege is shared by the Crown and the informant, and both must consent to waiving the confidentiality of the identity.

The concept of "information that may tend to identify the identity of the informer" needs some elaboration to see the importance the courts takes its role in protecting the informer. Information that even tends to merely narrow the pool of people who could be the informer, is sufficient justification for the Crown to withhold, or vet out the information, from the defence's disclosure.

The two privileges share a high standard by the courts to uphold the privilege above competing interests, with very narrow exceptions to extinguish it and a rationale based upon public policy to protect the free flow of valued information and trust in the communicative relationships required for an efficient justice system

CONCLUSION

In summary, solicitor-client privilege is an established and old rule of law. It has evolved over the centuries from protecting the lawyer's honour to now protecting the client. In fact, even recently it has been recognized that it is a fundamental right of justice—virtually akin to a *Charter* right for an accused. For there to be solicitor-client privilege it must follow the three-part test. It must be intended to be confidential. It must be done within the professional capacity of the lawyer, and it must be for legal advice. Despite its importance there are exceptions and limitations. For instance, the communication loses its privilege if it is in the furtherance of a crime. Finally, solicitor-client privilege is not only a substantive right, but is also an evidentiary rule of law. Solicitor-client information is inadmissible in a court of law.

Notes

[1] Sopinka, Lederman, Bryant, *The Law of Evidence in Canada*, 2nd ed. (Markham: Butterworths, 1999), at p. 728.

[2] *Smith v. Jones*, 1999 CarswellBC 590, 1999 CarswellBC 591, 1999 SCC 16, 22 C.R. (5th) 203, 132 C.C.C. (3d) 225, 169 D.L.R. (4th) 385, 60 C.R.R. (2d) 46, 62 B.C.L.R. (3d) 209, 236 N.R. 201, [1999] 1 S.C.R. 455, 120 B.C.A.C. 161, 196 W.A.C. 161, [1999] 8 W.W.R. 364 (S.C.C.) (S.C.C.), at para. 45.

[3] *R. v. Lavalle, Rackel & Heintz*, 2002 CarswellAlta 1818, 2002 CarswellAlta 1819, 2002 SCC 61, [2002] S.C.J. No. 61, 167 C.C.C. (3d) 1, 216 D.L.R. (4th) 257, 3 C.R. (6th) 209, 4 Alta. L.R. (4th) 1, 96 C.R.R. (2d) 189, [2002] 11 W.W.R. 191, [2002] 4 C.T.C. 143, [2002] 3 S.C.R. 209, 164 O.A.C. 280, 2002 D.T.C. 7267 (Eng.),

2002 D.T.C. 7287 (Fr.), 292 N.R. 296, 312 A.R. 201, 281 W.A.C. 201, 217 Nfld. & P.E.I.R. 183, 651 A.P.R. 183 (S.C.C.).

4   *Descôteaux c. Mierzwinski*, 1982 CarswellQue 13, 1982 CarswellQue 291, [1982] 1 S.C.R. 860, 28 C.R. (3d) 289, 1 C.R.R. 318, 44 N.R. 462, 141 D.L.R. (3d) 590, 70 C.C.C. (2d) 385 (S.C.C.)

5   *R. v. Lavalle, Rackel & Heintz, supra*, note 3, at para. 24.

6   *Smith v. Jones, supra*, note 2, at para. 51.

7   *R. v. Lavalle, Rackel & Heintz, supra*, note 3, at para. 36.

8   *R. c. Robillard*, 2000 CarswellQue 2576, 151 C.C.C. (3d) 296, 39 C.R. (5th) 189, [2001] R.J.Q. 1 (Que. C.A.).

9   *Descôteaux c. Mierzwinski, supra*, note 4.

10 *Stevens v. Canada (Prime Minister)*, 1998 CarswellNat 2311, 1998 CarswellNat 1051, [1998] F.C.J. No. 794, [1998] 4 F.C. 89, 147 F.T.R. 308 (note), 11 Admin. L.R. (3d) 169, 161 D.L.R. (4th) 85, 228 N.R. 142, 21 C.P.C. (4th) 327, 80 C.P.R. (3d) 390 (Fed. C.A.).

11 *R. v. Dorion*, 2007 CarswellNB 249, 2007 CarswellNB 250, 221 C.C.C. (3d) 97, 315 N.B.R. (2d) 205, 158 C.R.R. (2d) 299, 2007 NBCA 41, 815 A.P.R. 205 (N.B. C.A.).

12 *R. v. McClure*, 2001 CarswellOnt 496, 2001 CarswellOnt 497, 2001 SCC 14, 151 C.C.C. (3d) 321, 40 C.R. (5th) 1, 195 D.L.R. (4th) 513, 142 O.A.C. 201, 80 C.R.R. (2d) 217, [2001] 1 S.C.R. 445, 266 N.R. 275 (S.C.C.).

13 *R. v. Shirose*, 1999 CarswellOnt 948, 1999 CarswellOnt 949, 133 C.C.C. (3d) 257, 24 C.R. (5th) 365, 171 D.L.R. (4th) 193, (sub nom. *R. v. Campbell*) 237 N.R. 86, (sub nom. *R. v. Campbell*) 42 O.R. (3d) 800 (note), (sub nom. *R. v. Campbell*) 119 O.A.C. 201, (sub nom. *R. v. Campbell*) 43 O.R. (3d) 256 (note), (sub nom. *R. v. Campbell*) [1999] 1 S.C.R. 565 (S.C.C.).

14 See *Bisaillon v. Keable*, 1983 CarswellQue 384, 1983 CarswellQue 28, 7 C.C.C. (3d) 385, 37 C.R. (3d) 289, [1983] 2 S.C.R. 60, 2 D.L.R. (4th) 193, 51 N.R. 81, 4 Admin. L.R. 205 (S.C.C.); *R. v. Leipert*, 1997 CarswellBC 101, 1997 CarswellBC 102, 112 C.C.C. (3d) 385, 41 C.R.R. (2d) 266, 85 B.C.A.C. 162, 138 W.A.C. 162, 143 D.L.R. (4th) 38, 207 N.R. 145, 4 C.R. (5th) 259, [1997] 3 W.W.R. 457, [1997] 1 S.C.R. 281 (S.C.C.); and *Application to proceed in camera, Re*, 2007 CarswellBC 2418, 2007 CarswellBC 2419, 2007 SCC 43, 224 C.C.C. (3d) 1, [2008] 1 W.W.R. 223, 51 C.R. (6th) 262, 73 B.C.L.R. (4th) 34, 285 D.L.R. (4th) 193, 247 B.C.A.C. 1, 409 W.A.C. 1, (sub nom. *Vancouver Sun v. Canada (Attorney General)*) 368 N.R. 112, (sub nom. *Named Person v. Vancouver Sun*) [2007] 3 S.C.R. 253, (sub nom. *Named Person v. Vancouver Sun*) 162 C.R.R. (2d) 104 (S.C.C.).

15 *R. v. Scott*, 1990 CarswellOnt 65, 1990 CarswellOnt 1012, 2 C.R. (4th) 153, 61 C.C.C. (3d) 300, 116 N.R. 361, 1 C.R.R. (2d) 82, 43 O.A.C. 277, [1990] 3 S.C.R. 979 (S.C.C.).

25

Bans on Publication and Other Media Restrictions

*Dean Jobb**

Court proceedings have long been a staple of media reports. Detailed, often lurid accounts of murders and trials began appearing in England's earliest newspapers in the mid-1500s. "The journalists who were feeding the early printing presses," notes media historian Mitchell Stephens, "learned what all journalists have learned: that crime news is prime news."[1] Yet the rationale for publicizing criminal cases—from the well-documented prosecution in 1613 of the conspirators who poisoned Sir Thomas Overbury in the Tower of London to O.J. Simpson's murder trial on live television in 1995—goes beyond selling newspapers and boosting audience ratings. News accounts play an important role in apprehending criminals and may prompt witnesses to come forward to implicate or exonerate a suspect. Reports of the sentences judges mete out are crucial to the justice system's goal of deterring others from committing crimes. Most important, coverage of trials ensures the actions of judges, prosecutors, defence lawyers, and police investigators are exposed to public scrutiny.

It follows, then, that the business of the courts must be as publicly accessible as possible. An often-quoted proponent of openness was nineteenth-century English philosopher Jeremy Bentham, who feared judges exerted too great an influence over public life:

> [i]n the darkness of secrecy, sinister interest, and evil in every shape have full swing. Only in proportion as publicity has place can any of the checks applicable to judicial injustice operate, Where there is no publicity there is no justice. Publicity is the very soul of justice."[2]

Canada's courts have long acknowledged the media's role as a pub-

---

* B.A., Mount Allison University, Sackville, New Brunswick; M.A., Saint Mary's University, Halifax, Nova Scotia; Associate professor of journalism, School of Journalism, University of King's College, Halifax; author of *Media Law for Canadian Journalists*, 2nd ed. (Emond Montgomery Publications, 2010); Editor, Media Law section, J-Source/The Canadian Journalism Project website, www.j-source.ca.

lic watchdog. As the Ontario Court of Appeal declared in a 1983 judgment:

> [t]here can be no doubt that the openness of the courts to the public is one of the hallmarks of a democratic society. Public accessibility to the courts ... is a restraint on arbitrary action by those who govern and by the powerful.[3]

The Supreme Court of Canada has recognized that it is only through the media that members of the public can monitor what is happening in the nation's courtrooms. "Discussion of court cases and constructive criticism of court proceedings is dependent upon the receipt by the public of information as to what transpired in court," Justice Peter Cory wrote in 1989. "Practically speaking, this information can only be obtained from the newspapers or other media."[4] In the words of Justice Morris Fish in a 2005 Supreme Court ruling: "[w]hat goes on in the courts ought therefore to be, and manifestly is, of central concern to Canadians."[5]

CONTEMPT OF COURT

The media's right of access, however, is not absolute. Judges have inherent powers to control proceedings that are *sub judice*—"before a court or judge for consideration".[6] Journalists, editors, and news organizations that cross the line between informing the public and publishing information that could prejudice the right to a fair trial or interfere in the course of justice can be cited for contempt of court. Courts have imposed fines of up to $5,000 for contempt in recent years and, if the published information causes a mistrial, media organizations may be ordered to cover the costs of the failed court proceeding.[7]

Contempt has been defined as encompassing "any conduct which tends to undermine, or bring into disrepute, the authority and administration of justice."[8] While it remains an offence to interfere with the administration of justice, legal observers consider a form of contempt concerned with the reputation of judges—known as "scandalizing the court"—to have become extinct, as Canadian judges recognize that their rulings and their conduct must be open to scrutiny and criticism. In 1987, the Ontario Court of Appeal ruled the offence of scandalizing the court violates the guarantee of freedom of expression under s. 2(b) of the *Charter of Rights and Freedoms*. The courts, the ruling observed, "are not fragile flowers that will wither in the hot heat of controversy".[9]

The law of contempt also prevents or delays the publication of certain information that could "interfere with someone's right to a fair hearing before a court or other quasi-judicial body."[10] Reporting an accused person's criminal record, details of a confession, or other evidence that may never be admissible in court are the acts most likely to draw a citation for contempt. There is a greater risk of prejudice if the case is to be heard by a jury, since such information may influence the jurors ultimately chosen to decide the guilt or innocence of the accused. In 1999, the British Columbia Court of Appeal warned:

> [i]t is therefore a grave contempt for anyone, particularly the members of what is now called the media, to publish, before or during a trial, any statements, comments, or information which reflect adversely upon the conduct or character of an accused person, or to suggest directly or indirectly that he has been previously convicted of any offence. [11]

The test, the Court said, is whether the published information presents a real risk of prejudicing the right to a fair trial.

The distinction between legitimate reports of court proceedings and potentially contemptuous ones is not always clear. As an Ontario judge faced with a contempt charge against a newspaper once remarked, "It's a question of timing."[12] Information published at the time an offence is committed is unlikely to be fresh in the minds of jurors many months later, when a trial is held. Publication of the same information on the eve of trial may well pose such a risk and be punished as contempt. To add to the uncertainty, courts in different jurisdictions take different approaches. Alberta judges have found media outlets in contempt for revealing an accused person's criminal record at the time of arrest, long before trial. In contrast, the Ontario and Nova Scotia media routinely reveal the same information when a suspect is arrested and this practice is becoming common in other provinces.[13] Even Alberta has eased its hard-line approach: the province's Court of Appeal reversed a contempt conviction in 2003, noting a newspaper report on a suspect's criminal past appeared long before trial and few people read the paper in the community where the trial would be held.[14] As professors G. Stuart Adam and Robert Martin have noted:

> Technical breaches of the *sub judice* rule or other parts of the law of contempt will not inevitably lead to a prosecution. The timing and character of the breach, the size of the community, the place of publication or broadcast or whether the matter is to be decided by a judge or a judge and jury can all have a bearing.[15]

STATUTORY BANS

Parliament has created statutory bans on publication that apply to certain information or specific stages of a criminal prosecution. Introduced to the *Criminal Code* in the mid-1950s, these provisions temporarily restrict broadcasting or publishing information that could prejudice a defendant's future trial. They prevent media coverage of criminal records and confessions—information that has traditionally carried a risk of a citation for contempt—produced at pre-trial hearings. In the 1980s, new, permanent bans were introduced to protect the identities of complainants and young witnesses involved in prosecutions of sexual offences; these have since been extended and now any witness can ask a court to shield his or her identity. The *Young Offenders Act* of 1984 and its successor, the *Youth Criminal Justice Act*, have opened juvenile justice to public scrutiny, subject to a prohibition on identifying young persons accused or convicted of crimes.

Some general observations can be made about statutory publication bans. The media's right to cover proceedings held in open court means these restrictions are limited in scope. Judges have the discretion not to impose certain bans if they are sought by the Crown, but have no choice if the defendant makes the request. Most bans expire once charges are dismissed or a verdict is reached, since there is no longer a need to protect the defendant's right to a fair trial. This is not the case for *Criminal Code* bans on identifying complainants or witnesses or the *Youth Criminal Justice Act* ban on identifying young persons; unless lifted by order of a court or the youth agrees to be identified, these bans are permanent.

CRIMINAL CODE BANS

Identity of Crime Victims and Witnesses

Judges have the power under subs. 486(3) to bar the media from identifying complainants and witnesses under the age of 18 involved in prosecutions of sexual offences and charges of extortion or loan-sharking. The section, intended to encourage victims of these crimes to come forward with their accusations by sparing them from embarrassing publicity, bans the person's name and "any evidence that could disclose" his or her identity. This poses problems for journalists, since reporting seemingly innocuous details like age, sex, address and occupation may disclose, in combination, the person's identity to some readers, listeners, or viewers. While the courts recognize no right to seek a publication ban on the identity of an accused person,[16] this provision may prevent the media from naming a defendant who is relative or close associate of the complainant, since identifying who is charged could disclose the complainant's identity. Unless a judge later agrees to lift the ban at the request of the complainant or witness, the ban is permanent, even if the accused is acquitted.[17]

In 1999, Parliament broadened the scope of this ban, allowing victims and witnesses involved in crimes other than those set out in subs. 486(3) to ask the court for an order banning publication of any information that could reveal their identities. In January 2002, this provision, subs. 486(4.1), was amended to allow officials within the justice system to seek this ban in cases of alleged intimidation or offences relating to members of a criminal organization. Among those categorized as "justice system participants" eligible to request the ban are politicians, judges, lawyers, jurors, court administrators, police officers, prison guards, parole officials, informants, and customs officers.

The ban under subs. 486(4.1) is discretionary and the judge must take into account the *Charter* right to freedom of expression when deciding whether to shield identification. The applicant must notify "any other person affected by the order" (generally the media) that a ban is being sought. A judge may hold a hearing and must weigh a range of factors—including security concerns and alternatives to restricting publication—before agreeing to impose a ban. The judge may hold the hearing in private and the media can only report what happened if the ban is denied. If a ban is imposed, "the contents of the application" and the evidence and legal arguments presented at the hearing are banned from publication.

Media outlets have successfully opposed bans under this section. A Nova Scotia judge refused to ban publication of the identities of two young assault victims and the accused, their mother's boyfriend, noting that persons who report crimes must expect public scrutiny and "simple embarrassment" is not sufficient grounds for a ban.[18] An Ontario judge allowed the media to identify the owner of a building where a murder occurred, ruling the landlord's fear of financial loss did not justify a ban.[19]

Pre-Trial Proceedings

At bail (show cause) hearings, held shortly after arrest to determine whether an accused person will be released pending trial, the prosecution or defence can seek an order that "the evidence taken, the information given or the representations made and the reasons, if any, given or to be given by the justice shall not be published in any newspaper or broadcast".[20] The ban is far-reaching: reporters are barred from publishing the evidence presented, arguments advanced by lawyers, even the judge's reasons for or against granting bail. The precautions arise from the nature of the hearing, which allows the introduction of hearsay evidence that is inadmissible at trial. Details of criminal records and potentially prejudicial evidence about whether the accused is considered dangerous or likely to flee the jurisdiction are also aired. Courts have ruled that whether bail is granted or denied, and any conditions upon which it is granted, can be reported without violating the ban.[21] The Ontario Court of Appeal concluded in 2009 that this ban applies only to cases slated to be heard by a jury.[22]

The ban can be imposed at any time during the bail hearing and expires if the accused is discharged at a preliminary hearing or once the trial is over. This ban can also be imposed on an array of other bail-related proceedings: hearings to review a judge's order to grant or deny bail under subs. 520(9) and 521(10); superior court bail applications under subs. 522(5); applications to vary the terms of bail under subs. 523(3); hearings into violations of bail conditions under subs. 524(12); and reviews of detention orders under subs. 525(8).

At the preliminary hearing stage, the Crown can seek—and the defence has a right to invoke—a ban on publishing "the evidence taken" before the provincial court judge.[23] It covers the testimony of witnesses and any information contained in documents tendered as exhibits. The restriction is less sweeping than for show cause hearings, allowing the media to report procedural matters, legal arguments, and other courtroom statements that do not disclose evidence.[24] As well, there is an automatic ban on publishing details of any statement or confession from an accused person entered into evidence at the preliminary hearing. The ban even prohibits references to the fact a statement or confession exists.[25] Both bans expire when the trial is over or if the accused is discharged at the preliminary hearing.

Sexual History and Confidential Records

There is provision to ban publication of the details of a defence application to delve into the sexual history of a complainant.[26] The media can report that the defence has asked to present evidence of previous sexual conduct, but there is an automatic ban on the "contents of an application", the legal arguments presented, and any evidence of prior sexual activity produced. If a judge agrees to hear the application, the hearing must be conducted *in camera*. If the evidence is not found to be admissible, the media cannot disclose the outcome of the application for a hearing or the hearing itself, unless a judge rules otherwise. If the evidence is accepted, the outcome and the judge's decision can be reported. Evidence of previous sexual conduct can be reported in the media once it is presented at trial.

Similar provisions apply to applications for access to the private records of a complainant or witness. The list includes medical, psychiatric, therapeutic, counseling, education, employment, adoption and social services records, and personal journals and diaries. The media can report that an application has been made for access to such records, but the "contents of the application" and all other details are subject to a publication ban. A judge must hold an initial hearing to determine whether the records should be produced; if they are, the judge will review the records privately and may hold a second hearing to determine whether they should be provided to the defendant. The media is banned from publishing any evidence or legal arguments presented at these hearings, which must be held *in camera* in any event. There is a publication ban on the outcome at both stages—the initial decision whether to review the records, as well as any order that the records be produced or withheld—but a judge may allow the media to reveal these decisions after weighing the interests of justice against "the right to privacy of the person to whom the record relates".[27]

Trial

The *Criminal Code* includes a ban to prevent jurors from being exposed to news reports of *voir dire* proceedings, which are held in their absence to determine the admissibility of evidence or to decide legal motions. This wide-ranging ban, applied automatically, dictates that "no information regarding any portion of the trial at which the jury is not present shall be published ... before the jury retires to consider its verdict."[28] The ban expires once deliberations begin, since jurors are sequestered—and denied access to media reports—until they reach a verdict. In some cases, however, judges have issued an order extending the ban until a verdict is returned. Use of the word "information" in this section indicates that all court business transacted in the jury's absence is captured by the ban, evidence and legal argument alike. In one case, the media was found to have properly reported that the victim's father tried to attack the accused during a recess. Even though the jury was absent, the Court ruled the incident did not occur during a "portion of the trial", as required for the subs. 648(1) ban to apply.[29] Some courts have ruled this ban applies to pre-trial hearings, held under subs. 645(5) to deal with *Charter* arguments and other complex issues, even though jurors have yet to be chosen. In a Nova Scotia case, a judge ruled the word "information" should be given a narrow interpretation at the pre-trial hearing stage; the judge only banned publishing evidence or allegations of wrongdoing on the part of the prosecution or accused that could prejudice the upcoming trial.[30]

Penalties

A violation of any of these bans is a summary offence, punishable on conviction by a maximum $2,000 fine and six months in jail. Some breaches of publication bans are punished as a contempt of court.

Exclusion Orders

The *Criminal Code* enables judges to bar members of the public, including reporters, from certain proceedings. A judge can convene an *in camera* hearing if he or she "is of the opinion that it is in the interest of public morals, the maintenance of order or the proper administration of justice".[31] A similar provision enables the public's exclusion from preliminary inquiries if the judge believes "the ends of justice will be best served by so doing".[32] These powers are usually reserved for sexual assault cases, especially when victims or witnesses are children likely to be intimidated by the presence of spectators. Their use has declined in recent years because provision has been made for young victims to testify via videotape or shielded by screens.[33] Note these sections do not ban publication; they simply make it impossible for journalists to be present to report on the hearing as it takes place. Journalists may be able to reconstruct what occurred through interviews with participants or by consulting transcripts of the proceedings.

Proceedings to approve a search warrant under subs. 487(1) and to issue a summons or arrest warrant under subs. 507(1) must be held *in camera*. The media and public are also barred, under subs. 488.1(10), from a hearing to decide whether solicitor-client confidentiality prevents disclosure of documents seized by police. Under subs. 672.5(6), a court or review board deciding the fate of a person found unfit to stand trial, or not criminally responsible for an offence due to a mental disorder, can hold a hearing *in camera* if doing so is "in the best interests of the accused and not contrary to the public interest". If the hearing is open, subs. 672.51(11) bans publishing information disclosed when the accused is absent, or if a court or review board believes releasing the information would be "seriously prejudicial" to the accused and "protection of the accused takes precedence over the public interest in disclosure".

Search Warrants

While the courts have held that search warrant documents are open to public scrutiny once evidence has been seized,[34] judges have the right to order warrants and associated documents sealed if "the ends of justice would be subverted" by their disclosure. Grounds for sealing a warrant include the risk of compromising an ongoing investigation; the need to protect the identity of a confidential informant; prejudice to the interests of an innocent person; and the possibility a person engaged in intelligence-gathering operations will be endangered.[35] Media outlets have the right to apply at any time to the judge who sealed the warrant, asking that it be made public.[36] The Ontario Court of Appeal, in a 2003 ruling upheld by the Supreme Court of Canada, concluded that sealing a search warrant is a "significant intrusion" on freedom of expression. The court ruled warrants should be sealed only when there is a serious risk to the administration of justice or of prejudicing a trial.[37]

Subsection 487.2(1) of the *Code* was introduced in 1985 to prevent the media from identifying suspects or premises searched by police if no charges resulted. The prohibition would be lifted in the unlikely event those searched agreed to be identified. Appellate courts in three provinces have struck down the provision as an infringement on the media's right to freedom of expression. The section remains on the books but is considered to be of no force and effect.[38]

Wiretaps and Intercepted Cellular Calls

Reporters must tread carefully if they discover the existence of wiretaps or wiretap evidence, either through police sources or from examining search warrant documents. The *Criminal Code* forbids disclosing the existence of an intercepted conversation and its contents. This restriction does not apply to wiretap evidence presented in a criminal or civil case or published reports based on such evidence.[39] Nor does it include conversations broadcast over a police scanner or a Citizens' Band radio, because such communications are not private. As well, journalists can tape interviews they conduct over the phone without the knowledge or consent of the person being interviewed—the law requires only that one party (in this case the reporter) consent to interception of a private communication. It is an offence to wilfully use or disclose intercepted cell phone conversations, which can sometimes be heard over police scanners, unless one of the parties agrees to the disclosure.[40] Anyone convicted of violating either offence can be jailed for two years and ordered to pay punitive damages of up to $5,000 to the person whose privacy has been invaded.[41]

RESTRICTIONS ON YOUTH COURT PROCEEDINGS

Bans on Identifying Young Persons

The *Youth Criminal Justice Act*, like the *Young Offenders Act* it replaced in 2003, allows media scrutiny of criminal proceedings involving accused persons aged 12 to 17, subject to restrictions on identifying those involved. Sections 110 and 111 impose an automatic ban on publishing any information that would identify the accused, as well as crime victims and witnesses who are under the age of 18.

Under subs. 110(2), however, the media can identify convicted young offenders if a judge decides to sentence them as if they were adults. The ban also may be lifted for offenders over the age of 14 who have been convicted of so-called "presumptive offences". This classification of offences includes murder, attempted murder, manslaughter, aggravated sexual assault, as well as a serious violent crime if it is the young person's third conviction for such an offence. The media can identify youths who receive an adult sentence for a presumptive offence. But if the judge declines to impose an adult sentence for a presumptive offence, s. 75 of the Act allows a prosecutor or defence lawyer to apply for the identity ban to continue. For the ban to remain in place, the judge must be convinced that suppressing the offender's identify to aid in rehabilitation is more important than the public interest in publication. If the Crown chooses not to seek an adult sentence for a presumptive offence, s. 65 requires the judge to impose a ban on the identity of the offender. A Nova Scotia judge has ruled youths sentenced as adults are not entitled to have their names banned from publication while their case is under appeal, even though it's possible an appeal court may decide they should be sentenced under the *Youth Criminal Justice Act* and remain unidentified.[42]

Penalties

Under subs. 138 (1), a breach of the ban on identifying young persons subject to the Act can be prosecuted as an indictable offence, punishable by up to two years in prison, or as a summary offence.

Lifting Bans on Identifying Young Persons

The *Youth Criminal Justice Act* sets out situations in which young people can be identified in the media. To help apprehend a suspect who is considered dangerous, police can apply under subs. 110(4) for an order allowing the youth's identity to be publicized in the media for five days. Subsection 110(3) allows young persons prosecuted under the Act or the *Young Offenders Act* to authorize publishing their identity once they reach the age of 18, as long as the person is no longer in custody for a youth crime at that point. Other offenders can use subs. 110(6) to apply to a judge for an order lifting the ban. The judge must be satisfied that disclosure is not contrary to the person's "best interests or the public interest". Under subs. 111(2), young victims or witnesses involved in youth cases can also authorize the media to disclose their identities with the permission of their parents or once they reach the age of 18. If the young person is deceased, parents have the right to authorize identification in the media. Crime victims or witnesses under the age of 18 can ask a judge to lift the ban on identification under subs. 111(3). Again, the judge must find that disclosure is either in the person's best interests or in the public interest.

When a young offender, victim, witness or parent agrees to waive the ban, or a judge lifts it, s. 112 authorizes other media, once the identity has been made public, to re-publish the information without requiring permission or further court approval.

Access

Section 132 of the *Youth Criminal Justice Act* enables a youth court judge to bar any person from the courtroom for "all or part of the proceedings". Grounds for exclusion include: the presentation of information or evidence that could be injurious or prejudicial to the accused, a young witness, or a victim; the need to protect public morals; and the proper administration of justice. Section 119 restricts access to transcripts and other youth court records to lawyers, court officials, police officers, and other persons a judge deems to have a "valid interest" in the records. In a Nova Scotia case decided under a similar section of the *Young Offenders Act*, the media was found to have a valid interest in the transcript of a youth court trial and was granted access.[43] There are time limits on any application for access, which range from two months to five years after the completion of the case, depending on the outcome and the sentence imposed. If a youth has been convicted of a serious crime and sentenced to the same punishment as an adult, however, the court file is open to public scrutiny. In one case, after a youth was convicted of criminal negligence causing death, journalists were allowed to examine pre-sentence reports, psychological reports and reports on a youth's behavior while in custody.[44]

IMPACT OF *THE CHARTER OF RIGHTS AND FREEDOMS*

Since its inception in 1982, the *Charter* has had a profound impact on this legal landscape. It enshrined the right of persons accused of crimes to be presumed innocent until proven guilty "according to law in a fair and public hearing by an independent and impartial tribunal".[45] Simultaneously, the *Charter* declared "freedom of thought, belief, opinion and expression, including freedom of the press and other media of communication" to be fundamental to Canadian society.[46]

The latter freedom was hailed as the harbinger of fewer restrictions on publication in criminal cases.[47] In response, media organizations launched legal challenges to many *Criminal Code* bans in the 1980s; most, however, fell short of striking down statutory limits on publication. In general, courts have held that such provisions are reasonable limits on the media's right to free expression and justified under s. 1 of the *Charter*.[48]

COMMON LAW BANS

In addition to the statutory bans outlined above, judges have the power under the common law to impose other restrictions on publishing information that could prejudice the right to a fair trial. This power is often used when persons accused of the same crime stand trial separately; judges have banned evidence publication dealing specifically with co-accused who have yet to stand trial.[49] A similar approach is often taken when a person pleads guilty and is sentenced while one or more co-accused await trial. An example is an Ontario court's controversial 1993 decision to ban publishing Karla Homolka's sentencing for manslaughter while her estranged husband, Paul Bernardo, awaited trial on charges of first-degree murder in the deaths of two teenaged girls.[50] Courts have also temporarily banned media coverage of a change of venue hearing.[51]

The *Charter* guarantees of press freedom and freedom of expression have limited the number and scope of these bans. In a landmark 1994 ruling,[52] the Supreme Court of Canada put the media's right to freedom of expression on the same footing as an accused person's right to a fair trial. The ruling creates a test for judges to apply when asked to impose a common law ban or a discretionary statutory ban—the kind a judge may choose not to impose. (The reasoning in *Dagenais* does not apply to bans that are automatically in place or bans a judge must impose upon request.) The media, the Court held, has standing to challenge such bans and should be given notice of a motion to impose one. Judges must restrict the scope of any publication ban imposed. There must be a "real and substantial risk" to the fairness of the trial and the judge must be satisfied that alternative measures, such as screening jurors and moving the trial to another location, will not alleviate the risk. The benefits of imposing the ban must outweigh the harm caused by limiting freedom of expression. Finally, the party seeking the ban must show that the restriction on media coverage is justified.

The Supreme Court of Canada has ruled that the *Dagenais* precedent applies "to *all* discretionary court orders that limit freedom of expression and freedom of the press in relation to legal proceedings."[53] In follow-up rulings, the Supreme Court has said judges must consider the impact on freedom of expression even if the media chooses not to challenge the ban.[54] Before sealing documents presented as evidence, a judge must weigh the right of free expression and the principle of openness against demands to protect confidential information about businesses.[55] Media outlets have also used the Charter to establish their right to examine and copy documents, photographs, video footage and other exhibits presented in criminal trials.[56] It has become routine for judges to grant a brief adjournment so media counsel can argue against the imposition of a common law or discretionary ban. Courts in some provinces have established procedures to notify the media of applications for bans.[57]

Judges applying the *Dagenais* principles have rejected applications for bans outright or opted for lesser restrictions on what the media can report, fulfilling the *Charter*'s promise that our courts will remain open and accessible. "In any constitutional climate," Justice Morris Fish noted in 2005, "the administration of justice thrives on exposure to light — and withers under a cloud of secrecy."[58] It's clear the *Charter* will continue to reshape the competition between the right to a fair trial and the media's right to inform the public about what happens in the nation's courtrooms.

Notes

1   Mitchell Stephens, *A History of News* (Toronto: Harcourt Brace College Publishers, 1997), at p.99.

2   Cited by Dickson J. in *MacIntyre v. Nova Scotia (Attorney General)*, 1982 CarswellNS 21, 1982 CarswellNS 110, 26 C.R. (3d) 193, [1982] 1 S.C.R. 175, 49 N.S.R. (2d) 609, 40 N.R. 181, 96 A.P.R. 609, 132 D.L.R. (3d) 385, (sub nom. *Nova Scotia (Attorney General) v. MacIntyre*) 65 C.C.C. (2d) 129 (S.C.C.), at pp.144-145 [C.C.C.].

3   *Reference re s. 12 (1) of the Juvenile Delinquents Act (Canada)*, 1983 CarswellOnt 273, 41 O.R. (2d) 113, 146 D.L.R. (3d) 408, 3 C.C.C. (3d) 515, 6 C.R.R. 1, (sub nom. *R. v. Southam Inc.*) 34 C.R. (3d) 27, (sub nom. *R. v. Southam Inc.*) 33 R.F.L. (2d) 279 (Ont. C.A.), at para. 15.

4   *Edmonton Journal v. Alberta (Attorney General)*, 1989 CarswellAlta 198, 1989 CarswellAlta 623, 1989 SCC 133, [1989] 2 S.C.R. 1326, [1990] 1 W.W.R. 577, 64 D.L.R. (4th) 577, 102 N.R. 321, 71 Alta. L.R. (2d) 273, 103 A.R. 321, 41 C.P.C. (2d) 109, 45 C.R.R. 1 (S.C.C.), at 1340 [S.C.R.]. The contrast between the Canadian and American approaches to media access to the courts is explored in G. Stuart Adam, "The Thicket of Rules North of the Border: Canadian perspectives on a free press and fair trials" *Media Studies Journal* 12:1 (Winter 1998), at pp.24-30.

5   *Toronto Star Newspapers Ltd. v. Ontario*, 2005 CarswellOnt 2613, 2005 CarswellOnt 2614, 2005 SCC 41, [2005] 2 S.C.R. 188, 253 D.L.R. (4th) 577, 29 C.R. (6th) 251, 197 C.C.C. (3d) 1, 132 C.R.R. (2d) 178, 76 O.R. (3d) 320 (note), (sub nom. *R. v. Toronto Star Newspapers Ltd.*) 335 N.R. 201, (sub nom. *R. v. Toronto Star Newspapers Ltd.*) 200 O.A.C. 348 (S.C.C.), at para. 2.

6   John A. Yogis, *Canadian Law Dictionary*, 4th ed. (New York: Barron's, 1998), at p.256.

7   The Canadian Newspaper Association tracks prosecutions of the media for contempt and other legal issues affecting journalists in a series of bulletins entitled *The Press and the Courts*. Volume 17:1 (28 February 1998) reports that a newspaper in Vernon, British Columbia, was fined $5,000 in December 1997 for prejudicial reporting that caused a mistrial in a murder case.

8   Michael G. Crawford, *The Journalist's Legal Guide*, 4th ed. (Toronto: Carswell, 2002), at p.144. For a detailed examination of the law of contempt of court in Canada, see D. Jobb, *Media Law for Canadian Journalists* (Toronto: Emond Montgomery, 2006), at ch. 5.

9   *R. v. Kopyto*, 1987 CarswellOnt 124, 24 O.A.C. 81, 61 C.R. (3d) 209, 62 O.R. (2d) 449, 39 C.C.C. (3d) 1, 47 D.L.R. (4th) 213 (Ont. C.A.), at para. 5. One media law scholar has declared that "scandalizing the court is effectively dead in Canada. Its burial was long overdue." Robert Martin, *Media Law* (Concord, Ont.: Irwin Law, 1997), at p.79.

10 Crawford, *supra*, note 8, at p. 144. For more definitions of contempt, see Jeffrey Miller, *The Law of Contempt in Canada* (Toronto: Carswell, 1997), at pp.101-117; Martin, *ibid.*, at pp.72-75, 79-83.

11 *CHBC Television, Re*, 1999 CarswellBC 189, 1999 BCCA 72, 23 C.R. (5th) 135, (sub nom. *R. v. CHBC Television*) 132 C.C.C. (3d) 390, (sub nom. *R. v. CHBC Television*) 118 B.C.A.C. 267, (sub nom. *R. v. CHBC Television*) 192 W.A.C. 267 (B.C. C.A.), at para. 23, quoting from the B.C. Supreme Court's ruling in *R. v. Froese* (1979), 1979 CarswellBC 540, 50 C.C.C. (2d) 119, (sub nom. *R. v. Bengert*

(No. 18)) 15 C.R. (3d) 215 (B.C. S.C. [In Chambers]). See also *Manitoba (Attorney General) v. Groupe Quebecor Inc.* (1987), 1987 CarswellMan 203, 59 C.R. (3d) 1, 45 D.L.R. (4th) 80, [1987] 5 W.W.R. 270, 47 Man. R. (2d) 187, 37 C.C.C. (3d) 421, (sub nom. *A.G. for Man. v. Groupe Quebecor Inc.*) 31 C.R.R. 313 (Man. C.A.).

[12] *Bielek v. Ristimaki* (1979), unreported (Ont. H.C.). Reproduced in Stuart Robertson, *Courts and the Media* (Markham: Butterworths, 1981), at pp.287-292

[13] For instance, The *Sun* newspapers in Edmonton and Calgary were cited for contempt and fined $5,000 in April 2000 for revealing, at the time of arrest, that a man charged with murder had previously assaulted the victim. *R. v. Edmonton Sun*, 2003 CarswellAlta 23, 2003 ABCA 3, 170 C.C.C. (3d) 455, 221 D.L.R. (4th) 438, [2003] 8 W.W.R. 347, 320 A.R. 217, 288 W.A.C. 217, 12 C.R. (6th) 121, 12 Alta. L.R. (4th) 6, (sub nom. *Alberta v. The Edmonton Sun*) 104 C.R.R. (2d) 1 (Alta. C.A.). For an examination of the differing approaches to contempt across Canada, see Dean Jobb, "The New Court Coverage" *Canadian Lawyer* (February 2001), at pp.42-46.

[14] *Ibid.*

[15] Robert Martin and G. Stuart Adam, *A Sourcebook of Canadian Media Law* (Ottawa: Carleton University Press, 1989), at p.204.

[16] An order banning publication of the name of a clergyman charged with sexual assault, even if he was acquitted, was overturned on appeal. See *R. v. D. (G.)* (1991), 1991 CarswellOnt 83, 2 O.R. (3d) 498, 4 C.R. (4th) 172, 63 C.C.C. (3d) 134, 46 O.A.C. 1 (Ont. C.A.), leave to appeal refused (1991), 64 C.C.C. (3d) vi (note), 3 O.R. (3d) xiii (note) (S.C.C.). See also *R. v. Several Unnamed Persons*, 1983 CarswellOnt 1393, 44 O.R. (2d) 81, 8 C.C.C. (3d) 528, 4 D.L.R. (4th) 310 (Ont. H.C.), in which the court refused to ban publication of the names of defendants charged with gross indecency.

[17] The ban remains in force until varied by a court with jurisdiction to do so. See *R. v. K. (V.)*, 1991 CarswellBC 418, 4 C.R. (4th) 338, 68 C.C.C. (3d) 18 (B.C. C.A.).

[18] *R. v. Rhyno*, 2001 CarswellNS 277, 2001 NSPC 9, 193 N.S.R. (2d) 250, 602 A.P.R. 250 (N.S. Prov. Ct.).

[19] *R. v. Brown*, 1999 CarswellOnt 4704, [1999] O.J. No. 4870, 74 C.R.R. (2d) 164, [1999] O.T.C. 217 (Ont. S.C.J.).

[20] *Criminal Code*, subs. 517(1).

[21] *R. v. Forget*, 1982 CarswellOnt 1341, 35 O.R. (2d) 238, 65 C.C.C. (2d) 373 (Ont. C.A.).

[22] *Toronto Star Newspapers Ltd. v. R.*, 2009 CarswellOnt 301, 2009 ONCA 59, 66 C.R. (6th) 329, (sub nom. *Toronto Star Newspapers Ltd. v. Canada*) 94 O.R. (3d) 82, (sub nom. *Toronto Star Newspapers Ltd. v. Canada*) 245 O.A.C. 291, (sub nom. *Toronto Star Newspapers Ltd. v. Canada*) 302 D.L.R. (4th) 385, (sub nom. *R. v. Ahmad*) 239 C.C.C. (3d) 437, (sub nom. *R. v. Ahmad*) 184 C.R.R. (2d) 114 (Ont. C.A.), leave to appeal allowed 2009 CarswellOnt 4356, 2009 CarswellOnt 4357 (S.C.C.). This ruling is currently under review by the Supreme Court of Canada.

[23] *Criminal Code*, subs. 539(1).

[24] D. Jobb, "Driving Blind: The Gerald Regan sex case helped define how far reporters can push a publication ban" *Media* (The Magazine of the Canadian Association of Journalists) (Summer 1997), at p.6.

[25] *Criminal Code*, subs. 542(2).

[26] *Criminal Code*, subs. 276.1(3), 276.2(1) and 276.3(1)

27 *Criminal Code*, subs. 278.9(1). See also subs. 278.4(2) and 278.6(2).

28 *Criminal Code*, subs. 648(1). The ban on publication of *voir dire* proceedings also applies under the common law to civil cases heard before a jury. There is no statutory ban on publishing information produced at a *voir dire* in provincial court or when a superior court judge is hearing a case without a jury.

29 *R. v. Dobson*, 1985 CarswellOnt 1392, 19 C.C.C. (3d) 93, 7 O.A.C. 145 (Ont. C.A.), leave to appeal refused (1985), 59 N.R. 238 (note), 9 O.A.C. 400 (note) (S.C.C.).

30 *R. v. Regan*, 1997 CarswellNS 566, 124 C.C.C. (3d) 77, 159 D.L.R. (4th) 350, 174 N.S.R. (2d) 28, 532 A.P.R. 28 (N.S. S.C.), additional reasons at 1998 CarswellNS 398 (N.S. S.C.). See also D. Jobb, "Regan coverage ruling partial victory for media" *The [Halifax] Chronicle-Herald* (22 October 1997), at C2.

31 *Criminal Code*, subs. 486(1).

32 *Criminal Code*, para. 537(1)(h).

33 *Criminal Code*, subs. 486(2.1), (2.2).

34 *MacIntyre v. Nova Scotia (Attorney General)*, *supra*, note 2.

35 *Criminal Code*, subs. 487.3(1).

36 *Criminal Code*, subs. 487.3(4)

37 *Toronto Star Newspapers Ltd. v. Ontario*, *supra*, note 5; See also earlier Court of Appeal decision at 2003 CarswellOnt 3986, [2003] O.J. No. 4006, 178 C.C.C. (3d) 349, 17 C.R. (6th) 392, 232 D.L.R. (4th) 217, (sub nom. *R. v. Toronto Star Newspapers Ltd.*) 178 O.A.C. 60, (sub nom. *R. v. Toronto Star Newspapers Ltd.*) 110 C.R.R. (2d) 288, (sub nom. *R. v. Toronto Star Newspapers Ltd.*) 67 O.R. (3d) 577 (Ont. C.A.).

38 See *Canadian Newspapers Co. v. Canada (Attorney General)*, 1986 CarswellOnt 127, 29 C.C.C. (3d) 109, 55 O.R. (2d) 737, 32 D.L.R. (4th) 292, (sub nom. *Canadian Newspapers Co. v. Canada*) 53 C.R. (3d) 203 (Ont. H.C.), additional reasons at 1986 CarswellOnt 435, 12 C.P.C. (2d) 203, 56 O.R. (2d) 240, 32 D.L.R. (4th) 292 at 304, 27 C.R.R. 52 (Ont. H.C.); *Canadian Newspapers Co. v. Canada (Attorney General)*, 1986 CarswellMan 364, 28 C.C.C. (3d) 397, [1987] 1 W.W.R. 262, 31 D.L.R. (4th) 601 (Man. Q.B.); *Thibault c. Demers*, 2001 CarswellQue 356, 43 C.R. (5th) 161, [2001] R.J.Q. 579, (sub nom. *Girard v. Demers*) 82 C.R.R. (2d) 278, (sub nom. *Girard (informant) v. Ouellet*) 153 C.C.C. (3d) 217, (sub nom. *Girard (informant) v. Ouellet*) 198 D.L.R. (4th) 58 (Que. C.A.); and Crawford, *supra*, note 8, at pp.185-186.

39 *Criminal Code*, subs. 193(1). A British Columbia judge ruled the media could disclose that wiretap evidence was used to obtain a search warrant for the home of the province's premier. Stewart Bell, "Wiretaps 'integral part' of getting search warrants, media can report" *National Post* (14 August 1999), at A4.

40 *Criminal Code*, subs. 193.1(1).

41 *Criminal Code*, s. 194.

42 *R. v. Smith*, 2007 CarswellNS 412, 2007 NSCA 94, 226 C.C.C. (3d) 196, 258 N.S.R. (2d) 185, 824 A.P.R. 185 (N.S. C.A. [In Chambers]).

43 *R. v. S. (R.D.)*, 1995 CarswellNS 467, 98 C.C.C. (3d) 235, (sub nom. *Halifax Herald Ltd. v. Sparks, J.F.C.*) 142 N.S.R. (2d) 321, (sub nom. *Halifax Herald Ltd. v. Sparks, J.F.C.*) 407 A.P.R. 321 (N.S. S.C.). See also Barry Dorey, "Judge violated freedom of the press, court rules" *The Chronicle-Herald* (26 April 1995), at A4.

44 *Youth Criminal Justice Act*, s. 117. See also *R. v. B. (A.A.)*, 2006 CarswellNS 229, 2006 NSPC 16, 774 A.P.R. 90, 244 N.S.R. (2d) 90 (N.S. Prov. Ct.).

45 *Canadian Charter of Rights and Freedoms*, Part 1 of the *Constitution Act*, 1982, enacted by the *Canada Act 1982* (U.K.), c. 11, s. 11(d).

46 *Charter*, s. 2(b).

47 Among those espousing this view was M. David Lepofsky, *Open Justice: The Constitutional Right to Attend and Speak About Criminal Proceedings* (Markham: Butterworths, 1985), at chs. 5 and 6.

48 See, for instance, *Canadian Newspapers Co. v. Canada (Attorney General)*, 1988 CarswellOnt 1023, 1988 CarswellOnt 1023F, 65 C.R. (3d) 50, 43 C.C.C. (3d) 24, [1988] 2 S.C.R. 122, 52 D.L.R. (4th) 690, 38 C.R.R. 72, 65 O.R. (2d) 637 (note), 32 O.A.C. 259, 87 N.R. 163 (S.C.C.), which held the ban on identifying complainants under subs. 486(3) of the *Code* is a justifiable limit on freedom of the press under s. 1 of the *Charter*. In *R. v. Banville*, 1983 CarswellNB 19, 34 C.R. (3d) 20, 3 C.C.C. (3d) 312, 145 D.L.R. (3d) 595, 5 C.R.R. 142, 45 N.B.R. (2d) 134, 118 A.P.R. 134 (N.B. Q.B.), the same conclusion was reached with respect to subs. 539(1), which bans publishing evidence presented at preliminary hearings. Exceptions are Ontario, Manitoba and Quebec appellate rulings that struck down a restriction on publication of search warrant documents (see *supra*, note 40).

49 See, for example, *R. v. Wood*, 1993 CarswellNS 187, (sub nom. *R. v. Wood (No. 2)*) 124 N.S.R. (2d) 128, (sub nom. *R. v. Wood (No. 2)*) 345 A.P.R. 128 (N.S. S.C.).

50 The Homolka ban is discussed in Omar Wakil, "Publication Bans on Court Proceedings in Canada" Centre for the Independence of Judges and Lawyers *Yearbook*, vol. 4 (December 1995), at pp.101-110. In *R. v. Church of Scientology of Toronto*, 1986 CarswellOnt 925, (sub nom. *Church of Scientology of Toronto v. R. (No. 6)*) 27 C.C.C. (3d) 193 (Ont. H.C.), the Court also issued a temporary ban on the outcome of the proceeding involving the initial accused.

51 *Southam Inc. v. R. (No. 2)*, 1982 CarswellOnt 1380, 70 C.C.C. (2d) 264, 141 D.L.R. (3d) 349 (Ont. H.C.).

52 *Dagenais v. Canadian Broadcasting Corp.*, 1994 CarswellOnt 112, 1994 CarswellOnt 1168, 1994 SCC 102, 34 C.R. (4th) 269, [1994] 3 S.C.R. 835, 120 D.L.R. (4th) 12, 175 N.R. 1, 94 C.C.C. (3d) 289, 76 O.A.C. 81, 25 C.R.R. (2d) 1, 20 O.R. (3d) 816 (note) (S.C.C.). For an analysis of the ruling, see Crawford, *supra* note 8, at 177-179; Beverley Spencer, "S.C.C. lays down law on publication bans" *The Lawyers Weekly*, 14:32 (6 January 1995), at 1, 16-17.

53 *Toronto Star Newspapers Ltd. v. Ontario, supra*, note 5, at para. 7.

54 See *R. v. Mentuck*, 2001 CarswellMan 535, 2001 CarswellMan 536, 2001 SCC 76, 47 C.R. (5th) 63, 158 C.C.C. (3d) 449, 205 D.L.R. (4th) 512, 163 Man. R. (2d) 1, 269 W.A.C. 1, [2002] 2 W.W.R. 409, 277 N.R. 160, [2001] 3 S.C.R. 442 (S.C.C.); and *R. v. E. (O.N.)*, 2001 CarswellBC 2479, 2001 CarswellBC 2480, 2001 SCC 77, 47 C.R. (5th) 89, 158 C.C.C. (3d) 478, 205 D.L.R. (4th) 542, 279 N.R. 187, 97 B.C.L.R. (3d) 1, [2001] 3 S.C.R. 478, 160 B.C.A.C. 161, 261 W.A.C. 161, [2002] 3 W.W.R. 205 (S.C.C.).

55 *Sierra Club of Canada v. Canada (Minister of Finance)*, 2002 CarswellNat 822, 2002 CarswellNat 823, 2002 SCC 41, [2002] 2 S.C.R. 522, 44 C.E.L.R. (N.S.) 161, 40 Admin. L.R. (3d) 1, 287 N.R. 203, 223 F.T.R. 137 (note), 20 C.P.C. (5th) 1, (sub nom. *Atomic Energy of Canada Ltd. v. Sierra Club of Canada*) 18 C.P.R. (4th) 1, (sub nom. *Atomic Energy of Canada Ltd. v. Sierra Club of Canada*) 211 D.L.R. (4th) 193, (sub nom. *Atomic Energy of Canada Ltd. v. Sierra Club of Canada*) 93 C.R.R. (2d) 219 (S.C.C.).

[56] See D. Jobb, *Media Law for Canadian Journalists*, *supra*, note 8, at pp.242-244.

[57] D. Jobb, "Notes on Publication Ban Notices" *Canadian Lawyer* (October 2001), at pp.20-24.

[58] *Toronto Star Newspapers Ltd. v. Ontario*, *supra*, note 5, at para. 1.

26

Dangerous Offenders

*Paul Carver**

INTRODUCTION

It is a sad fact of life that there are individuals in our communities who are driven to commit crimes of horrendous physical or sexual violence. These offenders leave in their wake victims who are often physically, emotionally and psychologically scarred for life. Many of these criminals offend repeatedly, regardless of periods of custody they may have served or efforts to rehabilitate them. A first offender who commits a brutal, savage crime or repeat offenders with patterns of behaviour involving physical or sexual violence may find themselves designated by the courts to be a "Dangerous Offender" and sentenced to custody for an indeterminate period.

HISTORICAL BACKGROUND

The concept of a "dangerous offender" is not new. In fact the roots of the legislation can be traced back to the *Prevention of Crime Act*.[1] That legislation provided for the designation of "habitual criminals" and directed the courts to impose a minimum of five years and a maximum of ten years incarceration in addition to any other sentence.[2]

In 1938, a Royal Commission was established to examine the penal system in Canada. It examined the British experience and recommended that Canada pass legislation that would allow the identification of persistent criminals and empower the courts to segregate them from society. In 1947, the *Criminal Code* was amended to permit:

> the preventive detention "for the protection of the public" of "habitual criminals", defined essentially as persons having a record of three previous indictable offences and who are persistently leading a criminal life.[3]

* B.A. (Hon.), Dalhousie University; LL.B., Dalhousie Law School, 1992, Halifax, Nova Scotia; Crown Attorney, Public Prosecution Service, Halifax, Nova Scotia. Many thanks to Shauna MacDonald for her helpful suggestions and editorial comments. Special thanks to Cindy Barkhouse,and Lila Pettipas for preparing each successive draft of the manuscript.

The following year there were further amendments which introduced the term "criminal Sexual Psychopath". This term referred to a person:

> who by a course of misconduct in sexual matters has evidenced a lack of power to control his sexual impulses and who as a result is likely to attack or otherwise inflict injury, loss, pain or other evil on any person.[4]

In 1960, the term "Criminal Sexual Psychopath" was removed from the *Criminal Code* and replaced with "Dangerous Sexual Offender", that was defined as:

> a person who, by his conduct in any sexual matter, has shown a failure to control his sexual impulses, and who is likely to cause injury, pain or other evil to any person, through failure in the future to control his sexual impulses or is likely to commit a further sexual offence...[5]

This definition was later refined to remove from consideration whether the accused was "likely to commit a further sexual offence".[6]

The Report of the Canadian Committee on Corrections, the Ouimet Report, 1969, criticized the habitual offender provisions for being at once too inclusive, "by applying to non-dangerous offences (e.g. property offenders), and too exclusive, by requiring a recidivist history as a pre-condition of their application."[7]

In 1977, the habitual offendor and dangerous sexual offendor provisions were repealed. They were replaced with Dangerous Offender legislation.[8] In 1997, the Dangerous Offender provisions were further modified.[9] Parliament eliminated the courts discretion about whether an individual, upon being designated a dangerous offender, should receive a determinate or indeterminate sentence.[10] The provisions dictated that if an individual is designated a dangerous offender then an indeterminate sentence had to be imposed.

The 1997, amendments also introduced the concept of "long-term offender". If at the end of a dangerous offender application the court was not satisfied the designation was appropriate the court could consider whether the person meets the criteria to be declared a long-term offender. If the court found this to be so, a fixed sentence was imposed followed by a period of supervision which can last up to ten years.

On July 2, 2008, provisions of the *Tackling Violent Crime Act*[11] came into force. This legislation made significant procedural and substantive changes to the process by which individuals may be declared Dangerous Offenders. Of particular importance is the change which permits individuals who meet the Dangerous Offender criteria to be sentenced to a determinate period of custody that may or may not include a long-term period of supervision.

PURPOSE OF THE LEGISLATION

The fundamental purpose of any sentence imposed by the courts is to protect the safety of the public. This is as true for dangerous offender applications as it is for sentences for shoplifting.

In *R. v. Jones*, the Supreme Court of Canada described the purpose of a dangerous offender designation:

> The overriding aim is not the punishment of the offender but prevention of future violence through the imposition of an indeterminate sentence.[12]

This reasoning was consistent with an earlier ruling in *R. v. L. (T.P.)*, where it was stated the dangerous offender designation

> merely enables the court to accommodate its sentence to the common sense reality that the present condition of the offender is such that he or she is not inhibited by normal standards of behavioural restraint so that future violent acts can quite confidently be expected of that person. In such circumstances it would be folly not to tailor the sentence accordingly.[13]

The legislation is not intended to apply to every violent offender or violent sexual offender. This point was made very clear in *R. v. N. (L.)*:

> The legislation is targeted to apply to a very small group of offenders whose personal circumstances militate strenuously in favour of preventative incarceration.[14]

In dangerous offender applications you sometimes hear the question asked "Is the accused one of the worst of the worst?" While this question tends to over-simplify the criteria to be declared a dangerous offender it does seem to capture the spirit of the legislation. The designation is not for every accused but if they have committed violent crimes and have a behaviour pattern they cannot control, Parliament has ensured steps can be taken to protect the safety of the public.

GENERAL OVERVIEW

The dangerous offender provisions are interrelated and involve multiple, complex terms and legal elements. An accused must be convicted of a serious personal injury offence in order for the Crown to apply to have him declared a dangerous offender. The *Criminal Code* defines "serious personal injury offence" in s. 752.

granted the Crown application to declare the accused a dangerous offender and imposed an indeterminate sentence. This designation was overturned by the Ontario Court of Appeal which held:

> Although the previous sexual offences committed by the respondent were, at times, violent and extremely degrading ... the predicate offences were "not nearly as serious" and that the trial judge erred by failing to focus on the seriousness of the predicate offences themselves.[16]

The Supreme Court of Canada overruled the Ontario Court of appeal and reinstated both the designation of dangerous offender and the indeterminate sentence. In doing so Chief Justice Lamer (as he then was), writing for a unanimous court, reasoned:

> Indeed the respondent is asking the Court to alter or even reduce the definition of "serious personal injury offence". This alteration would, as the appellant notes, effectively guarantee that an accused who has committed an arguably less serious sexual predicate offence would never be declared a dangerous offender. I cannot imagine that Parliament wanted the courts to wait for an obviously dangerous individual, regardless of the nature of his criminal record and notwithstanding the force of expert opinion as to his potential dangerousness, to commit a particularly violent and grievous offence before he or she can be declared a dangerous offender.
>
> Does it defy reality, as the respondent submits, to treat all "serious personal injury offences" the same in applying s. 753(b)? In my opinion, it does not. This might be problematic if s. 753(b) were a one-stage test. Section 753(b) might not make sense if, for example, it were to provide, without qualification, that a trial judge may designate any person who commits a "serious personal injury offence" as a dangerous offender. But, it is crucial to recognize that the conviction for a "serious personal injury offence" merely triggers the s. 753(b) application process. There remains a second stage to s. 753(b), at which point the trial judge must be satisfied beyond a reasonable doubt of the likelihood of future danger that an offender presents to society before he or she can impose the dangerous offender designation and an indeterminate sentence.
>
> Parliament has thus created a standard of preventive detention that measures an accused's present condition according to past behaviour and patterns of conduct. Under this statutory arrangement, dangerous offenders who have committed "serious personal injury offences" can be properly sentenced without having to wait for them to strike out in a particularly egregious way. For example, suppose a known sexual deviate has been convicted of repeated offences for stalking and sexually assaulting young girls in playgrounds. He operates by offering them candy, touching their private parts, and if the children seem to comply or submit to his criminal advances, by taking them away where he violently sexually assaults them.

Now suppose that individual is at large in society and caught by a parent at a playground after having offered a child candy and improperly touching her. In this example, like the present case, the predicate offence is objectively less serious than a violent and invasive rape, but the trial judge need not justify the dangerous offender designation and an indeterminate sentence as a just desert for the isolated act of sexual touching. On the theory of s. 753(b), the offender has committed an inherently "serious personal injury offence". On a dangerous offender application, a trial judge is then entitled to consider his "conduct in any sexual matter" to determine if he presents a future danger to society. Otherwise, we would be saying that an offender's present condition is defined by the precise degree of seriousness of the predicate offences. That is equivalent to assuming that a dangerous individual will always act out, or be caught for that matter, at the upper limits of his dangerous capabilities.[17]

The notion of an "objectively serious" component to the serious personal injury office has not been completely put to rest by the decision in *Currie*. In *R. v. N. (L.)*, the accused and the victim were both prostitutes. The accused took the victim to a parking lot and cut off her clothes with a knife to punish her for some transgression. When the accused left she had some of the victims clothes with her. Since violence was used and property was taken the requirements for robbery were met. Robbery is an offence punishable by life imprisonment. The trial judge found the accused had committed a serious personal injury offence. In considering the requirements of s. 752(a) the Alberta Court of Appeal reasoned as follows:

[69] ... unlike s. 752(b) dealing with sexual offences whether the mere fact of conviction will do, s. 752(a) necessarily invites a qualitative assessment of the degree of violence or endangerment. Thus, in the context of this case, since robbery is an indictable offence exposing N. to a sentence of ten years or more, the only live issue is whether the robbery which N. committed satisfied the violence requirement under s. 752(a)(i) or the endangerment under s. 752(a)(ii). To determine whether it does, we must first consider precisely what is meant by violence or endangerment in the context of these two sections. Will any level of violence or endangerment do? That is the question.[18]

. . .

[74] ... violence in its everyday usage, contemplates an element of severity to the physical force that constitutes the violent act. Hence, interpreting s. 752(a)(i) to require that the violence be objectively serious is consistent with the legislative text.

[75] As for s. 752(a)(ii), we are of the view that the level of endangerment contemplated in this section must also meet an objective standard

of seriousness. We concede that generally, any conduct which reaches the extent of jeopardizing life or safety will fall within the endangerment contemplated by s. 752(a)(ii). However, while this may well be so in most cases, it does not follow that it will be true in all. The difficulty with this proposition is that it necessarily involves questions of degree. There may well be some acts where, for example, the threat to safety exists but the potential consequences, even if the risk were to be realized, would be relatively minor and outside the scope intended by Parliament. In our view, what is contemplated under this section is that the endangerment involve a likelihood of material harm, whether physical or psychological.

. . .

[86] For all these reasons, we have concluded that violence or endangerment as those terms are used under ss. 752(a)(i) and (ii) must be objectively serious before an offence qualifies as a serious personal injury offence under either of these sections. And perhaps most importantly, the requirement of objectively serious violence or endangerment also assists in shielding the legislation from the danger of arbitrariness, thereby ensuring constitutionality.

With great respect to the Alberta Court of Appeal the reasoning on the requirement of objective seriousness under s. 752(a) is troubling. First, it is difficult to reconcile with the Supreme Court of Canada's reasoning in *Currie*. The Alberta Court of Appeal dismisses the application of *Currie* by stating it applied to sexual offences and all sexual offences are objectively serious.[19] Cannot the same be said about all robberies? Even what courts may conclude are "technical" offences are very real to the victims. Introducing the requirement of "objectively serious" to s. 752(a) offences creates precisely the potential danger Chief Justice Lamer warned about in *Currie*.[20] It would require courts to wait until potential dangerous offenders commit violent crimes which meet the "objectively serious" standard before stepping in to consider removing them from society. This ensures names are added to lists of victims and does not protect the public. Parliament has set out the criteria to be met in s. 752(a). The criteria already establish certain limitations on the conduct and type of offences that will permit an application to be madepen.

PROCEDURAL REQUIREMENTS

Once an accused is convicted of a serious personal injury offence the Crown must decide whether it is appropriate to make a dangerous offender application. Some of the factors which will influence this decision include:

(a) circumstances of the offence;

(b) criminal record of the offender; and

(c) circumstances of the offender including psychiatric condition.

If the Crown decides to proceed with an application several procedural requirements must be met. The Crown must apply for a remand for assessment under s. 752.1 of the *Criminal Code* which states:

> **752.1** (1) Where an offender is convicted of a serious personal injury offence or an offence referred to in paragraph 753.1(2)(a) and, before sentence is imposed on the offender, on application by the prosecution, the court is of the opinion that there are reasonable grounds to believe that the offender might be found to be a dangerous offender under section 753 or a long-term offender under section 753.1, the court may, by order in writing, remand the offender, for a period not exceeding sixty days, to the custody of the person that the court directs and who can perform an assessment, or can have an assessment performed by experts. The assessment is to be used as evidence in an application under section 753 or 753.1.
>
> (2) The person to whom the offender is remanded shall file a report of the assessment with the court not later than fifteen days after the end of the assessment period and make copies of it available to the prosecutor and counsel for the offender.
>
> (3) On application by the prosecutor, the court may extend the period within which the report must be filed by a maximum of 30 days if the court is satisfied that there are reasonable grounds to do so.
> 1997, c. 17, s. 4; 2008, c. 6, s. 41.

The Crown may nominate an expert or may come to an agreement with the defence as to which expert should be nominated. Regardless of how it occurs, neither the Crown nor defence are limited to using the court-appointed expert. Each side is free to obtain additional assessments. The obligation is on the Crown, however, to prove that an assessment was ordered and the report is filed within the time specified by the Court (a maximum of 90 days after the assessment is ordered unless permission for up to a 30-day extension is obtained from the court).

In addition to the assessment, the Crown is also required to obtain the consent of the Attorney General of the Province to the making of the application. This consent usually consists of a one- or two-page document which can be filed with the court at the commencement of the dangerous offender hearing.

Under s. 752.01 of the *Criminal Code* a prosecutor has a duty to advise the court as soon as feasible of an intent to make a dangerous offender application. This duty arises where the accused has been convicted of a designated offence (as defined in s. 752 of the *Code*) and has prior convictions for designated offences, for which he was sentenced to two years in custody or more for each offence. The last procedural requirement is the Notice of Application. The Crown is required to prepare a written notice which sets out the basis upon which the application is brought (i.e., circumstances of the predicate offence or offences and which of the four definitions of dangerous offender under s. 753 the accused is alleged to satisfy). The Notice of Application should also provide sufficient details of the evidence the Crown intends to call so that the accused is aware of the case he has to meet. The Crown is not required to specify every witness who may be called to testify or every fact that may be proved in evidence.

A prudent Crown Attorney will err on the side of caution and include a great deal of information in the Notice of Application. The last thing the Crown would wish to see happen is the denial of a dangerous offender application because of a failure to disclose information in the Notice of Application.

The Notice of Application will often be served on the accused months in advance of the hearing. The *Criminal Code* requires at a minimum that the Notice of Application be served on the accused at least seven days before the hearing commences.[21]

Dangerous offender applications typically occur after a finding of guilt for a serious personal injury offence but prior to sentencing. Under certain circumstances, however, the Crown can make a dangerous offender application even after a sentence is imposed. Subsection 753(2) states:

> An application under subsection (1) must be made before sentence is imposed on the offender unless
>
>> (a) before the imposition of sentence, the prosecution gives notice to the offender of a possible intention to make an application under section 752.1 and an application under subsection (1) not later than six months after that imposition; and
>>
>> (b) at the time of the application under subsection (1) that is not later than six months after the imposition of sentence, it is shown that relevant evidence that was not reasonably available to the prosecution at the time of the imposition of sentence became available in the interim.

It is likely the Crown would have to prove strict compliance with the requirements of this section in order to proceed with a dangerous offender application after an accused is sentenced.

not destroy the pattern which covers all the other incidents in which the person assaulted was unknown beforehand to Dow.[26]

In *R. v. N. (L.)*, the Alberta Court of Appeal concluded, as part of its analysis on how to assess the existence of a pattern:

> Generally however, in order to meet the requirements of a pattern, the fewer the incidents, the more similar they must be. We do not suggest that the offences must be of the same kind, that is, for example, a number of robberies. Similarity, as noted, can be found not only in the types of offences but also in the degree of violence or aggression threatened or inflicted on the victims. This explains why the requirement for similarity in terms of kinds of offences is not crucial when the incidents of serious violence and aggression are more numerous.[27]

In *R. v. Langevin*,[28] the Court concluded a pattern of repetitive behaviour existed in the following circumstances:

> In my opinion, this element is not based solely on the number of offences but also on the elements of similarity of the offender's behaviour. The offences committed were remarkably similar. Two young girls were grabbed from behind by the appellant, a stranger, and both were taken to a secluded place and ordered to undress. Both were forced into anal as well as vaginal intercourse. The younger girl was forced to fellate the appellant. Both were threatened to assure their cooperation and were released only after assurances not to tell anyone were extracted from them. In the circumstances, these two offences were properly found to establish a pattern of repetitive behaviour.[29]

Most offenders do not go about committing crimes in precisely the same manner. This is particularly so when the offender has poor impulse control and lashes out in a variety of circumstances for a variety of reasons. The important thing is to not be distracted by the differences in the crimes but to look carefully for similarities. In *R. v. Shrubsall*,[30] the accused killed his mother in their home when he was a teenager.[31] Later in life, he beat and robbed a store clerk. He then violently and sexually assaulted a young woman after pulling her into a driveway late at night. A few weeks later he attacked a young woman in his home. These crimes were committed in very different circumstances and for a variety of motives. Yet, Justice Cacchione concluded:

> The violence used against all of the victims was excessive and beyond what was required to gain compliance. All of these victims suffered serious injuries to their head. Each offence contained fear inducing elements. All of the offences against women feature elements of control and domination.[32]

753(1)(a)(ii)—Pattern of Persistent Aggressive Behaviour

Subparagraph 753(1)(a)(ii) states:

> The court may, on application made under this Part following the filing of an assessment report under subsection 752.1(2), find the offender to be a dangerous offender if it is satisfied
>> (a) that the offence for which the offender has been convicted is a serious personal injury offence described in paragraph (a) of the definition of that expression in section 752 and the offender constitutes a threat to the life, safety or physical or mental well-being of other persons on the basis of evidence establishing
>
> . . .
>
>> (ii) a pattern of persistent aggressive behaviour by the offender, of which the offence for which he or she has been convicted forms a part, showing a substantial degree of indifference on the part of the offender respecting the reasonably foreseeable consequences to other persons of his or her behaviour...

Elements

The Crown must prove beyond a reasonable doubt:

1. The accused has been convicted of a serious personal injury offence under s. 752(a); and
2. The accused is a threat to the life, safety or physical or mental well-being of other persons based on evidence that:
   (a) shows a pattern of persistent aggressive behaviour by the accused;
   (b) the offence for which he or she is convicted forms a part of the pattern; and
   (c) the pattern of persistent aggressive behaviour shows a substantial degree of indifference by the accused to the reasonably foreseeable consequences to other persons of his or her behaviour.

Case Law

The case law referred to in the earlier section on "pattern of repetitive behaviour" is often used to interpret the requirements of this definition.

In practical terms the difference between the first and second definitions is of little consequence. If the Crown can apply under the first definition it is difficult to conceive of a situation where the second definition will not apply as well. I am unaware of any authority which applied the same facts to both definitions and concluded one was satisfied while the other was not.

753(1)(a)(iii)—Offence of a Brutal Nature

Subparagraph 753(1)(a)(iii) states:

> The court may, on application made under this Part following the filing of an assessment report under subsection 752.1(2), find the offender to be a dangerous offender if it is satisfied
>
> > (a) that the offence for which the offender has been convicted is a serious personal injury offence described in paragraph (a) of the definition of that expression in section 752 and the offender constitutes a threat to the life, safety or physical or mental well-being of other persons on the basis of evidence establishing
> >
> > . . .
> >
> > (iii) any behaviour by the offender, associated with the offence for which he or she has been convicted, that is of such a brutal nature as to compel the conclusion that the offender's behaviour in the future is unlikely to be inhibited by normal standards of behavioural restraint...

Elements

The Crown must prove beyond a reasonable doubt:

1. The accused has been convicted of a serious personal injury offence under s. 752(a); and
2. The accused is a threat to the life, safety or physical or mental well-being of other persons based on evidence:
   (a) showing that any behaviour of the accused associated with the offence for which he or she has been convicted is of a brutal nature; and
   (b) the brutal nature of the behaviour compels the conclusion that the offender's behaviour in the future is unlikely to be inhibited by normal standards of behavioural restraint.

Case Law

In *R. v. Langevin*, the Court concluded:

I am satisfied that the brutal nature of the conduct which must be established before the requirements of the subparagraph are satisfied does not necessarily demand a situation of "stark horror". . .

Conduct which is coarse, savage and cruel and which is capable of inflicting severe psychological damage on the victim is sufficiently "brutal" to meet the test.[33]

In *R. v. Antonius*,[34] the Court concluded:

The offence was of a brutal nature, not in the sense that remarkable physical violence was associated with it—although Mr. Antonius' assault was serious—but in that it clearly demonstrates such a low threshold of inhibition that I must conclude that Mr. Antonius poses a grave risk that his future behaviour will not likely be inhibited by normal standards of behavioural restraint.[35]

Of any of the four definitions the "offence of a brutal nature" test is most dependent on the facts of the predicate offence. This is of significance because it means that if an offence is horrific enough it could justify a dangerous offender designation regardless of whether there is a pattern of behaviour. Conceivably this means even a first offender could meet the test.

753(1)(b)—Failure to Control Sexual Impulses

Paragrapgh 753(1)(b) states:

The court may, on application made under this Part following the filing of an assessment report under subsection 752.1(2), find the offender to be a dangerous offender if it is satisfied

. . .

(b) that the offence for which the offender has been convicted is a serious personal injury offence described in paragraph (b) of the definition of that expression in section 752 and the offender, by his or her conduct in any sexual matter including that involved in the commission of the offence for which he or she has been convicted, has shown a failure to control his or her sexual impulses and a likelihood of causing injury, pain or other evil to other persons through failure in the future to control his or her sexual impulses.

Elements

The Crown must prove beyond a reasonable doubt:

1. The accused has been convicted of a serious personal injury offence under s. 752(b);

2. By his conduct in any sexual matter, including that involved in the offence for which he has been convicted, the accused has shown a failure to control his sexual impulses;

3. There is a present likelihood or high potential for the accused continuing to fail to control his sexual impulses in the future; and

4. If the accused does fail in the future to control his or her sexual impulses he is likely to cause injury, pain, or other evil to other persons through such failure to control his sexual impulses.

Case Law

In *R. v. Schwartz*,[36] the Court stated, at para. 27, an "accused may be found a dangerous offender although his "failure to restrain his sexual impulses" arises only in certain opportunistic circumstances."

In *R.v. Oliver*,[37] the trial judge concluded the test is not whether the appellant can control his sexual impulses but *whether he has failed to do so*. He concluded the accused "gets himself into these positions by reason of his failure to restrain his sexual impulses. That is the thing that it starts with. Whether he can stop it is not the test ... I am satisfied ... he has shown a failure to control his sexual impulses."[38] The Court agreed that "failure to control" involves a straight factual investigation. The Court concluded the accused had not restrained his impulses even though the complainant was clever enough to talk him out of committing the offence.

In *R. v. S. (C.W.)*,[39] the Court referred to the trial judges finding that "... although the fact the accused desisted from completing the offence of rape shows, in a sense, that he was able to control his sexual impulses, failure to restrain his sexual impulses is shown by his *commencing* to commit the offence of rape" [emphasis added].[40] The Court also concluded:

> In my view, the psychiatric evidence is of particular relevance to this issue. The psychiatric evidence indicates that the appellant suffers from an ongoing personality disorder, that he has low impulse controls, and that his conscience is defective in regulating his sexual behaviour. In my opinion, the trial judge was entitled to rely on the psychiatric evidence against the background of the appellant's sexual offences on this issue. It warranted her conclusion that the appellant in the future is likely to similarly fail to control his sexual impulses.[41]

In *R. v. Carleton*,[42] the Supreme Court of Canada affirmed the Alberta Court of Appeal's ruling that the section does not require a court to be satisfied the offender *will* cause injury in the future. The court need only be satisfied there is a *likelihood* of causing future injury:

> It is that existing conduct which the judge must consider in determining whether it is likely that injury may be caused to others in the future. The phrase is "by his conduct has shown a likelihood". It is the nature of that conduct which the judge must be satisfied is such that it is likely that the offender will cause injury to others in the future.

> It is that past conduct with which the judge is concerned, and he is to be satisfied beyond reasonable doubt that the conduct is such that it gives rise to the likelihood of future injury to others.

> The likelihood is not as to the probability of whether this offender will in fact offend again—the likelihood flows from the conduct of the offender up to the time of hearing.[43]

In *R. v. Larkham*,[44] the Court concluded, at p. 9, that the fact the accused

> committed four sexual assaults over a ten and one-half year period, during which he spent approximately four and one-half years in custody, itself indicates a likelihood that in the future he will fail to control his sexual impulses.

The term "other evil" includes the offence of sexual assault and does not require actual physical injury.[45] This expression has also been held to include psychological harm.[46]

THE DANGEROUS OFFENDER HEARING

The preceding sections have set out the various elements and tests which must be met if the court is to designate an accused a dangerous offender. The conduct of the application can be a long, drawn out affair as many aspects of the accused's past conduct and personal character are explored in detail.

The next few sections will discuss the general principles which apply in dangerous offender proceedings and the type of evidence which can be called.

General Principles

Typically, whenever a court renders a decision on a dangerous offender application there is a discussion of the general principles which govern these proceedings. From a review of the case law some of the general principles include:

1.   The public interest looms large at dangerous offender applications. The specific object is to protect society from the person who has been convicted of a serious personal injury offence and who has shown a propensity for violent crimes (sexual or otherwise);[47]

2.   The overriding aim of dangerous offender legislation is not punishment but the prevention of future violence;[48]

3.   The onus of proof is upon the Crown and the standard of proof is beyond a reasonable doubt;[49]

4.   The Crown need not prove beyond a reasonable doubt the offender will re-offend, only that there is a likelihood that he will inflict harm;[50]

5.   The strict rules which govern a trial do not apply at a sentencing hearing and it would be undesirable to have the formalities and technicalities characteristic of the normal adversary proceedings prevail. The hearsay rule does not govern the sentencing hearing. Hearsay evidence may be accepted where found to be credible and trustworthy. The judge traditionally has had wide latitude as to the sources and types of evidence upon which to base his sentence. He must have the fullest possible information concerning the background of the accused if he is to fit the sentence to the offender rather than to the crime;[51]

6.   Dangerous offender proceedings do not constitute a new trial but rather a sentencing phase of a trial. The balancing of *Charter* values in this context results in societal values for protection outweighing individual rights against self-incrimination;[52] The confession rule has been designed for proceedings where, broadly speaking, the guilt or innocence of a person is the matter in issue. The rule has not been established for proceedings related to the determination of sentence;[53]

7.   The offender cannot be punished for not fully participating in the assessment nor can the court make an adverse inference

with respect to his or her refusal to participate. At a dangerous offender application it is the Crown and not the defence who has put the accused's mental state in issue;[54]

8. If the court finds the Crown has proven the requisite statutory criteria beyond a reasonable doubt then it must find the accused to be a dangerous offender. The finding is, upon the attainment of the requisite degree of proof imperative and not discretionary.[55]

Evidence

The preceding sections have set out the specific legal requirements for designating an accused to be a dangerous offender. Arguing that these requirements have been met is often the end result of presenting a wide variety and vast amount of evidence. One does not call a victim to the stand and at the end of the testimony stand up and argue a pattern of repetitive behaviour has been proved.

It is difficult to try and relate the testimony of witnesses to the complex terms and elements set out in the *Criminal Code*. In other words, if a particular witness is called to the stand the Crown Attorney is not typically thinking to themselves "this is good evidence of a failure to control impulses". A simpler way to approach the evidence is to divide it into two categories:

a) the accused's past behaviour; and
b) the accused's psychiatric condition or psychological profile.

As a general rule, the more evidence presented in the first category the greater will be the confidence in the opinions expressed in the second.

Accused's Past Behaviour

Criminal history

An obvious starting point will be to prove the accused's criminal history. Prior offences involving violence may be relevant to establishing a pattern of behaviour. Prior offences involving violence or dishonesty could be relevant to assessing an individual's psychiatric condition (including the presence of an anti-social personality disorder or psychopathy) and risk for re-offence.

The Crown will also be permitted to call evidence of other crimes for which the accused was never charged or prosecuted. There are numerous examples in the case law where the Crown led evidence of other conduct for which the accused had not been convicted. The authorities establish that so long as the offender has not been acquitted, the Crown may call evidence of other criminal conduct provided it is relevant to the elements under the dangerous offender definitions.

In *R. v. B. (J.H.)*,[56] the Crown called extensive evidence concerning other criminal activity that was not the subject of the predicate offence or other charges. The Crown also introduced evidence of the accused's extensive collection of pornography and excerpts from his diaries. The Court of Appeal held the offender did not have to be convicted of a prior offence in order for it to be admissible at a dangerous offender hearing. Particular attention must be paid to the accused's past conduct and prior incidents may be of considerable importance in establishing a pattern of repetitive and persistent aggressive behaviour or a failure to control sexual impulses.[57]

The principles that allow for admitting this type of evidence are quite simple:

1. a Dangerous Offender Hearing is a sentencing. Courts are entitled to consider all relevant evidence at a sentencing;
2. the court has no power to punish an offender for past offences. All the court can do is determine if the offence occurred and, if so, how it factors into the analysis under the definition in para. 753(1)(a) or (b), if it fits at all; and
3. the circumstances must be proven beyond a reasonable doubt. If the Crown fails to meet that burden then the circumstances cannot be considered by the Court in its determination of whether the accused is a dangerous offender.

In *R. v. D. (D.E.)*,[58] the Crown was permitted to call evidence of previous offences where charges had not been prosecuted. There was also evidence in relation to outstanding charges for which the accused was pending trial.[59]

Character

The Crown may be permitted to call evidence of the accused's character or reputation. Section 757 *Criminal Code* states:

> Without prejudice to the right of the offender to tender evidence as to his or her character and repute, evidence of character and repute may, if the

court thinks fit, be admitted on the question of whether the offender is or is not a dangerous offender or a long-term offender.

Evidence of character and reputation will assist experts in formulating opinions about an accused's psychiatric condition and psychological profile. The diagnosis of personality disorders, psychiatric conditions or psychopathy depends on a broad range of information about how an accused behaves and relates to others in a variety of circumstances. Experts will be hesitant to formulate an opinion about an accused based solely on an individual's criminal activity. Experts will often want information about how an accused behaved in school, employment situations and interpersonal or family relationships.

Manner of proof

There are a variety of methods of introducing evidence of an accused's past behaviour. The Crown may rely on documentary evidence from old prosecution or police files including statements or photographs. The Crown may introduce penitentiary records including psychological assessments. Transcripts from previous court proceedings can be filed.

Introducing evidence by way of documents can be expedient. However, the Court must still assess what evidentiary weight will be given to this information. The Court retains the power to weigh the information in any document and accept it in full or in part or reject it altogether.

The most common method of introducing evidence about an accused's past will be through oral testimony from witnesses. Such evidence may relate to a prior conviction, an unproven allegation or to the accused's reputation or character.

In *R. v. Jack*,[60] the Crown called the victim of a previous rape who refused to talk about the incident but did acknowledge a previous statement she had given to police was accurate. A victim of another offence would not testify. The Court concluded:

> The Crown must, on a sentencing hearing, prove disputed facts beyond a reasonable doubt. That applies to all sentencing hearings including dangerous offender proceedings. Gonthier J. said in *R. v. Jones*, at p. 292:
>
>> As Lamer C.J.C. points out, this court held in *R. v. Gardiner*, [1982] 2 S.C.R. 368, that the Crown must prove disputed facts beyond a reasonable doubt during the sentencing hearing. However, in determining what facts are admissible at the sentencing stage, *Gardiner* reaffirmed the widely accepted principle that judges should have

access to the fullest possible information concerning the background of the accused. As Dickson J. stated, at p. 414:

> It is a commonplace that the strict rules which govern at trial do not apply at a sentencing hearing and it would be undesirable to have the formalities and technicalities characteristic of the normal adversary proceeding prevail. The hearsay rule does not govern the sentencing hearing. Hearsay evidence may be accepted where found to be credible and trustworthy. *The judge traditionally has had wide latitude as to the sources and types of evidence upon which to base his sentence. He must have the fullest possible information concerning the background of the accused if he is to fit the sentence to the offender rather than to the crime.* [The emphasis is that of Gonthier J.]

In this case, the circumstances of the prior offences were proved beyond any doubt. That applies to the 1973 and 1982 offences as much as to the others. The lack of cooperation by the two complainants left no visible gap in the proof.

It is, undoubtedly, a matter of importance that the Crown, on a dangerous offender hearing, prove not only the record of convictions, but also the circumstances of crimes which are relied upon as establishing dangerousness. But it does not follow that the Crown must call all the evidence which was called at the trial of those offences. In most cases, it should be possible to prove the circumstances beyond a reasonable doubt without calling the complainants. It is more than understandable that the 1973 victim would not wish to repeat "all that garbage" some 21 years later. Past victims should not have to relive the emotional trauma inflicted on them by past offences unless it is necessary to do so...

... In deciding what evidence to call at hearings of this kind, Crown counsel should keep in mind the wide latitude given to the court in sentencing hearings as to the sources and types of evidence which may be received. That latitude will not likely apply to evidence, such as that of the psychiatrists, which is specifically directed to the issue of future dangerousness. But it surely can apply to historical facts such as the circumstances of previous offences. If, as may be the case, the purpose of calling the victims of past offences is to emphasize the extent of the trauma suffered by those victims, that has scant ~relevance to the central issue in proceedings of this kind, that of future dangerousness, and is in any event a given.[61]

This decision provides compelling authority for not calling victims to testify. The difficulty which sometimes presents itself however is that the accused may deny or minimize the circumstances of his past behaviour. If that is the case it may be difficult for a court to reach specific conclusions about facts without hearing from witnesses to the events or victims of past crimes.

If past victims are willing to testify this evidence may be preferable to a documentary record unless the accused is prepared to admit fully to his prior conduct.

Psychiatric Condition or Psychological Profile of the Accused

A large portion of any dangerous offender application will consist of expert opinion evidence regarding the accused's psychiatric condition or psychological profile.

Before any forensic psychiatrist or forensic psychologist appears in court they have typically been provided with written material about the accused. This may consist of police reports or exhibits or witness statements or transcripts of evidence from previous crimes. There may be disciplinary, administrative or psychological reports from institutions where the accused has been incarcerated. There may be statements from witnesses about the accused's character and reputation. There may be other documents provided to experts including school or employment records.

As stated above, experts will be hesitant to formulate an opinion based solely on an accused's criminal history. They will want information about how an accused behaves and relates in a variety of circumstances.

Forensic psychologists may interview the accused or witnesses prior to formulating opinions. It is important to note that personal interviews are not essential and many experts can provide detailed, reliable opinions based on a review of documents alone. Forensic psychiatrists and forensic psychologists will typically prepare a written report which can be submitted and considered by the court in conjunction with oral testimony. Testimony from forensic psychiatrists and forensic psychologists can often be lengthy and detailed. There may be testimony about what material has been reviewed by the expert. They should be in a position to explain how the information was evaluated and what relevance was placed on the information when various opinions were formulated.

Experts will often testify about the general personality traits of an accused such as whether he is a callous or manipulative individual. There may be specific evidence about personality traits which support opinions that the accused suffers from a personality disorder, psychopathic traits or is, in fact, a psychopath. Experts may also testify about what drives an accused to offend. Some examples include a need for domination or control, sexual gratification or financial gain. Experts may testify about an accused's risk for offending in the future. This often involves an analysis of the accused's past behavior, his personality characteristics, his motivations for offending and his prospects for treatment. It may also involve testimony about various risk assessment tools which are particular tests that have been developed to assist in trying to predict the likelihood of an accused reoffending.

It is important to recognize that when experts testify about the risk for offending in the future it is in the context of the accused's demonstrated offending behavior. In other words, if an accused has an antisocial personality disorder and becomes frustrated when under stress and reacts by going out and robbing banks then that is what he is at risk to do in the future. If the accused is a psychopath and a sexual deviant who has a history of stalking and sexually assaulting children then he will be at risk for continuing that particular pattern of offending.

Assessing Expert Evidence

Experts obviously play a critical role in dangerous offender applications. The case law establishes that the court can rely on psychiatric opinion evidence to reach the conclusion that certain conduct amounts to a pattern of behavior or that the offender will not control his violent or sexual impulses in the future. However it is ultimately for the court and not the experts to make determinations of fact and draw conclusions about patterns of behavior or future conduct.

In R. v. N. (L.), the Alberta Court of Appeal devoted a great deal of attention to the assessment and use of psychiatric evidence by the trial judge. When assessing and evaluating psychiatric evidence the Court of Appeal suggested the following be considered:

1. the qualifications and practice of the psychiatrist;
2. the opportunity the psychiatrist had to assess the person, including: length of personal contact, place of contact, role with ongoing treatment, and involvement with the institution in which the person is a patient or prisoner;
3. the unique features of the doctor- patient relationship, such as hostility or fear by the patient (or the psychiatrist) arising from the personalities, the circumstances of the contact, and the role of the psychiatrist;
4. *specifically and precisely* what documents the psychiatrist hadavailable and reviewed, for example, from earlier court proceedings,institutional records, other medical consultations, or treatment;

5. the nature and scope of consultations (this could include: personal contact with third parties, information from other health care professionals, prison authorities, police, lawyers, family);

6. *specifically and precisely* what the psychiatrist *relies on* in coming to an opinion; and

7. the strengths and weaknesses of the information and material that is relied on.[62]

The Court's conclusions on this issue were summarized as follows:

1. "at all times the responsibility remains with the sentencing judge to assess and weigh the opinion evidence, to determine whether the behavioural thresholds have been met, and whether based on that past behaviour someone is a threat and if so, should be designated a dangerous offender... The experts do not become the judges and the expert opinion is not the judgment";

2. "it is the sentencing judge—not the psychiatrists, or the Crown, or the defence—who decides what the key elements of the pattern of conduct are";

3. "in assessing the *existence of a pattern*, psychiatric opinion evidence, admissible under s.755, must be used cautiously. Clearly, psychiatrists can opine on the interpretation of what is alleged to constitute a pattern of conduct, on whether that pattern of conduct is pathologically or substantially intractable and of course, on the issue of future dangerousness. But, quite apart from any other use of psychiatric evidence in dangerous offender hearings, while the psychiatrists may review past criminal conduct and then give an opinion on whether it forms a pattern, it is in the final analysis the court's responsibility and not the psychiatrists' to make the determination whether the evidence establishes the proscribed patterns."[63]

Expert opinions will always involve some use of secondary source material. In *R. v. Larkham*, the accused refused to be assessed but the Court concluded this "did not prevent Dr. Malcolm from forming an opinion as to Larkham's mental condition. Dr. Malcolm testified that a patient history is often more important than a clinical interview. After all, impulse control disorder is not demonstrated during an interview."[64]

Since psychiatrists will always rely to a certain degree on secondary source material their opinions can always be challenged. From the case law, it would appear that the weight to be given to an expert's opinion will be diminished by the degree to which it is dependant on unproven or questionable information. In *R. v. Kanester*, the Court concluded:

> The value of a psychiatrist's opinion may be affected to the extent to which it may rest on second-hand source material; but that goes to the weight and not to the receivability in evidence of the opinion, which is no evidence as to the truth of the information but evidence of the opinion formed on the basis of that information.[65]

The circumstances in *R. v. Knight*[66] stand as a warning about placing too much reliance on secondary source information. The Crown provided police documents and statements in relation to other incidents but went no further. The Court accepted that the psychiatrist had examined these documents but held the truth of their contents had not been proved. As a result, the trial judge stated:

> I must hold that in so far as the psychiatrists gave any effect to it, the scope and value of their opinions is correspondingly diminished. If I were not to attribute this debilitating result to its use, I would in effect be delegating to the psychiatrists my responsibility for finding facts of a rather crucial nature.[67]

The Court acknowledged that psychiatrists do deal with second hand source information and that, while ultimately their conclusions may rest in part on second hand source material, it is nonetheless an opinion formed according to recognized normal psychiatric procedures. However, in the circumstances of *R. v. Knight*, the trial judge concluded:

> I do not think that it is within the recognized scope of a psychiatrists professional activities, skill and training to evaluate the type of data in issue here and to make a finding as to what it adds up to in the simple realm of historical fact. Even if it were, I do not think I could rely on any consequent opinion based on inferences drawn therefrom, without these facts being independently proven before me.[68]

The trial judge was concerned that the expert could not form an opinion as to future likelihood without taking into account evidence which the judge ruled to be of no weight. The Crown application was denied.

It should be noted that even if the Crown has to rely substantially on secondary source material an argument could be made that the decisions in *R. v. Gardiner*[69] and *R. v. Jack*[70] support the admissibility of such material.

THE DANGEROUS OFFENDOR HEARING—DECISION AND SENTENCE

Once the evidence has been heard and closing submissions made by the Crown and the Defence, the court will decide the outcome of the application.

The *Tackling Violent Crime Act*, which came into force on July 2, 2008, contains several provisions of profound significance to the decision making process in dangerous offender applications.

Presumption of Dangerous Offendor Status

Subsection 753(1.1) of the *Criminal Code* now states that an accused is presumed to be a dangerous offender where certain criteria are met, unless the contrary is proven on a balance of probabilities. The criteria which must be established are:

1. the offence which led to the dangerous offender application is a primary designated offence as defined in s. 752 of the *Code*;
2. the appropriate sentence for the offence which led to the dangerous offender application is two years or more;
3. the accused has ben convicted in the past at least twice of a primary designated offence;
4. the accused was sentenced to at least two years in custody or more for at least two prior convictions for primary designated offences.[71]

The effect of the presumption is to create an evidentiary burden on the accused to disprove that he is a dangerous offender in certain circumstances.

Given the potential that an indeterminate sentence might be imposed, it is expected that there will be a constitutional challenge to the validity of the presumption. Any constitutional challenge will likely take years to litigate and will no doubt find its way to the Supreme Court of Canada. Until the Supreme Court has ruled on the validity of the presumption, Crown Attorneys would be well advised to proceed with caution. Indeed, if the Crown's case is strong, they might consider proceeding to argue the application without reliance on the presumption even where the criteria to do so are met.

Sentence Options

In years gone by, if the court concluded an accused was a dangerous offender, the only question was whether the sentence should be determinate or indeterminate. The 1997 amendments to the *Criminal Code* created a scheme whereby any accused found to be a dangerous offender had to be sentenced to an indeterminate sentence. The 1997 amendments also introduced the concept of a long-term offender. While a detailed analysis of the long-term offender provisions would be outside the scope of this chapter, briefly, the designation permits the imposition of a custodial sentence followed by up to ten years of supervision in the community.

Following the 1997 amendments, the Supreme Court of Canada ruled in *R. v. Johnson*[72] that the court retained a residual discretion not to declare an accused to be a dangerous offender even if all the criteria were met. This discretion was most often exercised in circumstances where the evidence established that "there is a reasonable possibility of eventual control of the risk in the community."[73]

The *Tackling Violent Crime Act* has changed the process once again. Section 753 now states:

> (4) If the court finds an offender to be a dangerous offender, it shall
> > (*a*) impose a sentence of detention in a penitentiary for an indeterminate period;
> > (*b*) impose a sentence for the offence for which the offender has been convicted—which must be a minimum punishment of imprisonment for a term of two years—and order that the offender be subject to long-term supervision for a period that does not exceed 10 years; or
> > (*c*) impose a sentence for the offence for which the offender has been convicted.
>
> (4.1) The court shall impose a sentence of detention in a penitentiary for an indeterminate period unless it is satisfied by the evidence adduced during the hearing of the application that there is a reasonable expectation that a lesser measure under paragraph (4)(*b*) or (*c*) will adequately protect the public against the commission by the offender of murder or a serious personal injury offence.

This section creates three sentencing options for the court if the accused is found to meet the dangerous offender criteria. The court can sentence the accused to an indeterminate period of custody or there can be a determinate sentence with or without a period of long-term supervision. Interestingly, this section creates the possibility that accused persons who are declared dangerous offenders may nevertheless be released into the community at the end of a determinate sentence. They may even not be subject to a supervision order.

The section makes clear that an indeterminate sentence should be imposed unless the court is satisfied there is a "reasonable expectation" that a lesser sentence will protect the public. The determination of the appropriate sentence will involve an analysis of the evidence of the risk for future violence balanced against the prospects for control of the risk through treatment or community supervision.

ASSESSING THE RISK OF FUTURE DANGEROUSNESS

How should a judge assess the risk posed by the accused in terms of whether his condition is intractable or whether there is a possibility of eventual control of the risk in the community? When assessing an accused's likelihood of failing to control or restrain behavior, the court should examine his past conduct and assess his present condition. Speculation as to what may occur in the future should be kept to a minimum.

I would suggest the evidence to be considered when assessing future risk can be broken into five general groups:

1. Accused's Psychiatric Condition;
2. Accused's Behaviour;
3. Accused's Attitude;
4. Characteristics of the Accused; and
5. Expert Opinion and Risk Assessment.

I will explain each in turn.

Accused's Psychiatric Condition

When considering an accused's psychiatric condition, the court should assess the expert opinion evidence regarding the presence or absence of any psychiatric or personality disorders. For example if an accused is a psychopath, a virtually untreatable condition at present, this would be a negative indicator for future control. The presence of a personality disorder resulting in a rejection of society's rules would also be of concern. The presence of sexual deviancy may also be a negative indicator for future control depending on any available treatment. Conversely, if an accused has few psychopathic traits or has no personality disorder or sexual deviancy these may be positive indicators that his behavior can eventually be controlled.

Accused's Behaviour

In contemplating the accused's behavious, I would suggest the court consider a variety of factors. The first is the method of offending. Was it impulsive or was there a degree of planning? Was the victim a stranger or were they groomed in some way? Was the violence instrumental for the purpose of committing another crime or was it excessive or sadistic? An accused who acts on impulse and uses violence on strangers may be less susceptible to external controls. For example, it would be very difficult to enforce a condition of release that required an accused to have no contact with young women. However if an accused only offends in certain contexts (i.e., domestic or family or as a result of alcoholic or drug use it may be easier to impose some external control to prevent offending).[74]

The court should carefully examine the accused's behavior to determine if there are any demonstrations of acceptance of responsibility for their offending. For example did the accused plead guilty or cooperate with the court-ordered assessment? Did the victim of any offences have to testify or were these facts admitted? Certain behavior can be a positive indicator of acceptance of responsibility and give rise to a hope for eventual control. It must be emphasized, however, that the absence of some of this behavior should not be used as a negative indicator for future control. For example, an accused has the right to plead not guilty or to decline to cooperate with the court ordered assessment. This behavior cannot be used against him.

Other behavior which is of particular interest includes how an accused has responded in the past to treatment or to court-ordered supervision such as probation. If an accused has offended following treatment or while under supervision this would be cause for concern about the possibility of controlling his behavior in the future.

Accused's Attitude

When considering the accused's attitude, the court should examine the accused's present condition. The court should consider whether the accused has insight into his own behavior. Does he have empathy towards his victims? Is he sincerely motivated to seek treatment? Is the accused remorseful? The presence of insight, empathy, motivation and remorse would be positive indicators for future control (provided there was confidence the accused is sincere and not engaging in manipulation). However if the accused engages in denial, rationalization, minimization and lacks sincere motivation to seek treatment then these would be negative indicators for future control of his behavior.

Characteristics of the Accused

The court should look beyond the circumstances of the accused's offending and psychological profile. One fact which may be of particular importance is the age of the accused. If he is relatively young (late teens to early twenties) it may be that his personality traits are more susceptible to change. Conversely an older accused (over 40) may begin to "burn out" in the sense of committing fewer offenses.[75]

Other facts which may be of significance include whether the accused has been able to establish stable relationships or maintain steady employment. These are positive indicators for future control. An accused who has become fully criminalized will be at a greater risk to return to this lifestyle if released back into the community.

Expert Opinion and Risk Assessment

The court should examine carefully the experts' assessment of the accused's risk to re-offend and in particular what may be required to bring it under some measure of control. For example, if an expert has testified there is a treatment available for the accused (i.e. medication to reduce sexual impulses) which would substantially reduce the risk for offending then this would be a positive indicator for future control. Conversely, if there is no treatment available and the only hope to reduce the risk is if the accused can somehow change his personality, a virtually impossible task, then this would be a negative indicator for future control.

The above discussion has been general in nature. The headings and factors I have identified are not intended to be comprehensive. Every accused is unique and some characteristics or conditions will be worthy of greater emphasis. Every accused will exhibit characteristics that are both positive and negative indicators for future control. The difficult task for the court is to identify and assess them all and determine if there is a likelihood the accused will fail to restrain his behavior and harm another victim in the future or is there a reasonable expectation that the risk can be controlled and the public protected through some lesser penalty than an indeterminate sentence.

REASONABLE EXPECTATION STANDARD

There is no doubt we face years of litigation as the courts interpret the meaning of "reasonable expectation" and the evidence required to satisfy this standard. I will go out on a limb and speculate that the "reasonable expectation" standard is no less than the "reasonable possibility" standard that is part of the long-term offender provisions.[76]

In *R. v. Little*,[77] the Ontario Court of Appeal overturned a trial judge's exercise of residual discretion to declare the accused a long-term offender despite concluding he satisfied the criteria for dangerous offender. Thr trial judge concluded there was a reasonable possibility of eventual control of the accused's risk in the community:

> in the circumstances of this case it is my opinion that the trial judge erred by imposing a determinate sentence in the absence of evidence either that Little could be meaningfully treated within a definite period of time, or that the resources needed to implement the supervision conditions that the trial judge concluded were necessary to eventually control Little's risk in the community were available, so as to bring Little's risk of future reoffending within tolerable limits.[78]

The Court further elaborated on this finding:

> to achieve the goal of protection of the public under the dangerous offender and long-term offender provisions in the *Code*, evidence of treatability that (i) is more than mere speculative hope, and (ii) indicates that the specific offender in question can be treated within an ascertainable time frame, is required. The requisite judicial inquiry on a dangerous offender application, mandated by *Johnson*, is concerned with whether the sentencing sanctions available under the long-term offender provisions of the *Code* are "sufficient to reduce [the offender's] threat to an *acceptable* level." [Emphasis added.] The determination of whether an offender's risk can be reduced to an "acceptable" level requires consideration of all factors, including treatability, that can bring about sufficient risk reduction to ensure protection of the public. This does not require a showing that an offender will be "cured" through treatment or that his or her rehabilitation may be assured. What it does require, however, is proof that the nature and severity of an offender's identified risk can be sufficiently contained in the community, a non-custodial setting, so as to protect the public.[79]

I would suggest that a "reasonable expectation" standard would require at least the same degree of confidence as required by the "reasonable possibility" standard as interpreted in *R. v. Little*.

RE-OFFENDING DANGEROUS OFFENDERS

There may be situations where an accused who has been declared a dangerous offender commits a further offence while on parole or while bound by a long-term supervision order. If the subsequent offence is a serious personal injury offence, then the Crown can request an assessment report. Upon the filing of the report, the Crown can apply to have the accused sentenced to an indeterminate period in custody. The court shall impose an indeterminate sentence unless it is satisfied a lesser penalty will protect the public.[80]

Essentially, this means that if an accused who has been declared to be a dangerous offender is released and commits a further serious personal injury offence, it will not be necessary to have another hearing to determine if he meets the criteria for the designation again. Rather, the case will proceed to a hearing to determine the appropriate sentence whether it is indeterminate custody or a fixed term with or without a long-term supervision order

EFFECT OF AN INDETERMINATE SENTENCE

When an accused is designated a dangerous offender and an indeterminate sentence is imposed, it must be understood that this does not amount to the legal equivalent of locking him up and throwing away the key. The *Criminal Code* provides:

> **761.** (1) Subject to subsection (2), where a person is in custody under a sentence of detention in a penitentiary for an indeterminate period, the National Parole Board shall, as soon as possible after the expiration of seven years from the day on which that person was taken into custody and not later than ever two years after the previous review, review the condition, history and circumstances of that person for the purpose of determining whether he or she should be granted parole unless Part II of the *Corrections and Conditional Release Act* and, if so, on what conditions.

The requirement for a review and the opportunity to apply for parole have been held to preserve the constitutionality of the dangerous offender provisions.[81]

In *R. v. Jones*, the Supreme Court concluded:

> An indeterminate sentence is not an unlimited sentence. If, in the case at hand, the psychiatrists testifying on behalf of the accused are correct in their assessment that Mr. Jones will be fit to be released in ten years, then he will be liberated at that time. The offender faces incarceration only for the period of time that he poses a serious risk to the safety of society. In the interim, it is hoped that he will receive treatment that will assist him in

controlling his conduct. To release a dangerous offender while he remains unable to control his actions serves neither the interests of the offender nor those of society.[82]

While it is true that an indeterminate sentence is not a life sentence and there are provisions requiring a regular review of every dangerous offender's situation, it is equally true that the possibility for release for many of these offenders is remote. From 1978 to 2008, a total of 455 accused were declared dangerous offenders. Of these, 394 are still alive, six are serving determinate sentences (meaning they were designated under the pre-1997 provisions) and 388 are serving indeterminate sentences. Of the 394 dangerous offenders still alive, 374 remain incarcerated, one has been deported and 19 are being supervised in the community. Significantly there are 18 accused who were designated as dangerous sexual offenders or habitual offenders under the pre-1977 provisions who are still incarcerated. A further 28 are being supervised in the community.[83]

CONCLUSION

Dangerous offender legislation is not new in Canada. It has a long history and continues to be the subject of legal debate and amendments. The provisions are complicated and the legal principles can be difficult to grasp. The evidence which can be presented is varied and complex. The hearing is often long and exhausting to all involved. This is appropriate. It should not be easy to declare an accused to be a Dangerous Offender. It is a designation which should be reserved for those who threaten the safety of the public, who ignore the fundamental rules of society and satisfy their own perverse needs by resorting to acts of horrendous physical or sexual violence.

Notes

[1] 1908, (U.K.), c. 59, ss. 10 to 16.
[2] *R. v. L. (T.P.)*, 1987 CarswellNS 41, 1987 CarswellNS 342, 37 C.C.C. (3d) 1, 80 N.R. 161, [1987] 2 S.C.R. 309, 44 D.L.R. (4th) 193, 82 N.S.R. (2d) 271, 61 C.R. (3d) 1, 32 C.R.R. 41, 207 A.P.R. 271 (S.C.C.), at p. 16 [C.C.C.)].
[3] *Ibid.*, at p. 17 [C.C.C.].
[4] *An Act to amend the Criminal Code*, S.C. 1948, c 39, s. 43.
[5] *An Act to amend the Criminal Code*, S.C. 1960-61, c. 43, s. 32.
[6] *Criminal Law Amendment Act, 1968-69*, S.C. 1968-69, c. 38, s. 76.
[7] *R. v. L. (T.P.)*, *supra*, note 2, at p. 17 [C.C.C.].
[8] *Criminal Law Amendment Act, 1977*, S.C. 1976-77, c. 53, s. 14.

⁹ *An Act to amend the Criminal Code (high risk offenders)*, etc., S.C. 1997, c. 17, s. 3.

¹⁰ An indeterminate sentence effectively orders an accused be kept in custody until the National Parole Board decides he can be released. There is no fixed date for release but there are requirements for regular review by the Parole Board.

¹¹ S.C. 2008, c.6.

¹² *R. v. Jones*, 1994 CarswellBC 580, 1994 CarswellBC 1240, 89 C.C.C. (3d) 353, [1994] 2 S.C.R. 229, 114 D.L.R. (4th) 645, 30 C.R. (4th) 1, 166 N.R. 321, 43 B.C.A.C. 241, 69 W.A.C. 241, 21 C.R.R. (2d) 286 (S.C.C.), at p.306 [C.C.C.].

¹³ *R. v. L. (T.P.)*, *supra*, note 2, at pp.22-23 [C.C.C.].

¹⁴ *R. v. N. (L.)*, 1999 CarswellAlta 595, 1999 ABCA 206, 137 C.C.C. (3d) 97, 71 Alta. L.R. (3d) 92, 237 A.R. 201, 197 W.A.C. 201, [1999] 11 W.W.R. 649 (Alta. C.A.), at p. 122 [C.C.C.].

¹⁵ *R. v. Currie*, 1997 CarswellOnt 1487, 1997 CarswellOnt 1488, 115 C.C.C. (3d) 205, [1997] 2 S.C.R. 260, 211 N.R. 321, 7 C.R. (5th) 74, 100 O.A.C. 161, 146 D.L.R. (4th) 688 (S.C.C.).

¹⁶ *Ibid.*, at p. 212 [C.C.C.].

¹⁷ *Ibid.*, at pp. 216-17 [C.C.C.].

¹⁸ *R. v. N. (L.)*, *supra*, note 14, at paras. 69-86.

¹⁹ *Ibid.*, at paras. 68-69.

²⁰ Chief Justice Lamer stated: "I cannot imagine that Parliament wanted the courts to wait for an obviously dangerous individual, regardless of the nature of his criminal record and notwithstanding the force of expert opinion as to his potential dangerousness, to commit a particularly violent and grievous offence before he or she can be declared a dangerous offender" (*R. v. Currie*, *supra*, note 15, at pp. 216).

²¹ The procedural requirements are set out in ss. 752.1, 753 and 754 of the *Criminal Code*.

²² *R. v. D. (D.E.)*, 1994 CarswellNS 581, [1994] N.S.J. No. 626, 140 N.S.R. (2d) 162, 399 A.P.R. 162 (N.S.S.C.).

²³ *Ibid.*, at para. 3.

²⁴ *R. v. C. (P.M.)*, 1998 CarswellBC 316, [1998] B.C.J. No. 32252 (B.C. S.C.), at para. 20.

²⁵ *R. v. Dow*, 1999 CarswellBC 592, 1999 BCCA 177, 134 C.C.C. (3d) 323, 120 B.C.A.C. 16, 196 W.A.C. 16 (B.C.C.A.).

²⁶ *Ibid.*, at paras. 22-26.

²⁷ *R. v. N. (L.)*, *supra*, at note 14, at para 113.

²⁸ *R. v. Langevin*, 1984 CarswellOnt 50, 11 C.C.C. (3d) 336, 45 O.R. (2d) 705, 39 C.R. (3d) 333, 8 D.L.R. (4th) 485, 3 O.A.C. 110, 9 C.R.R. 16 (Ont. C.A.).

²⁹ *Ibid.*, at p. 348 [C.C.C.].

³⁰ *R. v. Shrubsall*, 2001 CarswellNS 482, 2001 NSSC 197, [2001] N.S.J. No. 539, 199 N.S.R. (2d) 314, 623 A.P.R. 314 (N.S.S.C.).

³¹ *Ibid.* This was part of his criminal record. It was not a predicate offence for the Dangerous Offender Application.

³² *Ibid.*, at para. 11.

³³ *R. v. Langevin*, *supra*, note 28, at p.349 [C.C.C.].

³⁴ *R. v. Antonius*, 2000 CarswellBC 600, 2000 BCSC 429, [2000] B.C.J. No. 577 (B.C.S.C.).

³⁵ *Ibid.*, at para. 25.

36 *R. v. Schwartz*, 2000 CarswellBC 44, 2000 BCSC 40, [2000] B.C.J. No. 47 (B.C.S.C.).

37 *R. v. Oliver*, 1997 CarswellAlta 121, 114 C.C.C. (3d) 50, 48 Alta. L.R. (3d) 180, 193 A.R. 241, 135 W.A.C. 241 (Alta. C.A.).

38 *Ibid.*, at p. 56 [C.C.C.].

39 *R. v. S. (C.W.)*, 1987 CarswellOnt 1079, 37 C.C.C. (3d) 143, 20 O.A.C. 323 (Ont. C.A.).

40 *Ibid.*, at p. 157.

41 *Ibid.*

42 *R. v. Carleton*, 1981 CarswellAlta 286, 69 C.C.C. (2d) 1, [1981] 6 W.W.R. 148, 32 A.R. 181, 23 C.R. (3d) 129 (Alta. C.A.), affirmed 1983 CarswellAlta 303, 1983 CarswellAlta 319, [1983] 2 S.C.R. 58, 36 C.R. (3d) 393, 6 C.C.C. (3d) 480, 47 A.R. 160, [1984] 2 W.W.R. 384, 52 N.R. 293 (S.C.C.).

43 *Ibid.*, at p. 6 [C.C.C.].

44 *R. v. Larkham*, [1987] O.J. No. 1203 (Ont. H.C.), at p. 9.

45 *R. v. Schwartz*, *supra*, note 36, at para. 28.

46 *R. v. Dwyer*, 1977 CarswellAlta 200, 34 C.C.C. (2d) 293, [1977] 2 W.W.R. 704, 3 A.R. 96 (Alta. C.A.).

47 *R. v. L. (B.R.)*, 1987 CarswellMan 312, [1987] M.J. No. 263, 47 Man. R. (2d) 81 (Man. Q.B.).

48 *R. v. Schwartz*, *supra*, note 36, at para. 34.

49 *Ibid.*, at para. 35.

50 *Ibid.*, at para. 36.

51 *R. v. Gardiner*, 1982 CarswellOnt 90, 1982 CarswellOnt 739, 68 C.C.C. (2d) 477, [1982] 2 S.C.R. 368, 30 C.R. (3d) 289, 140 D.L.R. (3d) 612, 43 N.R. 361 (S.C.C.), at p. 514 [C.C.C.].

52 *R. v. Brown*, 1999 CarswellBC 2988, [1999] B.C.J. No. 3040, 70 C.R.R. (2d) 170 (B.C. S.C.), at paras. 38-39.

53 *R. v. Jones*, *supra*, note 12, at p. 375 [C.C.C.].

54 *R. v. Brown*, *supra*, note 52, at para. 34; see also *R. v. Teskey*, 1996 CarswellAlta 280, [1996] A.J. No. 344, 38 Alta. L.R. (3d) 246, 48 C.R. (4th) 267, 183 A.R. 55 (Alta. Q.B.), at para. 101.

55 *R. v. Schwartz*, *supra*, note 36, at para 38. There is some varying judicial opinion on this issue and some courts have found there exists a residual discretion to not declare an accused to be a dangerous offender even if all criteria are met. The issue will hopefully be resolved when the Supreme Court of Canada decides the aspect in *R. v. Johnson*, 2001 CarswellBC 2128, 2001 BCCA 456, [2001] B.C.J. No. 2021, 158 C.C.C. (3d) 155, 159 B.C.A.C. 255, 259 W.A.C. 255 (B.C.C.A.).

56 *R. v. B. (J.H.)*, 1995 CarswellNS 37, 101 C.C.C. (3d) 1, 144 N.S.R. (2d) 293, 416 A.P.R. 293 (N.S. C.A.).

57 *Ibid.*, p. 23 [C.C.C.].

58 *R. v. D. (D.E.)*, 1995 CarswellNS 485, (sub nom. *R. v. Dicks*) [1995] N.S.J. No. 159, 143 N.S.R. (2d) 81, 411 A.P.R. 81 (N.S.S.C.).

59 See *R. v. MacInnis*, 1981 CarswellNS 190, 64 C.C.C. (2d) 553, 49 N.S.R. (2d) 393, 96 A.P.R. 393 (N.S.C.A.); *R. v. Schwartz*, *supra*, note 36; *R. v. Teskey*, 1996 CarswellAlta 280, [1996] A.J. No. 344, 38 Alta. L.R. (3d) 246, 48 C.R. (4th) 267, 183 A.R. 55 (Alta. Q.B.); *R. v. Lewis*, 1984 CarswellOnt 1364, 12 C.C.C. (3d) 353,

46 O.R. (2d) 289, 4 O.A.C. 98, 9 D.L.R. (4th) 715 (Ont. C.A.); and *R. v. Kanester*, 1967 CarswellBC 201, [1968] 1 C.C.C. 351 (B.C.C.A.).

[60] *R. v. Jack*, 1998 CarswellBC 412, [1998] B.C.J. No. 458, 104 B.C.A.C. 175, 170 W.A.C. 175 (B.C.C.A).

[61] *Ibid.*, at paras. 38-41.

[62] *R. v. N. (L.)*, *supra*, at note 14, at para. 189.

[63] *Ibid.*, at para. 199.

[64] *R. v. Larkham*, *supra*, note 44, at p. 5.

[65] *R. v. Kanester*, *supra*, note 59 at p. 355 [C.C.C.], quoting from *R. v. Wilband*, 1966 CarswellBC 168, [1967] 2 C.C.C. 6, [1967] S.C.R. 14, 2 C.R.N.S. 29, 49 C.R. 193, 60 W.W.R. 292, [1966] 4 C.C.C. 8 (S.C.C.), at p. 11.

[66] *R. v. Knight*, 1975 CarswellOnt 1077, 27 C.C.C. (2d) 343 (Ont. H.C.).

[67] *Ibid.*, at p. 354 [C.C.C.].

[68] *Ibid.*, at pp. 354-355 [C.C.C.].

[69] *R. v. Gardiner*, *supra*, note 51.

[70] *R. v. Jack*, *supra*, note 60.

[71] Primary designated offences include crimes such as assault causing bodily harm, aggravated assault, sexual assault, sexual assault causing bodily harm, aggravated sexual assault, sexual interference, invitation to sexual touching and sexual exploitation.

[72] *R. v. Johnson*, 2003 CarswellBC 2354, 2003 CarswellBC 2355, 2003 SCC 46, [2003] S.C.J. No. 45, 19 B.C.L.R. (4th) 243, 308 N.R. 333, 186 B.C.A.C. 161, 306 W.A.C. 161, 177 C.C.C. (3d) 97, [2004] 2 W.W.R. 393, 230 D.L.R. (4th) 296, 13 C.R. (6th) 205, [2003] 2 S.C.R. 357 (S.C.C.).

[73] *Criminal Code*, para. 753.1(1)(c).

[74] In *R. v. Tremblay*, 2000 CarswellAlta 949, (sub nom. *R. v. T. (J.G.)*) [2000] A.J. No. 938, 2000 ABQB 551, [2001] 2 W.W.R. 722, 87 Alta. L.R. (3d) 229, 274 A.R. 203 (Alta. Q.B.), the accused typically offended against his partner after establishing a spousal relationship. As part of his long-term offender designation it was recommended the National Parole Board impose conditions of his supervision which prohibited the accused from establishing a relationship or living with any woman without the express knowledge and consent of his Parole Officer. It should be remembered external controls as part of a long-term offender designation are only in place for a maximum of ten years after release from custody. Therefore, in my view, courts should be cautious about placing too much reliance on external controls.

[75] The concept of "burn out" is not universally applicable and some accused will continue to offend throughout their lives regardless of age.

[76] *Criminal Code*, s. 753.1.

[77] *R. v. Little*, 2007 CarswellOnt 4808, [2007] O.J. No. 2935, 225 C.C.C. (3d) 20, 2007 ONCA 548, 226 O.A.C. 148, (sub nom. *R. v. L. (G.)*) 87 O.R. (3d) 683 (Ont. C.A.), leave to appeal to refused 2008 CarswellOnt 2329, 2008 CarswellOnt 2330, [2008] S.C.C.A. No. 39, 386 N.R. 396 (note), 253 O.A.C. 398 (note) (S.C.C.).

[78] *Ibid.*, para. 37.

[79] *Ibid.*, para. 42.

[80] *Criminal Code*, s. 753.01.

[81] *R. v. L. (T.P.)*, *supra*, note 2, at p. 31-32 [C.C.C.], and *R. v. D. (T.M.G.)*, 2000 CarswellBC 53, 2000 BCSC 69, [2000] B.C.J. No. 63 (B.C.S.C.), at para. 47.

[82] *R. v. Jones*, *supra*, note 12, at pp.396-397 [C.C.C.].

[83] Source: Corrections and Conditional Release Statistical Overview—2008, pp. 660-667 and 109-110, Public Safety Canada (see www.publicsafety.gc.ca).

27

Eyewitness Evidence

*Rory O'Day**

INTRODUCTION

The Eyewitness

Two ways exist for evidence to be introduced into a trial. One is by the introduction of some document or physical object, such as a murder weapon. The second is by the oral testimony of witnesses. This chapter will focus on a special type of witness, the eyewitness.

According to the Oxford English Dictionary, "eyewitness" is defined as:

> One whose evidence is of what he has seen with his own eyes; one who has seen a thing done or happen; and, the result of actual observation.

No more dramatic occurrence can transpire in a courtroom than the identification of a defendant by an eyewitness. In fact, research shows that the presence of an eyewitness sharply increases the likelihood of conviction.[1] Therefore, an eyewitness who can identify the defendant as the culprit is an invaluable asset to the prosecution of a case, and an almost certain liability for the defence.

Opposing Points of View

Psychologists who study human perception have long been interested in the use of eyewitness testimony, because of the significant differences of opinion between the scientific community and the judicial community regarding the value of eyewitnesses.

Many psychologists distrust the accuracy of eyewitness testimony.

* Professor of Social Work (recently retired), Dalhousie University, Halifax, Nova Scotia. Dr. O'Day received his Ph.D. from the University of Michigan in 1969. Since that date, he has taught at the following universities: University of Michigan, St, Mary's University, University of British Columbia, University of Waterloo, and Dalhousie University. Dr. O'Day has authored and co-authored numerous articles and book chapters pertaining to the field of psychology

On the other hand, the public and, most importantly, jurors seem to feel that eyewitnesses are generally accurate and trustworthy.

Use the References

Because of space limitations, much of the theory and research underlying the scientific conclusions presented with respect to eyewitness identification can be dealt with only briefly in this chapter. For more extensive and intensive treatments of theoretical and empirical issues, therefore, the reader is directed to the following texts:

Cutler, B.L. & Penrod, S.D. *Mistaken Identification: The Eyewitness, Psychology, and the Law* (New York: Cambridge University Press, 1995).

Deutscher, D. & Leonoff, H. *Identification Evidence* (Toronto: Carswell, 1991).

Loftus, E.F., *Eyewitness Testimony* (Cambridge, Mass.: Harvard University Press, 1979).

Loftus, E.F. & Doyle, J. *Eyewitness Testimony: Civil and Criminal*, 3d ed. (Charlottesville, VA: Lexis Publishing, 1997).

Payne, D. & Conrad, F. *Intersections in Basic and Applied Memory Research* (Mahwah, NJ: Erlbaum, 1997).

Ross, D.F., Read, J.D., & Toglia, M.P., eds. *Adult Eyewitness Testimony: Current Trends and Developments* (New York: Cambridge University Press, 1994).

Sporer, S.L., Malpass, R.S., & Koehnken, G. *Psychological Issues in Eyewitness Identification* (Mahwah, NJ: Erlbaum, 1996).

Thompson, C.P., Herrmann, D.J., Read, J.D., Bruce, D., Payne, D.G., & Toglia, M.P., eds. *Eyewitness Memory: Theoretical and Applied Perspectives* (Mahwah, NJ: LEA Publishers, 1998).

Wells, G.L. *Eyewitness Identification: A System Handbook* (Toronto: Carswell, 1988).

Wells, G.L. & Loftus, E.F., eds. *Eyewitness Testimony: Psychological Perspectives* (Cambridge: Cambridge University Press, 1984).

Yarmey, A.D. *The Psychology of Eyewitness Testimony* (New York: The Free Press, 1979).

Perhaps, over time, as knowledge of the consequences of DNA evidence becomes more imbedded in the public consciousness (i.e., overturning guilty verdicts), future jurors will be more skeptical about the validity of eyewitness evidence.[2]

THE PROBLEM

The problem, from the court's point of view, is that most lay people operate with a conception of human memory which blinds them to the various factors which, to one degree or another, can distort specific memories a person has about an event she witnessed. The answer is to permit expert testimony in cases involving eyewitness identification evidence, in order to instruct the court regarding the scientific model of human memory, and the various perceptual and memorial errors that can make such evidence inaccurate.

If eyewitness identification were always valid, assuming no ulterior motive on the part of the eyewitness, then there would be no problem. According to this scenario, if only one person said she saw you do something then you most surely did it, unless you can prove you were somewhere else at the time.

If, however, eyewitnesses can sometimes mistakenly identify alleged perpetrators, then there is room to argue about the validity of any particular eyewitness identification evidence. The issue then becomes one, not of blindly accepting eyewitness evidence as valid, but rather, of analyzing those general and specific personal and situational factors that may increase or decrease one's confidence in the validity of an individual's eyewitness identification evidence.

Inherent Dangers: The Legal Picture

Both American and Canadian courts have been aware for some time now of the dangers inherent in eyewitness testimony.[3] The United States Supreme Court listed five factors to be considered in determining eye witness identification accuracy:[4]

(1) The opportunity of the witness to view the criminal, at the time of the crime;

(2) The witness's degree of attention;

(3) The accuracy of the witness's prior description of the criminal;

(4) The level of certainty demonstrated by the witness at the time of confrontation (the manner of pre-trial identification of the criminal by an eyewitness and includes such procedures as line-ups, showups, photographs, and composite sketches); and

(5) The length of time between the crime and the confrontation.[5]

Wells and Murray, however, in their 1983 summary of both the anecdotal and scientific literature, to that point[6] argued that the *Neil v. Biggers* advice or criteria had limited usefulness in judging the accuracy of eyewitness identification evidence.

The eyewitness identification research that has been conducted over the past 20 years continues to support Wells and Murray's conclusions that, from a scientific point of view, it is extremely difficult to be confident about the veridicality of eyewitness identification evidence.[7]

Extreme Positions

The positions on the status of eyewitness testimony range, on the one hand, from those who would charge and convict solely on the evidence of one eyewitness to those, on the other hand, who would set free from investigation and trial all those for whom the only evidence against them is eyewitness identification.[8] These extreme positions see eyewitness identification either as incontrovertible or as without merit. The fact that such extreme positions co-exist with respect to the usefulness of such evidence indicates the need for a better understanding of the phenomenon of eyewitness identification.

It behooves all concerned with the criminal justice system, therefore, to examine both sides of the question regarding the validity of eyewitness identification so that it can assume its proper place among the variety of evidence that can be brought against an accused person. Too accepting an attitude about eyewitness identification runs the risk of convicting innocent people, while extreme skepticism runs the risk of freeing guilty people.

The Issue

The primary issue perhaps becomes one of determining whether a particular eyewitness identification is accurate and trustworthy. It is not automatically accepting all such evidence as gospel, or automatically rejecting it as fundamentally so flawed as to be at best useless information and at worst dangerous to the innocent.

The hope is that the conclusions regarding eyewitness identification and testimony arrived at in this chapter will cause all participants in the criminal justice system (police, prosecutors, defence lawyers, and judges) to re-examine their beliefs about eyewitness evidence in an honest effort to determine whether those beliefs are supported by expert knowledge.

Since the beliefs people have about the significance of such evidence give the evidence its significance, it is important for all involved in the criminal justice system to have well-informed knowledge about how much importance eyewitness identification evidence should be accorded, both generally and specifically. Erroneous conceptions about human memory and eyewitness testimony can lead to incorrect verdicts.

Effects of Informed Juries

Permitting experts in eyewitness research to inform the juries about the social psychological findings about eyewitness identification accuracy might lower jurors' confidence in eyewitnesses and yield fewer guilty verdicts.[9] Research has shown that jurors who hear expert testimony about the weaknesses of eyewitness testimony subsequently rely on it less.

The research indicates that jurors do not completely dispense with their belief in the accuracy of the eyewitness, but that they modify it. Even when faced with strong evidence and eloquent testimony on the part of an expert, however, jurors often decide trials based on their own notions of what is true and accurate.[10]

The Empirical Picture

Experts in human cognition can assist the courts with both general and specific testimony. General expert testimony can focus on the nature of human memory and the differences between the popular view and the scientific view. The expert can then examine specific eyewitness identification evidence using the scientific model to determine how wrong (or right), how accurate (or inaccurate) the evidence might be, given what factors are known to introduce error into human memories.

The Power of Eyewitness Evidence

While psychologists believe that eyewitness identification may be a rather untrustworthy kind of evidence of guilt under the criminal law, Brigham and Bothwell found that approximately 84 per cent of jurors overestimated the accuracy of eyewitnesses.[11] In this study, jury-eligible Floridians read descriptions of experiments in which a crime or crime-like event was staged and the unwitting witnesses were asked to identify the perpetrator from a photo-spread lineup. When asked to estimate the percentage of witnesses who made a correct identification in these experiments, the respondents consistently overestimated in comparison to the actual percentages.

Jurors tend to believe that eyewitness identification is the most persuasive evidence in helping them render a guilty or not guilty verdict. To jurors and prosecutors, eyewitness identification is the closest thing to being indisputable.[12]

In a controlled laboratory study at the University of Washington, Loftus presented mock jurors (students) with a hypothetical robbery-murder case with circumstantial evidence but no eyewitness testimony.[13] In this situation, only 18 per cent of the mock jurors voted for conviction.

Other mock jurors received the same information but with the addition of a single eyewitness. In this condition, 72 per cent of the mock jurors voted for conviction. For a third group, the eyewitness testimony was discredited (the witness had 20/400 vision and was not wearing glasses) but 68 per cent of the mock jurors still voted for conviction. That is heavy reliance indeed on eyewitness testimony.

In England and Wales in 1973, the total number of persons accused of and prosecuted for a crime that were identified by an eyewitness was 850.[14] Of those 850 accused persons, there were 347 for whom the only evidence of guilt was the identification. Seventy-four per cent of the 347 were convicted. That is an important figure. It says that when there was no evidence of crime other than eyewitness identification, that evidence was judged to be sufficient for conviction in 74 per cent of all cases.

What is it about eyewitness testimony that is so appealing to jurors and police and prosecutors?

THE POPULAR VIEW OF EYEWITNESS EVIDENCE

Model

In order to answer this question, in part, it is necessary to consider the model of human information processing utilized by lay people (and that includes almost everyone who has not made a systematic study of human cognition).

Most people subscribe to an intuitive, common sense model of human perception and memory which encourages confidence in eye witness identification, because it describes visual memory in terms of photographic images (still or moving) and auditory memory in terms of sound recordings. This intuitive model also assumes fixed (permanent and immutable) sights and sounds and this is conducive to thinking of perception and memory as the one-to-one transfer of information with no loss and no distortion. If someone can recall, therefore, what she saw and/or overheard, that memory is accepted as a veridical representation of the event in question.

Lay people tend to believe that information, once acquired by the human memory system, is unchangeable, and that errors in memory result either from an inability to find stored information or from errors made during the original perception of the event.

This latter point was dramatically portrayed in the well-known play/film, *Twelve Angry Men*. Here, the jury finally voted 12 to 0 for acquittal, after it became clear to all that the eyewitness to the murder could not have not have seen the defendant as she claimed, because she was not wearing her eyeglasses at the time she witnessed the crime. The corollary of this, of course, is that, had she been wearing her glasses, her eyewitness evidence would have been believed and the jury would have voted 12 to 0 for conviction.

This fits with the common assumption that eyewitness misidentification occurs only at the time of the original perception. This means that for most people, the only way that eyewitness testimony can be discredited is to show that the witness could not have had seen or heard what she claims, because of conditions existing at the time of the original observations (e.g., too dark, too far away, too noisy).

The Reality of Misperception

Eyewitness identification also has an intrinsic value based on everyone's personal experience which, independent of other factors, makes people want to believe it. After all, facial recognition is something everybody knows something about. The experience of most people is that their facial recognition memory is better than their recall memory (e.g., I can remember meeting you once even though I cannot remember your name, what you were wearing, or what you said).

People who utilize the common sense model of memory do not appreciate that the ability to recognize familiar faces differs from the ability to recognize unfamiliar faces because the common sense model does not consider facial familiarity an important factor.[15]

Generally speaking, eyewitnesses are asked to identify faces they have only seen once, at the time of the crime. Because the common sense model makes no distinction between recognizing familiar and unfamiliar objects, however, those who subscribe to it do not appreciate that it can take people quite a while to learn to recognize unfamiliar faces and, as a result, their accuracy for this kind of target can be quite low.

It seems that since people know they are accurate with respect to familiar faces and because they rarely get any feedback regarding their ability to identify unfamiliar faces, people tend to think they are more accurate in recognizing unfamiliar faces than they may, in fact, be.

Another factor contributing to jurors' inflated confidence in the accuracy of eyewitness facial identification seems to come in part from people's common experience of being better at remembering faces than remembering names.[16] In general, people seem to have more confidence in visual memory (theirs and others) than in auditory memory.[17] Specifically, we can often be more confident, based on only one exposure, of recognizing a person's face than we can be about recalling what the person said, or what the person's voice sounded like.

Jurors are impressed with confident eyewitnesses who can provide a lot of detail because such testimony presents them with memories they can believe are based on good recording of the original perceptions. The common sense model of human memory does not allow for the altering of memories once they are deposited and recorded in the memory bank.

So it would never occur to jurors, on their own, that the eyewitness's confident and detail-laden memories may have been developed more as a result of events subsequent to the one in question, than to the original perception. The thought that original perceptions might just be the germ of a full-scale memory, in a way similar to how artists work as they create a work of art, is foreign to most people's thinking about human memory.

The common sense model does not consider that human memories are almost always works of art, partly fact and partly fiction. This means that, for the lay person, it does not matter how the memories are retrieved because, once stored, they are permanent and unchangeable and no process of extraction (e.g., police interviews, interviews with prosecutors, line-ups, photo displays, hypnosis) will alter or damage those memories in any way.

The popular view is that you either remember what happened or you don't, but that what you remember is true and how you came to remember is irrelevant.

Eyewitness Confidence

If the eyewitness is confident, the testimony is even more believable to jurors.[18] In Wells, Leippe, and Ostrom, it was the perceived confidence of the witness that chiefly determined whether she would be believed or not; the correlation between jurors' ratings of witness confidence and their tendency to believe witnesses was strongly positive, meaning that a confident eyewitness is a believable eyewitness. This is true in spite of the fact that Deffenbacher's review of 43 studies revealed that the relation between witness accuracy and witness confidence was, on average, very weak.[19]

Practical, Cultural, and Social Considerations

In addition, the more detailed the description, the more believable the testimony is to the jurors, even though those details might well have been added subsequent to the original perception as the witness did her best to recall everything seen or heard and as others (police and prosecutors) did their best to improve the witness's memory of the incident.

Juries tend to believe eyewitnesses if they make themselves available for testimony, have good memories of the defendants' faces, and remember the incidents clearly.[20] Juries believe likeable eyewitnesses[21] and juries believe confident eyewitnesses even though confidence and accuracy may not be related to each other.[22]

The belief in eyewitness testimony seems also to be rooted in practical, cultural, and social considerations which are served by the common sense model of human perception and memory.[23] For example, for those having to decide whether someone is guilty or not guilty, there is enormous appeal to being able to solve the "whodunnit" question through the identification of the culprit by someone who saw what happened and who did it.

The question of guilt has always been problematic because the guilty know how to lie and because most crimes are committed when there are no witnesses other than the culprit or culprits themselves. So, when presented with a situation where someone says they saw what happened, that becomes incredibly valuable information to those deciding whether someone is guilty or not.

The Roots of Misperception

In addition, eyewitness testimony fits right into our story-telling tradition which has been the fundamental way from time immemorial by which we humans have learned about the world around us, since none of us will have the time to see everything with our own eyes or hear everything with our own ears. We, therefore, rely on the eyes and ears of others to help us appreciate that which we have not directly experienced ourselves. We can use this second-hand, never directly experienced knowledge to make decisions about our lives and the lives of others.

It has undoubtedly been of survival value to believe what someone else tells us they have seen or heard until we get a chance to see it for ourselves. And, if someone says they saw something in the past that will never happen again, there is pressure to believe it, because we are never going to be able to prove it wrong. The event is gone and it is not coming back.

Since it is not psycho-economically cost effective to quarrel over unresolvable matters because of the energy expended and the damage done to the web of human relationships, if someone says with confidence that they saw something, then what is to be gained from refusing to believe? Being able to believe in what others, with no apparent axe to grind, tell us is part of the important glue that holds human communities together.

The idea of truthful eyewitness testimony seems to appeal to the notion that life would be a lot simpler and safer if we could rely on each other's word and knew that people were looking out for each other.[24] There is something powerfully romantic and idealistic about the image of people being as good as their word, and observant about what is going on in their community.

Societal Examples

The inherent power of eyewitness identification can be seen in programs designed to deter criminal activities. For example, the assumption underlying the various Neighbourhood Watch Programs whose symbol is the big eye overlooking the neighbourhood and watching for lawbreakers, seems to be that criminals, like everyone else, are also impressed with eyewitness identification evidence. As a consequence, they will avoid neighbourhoods in which there is a good chance that a concerned citizen will eyewitness their crimes because they will be as good as convicted.

Similarly, convex mirrors are often positioned in stores so that potential shop-lifters are reminded by their reflections that if they can see themselves, then maybe they are visible to others who can identify them.

The obvious appeal of eyewitness identification evidence to jurors is based on a common sense model of human perception and memory.

What is it that experts in human cognition know that could possibly deter jurors from automatically accepting eyewitness identification evidence as accurate and truthful?

THE SCIENTIFIC VIEW OF EYEWITNESS EVIDENCE

One thing experts know that jurors might not is the fact that people have been wrongly convicted on the basis of eyewitness misidentification. At this point, we cannot know for sure how many unnecessary charges have been laid by police and prosecuted by the Crown or how many innocent people have been found guilty only, or largely, because of eyewitness testimony.

That some innocent people have been convicted on the basis of eyewitness identification has been documented elsewhere.[25] Borchard discussed 65 certain cases of wrongful conviction in the United States; of those 65 errors, 29 resulted from mistakes of eyewitness identification.[26] Rattner was able to identify 205 "pure" cases of wrongful conviction (innocent beyond doubt) in the United States, and 52 per cent involved errors of false eyewitness identification evidence.[27]

Such evidence raises the question about how many other cases involve false witness identification but are not easily documented.[28] However interesting such cases are, they can tell us little, from the scientific point of view, about the true nature of eyewitness behaviour because it is not known how representative these cases are, relative to the entire range of trials in which eyewitnesses testify.

Eyewitness Inaccuracy

Fortunately, again from the scientific point of view, psychological research in the field and in the laboratory has been able to show that, in fact, eyewitnesses are not very accurate.[29] Eyewitnesses have been shown to have an accuracy level less than chance.[30] Yarmey concludes that eyewitness misidentifications are the rule rather than the exception.[31] Goldstein suggests that even in face recognition laboratory studies where the conditions are favourable for accurate identifications—the lighting is good, there is no physical threat to the observer, and observers are prepared to identify someone—the error is still 30 per cent and rarely falls below 15 per cent.[32]

In the laboratory study of face recognition there are typically two steps:

(1) A single exposure to one or more target faces for some short period of time; and

(2) Exposure to a set of faces with instructions to say of each one whether or not it has been seen before.

Many experiments, varying the parameters of the task, permit generalizations such as:

(1) The larger the number of target faces, the more difficult the task;

(2) The shorter the initial exposure time, the more difficult the task;

(3) The longer the interval between exposure and recognition, the more difficult the task;

(4) The closer the resemblance between target faces and distracter faces in the recognition array, the more difficult the task.[33]

Goldstein concludes from laboratory face recognition studies using a variety of faces and a broad sample of observers that the average error rate is too high to justify the faith juries, prosecutors, and police officers have in eyewitness identification. He argues that laboratory studies of face recognition provide the observer with an easier task than do most real world eyewitness situations. Consequently, the 30 per cent error described above should be considered a minimal estimate, rather than an overestimation of eyewitness identification error.[34]

The laboratory face recognition task is considered an easier task than culprit identification because:

(1) The subject in the laboratory knows from the beginning that she is going to be recognizing faces she has observed; witnesses are not so forewarned;

(2) The initial exposure in the laboratory is usually to a photo identical with the photo later to be recognized; such is not the case in eyewitness identification where the initial exposure is to a living face; and

(3) Laboratory studies usually use recognition arrays that are a random set of faces, not a closely matched set like the photo layout used by the police.

At the University of Alberta, Gary Wells and his associates have documented mock jurors' inflated confidence in eyewitness identification.[35] A theft is staged in a highly credible way. Someone has left a calculator behind in an experimental cubicle, and a newly arrived subject (actually a confederate) pops it in her purse under the eyes of a witness (real subject) and quickly exits. The experimenter asks what has become of the calculator; the witness tells the story, and the experimenter asks the witness to pick out the thief in a set of six pictures. At this point deception ends and the witness is interrogated before a set of mock jurors.

In Wells, Leippe, and Ostrom, only 58 per cent of the eyewitnesses to the staged theft made correct identifications, but mock jurors believed that 80 per cent of the eyewitnesses were accurate.[36]

In a related study, the conditions in which a theft was committed were varied in such a way as to make accurate identification very improbable, moderately probable, or highly probable.[37] Mock jurors, in deciding whether to believe witnesses, showed some sensitivity to the varying circumstances, but the main effect was a simple tendency to be credulous. Even when the situation made accuracy improbable and, in fact, only 30 per cent of witnesses were accurate in the improbable circumstances, mock jurors still believed that 60 per cent of the eyewitnesses under perceptually adverse circumstances were accurate.

Brigham and Bothwell showed that 83.7 per cent of prospective jurors substantially overestimated the accuracy of eyewitness identification in their study of convenience store clerks' recognition of customer faces.[38]

A 1982 field study of how good convenience store clerks were at recognizing the faces of customers revealed that, even with unusually good opportunities to study the customers' faces, the overall rate of accurate recognition was 34.2 per cent, which is not very high considering that the chance level was 16.7 per cent.[39] If 24 hours passed between initial encounter and the photo identification, selections were not better than chance; that is, there was no evidence of any recognition at all.

With only the very short interval of two hours, there was some recognition.

However plausible eyewitness testimony might sound, research shows that:

(1)　The agreement of a large number of witnesses is no guarantee of eyewitness identification accuracy;

(2)　Friends and acquaintances of the person identified have sometimes made errors;

(3)　Trained observers (the police) have been in error;

(4)　No amount of confidence on the eyewitness's part precludes error; and

(5)　Errors have been made in capital cases (the death penalty) when one would have thought an eyewitness would feel some obligation to be cautious.[40]

Buckhout, using various staged crimes, has put together a consistent picture of eyewitness unreliability.[41] In some variations, he has found that an innocent bystander to a crime is almost as likely to be picked as the actual perpetrator. In Buckhout's 1980 study, which involved a 13-second film of a highly representative purse-snatching, it was found that only 14.1 per cent of over 2,000 viewers picked the actual mugger out of a lineup film of six men. This is slightly worse than a random guess with six possibilities, since 16.7 per cent should be correct by chance.

Caution

In Britain, the Devlin Report recommended that the trial judge be required to instruct the jury that it is not safe to convict upon eyewitness testimony alone except in exceptional circumstances (a close friend or relative) or when there is substantial corroborative evidence.[42] The thrust of the report is that prosecutions based on nothing but eyewitness identification should fail.

Just as it was necessary to understand lay people's confidence in eyewitness identification in terms of a common sense theory or model of human perception and memory, it is necessary to understand the model utilized by experts in human cognition if we are to appreciate further why they can be, and often are, skeptical about the veridicality of eyewitness identification evidence.

HUMAN INFORMATION PROCESSING

General

Generally speaking, human information processing (including eye-witness identification as a specific example) is understood by theoreticians and researchers in human cognition to be composed of three dynamic and interrelated phases:

(1) *The acquisition phase* during which an event is perceived and information about it is initially stored in short-term memory;

(2) *The retention phase* during which information about the event is transferred to long-term memory; and

(3) *The retrieval phase* during which the memory of the event is searched and pertinent information is recovered and communicated.

Figure 1 is a schematic representation of the scientific model of human memory.

Figure #1: A simple scheme for the memory process

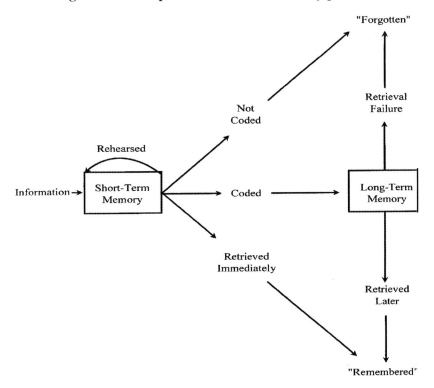

The Acquisition Phase

The first stage involved in perceiving and remembering an event (in particular, a crime) includes such conditions at the time the event occurs as:

(1) The length of time the event took;

(2) The amount and type of available light;

(3) The distance between the witness and the perpetrator;

(4) The perspective of the witness *vis-à-vis* the event;

(5) Any disguise the perpetrator might have been wearing;

(6) The witness's state of mind (interested, bored, terrified, angry); and

(7) Any distractions present in the situation.

All of this information has to be put within the context of the witness's personal history, the level of the witness's self-confidence, and the limits of this particular witness's information processing capabilities.

The witness brings to the situation particular human information processing capacities (attentional, perceptual, memorial, and descriptive) as well as a personal history which conditions a set of expectations of self and others through which the observations are filtered. In addition, the emotional and motivational state of the witness, brought on by the act of witnessing, will be a factor in what is perceived and remembered.

Situational demands (e.g., the actions of the alleged culprit, including the time involved, the distance involved, and the witness's perspective *vis-à-vis* the alleged culprit) also influence the perceptual and memorial abilities of the witness.

From a scientific point of view, it is necessary to consider all these issues, in order to clarify what exactly a particular eyewitness could actually have seen and overheard. That is, given who the eyewitness was and the circumstances surrounding the observed event, what kinds of perceptions is it likely that the eyewitness would have had? What information is it likely that the eyewitness acquired in the first place?

Here, we are interested in getting a fix on the likely nature of the original perceptions prior to any intention on the part of the witness to remember what was perceived.

As Wells has documented, this original perception is influenced by such event factors as exposure time and conditions and the seriousness of the crime.[43] In addition, there are witness factors such as stress, eye fixation, visual and auditory acuity, expectations, age, sex, race, alcohol and drugs which also influence what could have been seen or overheard. Finally, the nature of the original perception is a function of the cognitive limits of humans engaged in person perception.[44]

Innocent Bystander Bias

One startling example is that eyewitnesses even identify innocent bystanders as the culprit.[45] Loftus has called the phenomenon of identifying a person who had been present during the crime, but was, in fact, an innocent bystander "unconscious transference"[46] sometimes referred to as unconscious modification.[47] What seems to be happening here is that the witness integrates the face of the bystander, which is mildly familiar, into the memory of the crime. When presented with that face again, the witness is confident of the identification.

It is to be expected that during a crime, eyewitnesses are likely to be afraid, and thus are likely to be more concerned with their own safety than with carefully and dispassionately observing the criminal. Even in those situations in which the eyewitness's attention is riveted on the culprit, there is no guarantee the identification will be accurate.

Weapon Focus Hypothesis

If a weapon is involved, chances are that the eyewitness will focus on the weapon to the exclusion of everything else. Loftus, *et al.*, in support of the "weapon focus hypothesis", found that subjects who viewed an armed robbery.[48]

(1)   Spent a great deal of time looking at the weapon;
(2)   Were unlikely to correctly identify the person involved; and
(3)   Were unlikely to recall details about this individual.

Own Race Bias

Research has also shown that people are more likely to notice differences among the members of groups with which they are familiar, in comparison to differences among members of unfamiliar groups.[49] Given this tendency, it is not surprising that the race of the eyewitness and of the suspect is an important factor in eyewitness accuracy.

In a number of experiments, Brigham has shown an own-race identification bias in eyewitness identification, meaning that people are more accurate in identifying targets of their own race than targets of a different race.[50]

People seem to be aware of the facial cues that differentiate one member of their own group from the other, most likely because it is more important for them to do so, and because they interact with them more frequently.

The "other" group members seem all to "look alike" however, perhaps because people do not interact with them as often. People are just more familiar with the variety of facial features characterizing members of their own group. The own-race identification bias also suggests that the more cross-racial experience a person has, the less likely that person will be a victim of race bias in identifying people.[51]

Focus of Attention

The acquisition of information depends on both where and how a person attends. For example, when people have been asked to examine faces for the purpose of either making judgments of physical features (e.g., size of nose, type of mouth) or for the purpose of judging personality traits (e.g., honesty, kindness), those who made trait judgments were better at recognizing those faces subsequently.[52]

Expectations

The acquisition of information also depends on expectations. Photofit reconstructions of a face that people previously saw tended to be "swarthy" if the witness was led to believe that the person was a mass murderer rather than a lifeboat captain.[53]

Ongoing Process

The acquisition of information is an ongoing process. While acquisition can be thought of as occurring while the eyewitness is viewing the event, things that occur prior to the event can also affect acquisition to the extent that the prior events create expectations.

As well, new acquisitions occur continually after witnessing the event and these new acquisitions can alter what is represented in memory.

In one study, people watched a film of an auto accident and it was subtly suggested to some of them that the cars "smashed" while others heard the label "hit". These labels affected the viewers' estimates of speed and their later reports as to whether or not they saw broken glass.[54]

What the scientific research indicates is that the information that an eyewitness puts into short-term memory about an event is not necessarily accurate. This is in complete opposition to the popular view of perception held by most people. Furthermore, as we shall see, transferring the information from short-term to long-term memory (retention) often distorts the information as does the process of remembering (retrieval).

The scientific view is that most eyewitness identification evidence is based on initially flawed information stored in short-term storage which is further flawed as it is placed in long-term storage and then finally flawed by the process of recollection.

The Retention Phase

The second stage involved in perceiving and remembering an event, such as a crime, refers to the interval between when the crime was committed and when the eyewitness first attempts to recall in words what she observed and then to identify (recognize) the criminal from a live or photo lineup. This is the period of time during which the witness is transferring the information about the event from short-term memory into long-term memory. The length of the interval can range from a few minutes to several months or even years. This interval includes what rehearsal the witness does in order to fasten information about the event securely in long-term memory as well as whatever post-event information might influence the nature of the information retained.[55]

Loftus' work raises a number of questions about the whole process of questioning witnesses, whether by police investigators prior to trial or by counsel during trial. In both cases, the questions that are asked may deposit in memory information that radically alters subsequent testimony.

The information acquired during the acquisition phase and the information acquired during the retention phase can become inextricably integrated, and the person may, therefore, be unable to distinguish them at the retrieval stage.

Once the memory for some event is distorted by intervening events, the information acquired during perception of the original event may never be recovered.[56]

The Retrieval Phase

The third stage involved in perceiving and remembering an event, such as a crime, occurs when the person attempts to "retrieve" the image from memory in order to give a free recall narrative or answers to specific questions from a police interviewer, and then maybe recognize (identify) the criminal from lineup (live or photo). This phase includes how the manner of gathering the eyewitness evidence from the memory of the witness influences what is remembered about the event in question. The identification process is governed not only by memorial processes but also by extra-memorial factors.[57]

Lay Person's Model of Memory

The common sense model of human memory takes no notice of how the witness's memory was retrieved, just whether it was retrieved or not. The common sense model does not consider that the recovery of memories can in any way alter or distort the memories that were originally recorded. Therefore, it does not matter how one gets the memories out of storage because the memories, once recorded, are indestructible.

Expert's Model of Memory

The expert model of memory, on the other hand, as well as breaking down the process of human memory into three discrete but highly interactive phases, also assumes that perceptual and memorial information is highly malleable, and various factors can distort memories during all three phases (acquisition, retention, and retrieval), not just during acquisition as the common sense model implies.

Experts understand that stored information is unstable, highly malleable and subject to change and distortion by events (such as misleading questions or overheard conversations) occurring during the retention stage in addition to those factors that can distort memories during acquisition and retrieval.

From the expert's perspective, what is recalled cannot necessarily be considered a veridical portrayal of the original event, primarily be cause human perception, information processing, and memory are all elastic and malleable processes.

According to the experts' conceptualization of human perception and memory, there are many opportunities for honest misidentification from the acquisition of the information through its retention to its retrieval. Eyewitness error is thus a joint product of inherent human cognitive limitations and the methods that are used to obtain information from eyewitnesses.[58]

MEMORY RETRIEVAL METHODS

Police Interviews

The initial method of retrieving information from eyewitnesses to a crime usually involves a police interview. According to Fisher and

Geiselman, the standard police interviewing procedure makes two critical mistakes that can distort and interfere with a witness's memory.[59]

(1) The first mistake is the use of early and frequent interruptions by the interviewer with questions to get answers from the witness.

(2) The second mistake is to begin the interviewing of the witness with a preconceived notion of what happened and then try to get the witness to fill in the blanks.

This kind of interviewing encourages the witness to embellish (unconsciously) details in order to satisfy the demands of the interview.

Hypnosis

Even though there is no research evidence that eyewitness identification can be improved through hypnosis, hypnosis is used as an investigative tool by police in some jurisdictions. Hypnosis is currently big business in the American criminal justice system. Several thousand criminal justice personnel have had some training in it, usually via a three-day seminar.

The following guidelines have been utilized at the Los Angeles Police Department to help ensure that hypnosis interviews are conducted in a professional and ethical manner:[60]

(1) The hypnosis project director screens all requests for investigative hypnosis to determine appropriateness.

(2) The hypnosis session is conducted by a qualified hypno-investigator or health professional.

(3) Informed consent is obtained from the subject or guardian.

(4) The entire hypnosis session is recorded on audiotape or videotape.

(5) The person conducting the hypnosis session shall not be otherwise involved in the conduct of the investigation in which the subject was a victim or witness.

(6) Hypnosis interviews will be conducted with volunteer witnesses but not with suspects or defendants.

(7) The welfare of the hypnosis subject is primary and takes precedence over any other considerations.

Hypnosis involves a state of heightened suggestibility. It may also include "posthypnotic amnesia" in which, on instruction from the hypnotist, the events that occurred during hypnosis may be forgotten.

Hypnosis as a memory enhancer is very appealing to the popular conception of human memory of photographic images and sound recordings because people think of hypnosis as a process by which the photos are enlarged and the sounds are amplified, thereby clarifying identification.

The main reservations which experts have about using hypnosis are that:

(1) It is unreliable as a memory enhancer (see Smit[61] for a review);
(2) It leads to increased error or confabulation;[62] and
(3) It renders eyewitnesses hypersuggestible to leading questions.[63]

The Cognitive Interview

An empirically based alternative to both the standard police interview and hypnotism as a memory enhancer involves conducting cognitive interviews with witnesses.[64] The cognitive interview procedure is designed to enhance the recollection of eyewitnesses to crime. Although the cognitive interview is an information-gathering device for the prosecution (police), the technique should be equally useful for the defence as it is not biased toward eliciting exculpatory evidence.

Benefits

Although the cognitive interview has the potential to be an effective investigative instrument, its utility will vary from one situation to another. Its primary contribution is in cases like commercial robbery, assault or battery, where the bulk of the evidence comes from eyewitness reports, as opposed to crimes where there is an abundance of physical evidence.

The cognitive interview was designed to be used with cooperative eyewitnesses. Those who wish to withhold information intentionally will not be "broken" by the cognitive interview.

Drawbacks

A fair amount of time is required to conduct the cognitive interview properly. Thus, it cannot be used effectively when time is limited. The cognitive interview requires considerable mental concentration on the part of the interviewer. She must make more on-line decisions and show greater flexibility than is typically demanded in police interviews. It is thus more difficult to conduct the cognitive interview than the standard interview.

Summary

Research suggests that the cognitive interview leads to more information, fewer errors, fewer leading questions, and less influence from misleading information.[65]

Confrontations

Various confrontation procedures (lineups: live or video, show-ups, photo-displays, police sketches) have been developed to enable the eye witness to identify the culprit. The purpose of a confrontation is to uncover, in an eyewitness's recognition memory, information that was not available in recall.

Live lineups, videotaped lineups, or photo arrays do not seem to produce substantial differences in identification performance.[66] Based on what is currently known, therefore, identifications from photo arrays should not be given less weight in investigations or in trials than identifications from live lineups.

Although live lineups, videotaped lineups, and photo arrays are apparently comparable identification performances, they have different implications for legal procedure, such as the defendant's rights to counsel during the identification test (see, for example, Wells & Cutler).[67]

Research has shown that lineup procedures can be altered to reduce dramatically the probability of false identification.[68] One researcher goes so far as to suggest that highly biased lineups (using foils who are dissimilar in appearance to the suspect) are more likely the product of intentional police misconduct than either incompetence or indifference on the part of police.[69]

A more typical reason for why witnesses misidentify suspects is because they use a level of familiarity normally adequate for a recognition decision alone (e.g., "that face looks familiar") as the basis for an identification decision (e.g., "that is the person who robbed me").[70] Basically, the misidentification comes from the pressure of having to decide who looks familiar enough to be the suspect and believing that the suspect is in the lineup.

Accurate witnesses (reporting an externally generated memory of a face) appear to make their identification without much cognitive effort, as evidenced by the reaction time data and report of decision-making processes. By comparison, inaccurate witnesses (who reported an internally generated "false" memory) use a recognition strategy that requires more effort and time.[71]

Fair Lineups

Obviously, one way to reduce the number of eyewitness misidentifications is to attempt to be sure that the identification process, such as the lineup, is done fairly. Among other things, the non-suspects placed in the lineup (known as "foils" or "fillers") should resemble the target as much as possible to reduce the number of false-positive identifications.[72] Further, the witness should be given the option of saying "I don't know", thus lessening some of the pressure to make an identification.

Potential witnesses can also be trained to give more accurate identifications. Wells had witnesses see a lineup composed entirely of innocent people.[73] Those witnesses who were shown that they had incorrectly picked an innocent person in this false lineup were then much more accurate when shown the real lineup. The experience of being wrong made them much more careful.

Wells, *et al.*, recommend that the following procedures, based on empirical research results, should ensure fairer identification procedures.[74] They use the term lineup to include live and videotaped lineups as well as photo displays.

(1) Verbal descriptions of the culprit should be obtained from all eyewitnesses prior to conducting a lineup.

(2) A lineup should contain at least five appropriate distracters for every one suspect.

(3) Distracters should be chosen to match the eyewitness's verbal description of the culprit.

(4) In cases where the eyewitness's description of the culprit does not match the suspect's appearance, the suspect's appearance on the discrepant feature(s) should be used rather than the eyewitness's description of that (those) feature(s).

(5) The set of potential distracters who match the description should exceed the number of distracters needed, so that any who show undue resemblance to the suspect can be discarded from the set that is used.

(6) Separate lineups should be conducted for each eyewitness in multiple-witness cases. Minimally, the positioning of the sus-

pect and foils should be different for each lineup; in some cases different distracters should be used.

(7) The lineup administrator should not be aware of which person in the lineup is the suspect and which persons are distracters.

(8) The eyewitness should be told explicitly that the perpetrator might or might not be in the lineup. This statement should be made when the eyewitness is initially asked to view a lineup and again just prior to viewing the lineup.

(9) The eyewitness should first be asked to indicate whether or not the culprit is present in the lineup, and only if the eyewitness makes an affirmative response, should she be asked to indicate which lineup member is the culprit in question.

(10) If an eyewitness identifies someone from the lineup, the eyewitness should be asked how certain she is that the identified person is the culprit. This question should immediately follow the identification response so that no extraneous factors can influence the eyewitness's statement of certainty.

(11) All phases and aspects of the lineup should be meticulously recorded, preferably using videotape.

(12) Acceptable variations to the standard lineup procedure in which a suspect is embedded among distracters and the entire set of lineup members is presented at one time to the eyewitness include:

(i) The blank-lineup control procedure in which the eyewitness is presented with two lineups, one containing the suspect and the other not[75] and

(ii) The sequential lineup which presents one lineup member at a time and the eyewitness is asked to make a decision (is this person the culprit?) of yes or no for each person viewed at the time of initial presentation.[76] By forcing the eyewitness to make a yes or no decision for each lineup member without knowing what the remaining members look like, the eyewitness is forced away from relative judgments and made to rely more on an absolute comparison between the lineup member being viewed at the time, and her memory of the culprit.

EARWITNESS IDENTIFICATION

Although most of the focus in this chapter has been on eyewitness facial identification, a witness is entitled to give evidence of identity based on voice recognition. The weight to be afforded the evidence is an issue for the trier of fact. Some of the factors that might affect weight would be previous familiarity with the voice, the stress and attention level of the witness, any distinctive characteristics of the voice, and length of delay between time of exposure and time of identification.

In the same manner that facial identification may be wrong, so may voice identification. In fact, voice identification may be even more subject to error than facial identification, because of the limited number of distinguishing characteristics and the fact that voices change with variations in mood. It may be very easy to recognize the voice of a famous person, but describing that voice to another may be virtually impossible. The jury might therefore often be asked to accept on "blind faith" the assertion, "that is the voice". Earwitness (voice) identification appears to be even less reliable than eyewitness identification.[77]

Deutscher and Leonoff offer the following list of issues to be considered when trying to evaluate the accuracy of voice identification evidence:[78]

(1) Was the witness previously familiar with the voice?
(2) Is the voice distinctive in any way, in such things as tone or expression, so as to separate it from other voices?
(3) Were the circumstances where the witness identified the voice sufficiently similar to the circumstances where the voice was first heard to lead to the conclusion that the voice would show the same characteristics in both situations?
(4) Was the voice disguised?

As with eyewitness evidence, any evaluation of earwitness evidence has to also consider that an honest and confident witness may still be mistaken and that the witness's stress and attention level at the time of the event affects perception and memory as does the length of delay between the original encounter and the identification procedure. The matter of how best to judge what is seen and heard was summed reasonably well by Smokey Robinson when he sang, "Believe half of what you see and none of what you hear" ("I Heard It Through the Grapevine").

VISUAL REPRESENTATIONS

Verbal descriptions of suspects are frequently supplemented by portraits of their faces based on descriptions given by the witness. However, there is no generally accepted technique for producing a finished portrait, and different police forces utilize artists in different ways.[79]

Police Artists

In the United States, artists are employed by only 200 of 2,000 police departments. Most police artists are police officers who have shown an interest in this form of work. The normal mode of these artists' operation is to interact directly with the witnesses, gradually producing a portrait in their presence. While training courses and instruction manuals have been developed,[80] there is little consistency in the methods they advocate and empirical data concerning their success rate are not available.

Homa and Cormack both suggest that interviews by the artist should begin by eliciting a verbal description from the witness. The artist then attempts to establish more precisely the type of feature described, directing the witness's attention to reference material, such as photographs of representative faces (Homa) or freehand drawings of the ranges of a given facial feature (Cormack). Only at this point is a preliminary sketch improvised. After an approximate facial structure has been negotiated, hair, scars and similar details are added to provide the finished product.

Not all police forces advocate direct interaction between the witness and the artist. For instance, the Federal Bureau of Investigation employs a small number of highly trained artists at their headquarters in Washington, D.C. All interviews are conducted in the field, by agents who carry a set of some 2,000 reference photographs that are also kept in the Washington office.

Details are provided to the artists by telephone and form the basis of a sketch that is quickly transmitted from the headquarters to the field agent by facsimile. Using the telephone, the witness may then suggest necessary modifications to the artist, who then transmits the final drawing. No systematic assessments have been made of this procedure, but a 35 per cent clearance rate has been claimed.[81]

Composite Systems

Few police departments can justify the cost of employing a full-time police artist, and many rely upon commercially manufactured kits of facial components. The American Identikit and the British Photofit are the best known.[82]

Most composite systems advocate an initial interview with the witness, during which a detailed verbal description is elicited. The attention of the witness is then directed to facial components that seem most relevant to the description provided, and the witness is asked to select the most appropriate components.

The number of alternative features from which the witness selects varies greatly among the available systems. These facial features are supplemented with such accessories as hats, scars, and eyeglasses.

After the witness has made a selection of relevant components, the operator synthesizes these into a total "face" that can be shown to the witness for comment. Amendments can then be made, either by exchanging features or by modifying their appearance through the use of a wax pencil applied to the surface of the composite. Pencilled amendments to the hair components are frequently made.

The aim of many police artists is to produce a finished and lifelike portrait.[83] However, the philosophy underlying the original Identikit, and such successors as the Field Identification System[84] is to produce a schematic line drawing that illustrates a general facial type. On the other hand, Photofit and the Identikit II strive for a realistic impression by using components derived from photographs of actual facial features.

This search for realism has been carried a stage further by the introduction of colour in some of the more recent systems. The prototype Magnaface system assembles a composite picture from coloured photographs of facial features that are blended together, where the Videofit colours up a standard monochrome composite picture and removes intrusive boundary lines between features.[85]

Given the widespread use of these and similar systems in police investigations, it is surprising that little information exists on their operational effectiveness, in absolute terms or compared to that of the police artist. There are wide variations in the frequency with which different police forces utilize artist[86] and composite technicians.[87] The choice seems to be based on the particular experience and preferences of the investigating officers.[88]

Researchers have distributed follow-up questionnaires to investigating officers in cases where Photofit composites had been produced. Of the cases which had been successfully resolved after two months of investigation, officers estimated that composites had been "entirely responsible" (5 per cent) or "very useful" (17 pre cent) for solving the case. However, these figures must be interpreted in light of the 20 per cent of cases in which the composites had been of "no use at all".[89]

To judge from a more recent survey summarized by Bennett,[90] Photofit has not greatly improved the clearance rates for cases. The composites in these cases examined in the later survey were judged to be "good" likenesses of the suspect in seven cases, "fair" in three cases, and "poor" in four cases.

These results were based on the use of Photofit, but there is no reason to believe that they are unrepresentative of composite systems as a whole.[91] It is of interest to explain the apparent ineffectiveness of such devices.

Improving Composite Performance

The simplest explanation for the poor performance of subjects who used Photofit is that witnesses are not particularly good at remembering faces. Although recall of facial detail is indeed poor, this seems insufficient to explain the difficulties of producing accurate composites, since subjects are reasonably competent at recognizing faces under laboratory conditions.[92]

This suggests that certain facial information has been internalized, and Christie and Elli[93] demonstrated that the initial verbal descriptions provided by witnesses under laboratory conditions proved to be a better guide to likeness than the subsequent Photofit pictures themselves. In addition, they found no relationship between the accuracy of the description provided by witnesses and the quality of their composites.

Both results have since been replicated using samples of juvenile witnesses.[94] It appears that composite kits such as Photofit fail to transmit existing information effectively from the witness to the user of the created composite.

A second possibility is that existing composite systems are basically sound but are not being used effectively. Composite technicians and artists receive little in the way of formal training.[95]

A study that compared a novice to a highly experienced composite operator, suggested that the quality of the likeness achieved by the latter was significantly higher and resulted from differences in the techniques used to elicit information.[96] The experienced operator took much longer to establish the initial description and showed the witness a smaller ranger of features. Both strategies were associated with better composite quality.[97]

There is clearly room for improvement in existing equipment, and there is also a need for a more fundamental analysis of the problem of facial recall. Existing systems appear to be based on a logical rather than a psychological analysis of the process of composition of faces, and it is important to align more clearly any new system with the dynamics of facial perception and memory as revealed by experimental research. Some insight into these issues can be gained by consideration of some of the areas of conflict and controversy in the design and development of aids to recall of faces.

Type Likeness versus Realistic Portrait

One source of controversy for both artist and composite technician is the optimal level of realism to be attained. The debate between advocates of the schematic Identikit and the photograph-based Photofit is paralleled by the debate between artists who opt for a three-dimensional portrait appearance and those who advocate two-dimensional sketches.

At one extreme, unaccented and unshaded line drawings of the kind typified by the Identikit are extremely difficult to recognize, even when the face represented is a very familiar one.

Faces of celebrities presented in photographs are four times as likely to be recognized as the same pictures transcribed into line form.[98] Even the use of a professional caricature is not sufficient to rival the superiority of a monochrome photograph.[99]

It could be argued that photographs are veridical portraits, and it is of interest to determine whether they have advantages over the approximate likenesses more typically represented by police composites.

Davies identified two groups of Photofit pictures generated by volunteers in a previous laboratory study, one group consisting of good likenesses of target faces and the other of poor likenesses.[100] From these composites he derived a parallel set of line transcriptions of the Photofits to provide a level of detail that approximated the original Identikit.

These two sets of composites were then matched to a third group of artists' impressions. The latter were created by giving an experienced police artist each of the original Photofit pictures, along with their associated verbal descriptions, and asking her to create a portrait from them.

The three sets of materials varied in their degree of animation and realism, ranging from flat outlines represented by the line transcriptions of the conventional Photofit, to the realistic, shaded portraits produced by the police artist. Their relative effectiveness as cues to recognition was assessed by asking subjects to identify the original target faces previously presented in a mug file. Overall, the Photofit pictures emerged as the best guide to likeness, followed by the line transcriptions. The portraits ranked a poor third.

While all three sets of material were identified at above-chance levels, the comparative failure of the portraits may be attributed to the tendency of the artist to go beyond the information given to produce a comprehensive and lifelike picture construed by the witness as a specific individual rather than a general type. It appears that the elusive goal of the Photofit system to obtain realism without specificity was achieved.

The Artist as an Aid or Hindrance to Witness Memory?

Another area of lively debate among police personnel concerns the appropriate point at which the artist/technician should interview the witness; should it be a first priority or a last resort? Underlying this debate are concerns about the impact of the face recall interview itself on the memory of the witness and whether the demands of the task will bias subsequent testimony.

The impact of face recall on subsequent person identification has been the subject of a number of studies, the outcomes of which have been far from consistent. Mauldin and Laugher[101] contrasted the effect of verbal recall of a face and production of an Identikit picture on subsequent ability to recognize the person represented in a mug file. Identikit construction facilitated recognition of the target, whereas verbally describing the face produced no clear effect.

These findings should be contrasted with those of Davies, et al.,[102] who found no effect of Photofit reconstruction on subsequent identification, and with those of Hall,[103] who reported a significant impairment of recognition following production of an artist's impression of the target.

Subsequent studies have failed to clarify the issue. Thompson and Laughery[104] replicated the original facilitation effect for the Identikit, and Wogalter, Laughery, and Thompson[105] reported similar effects when the Field Identification System was employed. However, these positive findings contrast with the significant impairments to recognition reported by Comish[106] regarding Identikit construction and by Schooler[107] regarding description production.

Davies suggested that the solution to this conflict may lie in the quality of the resulting composites or descriptions, rather than in the production process itself.[108] Jenkins and Davies[109] have shown that observation of a misleading composite can impair subsequent recognition of a target face. If the subjects themselves generate the errors during production of their own composites, this seems likely to impair recognition.

In the 1987 Schooler study, a week elapsed between the observation and the request for a description. Conversely, facilitation has been observed with very short time delays between initial observation and recall, often no more than 30 minutes and never more than two days.

Under these conditions, opportunities for trace information to be impaired or otherwise suffer deterioration have been minimized. As Laughery and his colleagues have noted, the face recall task may provide the opportunity for additional rehearsal of the target image and thus facilitate subsequent recognition (see Read).[110]

If this interpretation is correct, then one might expect accuracy in composite production to be correlated with subsequent recognition preferences. This effect has been observed on some occasion[111] but not on others.[112] Moreover, an inverse relationship between recall and recognition could be the result of the differing encoding demands of the two retrieval tasks, rather than the carry-over of erroneous information from one task to the other.[113]

Aside from the particular interpretation, current findings underline the need for training and caution among those responsible for interviewing witnesses. Unlike a verbal description, production of a face demands recall of all major features that will maximize reconstructive error among witnesses whose memory for the face has begun to fade.

Sketches and Composites

There are many police officers who argue that the artist's impression is preferable to the composite method because of the superior quality of likeness achieved, despite the disparity in operational costs.[114] Support for such a view comes from a laboratory comparison of sketches produced by trained artists and results obtained by technicians using the original Identikit.

Volunteers who talked casually with a stranger for 7 to 8 minutes achieved with the artist, likenesses of the stranger that were rated higher than those who worked with the Identikit.[115] The sketches also served as a better guide to locate the targets in a mug file than did the composites.[116]

In a subsequent detailed analysis of the production demands of the two tasks, Laughery, *et al.*, suggested that the sketch artist elicited more information from the witnesses and gave the witnesses greater time and opportunity to arrive at final versions of each facial attribute.[117] These findings reflect a general characteristic of the sketch artist.

Unlike the composite technician, the artist has an unlimited repertoire of features, compared to the fixed number available in the kits. In this respect, the apparent superiority of the sketch over the composite parallels the superiority of the cued description over the prompted description.

However, in both instances this potential superiority must be qualified by practical considerations, such as the availability of an artist gifted enough to provide the necessary flexibility, and a witness with sufficient verbal fluency to describe the appearance of the suspect.

Computerized Composite Systems

In recent years, the availability of computer graphics at modest costs has encouraged a number of manufacturers to develop identification packages. Comphotofit allows the witness and operator to build a Photofit picture on the computer screen in much the same manner as the conventional Photofit system. Features stored in the computer can be stretched or reduced to improve the likeness. Skin tone adjustment ensures that boundary lines between features are eliminated, and a painting facility allows limited colouring of the synthesized face.

The final composite may be photographed or printed on a high-resolution graphics printer. Similar systems have been developed to take advantage of the graphics capabilities of the Apple MacIntosh computer.

As yet, little empirical research has been conducted on this new generation of composite systems. They seem to have advantages over more traditional composite methods, yet they depend on many of the same assumptions as their predecessors about how faces are stored and retrieved from memory.

Research on the original prototype computer system suggested that the similarity of likenesses achieved by volunteer witnesses was no better, or even slightly poorer, than those with the conventional Photofit.[118] It will be unfortunate if increased technological ingenuity is not accompanied by appropriate allowances for the psychological factors that underlie facial perception and recall.

UNJUSTIFIED CONFIDENCE

Expert testimony on eyewitness issues easily meets the legal criteria of admissibility. Most people, however:

(1) have little idea of how to evaluate the accuracy of an eyewitness identification;
(2) underestimate the importance of many relevant variables; and
(3) apply significantly wrong expectations regarding other variables.[119]

Lay people (e.g., anyone who is not a cognitive psychologist) have a faith in eyewitness identification which is not always justified. Eyewitness testimony has an enormous credibility in jury trials, in part at least because lay people (potential jurors) often have erroneous beliefs about human memory and eyewitness testimony that can lead to incorrect verdicts.

Few police officers, and even fewer jurors, are aware of the psychological findings about eyewitnesses. While some psychologists have given expert testimony as to the accuracy of eyewitnesses, such testimony has not yet been routinely used by the courts.[120]

The Role of the Expert

The role of the expert is to help the court assess the credibility of the evidence, if at all possible. Scientists do this by looking for factors that would cause them to doubt the veracity of the evidence. The more doubt, the less the credibility.

Scientists like to work with two competing hypotheses. In any particular case, the eyewitness memory is either highly positively correlated with the original event or it is not. It cannot be both.

The expert can then, for the benefit of the court, take apart the naturalistic field study (the crime, the police investigation and the prosecution of the case) that produced the memory in question, to determine what relationship the memory now bears to the precipitating event (the crime).

From a methodological point of view, the weaker the naturalistic field study, the poorer the data, which in this case, are the memories. This occurs because a memory is not just a product of a precipitating event, but also of other factors preceding and subsequent to that event. If it can be shown that nothing else could have influenced the memory, then maybe, just maybe, said memory is a product solely of the observed event itself.

Experts can provide, for the court, an overview of current empirical research on eyewitness testimony and identification accuracy, covering both theory and application. Three issues are important in this regard:

(1) First, what are the cognitive, social, and physical factors that influence the accuracy of eyewitness reports?

(2) Second, how should memory retrieval tasks be conducted (lineup construction and collection of testimony) to improve the chances of obtaining accurate information? and

(3) Third, whose testimony should be believed (i.e., are there differences between accurate and inaccurate witnesses, and can jurors make such a distinction)?

General Expert Testimony

In terms of general expert testimony, the expert can educate the court on the nature of human memory. As Loftus reports:[121]

> Memory does not work like a videotape recorder; people do not sit and passively take in information, recording it the way a videotape recorder would record it. Rather, they take in information in bits and pieces, from different sources, at different times, and integrate this information together. In a sense, people actually construct memories...
>
> Psychologists make a distinction between three major phases in the memory process: the acquisition phase, the retention phase, and the retrieval phase. During the acquisition phase, one actually witnesses some event, takes in information about it. This is followed by the retention phase, the period of time in which information resides in memory before it is needed. Finally, there is the retrieval phase, the time during which people are asked questions about their recollection and they respond. At this time the contents of the memory are revealed. Many factors come into play that affect the accuracy and completeness of an eyewitness's report at each of these three stages.

Basically, circumstances beginning with perceiving and continuing through remembering can influence what is remembered, whether the event happened or not.

Specific Expert Testimony

With regard to specific expert testimony, following the overview of human memory, the expert can discuss those relevant psychological factors affecting eyewitness testimony for the particular case under consideration. These factors might include the following:

(1)   The retention interval, the period of time between the incident and the witness's recollection of that incident.

(2)   Stress, presuming that witnessing certain crimes would be stressful.

(3)   Weapon focus, in the event that a weapon was used in the commission of the crime.

(4)   The cross-racial identification phenomenon.

(5)   The factor of post event information.

(6)   Unconscious transference.[122]

(7)   People's tendency to overestimate the duration of a complex event, which means that they had less time than they think to extract some information from the event.

(8) Misleading or suggestive questions can distort eyewitness memory, and eyewitnesses can come to believe in those "memories".[123]

(9) Biases in memory retrieval tasks (lineups, photo displays, interviews) can distort eyewitness identification.[124]

(10) Jurors' tendency to equate eyewitness confidence with eyewitness accuracy and ignore other more important distinctions between accurate and inaccurate eyewitness evidence.[125] Witnesses can exhibit strong belief in their memories, even when those memories are verifiably false.[126]

(11) Lay persons' lack of awareness of reality monitoring processes when assessing the validity of other people's memories. Consequently, the ability of people to discriminate accuracy from inaccuracy is measurable, yet poor.[127] Asking witnesses how they came to their decisions can improve the validity of individual eyewitness identification.[128]

(12) Confusion of memories from different sources, and related errors which have important practical and theoretical implications.[129]

(13) Potential fallibility of eyewitness identification of voice, body size, or shape, especially in comparison to facial identification.[130]

CONCLUSIONS

Distrusting the accuracy of testimonials in court by people who observed the crime comes from an understanding of the various factors that contribute to inaccurate eyewitness identification. For example, during the crime, eyewitnesses can be afraid, and understandably more concerned about their own safety, than about careful observation. As well, during the commission of the crime, eyewitnesses focus on certain details and are likely to recall other details only vaguely.

Difficulties arise before and during the trial, because the participants in the criminal justice system (police, prosecutors, judges, and jurors) may not realize that people:

(1) Do not recognize unfamiliar faces as easily as they recognize familiar faces;

(2) May not appreciate the fact that people are more accurate in identifying faces of their own race than those of a different race; and

(3) May not realize that an eyewitness's confidence can have

more to do with the repeated rehearsals of the testimony with police and prosecutors than it does with the accuracy of the identification.

These various factors of misidentification are set out in Figure 2.

The debate over the reliability of eyewitness and earwitness identification evidence is really between two different conceptions of human memory: the common sense and the scientific. The common sense conception of fixed and permanent sight and sound recordings stored in memory supports a belief in eye/earwitness evidence. The scientific conception encourages a great deal of skepticism about veridicality of such evidence even when the witness is fully confident about her memories.

Figure #2: Eyewitness misidentification and the jury

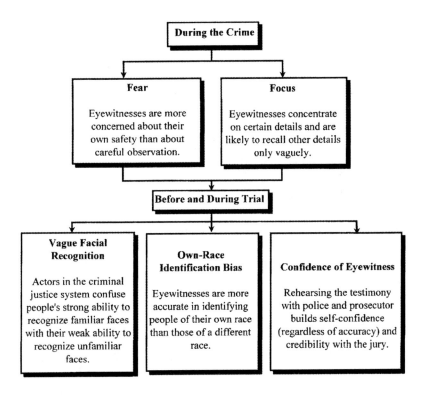

Many social psychologists distrust the accuracy of testimonials in court by people who observed the crime. Shown here are some reasons that eyewitnesses may be inaccurate and that jurors might tend to believe the testimony.

According to the scientific conception, memory is best construed as an interactive product of acquisition, storage (retention), and retrieval factors. Initial perceptions are influenced by expectations, attitudes and other social factors as well as generally shared errors (e.g., overestimating the time involved in the actual eyewitnessing).

Gaps exist in the acquisition of a witnessed event and these gaps may be filled in later by inferences, guesses, and so on.

There appears to be no scientific evidence to prove that long-term memory is permanent.[ ] Loss in memory accuracy over time seems to be more a function of new experiences that interfere with memory than a function of the passage of time *per se*.

The success of a retrieval task depends not only on the accuracy of initial perceptions, the adequacy of encoding strategies, and the minimization of interference during storage, but also the appropriateness of retrieval cues and retrieval strategies.

On eyewitness identification, there is a difference of opinion between the lay persons who become jurors and the psychologists who have studied identification of faces. Jurors typically give great weight to an eyewitness identification, sometimes convicting on such evidence alone.

Psychologists (and many legal authorities) believe that eyewitness identification in the case of a stranger's face seen briefly at one time and identified at a later time from an array of similar faces, is a very inaccurate process that should be given little weight as evidence.

It seems probable that the lay person overestimates the accuracy of eyewitness identification because she is thinking either of her experience in successfully recognizing highly familiar faces or else of certain vivid flashbulb memories that remain fresh for years because of their great emotional significance. But the eyewitness is not a video camera recording everything unselectively and accurately.

The witness is a fallible human being who perceives, encodes, stores, and retrieves with error, interpretation, and intrusion possible at every point. Consequently, eyewitness testimony cannot be taken as direct evidence, involving no inferential process, as the law has tended to take it.

In fact, eyewitness evidence needs expert interpretation just as much as does the evidence of fingerprints, voiceprints, the rifling patterns on a bullet, or the tracings of a polygraph (lie detection).

> Whether we are concerned with the identification of a person or the accurate recounting of the details of an event, there can be problems posed by evidence of eyewitness testimony. The problem can be stated rather

simply: on the one hand, eyewitness testimony is very believable and can wield considerable influence over the decisions reached by a jury; on the other hand, eyewitness testimony is not always reliable. It can be flawed simply because of the normal and natural memory processes that occur whenever human beings acquire, retain, and attempt to retrieve information.[132]

It is especially important to have the accuracy of eyewitness evidence evaluated by experts in human cognition during the initial police investigation, because it is at this stage that screening decisions are made regarding the admissibility of evidence, the likelihood of conviction, and the laying of charges.

The most important contributions that psychologists can make in the eyewitness area will result from developing techniques that increase the accuracy of eyewitness reports (for example, the Cognitive Interview,[133] or the accuracy of eyewitness identifications (for example, sequential lineups).[134]

The best way to reduce the tragedy of wrongful convictions based on eyewitness errors is to prevent those errors from occurring. Once the case is before the courts, it is probably too late![135]

POSTSCRIPT

The Cape Breton humorist, General John Cabot Trail, once described the joys of being a pensioner as being able to sit at the front of the bus, to sit at the back of the church, and to drive down the middle of the road.

The goal of this chapter has been to drive down the middle of the road between those who would unconditionally endorse eyewitness identification and those who would categorically reject it. The middle position argues that while eyewitness identification is subject to error, it should be admitted as evidence, in the absence of a satisfactory alibi (the suspect was elsewhere at the time of the offence). Once entered as evidence, the quality of the eyewitness identification can be assessed by clarifying the conditions under which information acquisition, retention, and retrieval occurred. The more those conditions could have introduced error in the memory of the original event, the less likely the memory is a veridical representation of that event.

Experts must not be "hired guns" for either the defence or the prosecution. Acquittal or conviction of the defendant is the business of the judge and jury, not of the expert. The expert's role is to bring the best factual (empirical) and theoretical information to the court in order to assist the trier of fact with the factors which would make a knowledgeable person have more or less confidence in the veracity of some particular eyewitness memorial evidence. No matter who is paying the expert, the expert must be prepared to drive down the middle of the road if that is what the assessment concludes.

The worst legal nightmare that some people imagine is having expert witnesses for the defence and the prosecution arguing with each other, leaving the poor jurors to decide between the two experts. How can a non-expert distinguish the capabilities of two experts and decide which expert is better?

If, other things being equal (qualifications, education, experience, etc.), two experts disagree, it is all right to ignore their opinions and decide for oneself. Rather than being overly impressed with expert opinion, jurors have to ask themselves if the experts helped clarify anything about the decision they have to make and if the experts did not do so, then their testimony is best ignored.

It is not possible to leave this debate without commenting on the ambiguity inherent in the legal concept of "reasonable doubt", the doubt a reasonable person is supposed to have under the circumstances. It is obviously a fluid concept with no fixed meaning for all people, all situations and all times. Each judge and each juror will have to decide individually whether the eyewitness identification evidence convinces her that the accused is guilty beyond a reasonable doubt. In order to arrive at this determination, it will be necessary for the court to use expert testimony to discuss the merits of the case in relationship to the quality of the eyewitness identification evidence.

Finally, the tenor of the times, in the sense in which the public sentiment is or is not tolerant of acquittal of the accused, in general or with regard to specific crimes (e.g., child sexual abuse), must be considered. Tolerance for acquittal means that society is saying that it is better to let a guilty person go free than it is to convict an innocent person. Intolerance for acquittal says that is better to convict an innocent person than let one guilty person go free.

Tolerance sets a higher standard regarding evidence for conviction than does intolerance. Basically this means that in intolerant times or with crimes that are not to be tolerated, accused individuals will more likely be convicted, on the basis of eyewitness evidence than otherwise, by juries serving as representatives of the society.

Notes

1. E.F. Loftus, "Experimental psychologist as advocate or impartial educator?" (1986) Law & Human Behavior 10, 63-78.

2. E. Connors, T. Lundregan, N. Miller, & T. McEwan, *Convicted by Juries, Exonerated by Science: Case Studies in the Use of DNA Evidence to Establish Innocence After Trial* (Alexandria, VA: National Institute of Justice, 1996); B. Scheck, P. Neufeld, & J. Dwyer, *Actual Innocence* (New York: Random House, 2000).

3. *R. v. Audy (No. 2)*, 1977 CarswellOnt 989, 34 C.C.C. (2d) 231 (Ont. C.A.); *United States v. Wade*, 388 U.S. 218 (1967).

4. *Neil v. Biggers*, 409 U.S. 188, 93 S. Ct. 375, 34 L. Ed. 2d 401 (1972).

5. *Ibid.*, at 199.

6. G.L. Wells & D.M. Murray, "What can psychology say about the *Neil v. Biggers* criteria for judging eyewitness accuracy?" (1983) Journal of Applied Psychology 68, 347-362.

7. D.F. Ross, J.D. Read, & M.P. Toglia, eds., *Adult Eyewitness Testimony: Current Trends and Developments* (New York: Cambridge University Press, 1994); B.L. Cutler & S.D. Penrod, *Mistaken Identification: The Eyewitness, Psychology, and the Law* (New York: Cambridge University Press, 1995); S.M. Kassin, V.A. Tubb, H.M. Hosch, & A. Memon, "On the 'general acceptance' of eyewitness testimony research" (2001) American Psychologist 56, 405-416; S.L. Sporer, R.S. Malpass, & G. Koehnken, eds., *Psychological Issues in Eyewitness Identification* (Mahwah, NJ: Erlbaum, 1996); C.P. Thompson, D.J. Herrmann, J.D. Read, D. Bruce, D.G. Payne, & M.P. Toglia, eds., *Eyewitness Memory: Theoretical and Applied Perspectives* (Mahwah, NJ: Erlbaum, 1998).

8. A.G. Goldstein, (1977) "The fallibility of the eyewitness: Psychological evidence" in B.D. Sales, ed., *Psychology in the Legal Process* (New York: Spectrum, 1977), at 223-247.

9. S.G. Fox & H.A. Walters, "The impact of general versus specific expert testimony and eyewitness confidence upon mock juror judgment" (1986) Law & Human Behavior 10(3), 215-228.

10. E.F. Loftus, (1986) "Ten years in the life of an expert witness" (1986) Law & Human Behavior 10(3), 241-264.

11. J.C. Brigham & R.K. Bothwell, "The ability of prospective jurors to estimate the accuracy of eyewitness identifications" (1983) Law & Human Behavior 7, 19-30.

12. J.C. Brigham & M.P. Wolfskeil, "Opinions of attorneys and law enforcement personnel on the accuracy of eyewitness identifications" (1983) Law & Human Behavior 7, 337-349.

13. E.F. Loftus, "Reconstructing memory: The incredible eyewitness" *Psychology Today* (December 1974), at 117-119.

14. The Honourable Lord Patrick Devlin (Chair) *Report to the Secretary of State for the Home Department of the Departmental Committee on Evidence of Identification in Criminal Cases* (London: Her Majesty's Stationery Office, 1976).

15. R. Brown, *Social Psychology: The Second Edition* (New York: The Free Press, 1986).

16. R. O'Day, "Some psychological, social, and cultural factors that account for the influence of eyewitness identification and testimony" (1995) [unpublished manuscript].

17. A.D. Yarmey, "Earwitness evidence: Memory for a perpetrator's voice" in D.F.

Ross, et al., *Adult Eyewitness Testimony: Current Trends and Developments*, *supra*, note 7, at 101-124.

[18] G.L. Wells, M.R. Leippe, & T.M. Ostrom, (1979) "Guidelines for empirically assessing the fairness of a lineup" (1979) Law & Human Behavior 3, 285-293; G.L. Wells, T.J. Ferguson, & R.C.L. Lindsay, "The tractability of eyewitness confidence and its implications for triers of fact" (1981) Journal of Applied Psychology 66, 688-696; R.C.L. Lindsay, G.L Wells, & C.H. Rumpel, "Can people detect eyewitness-identification accuracy within and across situations?" (1981) Journal of Applied Psychology 66, 79-89; S.D. Penrod & B. Cutler, "Witness confidence and witness accuracy: assessing their forensic relation" (1995) Psychol. Pub. Pol'y & L. 1, 817-845; S. Sporer, S.D. Penrod, D. Read, & B. Cutler, "Gaining confidence in confidence: a new meta-analysis on the confidence-accuracy relationship in eyewitness identification studies" (1995) Psychological Bulletin 118, 315-327.

[19] K. Deffenbacher, "Eyewitness accuracy and confidence: Can we infer anything about their relationship" (1980) Law & Human Behavior 4, 243-260.

[20] P.J. Lavrakas & L. Bickman, "What makes a good witness?" (Paper presented at the American Psychological Association, Chicago, 1975).

[21] L.T. Garcia & W. Griffitt, "Impact of testimonial evidence as a function of witness characteristics" (1978) Bulletin of the Psychonomic Society 11, 37-40.

[22] G.L. Wells, R.C.L. Lindsay, & T. Ferguson, "Accuracy, confidence, and juror perceptions in eyewitness identification" (1979) Journal of Applied Psychology 64, 440-448.

[23] R. O'Day, *supra*, note 16.

[24] *Ibid.*

[25] D. Deutscher & H. Leonoff, *Identification Evidence* (Toronto: Carswell, 1991); E.F. Loftus, *Eyewitness Testimony* (Cambridge, Mass: Harvard University Press, 1979); D.F. Ross, J.D Read, & M.P. Toglia, eds., *Adult Eyewitness Testimony: Current Trends and Developments*, *supra*, note 7; G.L. Wells, *Eyewitness Identification: A System Handbook* (Toronto: Carswell, 1988); G.L. Wells & E.F. Loftus, eds., *Eyewitness Testimony: Psychological Perspectives* (Cambridge: Cambridge University Press, 1984); A.D. Yarmey, *The Psychology of Eyewitness Testimony* (New York: The Free Press, 1979).

[26] E.M. Borchard, *Convicting the Innocent: Errors of Criminal Justice* (New Haven: Yale University Press, 1932).

[27] A. Rattner, (1983) *Convicting the Innocent: When Justice Goes Wrong* (Doctoral Dissertation, Ohio State University, 1983) [unpublished].

[28] E.M. Borchard, *Convicting the Innocent: Errors of Criminal Justice*, *supra*, note 26; A. Rattner, *Convicting the Innocent: When Justice Goes Wrong*, *Ibid.*; P.M. Wall, *Eyewitness Identification of Criminal Cases* (Springfield, Ill.: Charles C. Thomas, 1965); H.H. Wilder & P. Wentworth, *Personal Identification: Methods for the Identification of Individuals, Living or Dead* (Boston: R.G. Badger, 1918); F.D. Woocher, "Did your eyes deceive you? Expert psychological testimony on the unreliability of eyewitness identification" (1977) Stan. L. Rev. 29, 969-1030; E. Connors, T. Lundregan, N. Miller, & T. McEwan, *Convicted by Juries, Exonerated by Science: Case Studies in the Use of DNA Evidence to Establish Innocence After Trial*, *supra*, note 2; B. Scheck, P. Neufeld, & J. Dwyer, *Actual Innocence*, *supra*, note 2.

[29] J.C. Brigham, A. Maass, L.D. Snyder, & K. Spaulding, K., "Accuracy of eyewit-

ness identifications in a field setting" (1982) Journal of Personality and Social Psychology 42, 673-681; R. Buckhout, "Eyewitness identification and psychology in the courtroom" (1977) Criminal Defence 4, 5-10; R. Buckhout, "Nearly 2000 witnesses can be wrong" (1980) Bulletin of the Psychonomic Society 16, 307-310; D.F. Ross, et al., *Adult Eyewitness Testimony: Current Trends and Developments*, *supra*, note 7.

30 R. Buckhout, "Nearly 2000 witnesses can be wrong" *Ibid.*

31 A.D. Yarmey, *The Psychology of Eyewitness Testimony*, *supra*, note 25.

32 A.G. Goldstein, "The fallibility of the eyewitness: Psychological evidence," *supra*, note 8, at 223-247.

33 G.H. Bower & M.M. Karlin, "Depth of processing of pictures of faces and recognition memory" (1974) Journal of Experimental Psychology 103, 751-757; J. Chance, A.J. Goldstein, & L. McBride, "Differential experience and recognition memory for faces" (1975) Journal of Social Psychology 97, 243-253; I.F. Cross, J. Cross, & J. Daly, "Sex, race, age, and beauty as factors in recognition of faces" (1971) Perception and Psychophysics 10. 393-396; H.D. Ellis, G.M. Davies, & J.W. Shepherd, "Experimental studies of face identification" (1977) Journal of Criminal Defence 3, 219-234; A.G. Goldstein, B. Stephenson, & J. Chance, "Face recognition memory: Distribution of false alarms" (1977) Bulletin of the Psychonomic Society 9, 416-418; J. Hochberg & R. Galper, "Recognition of faces: I. An exploratory study" (1967) Psychonomic Science 9, 619-620; R.S. Malpass & J. Kravitz, "Recognition for faces of own and other race" (1969) Journal of Personality and Social Psychology 13, 330-334; K.E. Patterson & A.D. Baddley, "When face recognition fails" (1977) Journal of Experimental Psychology: Human Learning and Memory 3, 406-417; J.W. Shepherd, J.B. Deregowski, & H.D. Ellis, "A cross-cultural study of memory for faces" (1974) International Journal of Psychology 9, 205-211; R.K. Yin, "Looking at upside-down faces" (1969) Journal of Experimental Psychology 81, 141-145.

34 A.G. Goldstein, "The fallibility of the eyewitness: Psychological evidence," *supra*, note 8, at 223-247.

35 G.L. Wells, M.R. Leippe, & T.M. Ostrom, "Guidelines for empirically assessing the fairness of a lineup," *supra*, note 18; G.L. Wells, T.J. Ferguson, & R.C.L. Lindsay, "The tractability of eyewitness confidence and its implications for triers of fact," *supra*, note 18; R.C.L. Lindsay, G.L. Wells, & C.H. Rumpel, "Can people detect eyewitness-identification accuracy within and across situations?" *supra*, note 18.

36 G.L. Wells, M.R. Leippe, & T.M. Ostrom, "Guidelines for empirically assessing the fairness of a lineup," *supra*, note 18.

37 R.C.L. Lindsay, G.L. Wells, & C.H. Rumpel, (1981) "Can people detect eyewitness-identification accuracy within and across situations?" *supra*, note 18.

38 J.C. Brigham & R.K. Bothwell, R.K., "The ability of prospective jurors to estimate the accuracy of eyewitness identifications," *supra*, note 11.

39 J.C. Brigham, A. Maass, L.D. Snyder, &K. Spaulding, "Accuracy of eyewitness identifications in a field setting," *supra*, note 29.

40 P.M. Wall, "Eyewitness identification of criminal cases," *supra*, note 28.

41 R. Buckhout, "Eyewitness testimony" (December 1974) *Scientific American*, at 23-31.

42 The Honourable Lord Patrick Devlin (Chair), *Report to the Secretary of State for*

the Home Department of the Departmental Committee on Evidence of Identification in Criminal Cases, supra, note 14.

[43] G.L. Wells, *Eyewitness Identification: A System Handbook, supra*, note 25.

[44] *Ibid.*

[45] R. Buckhout, "Eyewitness identification and psychology in the courtroom," *supra*, note 29.

[46] E.F. Loftus, "Unconscious transference in eyewitness identification" (1976) Law & Psychol. Rev. 2, 93-98.

[47] G.L. Wells, *Eyewitness Identification: A System Handbook, supra*, note 25.

[48] E.F. Loftus, G.R. Loftus, & J. Messo, "Some facts about 'weapon focus'" (1987) Law & Human Behavior" 11(1), 55-62.

[49] B. Park & M. Rothbart, "Perception of outgroup homogeneity and levels of social categorization" (1982) Journal of Personality & Social Psychology 42, 1051-1068; D.A. Wilder, "Perceiving persons as a group: Effects of attributions of causality and belief" (1978) Social Psychology 1, 13-23; J.E. Chance & A.G. Goldstein, "The other-race effect and eyewitness identification" in S.L. Sporer, *et al.*, *Psychological Issues in Eyewitness Identification, supra*, note 7.

[50] J.C. Brigham, "Race and eyewitness identifications" in S. Worchel & W. G. Austin, eds., *Psychology of Intergroup Relations*, 2d ed. (Chicago: Nelson-Hall, 1986), at 260-282.

[51] *Ibid.*

[52] A.D. Baddeley, "Applied cognitive and cognitive applied psychology: The case of face recognition" in L.G. Nilsson, ed., *Perspectives on Memory Research* (Hillsdale, NJ: Erlbaum, 1979); G.H. Bower & M.M. Karlin, "Depth of processing of pictures of faces and recognition memory" (1974) Journal of Experimental Psychology 103, 751-757; G.L. Wells & B. Hyrciw, "Memory for faces: Encoding and retrieving operations" (1984) Memory & Cognition 12, 338-344; E. Winograd, "Elaboration and distinctiveness in memory for faces" (1981) Journal of Experimental Psychology: Human Learning and Memory 7, 181-190.

[53] J.W. Shepherd, H.D. Ellis, M. McMurran, & G.M. Davies, "Effect of character attribution on Photofit construction of a face" (1978) European Journal of Social Psychology 8, 263-268; D.J. Narby, B.L. Cutler, & S.D. Penrod, "The effects of witness, target, and situational factors on eyewitness identifications" in S.L. Sporer, *et al.*, *Psychological Issues in Eyewitness Identification, supra*, note 7, at 23-52.

[54] E.F. Loftus & J.C. Palmer, "Reconstruction of automobile destruction: An example of the interaction between language and memory" (1974) Journal of Verbal Learning and Verbal Behavior 13, 585-589.

[55] E.F. Loftus, *Eyewitness Testimony, supra*, note 25.

[56] *Ibid.*, at xiii

[57] C.A.E. Luus & G.L. Wells, "Eyewitness identification and the selection of distracters for lineups" (1991) Law & Human Behavior 15, 43-57.

[58] G.L. Wells, E.P. Seelau, S.M. Rydell, & C.A.E. Luus, "Recommendations for properly conducted lineup identification tasks" in D.F. Ross, et al., *supra*, note 7, at 223-244.

[59] R.P. Fisher & R.E. Geiselman, *Memory-enhancing Techniques for Investigative Interviewing* (Springfield, Il: Charles C. Thomas, 1992).

[60] M. Reiser, "Investigative Hypnosis" in D.C. Raskin, ed., *Psychological Methods in Criminal Investigation and Evidence* (New York: Springer, 1989), at 155.

[61] M. Smith, "Hypnotic memory enhancement of witnesses: Does it work?" (1983) Psychological Bulletin 94, 387-407.

[62] J. Dywan & K.S. Bowers, "The use of hypnosis to enhance recall" (1983) Science 222, 184-185.

[63] W.H. Putnam, "Hypnosis and distortions in eyewitness identification", (1979) International Journal of Clinical and Experimental Hypnosis 27, 437-448; R.S. Malpass, "Enhancing eyewitness memory" in S.L. Sporer, *et al.*, *Psychological Issues in Eyewitness Identification, supra*, note 7, at 177-204.

[64] R.P. Fisher & R.E. Geiselman *Memory-enhancing Techniques for Investigative Interviewing, supra*, note 59; R.P. Fisher, M.R. McCauley, & R.E. Geiselman, "Improving the eyewitness testimony with the cognitive interview" in D.F. Ross, *et al.*, *Adult Eyewitness Testimony: Current Trends and Developments, supra*, note 7, at 245-269.

[65] R.P. Fisher & R.E. Geiselman, *Memory-enhancing Techniques for Investigative Interviewing, supra*, note 59; R.P. Fisher, M.R. McCauley, & R.E. Geiselman, "Improving the eyewitness testimony with the cognitive interview," *Ibid.*, at 245-269; R.P. Fisher & M.L. McCauley, "Information retrieval: interviewing witnesses" in N. Brewer & C. Wilson, eds., *Psychology and Policing* (Hillsdale, NJ: Erlbaum, 1995), at 81-99; R.E. Geiselman & R.P. Fisher, "Ten years of cognitive interviewing" in D. Payne & F. Conrad, eds., *Intersections in Basic and Applied Memory Research* (Mahwah, NJ: Erlbaum, 1997), at 291-310.

[66] B.L. Cutler, G.L. Berman, S. Penrod, & R.P. Fisher, "Conceptual, practical, and empirical issues associated with eyewitness identification test media" in D.F. Ross, *et al.*, *Adult Eyewitness Testimony: Current Trends and Developments, supra*, note 7, at 163-181; G. Koehnken, R.S. Malpass, & M.S. Wogalter, "Forensic application of line-up research" in S.L. Sporer, *et al.*, *Psychological Issues in Eyewitness Identification, supra*, note 7, at 205-232; A.M. Levi, "Are defendants guilty if they were chosen in a lineup?" (1998) Law & Human Behavior 22, 389-408; Technical Working Group for Eyewitness Evidence, *Eyewitness Evidence: A Guide for Law Enforcement* (Washington, D.C.: United States Department of Justice, Office of Justice Programs, 1999); A.D. Yarmey, "Person identification in show-ups and lineups" in C.P. Thompson, *et al.*, *Eyewitness Memory: Theoretical and Applied Perspectives, supra*, note 7, at 131-154.

[67] G.L. Wells & B.L Cutler, "The right to counsel at videotaped lineups: An emerging dilemma" (1990) Conn. L. Rev. 22, 373-395.

[68] B.L. Cutler & S.D. Penrod, "Context reinstatement and eyewitness identification" in G.M. Davies & D.M. Thomson, eds., *Context Reinstatement and Eyewitness Identification* (New York: Wiley, 1988); B.L. Cutler & S.D. Penrod, "Improving the reliability of eyewitness identification: Lineup construction and presentation" (1988) Journal of Applied Psychology 73, 281-290; R.C.L. Lindsay, J.A. Lea, & J.A. Fulford, "Sequential lineup presentation: Technique matters" (1991) Journal of Applied Psychology 76, 741-745; R.C.L. Lindsay, J.A. Lea, G.J. Noseworthy, J.A. Fulford, J. Hector, V. Levan, & C. Seabrook, C., "Biased lineups: Sequential presentation reduces the problem" (1991) Journal of Applied Psychology 76, 796-802; R.C.L. Lindsay, H. Wallbridge, & D. Brennan, (1987) "Do the clothes make the man? An exploration of the effect of lineup attire on eyewitness identification accuracy" (1987) Canadian Journal of Behavioural Science 19, 464-478; R.C.L. Lindsay & G.L. Wells, "What price justice? Exploring the relationship of lineup

fairness to identification accuracy" (1980) Law & Human Behavior 4, 303-313; R.C.L. Lindsay & G.L. Wells, "Improving eyewitness identifications from lineups: Simultaneous versus sequential lineup presentation" (1985) Journal of Applied Psychology 70, 556-564; R.S. Malpass & P.G. Devine, "Eyewitness identification: Lineup instructions and the absence of the offender" (1981) Journal of Applied Psychology 66, 345-351.

[69] D.S. Lindsay, "Memory source monitoring and eyewitness testimony" in D.F. Ross, et al., *Adult Eyewitness Testimony: Current Trends and Developments, supra,* note 7, at 27-55.

[70] J.D. Read, "Understanding bystander misidentifications: The role of familiarity and contextual knowledge" in D.F. Ross, *et al., Adult Eyewitness Testimony: Current Trends and Developments, supra,* note 7, at 56-79.

[71] S.L. Sporer, "Decision times and eyewitness identification accuracy in simultaneous and sequential lineups" in D.F. Ross, *et al., Adult Eyewitness Testimony: Current Trends and Developments, supra,* note 7, at 300-327; G.L. Wells, M. Small, S. Penrod, R.S. Malpass, S.M. Fulero, & C.A.E. Brimacombe, "Eyewitness identification procedures: recommendations for lineups and photospreads" (1999) Law & Human Behavior 23, 603-647.

[72] G.L. Wells, "Applied eyewitness-testimony research: System variables and estimator variables" (1978) Journal of Personality and Social Psychology 36, 1546-1557.

[73] G.L. Wells, "The psychology of lineup identifications" (1984) Journal of Applied Social Psychology 14, 89-103.

[74] G.L. Wells, E.P. Seelau, S.M. Rydell, & C.A.E. Luus, "Recommendations for properly conducted lineup identification tasks," *supra,* note 58, at 223-244.

[75] G.L. Wells, G.L., "The psychology of lineup identifications" (1984) Journal of Applied Social Psychology 14, 89-103.

[76] R.C.L. Lindsay & G.L. Wells, (1985) "Improving eyewitness identifications from lineups: Simultaneous versus sequential lineup presentation," *supra,* note 68; G.L. Wells, (1984) "The psychology of lineup identifications," *Ibid.*; J.L. Tunnicliff & S.E. Clarke, "Selecting foils for identification lineups: matching suspects or descriptions?" (2000) Law & Human Behavior 24, 231-258.

[77] A.D. Yarmey, "Earwitness evidence: Memory for a perpetrator's voice" in D.F. Ross, *et al., Adult Eyewitness Testimony: Current Trends and Developments, supra,* note 7, at 101-124; R. Hammersley & J.D. Read, "Voice identification by humans and computers" in S.L. Sporer, *et al., Psychological Issues in Eyewitness Identification, supra,* note 7, at 117-152.

[78] D. Deutscher & H. Leonoff, *Identification Evidence* (Toronto: Carswell, 1991).

[79] G. Davies, "Capturing likeness in eyewitness composites: The police artist and his rivals," (1986a) Medicine, Science, and the Law 26, 283-290; J.W. Shepard & H.D. Ellis, "Face recall-methods and problems" in S.L. Sporer, *et al., Psychological Issues in Eyewitness Identification, supra,* note 7, at 87-116; S.L. Sporer, "Psychological aspects of person descriptions" in S.L. Sporer, *et al., Psychological Issues in Eyewitness Identification, supra,* note 7, at 53-86.

[80] G. Homa, *The Law Enforcement Composite Sketch Artist* (West Berlin, NJ: privately printed, 1983); S.J. Cormack, *The Police Artist's Reference* (Pewaukee, WI: Wakusha County Technical Institute, 1979).

[81] B.R. Clifford & G. Davies, "Procedures for obtaining identification evidence" in

D.C. Raskin, ed., *Psychological Methods in Criminal Investigation and Evidence* (New York: Springer, 1989), at 47-95.

[82] H. Allison, *Personal Identification* (Boston: Holbrook Press, 1973); G. Davies, "Face recall systems" in G. Davies, H. Ellis, & J. Shepherd, eds., *Perceiving and Remembering Faces* (London: Academic Press, 1981), at 227-250.

[83] S.J. Cormack, *The Police Artist's Reference*, supra, note 80.

[84] K. Laughery, V. Smith, & M. Yount, "Visual support devices: Evaluation of a new technique for constructing facial images" (Proceedings of the Human Factors Society, 24th Annual Meeting, New York, 1980), at 1-4.

[85] G. Davies, "The recall and reconstruction of faces: Implications for theory and practice" in H. Ellis, M. Jeeves, F. Newcombe, & A. Young, eds., *Aspects of Face Processing* (Dodrecht, The Netherlands: Martinus Nijhoff, 1986b), at 388-397.

[86] F. Domingo, (1984) "Survey to study the feasibility of conducting a national composite artist conference" (City of New York Police Department, 1984) [unpublished report].

[87] A. Kitson, M. Darnbrough, & E. Shields, "Let's face it" (1978) Police Research Bulletin 30, 7-13.

[88] P. Bennett, "Face recall: A police perspective" (1986) Human Learning 5, 197-202.

[89] M. Darnbrough, "The use of facial reconstruction methods by the police" (Paper presented at the Annual Conference of the British Psychological Society, Exeter, Devon, 1977).

[90] P. Bennett, "Face recall: A police perspective," supra, note 88, at 197-202.

[91] G. Davies, "Face recall systems" in G. Davies, H. Ellis, & J. Shepherd, eds., *Perceiving and Remembering Faces*, supra, note 82, at 227-250.

[92] H. Ellis, "Practical aspects of face memory" in G.L. Wells & E.F. Loftus, eds., *Eyewitness Testimony: Psychological Perspectives*, supra, note 25, at 12-37.

[93] D. Christie & H. Ellis, "Photofit reconstructions versus verbal descriptions of faces" (1981) Journal of Applied Psychology 66, 358-363.

[94] R. Flin, R. Markham, & G. Davies, "Making faces: Develop-mental trends in the construction and recognition of Photofit face composites" (1989) Journal of Applied Developmental Psychology.

[95] F. Domingo, "Survey to study the feasibility of conducting a national composite artist conference," supra, note 86; A. Kitson, M. Darnbrough, & E. Shields, E., "Let's face it," supra, note 87, at 30, 7-13.

[96] G. Davies, A. Milne, & J. Shepherd, "Searching for operator skills in face composite reproduction" (1983) Journal of Police Science and Administration 11, 405-409.

[97] K. Laughery, C. Duval, & M. Wogalter, "Dynamics of face recall" in H. Ellis, M. Jeeves, F. Newcombe, & A. Young, eds., *Aspects of Face Processing*, supra, note 85, at 373-387.

[98] G. Davies, H. Ellis, & J. Shepherd, "Face recognition accuracy as a function of mode of representation" (1978b) Journal of Applied Psychology 63, 180-187.

[99] B. Tversky & D. Baratz, "Memory for faces: Are caricatures better than photographs?" (1985) Memory and Cognition 13, 45-49.

[100] G. Davies, "Capturing likeness in eyewitness composites: The police artist and his rivals" (1986a) Medicine, Science, and the Law 26, 283-290.

[101] M. Mauldin & K. Laughery, "Composite production effects upon subsequent facial recognition" (1981) Journal of Applied Psychology 66, 351-357.

[102] G. Davies, H. Ellis, & J. Shepherd, "Face identification: The influence of delay

upon accuracy of Photofit construction" (1978a) Journal of Police Science and Administration 6, 35-42.

[103] D. Hall, "Obtaining eyewitness identifications in criminal investigations: Two experiments and some comments on the Zeitgeist in forensic psychology" (Paper presented at the American Psychology-Law Conference, Snowmass, Colorado, October 1977).

[104] B. Thompson & K. Laughery, "Facial memory: Effects of recall efforts on subsequent recognition" (Paper presented at the Annual Meeting of the Psychonomics Society, Phoenix, Arizona, 1981).

[105] M. Wogalter, K. Laughery, & B. Thompson, "Eyewitness identification: Composite construction on subsequent recognition performance" (University of Richmond, Virginia, 1987) [unpublished manuscript].

[106] S. Comish, "Recognition of facial stimuli following an intervening task involving the Identikit" (1987) Journal of Applied Psychology 72, 488-491.

[107] J. Schooler, (1987) "Verbalizing non-verbal memories: Some things are better left unsaid" (Doctoral Dissertation, University of Washington, Seattle, 1987) [unpublished].

[108] G. Davies, "Face recall systems" in G. Davies, H. Ellis, & J. Shepherd, eds., *Perceiving and Remembering Faces, supra*, note 82, at 227-250; G. Davies, "The recall and reconstruction of faces: Implications for theory and practice" in H. Ellis, M. Jeeves, F. Newcombe, & A. Young, eds., *Aspects of Face Processing, supra*, note 85, at 388-397.

[109] F. Jenkins & G. Davies, "Contamination of facial memory through exposure to misleading composite pictures" (1985) Journal of Applied Psychology 70, 164-176.

[110] J. Read, ("Rehearsal and recognition of human faces" (1979) Am. J. Psychol. 92, 71-85.

[111] M. Wogalter, "Face memory: Effects of verbal description and visual rehearsal" (University of Richmond, Virginia, 1987) [unpublished manuscript].

[112] M. Wogalter, K. Laughery, & B. Thompson, "Eyewitness identification: Composite construction on subsequent recognition performance," *supra*, note 105.

[113] G.L. Wells & B. Hryciw, "Memory for faces: Encoding and retrieval operations" (1984) Memory and Cognition 12, 338-344.

[114] G. Homa, "The law enforcement composite sketch artist," *supra*, note 80.

[115] K. Laughery & R. Fowler, "Sketch artist and Identikit procedures for recalling faces" (1980) Journal of Applied Psychology 65, 307-316.

[116] K. Laughery & V. Smith, "Subject identification following exposure to sketches and Identikit composites" (Proceedings of the Human Factors Society, 22nd Annual Meeting, Detroit, 1978), at 631-635.

[117] K. Laughery, C. Duval, & M. Wogalter, "Dynamics of face recall" in H. Ellis, M. Jeeves, F. Newcombe, & A. Young, eds., *Aspects of Face Processing, supra*, note 85, at 373-387.

[118] D. Christie, G. Davies, J. Shepherd, & H. Ellis, "Evaluating a new computer-based system for face recall" (1981) Law & Human Behavior 5, 209-218; M. Kovera, S.D. Penrod, C. Pappas, & D. Thill, "Identification of computer-generated facial composites" (1997) Journal of Applied Psychology 82, 235-246.

[119] R.C.L. Lindsay, "Biased lineups: Where do they come from?" in D.F. Ross, *et al.*, *Adult Eyewitness Testimony: Current Trends and Developments, supra*, note 7, at 182-200.

[120] E.F. Loftus, "Ten years in the life of an expert witness," *supra*, note 10.

[121] Loftus (1979a), at 213-214.

[122] When a witness looks at a photograph and is uncertain, and later looks at a new photograph of the same person and is suddenly more certain, it is possible that some sort of unconscious transference is taking place. The familiarity experienced with the second photograph might be mistakenly related by the witness back to the incident, rather than back to the prior viewing of photographs where it might belong. As a result, eyewitnesses can misidentify familiar but innocent persons (Lindsay, 1994; Read, 1994; Ross, Ceci, Dunning, & Toglia, 1994).

[123] K.R. Weingardt, H.K. Toland, & E.F. Loftus, "Reports of suggested memories: Do people truly believe them?" in D.F. Ross, et al., *Adult Eyewitness Testimony: Current Trends and Developments*, *supra*, note 7, at 3-26.

[124] J.C. Brigham & J.E. Pfeifer, "Evaluating the fairness of lineups" in D.F. Ross, *et al.*, *Adult Eyewitness Testimony: Current Trends and Developments*, *supra*, note 7, at 201-222; B.L. Cutler, G.L. Berman, S. Penrod, & R.P. Fisher, "Conceptual, practical, and empirical issues associated with eyewitness identification test media" in D.F. Ross, *et al.*, *Adult Eyewitness Testimony: Current Trends and Developments*, *supra*, note 7, at 163-181; R.P. Fisher, M.R. McCauley, & R.E. Geiselman, "Improving the eyewitness testimony with the Cognitive Interview" in D.F. Ross, *et al.*, *Adult Eyewitness Testimony: Current Trends and Developments*, *supra*, note 7, at 245-269; D.S. Lindsay, "Memory source monitoring and eyewitness testimony" in D.F. Ross, *et al.*, *Adult Eyewitness Testimony: Current Trends and Developments*, *supra*, note 7, at 27-55; G.L. Wells, E.P. Seelau, S.M. Rydell, & C.A.E. Luus, "Recommendations for properly conducted lineup identification tasks" *supra*, note 58, at 223-244.

[125] H. Hosch, "Individual differences in personality and eyewitness identification" in D.F. Ross, *et al.*, *Adult Eyewitness Testimony: Current Trends and Developments*, *supra*, note 7, at 328-347; M.R. Leippe, "The appraisal of eyewitness testimony" in D.F. Ross, *et al.*, *Adult Eyewitness Testimony: Current Trends and Developments*, *supra*, note 7, at 385-418; R.C.L. Lindsay, "Expectations of eyewitness performance: Jurors' verdicts do not follow from their beliefs" in D.F. Ross, *et al.*, *Adult Eyewitness Testimony: Current Trends and Developments*, *supra*, note 7, at 362-384; C.A.E. Luus & G.L. Wells, "Eyewitness identification confidence" in D.F. Ross, *et al.*, *Adult Eyewitness Testimony: Current Trends and Developments*, *supra*, note 7, at 348-361; S.L. Sporer, "Decision times and eyewitness identification accuracy in simultaneous and sequential lineups" in D.F. Ross, *et al.*, *Adult Eyewitness Testimony: Current Trends and Developments*, *supra*, note 7, at 300-327; L.B. Stern & Dunning, "Distinguishing accurate from inaccurate eyewitness identifications: A reality monitoring approach" in D.F. Ross, *et al.*, *Adult Eyewitness Testimony: Current Trends and Developments*, *supra*, note 7, at 273-299.

[126] K.R. Weingardt, H.K. Toland & E.F. Loftus, "Reports of suggested memories: Do people truly believe them?" in D.F. Ross, *et al.*, *Adult Eyewitness Testimony: Current Trends and Developments*, *supra*, note 7, at 3-26; C.A.E. Luus & G.L. Wells, "Eyewitness identification confidence," *supra*, note 125, at 348-361.

[127] R.E. Nisbett & T.D. Wilson, "Telling more than we can know: Verbal reports on mental processes" (1977) Psychological Review 84, 231-259.

[128] L.B. Stern & D. Dunning, "Distinguishing accurate from inaccurate eyewitness identifications: A reality monitoring approach" in D.F. Ross, *et al.*, *Adult Eyewit-*

ness Testimony: Current Trends and Developments, supra, note 7, at 273-299; J.W. Schooler, D. Gerhard, & E.F. Loftus, "Qualities of the unreal" (1986) Journal of Experimental Psychology: Learning, Memory, and Cognition 12, 171-181; M.R. Leippe, A. Romanczyk, & A.P. Manion, "Eyewitness memory for a touching experience: Accuracy differences between adult and child witnesses" (1991) Journal of Applied Psychology 76, 367-379; A.P. Manion, M.R. Leippe, & A. Romanczyk, "Discernibility of discrimination? Understanding jurors' reactions to accurate and inaccurate child and adult eyewitnesses" in G.S. Goodman & B. Bottoms, eds., *Understanding and Improving Children's Eyewitness Testimony* (New York: Guilford Press, 1994).

[129]   A witness asked to describe "what happened on the afternoon of Wednesday, March 23, 1995" may well include in his or her reply information suggested by others, memories of past thoughts or fantasies about the event in question, and ideas based on general knowledge and beliefs that come to mind in response to the question (Lindsay, 1994).

[130]   M.D. MacLeod, J.N. Frowley, & J.W. Shepherd, "Whole body information: Its relevance to eyewitnesses" in D.F. Ross, *et al., Adult Eyewitness Testimony: Current Trends and Developments, supra,* note 7, at 125-143.

[131]   E.F. Loftus & G.R. Loftus, "On the permanence of stored information in the human brain" (1980) *American Psychologist* 35, 409-420.

[132]   E.F. Loftus, *Eyewitness Testimony, supra,* note 25, at 6-7.

[133]   R.F. Geiselman, R.P. Fisher, D.P. MacKinnon, & H.L. Holland, "Eyewitness memory enhancement in the police interview: Cognitive retrieval memories versus hypnosis" (1985) Journal of Applied Psychology 70, 401-412.

[134]   B.L. Cutler & S.D. Penrod, "Context reinstatement and eyewitness identification," *supra,* note 68; B.L. Cutler & S.D. Penrod, "Improving the reliability of eyewitness identification: Lineup construction and presentation," *supra,* note 68, at 73, 281-290; R.C.L. Lindsay, J.A. Lea, & J.A. Fulford, "Sequential lineup presentation: Technique matters," *supra,* note 68, at 76, 741-745; R.C.L. Lindsay, J.A. Lea, G.J. Noseworthy, J.A. Fulford, J. Hector, V. Levan, & C. Seabrook, "Biased lineups: Sequential presentation reduces the problem," *supra,* note 68, at 76, 796-802; R.C.L. Lindsay & G.L. Wells, "Improving eyewitness identifications for lineups: Simultaneous versus sequential lineup presentation" (1985) Journal of Applied Psychology 70, 556-564; Levi, A.M. & Lindsay, R.C.L. (2001). Lineup and photospread procedures: Issues concerning policy recommendations. *Psychology, Public Policy and Law,* 7(4), 776-790; Loftus, E.F. (2003). Memory in Canadian courts of law. *Canadian Psychology/Psychologie canadienne,* 44(3), 207-212; Wells, G.L. & Loftus, E.F. (2002). Eyewitness memory for People and Events. (In) A. Goldstein (Ed.) *Comprehensive Handbook of Psychology: Volume 11, Forensic Psychology.* NY: John Wiley & Sons, 149-160; Wells, G.L. & Olson, E.A. (2003). Eyewitness Testimony. *Annual Review of Psychology,* 54:277-295; Yarmey, A.D. (2001). Expert Testimony: Does Eyewitness Memory Research have Probative Value for the Courts? *Canadian Psychology/Psychologie canadienne,* 42:2, 92-100; Yarmey, A.D. (2003). Eyewitness Identification: Guidelines and Recommendations for Identification Procedures in the United States and Canada. *Canadian Psychology/ Psychologie canadienne,* 44, 3:181-189.

[135] R.C.L. Lindsay, "Expectations of eyewitness performance: Jurors' verdicts do not follow from their beliefs" in D.F. Ross, *et al.*, *Adult Eyewitness Testimony: Current Trends and Developments*, *supra*, note 7, at 382.

28

How Judges Decide Cases:
Assessing Credibility

The Honourable Judge Alan T. Tufts*

INTRODUCTION

The vast majority of criminal cases in Canada are tried before a single judge either in a Provincial Court or in a Superior Court without a jury. While a trial judge is required to apply the law, much of a judge's task is to find facts. Witnesses testify and provide the judge, in many cases, with a whole host of different versions of an event or events which the judge is required to consider. Witnesses, of course, come from different perspectives and sometimes provide very different and contradictory accounts of a particular event. How does a trial judge therefore make findings of fact? How then does a judge know what and who to believe?.

This question, however, is not that simple. This is because a judge's role in a criminal trial is to decide if the Crown has proven guilt beyond a reasonable doubt, not just who and what to believe. A criminal trial is not just about belief, it is about proof and whether that proof has been established to the criminal standard. A judge, for example, may "believe" a complaining witness yet have a reasonable doubt whether an accused person is guilty?

Trial evidence will often include other evidence such as forensic evidence, fingerprinting and DNA analysis, expert reports and other objective evidence which will help to resolve conflicts in the testimony of different witnesses. Much of a judge's task, however, in finding facts, turns on assessing the credibility of the witnesses who appear at the trial and, in particular, assessing the credibility of witnesses who have an interest in the proceeding.

---

* Judge Tufts received his undergraduate education at Dalhousie University. He received his LL.B. from Dalhousie Law School in 1979. He was appointed to the Nova Scotia Provincial Court in 1998. Since 2004, Judge Tufts has lectured part-time at Acadia University in the Political Science Department.

WHAT IS CREDIBILITY?

Assessing and determining the credibility of witnesses is critical to a trial judge's role in the fact-finding process. Credibility has two different aspects: truthfulness or veracity on the one hand and accuracy—the ability to accurately observe and recall—on the other. The latter is often referred to as reliability, the former as credibility. A witness who is not credible cannot give reliable evidence whereas credibility is no proxy for reliability.[1] Sometimes a credible witness can give unreliable testimony. Some witnesses may honestly attempt to convey an accurate account of what they saw and heard but for various reasons may simply be incorrect while other witnesses are simply shading or slanting the truth or being deliberately deceptive. Justice Doherty of the Ontario Court of Appeal explains this in *R. v. Morrissey*:[2]

> Testimonial evidence can raise veracity and accuracy concerns. The former relate to the witness's sincerity, that is, his or her willingness to speak the truth as the witness believes it to be. The latter concerns relate to the actual accuracy of the witness' testimony. The accuracy of a witness' testimony involves considerations of the witness' ability to accurately observe, recall and recount the events in issue. When one is concerned with a witness' veracity, one speaks of the witness' credibility. When one is concerned with the accuracy of a witness' testimony, one speaks of the reliability of that testimony. Obviously a witness whose evidence on a point is not credible cannot give reliable evidence on that point. The evidence of a credible, that is, honest witness, may, however, still be unreliable.[3]

HOW TO ASSESS CREDIBILITY

Generally

Credibility assessment is not easy for trial judges. It is not a science.[4] Judges are expected to give reasons for their decisions explaining how they resolve credibility issues.[5] Yet the Supreme Court of Canada has recognized that it is difficult to "articulate with precision the complex intermingling of impressions that emerge after watching and listening to witnesses".[6] Appellate courts give considerable deference to trial judges when making findings of credibility.

In an adversarial system, witnesses are examined by the party that presents or leads that witness. Opposing parties then cross-examine or challenge the witness's testimony. There are rules of evidence which control how the examination and cross-examination is conducted and what evidence is admissible and how the evidence can be used by the trier of fact. This is particularly so when considering the testimony of the accused or evidence relating to the accused's credibility.[7]

Judges do not have a "divine insight into the hearts and minds of witnesses" who appear before them.[8] They cannot determine the absolute truth.[9] Judges are obliged to weigh and consider the truthfulness and reliability of witnesses that come before them. However, this is different from judging a witness' character. Character and honesty are distinct. Character is the "aggregate of the moral qualities which belong to and distinguish an individual... the moral traits of a person gleaned from his habitual conduct".[10] Saunders, J.A. pointed out in *R. v. P. (S.H.)*:[11]

> One is not judging character. The obligation is to ascertain the truthfulness and reliability of a person's testimony. Appearances alone may be very deceptive. A most reprehensible witness may well be telling the truth. A polished, well-mannered individual may prove to be a consummate liar.

Reliability depends in large measure on the witness' power or opportunity for observation, eyesight, perception, accuracy and emotional stability.[12] Also, a witness' judgment and memory is important to consider.[13] An eyewitness, for example, can give some of the most compelling and powerful testimony because the witness appears genuinely objective in his or her testimony. Yet his or her testimony can be completely wrong for a variety of different reasons.[14]

All witnesses come before the court with equal credit and their testimony should be treated equally without regard to personal characteristics such as race, religion, gender, occupation or nationality.[15] It is the assessment of the truthfulness of the individual witness' testimony which is necessary. A witness' own record for honesty, prior inconsistent statements, any partiality he or she displays, motive to lie, and other objective or verifiable evidence of the surrounding circumstances and context in which the events occurred is more telling of a witness' credibility. Trial judges need to examine and scrutinize all the evidence when considering the credibility of any single witness. In *R. v. S. (D.D.)*,[16] Saunders, J.A. said:

> [77] ... it would be wise to consider what has been said about the trier's place and responsibility in the search for truth. Centuries of case law remind us that there is no formula with which to uncover deceit or rank credibility. There is no crucible for truth, as if pieces of evidence, a dash of procedure, and a measure of principle mixed together by seasoned judicial stirring will yield proof of veracity. Human nature, common sense and life's experience are indispensable when assessing creditworthiness, but they cannot be the only guide posts. Demeanour too can be a factor

taken into account by the trier of fact when testing the evidence, but standing alone it is hardly determinative. Experience tells us that one of the best tools to determine credibility and reliability is the painstaking, careful and repeated testing of the evidence to see how it stacks up. How does the witness's account stand in harmony with the other evidence pertaining to it, while applying the appropriate standard of proof in a civil or a criminal case?

No Set of Rules

Credibility cannot be determined by following a set of rules.[17] However, juries have been instructed and trial judges have assessed credibility by using a number of guideposts or factors. In *R. v. Filion*,[18] Mossip, J. set out these factors:

> [30] In assessing the reliability and credibility of witnesses' testimony, I have considered factors that judges invite juries to consider such as:
> - Does the witness seem honest? Is there any particular reason why the witness should not be telling the truth or that his/her evidence would not be reliable.
> - Does the witness have an interest in the outcome of the case, or any reason to give evidence that is more favourable to one side than to the other?
> - Does the witness seem to have a good memory? Does any inability or difficulty that the witness has in remembering events seem genuine, or does it seem made up as an excuse to avoid answering questions?
> - Does the witnesses' testimony seem reasonable and consistent as she/he gives it? Is it similar to or different from what other witnesses say about the same events? Did the witness say or do something different on an earlier occasion.
> - Do any inconsistencies in the witness' evidence make the main points of the testimony more or less believable and reliable? Is the inconsistency about something important, or a minor detail? Does it seem like an honest mistake? Is it a deliberate lie? Is the inconsistency because the witness said something different, or because she/he failed to mention something? Is there any explanation for it? Does it make sense?
> - The manner in which a witness testifies may be a factor, and it may not, depending on other variables with respect to a particular witness.

Demeanour

What role does demeanor play in the assessment of credibility? Can any real indication be made from observing how a witness presents in the witness box and "honestly" and "sincerely" or otherwise relate their testimony? This is not an easy question to answer.

Firstly, what do we mean by demeanor? Black's Law Dictionary defines demeanor as "the tone of voice in which a witness's statement is made, the hesitation or readiness with which his answers are given, the look of the witness, his carriage, his evidence of surprise, his gestures, his zeal, his bearing, his expression, his yawns, the use of his eyes, his furtive or meaning glances, or his shrugs, the pitch of his voice, his self-possession or embarrassment, his air of candor or seeming levity". In *Laurentide Motels Ltd. c. Beauport (City)*,[19] Justice L'Heureaux-Dubé refers, at para. 232, to a trial judge's ability to observe a witness' "movements, glances, hesitations, trembling, blushing, surprise or bravado" when engaging in the difficult task of separating "wheat from the chaff".

The Supreme Court of Canada has recognized that trial judges will consider a witness' demeanor. In *R. v. Lifchus*,[20] Justice Cory said:

> [29] ... there may be something about a person's demeanor in the witness box which will lead a juror to conclude that the witness is not credible. It may be that the juror is unable to point to the precise aspect of the witness's demeanor which was found to be suspicious, and as a result cannot articulate either to himself or others exactly why the witness should not be believed. A juror should not be made to feel that the overall, perhaps intangible, effect of the witness's demeanor cannot be taken into consideration in the assessment of credibility.

In *R. v. Jabarianha*,[21] the Supreme Court of Canada commented on the trial judge's reasons for disbelieving a witness because the witness' demeanor "demonstrated signs of untruthfulness". The witness, the trial judge found, was "evasive at times or his eyes shifted around".

Appeal courts have recognized that trial judges are in a unique position of seeing and hearing the evidence of witnesses.[22] Trial judges can look at what was said and how it was said.[23] Indeed, one of the rationales for not receiving hearsay evidence is that the trial judge or jury do not have the advantage of observing the demeanor of the declarant when the out-of-court statement was made.

Yet appeal courts have repeatedly warned trial judges that demeanor cannot be the sole ground for credibility assessment in a criminal proceeding.[24] Credibility of an interested witness cannot be gauged solely on the basis of whether the demeanor of that witness carries a conviction of truth.[25] The appearance of honesty is of little assistance.[26] However, trial judges are not required to ignore demeanor when assessing a witness' credibility including the testimony of the accused and can use demeanor in their assessment along with other evidence.[27]

The difficulty with using demeanor as a basis for assessing a witness' credibility is that the trier of fact has no baseline or standard from which to measure a witness' truthfulness. Studies have shown that the average person can detect deceit no better than for fifty percent of the time and that professionals such as police, lawyers and judges are only slightly better.[28]

Paul Ekman, a researcher in lie detection identifies two errors when using demeanor in assessing credibility.[29] The *Othello Error*, named after the Shakespeare play, describes the mis-attribution of the cause of emotion which can appear to be a sign of deceit when in fact it may be attributed to other causes which are not apparent to the observer. The second error is called the *Brokaw Error*, named after the famous news anchor Tom Brokaw, who once said, "I can always tell when someone is lying because they...". No matter what follows, the statement is not correct. The reality is that body language, hand or eye movements or speech patterns alone say little about deception.

In the end, while a trial judge's role in seeing and hearing witnesses is critical, the demeanor of a witness cannot be the sole measure of a witness' credibility. The surrounding context and how the witness' testimony "stacks up"[30] against the whole of the evidence is a more reliable measure. It is perhaps best summed up by Justice O'Halloran in *Faryna v. Chorny*,[31] a case often relied on by judges, where he says:

> [10] The credibility of interested witnesses, particularly in cases of conflict of evidence, cannot be gauged solely by the test of whether the personal demeanour of the particular witness carried conviction of the truth. The test must reasonably subject his story to an examination of its consistency with the probabilities that surround the currently existing conditions. In short, the real test of the truth of the story of a witness in such a case must be its harmony with the preponderance of the probabilities which a practical and informed person would readily recognize as reasonable in that place and in those conditions.

Prior Consistent and Inconsistent Statements

A trial judge may hear evidence of what a complainant told other witnesses or what the complainant may have said when the complaint arose or when it was reported to the police. This evidence however cannot be used for the truth of its contents and is inadmissible for that purpose. However, this evidence is often included as narrative—evidence which helps a trial judge understand how the events unfolded. At first blush this might seem to enhance a witness' credibility. However this evidence is considered irrelevant and lacking in probative value.[32] This is because an account which is repeated does not gain strength. This evidence is self-serving, self-corroborative and superfluous.[33] The trial judge, therefore, cannot use the fact that a witness told another person previously the same "story" or account to bolster the credibility of the witness' testimony at trial.

However, prior statements can be used to rebut an allegation of recent fabrication,[34] where it is suggested the witness is "making up a story" or for removing a potential motive to lie. In *R. v. Stirling*,[35] the accused was charged along with another individual in causing death and bodily harm resulting from a motor vehicle accident. The main issue was whether the accused or the other individual, the witness, was driving. The other individual was cross-examined about a pending civil claim he launched and drug-related charges against him which were recently dropped. This raised the suggestion that the other individual had a motive to fabricate his testimony. The Supreme Court of Canada found that the trial judge did not err by using his prior statement to bolster the witness' credibility by removing the potential motive to lie. Justice Bastarache said,

> consistent statements have the impact of removing a potential motive to lie, and the trial judge is entitled to consider removal of this motive when assessing the witness's credibility.[36]

A witness' prior inconsistent statement, however, may be more telling.

Duty to Resolve Inconsistencies

Witnesses are often cross-examined on inconsistent prior statements. Different accounts of the same event by the same witness can seriously weaken a witness' credibility, particularly where the inconsistent account touches on a material aspect of the witness' testimony. A complainant who changes his or her account from what is said in a statement given to the police, for example, and what is said at trial can dramatically reduce the weight given to that witness' testimony. It is important, then, to look at the internal consistency of the testimony, the logic and common sense of it in terms of the circumstances described, the consistency of the that witness' evidence against the standard of prior statements of that witness and against other evidence and the exhibits. Judges must recognize and reconcile these inconsistencies particularly where they are present in a principal Crown witness.[37] While minor inconsistencies can be overlooked, a witness whose testimony presents with inconsistencies which are material and are not reconciled cannot be relied upon to support a conviction.

Areas of Caution

There are some witnesses where judicial experience has shown that considerable caution must be exercised if relying on that witness' testimony. Care needs to be taken when making credibility assessments of such witnesses.

Jailhouse Informants

In some cases other prisoners come forward and testify for the Crown. Judges and juries need to be extremely wary of these witnesses. In the Thomas Sophonow inquiry,[38] Justice Peter Cory warned in very strong words about relying on jailhouse informants. He said:

> Jailhouse informants comprise the most deceitful and deceptive group of witnesses known to frequent the courts. The more notorious the case, the greater the number of prospective informants. They rush to testify like vultures to rotting flesh or sharks to blood. They are smooth and convincing liars. Whether they seek favours from the authorities, attention or notoriety they are in every instance completely unreliable. It will be seen how frequently they have been a major factor in the conviction of innocent people and how much they tend to corrupt the administration of justice. Usually, their presence as witnesses signals the end of any hope of providing a fair trial.
>
> They must be recognized as a very great danger to our trial system... Perhaps, the greatest danger flows from their ability to testify falsely in a remarkably convincing manner... Jailhouse informants are a festering sore. They constitute a malignant infection that renders a fair trial impossible. They should, as far as it is possible, be excised and removed from our trial process.

Justice Kaufman, in the Morin Inquiry,[39] made similar recommendations. In both of these cases the jailhouse informants gave convincing, yet false, testimony.

Accomplice and Unsavoury Witnesses

When a witness testifies for the Crown who is an accomplice or an unsavoury witness, a trial judge needs to take particular caution. However, the Supreme Court of Canada tells judges they should not pigeonhole witnesses into categories and that whether a witness is deserving of caution is to be determined on a case by case basis.[40] This unsavoury characterization may come from the fact that the witness is an accomplice, an informant, has a significant criminal record, or has a significant interest in the case. In a jury trial, the trial judge must consider the credibility of the witness and the importance of the witness' testimony to the Crown's case before determining whether a caution should be given. If the trial judge then determines the jury should be cautioned, the trial judge gives what is referred to as a *"Vetrovec"* warning.[41]

A *Vetrovec* warning cautions a jury about relying on that witness' testimony to convict the accused without more corroborating or confirming evidence. Justice Fish, in *R. v. Khela*,[42] explains why such a warning is necessary:

> [4] ... It is meant to bring home to lay jurors the accumulated wisdom of the law's experience with unsavoury witnesses. Judges are alert to the concern that unsavoury witnesses are prone to favour personal advantage over public duty.

Confirmatory evidence does not, however, have to implicate the accused or confirm the Crown witness' testimony in every aspect. It is sufficient if the evidence is capable of restoring the trier of fact's faith in the relevant aspects of the witness' account.[43]

Eyewitness Identification Testimony

A witness who testifies that he or she witnessed the accused commit the alleged offence can be a very compelling witness and give what appears to be very credible testimony because the witness often appears very honest and sincere. Yet eyewitness testimony can sometimes be the most dangerous of all witnesses. This is because a witness pointing to the accused in court can have a powerful effect out of proportion to the import of the testimony. In *R. v. Hibbert*,[44] Justice Arbour explained the frailties of an in-court identification of an accused and that it should be given little weight.

Justice Cory, in the Sophonow Inquiry, highlighted the tragedy of false eyewitness identification testimony. The strength of an eyewitness is better determined by the quality of the procedure which the police used initially for the witness to identify the accused as the perpetrator. Again, Justice Cory made recommendations on how a proper police lineup should be conducted to ensure its fairness and impartiality. However even if the lineup procedure is not perfect the eyewitness testimony can provide reliable testimony.[45]

Other

There are other aspects of a witness' circumstances which may give rise to caution. Section 12 of the *Canada Evidence Act* allows a witness to be questioned about his or her criminal record. A criminal record related to a crime of dishonesty is more important, clearly, to assessing credibility. However evidence of bad character can be taken into account when a trial judge assesses the credibility of a witness other than the accused. Special rules apply to the accused. For example, a witness who has lied to authorities previously or has been dishonest in the past will receive very careful scrutiny of his or her testimony.

Obviously, witnesses who demonstrate a bias or partiality to any of the parties, have an interest in the outcome, have or show animus towards the accused or others, have possibly colluded with another witness, or where there have been glaring inconsistencies between their in-court testimony and their prior statements, may be given reduced weight when considering their testimony.

Also, certain evidence of character traits is admissible to show that a witness lacks credibility. Chief Justice Dickson, in *R v Corbett*,[46] approved this passage from *State* v. *Duke*:[47]

> What a person is often determines whether he should be believed. When a defendant voluntarily testifies in a criminal case, he asks the jury to accept his word. No sufficient reason appears why the jury should not be informed what sort of person is asking them to take his word. In transactions of everyday life this is probably the first thing that they would wish to know. So it seems to us in a real sense that when a defendant goes onto a stand, "he takes his character with him."[48]

However, it is only when the particular evidence is relevant to credibility assessment that the judge can use this evidence and then only for that purpose.

Motive to Lie

Clearly where a witness has a motive to lie that witness' credibility requires close scrutiny and may be weakened as a result. However, a lack of motive to lie or an absence of a motive to lie of a complainant cannot be used necessarily to bolster the complainant's credibility. It does not logically flow that because there is no apparent reason to lie a witness must be telling the truth.[49] While the lack of any motive may appear relevant it cannot be used as a dominant reason for rejecting an accused's testimony nor can an adverse inference be drawn against the accused for his or her failure to provide a motive as to why the complainant may be lying.

Appellate courts have been clear that any suggestion that the reasoning, "Why would the complainant lie?" was used, in effect amounts to reversing the burden of proof and undermines the presumption of innocence and is reversible error.[50] In fact, an accused cannot be asked on cross-examination why the complainant would lie[51] nor is it proper for a trial judge to ask the accused's counsel why a complainant would lie.[52] This type of reasoning is consistent with treating the testimony of the complainant and the accused as a "credibility contest" which the Supreme Court of Canada and other appeal courts have consistently indicated is not proper.

At the same time, a trial judge must be careful about assessing the accused's credibility on the basis that he or she clearly has an interest in not being convicted. This cannot be the primary basis for a rejection of the accused's testimony.[53] Isolating the issue of the accused's interest in the trial outcome again tends to undermine the Crown's burden and the presumption of innocence.[54]

Child Witness

In the past, the common law and the *Criminal Code* viewed the testimony of children with suspicion. However the law has now been developed through legislative amendments[55] and evolving jurisprudence to view child testimony differently. A child's testimony does not need to be corroborated[56] and the rules respecting recent complaint are abrogated.[57] The courts have now taken a more enlightened approach to a child witness' testimony. The Supreme Court of Canada has recognized that children have been subjected to certain myths and stereotypes concerning their complaints, particularly about allegations of sexual assault. In *R. v. Find*,[58] Chief Justice McLachlin said:

> [102] Child complainants may similarly be subject to stereotypical assumptions, such as the belief that stories of abuse are probably fabricated if not reported immediately, or that the testimony of children is inherently unreliable...

> [103] These myths and stereotypes about child and adult complainants are particularly invidious because they comprise part of the fabric of social "common sense" in which we are daily immersed. Their pervasiveness, and the subtlety of their operation, create the risk that victims of abuse will be blamed or unjustly discredited in the minds of both judges and jurors.

In *R. v. B.(G.)*,[59] the Supreme Court of Canada found that a "common sense" approach to children's testimony is more appropriate. The Court cautioned not to impose the same exacting standard to the testimony of a child as one would apply to that of an adult. For example, a flaw in a child's testimony such as a contradiction may not have the same significance as in the testimony of an adult. A child experiences the world differently and new sensitivity to how children relate their experiences is necessary.[60]

A child's perception of time, sequence of events and other circumstantial details may be quite different from that of an adult. Consequently, internal inconsistencies or even inconsistencies between a child's testimony and other independent and objective evidence may not be so significant as if the same existed with an adult witness. The previous law, that a child's testimony is inherently unreliable is gone.[61] A trial judge or jury cannot simply apply adult standards to measure the credibility of a child witness. However, while the standard to measure credibility may be different, the standard of proof is the same—proof beyond a reasonable doubt. Therefore, in cases where a child's testimony is the primary evidence against the accused, the burden of proof is no less simply because the evidence comes from a child witness.

Even though corroboration is no longer required for a child witness, it may still be necessary in appropriate cases for a trial judge to be cautious about the frailties of a child's testimony and the danger of convicting on the testimony of a single witness.[62] In commenting on a child's competency to testify the Supreme Court of Canada noted three factors:[63]

1. the child's capacity to observe or perceive;
2. the child's capacity to recollect; and
3. the child's capacity to communicate.

While competency is different from credibility and these factors do not ensure credibility, they are factors which a judge can consider when assessing a child's credibility.

There is no fixed or precise formula on how to determine when to be cautious of a child's testimony. The same principles which apply to assess credibility of other witnesses can be used, however, with sensitivity to a child's different experience and perspective.

Expert Opinion on Credibility and Oath Helping

As a general rule neither the Crown or the Defense can call evidence which bolsters the credibility of its own witness until the opposite party attempts to impeach the witness' credibility. This is called oath-helping and a judge cannot admit or use this evidence to find a witness credible.[64]

The Crown cannot call experts to comment on the veracity or truthfulness of a particular witness. In child abuse cases the Crown has attempted to lead evidence of an expert indicating the child's explanation is true and that evidence offered by the accused is not. In *R. v. Marquard*,[65] Justice McLachin explained why this evidence is inadmissible:

> [49] It is a fundamental axiom of our trial process that the ultimate conclusion as to the credibility or truthfulness of a particular witness is for the trier of fact, and is not the proper subject of expert opinion... A judge or jury who simply accepts an expert's opinion on the credibility of a witness would be abandoning its duty to itself determine the credibility of the witness. Credibility must always be the product of the judge or jury's view of the diverse ingredients it has perceived at trial, combined with experience, logic and an intuitive sense of the matter... Credibility is a matter within the competence of lay people. Ordinary people draw conclusions about whether someone is lying or telling the truth on a daily basis. The expert who testifies on credibility is not sworn to the heavy duty of a judge or juror. Moreover, the expert's opinion may be founded on factors which are not in the evidence upon which the judge and juror are duty-bound to render a true verdict. Finally, credibility is a notoriously difficult problem, and the expert's opinion may be all too readily accepted by a frustrated jury as a convenient basis upon which to resolve its difficulties. All these considerations have contributed to the wise policy of the law in rejecting expert evidence on the truthfulness of witnesses.

However, an expert may testify as to how a child who has been abused may respond and why there is a delay in reporting abuse. The Supreme Court of Canada has cautioned, though, that there is a danger that, faced with this type of evidence, a jury or trial judge could abdicate its role as fact-finder and rely simply on the expert's opinion. The duty to assess credibility and find facts belongs to the trial judge in a judge alone case or, in a trial by judge and jury, to the jury.

ACCUSED AS A WITNESS

Accused's Record and Character

There are special rules when the accused testifies. Firstly, the Crown cannot cross-examine the accused on his character or put evidence of the accused's bad character into evidence unless the accused himself raises his character as an issue. However, in this latter case the Crown can only use the accused's bad character or prior bad acts to rebut evidence of the accused's good character.[66] Evidence of the accused's bad character or prior bad acts cannot, however, be used to infer guilt. Generally, a judge or jury cannot infer that because the accused had done something previously, even if it is similar to the crime with which the accused is charged, that the accused is guilty. There are special rules which govern the admissibility of "similar fact evidence".

The accused is permitted to lead evidence of good character whether or not the Crown attempts to impeach the accused's credibility. This evidence may be about the accused's reputation for veracity in community, although witnesses cannot be asked opinions as to whether or not they would believe the witness under oath.[67]

Similar rules apply regarding the accused's record. Any witness can be cross-examined about his or her criminal record,[68] including the accused. A cross-examination is limited to the fact of the conviction[69] but cannot extend to whether the accused stood trial or testified[70] or to details underlying the conviction.[71] It can however include the type of offence, where it occurred and the sentence imposed.[72] A record for crimes of dishonesty is the most relevant because the accused's record can only be used to attack the accused's credibility and cannot, like character evidence, be used to infer guilt of the crime charged.

In a trial by judge and jury, the Crown must seek permission before the accused testifies to determine if it can cross-examine the accused about his or her record.[73] Because the accused's record is relevant only to credibility, the Crown will generally be limited to cross-examination regarding non-violent crimes of dishonesty. Convictions which risk the jury finding that the accused had a propensity to the crime charged will most likely be off limits to the Crown.

Accused's Credibility

In a criminal trial the Crown bears the burden or onus to prove the particular allegation beyond a reasonable doubt. This means the Crown presents its case first. The Crown witnesses testify and are cross-examined by the defense. It is only after the Crown has completed its evidence is the accused called upon to present a defense.

In cases where the accused testifies, there is a risk that the accused's testimony will be compared or measured against the testimony of the Crown witnesses, especially in cases where the Crown witnesses appear to be credible. It is often the case that there is only one principal Crown witness and in some cases there is very little or no other objective or independent evidence—the so-called "he said - he said" or "he said - she said" case.

The Supreme Court of Canada and appeal courts across the country have repeatedly emphasized that such cases are not credibility contests[74] and that finding the complainant credible does not require the trier of fact to disbelieve or reject the accused's testimony to the contrary. The Supreme Court of Canada has reminded trial judges that the burden of proof remains on the Crown and never shifts to the accused. Where the accused testified the trier of fact must be instructed in accordance with Justice Cory's direction in the often cited case of *R. v. W.(D.)*, where he said:

> A trial judge might well instruct the jury on the question of credibility along these lines:
>
> First, if you believe the evidence of the accused, obviously you must acquit.
>
> Second, if you do not believe the testimony of the accused but you are left in reasonable doubt by it, you must acquit.
>
> Third, even if you are not left in doubt by the evidence of the accused, you must ask yourself whether, on the basis of the evidence which you do accept, you are convinced beyond a reasonable doubt by that evidence of the guilt of the accused.[75]

This does not mean that the accused's evidence is necessarily assessed in isolation. All witnesses must be assessed in the context of all other evidence including the testimony of other witnesses. This will necessarily mean a weighing and re-weighing of the evidence. Justice Cory's direction reminds trial judges that the presumption of innocence and the burden of proof applies to the issues of credibility particularly where the case turns on this critical issue.

It means that, even where the complainant is believable or credible and the accused's testimony is not believed, the trier of fact must look beyond that to see if a reasonable doubt is present either from the accused's testimony or from examining the whole of the evidence. It is not necessary to find just that the accused's evidence might reasonably be true,[76] it is enough if his or her evidence raises a reasonable doubt.

Appeal courts have criticized trial judges for failing to scrutinize the Crown's evidence adequately or applying different degrees of scrutiny to the evidence of the accused than to the evidence of the Crown.[77] In the end, the trier of fact must look at all of the evidence to determine whether the Crown's case has been proven beyond a reasonable doubt.

REASONS FOR JUDGMENT

Trial judges are required to give reasons for their findings in a criminal trial[78] including findings of credibility.[79] Judges must show a path of reasoning for their conclusions, in part so that an appeal court can assess the legality and reasonableness of the judge's findings. Justice Laskin reminds judges that the well-known phrase "sometimes it just won't write" may be a signal that the judge's conclusions will not stand up to reasoned analysis.[80] Judges know it is important for them to provide reasons so their analysis can be understood[81] and if necessary scrutinized by appeal courts. Crafting reasons helps judges apply the proper principles and avoid improper reasoning.

However, the Supreme Court of Canada has acknowledged that it may be difficult for a trial judge "to articulate with precision the complex intermingling of impressions that emerge after watching and listening to witnesses and attempting to reconcile the various versions of events".[82] It is not necessary to detail every landmark in the path of reasoning or provide a detailed account of the conflicting evidence as long as it is apparent why the judge made the particular finding.[83]

CONCLUSION

Assessing credibility is a difficult task for trial judges. It can be complex and complicated. Judges do not have crystal balls nor do they have any unique insight into the hearts and minds of witnesses. They cannot act as detectives. In the end they must use logic, common sense, and their own knowledge of human behaviour to apply the "time honoured" means to determine whether an allegation has been proven to the standard that is the only one acceptable in criminal law, that being "beyond a reasonable doubt",[84] the golden thread that weaves its way through our criminal law.[85]

Notes

[1] See *R. v. C. (H.)*, 2009 CarswellOnt 202, 2009 ONCA 56, 241 C.C.C. (3d) 45, 244 O.A.C. 288 (Ont. C.A.).

[2] *R. v. Morrissey*, 1995 CarswellOnt 18, [1995] O.J. No. 639, 38 C.R. (4th) 4, 22 O.R. (3d) 514, 97 C.C.C. (3d) 193, 80 O.A.C. 161 (Ont. C.A.).

[3] *Ibid.*, at para. 33.

[4] See *R. c. Gagnon*, 2006 CarswellQue 3559, 2006 CarswellQue 3560, 2006 SCC 17, [2006] 1 S.C.R. 621, 37 C.R. (6th) 209, 347 N.R. 355, (*sub nom. R. v. G. (L.)*) 207 C.C.C. (3d) 353, 208 C.C.C. (3d) vi (note), (sub nom. *R. v. G. (L.)*) 266 D.L.R. (4th) 1 (S.C.C.), at para. 20; and *R. v. S. (R.D.)*, 1997 CarswellNS 301, 1997 CarswellNS 302, [1997] 3 S.C.R. 484, 161 N.S.R. (2d) 241, 477 A.P.R. 241, 151 D.L.R. (4th) 193, 118 C.C.C. (3d) 353, 10 C.R. (5th) 1, 218 N.R. 1, 1 Admin. L.R. (3d) 74 (S.C.C.).

[5] *R. v. McCullough*, 1969 CarswellOnt 919, [1969] O.J. No. 1536, [1970] 1 O.R. 785,

[1970] 1 C.C.C. 366 (Ont. C.A.); see also *R. v. Maharaj*, 2004 CarswellOnt 1921, (sub nom. *R. v. Y.M.*) [2004] O.J. No. 2001, 186 C.C.C. (3d) 247, 187 O.A.C. 101, (sub nom. *R. v. M. (Y.)*) 71 O.R. (3d) 388 (Ont. C.A.).

6   *R. c. Gagnon, supra*, note 4, at para. 20.

7   *Infra*: "Accused as a Witness: Accused's Credibility".

8   *R. v. Pressley*, 1948 CarswellBC 123, [1948] B.C.J. No. 63, 7 C.R. 342, [1949] 1 W.W.R. 692, 94 C.C.C. 29 (B.C. C.A.), at para. 13.

9   *R. v. M. (M.E.)*, 1998 CarswellNWT 22, [1998] N.W.T.J. No. 50 (N.W.T. S.C.), para. 1.

10   H.C. Black, *Black's Law Dictionary* (rev 6th Ed.) (St. Paul Minn. West Publishing Co.).

11   *R. v. P. (S.H.)*, 2003 CarswellNS 182, 2003 NSCA 53, 176 C.C.C. (3d) 281, 215 N.S.R. (2d) 66, 675 A.P.R. 66 (N.S. C.A.), at para. 29.

12   Judicial Fact Finding and a Theory of Credit, Judge Gerald T.G. Seniuk, (1992), 56 Sask L.Rev. 79.

13   *R. v. White*, 1947 CarswellOnt 8, [1947] S.C.R. 268, 3 C.R. 232, 89 C.C.C. 148 (S.C.C.), relying on *Raymond v. Bosanquet (Township)*, 1919 CarswellOnt 21, 59 S.C.R. 452, 50 D.L.R. 560, 17 O.W.N. 295 (S.C.C.).

14   *Infra*: "How to Assess Credibility: Areas of Caution: Eyewitness Identification Testimony".

15   *R. v. S. (R.D.), supra*, note 4, at para. 131; juries can however use their knowledge of human behaviour to assess credibility and to draw inferences from proven facts (see *R. v. Pan*, 2001 CarswellOnt 2261, 2001 CarswellOnt 2262, 2001 SCC 42, [2001] 2 S.C.R. 344, 155 C.C.C. (3d) 97, 200 D.L.R. (4th) 577, 43 C.R. (5th) 203, 270 N.R. 317, 147 O.A.C. 1, 85 C.R.R. (2d) 1 (S.C.C.)).

16   *R. v. S. (D.D.)*, 2006 CarswellNS 109, 2006 NSCA 34, [2006] N.S.J. No. 103, 207 C.C.C. (3d) 319, 770 A.P.R. 235, 242 N.S.R. (2d) 235 (N.S.C.A.).

17   *R. v. White, supra*, note 13.

18   *R. v. Filion*, 2003 CarswellOnt 3286, [2003] O.J. No. 3419 (Ont. S.C.J.).

19   *Laurentide Motels Ltd. c. Beauport (Ville)*, 1989 CarswellQue 53, 1989 CarswellQue 105, [1989] 1 S.C.R. 705, 94 N.R. 1, 45 M.P.L.R. 1, 23 Q.A.C. 1 (S.C.C.).

20   *R. v. Lifchus*, 1997 CarswellMan 392, 1997 CarswellMan 393, [1997] 3 S.C.R. 320, 118 C.C.C. (3d) 1, 216 N.R. 215, 150 D.L.R. (4th) 733, 9 C.R. (5th) 1, 118 Man. R. (2d) 218, 149 W.A.C. 218, [1997] 10 W.W.R. 570 (S.C.C.).

21   *R. v. Jabarianha*, 2001 CarswellBC 2500, 2001 CarswellBC 2501, 2001 SCC 75, [2001] 3 S.C.R. 430, 159 C.C.C. (3d) 1, 206 D.L.R. (4th) 87, 158 B.C.A.C. 82, 258 W.A.C. 82, 88 C.R.R. (2d) 1, 96 B.C.L.R. (3d) 211, 47 C.R. (5th) 97, 277 N.R. 388, [2002] 2 W.W.R. 599 (S.C.C.), at para. 29.

22   *R. c. Gagnon, supra*, note 4; *R v. Howe*, 2005 CarswellOnt 44 [2005] O.J. No. 39, 192 C.C.C. (3d) 480 (Ont. C.A.); *R. v. François*, 1994 CarswellOnt 1160, 1994 CarswellOnt 86, [1994] 2 S.C.R. 827, 31 C.R. (4th) 201, 169 N.R. 241, 73 O.A.C. 161, 91 C.C.C. (3d) 289, 116 D.L.R. (4th) 69, 19 O.R. (3d) 322 (note) (S.C.C.).

23   *R. v. Howe, supra*, note 22.

24   See *R. v. Owen*, 2001 CarswellOnt 3852, [2001] O.J. No. 4257, 150 O.A.C. 378 (Ont. C.A.); *R. v. Norman*, 1993 CarswellOnt 140, [1993] O.J. No. 2802, 26 C.R. (4th) 256, 16 O.R. (3d) 295, 87 C.C.C. (3d) 153, 68 O.A.C. 22 (Ont. C.A.); *R. v. De Haan*, 2002 CarswellOnt 229, [2002] O.J. No. 430, 155 O.A.C. 358 (Ont. C.A.);

and *R. v. G. (G.)*, 1997 CarswellOnt 1886 [1997] O.J. No. 1501, 99 O.A.C. 44, 115 C.C.C. (3d) 1 (Ont. C.A.).

25 *R. v. De Haan, supra,* note 24.

26 See *R. v. Norman, supra,* note 24; for example, in *R v. E. (T.),* 2007 CarswellOnt 8206, 2007 ONCA 891, [2007] O.J. No. 4952 (Ont. C.A.), the trial judge referred to the accused's passivity and failure to make eye-contact when assessing his credibility and rejecting his testimony, without explaining why and without acknowledging any cultural differences (accused was from Sudan) - a new trial was ordered.

27 See *R. v. Boyce,* 2005 CarswellOnt 4970, [2005] O.J. No. 4313 (Ont. C.A.); and *R. v. Hull,* [2006] O.J. No. 3177, 2006 CarswellOnt 4786 (Ont. C.A.).

28 Ekman, P. & O'Sullivan, M (September 1991) Who Can Catch a Liar? American Psychologist.

29 Ekman, P. (1992) Telling Lies 2nd Edition, New York: Norzon & Co.

30 *R. v. S. (D.D.), supra,* note 16, at para. 77.

31 *Faryna v. Chorny,* 1951 CarswellBC 133, 4 W.W.R. (N.S.) 171, [1952] 2 D.L.R. 354, [1952] 4 W.W.R. 171 (B.C. C.A.).

32 See *R. v. Evans,* 1993 CarswellBC 1263, 1993 CarswellBC 495, [1993] 2 S.C.R. 629, 153 N.R. 212, 82 C.C.C. (3d) 338, 104 D.L.R. (4th) 200, 28 B.C.A.C. 81, 47 W.A.C. 81, 21 C.R. (4th) 321 (S.C.C.); *R. v. Curto,* 2008 CarswellOnt 1238, 2008 ONCA 161, [2008] O.J. No. 889, 230 C.C.C. (3d) 145, 234 O.A.C. 238, 54 C.R. (6th) 237 (Ont. C.A.); and *R. v. C. (G.),* 1997 CarswellOnt 1634, [1997] O.J. No. 1817, 8 C.R. (5th) 61, 27 O.T.C. 335 (Ont. Gen. Div.), which explains the scope of the admission of prior complaint evidence as narrative.

33 *R. v. C. (G.), supra,* note 32.

34 *R. v. Curto, supra,* note 32.

35 *R. v. Stirling,* 2008 CarswellBC 506, 2008 CarswellBC 507, 2008 SCC 10, 59 M.V.R. (5th) 1, [2008] 5 W.W.R. 579, 77 B.C.L.R. (4th) 1, 371 N.R. 384, [2008] 1 S.C.R. 272, 420 W.A.C. 62, 251 B.C.A.C. 62, 54 C.R. (6th) 228, 229 C.C.C. (3d) 257, 291 D.L.R. (4th) 1 (S.C.C.).

36 *Ibid.,* at para. 10.

37 See *R. v. D. (N.K.),* 1997 CarswellOnt 4502, [1997] O.J. No. 3877 (Ont. Gen. Div.); *R c. Dinardo,* 2008 CarswellQue 3451, 2008 CarswellQue 3452, 2008 SCC 24, [2008] 1 S.C.R. 788, 374 N.R. 198, 57 C.R. (6th) 48, 293 D.L.R. (4th) 375, 231 C.C.C. (3d) 177 (S.C.C.) ; and *R v R. (D.),* 1996 CarswellSask 448, 1996 Carswell-Sask 449, [1996] S.C.J. No. 8, EYB 1996-67935, 144 Sask. R. 81, 124 W.A.C. 81, [1996] 2 S.C.R. 291, 197 N.R. 321, 107 C.C.C. (3d) 289, 136 D.L.R. (4th) 525, 48 C.R. (4th) 368 (S.C.C.); although there is no rule when inconsistencies may raise a doubt (see *R v. B. (R.W.),* [1993] B.C.J. No. 758, 1993 CarswellBC 943, 24 B.C.A.C. 1, 40 W.A.C. 1 (B.C. C.A.)).

38 Re Inquiry Regarding Thomas Sophonow www.gov.mb.ca/justice/publications/sophonow.

39 Report of the Kaufman Commission on Proceedings Involving Guy Paul Morin, www.attorneygeneral.jus_ca.gov.on.ca/english/about/pubs/morin.

40 See *R. v. Brooks,* 2000 CarswellOnt 292, 2000 CarswellOnt 293, 2000 SCC 11,, [2000] 1 S.C.R. 237, 141 C.C.C. (3d) 321, 182 D.L.R. (4th) 513, 30 C.R. (5th) 201, 129 O.A.C. 205, 250 N.R. 103 46 O.R. (3d) 640 (headnote only) (S.C.C.).

41 Named after the case of *R. v. Vetrovec,* 1982 CarswellBC 663, 1982 CarswellBC

682, [1982] 1 S.C.R. 811, [1983] 1 W.W.R. 193, 27 C.R. (3d) 304, 136 D.L.R. (3d) 89, 41 N.R. 606, (sub nom. *R. v. Gaja*) 67 C.C.C. (2d) 1 (S.C.C.).

[42] *R. v. Khela*, 2009 CarswellBC 69, 2009 CarswellBC 70, 2009 SCC 4, 62 C.R. (6th) 197, 238 C.C.C. (3d) 489, 301 D.L.R. (4th) 257, 383 N.R. 279, 265 B.C.A.C. 31, 446 W.A.C. 31, [2009] 1 S.C.R. 104 (S.C.C.), at para. 4.

[43] See *R. v. Kehler*, 2004 CarswellAlta 94, 2004 CarswellAlta 95, 2004 SCC 11, 23 Alta. L.R. (4th) 1, 19 C.R. (6th) 49, [2004] 5 W.W.R. 1, [2004] 1 S.C.R. 328, 346 A.R. 19, 320 W.A.C. 19, 317 N.R. 30, 181 C.C.C. (3d) 1 (S.C.C.).

[44] *R. v. Hibbert*, 2002 CarswellBC 847, 2002 CarswellBC 848, 2002 SCC 39, 287 N.R. 111, 50 C.R. (5th) 209, 163 C.C.C. (3d) 129, 211 D.L.R. (4th) 223, 165 B.C.A.C. 161, 270 W.A.C. 161, [2002] 2 S.C.R. 445 (S.C.C.). See also *R. v. Henemaayer*, 2008 CarswellOnt 4698, 2008 ONCA 580, 239 O.A.C. 241, 234 C.C.C. (3d) 3 (Ont. C.A.).

[45] See *R. v. Doyle*, 2007 CarswellBC 2853, 2007 BCCA 587, 412 W.A.C. 307, 248 B.C.A.C. 307 (B.C. C.A.).

[46] *R. v. Corbett*, 1988 CarswellBC 756, 1988 CarswellBC 252, [1988] 1 S.C.R. 670, [1988] 4 W.W.R. 481, 85 N.R. 81, 28 B.C.L.R. (2d) 145, 41 C.C.C. (3d) 385, 64 C.R. (3d) 1, 34 C.R.R. 54 (S.C.C.).

[47] *State* v. *Duke*, 123 A. 2d 745 (1956, N.H.).

[48] *R. v. Corbett*, *supra*, note 46, at para. 27.

[49] *R. v. B. (R.W.)*, *supra*, note 37; *R. v. S. (D.D.)*, *supra*, note 16.

[50] See *R. v. Kozy*, 1990 CarswellOnt 113, 74 O.R. (2d) 545, 80 C.R. (3d) 59, 58 C.C.C. (3d) 500, 41 O.A.C. 27 (Ont. C.A.).

[51] See *R. v. Rose*, 2001 CarswellOnt 955, 53 O.R. (3d) 417, 143 O.A.C. 163, 42 C.R. (5th) 183, 153 C.C.C. (3d) 225 (Ont. C.A.); and *R v. S. (W.)*, 1994 CarswellOnt 63, [1994] O.J. No. 811, 29 C.R. (4th) 143, 18 O.R. (3d) 509, 90 C.C.C. (3d) 242, 70 O.A.C. 370 (Ont. C.A.).

[52] *R. v. Boyd*, 2005 CarswellMan 227, 2005 MBCA 80, [2005] M.J. No. 209, 199 C.C.C. (3d) 185, 195 Man. R. (2d) 97, 351 W.A.C. 97 (Man. C.A.).

[53] *R. v. B. (L.)*, 1993 CarswellOnt 109, [1993] O.J. No. 1245, 22 C.R. (4th) 209, 82 C.C.C. (3d) 189, 64 O.A.C. 15, 13 O.R. (3d) 796 (Ont. C.A.).

[54] *R. v. Trombley*, 1998 CarswellOnt 2749, 126 C.C.C. (3d) 495, 110 O.A.C. 329, 40 O.R. (3d) 382 (Ont. C.A.).

[55] *Criminal Code*, ss. 275 and 659, as amended. Section 16.1 of the *Canada Evidence Act* now provides that a child under age fourteen shall not take an oath or affirmation and their testimony will be received if they are able to understand and respond to questions and the child need only promise to tell the truth.

[56] *Criminal Code*, s. 659 provides that any requirement for a court to give the jury a warning about convicting an accused on the evidence of a child is abrogated.

[57] *Criminal Code*, s. 275, as amended R.S.C. 1985, c. 19 (3rd Supp.), s. 11; 2002, c. 13, s. 121.

[58] *R. v. Find*, 2001 CarswellOnt 1702, 2001 CarswellOnt 1703, [2001 SCC 32, 269 N.R. 149, 42 C.R. (5th) 1, 154 C.C.C. (3d) 97, 199 D.L.R. (4th) 193, 146 O.A.C. 236, [2001] 1 S.C.R. 863, 82 C.R.R. (2d) 247 (S.C.C.), at paras. 102 and 103.

[59] *R. v. B. (G.)*, 1990 CarswellSask 20, 1990 CarswellSask 410, [1990] 2 S.C.R. 30, 77 C.R. (3d) 347, 56 C.C.C. (3d) 200, 111 N.R. 31, 86 Sask. R. 111 (S.C.C.).

[60] *R. v. W. (R.)*, 1992 CarswellOnt 90, 1992 CarswellOnt 991, [1992] 2 S.C.R. 122, 13 C.R. (4th) 257, 137 N.R. 214, 54 O.A.C. 164, 74 C.C.C. (3d) 134 (S.C.C.).

⁶¹ *Ibid.*

⁶² *R. v. Camp*, 1977 CarswellOnt 18, [1977] O.J. No. 2366, 36 C.C.C. (2d) 511, 17 O.R. (2d) 99, 39 C.R.N.S. 164, 79 D.L.R. (3d) 462 (Ont. C.A.), at para. 21.

⁶³ *R. v. Marquard*, 1993 CarswellOnt 995, 1993 CarswellOnt 127, [1993] 4 S.C.R. 223, 66 O.A.C. 161, 25 C.R. (4th) 1, 85 C.C.C. (3d) 193, 108 D.L.R. (4th) 47, 159 N.R. 81 (S.C.C.).

⁶⁴ See *R. v. Clarke*, 1998 CarswellOnt 3447, [1998] O.J. No. 3521, 129 C.C.C. (3d) 1, 18 C.R. (5th) 219, 112 O.A.C. 233 (Ont. C.A.). For example, polygraph evidence is not admissible because it is considered to be oath-helping (see *R. c. Béland*, 1987 CarswellQue 14, 1987 CarswellQue 96, [1987] 2 S.C.R. 398, 79 N.R. 263, 9 Q.A.C. 293, 36 C.C.C. (3d) 481, 60 C.R. (3d) 1, 43 D.L.R. (4th) 641 (S.C.C.).

⁶⁵ *R. v. Marquard*, *supra*, note 63, at para. 49.

⁶⁶ See *R. v. Morris*, 1978 CarswellQue 38, 1978 CarswellQue 150, [1979] 1 S.C.R. 405, 6 C.R. (3d) 36, 43 C.C.C. (2d) 129, 91 D.L.R. (3d) 161, 23 N.R. 109 (S.C.C.).

⁶⁷ See *R. v. Clarke*, *supra*, note 64.

⁶⁸ *Canada Evidence Act*, s. 12, as amended 1992, c. 47, s. 66.

⁶⁹ See R. v. Ménard, 1996 CarswellOnt 2574, [1996] O.J. No. 2453, 108 C.C.C. (3d) 424, 92 O.A.C. 43, 29 O.R. (3d) 772 (Ont. C.A.).

⁷⁰ See *R. v. Geddes*, 1979 CarswellMan 228, [1979] M.J. No. 125, 2 Man. R. (2d) 339, 52 C.C.C. (2d) 230 (Man. C.A.).

⁷¹ See *R. v. Wells*, 1998 CarswellNfld 174, [1998] N.J. No. 205, 165 Nfld. & P.E.I.R. 346, 509 A.P.R. 346, 127 C.C.C. (3d) 403 (Nfld. C.A.).

⁷² *R. v. R. (S.A.S.)*, 1996 CarswellOnt 4283, [1996] O.J. No. 3736, 94 O.A.C. 307, 111 C.C.C. (3d) 305, 2 C.R. (5th) 340 (Ont. C.A.).

⁷³ *R. v. Corbett*, *supra*, note 46.

⁷⁴ *R. v. W. (D.)*, 1991 CarswellOnt 80, 1991 CarswellOnt 1015, [1991] 1 S.C.R. 742, 3 C.R. (4th) 302, 63 C.C.C. (3d) 397, 122 N.R. 277, 46 O.A.C. 352 (S.C.C.).

⁷⁵ *Ibid.*, at p. 758 [S.C.R.].

⁷⁶ See *R. v. Tyhurst*, 1992 CarswellBC 818, [1992] B.C.J. No. 2770, 79 C.C.C. (3d) 238, 21 B.C.A.C. 218, 37 W.A.C. 218 (B.C. C.A.); and *R. v. K. (S.)*, 2008 CarswellOnt 2173, 2008 ONCA 285, [2008] O.J. No. 1481 (Ont. C.A.).

⁷⁷ See *R. v. Owen*, *supra*, note 24; *R. v. F. (J.)*, 2003 CarswellOnt 3135, [2003] O.J. No. 3241, 177 C.C.C. (3d) 1, 16 C.R. (6th) 317 (Ont. C.A.); *R. v. Gostick*, 1999 CarswellOnt 1952, [1999] O.J. No. 2357, 121 O.A.C. 355, 137 C.C.C. (3d) 53, 26 C.R. (5th) 319 (Ont. C.A.); and *R. v. De Haan*, *supra*, note 24.

⁷⁸ See *R. v. Sheppard*, 2002 CarswellNfld 74, 2002 CarswellNfld 75, 2002 SCC 26, [2002] 1 S.C.R. 869, 50 C.R. (5th) 68, 211 Nfld. & P.E.I.R. 50, 633 A.P.R. 50, 210 D.L.R. (4th) 608, 284 N.R. 342, 162 C.C.C. (3d) 298 (S.C.C.).

⁷⁹ See *R. v. McCullough*, *supra*, note 5.

⁸⁰ *R. v. Maharaj*, *supra*, note 5, at para. 22; see also *R. v. D. (S.)*, 2004 CarswellOnt 2123, [2004] O.J. No. 2142, 186 C.C.C. (3d) 304, 187 O.A.C. 19 (Ont. C.A.).

⁸¹ See *R. v. M. (R.E.)*, 2008 CarswellBC 2037, 2008 CarswellBC 2038, 2008 SCC 51, [2008] 3 S.C.R. 3, [2008] 11 W.W.R. 383, 83 B.C.L.R. (4th) 44, 235 C.C.C. (3d) 290, 60 C.R. (6th) 1, 297 D.L.R. (4th) 577, 380 N.R. 47, 439 W.A.C. 40, 260 B.C.A.C. 40 (S.C.C.).

⁸² *R. c. Gagnon*, *supra*, note 4, at para. 19; see also *R. v. S. (J.H.)*, 2008 CarswellNS 270, 2008 CarswellNS 271, 2008 SCC 30, 293 D.L.R. (4th) 257, 57 C.R. (6th) 79,

375 N.R. 67, [2008] 2 S.C.R. 152, 265 N.S.R. (2d) 203, 848 A.P.R. 203, 231 C.C.C. (3d) 302 (S.C.C.).

[83] See *R. v. M. (R.E.)*, *supra*, note 81.

[84] *R. v. M. (M.E.)*, *supra*, note 9.

[85] *Woolmington v. Director of Public Prosecutions*, [1935] A.C. 462, 25 Cr. App. R. 72 (U.K. H.L.).

Appendix

Examples of Offences

EXAMPLES OF INDICTABLE OFFENCES

Section 47	High Treason
Section 74	Piracy
Section 76	Hijacking
Section 77	Endangering Aircraft
Section 82	Possessing Explosives
Section 87	Possession of a Weapon or an Imitation Thereof Dangerous to the Public Peace
Section 121	Fraud Upon the Government
Section 123	Municipal Corruption
Section 131	Perjury
Section 145(1)	Escaping Lawful Custody
Section 155	Incest
Section 181	Spreading False News
Section 210(1)	Keeping a Bawdy-House
Section 220	Death by Criminal Negligence
Section 221	Bodily Harm by Criminal Negligence
Section 235	Murder
Section 236	Manslaughter
Section 237	Infanticide
Section 239	Attempted Murder
Section 240	Accessory After the Fact to Murder
Section 241	Aiding Suicide
Section 264.1(a)	Uttering Threats
Section 268	Aggravated Assault
Section 272	Sexual Assault With Weapon
Section 273	Aggravated Sexual Assault
Section 279	Kidnapping
Section 280	Abduction of Person Under 16

Section 281	Abduction of Person Under 14
Section 291	Bigamy
Section 334(a)	Theft Over $5,000
Section 336	Criminal Breach of Trust
Section 344	Robbery
Section 346	Extortion
Section 348	Break and Enter With Intent or Breaking Out
Section 349	Unlawfully Being in a Dwelling-house
Section 351	Possession of House-breaking Tools
Section 356	Theft From Mail
Section 362(1)(a)	False Pretences
Section 367	Forgery
Section 368	Uttering a Forged Document
Section 372(1)	False Messages
Section 380(1)(a)	Fraud in Excess of $5,000
Section 430(2)	Mischief
Section 433	Arson— Disregard for Human Life
Section 434	Arson— Damage to Property
Section 449	Making Counterfeit Money
Section 450	Possession of Counterfeit Money

EXAMPLES OF SUMMARY CONVICTION OFFENCES

Section 173	Indecent Acts
Section 174	Nudity
Section 175	Disturbances
Section 177	Trespass at Night
Section 201	Keeping Gaming or Betting House
Section 210(2)	Using Bawdy-House
Section 335	Taking Motor Vehicle or Vessel Without Consent
Section 364	Fraudulently Obtaining Food and Lodging
Section 372(2), (3)	Alarm or Harass by Telephone
Section 423	Intimidation
Section 649	Disclosure of Jury Proceeding

EXAMPLES OF DUAL PROCEDURE OFFENCES

Section 86(1)	Pointing a Firearm
Section 90	Carrying a Concealed Weapon
Section 91	Possession of a Prohibited Weapon

Section 129	Obstructing of Officer in Execution of His Duty
Section 139	Obstructing Justice
Section 140	Public Mischief
Section 151	Sexual Interference
Section 152	Invitation to Sexual Touching
Section 153	Sexual Exploitation
Section 159	Anal Intercourse
Section 160	Bestiality
Section 249	Dangerous Operation of Motor Vehicle, Vessel or Aircraft
Section 252	Hit and Run
Section 253(a)	Driving While Impaired
Section 253(b)	Driving With More Than 80 mg of Alcohol per 100 mL of Blood
Section 254(5)	Refusing a Breathalyzer or A.L.E.R.T.
Section 266	Assault
Section 267	Assault With a Weapon
Section 269	Unlawfully Causing Bodily Harm
Section 270(1)	Assaulting a Peace Officer
Section 334(b)	Theft Under $5,000
Section 355(b)	Possession of Property Under $5,000
Section 362(2)(b)	Fraud Under $5,000
Section 437	False Fire Alarm

Glossary of Frequently Used Legal Words in the Criminal Justice System

Abet. A French word combined of two words "a" and "better"—to bait or excite an animal; it includes knowledge of the wrongful purpose of the perpetrator and counsel and encouragement in the crime.

Accessory. Any one contributing to, or aiding in, the commission of a crime.

Accessory Before the Fact. One who, although being absent at the time a crime is committed, assists, procures, counsels, incites, encourages, induces, engages, or commands another to commit it.

Accessory After the Fact. One who, having full knowledge that a crime has been committed, conceals it from the magistrate, and harbors, assists or protects the person charged with, or convicted of, the crime.

Accomplice. A person who knowingly, voluntarily, and with common intent with the principal offender, unites in the commission of a crime.

Acquittal. The legal and formal certification of the innocence of a person who has been charged with a crime; a deliverance or setting free a person from a charge of guilt.

Actus Reus. The wrongful act or crime.

Admission. The avowal of a fact or of circumstances from which guilt may be inferred, but only tending to prove the offence charged, and not amounting to a confession of guilt.

Adjournment. A putting off or postponing of business or of a session until another time or place.

Adversary Proceeding. One having opposite parties; contested, as distinguished from an ex parte application. Via direct examination, cross-examination, redirect examination, the trier of fact tries to determine the truth of the matter.

Aiding. To support, help, assist or strengthen.

Alternative Measures. Measures other than judicial proceedings under the *Criminal Code* used to deal with a person who is eighteen years of age or over and alleged to have committed an offence.

Appeal. To resort to a higher court or tribunal to consider a judgment of a lower court.

Appearance Notice. A notice prescribed by the *Criminal Code* of Canada and issued by a peace officer to compel one's attendance before a court.

Arraignment. To bring a prisoner to the bar of the court to answer the matter charged upon him or her in an information or indictment.

Arrest. To deprive a person of his or her liberty by legal authority.

Attorney General. The chief law enforcement officer in the province.

Autrefois Acquit. The name of a plea in bar to a criminal action, stating that the defendant has been once already indicted and tried for the same alleged offence and has been acquitted.

Autrefois convict. A plea by a criminal in bar to an indictment that he or she has been formally convicted of the same offence.

Bail. To procure the release of a person from legal custody, by undertaking that he or she shall appear at the time and place designated and submit him or herself to the jurisdiction and judgment of the court.

Best Evidence Rule. A rule of evidence applying only to documents, which requires that, if an original document is available in your hands, you must produce it, i.e., that evidence should be the best that the nature of the case will allow (*R. v. Cotroni*, 1977 Carswel-lOnt 1180, (*sub nom. R. v. Swartz*) 37 C.C.C. (2d) 409 (Ont. C.A.)).

Challenge for Cause. To object to a potential juror on the ground that the name of the juror does not appear on the panel, a juror is not indifferent between the Queen and the accused, a juror has been convicted of an offence to which he or she was sentenced to a term of imprisonment exceeding 12 months, a juror is an alien or a juror is physically unable to peform properly the duties of a juror.

Circumstantial Evidence. The term includes all evidence of an indirect nature; it means that existence of principal facts is only inferred from circumstances.

Civil Law. Deals with the exposition and enforcement of civil rights as distinguished from criminal law. It is a convertible phrase with roman law.

Common Law. As distinguished from law created by the enactment of legislatures, the common law comprises the body of those principles and rules of action relating to the government and security of persons and property which derive their authority solely from usages and customs of immemorial antiquity, or from the judgments and decrees of the courts recognizing, affirming and enforcing such usages and customs.

Conditional Sentence. A "conditional sentence" is available where a person is convicted of an offence, except an offence that is punishable by a minimum term of imprisonment, and the court (a) imposes a sentence of imprisonment of less than two years, and (b) is satisfied that serving the sentence in the community would not endanger the safety of the community. The court may, for purposes of supervising the offender's behaviour in the community, order that the offender serve the sentence in the community, subject to the offender's complying with the conditions of a conditinal sentence order (s. 742.1 of the *Code*).

Confession. A voluntary statement made by a person charged with a commission of a crime or misdemeanor, communicated to another person, wherein he or she acknowledges himself or herself to be guilty of the offence charged, and discloses the circumstances of the act or the share in participation which he or she had in it.

Counselling. Giving advice by one to another in regard to a proposed line of conduct, claim or contention.

County Court Judge (District Court Judge). A judge appointed by the Governor General in Council; has powers to deal with most indictable matters and most summary conviction appeals.

Credibility. Worthiness of belief; that quality in a witness which renders his or her evidence worthy of belief.

Criminal Law. That branch or division of law which treats of crimes and their punishments.

Criminal Prosecution. An action or proceeding instituted in a proper court on behalf of the public, for the purpose of securing the conviction and punishment of one accused of crime.

Criminal Record. The formal conviction of a person convicted of a crime.

Crown Attorney. The appointee of the Crown who conducts the Crown's case in a criminal matter.

Direct Evidence. That means of proof which tends to show the existence of a fact in question, without the intervention of the proof of any other fact, and is distinguished from circumstantial evidence which is often called indirect evidence.

Direct Examination. In practice. The first interrogation or examination of a witness, on the merits, by the party on whose behalf he is called.

Dismissal. An order or judgment finally disposing of an action.

Due Process of Law. Law in its ordinary course of administration through courts of justice.

Election of Court. The choice that an accused has in a criminal trial as to how he or she wishes to be tried.

Electronic Surveillance. Any means whereby a third party clandestinely overhears, by means of any electromagnetic, acoustic, mechanical or other device, oral communications or telecommunications between two or more other persons.

Entrapment. The conception and planning of an offence by a peace officer, and his procurement of its commission by one who would not have perpetrated it except for the trickery, persuasion, or fraud of the peace officer.

Ex Parte. On one side only; by or for one party; done for, in behalf of, or on the application of, one party only.

Exculpatory. Clearing or tending to clear from alleged fault or guilt; excusing.

Exhibit. A paper or document produced and exhibited to a court during a trial or hearing, in proof of facts, or as otherwise connected with the subject-matter, and which, on being accepted, is marked for identification and filed in the record as part of the case.

Extrajudicial Measures. Measures other than judicial proceedings under the *Youth Criminal Justice Act*, used to deal with a young person alleged to have committed an offence. Include extrajudicial sanctions.

Extrajudicial Sanction. A sanction that is part of a program referred to in s. 10 of the *Youth Criminal Justice Act.*

Habeas Corpus. The name given to a variety of writs, having for their object to bring a party before a court or a judge. The sole function of the writ is to release from unlawful imprisonment.

Hearsay. Evidence not proceeding from the personal knowledge of the witness, but from the mere repetition of what he or she has heard others say. That which does not deprive its value solely from the credit of the witness, but rests mainly on the veracity and competency of other persons. The very nature of the evidence shows its weakness, and it is admitted only in specified cases from necessity.

Hybrid Offence. A crime which is punishable either by indictment or summary conviction.

Included Offences. An included offence is a part of an offence that has been charged in an indictment. Where the commission of the offence charged includes the commission of another offence, the accused may be convicted of an offence so included that is proved, notwithstanding that the whole offence that is charged is not proved (s. 6621(1)(a) of the *Code*) or an attempt to commit an offence so included that is proved (s. 662(1)(b)).

Inculpatory Statement. Going or tending to establish guilt.

Indictable Offences. Crimes which are punishable by two, five, ten or fourteen years, or life imprisonment, whereby the accused has an election as to how he or she wishes to be tried except those indictable offences mentioned in s. 553 of the *Code*.

Indictment. An accusation in writing setting out the charge against an accused person where a person is charged with a criminal offence punishable by indictment and elects to be tried by District or County Court Judge and/or Judge and jury.

Information. An accusation exhibited against a person for some criminal offence which is read to him or her upon his or her arraignment in court at first instance.

Judicial Interim Release. The judge's setting free the accused between committal for trial and the trial's completion.

Jurisdiction. The authority by which a court and judicial officers take cognizance of and decide cases.

Jury. A certain number of men or women selected according to law, and sworn to inquire of certain matters of fact, and declare the truth upon evidence to be laid before them.

Law. That which is laid down, ordained or established by government, the violation of which will cause one to be penalized.

Mandamus. This is the name of a writ which issues from a court of superior jurisdiction, that is directed to a private or municipal corporation, or any of its officers, or to an executive, administrative or judicial officer, or to an inferior court, commanding the performance of a particular act therein specified, and belonging to his or her or their public, official or ministerial duty, or directing the restoration of the complainant to rights or privileges of which he or she has been illegally deprived.

Mens rea. A guilty mind; a guilty or wrongful purpose; a criminal intent.

Oath. Any form of attestation by which a person signifies that he or she is bound in conscience to perform an act faithfully and truthfully.

Officer in Charge. Means the officer for the time being in command of the police force responsible for the lockup or other place in which an accused is taken after arrest or a peace officer designated by him or her for this purpose.

Pardon. An act of the Crown which releases a person from the punishment that person has incurred for some offence. A pardon may be granted before, during or after a prosecution.

Parole. Release of convict from imprisonment on certain conditions to be observed by him or her, and suspension of sentence during liberty thus granted.

Person in Authority. A person who may promise, threaten, or induce a person who has committed a criminal offence and who the person having committed the criminal offence believes can carry out those promises, threats and/or inducements.

Plea. When appearing before the court that is going to try an accused a person is either not guilty or guilty or pleads one of the special pleas available to him or her.

Precedent. An adjudged case or decision of a court or justice, considered as furnishing an example or authority for an identical or similar case afterwards arising or a similar question of law.

Pre-hearing Conference. A conference between the prosecutor and the accused or counsel for the accused to consider such matters as will promote a fair and expeditious hearing or trial.

Preliminary Hearing. Synonymous with preliminary examination— the examination of a person charged with a crime before a Provincial Court Judge who will make a determination as to whether or not there is sufficient evidence upon which the accused should stand his or her trial.

Pre-emptory Challenge. The right of an accused to stand aside a potential juror without giving any reason.

Pre-sentence Report (P.S.R.). A report prepared for the court prior to the sentencing of an accused which sets out the accused's background. In the context of the *Youth Criminal Justice Act*, a report on the personal and family history and present environment of a young person made in accordance with s. 40 of the Act.

Presumption. An inference, affirmative or non-affirmative, of the truth or falsehood of any proposition or fact drawn by a process of probable reasoning in the absence of actual certainty of its truth or falsehood, or until such certainty can be ascertained.

Promise to Appear. Is a form given to the accused, signed by him or her, by the officer in charge at the time of his or her release from custody.

Provincial Court Judge. A person who presides over the Provincial Court and is appointed by the Lieutenant Governor in Council upon the recommendation of the Provincial Government.

Reasonable and Probable Grounds. Such grounds as justify anyone suspecting another of a crime.

Recognizance. A form used by the officer in charge or a justice or a judge at the time of the release of a person who is in custody.

Relevancy. That quality of evidence which renders it properly applicable in determining the truth and falsity of the matters in issue between the parties to a suit.

Remand. To send back.

Search Warrant. An order in writing, issued by a justice in the name of the state directed to the police to search a specific house, shop or other premises, for personal property alleged to have been stolen or unlawful goods and to bring the same, when found, before the Provincial Court Judge or Justice and usually also the body of person occupying the premises, to be dealt with according to law.

Sentence. The judgment formally pronounced by the court or a judge upon the defendant after his or her conviction in a criminal prosecution awarding the punishment to be imposed.

Show Cause Hearing. A proceeding held prior to the granting of bail where the Crown has an opportunity to try to keep the accused in custody.

Stare Decisis. To abide by, or adhere to, decided cases.

Statute. An act of the legislature declaring, commanding, or prohibiting something; a particular law enacted and established by the will of the legislative department of government; the written will of the legislature, solemnly expressed according to the forms necessary to constitute it the law of the state.

Subpoena. A document requiring a person to attend as a witness.

Summary Conviction. The conviction of a person (usually for a minor misdemeanor) as a result of his trial before a Provincial Court Judge. The punishment for same is six months in jail or a fine of up to $2,000 or both, unless otherwise stated.

Summons. To cite a defendant or an accused to appear in court to answer to a charge.

Supreme (Superior Court). The courts of the highest and most extensive jurisdiction.

Surety. One who undertakes to pay money or to do any other act in the event that his or her principal fails therein.

Undertaking. A promise, engagement or stipulation. A promise or security in any form.

Unfit to Stand Trial. Unable on account of mental disorder to conduct a defence at any stage of the proceedings before a verdict is rendered or to instruct counsel to do so, and, in particular, unable on account of mental disorder to (a) understand the nature or object of the proceedings, (b) understand the possible consequences of the proceedings, or (c) communicate with counsel.

Voir Dire. Trial within a trial. Used to determine the admissibility of evidence.

Warrant. A writ from a competent authority in pursuance of law, directing the doing of an act, and addressed to an officer or person competent to do the act, and affording him or her protection from damages.

Index

References given are to page numbers.